The Europeans

The
Europeans

THREE LIVES AND THE MAKING OF
A COSMOPOLITAN CULTURE

Orlando Figes

METROPOLITAN BOOKS

HENRY HOLT AND COMPANY   NEW YORK

Metropolitan Books
Henry Holt and Company
Publishers since 1866
120 Broadway
New York, New York 10271
www.henryholt.com

Library of Congress Cataloging-in-Publication data is available.

ISBN: 9781627792141

Our books may be purchased in bulk for promotional, educational, or
business use. Please contact your local bookseller or the Macmillan Corporate and
Premium Sales Department at (800) 221-7945, extension 5442, or by e-mail at
MacmillanSpecialMarkets@macmillan.com.

First U.S. Edition 2019

Printed in the United States of America

1 3 5 7 9 10 8 6 4 2

For my sister, Kate

When the arts of all countries, with their native qualities, have become accustomed to reciprocal exchanges, the character of art will be enriched everywhere to an incalculable extent, without the genius peculiar to each nation being changed. In this way a European school will be formed in place of the national sects which still divide the great family of artists; then, a universal school, familiar with the world, to which nothing human will be foreign.

Théophile Thoré, '*Des tendances de l'art au xix*^e *siècle*' (1855)

Money has emancipated the writer, money has created modern literature.

Émile Zola, '*Money in Literature*' (1880)

'*You are a foreigner of some sort,*' *said Gertrude.*

'*Of some sort – yes; I suppose so. But who can say of what sort? I don't think we have ever had occasion to settle the question. You know there are people like that. About their country, their religion, their profession, they can't tell.*'

Henry James, *The Europeans* (1878)

Contents

A Note on Money

I have given monetary figures in their original currencies but have added in parentheses a French-franc equivalent where this may be useful for comparison. The French franc was the currency most widely used in Europe in the nineteenth century, and it was in francs that the people at the centre of this book mostly handled their affairs.

The exchange rates between Europe's major currencies remained relatively stable for most of the nineteenth century. They depended on the metal content of the coins. The key stabilizing factor was the British pound, which was on the gold standard. Other currencies established stable exchange rates with the British pound by moving to the silver standard (as did most of the German and Scandinavian states) or the bimetallic (gold and silver) standard (as did France and Russia). From the 1870s there was a general European move towards parity with gold.

In the middle decades of the nineteenth century 100 French francs were worth roughly

4	British pounds
25	Russian silver roubles*
90	Milanese (Austrian) lire
19	Roman scudi
23	Neapolitan ducats
38	Austrian gulden

* There were two types of rouble in circulation until 1843: the silver rouble (worth then about four French francs), used for foreign payments, and the assignat or paper rouble, which could be exchanged for the silver rouble at a rate of 3.5 to 1. In 1843, the paper rouble was replaced by State credit notes.

27 Prussian thaler
100 Belgian francs
20 US dollars

As an indicator of value the simple conversion of currencies can be misleading because it fails to take into account differences in purchasing power. The cost of living in Britain was generally higher than on the Continent, although some items (such as cotton) were cheaper because of the benefits of industrialization and empire. Higher costs were reflected in higher wages in Britain too. The British professional classes were paid significantly more than their confrères on the Continent. In 1851, the salary of a British judge in the Court of Appeal was £6,000 (around 150,000 francs), twice the annual income of his French equivalent. The fellow of an Oxford college had a basic income of £600 per year (around 15,000 francs), more than a professor at the Sorbonne earned (around 12,000 francs a year). Lower down the social scale the differential was less significant. A 'middling' British family would generally have an annual income of around £200 (5,000 francs) in the 1850s, an income at least equalled by the vast majority of bourgeois families in France, where dowries continued to supplement the household income more substantially than in Britain. A French mechanic or junior engineer earned anything between 3,000 and 7,000 francs a year. A skilled urban labourer or clerk had an annual salary of anything between 800 francs and 1,500 francs. At this end of the social scale British salaries were similar.

In the arts incomes were extremely variable. In monetary terms the writers, artists and musicians featured in this book were located on the scale described above anywhere between the best-paid judge and the worst-paid mechanic. A few examples must suffice to illustrate the variations in income. At the peak of his career, in the 1850s, the painter Ary Scheffer earned between 45,000 and 160,000 francs per year; but many artists, such as Scheffer's protégé, Théodore Rousseau, meanwhile made less than 5,000 francs a year. Before 1854, the writer Victor Hugo received from his writings, on average, 20,000 francs per year. George Sand and Ivan Turgenev earned about the same amount – the latter getting as much money again from his estates in Russia. Between 1849 and 1853 the composer Robert Schumann earned, on average, around 1,600 Prussian thalers (6,000 francs) from his compositions every year, an income supplemented by his salary as music director in Düsseldorf, which paid 750 thalers (approximately 2,800 francs) per year.

It is almost impossible to translate these figures into today's terms. The cost of goods and services was very different in the nineteenth century. Labour was a lot cheaper (and in Russia free for landowners owning serfs); rent was far less costly too; but food was relatively expensive in the cities. To help readers get a general sense of monetary values in the mid-nineteenth century: a million francs was a large fortune, purchasing goods and services worth around £5,000,000 ($6,500,000) in today's terms; 100,000 francs was enough to buy a château with extensive land (such as the one at Courtavenel purchased by the Viardots); while 10,000 francs, worth approximately £50,000 ($65,000) today, was the price the Viardots paid for an organ made by the famous organ-builder Aristide Cavaillé-Coll in 1848.

List of Illustrations

PLATES

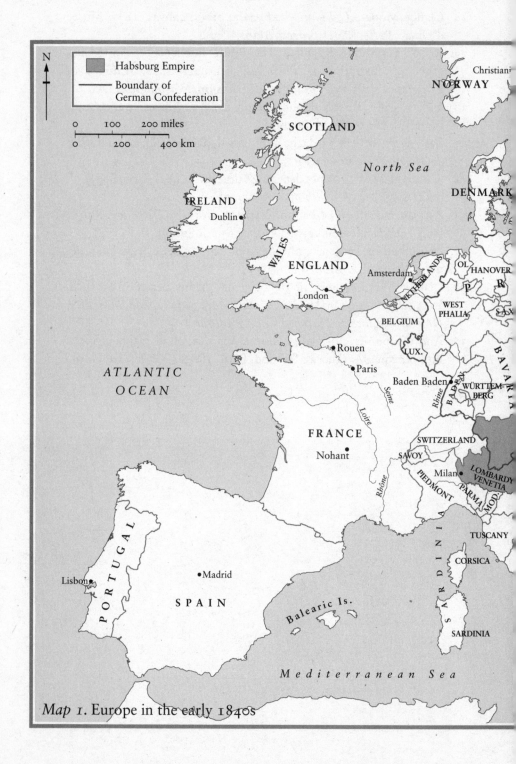

Map 1. Europe in the early 1840s

St. Petersburg

Stockholm

Moscow

SWEDEN

Baltic Sea

Riga

Dvina

Spasskoe

Oryol

Copenhagen

Nieman

Wilno

Danzig

EAST PRUSSIA

R U S S I A

Don

POMERANIA

Berlin

BRANDENBURG

Warsaw

R U S S I A N   E M P I R E

U

NY

K. OF SAXONY

SILESIA

Oder

REP. OF KRAKOW

Vistula

Kiev

BOHEMIA

Prague

Krakow

Dnieper

MORAVIA

THE HAPSBURG EMPIRE

Dniester

Vienna

Buda

Pest

HUNGARY

Black   Sea

Danube

BOSNIA

DALMATIA

PAPAL STATES

Adriatic Sea

Rome

K. OF THE TWO SICILIES

Île de France

Bougival

Paris

SEINE-ET-MARNE

SEINE-ET-OISE

Courtavenal

Barbizon

Seine

0   5   10   15 miles

0   10   20   30 km

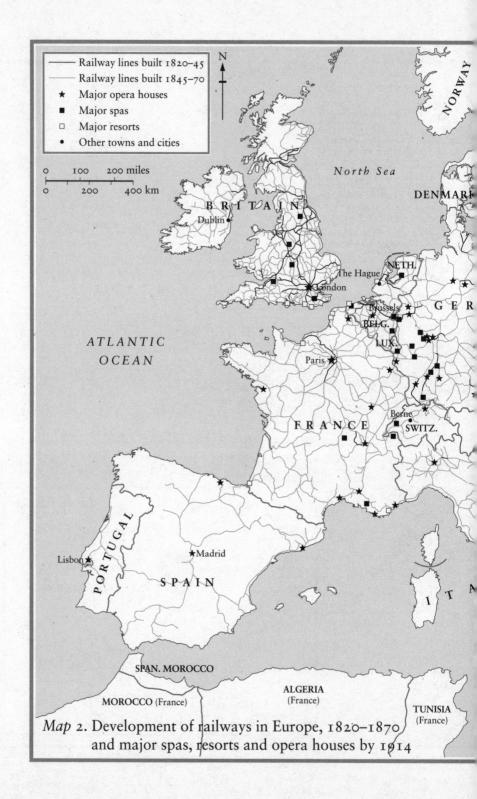

Map 2. Development of railways in Europe, 1820–1870 and major spas, resorts and opera houses by 1914

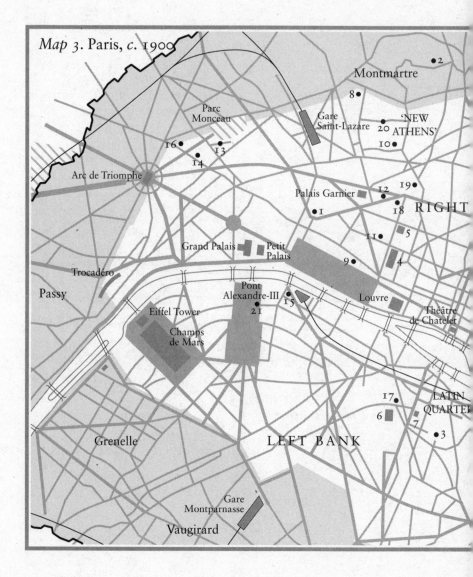

Map 3. Paris, *c.* 1900

Montmartre

2

8

Parc
Monceau

Gare
Saint-Lazare

'NEW
ATHENS'

20

10

16

13

14

Arc de Triomphe

19

12

Palais Garnier

18

RIGHT

1

5

11

Grand Palais

Petit
Palais

4

9

Trocadéro

Passy

Pont
Alexandre-III

Louvre

15

Théâtre
de Chatelet

21

Eiffel Tower

Champs
de Mars

17

LATIN
QUARTE

6

7

Grenelle

LEFT BANK

3

Gare
Montparnasse

Vaugirard

BANK

Gare du Nord

Gare de l'Est

Place de la République

Hôtel de Ville

Place de
la Bastille

Gare
d'Austerlitz

N

| 0 | | 500 yards |
| 0 | | 500 metres |

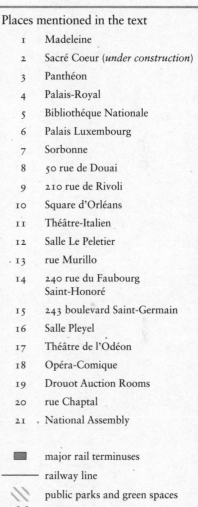

Places mentioned in the text

1	Madeleine
2	Sacré Coeur (*under construction*)
3	Panthéon
4	Palais-Royal
5	Bibliothéque Nationale
6	Palais Luxembourg
7	Sorbonne
8	50 rue de Douai
9	210 rue de Rivoli
10	Square d'Orléans
11	Théâtre-Italien
12	Salle Le Peletier
13	rue Murillo
14	240 rue du Faubourg Saint-Honoré
15	243 boulevard Saint-Germain
16	Salle Pleyel
17	Théâtre de l'Odéon
18	Opéra-Comique
19	Drouot Auction Rooms
20	rue Chaptal
21	National Assembly

■ major rail terminuses

— railway line

▨ public parks and green spaces

▨ cemetery

Introduction

The first steam engine pulled out of the Gare Saint-Lazare on its pioneering journey to Brussels at 7.30 in the morning, on a sunny Saturday, 13 June 1846. Two more locomotives followed it in sequence while the crowd cheered and the band played to send them on their way. Each of the three trains was made up of twenty open carriages decked out in the French and Belgian tricolours. Their 1,500 passengers had been invited by Baron James de Rothschild to celebrate the opening of the Paris–Brussels railway, which his company, the Chemins de Fer du Nord, had recently completed with the building of the line from the French capital to Lille.

It was not the first international railway. Three years earlier, in 1843, the Belgians had inaugurated a railroad from Antwerp to Cologne in Prussia's Rhine province. But the Paris–Brussels line was especially important because it opened up a high-speed connection linking France and the Low Countries, Britain (via Ostend or Dunkirk) and the German-speaking lands. The French press heralded the new railway as the beginning of Europe's unification under the cultural dominance of France. 'Inviting foreigners to see our arts, our institutions, and all that makes us great is the surest way to maintain the good opinion of our country in Europe,' reasoned the commission that approved the building of the line to Lille.[1]

The first train carried the official dignitaries, the Ducs de Nemours and Montpensier, sons of the French king, accompanied by French and Belgian ministers, police chiefs and various celebrities, among them the writers Alexandre Dumas, Victor Hugo and Théophile Gautier, as well as the painter Jean-Auguste-Dominique Ingres. Travelling from Paris at the unheard-of speed of thirty kilometres per hour, the advance party reached Lille in the sweltering heat of the afternoon. With their windswept hair and fine clothes covered in dust from the open-air journey, the travellers descended at a temporary station outside the medieval walls, where they were met by the city's leaders, the Archbishop of Cambrai, and a mounted guard of honour bearing French and Belgian flags. After the playing of the national anthems by a military band, the dignitaries walked in procession through the decorated streets, where such large crowds had assembled that the National Guard struggled to maintain order. Thieves were everywhere, there were scenes of chaos when the drinks ran out, and alarms were raised as a fire broke out in the Palace of Justice.[2]

The festivities began with a magnificent banquet given by Rothschild for 2,000 people in a vast marquee on the site of the future railway station, at that time being built inside the medieval walls. Sixty cooks and 400 waiters served up generous helpings of poached salmon in white sauce, York ham with fruits, quails *au gratin*, partridges *à la régence*, creamed beans, cheeses, desserts and French wines, whereupon the toasts began: 'To the unity of France and Belgium!' 'To international peace!' Rothschild made a heartfelt speech about the railways bringing Europe's nations together.[3]

As evening drew in there was a 'monster concert' on the esplanade, where Berlioz conducted a first performance of his *Grande Symphonie funèbre et triomphale* by 400 bandsmen from the local garrisons. The organizers had insisted on adding twelve cannons to the orchestra which were meant to fire on the final chords of the Apotheosis. But when the moment came they could not be fired because the lighters had been lost, although two were lit with a cigar, which caused their fuses to fizzle in the air, fooling some of the audience into thinking that had been intended all along.[4]

Berlioz had been commissioned to compose a cantata, *Le Chant des chemins de fer*, to a text by the writer Jules Janin celebrating international peace and brotherhood, ideals which the railways inspired. Composed for a tenor soloist, orchestra and several choirs, the cantata was performed at a banquet in the Hôtel de Ville following the concert on the esplanade. 'The cantata was sung with uncommon verve and fresh voices,' Berlioz reported to his sister Nanci. 'But while I was in conversation in the adjoining room with the Ducs de Nemours and Montpensier, who had asked for me, my hat was stolen, along with the music of the cantata.'[5] The score was recovered, but the hat was not.

At two o'clock in the morning, the convoy of revellers continued on their journey to Brussels. At Kortrijk, the first Belgian town, the whole population appeared at the station to greet the extraordinary trains from France. At Ghent there was a military parade with a cannonade. For the last stretch of the route, from Mechelen, the front two trains progressed in parallel, entering the station in Brussels, to cheers from the assembled crowd, at the same time. The French princes were received on the platform by Léopold, the Belgian king, and his French wife, Louise of Orléans, the princes' elder sister. There was a banquet in the Grand Palace, and a ball given by the Belgian Railways in the newly opened Gare du Nord. The station was converted into a ball-room by constructing a wooden floor above the tracks, suspending chandeliers from the glass roof, and importing tulips by the wagonload from Holland. 'We have never seen a ball as magnificent as this,' claimed the correspondent of Le National.[6]

In the early hours of the next morning, the visitors from France began their return to Paris. The 330-kilometre journey took just twelve hours – a quarter of the time it usually required to make the trip by stagecoach, the fastest mode of transport before the railway.

Soon national boundaries were being crossed by railways every-where. A new era for European culture had begun. Artists and their works could now move around the Continent much more easily. Berlioz would travel on the line from Paris to Brussels on his way to Russia for a concert tour in 1847 (at that time he could only get as far as Berlin by railway, but on his second tour of Russia, twenty years later, he could travel all the way from Paris to St Petersburg by train). From these dec-ades, the railways would be used by orchestras and choirs, opera and theatre companies, touring exhibitions of artistic works, and writers on reading tours. The formidable weight of many artistic enterprises, which would have required incredible numbers of horses and carriages, was relatively effortlessly moved by steam power. An international market would be opened up for cheap mass reproductions of paintings, books and sheet music. The modern age of foreign travel would begin, enabling Europeans in much greater numbers to recognize their com-monalities. It allowed them to discover in these works of art their own 'Europeanness', the values and ideas they shared with other peoples across Europe, above and beyond their separate nationalities.

How this 'European culture' was created is the subject of this book. It sets out to explain how it came about that by around 1900 the same books were being read across the Continent, the same paintings re-produced, the same music played at home or heard in concert halls, and the same operas performed in all the major theatres of Europe. How, in sum, the European canon – which forms the basis of today's high culture not just in Europe but all around the globe where Europeans settled – was established in the railway age. An élite international culture had existed in Europe since at least the Renaissance. It was built on Christianity, Classical literature, philosophy and learning, and had spread through Europe's courts, academies and city states. But it was only in the nineteenth century that a relatively integrated mass culture was able to develop right across the continent.

The Europeans is an international history. It looks at Europe as a whole, not divided into nation states or geographic zones, as in the majority of European histories, which have mostly focused on the role of culture in the nationalist movements and nation-building projects of the nineteenth century rather than on the arts as a unifying force between nations. My aim is to approach Europe as a space of cultural transfers, translations and exchanges crossing national boundaries, out of which a 'European culture' – an international synthesis of artistic forms, ideas and styles – would come into existence and distinguish Europe from the broader world.[7] As Kenneth Clark once said, nearly all the great advances in civilization – and the glittering achievements of European culture in the nineteenth century undoubtedly were one – have been during periods of the utmost internationalism, when people, ideas and artistic creations circulated freely between nations.[8]

In many ways the book is an exploration of the railway age as the first period of cultural globalization – for that is in effect what the creation of a European market for the arts in the nineteenth century represents. There were many who opposed this process from the start – nationalists, most obviously, who feared that the international flow of cultural traffic would undermine their nation's distinct culture and originality – but nobody was capable of stopping it. In ways beyond the political control of any nation state, the great technological and economic transformations of the nineteenth century (the revolution in mass communications and travel, the invention of lithographic printing and photography, the ascendancy of the free-market system) were the hidden motive forces behind the creation of a 'European culture' – a supranational space for the circulation of ideas and works of art stretching right across the Continent.

At the heart of the book is the new relationship between the arts and capitalism which developed in the nineteenth century. There is as much in it about the economics of the arts (technologies of production, business management, marketing, publicity, social networks, the problem of combating piracy) as there is about the works of art themselves. My focus is on forms of art that were most engaged in the capitalist system through their printed reproduction for the marketplace (the main source of profit for literature, music and painting) or because they functioned as a business once they lost State subsidies (e.g. opera). Sculpture and large public works of art are of less significance for my thesis. In the end it was the market that determined the European canon, deciding which works would survive, and which (a much greater number) would be lost and forgotten.

Three people stand at the centre of this book: the writer Ivan Turgenev (1818–83), the singer and composer Pauline Viardot (1821–1910), with whom Turgenev had a long and intimate relationship, and her husband, Louis Viardot (1800–1883), a now forgotten but in his time important art critic, scholar, publisher, theatre manager, republican activist, journalist and literary translator into French from both Russian and Spanish (everything, in other words, that is not the artist but on which the artist depends). Their biographies are woven through the narrative, which follows them around Europe (between them they lived at different times in France, Spain, Russia, Germany and Britain, and travelled widely through the rest of it), engages with those people whom they knew (almost everyone of any real importance on the European cultural scene), and explores those issues that affected them as artists and promoters of the arts.

In their different ways, Turgenev and the Viardots were figures in the arts adapting to the market and its challenges. Pauline had been born into a family of itinerant singers, so commercial enterprise was in her blood; but she was extremely skilful in her exploitation of the new economy and, as a woman, unusually independent for this patriarchal age. Louis acted as her manager in the early years of their marriage. As the director of the Théâtre Italien, one of Europe's major opera houses, he had quickly learned how to operate in a free market, but his business acumen was always moderated by an academic temperament. As for Turgenev, he had been born into the Russian aristocracy, whose sons were expected to enter public service and live off their estates. He had no head for business when he started out as a writer.

Through their international connections, Turgenev and the Viardots were important cultural intermediaries, promoting writers, artists and musicians across Europe and helping them establish foreign markets for their work. The people who attended their salons at various times in Paris, Baden and London represent a *Who's Who* of the European arts, high society and politics.

This was an international culture that vanished on the outbreak of the First World War. Turgenev and the Viardots were cosmopolitans, members of a European cultural élite, capable of living anywhere on European soil, provided it did not compromise their democratic principles, without losing any of their nationality. They found their home in 'European Civilization'. Burke's famous phrase – that 'No European can be a complete exile in any part of Europe'[9] – might have been designed for them.

I

Europe in 1843

*Space is killed by the railways, and we are left with time
alone . . . Now you can travel to Orléans in four and a half
hours, and it takes no longer to get to Rouen. Just imagine
what will happen when the lines to Belgium and Germany are
completed and connected up with these railways. I feel as if the
mountains and forests of all countries are advancing on Paris.
Even now, I can smell the German linden trees; the North Sea
breakers are rolling against my door.*

Heinrich Heine, 1843

I

At eight o'clock in the evening of 3 November 1843, a full house at the
Bolshoi Theatre in St Petersburg waited in excitement for the curtain to
go up. The house was packed to see the great soprano Pauline Viardot
make her Russian debut as Rosina in *The Barber of Seville*. In the front
rows of the stalls, seated in armchairs, were the highest-ranking dignitaries of the Russian Empire, all dressed in tailcoats, alongside their
wives and daughters, mostly dressed in white, the colour of the season;
behind them were ministers in evening dress and officers in uniforms. There was not a spare seat to be had, neither in the *bel-étage* nor
in any of the private boxes in the four lower tiers, where the nobility
was all turned out, diamonds twinkling in the light from the oil-lamps
of the immense chandelier. In the cheapest seats on the fifth and highest
tier, above the level of the chandelier, students, clerks and serious music
lovers squeezed up tight on the benches and strained their necks to see

the stage. The auditorium was buzzing with excitement as the late arrivals took their places and the overture began. The imminent appearance of the famous singer with Giovanni Rubini and his Italian company of singers had been the only compelling subject of salon conversation in St Petersburg for many weeks. The press build-up was so intense that one newspaper tried to jump the gun by publishing a piece about Viardot's first performance – complete with descriptions of the wild applause – two days before it took place.[1]

Viardot-Garcia, as she was then known, struck everybody by her appearance. With her long neck, large protruding eyes and heavy lids, she looked exotically unusual, some would even say horsey; but her gracious smile and hazel eyes, sparkling with intelligence, and the liveliness of her expressions, which reflected her vivacious character, gave an alluring interest to her face. 'Richly ugly' was how she was described by the Russian Foreign Minister, Count Karl Nesselrode, on her debut in St Petersburg. The poet Heinrich Heine, a famous wit, thought she was so unattractive that she was 'almost beautiful'.[2]

Her voice was the key to her spellbinding presence on stage. It had a tremendous force, extraordinary range and versatility.* It was not a soft or crystal voice – some thought it was guttural – but had a dramatic power, an emotional intensity, that suited it equally to tragedy or to the Spanish gypsy songs she often sang (Camille Saint-Saëns compared it to the taste of 'bitter oranges').[3] Clara Schumann, who heard her sing in Paris in August 1843, thought she had 'never yet heard a woman's voice like that'.[4] The Russians agreed. 'We have heard many first-rate singers but none has overwhelmed us in this way,' wrote one critic of that first performance in St Petersburg. 'The astonishing range of her voice, its unrivalled virtuosity, its magical, silvery tonality, those passages which even the trained ear could barely follow – we have not heard anything like it before.'[5] After the final curtain had gone down, she was called out nine times by the audience, which remained standing in the theatre, not one person heading to the exits, for a full hour.

---

* Technically, by today's standards, Viardot was a mezzo-soprano, but that term was not commonly used until the late nineteenth century, so she would have been billed as a soprano. The Rosina role in *The Barber of Seville* was originally written for a contralto but is now known as one of the staple roles for a mezzo-soprano.

The Russian public was passionate about opera. It displayed a spontaneous enthusiasm which delighted Viardot.[6] She brought the house down on the second night when she sang a well-known Russian air in the Act II lesson scene. She had taken Russian lessons to get the diction right. It was a piece of showmanship she often used to win the hearts of an audience abroad. Tsar Nicholas was so delighted that he led the exuberant applause, received the singer in the Imperial box, and the next morning sent her a pair of diamond earrings, which Pauline at once had valued.[7]

Levels of excitement reached new heights with each fresh performance. Viardot herself felt her voice improving every night as she worked through the season's repertoire, following her debut in *The Barber of Seville* with equally sensational performances in Rossini's *Otello*, Bellini's *La Sonnambula* and Donizetti's *Lucia di Lammermoor*. Every aria was applauded with cries of '*Brava!*' Every act ended with a dozen curtain calls, most of them for Viardot. At the final curtain of *La Sonnambula* there were fifteen calls for her alone. The Tsarina, seated in the side box by the curtain, threw a camellia that landed by the prima donna's feet. The gesture broke an Imperial interdiction against throwing flowers on the stage. From the next night, after every aria by Viardot, flowers were thrown on the stage. Florists did a roaring trade. Every available bouquet was bought up by 'fanatics' of the opera – the new ritual itself became the subject of a contemporary vaudeville, *Bouquets*, by Vladimir Sologub.[8]

This was the height of the Russian craze for Italian opera. Few other operas could get a hearing in St Petersburg. In the 1843–4 season there were almost twice as many performances of Italian operas than there were of Russian ones. Even Mikhail Glinka, the 'inventor of the Russian opera', whose *Ruslan and Liudmilla* and *A Life for the Tsar* had filled the Bolshoi Theatre almost every night in the early months of 1843, found his works demoted to Sundays and then despatched to the provinces once Rubini's company had arrived. Glinka was in fact long accustomed to the domination of Italians. He had lived in Italy in the early 1830s and could not help but adapt his music to the fashionable Italian style with its cheerful melodies and virtuoso thrills. His most 'Russian' work, *A Life for the Tsar* (1836), positively 'reeked of Italianism', as he later acknowledged.[9]

This Italomania was relatively new. Although the tsarist court had kept a resident Italian opera in the eighteenth century, there was none in Russia after 1801, except in the Black Sea port of Odessa, where many non-Russians lived. The exiled poet Alexander Pushkin heard a mediocre touring company perform Rossini operas in Odessa in the 1823–4 season. The experience inspired these lines in Pushkin's verse novel *Eugene Onegin* (1825), in which the bored narrator lets his lorgnette rove around the opera house:

> And what of other fascinations?
> And what of keen lorgnettes, I say?
> And in the wings . . . the assignations?
> The prima donna? The ballet?
> The loge, where, beautiful and gleaming,
> A merchant's youthful wife sits dreaming,
> All vain and languorous with pride,
> A crowd of slaves on every side?
> She heeds, and doesn't heed the roses,
> The cavatina, heated sighs,
> The jesting praise, the pleading eyes . . .
> While in the back her husband dozes,
> Cries out from sleep *Encore!* – and then
> Emits a yawn and snores again.[10]

Italian opera came back into fashion in St Petersburg only after 1836, when a Russified Venetian, Catterino Cavos, the director of the Bolshoi Theatre, made a splash with a production of Rossini's *Semiramide*.

Russia was the last European country to be swept up in this international craze. It attracted ageing stars eager to cash in on their past fame. In 1841, the great Giuditta Pasta, then at the end of her career, her voice almost completely gone, appeared with the Russian opera in the title role of Bellini's *Norma*, a part she had sung in the opera's first performance ten years earlier. Soon afterwards the Russians welcomed the 'greatest tenor of the age', Rubini, now aged forty-nine, who had been advised by Liszt, the virtuoso pianist and composer, to follow his example and make a tour of Russia for the piles of cash the naive Russians were prepared to pay for 'civilization'. Keen to put St Petersburg on a cultural par with Paris, Vienna and London, the Tsar paid Rubini a fortune (80,000 paper roubles, or 90,000 francs) as his fee for bringing an Italian opera troupe to St Petersburg in the 1843–4 season. Viardot, alone, received 60,000 roubles as well as half the earnings from other concerts she was free to give.[11] It was a level of remuneration few opera singers had received before. Such expenditure was fully justified by the prestige the troupe brought to the Russian capital, according to the Tsar's own spokesman, the editor Faddei Bulgarin, who wrote in his newspaper, *The Northern Bee*, during that first season:

> Let's admit it: without an Italian opera troupe it would always seem as if something were missing in the capital of the foremost empire in the world! There would seem to be no focal point for opulence, splendour, and cultivated diversion. In all the capitals of Europe the richest accoutrements, the highest tone, all the refinements of society are concentrated at the Italian Opera. This cannot be changed, nor should it be.[12]

In Western Europe opera had flourished since the seventeenth century. From its origins as a private court event, opera was soon transformed into a public spectacle, first in Venice and then throughout Italy. Unlike in France, where opera was under royal control, every major town in Italy had its own theatre and a group of nobles or rich merchants and professionals to manage it (the first Italian national census in 1868 recorded 775 opera houses in active existence).[13] The business model was fairly uniform throughout the peninsula. Forming a consortium of boxholders, the owners of the theatre would contract with an impresario, usually a former singer or musician, who employed a company for a season (few provincial theatres could afford to keep a troupe). The impresario would receive an advance from the owners and would take the profits from the sale of tickets in the stalls, while the theatre earned its income from leasing private boxes for an annual fee.[14] The small size of the audience, drawn from the élite of a single town, obliged companies to tour constantly to reach a larger audience. Opera thus became a unifying element of the various states in Italy, its language understood even where the people spoke a dialect rather than Italian.

Touring companies exported opera from Italy to the European courts. New theatres were built for its needs in every European capital. Where opera took root in the eighteenth century – in Handel's London or Gluck's Vienna – it did so in a style that was essentially Italian. Such was the domination of Italian opera that composers of every nationality were drawn into writing it: the German Simon Mayr composed over fifty operas for Italian opera houses between 1795 and 1820; Mozart, as a teenager, wrote three operas for La Scala in Milan, as well as going on to write many others in Italian for Austrian theatres. But it was Rossini who first cornered an international market for Italian opera. Conquering theatres across Europe and the wider world, he was a musical Napoleon, in the estimation of Stendhal, his earliest biographer: 'Napoleon is dead; but a new conqueror has already shown himself to the world; and from Moscow to Naples, from London to Vienna, from Paris to Calcutta, his name is constantly on every tongue. The fame of this hero knows no bounds save those of civilization itself.'[15]

The employment of Rossini was a virtual guarantee of making money for an opera house. His tuneful and lighthearted operas would prove ideally suited to the mood of the Restoration period, when frothy entertainment was the order of the day. Following the dazzling successes of his early operas, especially *Tancredi* (1813), Rossini was employed as musical director of the San Carlo in Naples, at that time the leading theatre in the world. Its manager was Domenico Barbaja, an astute businessman turned impresario, who had stumbled on a novel method to make opera pay.

Barbaja had started his career as a waiter in a café near La Scala in Milan. He had made a killing by delivering refreshments to people in their boxes at the opera and by inventing a new type of coffee mixed with cream and chocolate (a type of mocha) that became all the rage. During the French occupation of Milan (from 1796 to 1815), the previous Austrian ban on gambling in the theatres was lifted. Barbaja won the lucrative concession to run the roulette tables (a game brought to Italy by Napoleon's officers) in La Scala's entrance hall. His gambling empire quickly spread to other cities conquered by the French. The organizing skills Barbaja had developed to run his gaming syndicate were easily transferred to opera management, where large amounts of cash were also regularly moved around. In Naples, where he was in charge of not only the San Carlo but the smaller Teatro dei Fiorentini, Barbaja used the profits from his roulette wheels to hire the best singers for the opera. As musical director of the San Carlo from 1815 to 1822, Rossini was contracted to write two operas every year, for which he was paid a salary of 12,000 French francs and received a share of all Barbaja's takings from the roulette wheels – considerably more than Rossini earned from his music.[16]

With the international triumph of *The Barber of Seville* (1816) and *La Cenerentola* (1817) Rossini became a global phenomenon. When Barbaja took over the Vienna Opera in 1822, he employed Rossini there. The Viennese nobility soon succumbed to the Italian craze, in spite of the nationalist critics who opposed this 'foreign invasion' and rallied their supporters behind Carl Maria von Weber's *Der Freischütz* (1821), a work they championed as a 'German national opera', mainly on account of its folk motifs and language (in fact its style was largely French and its setting in Bohemia). Likewise, in London, where Rossini spent five months in 1823, he was greeted as an international celebrity. Rossini's every movement was reported in the press, if only to remark on his fat and jolly figure walking to his rooms in the Quadrant, Regent Street, then just completed by John Nash. Popular demand for his music was insatiable. All three London opera houses (the King's Theatre, the Drury Lane Theatre and the Theatre Royal in Covent Garden) catered to the craze for Rossini's operas.[17]

But it was in Paris that Rossini had his biggest impact on the opera world. In 1824, he became director of the Théâtre Italien, one of the city's three main opera theatres under royal control, the others being the Paris Opéra and the Opéra-Comique. Rossini's contract was lucrative. Following his triumph in London, the French court was willing to

The Théâtre Italien, engraving, c. 1840.

accept the composer's extravagant demands: 40,000 francs for the first year, when he was meant to write two operas, and the recognition of his copyright on an equal basis with all citizens under French law, the most advanced protection in Europe at that time.[18] Over the six years of his directorship, the Théâtre Italien became one of the leading opera houses in Europe. The Paris Opéra was in the doldrums by comparison. People had grown tired of the old French operas – now long lost or forgotten works by the likes of Christoph Gluck, André Grétry or Nicolas Dalayrac – which made up so much of its repertoire. They flocked instead to the 'Italiens', as it was fondly called, where Rossini reigned, in the words of Stendhal, as a 'citizen monarch'.

The Salle Favart, its auditorium, was not just a theatre but a way of life ('as much a salon as an opera house', according to Gautier). Exclusively devoted to the Italian repertoire, it was a place for elegant society, for opera fanatics (the 'tribe of *dilettanti*' who posed as cognoscenti), serious music lovers and intellectuals, as opposed to the more stately public of the Opéra's Salle Le Peletier. The novelist George Sand, the poet Alfred de Musset and the painter Eugène Delacroix were regulars at the Italiens. Because the stalls were barred to women, Sand appeared dressed as a man, wearing a long military coat with trousers and a waistcoat, the fashion of the day, cravat and hat and hobnailed boots, an outfit which she also wore elsewhere. Among the French Romantics only Berlioz, a devotee of the Gluck school, despised the cult of Italian opera and 'more than once debated with myself the possibility of mining the Théâtre Italien and blowing it up one evening, along with all its congregation of Rossinians'.[19] In contrast to the city's other music theatres, where the public talked throughout the performance, the audience at the Italiens listened more attentively: they were stilled and silenced by maestro Rossini when he knocked three times to signal the beginning of the overture.

In the early nineteenth century, the opera industry was an international business of itinerant tradesmen. The young Rossini earned his living until 1810 as a vocal coach (répétiteur) and harpsichord accompanist, both important music trades. He was then hired as a composer at the Teatro del Corso in Bologna. His contracts stipulated that he was a 'trader in music' (*mercante di musica*). Musicians still had a lowly status in the palaces and salons of the aristocracy, despite the efforts of composers such as Mozart to elevate their position. They appeared 'on the footing of inferiors', wrote Countess Marie d'Agoult, who lived with Liszt:

> If someone wanted to give a fine concert, he sent to Rossini, who, for a recognized fee – it was small enough, only 1500 francs if I recollect correctly – undertook to arrange the programme and to see to its carrying out, thus relieving the master of the house of all embarrassments in the way of choice of artists, of rehearsals and so on . . . At the appointed hour [the musicians] arrived in a body, entering by a side door; in a body they sat near the piano; and in a body they departed, after having received the compliments of the master of the house and of a few professed dilettantes.[20]

Typically, in the opera business, a composer would be engaged by an impresario to compose the music for a libretto, oversee the rehearsals, and conduct the first three performances as the player of the harpsichord. For his services he would receive a one-off fee that put him at the level of a master artisan. Once he had fulfilled his contract, the composer was free to leave and ply his trade in the next town. The production of an opera tended to be very quick, so it was possible to mount several operas in a year. *The Barber of Seville* received its first performance within a month of Rossini starting on the score. The singers were still learning their parts on the day of the premiere, which may in part explain why it ended in fiasco, with whistling and hissing from the audience, following a series of accidents on stage at the Teatro Argentine in Rome.

Rossini churned out operas at a furious rate – sixteen in his first five years of composing – many of them made up of recycled bits from his earlier works. This recycling was still a common practice by opera composers in the early nineteenth century, when people did not travel far: it was easy to pass off a rehashed work as something new in a distant town. Donizetti did so famously (he was caught and criticized for it). The pressure to compose quickly was the main reason why he reused music from his own previous scores. In 1832, when he had just a few weeks to compose *L'elisir d'amore*, Donizetti borrowed whole chunks of his *Alahor in Granata* (1826) and *Elizabeth at Kenilworth Castle* (1829).[21] Underlying this practice was the economy of opera production before the railway age, when theatres drew their public from a narrow geographic area and needed several new works every year to keep it entertained. Working in this industry did not always give composers time to write original material. In 1827, for example, Donizetti signed a contract with Barbaja in Naples to write twelve operas in the next three years, during which he would be paid a monthly salary of 400 ducats (approximately 2,100 francs). Nothing in the contract stipulated that the music of each opera should be new; as long as he produced enough in quantity, Donizetti would be paid.[22]

The leading singers earned more than the composers. People came to the opera to hear the star performers, and the music played a supporting role to showcase their talents. All the main composers would write for particular singers or adapt their scores to suit their vocal qualities. The fees paid to the prima donnas were astronomical. With the disappearance of the treasured *castrati* in the early decades of the nineteenth century, female singers were the highest paid in opera. It was not unusual for half an opera's production costs to go into the fees of the leading soloists, especially if these included famous divas like Giuditta Pasta or Maria Malibran, Viardot-Garcia's elder sister. They bargained hard for better pay and conditions, sometimes using agents, sometimes negotiating by themselves, but always with an eye to what their rivals were earning.[23]

Increasingly, the leading soloists were spending time on international tours, travelling wherever they could earn the highest pay. Improvements in road transport, steamships from the 1820s and railways later, pushed up fees, as more theatres were able to compete for their services. For the London season in 1827, for example, Pasta earned £2,365 (60,000 francs) – thirty times as much as any of the other soloists – for forty-five performances. In the early 1830s Malibran was paid even higher fees – £1,000 for just twelve performances at Covent Garden and £3,200 for forty nights at Drury Lane, not including earnings from a series of benefit concerts guaranteed to net £2,000. For a two-year contract in New York, from 1834, she was offered a fortune, 500,000 francs (£20,000), but turned it down.[24]

The concert tours by Liszt or Paganini were the only real comparison to the financial success of the leading divas. In 1831, according to one reckoning, Paganini earned 133,107 francs from just eleven concerts during March and April in Paris, and then in London, from May to July, was paid £10,000 (250,000 francs), enough to buy a mansion in Mayfair. People paid enormous sums to hear the virtuoso violinist play – a whole guinea for a stalls seat in the King's Theatre, almost three times the usual price. Ticket prices were inflated by extravagant accounts of his strange appearance and demonic personality, of his sexual conquests, and the hypnotic powers he was said to exercise through his playing – rumours Paganini encouraged by playing ever more wildly. Everything in his performance was calculated for sensational effect and spectacle. But he approached his tours as a businessman, keeping detailed accounts of his income and expenses in a 'secret book'. He employed concert managers to act as agents and handle the expenses for a share of the receipts – an innovation in the music industry, where composers had previously managed themselves. With his manager, Paganini controlled every aspect of his concerts, from finding venues to placing adverts in the press, hiring orchestras, employing ticket agents, and sometimes selling tickets at the door himself. He developed his own merchandising: print engravings, 'Paganini cakes' and other souvenirs of his concerts.[25]

Liszt took a leaf out of Paganini's book. Much of his early career was spent touring, from which he learned how to cultivate his own celebrity to attract an audience. Touring Europe with his father in 1823–4, Liszt had drawn enormous interest as a teenage prodigy. Reproduction prints of the precocious pianist were sold in Paris shops. His father charged 100 francs for his son to play in private homes. After his father's death in 1828, Liszt gave up on concert tours (he compared them to being a 'performing dog') and tried to make a living as a piano teacher. But then, in 1831, he heard Paganini play at the Paris Opéra. Liszt set out to create a new kind of piano repertoire by emulating the effects of Paganini's violin, its tremolos and leaps and glissandi. It was a type of virtuoso playing that set him on a highly profitable course of concert tours across Europe – from Spain and Portugal to Poland, Turkey and Russia – between 1839 and 1847. Whereas previous composers had mostly toured to enhance their reputation and win patrons, Liszt thought of his tours as a business venture whose purpose was to make him 'capital' – a word he used himself.[26] He employed an agent, Gaetano Belloni, who managed his accounts and worked with him on his public image for these tours. Liszt's flamboyant stage behaviour gave him an emotional appeal, encouraging his listeners to respond to his performance with strong emotions in the concert hall. 'Lisztomania' (a term coined by Heine) swept through Europe from 1843. Fans would swarm around the virtuoso pianist. Women in the front rows of his audience would fight to get the handkerchiefs or gloves which he dropped deliberately before seating himself at the piano. His cigar ashes were jealously guarded as 'relics'.[27] Thousands of his fans would buy the music of his most demanding pieces, even if they had no chance of ever being able to play them, solely for the reason that they wanted to possess a memento of the Liszt phenomenon.

The opera industry had many families and even dynasties of singers, dancers, instrumentalists, who toured around the theatres of Europe together. But the Garcias were the most talented, prolific and successful of them all. Liszt, who was a close friend of the Garcias, once wrote that Pauline had been 'born into a family where genius seemed to be hereditary'.[28]

Manuel Garcia, Pauline's father, was born in Seville in 1775, only five years after the last victim of the Spanish Inquisition was burned at the stake there as a heretic. For a long time it was thought that he had gypsy origins (Pauline believed it) but he probably invented this himself to add a Romantic aura to his stage personality. Garcia belonged to the first generation of professional singers independent of any patronage (by State, Church or aristocracy) and dependent on the market to make a living.[29] His voice had an extraordinary range, allowing him to sing both baritone and tenor roles. He had started as a singer and composer in Cadiz, where he married Manuela Morales, a bolero dancer, and then moved to Malaga, a centre of Italian opera in Spain, before becoming the musical director of the royal theatres in Madrid, where he took up with the singer Joaquina Briones, whom he married too.

Garcia composed in a Spanish style, incorporating folk songs and dances into his operettas, or *zarzuelas*. Later Spanish composers saw him as the founder of Spanish opera.[30] In Madrid there was little cultural space for the national tradition. The theatre there was given over to performing mainly French and Italian works. Abandoning Morales and their two small daughters, whom he continued to support financially, Garcia left for Paris with Joaquina, who had already given birth to Manuel's son, named after him. In 1807, he made his debut in the Théâtre Italien, where he soon became the leading tenor, celebrated for his brilliant virtuoso improvisations then deemed part of the Romantic singing style (the comparison between Paganini and Garcia would frequently be made).

A good-looking man with dark curly hair and 'gypsy' features, Garcia had a fiery and rebellious temperament. Much of his violence was taken out on Joaquina, who bore not only his beatings but the shame of passing for his mistress in public to conceal his crime of bigamy.[31] His tempestuous character often led to conflicts with the authorities (in Madrid he was even once imprisoned on the orders of the theatre management for refusing to perform). Garcia's solution to these conflicts was always to move on to a new place. Three years after the birth of their second child, Maria, in 1808, the Garcias left for Naples, where Manuel met Rossini, and then moved to Rome, where he sang the part of Count Almaviva – a role created especially for him – in the first performance of *The Barber of Seville*. From Rome they went to London, where the eight-year-old Maria was put into a convent school in Hammersmith. The Garcias then returned to Paris, where Pauline, their third child, was born in 1821.

From an early age the Garcia children were taught to sing by their father. He was a hard taskmaster and was said to hit them when they did not get their repetition right. Maria, who was as fiery as her father, suffered most on this account. Pauline, the youngest and his favourite, claimed years later that he had only hit her once, rightly she believed, and denied that he was cruel. He was in any case a first-class teacher and had his tried-and-tested pedagogic methods – based on hard work, discipline and exercises for the training of the voice – which he passed down to his children, enabling them to become famous singing teachers in their turn.

At the age of just fourteen Maria made her debut as Rosina in *The Barber of Seville* at the King's Theatre in London. Manuel sang the Almaviva role. He had fled Paris, where Morales had turned up, demanding money and threatening to expose him as a bigamist. Maria caused a sensation. Her voice was extraordinary, rich in tone, with a range of over three octaves that enabled her to sing both soprano and contralto roles. Manuel assumed the office of his daughter's manager, demanding higher fees for her than those earned by even well-established prima donnas. The English critics became hostile, so Manuel moved on again.

In 1825, he accepted a profitable offer to take his family and a company of singers to New York, where a group of wealthy men, who had fallen in love with Italian opera, were ready to support the trip. The 1820s saw a marked increase in the number of Italian opera troupes touring the Americas: the new wealth of cities such as Buenos Aires and New York acted as a magnet to adventurous touring groups.[32] Pauline, who was then aged four, learned to sing on the long sea voyage across the Atlantic. 'It was on a sailing boat that I was taught, without a piano, at first singing on my own, then with two voices and with three,' she recalled many years later. 'My father wrote some small canons, we sang them daily, in the evenings on the bridge, to the delight of the crew.'[33]

There was great excitement in America about the arrival of Italian music – much of it drummed up by no less a figure than Lorenzo da Ponte, Mozart's great librettist, who was then living in New York and teaching at Columbia College. The New York season opened with *The Barber of Seville* on 29 November 1825 (the first time an opera had been sung in Italian in the New World) before an audience that included Joseph Bonaparte, the exiled former King of Spain, and James Fenimore Cooper, who was just about to publish *The Last of the Mohicans*. The opera was a great success. Maria was hailed as a star. The season continued with Mozart's *Don Giovanni* – performed for the first time in the United States by four of the Garcias (the two Manuels, Maria and Joaquina) in the presence of da Ponte. But the opera-going public was too small – and there were no kings or noble patrons – to make opera a profitable venture in New York. The Garcias faced a more immediate problem when the seventeen-year-old Maria decided to escape her domineering father by marrying a New York banker of French origin by the name of Eugène Malibran. The banker paid a fortune, said to be as much as $50,000 (250,000 francs), to compensate Garcia for the loss of his lead singer.[34]

Without Maria, the Garcias left for Mexico, where at least people spoke Spanish. But it was virgin territory for opera. There were no real theatres in the European sense, and audiences were too small to make any money out of opera. In 1828, the family gave up and returned to Paris. On their way to Vera Cruz, the first part of their long trek back to Europe, their convoy was attacked by brigands operating in collusion with the convoy's escort of soldiers. The masked bandits forced the travellers to lie face downwards on the ground and robbed them of everything – 'down to our clothes', as Pauline would recall – a story she retold in the same vivid detail right until the end of her long life.[35]

'God created me for travelling. It was in my blood from before I was born,' Pauline wrote many years later.[36] The constant movement of her early years, combined with the rigour of her father's teaching, imbued in her a steely stoicism and determination to succeed. It also made her talented at languages. Adding to the Spanish which she spoke at home, she was completely fluent in French, Italian and English from childhood, and in German from a little later on. There were, it seems, no mental barriers between her many languages: in her diaries and letters she expressed herself with natural ease in all of them, often shifting in mid-sentence from one language to another if it contained a better word.

In 1827, Pauline's elder sister had returned to Paris, where she made her debut in Rossini's *Semiramide* at the Théâtre Italien, launching her spectacular career in Europe. The extraordinary power of her voice, so simple in expression, her exotic Spanish looks, her passionate performance style and general air of melancholy perfectly embodied the Romantic spirit of the times, quickly winning for her a cult status among young Parisians. Malibran had left her banker husband in New York and taken up with Charles de Bériot, a Belgian violinist, living with him near Brussels and bearing him two children, only one of whom survived. Manuel refused to see Maria any more, declaring that her conduct 'offends and dishonours her entire family' (as if his own bigamy had not done so already).[37] Maria continued to send the family money, several thousand francs a year. She wrote to her mother asking her for news, but 'dared not' write to her father, because she was afraid that he would not reply. 'Let him know that he can be content with his daughter' was all that she would say.[38]

Manuel Garcia died of a sudden heart attack at the age of fifty-seven on 10 June 1832. Pauline and her mother joined Maria in Brussels (her brother Manuel had enrolled in the French expedition to Algeria two years earlier). Following her husband's death, Joaquina carried on the role of Pauline's coach and general manager. Pauline had shown a precocious talent for singing. At the age of four she had sung for the Duke of Wellington, and at eight for Rossini.[39] In Paris she was sent to study composition with Anton Reicha, the Czech-born composer and friend of Beethoven, whose pupils had included Berlioz and Liszt. At this stage Pauline seemed set on a career as a concert pianist – the piano, harp or voice being at that time the only instruments deemed fit for women performers. She had taken lessons from the cathedral organist in Mexico City and now, at the age of twelve, was taught by Liszt, who was then in his twenties. Naturally she fell in love with him. Getting dressed to go to her Saturday lessons, Pauline's hands would tremble so much from emotion that she could not tie the laces on her boots, she recalled many years later. 'When I knocked on his door, my blood would freeze; when he opened it, I would burst into tears . . . But what joy it was when we played together Herz's variations for four hands.'[40]

It was her mother who insisted that Pauline become a singer – a decision reinforced by Maria's death, at the age of twenty-eight, in 1836. She had fallen from her horse in Regent's Park in London two months earlier but had struggled on with her concert engagements until she finally collapsed and died in Manchester. In the last years of her short life she had been at the height of her international fame. Huge crowds would gather wherever she performed. At La Scala, where her performance of *Norma* had given Malibran an almost divine status, fans would stand for several hours just to see her enter the theatre. Her death sent shock waves around the opera world. Gautier and Musset both wrote poems to express their grief. The impact on the Garcias was obviously even more immense, coming as it did so shortly after Manuel's death. For Pauline it was decisive, determining that she would follow in the footsteps of Maria. To Joaquina it was inconceivable that there should be no Garcia singing on the stage.

Charles de Bériot took Pauline under his wing, organizing concerts for them both. In August 1836, three weeks after turning fifteen, Pauline made her concert debut with him in Liège. By coincidence, the composer Meyerbeer – who would go on to play a crucial role in her career – was in the audience.[41] From the start, she included Spanish songs as part of her repertoire. She had sung these songs since her childhood – many had been written by her father – and these 'party pieces' must have come across as charmingly original to audiences in northern Europe, where Spanish music was still then unknown. Pauline's first public performance was a triumph. During the next eighteen months, she appeared with Charles in several concerts in Brussels (once in the presence of the Belgian royal couple), as well as in Berlin, where the Prussian king, Friedrich Wilhelm III, was so enchanted by her singing that he presented her with an emerald necklace and several times invited her to meet his family at Charlottenburg palace. It was during these visits that Pauline began her long friendship with Princess Augusta, the future Prussian queen.[42]

Inevitably, Pauline was compared to Malibran. It was a comparison she exploited. At her Paris concert debut, in December of that year, Pauline wore the same costume, a simple white dress with a black diamond, that Malibran had always worn. 'It is her sister come alive again,' wrote one critic. 'The same voice, the same singing method, the same style, a resemblance of talent that confounds, and yet not the slightest hint of imitation!' The poet Musset, the archpriest of the cult of Malibran, thought the resemblance 'so striking that it appears supernatural'.[43]

What Musset had idealized in Malibran he now saw in her sister: her exotic Spanish origins; her fiery, melancholic temperament; her freedom of expression; her natural appearance; and, above all, the purity of her singing, without any excess of virtuosity or Romantic effect. 'She abandons herself to inspiration with that easy simplicity which gives everything an air of grandeur,' Musset wrote. 'She sings as she breathes.'[44] Musset fell in love with her, and courted her relentlessly. He had met Pauline at a musical soirée organized by Madame Caroline Jaubert, one of Musset's former mistresses, and pursued the young singer. In the *Revue des deux mondes*, where he was a regular writer, Musset praised her singing to the skies. Using his connections, he opened doors for her to the most important salons of Paris.

The relatively small size of the music world, even in a city like Paris, meant that artists were heavily dependent on influential critics and patrons to promote their talent. Madame Jaubert's lively salon was one of a growing number in the fashionable Faubourg Saint-Germain to favour musical performances and conversations about art and music over political gossip. The weekly salon was attended by well-connected intellectuals, among them Prince Belgiojoso, the sculptor Jean-Auguste Barre and the Mussets, Alfred and his brother Paul, who shared a love of music, and adored Pauline. They organized her Paris concert debut in the Salle Ventadour on 15 December 1838, and spread in conversation and writing the conviction that she was a rising star.[45]

On the back of her success, Pauline spent the next spring in London, where she performed in two private concerts for Queen Victoria and made her opera debut as Desdemona in Rossini's *Otello* at Her Majesty's Theatre on 9 May 1839. Her mother had negotiated a very handsome fee, 6,000 francs (around £240) for her six performances, more than any other singer had ever been paid for a first appearance in London.[46] 'The public received me as if I were a returning favourite rather than a foreigner performing for them for the first time,' Pauline wrote to a friend on 13 May.

> I was so emotional that my voice choked during the first act. But in the second, as their interest grew, I gained in strength and confidence, and by the end I was no longer terrified of the public . . . I was called back many times and repeated several airs. At the end of the [second] act, the whole of the stalls were on their feet, waving their cravats and hand-kerchiefs with frenetic cheers.[47]

The press reviews were ecstatic. 'There could be no doubt in anyone who saw that Desdemona on that night,' wrote the *Athenaeum* critic Henry Chorley of 'this new Garcia', that 'another great career was begun'.[48]

In London she received a visit from a certain Louis Viardot, a well-known journalist and man of letters, art collector and critic, Spanish expert and historian, who had recently become the director of the Théâtre Italien. A handsome and distinguished-looking man, then just turning forty, with finely barbered sideburns and moustache, Viardot had come to see if she would sing for his theatre. He seemed prepared to satisfy her monetary demands, declaring his belief in her talent as the equal of her sister's, whom he had known. On his appointment to the Théâtre Italien he had received a letter from Charles de Bériot rec-ommending Pauline in such high terms that he thought at once of signing her as his new star.[49]

Louis Viardot was born in 1800 in Dijon, where his father was the Procurator General in the Court of Appeal. As a law student at the Sorbonne, he became an opera fan, spending every sou he could afford at the Théâtre Italien. It was there, in 1819, that he first heard Manuel Garcia sing in *Don Giovanni*. He skimped on meals to save for a ticket in the second balcony. For the next three years he did not miss a performance by Garcia or his family. He became a trusted friend and adviser to Malibran, who turned to him in her despair when she became pregnant with the child of Charles de Bériot in 1830 and needed legal help in seeking a divorce from Eugène Malibran.[50] Viardot was level-headed, kind and principled, with a fierce commitment to individual liberty, including the promotion of women's equal rights. He was the best man possible for Malibran to turn to in her desperate plight.

Viardot's attraction to the Garcias was strengthened by his interest in Spain. In 1823, a French expeditionary force of 60,000 troops was mandated by the five great powers at the Congress of Verona to invade Spain and restore the absolutist power of King Ferdinand VII, who had been imprisoned for the past three years by the leaders of a parliamentary government. Having graduated from law school, Viardot joined the expedition, considering it an 'opportunity to see the world'. Later he would come to view the restoration as a 'crime against the nascent constitutionalism of Spain'. But at the time he reconciled the trip with his democratic conscience by serving not as a soldier but as a provisioner to the French troops in Seville. He was proud of his military title ('*garde-magasin de liquides*'), because at the time of the Spanish Armada, in 1588, Cervantes had also worked as a supplier to the fleet based in Seville.[51]

The two years he spent in Seville began a life-long engagement with Spanish art and literature – one that would be shared by several generations of Frenchmen – and turned him from a lawyer into a writer. In the first of many books on Spain, *Lettres d'un Espagnol*, an epistolary novel published in two volumes in 1826, Viardot's impressions of the country animated his account of a French officer journeying through Andalusia – one of the 'most backward parts of Europe', ruined by the power of feudal institutions and the Church (and the French occupation), which 'needed to be opened to the influence of other European cultures for its civilization to develop'.[52] It was a founding statement of his cultural philosophy of internationalism.

Back in Paris, Viardot turned more and more to writing political commentary. Under the pseudonym of 'Y . . .' he appeared regularly in *Le Globe*, a literary journal that became increasingly vocal in its opposition to the reactionary French king, Charles X.[53] From 1830, *Le Globe* became the organ of the Saint-Simonians, an early socialist movement to which Viardot was loosely connected.

Viardot would not only write but take action too. He participated in the 1830 July Revolution, which replaced Charles with his more liberal cousin, Louis Philippe, the Duc d'Orléans, at the head of the July Monarchy. On the morning of 30 July, the last of the three days of the uprising, Viardot was in the offices of *Le Globe* preparing the first bulletin on the victory of the Revolution, when a young journalist charged by the Commission of the Hôtel de Ville to take control of the *préfecture de police* came in search of help. The two men went armed with rifles to the prefecture, which they occupied for the next twenty-four hours, getting the administration back to work and restoring the free movement of goods into Paris, which had been blocked by the militias during the fighting.[54]

In August 1830, the liberal Spanish exiles in Paris nominated Viardot as the leader of a 'revolutionary committee' to promote democracy in Spain. Louis Philippe had supported the initiative but his appointed government, led by Casimir-Pierre Périer (1831–2), turned out to be more conservative: it renounced foreign intervention, in the name of revolution in particular, and closed down Viardot's committee. Viardot joined the opposition to the July Monarchy. He became a journalist for radical republican journals, writing mainly about opera, theatre, art and politics, and worked as an editor of *La Revue républicaine*.[55] By the end of the 1830s, he was considered one of the major figures in the intellectual circles of Paris.

A fire started by an overheated stovepipe swept through the Théâtre Italien on 14 January 1838. The Salle Favart was destroyed. One of the directors of the theatre, Carlo Severini, burned to death.[56] Viardot stepped in to get the theatre back onto its feet, moving it to temporary quarters in the Théâtre de l'Odéon, and in June he was appointed its director on a salary of 12,000 francs a year. Viardot was respected for his business acumen – in addition to his journalism he also ran a city transport company which he called a 'social enterprise'.[57] But the key to his appointment was his friendship with the Spanish banker Alejandro Aguado, the Marquis de Las Marismas, a major power in the European opera world.[58]

Born in 1784 into one of Seville's leading noble families, Aguado had enrolled in the Spanish army, but went over to the French in 1810, when Napoleon's forces conquered Andalusia. He became an aide-de-camp to Marshal Soult, helping him in the wholesale pillaging of Spanish art and exporting it to France. When the French troops were expelled from Spain, he left with them and set up as a merchant in Paris, later becoming a financial broker for Spanish investors in France. His breakthrough came in 1823, when the heavily indebted Spanish government was forced to take a loan from France, its main protector following the intervention of that year. As one of the key players in setting up the loan, Aguado made a profit of around 5 million francs. From this point he acted as the Spanish government's banker, securing loans for it from the financial markets in Paris, and by the end of the 1820s he had amassed a fortune of over 20 million francs. He owned several mansions in Paris, the Château de Petit-Bourg in Évry-sur-Seine, a hunting estate at Grossouvre in the Cher, and in 1835, when he was even richer from securing loans for Algeria and Greece, he bought Château Margaux, the famous wine estate.[59]

Eager to convert his immense wealth into 'symbolic capital', Aguado bought up newspapers and amassed a collection of 400 paintings by the old masters (including 17 by Velázquez, 55 Murillos, 13 Zurbaráns, and 4 Rembrandts), which he opened to the public in 1837. Spanish art was little known in France until that time, but the opening of Aguado's gallery coincided with a growing interest, reflected in the founding of the Musée Espagnol by Louis Philippe in 1838. To publicize his gallery, Aguado commissioned Viardot, recognized as a connoisseur of Spanish painting, to write a study of the masters it contained for a book of engravings.[60]

Opera was Aguado's biggest interest and the focus of his lavish spending in Paris. A close friend of Rossini, he commissioned works from him, gave him large amounts of money, showered him with gifts, and opened up his palaces to him (Rossini wrote his operas Le Comte Ory and William Tell during his extended stays at Petit-Bourg in 1828–9).[61] It was through Rossini that Aguado became more involved in managing the Théâtre Italien and the Paris Opéra.

The Théâtre Italien was the first to fall to his control. In July 1829, the royal court signed a contract with Édouard Robert to run the theatre as a private enterprise for a period of fifteen years. Recommended by Rossini, Robert was Aguado's man, his 'pawn' (prête-nom), as he was described by the Paris prefect of police, who oversaw the royal theatres. The contract set a number of conditions for the director-entrepreneur to maintain the theatre in its 'present state of glory', for which the court would pay him an annual subsidy of 70,000 francs. His side of the contract was guaranteed by a surety (cautionnement) of 100,000 francs deposited by Aguado.[62]

The model set by this contract was then extended to the Opéra in a reform of February 1831. The July Revolution had added force to the idea that the theatre should be run as a business without burdening the public purse. The Opéra had amassed colossal debts, despite its growing subsidies during the 1820s. Its privileged position became a target for the liberal opposition, which also called for a renovation of its conservative repertoire. In February 1831, the government appointed a 'director-entrepreneur' to run it as a business for the next six years with an obligation to maintain it 'in the state of magnificence and splendour' appropriate for a national theatre. It was a form of public–private partnership. The director would receive a subsidy, which would be reduced as he brought the Opéra back into profit. The man chosen for this role was Louis-Désiré Véron, a doctor, journalist and businessman, who had made a small fortune by marketing a chest ointment for common colds. Like Robert, he was placed in the office by Aguado, who paid 200,000 of the 250,000 francs required as a surety.[63]

For the next ten years, Aguado effectively controlled the two main opera houses in Paris. He paid the surety for every director and spent a fortune on financing them.[64] The theatres' running costs were far higher than their subsidies and receipts from ticket sales: they depended on the Spanish banker to survive. Aguado's losses were considerable (at least 50,000 francs a year), but they were more than compensated for by the prestige which he gained. At the Salle Le Peletier he sat in the royal box, which had a sumptuously furnished antechamber and a private toilet (*lieu à l'anglaise*) for the king and queen. On the marriage of Ferdinand-Philippe, the Duc d'Orléans and heir to the throne, to the Duchess Hélène of Mecklenburg–Schwerin in 1837, Aguado gave his box as a wedding gift to the royal couple (and then had a similar but bigger suite converted from two other boxes for himself). After each performance, that night's takings were counted on a table placed outside Aguado's box, where he waited for the sum to be announced. Such was the banker's influence that at the Opéra, where a ballet was mandatory in any production, the costumes worn by the dancers were fashioned in a Spanish style and their fabrics put on sale in the theatre's shop, the *Garde-robe d'Aguado*, which opened in 1838. Fashionable members of the audience started coming dressed *à l'espagnol*.[65]

On his appointment by Aguado to the Théâtre Italien, Viardot looked for ways to bring it back into profit. One way of making opera pay was to combine the management of several theatres and share the singers between them. Barbaja had successfully combined the running of La Scala with the Italian season at the Kärntnertortheater in Vienna during the 1820s. Rossini had encouraged Aguado to think of Paris, London and Naples as the basis of an opera empire which he might build up by running them together as a single enterprise. Covent Garden and the San Carlo theatres were both in financial crisis in the 1830s, so their leases might be cheaply acquired. Viardot wrote a memorandum for the Spanish banker in which he proposed a merger of the two Paris opera houses with Covent Garden. It would save on costs, because the same singers could be used in both cities (the Paris season ended in the spring before the beginning of the season in London); and it could make handsome profits if a larger theatre was constructed on the site of the Salle Le Peletier to increase the audience capacity. A good case could be made to the government that France's glory would be served by a bigger opera house.[66]

In May 1839, Viardot left for London with instructions from Aguado to buy the Covent Garden lease. On 1 June, Viardot reported that the trustees would not sell; they had already rejected three offers in excess of £80,000, and were holding out, he had been told, for £90,000 (2.26 million francs). He thought that at that price a purchase still made business sense. The failing London theatre could be turned around, bringing in a profit of perhaps £6,000 (150,000 francs) a year, if it was combined with the Opéra and the Théâtre Italien. 'But for that,' he concluded, 'we must first put our affairs in Paris in order.'[67]

The fire at the Salle Favart had been a major setback for the Théâtre Italien. Its new home at the Odéon was less well located on the left bank of the Seine for its mainly right-bank clientele. To boost ticket sales for the coming autumn season, Viardot purchased three new Donizetti operas, and it was then, after hearing Pauline sing in London, that he called on her to see if she would sign for the Théâtre Italien.

His negotiations with her mother, then still acting as her manager, proved difficult. Joaquina was no fool. She knew what price she could earn for her daughter and did not hesitate to turn down any offer if it fell short.[68] The deal she struck with Viardot was expensive for the Théâtre Italien. Pauline would be paid 4,500 francs a month, 27,000 for the whole season, and take half the profits from a benefit, a sum guaranteed by the management to be at least 5,000 francs. 'I do not know if the financial conditions will appear to you a little hard,' Viardot wrote to Aguado on 1 June,

> but I have always thought, and you have shared my opinion, that we need to engage Pauline Garcia, at any price, whatever success she may have or not in the future. In effect, more than staying at the Odéon, what matters most is to push up sales of season tickets so as to ensure the theatre's income independently of the artists' or productions' chances of success. The best way for certain is to pique in advance the curiosity of your *parroquianos* [parishioners] by promising them a new and already celebrated talent.[69]

Pauline returned to Paris on her own to begin rehearsals at the Théâtre Italien in September. She wrote to Joaquina in Brussels saying how she wished she was in Paris for her debut there and that she had kept a room for her in case she came. She felt let down that Charles de Bériot had left Paris on a concert tour days before her premiere.[70] In the absence of her mother and Charles she must have become more dependent on Viardot. She needed the protection of a manager against rival prima donnas, jealous of the highly paid and heavily promoted newcomer. Despite the malicious rumours which they circulated against her, Pauline made a brilliant debut in the part of Desdemona in Rossini's *Otello* on 8 October.

Musset praised her to the skies in the *Revue des deux mondes*. 'The whole of Paris was drawn to the Odéon' for the first night, he wrote. 'There was a moment of silence when Mlle Garcia entered on the stage. The young artist was visibly moved, she hesitated, but before she was able to open her mouth, she was greeted by unanimous applause from all parts of the theatre. Was it the memory of her sister that had moved us to do that?' Whereas Malibran had played Desdemona as a 'Venetian heroine – love, anger, terror, everything about her was exuberant,' Musset wrote, her younger sister played her in a manner that was truer to Rossini, 'as a girl who loves naively, who wishes to be pardoned for her love, who weeps in the arms of her father at the very moment when he is about to curse her, and has courage only at the moment of her death'. The public was delighted by her innocent appearance (she wore a plain white dress to conjure memories of her sister), by the naturalness of her acting, without grand dramatic gestures, and by the purity of her singing. Some were bemused by the freshness of her performance, the likes of which had not been seen before. Marie d'Agoult was ill-disposed towards Pauline. She wrote to Liszt that the young singer was 'ugly, badly dressed, and ungainly'. Yet even she acknowledged that she had a 'magnificent voice', which elevated her role to tragic heights in spite of these 'blemishes'. Pauline had the air of 'a proud and noble woman with an immense future before her', d'Agoult reluctantly concluded. Two decades later, in his history of the nineteenth-century French theatre, Gautier wrote about her debut that 'no one could forget her adorable gaucherie and naiveté worthy of the frescoes of Giotto'.[71]

Pauline's debut was the talk of Paris, and everybody wanted to meet her. Viardot introduced her to George Sand, who had recently returned from her country house at Nohant in central France with the composer Chopin, her lover. A great fan of Malibran, Sand went to hear her sister sing, and at once pronounced her to be 'the first, the only great and true singer', a 'priestess of the ideal in music'. Sand befriended the young star. Old enough to be her mother (she was thirty-five), Sand became her champion and counsellor, her 'maternal and dearest friend', as Pauline addressed her in their many letters during the 1840s. 'It seems to me,' Sand wrote in her diary, 'that I love Pauline with the same sacred love I have for my son and daughter, and to all those tender feelings I add enthusiasm inspired by her genius.'[72]

The writer saw Pauline as the embodiment of her feminist ideal of artistic freedom and autonomy. She would use her as the model for her heroine in *Consuelo*, a romantic saga serialized in 1842–3 in *La Revue indépendante*, a left-wing journal she had founded with Louis Viardot and Pierre Leroux in 1841.[73] Consuelo is a simple Spanish girl with a divine operatic gift. She arrives in Venice in the 1750s, becomes a leading singer in the courts of Europe, and, because she is devoted to her art, refuses to be tied down by any man or marriage, although in a sequel, *The Countess of Rudolstadt* (1843), she is reunited with Albert, a loyal spiritual companion, and eventually marries him. Sand based her heroine on what she wanted Pauline to become. She tried to shape the real life of her young friend and protégée, as she had shaped the story of her heroine.

Sand was determined to protect Pauline from the amorous attentions of Musset, who ended up proposing to the young singer.[74] Sand's own stormy love affair with the romantic poet had left her deeply wounded, not least by his treatment of her infidelities in his auto-biographical novel, *The Confession of a Child of the Century* (1835). Knowing him to be a womanizer and libertine, Sand thought that Musset was unsuitable as a suitor for Pauline, who needed a more stable and undemanding husband to pursue her career (a view shared by Pauline's other female patron, Caroline Jaubert).[75] Sand had in mind her old friend Louis Viardot, who was in any event already showing a keen interest in Pauline, inviting her and Joaquina to his house for dinner with Aguado, Donizetti and the painter Ary Scheffer.[76]

Viardot had all the qualities required to fulfil the role of Pauline's husband, manager, protector, friend and spiritual companion. Old enough to be her father, he was not driven by the egotism of a younger and artistic man such as Musset, and would not have any problem putting her career first, supporting it indeed with his business skills in theatre management. He had excellent connections in society, in the artistic, literary and theatre worlds. By taking on the role of Pauline's manager, he could promote her career more effectively than her mother Joaquina, who as a woman was at a disadvantage in the opera business, despite her undoubted strengths. Viardot, in addition, would give Pauline the respectability that her sister never had because of her scandalous affair with Charles de Bériot. Since the death of Malibran there had been malicious rumours that Bériot, who had led Pauline's concert tours to London, Brussels, Leipzig and Berlin, had in turn been having an affair with her and was about to marry her.[77] Worried that such gossip might ruin her career in its infancy, Sand urged Pauline to accept Viardot's offer of marriage, and recommended him to Joaquina as not just her daughter's husband but her manager.

This was not to be a marriage of passion. Louis was a decent, kind and intelligent man. He stirred deep feelings of friendship and affection in Pauline but not strong romantic emotions. She depended on his advice and support (without them she would have been lost) and felt blessed to have him as her husband. But she was 'unable to return his deep and ardent love, despite the best will in the world', as she herself once confessed.[78]

In a revealing letter to her confidante and friend, the German composer and conductor, Julius Rietz, in 1858, Pauline introduced her husband thus:

You will get to know him as an admirable man with a sensitive soul. He looks very cold, but is not so. His heart is warm and good, and his mind is far superior to mine. He worships art, and thoroughly appreciates the beautiful and the sublime. His only fault is that he lacks the childlike element, the impressionable mood. But is that not splendid to have *just one* fault! Perhaps in his youth he did not even have that fault. I did not know him yet when he was a young man – too bad – I was not born then.[79]

To write about her husband to another man like that suggests that Pauline felt a high degree of emotional freedom. She had no internal brake to prevent her from developing – as she would in the years to come – a series of intimate relationships with men more suited than Louis to her passionate and playful temperament. Louis was too calm and sensible, too reasonable and staid, to satisfy what she herself described as her 'demonstrative and southern character'. She was capable of loving Viardot, according to Sand, 'only in a certain way, tenderly, chastely, generously, greatly without storms, without intoxication, without suffering, without passion in a word'.[80]

They were married on 18 April 1840 in a civil ceremony at the Mairie of the 2nd *arrondissement*. Pauline was eighteen and Louis thirty-nine. Musset was sour about losing out, and claimed to friends he had been treated badly both by Pauline and by Sand. He drew a cruel satirical cartoon strip of Viardot's courtship of Pauline and their wedding: the theatre manager is handicapped by his gigantic nose, which turns to dust when Sand makes a speech on his behalf to win him the consent of Pauline's mother for her hand. The image of Viardot was henceforth to be linked to this mythically proportioned nose, which frequently appeared in drawings of him in the press.

They spent an extended honeymoon in Italy, a popular destination for well-off newlyweds, where Louis was commissioned by the government to write a report 'on the state of the theatres and the arts'. They travelled to Milan, Bologna, Venice, Florence and then Rome, where they visited the Villa Medici, the French Academy in Rome, then under the direction of Ingres, where they met a young Charles Gounod, who had just received the Prix de Rome.

Later that summer they returned to Paris, where they set up home in rue Favart, a few steps from the old Théâtre Italien. The next year they

Part of Musset's cartoon satirizing Louis Viardot's courtship of Pauline. The captions read (in English): *left panel*: 'Superb lecture by Indiana [the heroine of George Sand's first novel] that proves as two and two equal four that the more a man has nothing, the more one must give one's daughter to him. Mr V. rests his nose on the backgammon table'; *right panel*: 'The nose of Mr V crumbles into dust at the end of Indiana's speech'.

moved to square d'Orléans, a secluded residence of Nash-style mansions built in 1829 by the English architect Edward Cresy, where Sand and Chopin lived in separate apartments.[81]

On their marriage Louis had announced his resignation as director of the Théâtre Italien, a post he felt he could not hold without a conflict of interest. He now took on the role of Pauline's business manager, negotiating all her fees and contracts, and handling all her earnings and her property, for which, as her husband, he was legally responsible in most countries in Europe.[82] Until 1852, all her contracts were 'duly authorized by her husband' and signed by him. Later contracts were signed by herself but even then it was noted that she had been 'duly assisted by her husband'.[83] Because of the theatre's reputation for immorality, the laws for married women on the stage tended to be stricter in subordinating them to the control of their husbands than they would be otherwise. Under the Napoleonic Code, which ruled in France and strongly influenced the laws of other countries in the nineteenth century, women could not sign a contract without the consent of their husband, but they were allowed to act in business on their own. Jurists argued, however, that in the case of women in the theatre business a husband should retain the right to break a contract he had previously approved on grounds of morality and the protection of his family.[84]

Being the wife of Louis Viardot, an influential man in the theatre world with close links to Aguado, was not the ticket to success Pauline's supporters had imagined it would be. Aguado might have helped her on the Paris stage, but in 1840 his influence was cut by the government, which opposed his merger plans and forced him to accept its own choice of director at the Opéra, Léon Pillet, a man Aguado could not stand (he immediately reduced his investment there from 300,000 francs to 150,000 francs a year). Then, in 1842, Aguado died in a carriage accident in Spain, whereupon his widow sold his opera interests.[85]

Once the power of Aguado was removed, the opera world of Paris descended into a welter of petty rivalries. Pauline found her career blocked by rival prima donnas and their supporters. At the Opéra, she was obstructed by Rosine Stolz, a singer known for her passionate excess, who was the mistress of Pillet.[86] Too weak to resist her influence, Pillet would not let an opera be staged without his mistress in the leading role. Stolz employed a claque to organize applause and cheering for herself. She intrigued against Pauline, paying journalists to spread the rumour that she was too mercenary to reach an agreement with the Opéra's management. Louis became so frustrated that he launched an attack on the Opéra, accusing it of bias and incompetence, in *La Revue indépendante*, in December 1841. It was not the most effective way of promoting Pauline's cause.[87]

Meanwhile at the Théâtre Italien the new management was reluctant to employ Pauline for fear of alienating their own prima donna, Giulia Grisi, the Italian soprano, then at the height of her powers. Grisi was ten years older than Pauline, and feared her as a rival. When at last Pauline was engaged for one season, beginning in October 1842, Grisi employed a claque to greet her own arias with loud applause and *brava*s while hissing at Pauline's. Grisi also bribed the leading critics to heap lavish praise on her own performances and scorn on those of her competitor. The critics of the *Revue des deux mondes*, the *Revue de Paris*, *Le Ménestrel* and *Le Moniteur* were all in her pay. The most vicious attack came from Henri Blaze de Bury in the *Revue des deux mondes* on 1 December. The real target of the article was not only Pauline but her husband, one of the founders and main financier of *La Revue indépendante*, the rival publication to the *Revue des deux mondes*.[88] Feeling honour-bound to defend his wife, Louis wrote a pompous letter to the newspaper *Le Siècle*, explaining the real motive of Blaze de Bury, who only three years previously, on her debut at the Théâtre Italien, had praised Pauline to the skies. 'There are good-hearted people who strike a woman in order to wound a man,' concluded Viardot.[89]

Blocked in Paris, Pauline was obliged to tour abroad. In 1841, she spent a second season in London, a city she disliked, complaining to George Sand that its citizens were dull and over-formal, and 'one had to flatter their bad taste'.[90] The next summer, following the birth of their first child, Louise, Pauline went on a concert tour of Spain accompanied by Louis as her manager. The reception she received was ecstatic. In Granada, in the stifling heat, huge crowds thronged outside the theatre, pushing at the door in desperate efforts to get in. Black-market ticket prices soared.[91] It was the first time she had visited the country of her parents. As she recalled many decades later, it all seemed strangely familiar to her: 'Everything I saw, it seemed, I had seen before, everything I heard I thought I had heard before . . . the people I encountered seemed to reappear from my own dreams . . . I felt as if this was my true homeland. But that did not mean that I wanted to live there.'[92]

Sand wrote that she was following her tour in the newspapers with Chopin and Delacroix at Nohant, where she was also taking care of the baby Louise. 'You have your foot in one stirrup, that is Spain. You need to put your foot in a second stirrup, which will be Italy, and then you will ride through France and England at a great gallop.' The three friends agreed, she reported, that Pauline was the greatest singer in the world, that one day it would be obvious, 'to the vulgar as well as the connoisseurs', that she had made rapid progress before suffering a set-back (her exclusion from the Paris Opéra), and that to advance she needed to adopt a different route. She was sure that 'our Loulou [Louis], once he had reflected and discussed it with you, would give you the same advice':

The fact is that France and England are too *blasé* and their taste is too corrupted not to stifle – so far as they are able – the development of a young artist, above all when that artist is a woman, faithful and modest, devoid of intrigue or impropriety. You must return to these cold countries with a renown so well-made abroad that the cabals against you only serve to strengthen you. It must be that the newspapers with their ignorant and petty, pedantic criticism in bad faith, do not come every morning to push you right and left. You must by enthusiasm reign in the less sceptical and less dogmatic countries, and for a few years *the newspaper countries* [Sand's emphasis] must only record and draw attention to your successes, without being able to analyse them and pick them to pieces. It must come about, in sum, that the imbecile public, which thinks itself such a great connoisseur but is so far from it, because of its lack of heart, desires you, calls for you, demands that you return.

The conclusion was that Pauline should continue on her tours, and not return to Paris until her fame forced her enemies to give way. 'Paris without an engagement at the theatre would be like a grave for you.'[93]

The Viardots agreed, and, as Pauline's manager, Louis soon began negotiations with La Scala and Berlin. The next spring, from April to

Meyerbeer, 1847.

July, they were in Vienna, where Pauline triumphed as Rosina in *The Barber of Seville* and as *La Cenerentola*. On the opening night there were no fewer than a dozen curtain calls; each time flowers were thrown onto the stage, which was completely covered by them, as she herself reported to George Sand. The Viennese had 'not heard anybody sing like that before', recalled Princess Metternich in her memoirs. From Vienna they travelled on to Prague, where Pauline found the public to be 'very intelligent and very enthusiastic', and from there continued to Berlin. On her previous concert tours she had struggled to make an impression on the Prussians, who were known for their relative decorum as theatre-goers. But this time she was able to report to Sand: 'the cold Berliners have suddenly become as hot as the Viennese'.[94]

It was in Berlin that Pauline first met the composer Meyerbeer, a powerful figure in the European music world whose spectacular *Robert le diable* (1831) and *Les Huguenots* (1836) had been huge hits throughout the Continent. Meyerbeer was the *Kapellmeister* (musical director) at the Prussian court and (from 1843) the *Generalmusikdirektor* of the Berlin Opera. A keen admirer of Pauline's voice and acting qualities, he arranged for her to sing at Potsdam for the Prussian king, Friedrich Wilhelm. Meyerbeer believed that Pauline should become the prima donna at the Paris Opéra. He promised her that he would not allow his operas to be put on there unless she appeared in them. 'Meyerbeer has plans for me,' Pauline wrote excitedly to Sand in August 1843. 'He tells anybody he can get to listen that for him I am the greatest artist in the universe, that it is me he wants at the Opéra.'[95]

Meyerbeer was a powerful ally, but even his support was not enough to overcome the opposition in Paris. As a result, shortly after their return to the French capital, in September 1843, the Viardots accepted the contract for the coming autumn season in St Petersburg. 'I can announce with heated excitement that the engagement for St Petersburg was signed an hour ago and we are all *very* happy,' Pauline wrote to Sand on 20 September, 'all the more because this *grand parti* is advantageous in a thousand different ways.'[96] Their motives for the trip were commercial: the money she was offered by the Russians was just too good to refuse. Russia was a lucrative new market for Italian opera, and Pauline needed it, not just for the huge fees she would earn, but because, as George Sand had advised, she needed more successes to draw attention to herself in the 'newspaper countries' such as France.

In the first week of October, the Viardots departed on the long and arduous journey from Paris via Berlin to St Petersburg. The French railways were only just beginning to be built, so from Paris to the Belgian border they had to travel by stagecoach. But from there they could connect to the newly finished railway between Antwerp and Cologne. Crossing western Prussia by mail coach, they reached Hanover on their sixth day on the road. From there they could go by train to Magdeburg, continuing their journey by horse and carriage to Potsdam, where there was a rail link to Berlin. There was no railway for the last part of their journey from the Prussian capital, so they travelled the remaining 1,600 kilometres to St Petersburg by *Schnellpost*, the fastest German carriage, as far as the Russian frontier, and then by *kibitka*, a closed wagon drawn by horses over muddy, bumpy roads.

2

The first international railway, between Antwerp and Cologne, had only just opened, and the Viardots must have been among the first to travel on the line. The new railway was a vital boost to international trade. Goods from lands with access to the Rhine could now be transported via Aachen and Liège to Antwerp's harbour on the River Scheldt, and from there by ship to the rest of the world.

There were festivals to mark its opening in Cologne, Aachen and Antwerp, where the main theme was the unity of Belgium with Prussia's Rhine province. 'Our customs, habits, desires, our interests are the same. We feel the same impulse to business, and we are inspired by the same love for art and science,' declared the Mayor of Antwerp at a banquet for 500 people in his city's Stock Exchange.[97]

The King of Prussia was not there. As a member of the Holy Alliance, established by the three great conservative powers (Russia, Austria and Prussia) at the 1815 Congress of Vienna, Friedrich Wilhelm would not recognize the Belgian state, founded by a revolution in July 1830, and saw it as a growing threat to Prussia's Rhineland interests, not least through its 'ultramontane' movement linking Belgian Catholics with Rhenish Catholics. He feared that the railway between Antwerp and Cologne might unify the Rhineland with Belgium and prise it away from Prussia. The Rhenish bourgeoisie admired Belgium's freedoms. It invested heavily in the international line, wanting closer trade links with Belgium. From its very start, the railway weakened national frontiers.

With a second railway from Antwerp via Brussels to Mons in the south, Belgium was soon crossed by two main routes – one from east to west, the other north to south – connecting its main cities, ports and industrial regions. The network also opened Belgium to its four neighbours: Britain, France, the Netherlands and the patchwork of independent states that made up Germany.

Within a few years of the opening of the Cologne–Antwerp line, national boundaries were being crossed by railways everywhere. In 1846, the line from Paris to Brussels was completed when the Compagnie des Chemins de Fer du Nord opened the French section as far as Lille. The Chemin de Fer du Nord soon connected Paris to the Channel ports of Boulogne, Dunkirk and Calais, from which a steamer took only three hours to reach England. By 1848, there were railways linking France to Switzerland, Switzerland to Baden and Hesse, Bavaria to Saxony and Prussia, Brunswick to Hanover and Holland. The Austrians had a railway from Vienna to Prague and were building another through the Semmering mountains to Trieste, their only seaport. The Russian Empire had a railway line from Warsaw to the Austrian border, where trains went through to Vienna.

The railway was *the* symbol of industrial progress and modernity. It defined the 'modern age', consigning horse-drawn transport to the 'old world'. 'We who lived before the railways and survive the ancient world are like Father Noah and his family out of the Ark,' declared William Makepeace Thackeray.[98] The railways brought about a revolution in the European sense of space and time. Broad new vistas opened up and countries seemed to shrink in size as remote hinterlands were brought closer to cities. 'I feel as if the mountains and forests of all countries are advancing on Paris. Even now, I can smell the German linden trees; the North Sea breakers are rolling against my door,' Heine wrote on the opening of two lines from Paris (one to Orléans, the other to Rouen) in 1843.[99]

The power of the railways to unite people was seized upon immediately. They were seen as a democratic force. Reflecting on a train ride from Versailles to Paris, Jules Michelet, the historian, wrote that, where the palace was the caprice of a king, the railways were 'for everybody's use, bringing France together, uniting Lyon with Paris'.[100] Reactionaries feared the railways' democratic influence. Pope Gregory XVI banned them in the Papal States for this reason, while the Crown Prince of Hanover was equally opposed to them because he did 'not want every shoemaker and tailor travelling as fast' as him.[101]

Goethe saw the railways as a unifying force for Germany, a vision shared by the German economist Friedrich List in his influential work, *The National System of Political Economy* (1841). List envisaged a railway system for the whole of Germany, with six lines radiating out of Berlin to Munich, Basel, Cologne, and connecting Germany to neighbouring countries. The railways, he maintained, were the driving force of national development, allowing trade and industries to grow, promoting a common culture, and weakening provincial isolation and narrow-mindedness. He even thought the railways would facilitate the development of a Europe-wide economy.

List was not alone in seeing the potential of the railways to unite Europe. Camillo Cavour, the Minister of Finance, who oversaw the building of the railways in Piedmont, believed more broadly in their cultural mission to 'raise the civic spirit of the backward nations of Europe', by which he largely meant the rest of the Italians.[102] In France, Victor Hugo spoke about them as the locomotive of progress, leading to a global culture with a single language, French: *'On va en wagon et l'on parle français.'* In Britain there were predictions that the railroad would transform the world of nations into 'one large family speaking one language and worshiping a single God'.[103]

But no one believed in the unifying force of the railways more than the Saint-Simonians, who saw in them the realization of the French Revolution's ideals of fraternity between nations. 'To foreshorten for everyone the distances that separate localities from each other is to equally diminish the distances that separate men from one another,' wrote the Saint-Simonian thinker Constantin Pecqueur in a book of 1839 whose central argument – that changes in material conditions produce changes in the cultural sphere – was a major influence on Marx's materialist philosophy.[104]

Marx himself was keenly conscious of the railways' impact on the circulation of commodities. In the *Grundrisse* (1857–8) he analysed the 'annihilation of space by time' through the railways, steamships and the telegraph, enabling commerce to be globalized. By cutting transport costs, the railways opened new markets to a whole range of products: fresh fish could now reach inland towns; wines from France or Italy became known throughout Europe. During the previous 300 years, the volume of world trade had risen slowly at less than 1 per cent per year; but between 1820 and 1870 it shot up by 4.18 per cent every year.[105]

It was not just commodities that circulated wider and faster, but people, letters, news and information, leading to a widening public sense in all the railway nations of belonging to 'Europe'. The connection between the growth of international commerce and the development of a pan-European or 'cosmopolitan' culture was indeed emphasized by many leading thinkers, including Kant, Goethe and Marx. Before the railways it was not uncommon for citizens to spend their whole lives in the town where they were born. 'A journey of a hundred miles,' recalled an English writer in the 1890s, 'was then looked upon with greater apprehension than a journey round the globe is at present.'[106] The fastest mode of long-distance travel was by stagecoach or diligence, which even on macadam roads could not go faster than 10–12 kilometres an hour, allowing time for horses to be changed.

The arrival of the railways did not transform times of travel overnight. It took years for lines to be completed, so passengers were forced to switch from train to carriage for those sections of their journey where the railway was not yet built, as the Viardots had done on their first voyage to St Petersburg. Similarly, in July 1849, an Italian diplomat took more than a week to reach Genoa from Ferrara, a distance of 300 kilometres as the crow flies, despite using the newly opened railway between Florence and Livorno. To reach Florence he had to cross the Apennines in a carriage, and then take another one from Pisa to Genoa.[107]

Nonetheless, the speed of railway travel was experienced as a revolution. The first trains travelled at between thirty and fifty kilometres per hour, with some reaching speeds of up to eighty kilometres per hour, causing many passengers to both marvel and take fright.[108] Before 1843, George Sand needed two days, sometimes more, to travel by mail-coach from Paris to her home at Nohant, a journey of 280 kilometres; but the opening of the railway to Orléans cut the journey time by half.[109] Five years later, in 1848, Chopin took just twelve hours to go by train from London to Edinburgh, a journey of 650 kilometres which only ten years earlier had lasted two days and a night by the fastest coach on turnpike roads.[110] Letters which had taken weeks to travel across Europe by mail-coach now arrived in a few days, and with the telegraph, which ran along the railways, news could reach the major cities in minutes. National daily newspapers were a product of the railways, which could get an evening edition from the capital to most provincial towns by the following morning. Regional newspapers were a product of the telegraph, which transmitted the main national and international headlines in a matter of seconds, so that they could report them in the paper locally.

Spreading right across the Continent, the railways also powered the international circulation of European music, literature and art. They brought about a revolution in the cultural marketplace.

A market for creative works had existed in the eighteenth century, when a public sphere developed in the form of concerts, newspapers and periodicals, private galleries and museums, enabling writers, artists and musicians to free themselves from their previous dependence on powerful patrons and sell their works to a wider society.[111] But this market was still quite small and localized. In the visual arts and music it was dominated by the networks organized around a group of noble connoisseurs, an academy of arts or opera house, and artists still depended on these personal connections to pursue their trade. The situation did not change substantially in the early decades of the nineteenth century. It was only with the arrival of railways, telegraphs, a national press and cheap methods of mass printing that the arts began to function in a more impersonal marketplace – one in which producers sold their works in forms that could be reproduced and distributed internationally.

The impact of the railways was transformational, especially in the book trade, where transport costs were cut dramatically. The international export of books from France, for example, more than doubled in volume between 1841 and 1860. For the first time the market for French books became truly global, one third of the exports going beyond Europe by 1860, when steamships made it economical to transport books to francophone Canada.[112] In the German-speaking world, the publishers of Leipzig and Berlin enjoyed a similar export boom thanks to their excellent rail connections, which cut transport costs by three quarters between 1845 and 1855.[113]

The speed with which a new creative work was now able to cross national boundaries was phenomenal. Nothing like it had been seen before. For example, on 1 September 1843, the Théâtre du Palais-Royal in Paris premiered a vaudeville about the newly opened railways, entitled

Paris, Orléans, Rouen. Published in the *Magasin théâtral*, it was adapted by the Austrian actor Johann Nestroy as *Railway Marriages, or Vienna, Neustadt, Brünn,* whose first performance took place at the Theater an der Wien only four months later, on 3 January 1844.[114]

The cultural map of Europe was redrawn by the railways. Provincial towns were drawn into the orbit of big cities, whose growth went hand in hand with the development of the railways. For Lille, for instance, the opening of the line from Paris meant more visits by touring artists from the capital (the Théâtre Italien did a season there in 1856, and again in 1865).[115] Cities with an international link became important cultural hubs in their own right. Brussels was transformed from a Flemish-speaking Brabant town into a cosmopolitan European city by its rail connections to France and Germany. The opening of the Paris–Brussels line brought in 20,000 foreign immigrants, mostly French, between 1843 and 1853.[116] The French emerged as the city's cultural élite, running theatres and museums, writing for the press, or working there as writers and artists. Because of its position between the francophone and German-speaking worlds, Brussels became an important channel for the German arts in France (many of the operas of Wagner, for example, were performed in Belgium before they were in France).

The railways also brought a new provincial public into the cities. Hotels, restaurants, shops and cafés sprang up near the railway terminals. The impact on the entertainment business was extraordinary. Previously, in the age of carriage travel, when a theatre would depend on the population of a single town and its environs, managers relied on selling season tickets to the box-holders. To keep this local public entertained, they needed constant novelty. An opera would last for a season – or less – before being dropped and forgotten. Few productions maintained their powers of attraction to survive much longer than a year or warrant a revival later on, so they simply disappeared. At La Scala, for example, 298 different operas were produced in the first four decades of the theatre's existence (from 1778 to 1826), but only thirty were repeated in a second season, and just eight in a third. Paisiello's *Barber of Seville* (1782) was the only opera to be staged in five seasons.[117] With the coming of the railways a new type of market for the theatre developed. Theatre-goers came into the cities from a wider catchment area, from distant provinces and foreign lands, pushing up demand for single-performance tickets. Released from their dependence on selling

season tickets, managers could put on longer runs of the most successful works, or bring back old productions for a second run, so that
something like a stable repertory or canon began to emerge.

The railway also made it possible for touring companies and musicians to reach a wider audience. For Pauline Viardot, who had toured
by coach and boat for years, the railways opened up exciting possibilities. She could now return to France between seasons or performances
in Germany or England, both of which had fast rail links. At the same
time, the railways made it possible for her to make money from provincial tours. Travelling on the newly opened Great Western Railway on
their way to the Three Choirs Festival at Gloucester in September 1841,
the Viardots marvelled at the 'huge horses of civilisation devouring
coal and spewing flame', as Louis called the locomotive trains.

> Peacefully seated in a vast armchair, without jolting or jarring, without
> pitching or rolling, one looks out through the window at a moving pan-
> orama, whose points of view change every second, and renew themselves
> incessantly. Villages and towns, manor houses, cottages and farms dotted
> over every hill and valley – they all flew past. We had for our journey one
> of those days interspersed with sun and rain, which allowed us to observe
> things in all their aspects of light and shade.[118]

Johann Strauss was delighted by the possibilities of railway travel in
Britain. In 1838, his orchestra performed in over thirty British towns
between April and July – a rate of travel that would have been impossible in Austria or France, where railway-building lagged behind. 'I
found myself in a different town almost daily,' Strauss wrote to the
conductor Adolf Müller at the end of his British trip, 'as one may travel
here exceedingly quickly by virtue of the good horses and excellent
roads. In particular, of great advantage to the traveller are the railways,
which mode of transport I have used extensively, e.g. in Liverpool,
Manchester, Birmingham, etc . . .'[119]

Musicians had been forced to travel constantly to make a living long
before the arrival of the railways. But the time spent on travelling by
coach, not to speak about the dangers and discomforts, ate into their
profits heavily. Berlioz would frequently complain about the 'ruinous
costs' of transporting heavy boxes of sheet music by boat and horse-
drawn carriage over pot-holed roads, claiming that they wiped out any
profit from his concert tours. But he was encouraged by the coming of

the railways to set off on a series of ambitious tours of Germany, beginning in the winter of 1842–3, taking advantage of the newly opened lines between Berlin, Magdeburg, Brunswick and Hanover. In his memoirs, Berlioz recalls an 'unusual success' at Magdeburg, where a mail office clerk, on registering his luggage, would not believe that he was the famous composer:

> No doubt the good man had imagined that this fabulous musician would be bound to travel, if not mounted in a hippogriff in a whirlwind of flame, at least with a sumptuous baggage-train and a small army of flunkeys in attendance; instead of which, here was a man who looked like any other man who has been at once smoked and chilled in a railway carriage, and who saw to the weighing of his trunk, walked by himself, did his own talking, in French, spoke no word of German but 'Ja', and was clearly an impostor.[120]

Rossini, famously, was scared of trains. It had not always been that way. On his first rail journey, between Antwerp and Brussels in 1836, he had marvelled at the speed of the train and had told his mistress, Olympe Pélissier, that he felt no fear. But something must have happened after that, an accident perhaps, because from the 1840s he refused to board a train again and travelled everywhere by horse-drawn carriages. His inability to move with modern times was symbolic. Rossini's music was firmly rooted in the world before railways: it was small-scale, it went along with the light clip-clop of a horse and carriage, and was designed for the economies of a provincial or court theatre whose public did not travel far. The composer was unable to adapt to the new conditions of the railway age, when theatres also catered to a broader middle-class public, demanding large-scale entertainments with bigger orchestras and choruses, sumptuous stage designs and spectacular effects – namely the Grand Operas, the five-act music dramas favoured by the Paris Opéra. Rossini tried but could not work with this new form. After *William Tell* (1829), his first and last attempt at it, he gave up writing operas altogether and went into retirement, settling down in Bologna. Seeking to explain his decision to retire, Rossini later wrote that opera, like any type of art, was 'inseparable from the times in which we live', that the 'idealism and sentiment' which underpinned his art had become outdated in the modern age of 'steam' and 'barricades'.[121] It is no accident that Meyerbeer, the first great composer of

Grand Opera, embraced the industrial age. He travelled on the railways all the time; he composed on trains. You can hear their pulse in his music. Meyerbeer had been a protégé of Rossini. The two men were friends, colleagues and contemporaries, but their music was the voice of two entirely different worlds.

The railways underpinned the optimism of the nineteenth century, the belief in moral progress through science and technology. Along with photography and mechanical technologies, they helped to generate a modern understanding of reality, a new sense of the 'here and now', of a world made up of movement, constant change, where everything was momentary. 'Modernity is the transient, the fleeting, the contingent', as Baudelaire put it.[122] Fresh art forms were needed to reflect this contemporary reality: an art that made sense of the modern world as it was experienced by the city dweller; an art that showed things as they actually were, not Romantic fantasies. As Theodor Fontane wrote in 1843, 'Romanticism is finished on this earth, the age of the railway has dawned.'[123]

3

Eugène Sue's *Les Mystères de Paris* was published in *Le Journal des débats* over seventeen months from June 1842 to October 1843. Set in the criminal underworld of Paris, where its hero, Prince Rodolphe, ventures on a mission to help the urban poor, the melodrama proved so popular that its serialization boosted the newspaper's sales by several thousand in only a few weeks. The number of its readers was far higher than those who could afford to pay the 80-franc subscription to *Le Journal des débats*. By some estimates, anything between 400,000 and 800,000 people read the story between 1842 and 1844. In that time there were ten translations of the novel, including six in English, at least doubling its readership. Tens of thousands of its poorest French readers bought the novel in fifty-centime instalments. Others kept up with its weekly episodes in public reading rooms, the *cabinets de lecture*, where books and journals could be read for a small fee, although demand for *Le Journal des débats* was so high that in many *cabinets* access to it needed to be timed. 'In the cafés,' noted Charles Sainte-Beuve, the literary critic, 'they fight over the *débats* in the morning;

they charge as much as ten sous for the time it takes to read the episode of Sue's story.' Groups of workers assembled in their workshops to hear the next instalment read. They wrote to Sue with comments on his passages describing the conditions of the poor, and made suggestions for plot development. The novel's characters were household names. 'Everyone is talking about your mysteries,' wrote one reader to the novelist.

> Your work is everywhere – on the worker's bench, on the merchant's counter, on the little lady's divan, on the shop-girl's table, on the office worker's and magistrate's desk. I am sure that of the entire population of Paris, only those people who cannot read do not know of your work.[124]

For middle-class subscribers of *Le Journal des débats* the novel's dark descriptions of the backstreets of Paris tapped into their fears of the city's poor. *Les Mystères de Paris* transposed the horrors of a Gothic novel to the urban underworld. It also offered hope of reconciliation between rich and poor (a point on which Marx took serious issue with Sue's politics). The novel had a popular appeal to a new class of readers created by the Guizot law of 1833, which obliged every commune or municipality to maintain a public school. What the novel meant to the newly literate shopgirl or worker is hard to tell; though, judging from the letters that many of them wrote to its author, they liked its exciting episodes, the story's twists and turns, and its characters from humble backgrounds like themselves.

The serialized novel was a cheap alternative to the standard hardbound novel format, which was too expensive for these new readers. For the newspapers it represented a marketing technique in their quest for a mass readership. The first novel to be serialized in a French newspaper was Balzac's *La Vieille Fille*, which came out in twelve daily episodes in *La Presse*, starting on 23 October 1836 – the same year as Dickens's *Pickwick Papers* began to appear in monthly shilling instalments. *La Presse* was the brainchild of Émile de Girardin, one of a new breed of commercial publishers to take advantage of the mass demand for reading matter. He worked out that subscription prices could be lowered if a bigger readership succeeded in attracting increased advertising revenue. Launched in July 1836 with an annual subscription price of only forty francs, *La Presse* tripled its daily circulation by 1845, doubling its advertising income during the same period. Adverts appeared on every page. The serialized novel, or *roman feuilleton*, was the paper's major draw. Girardin was ready to pay writers handsomely. He had been lucky to discover Sue at the lowest point of his literary career, when he had fallen into debt after his first stories had been given bad reviews. Girardin paid him by the page for his first success, *Mathilde: The Memoirs of a Young Woman*, published in *La Presse* from December 1840. It was followed by three more serials in 1842.[125]

By this time, every major newspaper was in the market for serial stories to increase circulation. Technical improvements in lithography enabled them to publish them cheaply in mass print-runs with illustrations, which added to their popularity. Editors competed for the best authors. *Le Journal des débats* had paid 26,500 francs for Sue's *Mystères*, a huge sum for a novel, but the boost it gave to the newspaper's sales meant that bids were even higher for his next novel, *Le Juif errant*. The editor of *Le Constitutionnel*, Louis Véron (the former director of the Opéra), won with a payment of 100,000 francs for Sue's family saga, reckoning that he would earn it back just by increasing subscriptions. By Véron's calculations, *Le Constitutionnel* would need to double its 40-franc subscriptions, but in fact the number rose from 3,600 to 25,000 while the story ran on its pages, and went on rising to 40,000 in the next few years as the continued popularity of *Le Juif errant* in cheap book formats and theatrical adaptions brought prestige to *Le Constitutionnel* as a source of popular fiction.[126]

Many of the most successful writers made their fortunes from the *roman feuilleton*. From *Pickwick Papers* (in 1836–7) to *Bleak House* (in 1852–3), Dickens published his bestsellers in monthly shilling instalments, switching to a weekly format for *Hard Times* in 1854. Balzac wrote on an industrial scale for the *feuilletons*. He was preoccupied with making money, because he was constantly in debt. Over twenty Balzac novels (including *Cousin Pons* and *Cousin Bette*) appeared first in newspapers between 1836 and 1850, all of them reprinted in book form. In 1847 alone, he had novels being serialized in three different newspapers. George Sand published *Consuelo* in instalments in *La Revue indépendante* between 1842 and 1843. Its appearance helped to keep the struggling journal going at a time when Louis Viardot, as the journal's financial guarantor, might have been bankrupted otherwise (this was an extra incentive for the Viardots to accept the lucrative contract for St Petersburg in 1843). In the next four years Sand wrote seven novels in serialized form – the first, *Jeanne* (1844), for *Le Constitution-nel*, which paid her handsomely, although she disliked the monthly deadlines and the need to write to the same format, complaining to Véron that she felt like his *bouche-trou* (column-filler).[127]

No one filled more column inches than Alexandre Dumas, whose long novels, *The Three Musketeers* and *The Count of Monte Cristo*, were both published in serial form, the first in *Le Siècle* from March to July 1844, the second in *Le Journal des débats* from 1844 to 1846. Dumas needed to finance an extravagant lifestyle. He had several mistresses and at least four children to support. Because they were paid for fiction by the line, writers were encouraged to string out stories by adding characters and episodes, and editors were happy to keep on printing them, as long as they sold their newspapers. *The Count of Monte Cristo* proved so popular that Dumas was able to spin it out for 139 episodes, earning him 200,000 francs at 1.5 francs per line. By the mid-1840s, he was writing several novels simultaneously for different newspapers. Nobody could work out how he found the time to churn out so much prose. The cartoonist Émile Marcelin drew Dumas at a table holding four pens between the fingers of his hands while a waiter fed him soup.[128]

Able to make do with very little sleep, Dumas would write from the morning until late at night. He composed extremely quickly, producing up to twenty large sheets every day, and leaving it to secretaries to add the punctuation to his flowing prose. He relied heavily on assistants – the most important of them being a young aspiring writer and historian, Auguste Macquet, who met Dumas in 1838. Macquet helped him with his major novels, usually writing the first draft on an idea from Dumas, and often adding his historical research, before Dumas rewrote it in finished form. Although Macquet was well paid, his name did not appear on the title page, on the insistence of the publishers, who were interested only in the Dumas brand. But rumours spread, and soon Dumas was accused of not writing everything in his own name. 'Everyone has read Dumas, but nobody has read everything of Dumas's, not even Dumas himself,' commented one wit. There were unfair claims that Dumas bought up manuscripts from literary hacks and put his name to them to profit from his popularity. One critic, a jealous rival called Eugène de Mirecourt, wrote a pamphlet (*Fabrique de romans* [The Novel Factory]: *Maison Alexandre Dumas et Compagnie*) accusing him of running a literary sweatshop in which his hired scribblers were reduced to the condition of 'black slaves working under the whip of a half-caste overseer' – a malicious reference to Dumas's own ancestry, for his grandmother was of African descent and had been enslaved on a French plantation in Haiti. Dumas won a libel case against the pamphleteer.[129] Yet the critics did not go away. What they objected to was not so much the provenance of Dumas's stories as the monetary profits which they made. Commercially successful literature was seen almost automatically as bad literature. The idea that a writer would debase himself as a 'literary merchant' – as Thackeray accused Sue of doing in a critical review of *Les Mystères* – was anathema to those who held that literature should aspire to the ideals of pure art. Among them was Sainte-Beuve, who wrote a blistering attack, 'On Industrial Literature', claiming that it transformed writing into a form of business where success was measured not by artistic merit, but by profit and celebrity. 'Money, money, money,' the critic lamented, 'we cannot overemphasize how it has become the nervous system and the god of literature today.'[130]

It was not just in the newspapers that fiction boomed. There was also a revolution in the publication of books.

At the beginning of the nineteenth century the making of a book was still a craft. The main production processes – paper-making, typecasting, composition, inking and binding – were all done by hand. Hard-bound books were expensive. In England novels were often published in three volumes – a format designed to enable libraries to lend the parts out separately – with each volume costing between five and six shillings. Since the average weekly earnings of a skilled worker were not much more than twenty shillings, or a pound, the purchase of a novel was a luxury. The restricted size of the market meant that publishers were risk-averse. They were small-scale businesses. Without capital, they were unable to make long-term investments in a book; nor could they afford to do so without effective laws of copyright, for pirate reprinters of anything successful soon ate into their profits. Instead they published small print-runs in the hope of making profits on a quick turnover, and reprinted only if the book caught on. Even when it did, they were more likely to increase its price than to sell it cheaply in a bigger print-run. The publisher of Walter Scott, Archibald Constable, cashed in on his popularity by charging the enormous sum of 10s 6d (roughly fourteen francs or $11) for each volume of his works.[131]

There had always been cheap books. Bibles, prayer books, catechisms, ballads, almanacs and popular abridgements of classic tales were sold by pedlars in large numbers. What was new in the 1830s and 1840s was the development of a commercial strategy by publishers in Britain, France and Germany to make literary works affordable to a mass readership by exploiting new technologies and increasing the print-run to achieve a lower unit cost. Between 1828 and 1853 the price of books in England came down by 40 per cent, on average, but the biggest reduction was in the price of fiction for the new mass market of readers. The novel published in three leather-bound volumes gave way to cloth or paperback editions in one volume which were cheaper to produce and easier to sell. The eighteen-shilling 'three-decker' novel in Britain was replaced by the two-shilling or 1s 6d book. In France the twenty-two-franc novel in three octavé volumes gave way to the pocket-sized editions of the Bibliothèque Charpentier and other series published by the likes of Lévy or Hachette where the whole text was contained in a single volume costing only 3.5 francs. In Germany the new (16mo) format was introduced by the publishing house of J. G. A. Cotta in its cheap twelve-volume pocket edition of Schiller's works (1837–8), which sold 100,000 copies, an unheard-of figure for German publishing at that time.[132]

The revolution in trade publishing was driven by a series of developments. The popular demand for cheaper books was a result of the growth of literacy in the middle decades of the nineteenth century. In France the number of adult readers rose by 21 per cent in the 1830s, by a further 18 per cent in the next decade, and by 21 per cent again during the 1850s.[133] More people had a bit of extra cash to spend on books. A middling British family with an annual income of around £200 (5,000 francs) could afford to spend a pound or two on books and music every year. Leisure time increased. The introduction of gas lighting had a transformative effect, making it much easier to read or play the piano in the evenings, turning these home entertainments into the main leisure activities of 'respectable' families.

New technologies made book production cheaper: paper-making was increasingly mechanized, reducing its cost by around half in the early decades of the nineteenth century; hand-sewn leather bindings were replaced by machine-bound cloth covers; and steam-powered presses made large-scale printing possible. The real breakthrough in mechanized printing was the revolving cylinder machine, the basis of the rotary press, invented in 1843, which used a curved stereotype to move back and forth across the inked printing plate. Cast from a papier-mâché mould, the stereotype was more durable than moveable print and could last for thousands of impressions before it needed recasting. The mould could be stored and used for reprinting, allowing publishers to respond to demand if sales were good from the first print-run, rather than having to reassemble the type. Stereotypes also made it easy to reprint the instalments of serialized novels and bind them as a book, a form of publishing which flourished during the 1840s.

The boom in book production was astonishing. So many books were being published that some people feared the market would be swamped. One writer estimated that the books produced in France in a single year would go round the world if they were placed end to end. The number of new titles registered in the *Bibliographie de la France* rose by 81 per cent between the 1840s and 1860s.[134] In Britain the number of new titles increased by two and a half times, while in the German lands it quadrupled. In all three countries there was a steep rise in print-runs. The most popular titles sold in larger numbers than before, with some 'classics', such as the collected works of Walter Scott, Goethe's *The Sorrows of Young Werther* and La Fontaine's *Fables*, reaching annual sales in the hundreds of thousands.[135]

With the expansion of the industry the production process became more specialized and the publisher emerged as a new figure alongside the printer and the bookseller, who, between them, had run the trade before. The publisher now became the major intermediary between the author and the public. He took on the tasks of buying manuscripts, editing them, distributing them to booksellers, and publicizing them with marketing techniques which aimed to give his books an edge over their competitors. Whereas the printer was an artisan, and the bookseller a merchant, the publisher was identified as a professional entrepreneur.

The pioneers of this revolution were mostly new to the book trade. They were self-made men with little or no family background in the industry, and in some cases no actual interest in books except for the money they could make from them. Pierre-François Ladvocat was the son of an architect who entered the book trade by marrying the owner of a *cabinet de lecture*. The most successful of the Paris booksellers and publishers, Ladvocat was the prototype for Dauriat, the despotic publisher in Balzac's *Lost Illusions,* who describes himself as a 'speculator in literature'. Pierre-Jules Hetzel, the publisher of Balzac, Hugo, Zola and Jules Verne, had been born into the family of a master saddler in the First Lancers' Regiment and studied law in Strasbourg before dropping out of university to set up his business in 1837. Gervais Charpentier, the pioneering publisher of the cheap mass editions of the Bibliothèque Charpentier, was the son of a soldier who had started out as a bookseller's clerk, working for a while with Ladvocat, before opening his own bookshop and *cabinet de lecture* in Paris. Louis Hachette's father was a pharmacist, while his mother came from a textile-manufacturing family. Of the men who would transform the European book trade in the 1830s and 1840s, only Bernhard Tauchnitz and Michel Lévy came from backgrounds in the industry; Tauchnitz hailed from a family of publishers in Leipzig, while Lévy's father was a *colporteur,* or pedlar of books.

Behind the success of all these publishers was their use of innovative marketing techniques. The most important was the 'Library' – a series of cheap books in small formats with uniformly coloured cloth or paper covers, standard prices and the same familiar brandmark on the cover, which made them easily recognizable and collectable as commodities to furnish the cultured home. The idea was developed by publishers across Europe during the 1840s. First off the mark was the Leipzig publisher Anton Philipp Reclam with his Wohlfeile Unterhaltungsbibliothek für die gebildete Lesewelt (Inexpensive Entertainment Library for the Educated Reading World), launched in 1844, which quickly grew to sixty cheaply priced volumes before folding after just three years.[136] In 1847, the Belfast firm of Simms and McIntyre introduced its Parlour Library of fiction reprints in distinctive green covers which sold for a shilling each. It was soon followed by Thomas Hodgson with his Parlour Library, and, from 1849, by George Routledge with his Railway Library, whose shilling novels and adventure stories had bright green or yellow covers ('yellow-backs') to attract attention at bookstalls. In France the same approach was taken by the Bibliothèque Charpentier, whose novels all appeared in yellow cloth covers from 1838. The Collection Michel Lévy, launched in 1856, had different colours for each category and price of book (green-covered paperbacks at one franc;

blue-covered hardbacks at 1 franc 50 centimes, and so on), though all had the 'M.L.' logo on the back.[137]

These libraries were an early indication of how market forces and technologies would create a canon of standard literary works in the nineteenth century. The rationale of their publishers was to make the classics accessible to all. Launching his Panthéon Littéraire in 1839, Girardin, for instance, declared his aim to be the publication of a 'universal collection of masterpieces of the human spirit' at prices any household could afford.[138] The economics of the mass market obliged these collections to concentrate on books with an established popularity. The main 'interest of the public is the price', explained Lévy: 'this is why we have decided to publish only successful works so that we can sell more and reduce the price.' At the same time, this commercially driven canon comprised not just classic works, the oeuvres complètes of dead writers, but also contemporary works, the 'modern classics', or oeuvres durables, as Charpentier called them, which publishers selected for their collections because they thought, as he put it, that they would stand the test of time and 'enter literary history'.[139]

Other shrewd techniques of marketing included catalogues, advertising posters, and bills and notices in periodicals; some publishers even paid for favourable reviews and articles in newspapers. One or two started giving away a lottery ticket with each book. Charpentier was the most advanced, pioneering many of the basic strategies of publishers today. He employed agents to pre-sell books to booksellers; used wholesalers as intermediaries; and sold in bulk at extra discounts to the shops on condition that they placed his books in their window or displayed them prominently on tables. He was the first publisher to perfect the modern system of selling books by mail or telegraph order (a sort of nineteenth-century Amazon) by holding large amounts of stock in warehouses near the railway stations in Paris.[140]

The railways once again were key to these developments. They enabled publishers to reach small towns and rural areas where readers had before been served only by the colporteur's cartload of religious books, cheap pamphlets and almanacs. Colportage was a thriving rural business throughout Europe in the early nineteenth century. In France alone there were 3,000 licensed colporteurs, each one travelling an average of thirty kilometres a day by horse and cart, and all of them together selling every year an estimated 9 million francs' worth of books and almanacs. The arrival of the railway gradually drove them out of business by enabling bookshops in provincial towns to supply readers quickly with editions from Paris, although some *colporteurs* managed to survive by using the branch lines to distribute their books to smaller communities on the periphery of the market. The growth of bookshops in provincial towns took off in line with the spread of the railways. Between 1850 and the 1870s the number of bookshops in France more than doubled, to over 5,000, mostly on the railway network around Paris, in the north-east around Lille and the south near Lyons, areas where the railways were most advanced.[141]

Through the railways publishers were able to connect directly to their customers in the provinces. They sent sales reps with samples of their books to drum up interest in them among provincial booksellers. Lévy was the first to use the railway in this way. In 1847, he toured provincial France to promote his books to booksellers. Two years later, he made a second lightning tour, travelling by rail and coach to Chartres, Tours, Blois, Poitiers, Angoulême, Bordeaux, the Midi and the Rhone valley before crossing into Switzerland. From these tours, which would have been unthinkable before the railway, he gained a better sense of the literary tastes of provincial readers that would stand him in good stead.[142]

Railways also fuelled the boom in cheap fiction. Travellers on trains were a large market, especially for entertaining literature. The train was smoother than a horse-drawn carriage on a bumpy road, enabling passengers to read a book more easily. Reading was a good way to relieve the boredom of a long journey as well as to avoid the embarrassment of constant eye contact with the person sitting opposite (in most European trains the seats were arranged, as they had been on the stagecoach, facing each other).

The short-story form was made for these journeys. It is no coincidence that it came into its own with the growth of railway travel in the nineteenth century. New types of publishing for railway readers began to appear: adventure and detective tales, known as penny dreadfuls, as well as miscellanies of fiction, humorous incidents and anecdotes mixed with travel guides and information for the traveller. Carlo Collodi, the creator of Pinocchio, had his first success with *Un romanzo in vapore*

(A Novel in Steam, 1856), a book of comic tales with a guide to Florence, Pisa and Livorno, which sold in railway stations on the Florence–Livorno line.[143] Many of the biggest publishers in Europe – Longman and Routledge in Britain, Albert Hofmann in Berlin, Hachette in France – brought out cheap mass editions of novels, stories, travel books and guides in standard pocket formats well suited to a travel bag.

Every station had a lending library or bookstall. A licence to sell books in the stations was practically a guarantee of big profits. In Germany, station bookshops were as old as the railroads themselves. The three main lines – between Berlin, Hamburg and Munich; Frankfurt am Main and Basel; and Mannheim and Cologne – all had bookstores before 1848.[144] Britain followed close behind. In 1848, William Henry Smith secured a concession from the London and North Western Railway to open a bookstall at Euston Station. Born into a family of London booksellers, Smith had used the railways to deliver newspapers to provincial towns. A pious businessman, he had won the Euston franchise by promising to offer travellers a more wholesome diet of improving literature than the previous tenant of the stall, who had sold smutty books along with blankets, cushions, candles and other useful items for their journey. Smith had the support of the major publishers of cheap books and pamphlets for the railway traveller: Simms and McIntyre and Chapman and Hall with their Parlour Libraries, Longman and Routledge with their Railway Libraries, and G. W. M. Reynolds with his *Miscellany* – all of which were found in the seventy bookstalls established by W. H. Smith in station halls by the end of 1851.

The Great Exhibition of 1851 brought millions of railway travellers to London. One of them was the publisher Hachette, who was more impressed by Smith's bookstalls in the stations than by any of the exhibits in the Crystal Palace in Hyde Park. Born in 1800, Hachette had attended Guizot's classes at the École Normale Supérieure and trained as a lawyer before starting up as a publisher of school textbooks and dictionaries – a market then, in the mid-1820s, in a backward state. After Guizot's law mandated primary schooling, Hachette was ideally placed to expand his business: his schoolbooks were commissioned by Guizot's ministry. One million copies of his ABC were published in 1833 alone, while his reading books practically had a monopoly in French schools in the 1830s and 1840s. By 1851, Hachette had moved into general publishing. He was looking to increase his market share, and W. H. Smith with its bookstalls in stations offered him that opportunity.

In 1852, Hachette won his first concession from the Compagnie des Chemins de Fer du Nord. He promised to fill his railway bookstalls with a library of 100 books, increasing to 500 in the next few years. They would appear in seven different series, each with their own colour-coded jackets (travel guides in red, histories in green, French literature in a sort of cream, children's books in pink, etc.), all in the same pocket-size format and easily affordable to railway travellers at just two francs each. The five-year contract was soon followed by deals with other railway companies. By 1854, there were sixty bookstalls filled with the titles of Hachette in France, and by the 1870s the number had increased to 500, a national distribution network for the publisher, which had a monopoly on all the country's major lines.[145] The railways had transformed the company from a niche publisher to one of the biggest in the world.

4

A long-term sufferer from gonorrhoea, Rossini came to Paris in May 1843 to consult France's most acclaimed urologist, Jean Civiale, who kept him under observation for three months. During his stay, Rossini sat for a portrait by Ary Scheffer (1795–1858) in the artist's studio in rue Chaptal. It was to become one of the most celebrated pictures of the composer (of which there were many). It shows Rossini at the age of fifty-one, at the height of his international fame, a man at ease and enjoying life in his long retirement from composing operas. Throughout that summer in Paris he was still living with Olympe Pélissier, an artist's model, in the place de la Madeleine.

Rossini was a frequent visitor to Scheffer's studio. He had been going there since the 1830s, when it was a meeting place for artists and intellectuals: George Sand, Chopin, Liszt, Ernest Renan and the Viardots were there on a regular basis. Born in Dordrecht, Holland, in 1795, Scheffer came to Paris to study in the workshop of the painter Pierre-Narcisse Guérin. He quickly came to the attention of the French Academy with his portraits in the Ingres style. The Duc d'Orléans became his patron, appointing him as the art tutor to his ten children and granting him commissions at Versailles.[146]

Scheffer was a good friend of the Viardots. He had known Louis since the 1820s, when he taught his younger brother Léon Viardot, one of the many now forgotten painters who made a modest living in Paris. Scheffer had a gruff exterior, but he was loyal and generous to friends. He was devoted to Pauline. When Louis introduced the painter to his bride in 1840, he asked him his opinion: 'Dreadfully ugly,' replied Scheffer, 'but if I were to see her again, I would fall madly in love with her.' Scheffer's portrait of Pauline (ill. 1), painted around 1841, is, according to Saint-Saëns, 'the only one to show this unequalled woman truthfully and give some idea of her strange and powerful fascination'.[147]

Rue Chaptal was at the heart of the 'New Athens' area leading up to Montmartre – at that time a quiet part of Paris where many artists had their studios. Eugène Delacroix, Horace Vernet, Paul Delaroche, Paul Gavarni and the sculptor Jean-Pierre Dantan were all neighbours of Scheffer. Soon they would be joined by Adolphe Goupil and his family, art dealers and print sellers, whose gallery in rue Chaptal became a meeting place for artists, some of whom had rented studio spaces on the upper floors. Scheffer, Vernet and Delaroche were the founding artists of the Goupil business, one of Europe's first commercial dealers in contemporary art.

Old Masters had been sold by private dealers since the seventeenth century.[148] But a commercial market for contemporary art was something new in the 1840s, when private galleries like Goupil's first emerged as a space for living artists and their buyers outside the Academy system, which had previously controlled the art market.[149] In France this meant the École des Beaux-Arts, whose annual Salon was the main way for an artist's works to be known and sold. The Salon's jury selected entries exclusively from graduates of the École. The system was based on an academic hierarchy of genres, in which history paintings, and mythological and religious subjects, occupied the highest positions, while still-lifes and landscapes found themselves at the bottom. Innovative pieces were nearly always rejected.

Scheffer was one of many painters to become frustrated with the Salon's academic rules. Public taste in art was changing, the demand for genre and landscape painting was on the rise, but the jury did not change its selection criteria. Scheffer did not submit any of his works to the Salon after 1846. Instead he turned his studio into a private gallery for Delacroix, Rousseau, Corot, Dupré and other landscape painters, all of them rejected at some point by the Salon. He formed them into an association of 'free artists'. The next year, he joined a larger group of independent-minded artists, including Théodore Rousseau, Honoré Daumier and the sculptor Antoine-Louis Barye, who established a *salon indépendant* to exhibit and sell their works.[150]

There were many such initiatives. In 1843, a gallery was opened on the top floor of the Bazar Bonne-Nouvelle, one of the first department stores in Paris, where artworks rejected by the Salon could be hung and sold in exchange for a small rent or commission. Delacroix had three paintings at the Bonne-Nouvelle, including *Tasso in the Madhouse* (1839), which was sold, and his superb *Execution of the Doge Marino Faliero* (1825–6), which was not. Inspired by Byron's play, the *Execution* was the picture Delacroix himself was most proud of, but it was attacked for flouting all the academic laws of history painting.[151]

Meanwhile, private dealers were setting themselves up as intermediaries between artists and their customers. In the early years of the picture trade there was little clear distinction between art dealers and print sellers, merchants of artists' supplies and stationery, sellers of antiques and luxury goods. In the 1840s, Goupil & Vibert, as the company was known, combined selling prints with representing artists in its gallery. Ernest Gambart, the London dealer, started as an agent of Goupil selling reproductions of French art and engravings of celebrities, before setting up his own gallery in Berners Street in 1845. Jean-Marie Durand-Ruel (father of the Impressionist dealer Paul Durand-Ruel) began as a trader in artists' paper and materials in the Latin Quarter, home to poor art students, before establishing his fine-art gallery near the Palais-Royal in Paris in 1833. In 1846, to be even closer to his wealthy clientele, he opened a new gallery on the fashionable boulevard des Italiens, where stockbrokers and opera-goers mixed with foreign visitors.

A range of new art buyers were appearing on the scene, from connoisseurs, like Louis Viardot, to wealthy bankers and industrialists, like Aguado, who depended on the expertise of dealers and advisers to guide them in their purchases.

As Aguado's main adviser in the Paris art market, Viardot had acquired a deep knowledge of not only Europe's major public galleries but also of the smaller private collections when he started buying art in 1845. Old Masters were readily available on the market, but buying them involved a relatively high level of risk because their provenance was not always established. There were many forgeries. The market was unsettled at this time by a series of scandals, one of which involved a whole London 'Canaletto manufactory'. Viardot had a limited budget. He started out with only a few hundred francs. But his expert knowledge of European painting, Spanish, French and Dutch art, in particular, enabled him to build up and improve his collection by buying and reselling constantly. Over the years he would amass almost 200 paintings, mostly Dutch and Spanish Old Masters, portraits, landscapes and genre paintings from the seventeenth century, though he also bought some modern art – paintings by Scheffer, the Swedish artist August Hagborg and Antoine Chintreuil, including his *Pommiers et genêts en fleurs* (c. 1870: now in the Musée d'Orsay). It was in many ways a typical collection of the nineteenth-century connoisseur – not too large, with a small number of acknowledged masterpieces that would later go to museums, but made up mainly of first-rate works by artists such as Jacques Stella, Govaert Flinck, Salomon Ruysdael or Philips Wouwerman, whose names might have been forgotten had collectors such as Viardot not recognized their worth. He bought from private sales and galleries, from other collectors and increasingly from public auctions, while his contemporary paintings came mainly from the Salon, where he was a member of the jury in the 1860s and 1870s. Viardot's most successful buys were a handful of neglected masterpieces that he picked up for a song because no one else had recognized their value: Ferdinand Bol's *Portrait of a Woman* (1642: now in the Metropolitan Museum in New York) and Rembrandt's *Slaughtered Ox* (1655: now in the Louvre). His expertise enabled him to stay clear of forgeries, although he did make some mistakes. Having bought a painting of an old bearded rabbi signed by Rembrandt, he later came to the conclusion that it was the work of one of Rembrandt's pupils and consigned the picture to the darkest corner of his collection.[152]

Among other art buyers, especially the new industrialists who did not have much knowledge of the Old Masters, the fear of losing money on a forgery was a powerful incentive to invest in modern art instead. The growth in the market for contemporary art was strongest in Britain, where the Industrial Revolution had created a wealthy manufacturing and commercial class of art collectors – men like Joseph Sheepshanks, a Leeds textile manufacturer who made his fortune from supplying fabrics for army uniforms during the Napoleonic Wars; Elhanan Bicknell, a sperm-whale oil manufacturer who sold his art collection for £80,000 in 1863; John Allnutt and John Ruskin, both wine merchants and collectors of Turner; Henry McConnell, a cotton manufacturer from Manchester, who commissioned Turner's *Keelman Heaving in Coals by Moonlight* (1835), one of his few industrial scenes; Joseph Gillot, a pen manufacturer from Birmingham, who built a large collection of English landscapes; and Robert Vernon, a London hackneyman, who left his stock of modern British art, on which he had spent £150,000, to the National Gallery.[153]

There were many reasons for this growing interest in contemporary art, aside from worry about forgeries. In France an example had been set by the Duc de Berry and the Duc d'Orléans, who after 1815 had both switched their attention from the Flemish Old Masters to modern French works as a patriotic act. The opening of the Musée du Luxembourg, the first public gallery of contemporary art, in 1818, reinforced this trend. The big French bankers who collected art from the 1820s (Benjamin Delessert, Casimir-Pierre Périer, Jacques Lafitte, Isaac Péreire) all bought a growing share of their collections from living French artists. It enabled them to act as patrons, a prestigious role traditionally performed by the aristocracy. Perhaps most importantly, contemporary art was not only cheaper but offered better prospects of speculative profit than old paintings. 'I always buy a few moderns, because it is more reliable,' Péreire told the Goncourt brothers, Edmond and Jules, the famous diarists of Parisian cultural life. 'And its price will always rise.'[154]

This was the moment when the work of art began to play the role it has today: a financial investment. Not all artists liked the change. Many thought that the workings of the market were destroying the ideals of art. 'Here in France there are no longer art collectors,' complained the French sculptor and painter Antoine Étex in 1855. 'One cannot give such a title to that group of stock-market speculators who only encourage and buy minor paintings, little pictures worthy of decorating the boudoirs of their mistresses, and who, even in buying them, hope to turn a profit by later reselling them to foreigners.'[155]

Certain painters were gilt-edged. Enormous prices were paid for the highly detailed genre paintings and 'Oriental' scenes of Alexandre-Gabriel Decamps (1803–60), a self-taught artist, rejected all his life by the Academy. The jewel-like appearance of these miniatures made them luxury objects for the bourgeois living room. The genre paintings of Ernest Meissonier (1815–91), inspired by the interiors of the old Dutch masters, were collected by the richest bankers and businessmen of Europe, who prized them for their polished craftsmanship and investment potential. Meissonier's prices soared. *The Chess Game*, for example, which Périer had bought for 2,000 francs from the Salon of 1841, was resold six years later for 5,000 francs to Delessert, and in 1869 to the financier François Hottinguer for 27,000 francs – the sort of money paid for a Rembrandt. Meissonier's paintings became financial assets, often changing hands in business deals. For those who deplored the commodification of artworks they became a symbol of 'bourgeois vulgarity'. Baudelaire was disgusted by the stupidity of those bankers who paid ten or twenty times as much for a Meissonier as they would for a painting by his hero, Delacroix.[156]

The merchants, bankers and industrialists who dominated this new art market did not have a detailed knowledge of the classics and mythology, nor an acquaintance with the cultural sites of the Grand Tour – all things acquired by the aristocracy and usually required to interpret academic art. They wanted paintings which they could enjoy and understand: scenes they recognized from everyday modern life; narrative and landscape paintings; family portraits; pictures small enough to ornament their homes as symbols of their culture and standing. As Wilkie Collins wrote in 1845:

> Traders and makers of all kinds of commodities . . . started with the new notion of buying a picture which they themselves could admire and appreciate, and for the genuineness of which the artist was still living to vouch. These rough and ready customers . . . wanted interesting subjects; variety, resemblance to nature; genuineness of the article, and fresh paint; they had no ancestors, whose feelings, as founders of galleries, it was necessary to consult; no critical gentlemen and writers of valuable works to snub them when they were in spirits; nothing to lead them by the nose except their own shrewdness, their own interests, and their own tastes – so they turned their backs on the Old Masters, and marched off in a body to the living men.[157]

Whether they liked it or not, artists were obliged to adapt their work to this growing market for small ('cabinet') paintings. Larger works were difficult to sell: they had no place in the new commercial galleries, as Goupil underlined to his artists. Scheffer followed his advice. With no personal fortune, only what he earned from his painting, he was always short of money in the early stages of his career. After he had signed up with Goupil, around 1835, Scheffer turned away from large religious paintings, most of which remained unsold, and concentrated rather on small portraits, which sold well as originals and reproductions (engravings of his portrait of Rossini sold in thousands of copies). He also made reductions of his large paintings which could be sold more easily because they were more affordable. Scheffer's prices rose. By the end of the 1840s, he could earn as much as 50,000 francs from a single painting by selling the engraving rights. The biggest share of his income came from portraits and small copies of his larger works.[158]

Delacroix would also make reductions of his larger works, or get assistants to do them and finish them himself for sale to dealers and private buyers in various formats (copies in the classic 'sofa size', around 50 × 80 centimetres, fetched the highest prices).[159] Like Scheffer, Delacroix had been trained in the neo-classical school in the Guérin studio and had started his career as an artist working for the court. He had won important commissions from Louis Philippe in the 1820s and 1830s, benefiting from the powerful support of Adolphe Thiers, one of the first critics to write about his work, who was twice Prime Minister under the July Monarchy. His livelihood depended on these commissions, for his work was little understood or valued by the critics and public. From the 1840s, however, Delacroix depended more on sales to connoisseurs and dealers, such as Goupil and Durand-Ruel, who bought his works at the Salon, at auctions or directly from his studio. He adapted his work to this new market, producing smaller pictures with subjects that would sell – animal paintings, 'Oriental' scenes and landscapes. He accepted requests from dealers and clients who wanted pictures on particular subjects, and even followed their instructions on the way his paintings should appear. For example, in *Bathers* (also known as *Turkish Women Bathing*: 1854), it was the patron who had decided on the subject, on the position of the figures, and even on the style, which was meant to resemble that of other painters named by him in his letters to Delacroix.[160]

During this late period of his career, Delacroix became more and more involved in the reproduction of his works, recognizing that the print engraving was a major source of income and an effective way to promote his paintings to a broader audience. He delighted in the modest popularity which he obtained through these initiatives, and took it as a belated vindication of his work. 'Happiness always comes too late,' he wrote in his journal in 1853. 'It is like the little vogue for my pictures; after despising me for so long, the patrons are going to make my fortune.'[161]

Some critics were uncomfortable with the way that art was shaped by the imperatives of furnishing a living room. 'Genre painting, which fits small frames and hangs easily in the small rooms in which we live, is pushing history painting out of existence,' complained Maxime du Camp, the writer and photographer, in a review of the 1857 Salon.[162] But artists were subjects of the market by this time: there was no escaping its imperatives. John Everett Millais, the Pre-Raphaelite, bemoaned the fact that there was no demand for the large ambitious canvases he wanted to produce. In 1857, he wrote about a visit from Thomas Combe, the publisher and printer, whose portrait he had painted seven years before: 'He wants me to paint him a picture about the size of the *Heretic* (*anything larger than that size is objected to*). There is no encouragement for anything but cabinet pictures. I should never have a small picture on my hands for ten minutes, which is a great temptation to do nothing else.'[163]

Once the rules of art had been reset by the market there was no longer any clear distinction between the painting as a 'work of art' and as part of a room's furnishing. Later artists, such as the Impressionists, who sold exclusively to this domestic market, embraced this aspect of their art, painting decorative panels and pictures for specific places in a room on the request of patrons. Because of the critical attention their paintings have received in the history of the avant-garde, the function of their work in simply furnishing interior spaces has been largely lost from sight.[164]

5

In 1843, the Marquis de Custine published an account of his travels in Russia. *La Russie en 1839* probably did more than any other publication to shape European attitudes towards Russia in the nineteenth century.

Within a few years of its publication, the entertaining travelogue went through at least six French editions, came out in several pirated editions in Belgium, was translated into German, Dutch and English, and appeared in pamphlet form in various European languages.

Custine had travelled to Russia in 1839 with the express aim of writing a popular travel book to make his name as a writer. He had previously tried his hand at novels, plays and melodramas without success, so travel literature, an increasingly popular genre, was, he thought, his final chance to make a reputation for himself.

La Russie was not his first attempt in this genre. After the July Revolution, Custine had travelled to Spain in search of validation of his legitimist Catholic principles. He had been struck by the 'Oriental' feel of southern Spain, rooted in the culture of its Moorish past. The experience made him think more generally about 'European civilization', its core countries and peripheries. At the end of his book, *L'Espagne sous Ferdinand VII* (1838), Custine had reflected on what defined 'Europe' and arrived at the idea of travelling to Russia, Europe's other 'Orient', to see better what it was:

> I have travelled almost everywhere in Europe, and of all the ways of living that I have observed in this part of the world, those of the people of Seville seem to me the most natural, the most simple, the closest to the ideas I have always had of the social good . . . In vain have I searched for traces of this right-mindedness in other peoples of Europe. Austria is prosperous, it is calm, but it is the skill of its rulers, more than the spirit of its people, to which I attribute the good fortune of this monarchy. I cannot talk of Russia, which I do not know, and which I would like to know well; they are also Asiatics, at least as much as the peoples with whose blood the Spanish have been mixed. Also I would be interested to compare Russia to Spain; both hold more immediately to the Orient than any other nations of Europe, of which they form the two extremities.[165]

The comparison between Spain and Russia, the two 'Oriental' peripheries of Europe, was not entirely new. The French in 1812, struggling with their military campaigns in both countries, had compared the *barbares du Nord* (the Russians) with the *barbares du Sud* (the Spanish). But by the 1840s it had become something of a commonplace. It was to be found, for example, in Vasily Botkin's *Letters From Spain* (1847–9), in which the Russian writer compared the Moorish impact on Spanish culture to that of the Mongols on Russia. Louis Viardot similarly noted in 1846 that 'the Orient has penetrated Europe from its two extremes. Is it not the case that the Arabs brought it into Spain and the Mongols into Russia?'[166]

What the Marquis found in Russia reinforced his belief in European freedoms and values. Everything about the country filled the Frenchman with contempt and dread: the despotism of the Tsar; the lack of individual liberty and human dignity; the contempt for truth that corrupted society; the servility of the aristocracy, who were no more than slaves; their pretentious European manners, which were just a thin veneer of civilization to hide their Asiatic barbarism from the West. 'It must never be forgotten that we are on the confines of Asia,' he maintained. As for the comparison to Spain, Custine ended with this famous warning:

> In sum, the two countries are the very opposite of each other; they differ as do day and night, fire and ice, north and south.
>
> To have a feeling for the liberty enjoyed in the other European countries, whatever form of government they may have adopted, one must have sojourned in that solitude without repose, in that prison without leisure, that is called Russia . . . If ever your sons should be discontented with France, try my recipe: tell them to go to Russia. It is a journey useful to every foreigner; whoever has well examined that country will be content to live anywhere else.[167]

The key to the success of Custine's book was its articulation of fears and prejudices about Russia widely held in Europe at that time. In the early decades of the nineteenth century a large number of books and articles had built up the perception of Russia as an Asiatic power, aggressive and expansionist by nature, a 'menace' to European liberties and civilization. It was an impression reinforced by the Tsar's brutal repression of the Polish uprising in 1830–31, forcing many Polish noblemen and intellectuals into exile in Paris, where they had a major influence on Western thinking about Russia, not least through their contacts like Custine. Viardot was a rare exception in choosing not to join this Russophobic chorus in his *Souvenirs de chasse* (1846), which contained a positive account of his Russian hunting trips. It was a choice dictated by his need to keep the door to Russia open to Pauline, as he explained to George Sand when she reproached him for criticizing Custine's book (and, by implication, compromising his republican convictions by doing business with the 'gendarme of Europe', as Nicholas I was known).[168]

But *La Russie* was doing something more than stoking Western Russophobia. By focusing on Russia's Asiatic 'otherness', it was inviting its readers to recognize their 'Europeanness'.

The idea of 'Europe' had always been defined by this cultural contrast with the 'Oriental' world. In the European imagination the 'Orient' was primitive, irrational, indolent, corrupt, despotic – an intellectual construction underpinning Europe's domination of the colonial world.[169] The 'Orient' was not a geographic category. It was not just located in the Middle East, Asia or North Africa, but was inside Europe too, in the continent's periphery in the south and east, where the influence of Arab and Islamic cultures remained strong.[170]

In *The Spirit of the Laws* (1748) Montesquieu divided Europe into a progressive North and a backward South, Spain and Sicily, which as former Muslim colonies had never been entirely Europeanized. Arguing that cultures are shaped by climate and geography, Montesquieu defined the edge of Europe at that point in southern Italy where the sirocco wind holds sway.

> There is, in Italy, a southern wind, called Sirocco, which passes through the sands of Africa before reaching Italy. It rules that country; it exerts its power over all spirits; it produces a universal weightiness and slowness; Sirocco is the intelligence that presides over all Italian heads, and I am tempted to believe that the difference one notices between the inhabitants of northern Lombardy, and those of the rest of Italy, derives from the fact that Lombardy is protected by the Apennines, which defend her from the havoc of the Sirocco.[171]

Voltaire built on Montesquieu's idea, adding a secondary distinction between the progressive heart of European civilization in the Western capitals (the Republic of Letters) and the semi-Asiatic East. Drawing on these divisions, Hegel constructed a schema of historical progression from the infancy of European civilization in the South, Ancient Greece and Rome, to the German-centred Europe of the North (Hegel's 'end of History'). By the mid-nineteenth century, a distinct cultural map had thus emerged, with the core of 'Europe' in the north-west of the continent, in France, the Low Countries and the German lands, while on its periphery, from Spain to the Black Sea, there was an internal 'Orient'. The vice-president of the French Oriental Society wrote in 1843:

> Our Orient comprises all the countries of the Mediterranean basin which are related to the African and Asian countries on the shores of that sea: Greece and its islands; Turkey and its annexed territories, Wallachia, Moldavia; the Austrian possessions on the Adriatic; the English possessions, Malta and the Ionian islands; Southern European Russia, which dominates the Black Sea and the Sea of Azov. Everything that depends on what we still call today the trade with the Orient . . .[172]

In the early decades of the nineteenth century, interest in the exploration of South and Eastern Europe encouraged travel writers to reflect again on the idea of 'Europeanness'. During their travels in Albania, a virtually unknown part of Europe, in 1809–10, Lord Byron and his friend John Hobhouse wondered whether the Albanians and Turks, or indeed the Russians and the Greeks, could be counted as Europeans at all. Hobhouse thought that the Turks were closer to the English than the Greeks, whom he categorized as 'Orientals' rather than descendants of the ancient Hellenic culture idealized by philhellenics like Byron. For Byron the Albanians were a hybrid tribe, half Asiatic, but capable of being Europeanized, a position with which he identified himself when he posed for his famous portrait in Albanian dress.[173]

Travellers in Spain were equally aware of exploring Europe's edge. The Iberian peninsula was a relatively unknown part of Europe until the Napoleonic Wars. Travelling was slow and difficult, without any railways until 1848 and few well-made roads. From the 1820s Andalusia was 'discovered' by the French Romantics. Impressed by its Jewish and Moorish heritage, they projected onto it their own exotic myths of 'oriental' colour and passion. In his *Voyage en Espagne* (1843), which remained popular throughout the nineteenth century, Gautier assembled an image of 'Arabian Andalusia' out of scenes of gypsy life, flamenco dancing and picturesque descriptions of the Alhambra. 'Spain, which borders Africa as Greece borders Asia, is not designed for European ways. The spirit of the Orient penetrates it in all its forms,' Gautier wrote. 'South of the Sierra Morena, the nature of the country changes completely: it is as if one were passing suddenly from Europe to Africa.'[174]

The 'otherness' of Spain was one of its attractions to Louis Viardot. He was fascinated by the cultural traces of the Jews and Moors in Spain. In Andalusia he saw a country linked by history to the ancient civilizations of North Africa and the Near East. It reminded him that Europe was neither closed nor self-contained: it was a culture in progress, constantly evolving through its interaction with the world beyond, its periphery permeated by the Orient. In his *Lettres d'un Espagnol* Viardot maintained that the Comte de Volney, the eighteenth-century Orientalist, had scarcely 'needed to leave Europe, to cross the seas and follow Arab nomads across the desert, to go in search of the great lessons of the ancient ruins in the Syrian sands, when he could have found such traces in the Iberian peninsula'.[175]

Viardot explored the impact of the Moors on European culture in *L'Essai sur l'histoire des Arabes et des Mores d'Europe* (1833). He wrote many articles on Spanish art and literature that emphasized this legacy. His translation into French of *Don Quixote* (1837), in which he gave full expression to the novel's ethnographic details and colour to create a vivid sense of Spain, was vitally important for the Romantic discovery of Spanish literature (it was read by Prosper Mérimée, the author of *Carmen*, whose love of the translation was the starting point of his interest in Spain). Viardot's version of Cervantes's masterpiece became a bestseller. Reissued many times, it served as the basis for subsequent translations into other languages.[176]

No doubt part of Viardot's attraction to Pauline was her Spanish ancestry. Just as he was drawn to the 'otherness' of Spain, so he fell in love with a woman who, in Heine's words, 'recalls not the civilized beauty and domesticated grace of our European homeland, but the wild splendour of an exotic landscape in the desert'.[177]

As the Viardots travelled to St Petersburg, in October 1843, they might have been forgiven for thinking they were leaving Europe for Asia. Russia was an unknown territory to all but a tiny number of European travellers. St Petersburg and Moscow were the only parts of it that people ever visited. Travelling conditions were extremely difficult. The trek from Paris to St Petersburg took a minimum of sixteen days. There was no railway for the last part of the journey from Berlin – the only finished railroad in the Russian Empire at that time was the short line from the capital to the Tsar's residence at Tsarskoe Selo and the nearby resort of Pavlovsk.

In St Petersburg only the main avenues had 'wooden pavements' for the carriages. Beyond these the streets were all unpaved. Muddy in the spring, hot and airless with the stench of sewers in the summer, always bustling with labourers and traders, these back streets and alleys remained unchanged when Dostoevsky described them in *Crime and Punishment* (1866). A stone's throw from the elegant neo-classical façades of the Nevsky Prospekt, where the Viardots were staying in the Demidov Palace, a different world of poverty and squalor could be found.

The reading public of this world was limited to the cultural élite. Shopfronts were decorated with pictures to show the unlettered what they could obtain inside. There were few bookshops. In Kharkov, the biggest city in Ukraine, there were only four in 1843, 'three Russian [shops] where they sell books by the pound', according to a travel guide, 'and one French, whose owner boasts of valuing his intellectual wares by their intrinsic worth'.[178] There was a vibrant literary life in St Petersburg and Moscow, however. The small and bookish circle of the intelligentsia was almost totally confined to these two capital cities. The 1840s were an extraordinary decade of intellectual ferment, when Slavophiles and Westernists debated whether Russia should be part of Europe or follow its own native traditions, and a stellar range of writers (Gogol, Nekrasov, Turgenev, Dostoevsky) emerged on the European scene.

In these circles there was an enormous appetite for any new ideas or books from Europe, from which the intelligentsia was cut off by geography and censorship. Among the progressive Westernists – for whom Europe was the solution to all of Russia's problems – there was a particular interest in the writings of George Sand. Somehow her works had managed to escape the attentions of the censors and appear in Russian periodicals. The Russian socialist Alexander Herzen maintained that through these journals she was even read as far afield as Omsk and Tobolsk, Siberian towns with large contingents of political exiles.[179] Idolized as the embodiment of the Westernist ideals of human liberation and democracy, Sand was the most translated foreign author in Russia at that time, although she would soon be overtaken by Dickens. There were as many translations of her work in Russian as there were of Balzac, Paul de Kock, Sue and Dumas together. 'Here you are the first writer, the first poet of our country,' Louis wrote to her on

18 November 1843. 'Your books are in everybody's hands, your portrait is everywhere; they talk constantly to us of you, congratulating us on our good fortune to be your friends.'[180]

After their arrival in St Petersburg the Viardots were soon immersed in these circles. They were frequent guests of Count Michał Wielhorski, an amateur composer and noble scion of a Polish family with a position at the court. Wielhorski's palace in St Petersburg was an unofficial ministry of European culture with musical soirées attended by the leading members of the Russian aristocracy and intelligentsia, including the composer Mikhail Glinka, the poet Prince Vyazemsky, the philosopher and music critic Prince Vladimir Odoevsky, the painter Karl Bruillov, the Ukrainian poet Taras Shevchenko and the writer Nikolai Gogol. But the longest-lasting Russian friendship the Viardots would make did not originate in these illustrious circles.

On 9 November 1843, Louis met a nobleman, tall and handsome with long hair and a beard, gentle manners and, surprisingly for his gigantic size, a relatively high-pitched voice, who on that day was celebrating his twenty-fifth birthday. There was a party for him in the house of Major A. S. Komarov, a figure on the margins of the literary circles of St Petersburg, who had taken it upon himself to introduce the Frenchman to some of his hunting friends. The young nobleman was obviously keen to meet Pauline, whose every performance he had seen. He invited Louis to join him the next day on a hunting trip, and a few days later, on 13 November, called on him at the Demidov Palace in the hope that Pauline was at home. He was in luck. The admirer was introduced to her, as she recalled, as a 'young Russian landowner, a good hunter and a bad poet'.[181] His name was Ivan Turgenev.

6

Turgenev had published his first work, a long poem called *Parasha*, in April 1843, and by the time he met Pauline four more poems had appeared with his signature 'T.L.' (Turgenev Lutovinov) in *Annals of the Fatherland* (*otechestvennye zapiski*), a liberal monthly journal in St Petersburg. The journal's editor, the influential critic Vissarion Belinsky, had published a review of *Parasha* in the April issue of *Annals of the Fatherland* and had praised it as the work of a new poetic star in

Russia following the deaths of Alexander Pushkin in 1837 and Mikhạil Lermontov in 1841. Turgenev, then, was clearly seen as a young upcoming writer when he met Pauline, not as the 'bad poet' who was introduced to her, though in later years he would look back on his early verse with 'physical repulsion' and embarrassment.[182]

The idea of becoming a writer had developed in Turgenev's thinking only during the last year. In 1843, he was employed as a civil servant in the Agronomic-Economic Department of the Ministry of the Interior, mainly tasked with reviewing various proposals for the reform of serf-dom. Before that he had wanted to become a professor of philosophy. Turgenev turned his hand to writing only after the Tsar had frozen new appointments in philosophy, a potentially seditious subject. But at this stage writing was no more than his hobby. He had no need to make it pay. He lived on an allowance from his mother, Varvara Petrovna Lutovinova, who disapproved of literature as a career for a nobleman.

Turgenev's mother was a wealthy landowner with 5,000 serfs on several estates in Kursk, Tula, Orel and Tambov provinces inherited from her uncle. In 1816, she married Sergei Nikolaevich Turgenev,

Turgenev's mother, Varvara Petrovna Lutovinova, daguerreotype, c. 1845.

a handsome cavalry officer, seven years her junior, who owned 140 serfs on his small estate, Turgenevo. The main family house was at Spasskoe, not far from Mtsensk in Orel province, 350 kilometres south of Moscow. The residential buildings were laid out in a horseshoe shape, with two curved wings stretching out from either side of the large central palace, a two-storeyed wooden house at the end of each wing, formal gardens and a park. The estate had its own hospital, police station, serf theatre and orchestra. Varvara Petrovna was an old-style Russian landowner, strict and orderly, careful in the running of her estates, not without a sense of charity, but generally tyrannical and cruel to her serfs. Once she sent two household serfs into penal exile in Siberia for the sole reason that they had failed to remove their caps and bow to her in the appropriate manner. Widowed by the death of her philandering husband in 1834, Varvara Petrovna became even more controlling and demanding of her sons. 'I have no happy memories of my childhood,' Turgenev recalled. 'I feared my mother like fire. She punished me for nothing, treating me like a recruit in the army. Few days passed without the stick; if I should dare to ask a question, she would punish me for it, declaring categorically: "You should know the answer better than I, work it out for yourself."' His mother's cruelty shaped Turgenev's liberal attitudes, his feelings of revulsion from serf-dom, as well as the softness of his character. Throughout his adult life he craved affection from women. For him there was nothing higher than a woman's love. According to his closest friend, the literary critic Pavel Annenkov, the young Turgenev

> was an unhappy man in his own eyes: he lacked the love and attachment of a woman which he sought from his early youth. It was not for nothing that he repeatedly remarked that the company of men without the presence of a kind and intelligent woman was like a great cart with ungreased wheels, which shatters the eardrums with its unbearable, monotonous screech.[183]

In 1838, at the age of nineteen, Turgenev went to Berlin University, promising his mother that he would return within two years to take up a position as professor of philosophy at Moscow University. He was already fluent in German from his studies at school and university in Moscow and St Petersburg. In Berlin, where he studied at the same time as Karl Marx, he embraced the whole of European culture, reading broadly in the classics, philosophy and German literature, and meeting a wide range of German intellectuals, including Alexander Humboldt and Bettina von Arnim. These years in Berlin were crucially important for Turgenev's intellectual development. The poetry of Goethe, much of which he knew by heart, set him on his literary path. In his way of thinking, sensibility and character, Turgenev was a European cosmopolitan. He was permanently shaped by the Westernism of the friends he made in his student years, above all Belinsky, whom he revered.[184] Turgenev believed in Europe as the source of moral progress, freedom and democracy. It was the only place where he felt able to fulfil himself as a writer and a human being. His path to it was via Germany, which remained his 'second homeland', as he himself would later acknowledge.[185]

In the Prussian capital, Turgenev lived a bohemian lifestyle with his fellow Russians Timofei Granovsky, the future medievalist, Nikolai Stankevich, the future poet, and Mikhail Bakunin, at that time not yet showing any signs of becoming a revolutionary anarchist. Careless with their money, they spent it all on tailored clothes, tickets to the opera, restaurants, wines, gambling and prostitutes, and then lived without a pfennig until they received their next allowance from their families. Turgenev's spending was particularly high: 20,000 assignat roubles were sent to him during his first year in Germany – twice his normal annual allowance from his mother. Varvara Petrovna became increasingly exasperated by her son's extravagant lifestyle, as reported to her by his manservant, whom she employed as a spy. She was horrified by the Russian company Turgenev was keeping (Bakunin was a 'monster', she told him).[186] She tried to tighten the purse strings, and threatened to stop payments altogether when she learned about his losses at the roulette wheels and the nightly visits to the theatre (which she supposed could only be to meet the actresses). Turgenev's spendthrift habits were a real drain on the family estate, where there was a series of bad harvests during his years in Berlin. The main residence at Spasskoe was destroyed in a fire, leaving only a two-storeyed wooden house. His mother exploited the situation to put moral pressure on Turgenev to return to Russia and take up a position in the military or civil service, which she believed were the only occupations fitting for a nobleman.

Turgenev did return, in the spring of 1841, having run out of money. Denied an allowance, he lived at home in Spasskoe or stayed with friends, surviving on loans from his brother Nikolai, who had joined an artillery regiment and was also still supported by Varvara Petrovna. For the next two years, Turgenev pursued his ambition of a university career, first in Moscow, where he briefly fell in love with Bakunin's sister, and then in St Petersburg, where he passed his exams but failed to write his dissertation for a master's degree. Throughout this time it was a struggle to get by. According to Annenkov, Turgenev was penniless, as everybody knew, but too proud to admit it; he kept up appearances by dressing like a dandy, which made him come across as insincere. 'A Khlestakov [Gogol's foppish anti-hero in *The Government Inspector*], educated, clever, superficial, with a desire to express himself and *fatuité sans bornes* [boundless fatuity]' was Herzen's first impression of him when they met around this time. At six foot three in height, Turgenev cut a striking figure at the Bolshoi Theatre with his fine tailsuit, white waistcoat, top hat, lorgnette and cane. But he did not have the money to buy his own ticket and had to cadge a seat in the box of friends.[187]

Eventually, in 1843, Turgenev gave up his pursuit of a professorship and dutifully took up his position as a civil servant in the Ministry of the Interior. His principal concern was to please his mother and assure his inheritance. He worked 'very badly' in the ministry, as he himself acknowledged, arriving late for work and spending most of the day with his nose in a novel, if not writing poetry. One of his duties was to process the paperwork for corporal punishments meted out to the peasants: in copying them out for execution he would change the harshest sentences (with the deadly knout) to make them softer (with the lash).[188]

Varvara Petrovna was disturbed by his lack of diligence. 'My son,' she wrote to him,

> you are entering an age when a man should make himself useful to others and aspire to join society. The time of selfish fantasies, of early youth's unlimited freedom, of rootless wandering for the body and the soul has passed for you, I would even say you have spent too long in this state of laziness and irresponsibility, which only sickness or extreme youth can justify.

She was opposed to the idea of his becoming a writer, an occupation she equated with a 'penpusher', and asked 'who reads Russian books in any case?' Yet she softened on the publication of *Parasha*. In a letter to

Turgenev on 28 May, she began with an opening position of hostility, but then could not conceal her pride:

> What is a poem? You can be like Pushkin, a good poet, but that brings nothing to a mother. My happiness consists in your love for me, in your obedience and respect. I do not know anything about poetry but I fear that you will suffer from the envious . . . Pushkin was attacked, they found fault in him, coldness, etc. May the Lord protect you from the grief of reading your critics . . .
>
> Do send me some copies of *Parasha* and tell me who is the publisher, and how many copies are printed. And how much it sells for, and if it can be purchased in Moscow.[189]

From his first encounter with Pauline, Turgenev was in love. He begged and borrowed all he could to hear her every performance. He applauded her so ostentatiously that he annoyed all the nearby members of the audience.[190] Every day he called upon the Viardots, engaging Louis in conversations about literature, offering to help him write books on the Hermitage, or on hunting in Russia, though his real aim was to catch sight of Pauline, to whom he offered himself as a teacher of Russian. Pauline did not take Turgenev's admiration very seriously. There is certainly no sign that she returned his affections at this time. The young writer was not even invited to receptions at the Viardots'.

She had many other young admirers. Among them was Stepan Gedeonov, an expert on music and the son of the director of the Imperial Theatre in St Petersburg, who arranged a private room beneath the stage where Pauline would retire after every performance and be entertained by four young men, her ardent fans, Gedeonov, Turgenev, P. V. Zinoviev (on whose estate Louis had been taken hunting by Turgenev) and Wielhorski's son. On one occasion the four men brought her the skin of a bear they had shot. Pauline had it made into a rug with golden claws. Relaxing after a performance, she would lie on it, while her four admirers were each assigned a paw on which to sit. Gossips called them 'the four paws'.[191]

The operatic season in St Petersburg ended with a week of carnival performances during the Shrovetide celebrations – with the start of Lent all theatres closed. Rubini and his company of singers left with promises to return for the next season. Just as they were about to leave, in March 1844, Clara and Robert Schumann arrived for a three-week concert tour, the latest European musicians to brave the long and uncomfortable journey to St Petersburg for the large amounts of money to be made. They were at once received 'in the most friendly way' by the Viardots, Clara noted in her diary. 'Pauline showed me her beautiful presents – sable, Turkish shawl, and lots of cut diamonds, everything from the court, chiefly from the Imperial couple.' Not long after, at their first concert, the Schumanns made a clear profit of 1,000 roubles (around 4,000 francs). 'In those days,' recalled the nationalist critic Vladimir Stasov, 'the Russian rouble had a good clink to German ears.'[192]

The Viardots returned for a second season in St Petersburg and Moscow, beginning in the autumn of 1844. Pauline's contract was improved: her fee was raised to 65,000 assignat roubles (75,000 francs), and she was guaranteed to take home a further 15,000 roubles (17,000 francs) from a benefit performance.[193] The centrepiece of the season was Bellini's *Norma* with Pauline in the title role. The demand for tickets was so great that the number of performances was increased from forty to sixty in two different subscription series, although including benefit nights the actual number was seventy-six. A larger troupe of singers had to be employed to cope with the strain. This was the height of the Russian mania for Italian opera. The public divided into warring factions over Viardot and her rival prima donna, Jeanne Castellan. Flower frenzy was at fever pitch. Fanatics paid the claques, including poor Turgenev, who spent all he had to rent a group of claqueurs in the top ring of the theatre for Pauline ('One cannot do without them, one must warm up the audience!' he explained to a friend).[194]

Satirists had a field day. 'Never mind the Bolshoi auditorium,' Nekrasov wrote in March 1845,

> wherever you may be you will hear the names of Rubini and Viardot; in every corner of the town you will hear roulades and trills; in a word, Petersburg has been turned into one gigantic organ performing only Italian motifs.
>
> Everyone has begun to sing!
>
> You take a walk down the Nevsky – 'U-na for-ti-ma lag-rima uu-na' [sic] booms out behind you; you look into a coffee shop – roulades à la Tamburini meet you already on the stairs; you drop in on a friend's

family, even one that lives on the Vyborg side, and they immediately sit their daughter down at the piano and force her to squeak her way through an aria from *Norma* or some other opera. You turn into the smallest alley, and barely ten steps in you come across an organ-grinder, who, having seen you from afar, has lost no time in striking up the finale to *Pirata* [an opera by Bellini] in full expectation of a generous reward.[195]

How far Nekrasov was exaggerating is difficult to tell. Certainly, through sheet music sales and constant repetition by orchestras and bands and street musicians, it did not take a long time for the latest opera hits to become widely known.

At the end of her second season, in March 1845, Pauline received a delegation of merchants with a German interpreter who, as she recounted in a letter to George Sand, 'begged me to accept the respects of the simple Russian peasants, in the same manner as I had accepted them from the Russian aristocracy'. Pauline had received a magnificent *porte-bouquet* from the St Petersburg nobility. Because the humble merchants had not been invited to join the subscription for this gift, they presented her with a diamond bracelet, financed entirely by their own modest contributions, 'to prove to me that they too possessed ears to hear and hearts to feel'.[196]

The Viardots returned to Paris in the spring of 1845. Turgenev went to them. He was hopelessly in love and would do anything to be close to Pauline. Resigning from his post in the ministry on grounds of poor eyesight, he received permission from the Tsar to travel to Europe for medical treatment. Turgenev spent the summer with the Viardots at Courtavenel, their château on the plains of Brie, south-east of Paris, which they had bought from Pauline's earnings in Russia. During the summer Turgenev and Pauline became more intimate in their relationship. He felt that she was starting to return his affections.* Although

---

* He was not the first young man to win Pauline's heart since her marriage. In the summer of 1844 Pauline fell in love with Maurice Sand, George Sand's son, a talented painter two years her junior, who spent a week with Pauline at Courtavenel. Realizing that the situation was impossible, Pauline wrote to George Sand after his departure: 'We promised each other to be brave ... I cannot say more about it at the moment ... I love him very seriously ... Write to me soon – a *double-entente* if possible [to avoid arousing the suspicions of Louis Viardot]' (*Correspondance de George Sand*, vol. 6, p. 632). In an earlier letter, on 11 August, George Sand had advised Pauline in *double ententes* to break off the love affair, even if she could have got away with it as far as Louis was concerned:

no kisses had yet been exchanged, there was the exciting possibility of deeper emotional connection. Turgenev would recall this summer as the 'happiest time of my life'.[197]

In the autumn the Viardots returned to St Petersburg for a third Russian season. Turgenev followed them. Louis's account of their hunting parties in Russia had been published in *L'Illustration* in 1844 and had been read in Russia, making him a person of real interest there. He was invited to hunt everywhere. By this time he was also acting as an intermediary between the Imperial Theatre in St Petersburg and those artists in Europe the Russians were attempting to recruit, among them Meyerbeer and the librettist Eugène Scribe.[198]

Pauline, by contrast, was not as popular as she had been before. The craze for Italian opera was on the wane. Houses were half-empty. So few tickets were sold for some of the Moscow performances that these had to be cancelled. One literary journal explained this cooling-off as the public waking from a dream: 'someone sang and played while we slept, an unknown feeling of sweetness swept all over us, we felt happiness, and then we woke to silence and emptiness.'[199]

The season was cut short because Louis became ill with gastric fever, while the young Louise, who accompanied her parents for the first time on a tour, developed whooping cough. As soon as they were fit to embark on the arduous voyage overland, the Viardots departed by carriage for Berlin, where Pauline had her next engagements in March 1846. It was a terrible three-week journey in freezing temperatures and snow blizzards. By the end, the 'coach was literally breaking into bits', Louis wrote to Turgenev. 'I don't think it could have done another leg.'[200]

Perhaps three seasons were enough. The market was not big enough to sustain another year of interest in Italian opera. But these seasons would be long remembered in Russia: for years the press would follow the career of 'our Viardot' and publish memoirs about her. Pauline herself recalled her visits to Russia with gratitude.[201] They had been the making of her career. But now she had to find a bigger stage.

'While your husband would let you do whatever you wanted, your mother [i.e. Sand herself] would advise you not to follow the inspiration of your friendship' (George Sand, *Lettres retrouvées*, ed. Thierry Bodin (Paris, 2004), p. 55).

2

A Revolution on the Stage

I said to myself: 'The July Revolution is the triumph of the bourgeoisie: this victorious bourgeoisie will want to cut a dash and be entertained. The Opéra will become its Versailles, it will flock there to take the places of the banished court and nobles.' The idea of making the Opéra at once magnificent and popular seemed to me to have a good chance of success.

Louis-Désiré Véron, *Mémoires d'un bourgeois de Paris* (1857)

I

At the end of April 1846, the Viardots began their long trip back from Berlin to Courtavenel. They would spend the summer there while Pauline made up her mind where she would appear in the coming autumn season. Turgenev wrote to Pauline frequently. His correspondence was conversational, full of news and observations, witty, light in tone. Knowing that his letters would be shown to Louis, he composed them with this in mind, but if she read between the lines, Pauline would have understood his emotions. At his most passionate Turgenev would switch from French to German, a language Louis did not speak at all.[1]

Turgenev longed for her to return to Russia that autumn. 'As regards the next season,' he wrote to her in May, 'you will be the best judge of that yourself. I am persuaded in advance that your decision will be well made, but I must tell you that your absence here this winter (if that is the outcome, which I still do not want to accept) will sadden many people. *Ich bin immer der selbe und werde es ewig bleiben* ['I am still the same, and always will be'] . . . In any case, do me the goodness of informing me of your decision. Farewell, be healthy and happy . . . come back; you will find *everything* here as you left it.'[2]

Louis was reluctant to return to Russia. He could not tolerate its cold climate, and felt himself at odds with the tsarist government because of his left-wing views (an article on Moscow he had published in the journal *L'Illustration* had been censored in Russia).[3] Berlin was the obvious alternative. Meyerbeer, the *Generalmusikdirektor* of the Berlin Opera, was a keen admirer of Pauline's voice and wanted her to sing the leading role in *Le Prophète*, his next opera, which he had been working on since 1838. Meyerbeer had shelved the opera in 1843 after Léon Pillet, the director of the Paris Opéra, had rejected his request that Pauline sing the leading female role. Pillet wanted the part for Stolz, the prima donna at the Opéra, who was also his mistress, but Meyerbeer would have nothing to do with the overrated soloist. From that moment, as the music critic Eduard Hanslick quipped, the composer carried his opera 'back and forth between Berlin and Paris in his suitcase, possibly in an effort to determine whether prophets may travel customs-free'.[4]

Meyerbeer believed that an opera's success depended above all on the leading singers' vocal and dramatic skills. He travelled throughout Europe looking for the best singers. In Pauline he had found the range of voice and acting qualities that made her perfect for the all-important role of Fidès, the prophet's mother, on which the tragic power of his opera would depend. He wrote the part for her.[5]

In 1845, he persuaded her to come to Stolzenfels, the neo-Gothic castle near Koblenz where the Prussian king, Friedrich Wilhelm, marked the completion of rebuilding works with a gala concert for the visit of Queen Victoria at which Pauline performed Gluck and Handel arias. The next year, he lured her to Berlin, a major capital of the 'newspaper countries', where George Sand had insisted her career would be made.[6] In Berlin, Viardot could strengthen her credentials for the Paris Opéra, where she still had not appeared, by taking on the part of Valentine in Meyerbeer's *Les Huguenots*, the first time she had sung Grand Opera. After ten years of singing only the Italian repertoire, it required a great deal of effort to learn to sing in German and prepare her voice for this demanding role. 'The day after tomorrow I sing for the first time . . . *in German!!!!!!*,' she wrote to Sand on 22 January 1847.

> You would not believe how hard I have had to work. First you have to prune the text of words too harsh and ugly to sing. When you have finished with the text you have to learn it all over again, then make it fit your tongue, and then your voice. It's a terrible labour. They say my pronunciation isn't bad, and I believe it, given all the work I have put in.[7]

Pauline triumphed in *Les Huguenots*. The critics were ecstatic. The Berlin public 'boiled with enthusiasm' for the singer who could sing with equal conviction 'all the repertoires in every language', as Louis reported to George Sand on 22 February.[8] From March, Pauline sang the role of Alice in *Robert le diable*, another Meyerbeer Grand Opera. The production was extended for two months, such was the demand to hear her sing. On one famous evening, when another singer fell ill at the last moment, Pauline amazed everyone by singing both the female parts.

Turgenev could only read about her triumphs in the press, which he scoured every day. 'I read all the articles about you in the Prussian newspapers,' he wrote to her from St Petersburg in November. 'You have made progress, by which I mean the progress that a master makes and never stops to make until the end. You have now mastered the *tragic* element, the only element that you had not entirely mastered yet.'[9] Turgenev was too restless and too obsessed with Pauline to remain an armchair follower. In January 1847, he left Russia to join her in Berlin. He spent the last of his allowance from his mother on his travel costs. For the next three months he religiously attended her performances. The painter Ludwig Pietsch, who would become a good friend, met him for the first time in a beer hall in Berlin. 'Buttoned up in a fur coat', Turgenev's 'impressive figure' reminded Pietsch of the young Tsar Peter the Great, 'although he had nothing in common with the semi-wild and unchecked nature of the founder of the modern Russian state. His massive head and body contained the finest intellect and the softest, kindest temperament.'[10]

Turgenev followed the Viardots to Dresden, where Pauline was engaged for a series of recitals during May, and that autumn went with them to London, where she had a two-month contract to sing at Covent Garden, worth £1,000 (25,000 francs), the highest level of remuneration she had yet achieved outside Russia.* She was at the height of her powers and could virtually dictate her conditions to any opera house. At Covent Garden she was able to insist that her jealous rival Grisi should not be employed at the same time. Only the Paris Opéra was yet to be conquered by Pauline. 'Why have you not been engaged yet in Paris?' George Sand wrote to her on 1 December. 'I don't understand. Grisi is collapsing in ruins and you are the greatest singer in the world.'[11]

By this time, in fact, things were opening up for Pauline at the Opéra. The director, Pillet, was at last forced out, his mistress, Stolz, had gone following some terrible performances when she had been hissed off the stage, and the new directors, Nestor Roqueplan and Henri Duponchel, were now looking for a blockbuster to pay off the huge debts Pillet had amassed. Verdi's opera *Jérusalem*, a reworking of *I Lombardi*, premiered in November, but was no more than a moderate success, with only thirty-five performances. So they turned to Meyerbeer, promising to secure special funds from the Ministry of the Interior to meet the costs of the expensive scenery and technical effects which his Grand Operas demanded, as well as to secure the services of Pauline Viardot, who wanted 75,000 francs to sing in *Le Prophète* for a season. Without her Meyerbeer would not let them have his long-awaited opera.[12]

Only Meyerbeer was capable of setting terms like this. To put on one of his operas was an almost certain guarantee of big profits. Born in Berlin to a Jewish banking family, he changed his name from Jacob Beer to Meyerbeer on the death of his grandfather, Liebmann Meyer (Jacob was changed to Giacomo during his years in Italy between 1816 and 1826). At that time he was composing in the Italian style of Rossini, a friend and supporter, who encouraged Meyerbeer to follow him to Paris after his appointment as musical director of the Théâtre Italien.

Paris was the key to Meyerbeer's success. It was a truly international metropolis, the 'great European and cosmopolitan capital par excellence', in the words of one of its nineteenth-century historians, a city with more foreign residents than any other on the Continent.[13] Meyerbeer's music was perfectly adapted to this cosmopolitan environment. It was

---

* She sustained this level until 1855, when Frederick Gye, the manager of Covent Garden, found that 'her name did not draw as formerly' and offered her £1,000 for a season of four months (the Viardots 'turned their noses up at this', he noted in his diary). After long negotiations they settled on £1,200 for a season of three months (ROH, Gye Diaries, 13 and 18 Mar. 1855).

an eclectic mix of German harmony, French rhythm and orchestration, and the Italian bel canto style. The critic Blaze de Bury explained Meyerbeer's success by his ability to assimilate these diverse elements into a distinctive 'French system' – a synthesis of the German and Italian – that had characterized the development of opera in Paris under Gluck and Rossini. His eclectic style sounded natural to Parisian society.[14]

'Would I be interested in composing for the French stage, you ask?' Meyerbeer had written to the Paris Opéra in 1823. 'I assure you that it would be a much greater honour for me to write for the French opera than for all the Italian theatres put together ... Where else but in Paris can one find the immense resources that French opera offers to the composer who longs to write truly dramatic music?'[15]

Paris at that time was the capital of the operatic world. Success in Paris made an opera likely to succeed in theatres all around the Continent. The greatest stage composers – Rossini, Meyerbeer, Bellini, Donizetti, Wagner and Verdi – were all keen to work in the French capital. The advanced protection of copyright in France, where laws of 1791 and 1793 had given artists lifetime rights of property in their own work, were a major draw. Whereas in Italy or Germany a composer earned a one-time fee for writing an opera, in Paris he received a royalty not only for the score but for every performance of his opera, provided its libretto was in French. Until the 1840s, France was the only European country where performance royalties were not only recognized in law but effectively enforced – a system introduced in 1776 but strengthened by the law of 1793. 'If you are worth one thousand, you receive one thousand, if one hundred thousand, one hundred thousand,' Bellini wrote in praise of the French laws in 1834.[16]

Paris was the ideal legal environment for Meyerbeer, the first composer to take full control of the creative elements that went into the making of an opera and profit from them in commercial terms. He reversed the old relationship between the impresario, the librettist and the composer: where previously an impresario would employ the composer to write the music for a libretto, Meyerbeer employed a librettist (usually Scribe) to write the words for his scenario and score. It was Meyerbeer alone who shaped the work. He gave the librettist detailed comments on the changes he required, and in the latter stages, when Scribe's patience would run out, employed a second and even third librettist to make the final modifications.[17] Where Rossini had been a tradesman working for an impresario, Meyerbeer had made himself the boss of his own opera business, employing the librettist as an artisan to make a work to order for a theatre and his publisher.

The Paris Opéra was Meyerbeer's ideal stage. It was a large-scale entertainment business with high expectations of 'magnificence' which came with its licence from the crown. Where else could Meyerbeer expect to find the 'immense resources' he needed for Grand Opera?

Grand Opera was the largest form of music drama before Richard Wagner's revolution on the operatic stage. Technically, it meant a five-act opera with a ballet and, in contrast to the Opéra-Comique, which had dialogue, without any spoken words. It was characterized by large-scale human dramas, choruses on stage, sumptuous sets and costumes, and spectacular effects. First developed in Paris, the model quickly spread to Germany and Italy; it would be emulated and adapted by composers throughout Europe in the nineteenth century; but however global it became, Grand Opera remained in essence a Parisian phenomenon.[18]

It had its roots in the 1831 reform intended to put the Paris Opéra on a more commercial footing and reduce its debts. By the middle of the 1820s, the Opéra was heavily indebted, despite growing subsidies. Its privileged position became a target for the liberal opposition, which also called for a renovation of its conservative repertoire. The public had grown tired of Gluck and Spontini. It wanted dramas with themes more relevant to the present. It wanted to see elements of spectacle such as it could see in the boulevard theatres, where all kinds of special effects (revolving panoramas, light changes and optical illusions of visual depth) were borrowed from the dioramas of Daguerre (who worked in the theatre before turning his attentions to the invention of the daguerre-otype, a form of photography). It was in response to these demands that in 1828 the Opéra commissioned Daniel Auber's five-act opera, *La Muette de Portici*, technically the first Grand Opera, based on the story of a popular uprising against Spanish rule in seventeenth-century Naples. The stage designer, Charles Ciceri, who had worked with Daguerre in the boulevard theatres, created a series of visually stunning sets, and produced spectacular effects, culminating in the use of gas lighting for the eruption of Vesuvius at the end of the fifth act. Auber's opera was seized upon as a symbol of rebellion. Its heroic depiction of the people in the chorus emboldened revolutionaries, especially in Belgium, where its performance on 25 August 1830 became the signal for revolt against King Willem of the Netherlands.[19]

Following the July Revolution in Paris, the Opéra was turned over to Véron, its first entrepreneur-director. Financed by Aguado, Véron saw himself as the leader of a bourgeois revolution in the theatre. In his *Mémoires d'un bourgeois de Paris* (1857), Véron later claimed that on taking over at the Opéra his revolutionary business plan had been to turn the theatre into the Versailles of the bourgeoisie, which would 'flock there to take the places of the banished court and nobles. The idea of making the Opéra at once magnificent and popular seemed to me to have a good chance of success.'[20] Much of this was myth-making. It was not yet the case that the bourgeoisie was replacing the aristocracy at the Opéra, whose public continued to be dominated by the old élite, even if there was a growing contingent of bankers, businessmen and their families in the most expensive seats.[21] But Véron's words can certainly be taken as a statement of intent. Without compromising on the splendour of the opera house, he introduced a series of reforms to make the Salle Le Peletier, the Opéra's auditorium, more accessible to the bourgeois élites of the July Monarchy. He increased the number of small boxes (with four seats) by taking out the larger (six-seat) boxes on the upper circles. He opened two new boxes by the stage, furnished in the style of the gentlemen's clubs which were springing up in Paris at that time, where 'luxury and pleasure' (by which he meant a close view of the ballerinas' legs) 'could be purchased inexpensively'.* He added more rows to the stalls, where tickets could be bought for a single performance, and upgraded them from benches into comfortable armchairs, appropriate for women, who were now admitted to this area. He lengthened the season, extending it into the summer break, when the aristocracy left Paris for the countryside, making it easier for others to get tickets for this period (the Salle Le Peletier was 'invaded' by provincial doctors and their families in the summer, according to the memoirist Tamvaco). Finally, he made the start of performances an hour later, at 8 p.m.,

---

* One of his reforms was to allow patrons into the *foyer de la danse*, where they could watch the ballerinas warming up. At the Salle Le Peletier, access to the *foyer de la danse* had previously been reserved for members of the court. The doors to it were guarded by the king's troops. Degas's painting *Le Foyer de la danse à l'Opéra de la rue Le Peletier* (1872) captures the voyeurism of this scene.

allowing more time for business people and professionals to get to the theatre after work.

The idea was not in any way to downgrade the Opéra. No expense was spared on the smallest details to maintain the theatre's opulence (even the tickets cost a fortune to produce).[22] Rather, his aim was to make the Opéra more attractive to the newly moneyed bourgeoisie, which he believed would be a growing source of revenue. 'The taste for music, or to be more exact, for opera, has seized everyone,' wrote the critic Charles de Boigne. 'Each wants his box at the Opéra, some once, others twice, and still others three times a week. The solicitors, attorneys, and stockbrokers, who wish to show their rank, appear on two nights: on Monday, the *petit jour*, with their wives, and on Friday, the *grand jour*, with their mistresses.'[23]

To entertain this market Véron realized that he had to come up with a fresh repertoire. What this public wanted was entertainment, pleasure and distraction from their daytime business. They wanted music dramas they could understand, enjoy, without knowledge of mythology, or recourse to printed librettos where all this was explained. In Grand Opera he had found the medium to give them that.

In his *Mémoires* Véron talked about the main ingredients which he believed were needed for the success of Grand Opera as a commercial enterprise:

> An opera in five acts must have a very dramatic action, bringing into play the grandest human emotions with powerful historical interests. This dramatic action, however, must be capable of being understood by the eyes alone, as in the action of a ballet; the chorus has to be impassioned and play an active role in the drama. Each act must have different sets, costumes and above all scenes . . . When you have at your disposal a vast stage with fourteen depths, an orchestra of over eighty musicians, a chorus of the same size . . . and a team of sixty machinists to move the scenery, the public expects and demands great things from you.[24]

Grandeur, luxury and spectacle – all these contributed to the success of Meyerbeer's *Robert le diable*, Véron's first production for Paris, which packed the Salle Le Peletier, earning an impressive 10,000 francs per night from its premiere in November 1831. The box office triumph saved the Paris Opéra from bankruptcy.[25]

There had been Grand Operas before – *La Muette de Portici* and *William Tell* were both in that category – but *Robert le diable* was the first to qualify on all the elements outlined by Véron. It was truly a spectacular event. The smaller, three-act operas of Rossini could no longer compete with its huge scale and dramatic power, nor with its popularity. According to Liszt, it was the success of *Robert le diable* that finally persuaded the Italian to give up writing operas.[26] Within three years of its premiere, it had been produced by seventy-seven different companies in ten countries around the world, from New York to St Petersburg, and had made more money than any other opera until that time. At the Paris Opéra, alone, it brought in 4 million francs during its first quarter of a century; it was the first opera to become a constant fixture in its repertoire, with 470 performances by 1864, when Meyerbeer died.[27] More than any other work, *Robert le diable* became the model of what Grand Opera should be.

Loosely based on the medieval legend of Robert the Devil, a Norman knight who discovers that his father is Satan, the opera tells the story of Robert's struggle to obtain the hand of his beloved Princess Isabelle. In scene after scene, Robert veers between his virtuous desires and the influence of his companion, Bertram, the embodiment of Satan, whose real purpose is to get Robert to sign away his soul to the Devil in exchange for magic powers to help in his quest. Bertram fails, he is pulled down into Hell at the stroke of midnight, and Robert wins the hand of Isabelle.

The Faustian parallels of Eugène Scribe's libretto explain part of the opera's appeal. 'Faustmania' was at its height in the early 1830s. There had been numerous productions of Goethe's story in the boulevard theatres, from which Scribe (who had worked in vaudeville and learned from it what was required to hold an audience) derived many of the opera's most striking scenes, narrative techniques and characters. Despite the opera's medieval setting, Scribe's Robert is a psychologically complex and 'modern' character, 'the hero who does not know precisely what it is he wants', as Heine put it, 'in perpetual conflict with himself' – in short a 'veracious portrait of the moral uncertainties of the epoch'. He was a character in which a bourgeois public was able to see itself.[28]

Robert derived much of its popularity from its historical drama – a defining element of Grand Opera where stories of individuals caught up in the turmoil of historical events replaced the classical and mythological subjects of eighteenth-century *opera seria*. History was at the heart of the Romantic imagination, in particular the Gothic and medieval themes that Meyerbeer and Scribe presented in their opera. The international craze for Walter Scott was an expression of this interest. Translations of his historical novels sold in mass editions right across the Continent. He had imitators everywhere, from Victor Hugo, whose *Notre-Dame de Paris* (1831) borrowed from a range of his Waverley books, to Mickiewicz in Poland, who compared his own work to a 'few pages torn from Walter Scott'. There were numerous adaptions of Scott's novels for the stage, with no fewer than fifty operas in the nineteenth century.[29]

But the main appeal of *Robert le diable*, according to Véron, was the spectacle created on the stage – a feast of movement, light and colours – and the splendour of its costumes, scenery and technical effects. The visual highlight was the 'Ballet of the Nuns': white-clad ghosts rise from their graves to dance erotically by moonlight – an effect made even more ghostly by the use of gas lighting and the veils attached to the dancers' bodices (the origin of the tutu). Chopin, who was in the audience for the opera's opening night, described its stunning impact in a letter to his friend from Warsaw, Tytus Woyciechowski:

> I don't know whether there has ever been such magnificence in a theatre, whether it has ever attained the pomp of the new 5-act opera 'Robert le Diable' by Mayerbeer [sic] . . . It is a masterpiece of the new school, in which devils (huge choirs) sing through speaking-trumpets, and souls rise from graves . . . in groups of 50 and 60; in which there is a diorama in the theatre, in which at the end you see the *intérieur* of a church, the whole church, at Christmas or Easter, lighted up, with monks, and all the congregation on the benches, and censors – even with the organ, the sound of which on the stage is enchanting and amazing, also it nearly drowns out the orchestra; nothing of the sort could be put on anywhere else. Mayerbeer has immortalized himself![30]

The dramatic novelty of these effects can only be compared to the introduction of sound and colour to the silent films of Hollywood. As one reviewer put it, 'no longer must we suffer with the ancient palaces disturbed by the last glimmerings of a dying Argand lamp, or the antique relics and flimsy columns which tremble at the slightest touch of a Venus in curlpapers or a Cupid in ballet shoes.'[31] Opera had entered the industrial age.

*

The box office triumph of *Robert le diable* also owed a great deal to publicity and marketing, aspects of the opera business in which Véron excelled. He maintained close relations with music publishers, journalists and agents, who were often journalists or publishers themselves, and used the proliferating music press to publicize his productions. His most important connection was with Maurice Schlesinger, the editor and owner of the influential *Revue et Gazette musicale de Paris*, who also owned the publication rights to *Robert le diable*.

Born in Berlin, Schlesinger had moved to Paris as a young man during the 1820s. Following in the footsteps of his father, Adolf Schlesinger, the founder of the *Berliner Allgemeine Musikalische Zeitung*, he moved into music publishing, buying mainly German works, and, in 1834, launched the music journal *Gazette musicale de Paris* to promote that business. Within a year the *Gazette* had taken over its main rival, the *Revue musicale*, and renamed itself the *Revue et Gazette musicale de Paris*, for which he secured the services of writers such as Scribe, Sand, Dumas and Balzac by paying handsome fees. Their fame helped him to attract composers to his publishing house. Young composers accepted low fees for their works because they knew that Schlesinger could help them get established in Paris. An eye for the value of publicity was not his only business skill.* Schlesinger was quick to adapt to the new realities of the capitalist system, in which publishing was part of a multi-media industry. It did not unduly worry him that the *Revue* operated at a loss, because he saw it as a means of promoting those composers, such as Meyerbeer, whose works he also published. There were larger profits to be made from the publication of the musical arrangements of opera arias than he could make from a music periodical. It was an early example of what today would be called a loss-leader. Seizing on the new popularity of serialized fiction, Schlesinger commissioned a wide range of stories to promote his published music list in the *Revue*, including Balzac's *Gambara*, which centres on a long and largely positive conversation about *Robert le diable* (albeit with some of the usual

---

* Many of his traits would reappear in the character of Jacques Arnoux, the publisher of *L'Art industriel*, in Gustave Flaubert's novel *Sentimental Education* (1869). Flaubert had known Maurice Schlesinger as a young man. At the age of fifteen, on holiday in Trouville, the seaside Norman town, Flaubert had fallen hopelessly in love with the publisher's mistress, who would soon become his wife, Élisa Schlesinger. Flaubert had struck up a friendship with the couple which would provide the basis of his novel's plot.

reservations about Meyerbeer's eclectic style and commercialism, which would haunt him later on).[32]

Schlesinger's *Revue* was partisan in its support of his composers and attacks on rivals such as Verdi, who was published by another house. There was no such thing as impartial music criticism in the nineteenth century: the major music journals were too closely tied to the publishing and concert businesses, and the critics of the time, who were not usually musicians,* generally wrote their musical reviews to promote the journals' interests.[33] The largest of them all, the *Allgemeine Musikalische Zeitung*, was produced as an in-house magazine by the Leipzig music publisher Breitkopf & Härtel, and rarely published positive reviews of works not in its catalogue. The smaller periodicals were notoriously venal and would publish anything if they were paid. The Bologna journal *L'Arpa* even printed on its masthead the instruction, 'Articles for insertion must be paid for in advance'.[34] Music journals depended heavily on subscriptions, so publishers and agents would subscribe to them to guarantee a puff for their clients (according to the impresario Alessandro Lanari, it was difficult to get a mention otherwise). Bribing journalists for favourable reviews was common practice. The critic Jules Janin was said to earn up to 8,000 francs from a premiere. Charles Maurice, the editor of *Courier des théâtres*, ran his journal as a protection business. Famous for his critical reviews and sharp put-downs, Maurice received fawning letters accompanied by money from artists.[35] Even the high-minded Berlioz, who relied on music journalism, much of it in Schlesinger's *Revue*, was not beyond corruption – although in his case writing good reviews was motivated less by monetary gain than by the need to protect himself as a composer, and perhaps the hope of winning favours from the powerful. Wanting a commission from the Paris Opéra for his opera *Benvenuto Cellini* (1838), Berlioz could not afford to give a bad review to Meyerbeer's *Les Huguenots*, first performed at the Opéra two years before.[36] What he published in the musical reviews was often far removed from what he really thought. He praised Halévy's opera *La Juive* (1835) in *Le Journal des débats* but poured scorn on it in conversations with his friends.

Véron was particularly active in making sure that *Robert le diable*

* Berlioz, Ernest Reyer, Victorin de Joncières, Schumann and Saint-Saëns were exceptional among composers in writing music reviews for the press.

received a welcome reception. He paid for mentions in the press to build interest in the production, spent large sums on taking critics out to lunch before the opening night, and gave them boxes and passes to the *foyer de la danse*.[37]

He also employed a claque, a long-established institution of organized applause which he regarded as a 'business necessity . . . as much a part of the production scheme as anything that took place on the stage'. The organizer of the Opéra claque was Auguste Levasseur, an intimate of all the best-known Parisian singers, actors and musicians, who was paid by them to arrange cheering for their performances and drown out the boos of rival claques. Véron gave him a hundred tickets for a premiere, more for the next performances if a production needed extra help. Levasseur would sell these tickets to his claque. Their work was planned carefully. Levasseur attended the rehearsals and discussed with Véron where loud applause was needed most. The positioning of the claque was critical: it had to surround the audience from all sides to galvanize them into more applause. Levasseur, a tall figure dressed in bright colours, would coordinate it from the stalls. 'I have seldom seen a more majestic demeanour than his,' wrote Berlioz. 'Never was there a more intelligent or braver dispenser of glory enthroned in the pit of a theatre.' Véron called Levasseur his 'director of success' and justified his employment as essential for the creation of an atmosphere. The critic Gautier agreed. A claque, he argued,

> renders as much service to the public as to the administration of a theatre. If it has at times protected mediocrity, it has often sustained a new, adventurous work, swayed a hesitant public, and silenced envy. In delaying the failure of a piece that has necessitated much expense, it has prevented the ruin of a vast enterprise and the despair of a hundred families. The claque enlivens performances that without it would be dull and cold.[38]

Meyerbeer was also a believer in publicity campaigns to support a new production, particularly during the first performances, when a cool reception could spell financial disaster. He courted the critics, invited them to dinners in expensive restaurants, gave them complimentary tickets, and often loaned them money which was not repaid.* It

---

* One loan was to Heinrich Börnstein to help him start the weekly journal *Vorwärts* with Karl Marx in 1844.

was said that he bribed journalists for good reviews, but there is little evidence to support the rumour, which was fuelled by resentment of his wealth and anti-Semitic prejudice. Meyerbeer had the insecurity of an outsider. He was deeply sensitive to any criticism. Despite his immense success, he was always anxious about the reception of his latest work, and fussed neurotically about every detail of its production. Heine wrote of him in the 1830s that 'he lacked a winner's self-belief, he showed his fear of public opinion, the slightest adverse comment frightened him.'[39]

Meyerbeer was modern in his media management. Others took a more old-fashioned view. 'Nowadays,' wrote Verdi, 'what an apparatus for an opera!? Journalists, artists, choristers, conductors, musicians, etc. etc., each of them has to bring his own stone to the edifice of publicity, creating in this way a miserable little frame that adds nothing to the merits of an opera.'[40] But the growing power of the press made it hard for anyone involved in opera production to neglect these aspects of the business.

The chief source of profit from *Robert le diable* was the publication of various arrangements for the domestic market in the form of sheet music. Although an opera had to make a profit for the house, the real money came from its spin-offs. Meyerbeer would make his fortune from these reductions of his operas. They sold many thousands of copies and, from each, he earned a royalty. The law in France gave artists rights of property in their own work, including foreign artists if their work appeared there first in French.

There was a mutual dependence between the commercial success of an opera and the publication of these *morceaux détachés*. Melodies from *Robert le diable* were published in a large variety of arrangements (for voice and piano, piano duet, violin and piano, string quartet, wind ensemble, even for small orchestra), and these in turn became important for the opera's longer-term success. The public was more likely to attend a performance at the opera house when it already knew the music from playing it at home or hearing it performed in a concert.

This connection was not new. Stendhal claimed that *The Barber of Seville* had owed much of its success 'to the abundance of waltz-tunes and quadrilles it has supplied to our dance orchestras! After the fiftieth or sixtieth society-ball,' he wrote in 1824, 'the *Barber* suddenly begins to sound strangely familiar, and *then* a visit to the Théâtre Louvois becomes a real pleasure.[41] From the 1830s, however, there was a boom in music publishing, driven by the growing popularity of music-making in the home, which accelerated this cycle. The invention of lithography made it possible to print cheap mass editions of sheet music. Published opera arias migrated from the theatre to the living room, the salon, ballroom, music hall and tavern; they were played by bands in parks, by street musicians, until everybody could sing them; and once they knew these tunes, they wanted to find out where they came from. A virtuous circle was thus formed between the production of an opera and the reproduction of its music through sheet music sales with each side of the business adding to the success of the other. This was the moment when the music business became part of the modern capitalist economy.

There were arrangements of *Robert le diable* for every level of musical proficiency. Liszt and Chopin both wrote virtuoso pieces based on extracts from the opera, but there were also fantasies and variations by Sigismond Thalberg, Adolphe Adam and Carl Czerny easily playable by amateurs. All these sold in Schlesinger editions in enormous quantities. By 1850, the *Revue et Gazette musicale* listed more than thirty piano pieces from *Robert le diable* that could be bought from its publishing division for a few francs each. Thirty years later there were more than 160 transcriptions, variations and other arrangements for military bands, dance orchestras, piano, voice and other instruments.[42]

Music publishers were always on the look-out for playable arrangements from successful operas – and for composers it was an easy way to make some cash. Mozart and Beethoven both paid their rent by composing simple variations on well-loved opera tunes. The Viennese composer Josef Gelinek, a 'one-man wholesale piano-variation factory' with export sales throughout Europe, amassed an estate of 42,000 gulden (110,000 francs).[43] The pianist and composer Henri Herz churned out more than 100 opus numbers based on opera melodies. Czerny was even more industrious. In 1848, his English publisher, Robert Cocks and Co., issued a list of Czerny's printed works to date. Of his 798 opus numbers published so far, 304 were based on melodies from some eighty-seven operas. Three years earlier the London concert manager John Ella had seen how Czerny worked in his Vienna studio: he had four desks set up with a different composition on each one, allowing him to write the music on one page and turn to the next desk while the ink dried on the previous manuscript.[44]

Underlying this new industry was the tremendous growth of piano ownership in the early decades of the nineteenth century. In the eighteenth, the pianoforte was an expensive novelty. Delicately built, like a harpsichord, it lacked the power or range of notes and volume to play large-scale works. But technical improvements by makers such as Sébastien Érard in Paris and John Broadwood in England made the piano much more robust, with a heavier action and foot pedals producing a bigger sound, longer sustained notes and a more extensive range – improvements which enabled Beethoven to write his mature piano works.

By the end of the 1810s, Broadwood was manufacturing pianos on a factory scale and selling basic models for as little as £40.[45] In Jane Austen's *Pride and Prejudice* (1813), the piano was an item found not only in the homes of the upper landed gentry such as Lady Catherine De Bourgh, but also in the Bennet household and other minor houses in Longbourn – in the Lucas household and the Bingleys' leased mansion, though not in the home of the less prosperous Uncle Philips, where card-playing had to take the place of music as the main form of evening entertainment.[46] By the 1840s, piano ownership had become widespread in Britain: 200 firms were producing pianos, totalling 23,000 pianos per year, 10 per cent of these by Broadwood alone. Britain led the world in piano manufacturing.[47] But French and German piano-makers were catching up, particularly Érard and Pleyel, the two most prestigious French makers, whose export business benefited most from the development of the railways (unlike the English, they did not have to ship their pianos across a sea). The French manufacturers also profited from promotional European tours by virtuoso pianists such as Liszt (who played for Érard) and Thalberg (for Pleyel), which allowed these companies to advertise their pianos and show what they were capable of producing in the best hands (perhaps one of the earliest examples of celebrity branding). In 1845, there were an estimated 60,000 pianos and 100,000 people playing them in Paris, a city with a population of about a million people. 'There is not a home, even of the smallest bourgeois, where one does not find a piano,' wrote Édouard Fétis, with some exaggeration, in 1847. 'The instrument forms, in all necessity, a part of the furniture of every family; you will find it even in the concierge's lodge.' Heine complained that 'one drowned in music, there is almost not a single house in Paris where you can be saved as in the ark before the flood.'[48]

Piano ownership was also common further east. 'There is almost no house where the thumping of a piano is not heard,' claimed the *Warsaw Courier* in 1840. 'We have pianos on the ground, first, second and third floors. Young ladies play the piano, mothers play the piano, children play the piano.' Eight years later the same newspaper was more sober in its estimate of perhaps 5,000 pianos in Warsaw – that is one for every thirty people in a city with a population of around 150,000 – which is impressive enough. Most of the pianos in Warsaw were imported from Vienna or Leipzig.[49]

In Moscow and St Petersburg, by contrast, there were at least a dozen piano manufacturers protected by restrictive tariffs on imports. A grand piano made in Moscow could be bought for 800 roubles (920 francs), a quarter of the sum it would cost to import a Broadwood or Pleyel, and affordable to the landed gentry and wealthier merchants with an annual income of 3,000–4,000 roubles (3,500–4,600 francs).[50] By the 1840s, upright pianos were found in many homes. Manufacturers marketed the piano as a symbol of respectability, and piano tutors were in high demand as younger generations of the Russian gentry sought to acquire the trappings of Western civilization.

In Turgenev's novel *Home of the Gentry* (1859), set in provincial Russia in 1842, the piano appears frequently to illustrate the artificial manners of the aristocracy, as in this scene, where Panshin, an official from St Petersburg assigned to the local town, and Varvara Pavlovna, the daughter of a retired major-general from the Russian capital, sing a duet from Rossini's *Soirées musicales* (1835):

> Varvara Pavlovna sat down at the piano. Panshin stood beside her. They sang the duet in a low voice, with Varvara Pavlovna correcting him a number of times, and then they sang it aloud and twice repeated. '*Mira la bianca lu . . . u . . . una.*' Varvara Pavlovna's voice had lost its freshness, but she used it very cleverly. Panshin was diffident at first and slightly out of tune, then he carne into his own and, if he did not sing irreproachably, he at least made his shoulders quiver, swayed his whole body and raised his hand from time to time like a real singer. Varvara Pavlovna played two or three pieces by Thalberg and coquettishly 'spoke' a French ariette.[51]

Throughout Europe the piano was perceived as a key marker of gentility. Playing it was deemed one of the 'accomplishments' for a young woman that made her worthy of marriage.[52] Nineteenth-century fiction is full of courtship scenes in which a romantic heroine and her young suitor play duets – the touching of their hands being just about as close as they could get without kissing. Along with the harp, the piano was the instrument deemed most physically appropriate for women – woodwind instruments forcing them to purse their lips, violins to twist their bodies, and cellos to spread their legs; whereas at the piano they sat with their feet together, preserving decorum. Compared to woodwind or stringed instruments, on which players were required to make the notes themselves, the piano was considered relatively 'easy' and accessible to women, who needed only an ability to hit the right keys.[53] There is no plausible means by which one can measure the impact of the piano on women's lives, but it was clearly an important cultural and societal shift. Where women had once been the silent members of the family, meekly doing needlework in the salon, they now had a central role in music-making in the home.

The ease with which the piano could be played accounts for its popularity. Its upright design was important too, enabling the piano to be fitted in the smallest living rooms by placing it against a wall. Any family that owned a piano could now entertain itself at home. Whereas opera or concert tickets were too expensive for middling families to buy on a regular basis, sheet music was easily affordable, and weekly piano lessons were not beyond the means of a reasonably well-off family.

There was a whole industry of second-rank composers who churned out piano albums and arrangements for this new market. Thalberg, Herz, Franz Hünten, Tekla Bądarzewska-Baranowska – these and many others made their names from the sort of pieces (sentimental, easy on the ear, with brilliant effects, but not too hard to play) that gave the piano popular appeal. One of the most common forms of sheet music was the four-hand piano transcription. It swept aside the string quartet or trio as the main means of making music in the home. No other medium was so important to the dissemination of the opera, choral and orchestral repertory until the invention of the phonograph and radio. With four hands the full sound of a large-scale work could be reproduced; while such works would be hard for pianists to manage on their own, with two players the difficulties could be shared. The range of music for four hands was staggering: in Germany alone, a Hofmeister catalogue of

1844 listed almost 9,000 different works, including 150 entries for Beethoven, with all his symphonies, overtures, masses, concertos and chamber music, along with his opera, *Fidelio*.[54]

Such was the demand for duet transcriptions of the latest opera arias that publishers employed their own in-house arrangers to turn them out as fast as possible (in 1840, Schlesinger paid 1,000 francs to the young Richard Wagner – at that time trying to make his name in Paris – for what Wagner called the 'shameful labour' of making a whole series of arrangements of Donizetti's opera *La Favorite*).[55] Some composers undertook their own transcriptions, or employed assistants to do them, as Verdi did with Emmanuele Muzio, starting with *Macbeth* in 1846. As publishers and composers both realized, the rapid publication of multiple arrangements of a new opera was the most effective way to promote that work, disseminating knowledge of its winning tunes and stimulating interest in its performance. It was the public's familiarity with an opera's tunes that drew them to the opera house.

The sheet music industry changed the way composers earned their living in the middle decades of the nineteenth century.

In the eighteenth century, composers were the servants of their employers, who often assumed the ownership of their music. When Haydn went to work for Prince Anton Esterházy in 1769, his contract stipulated that he was obliged to 'compose such pieces of music as His Serene Princely Highness may command, and neither to communicate such new compositions to anyone, nor to allow them to be copied, but to retain them wholly for the exclusive use of his Highness'. The pirate publication of his works in Paris led to this restriction being dropped when the contract was renewed in 1779. This allowed Haydn to develop his relations with music publishers in Vienna, Germany, France and Britain, where his works were well known when he arrived in London in the 1790s.[56]

In the opera world, meanwhile, as we have seen, composers would receive a one-time fee for their music. Once they had sold the score to a theatre or an impresario, they earned no more if it was resold or copies of it were made for other impresarios. Nor was there any money to be earned from other theatres putting on their work, unless the composer was a citizen of France, the only country to recognize performance rights in law before the 1840s, or had their work performed in French in that country.*

The development of music publishing opened up a new source of income, enabling composers to become the owners of their music and collect a fee or royalty for the right to publish it. For all but the most commercial composers it took many decades before such earnings came close to their earnings from performing and teaching. As late as the mid-1850s, the young Brahms (who would later make a comfortable living from his published works) was paid more for a single piano recital than he received from his publisher, Breitkopf & Härtel, for his *Four Ballads* (Op. 10).[57] In the early decades of the century the money to be made from publishing was insignificant: the market was too small, and there were too many pirate copies of a newly published work. Mozart earned extremely little from his published scores, but lost a lot to piracy, mostly by his copyists. He tried to contain the problem by making them work in his apartment, where he could keep an eye on them. Beethoven was more organized. He would protect himself by copying out the last few pages of his works himself.

Beethoven struggled to achieve economic independence through his music. As a freelance composer, he scraped a modest living by various means: teaching; concerts; composing on commission; soliciting donations from wealthy men and women by dedicating works to them; and selling scores to publishers. He was a competent and at times artful businessman, pushing hard for higher fees from publishers, and in his last years, as he became increasingly indebted, even double-dealing between them. To counteract the problem of international piracy, he would sell the same work to several publishers in different countries and try to coordinate the publication simultaneously – a difficult operation before the railway and the telegraph but the most effective policy without laws of copyright. Beethoven's earnings from these publications were modest. For the Fifth and Sixth Symphonies, the Op. 69 Cello Sonata and the two Piano Trios of Op. 70, Breitkopf and Härtel paid him just 400 gulden (1,050 francs), enough for him to live on for three months.[58] His highest fees were earned from easy piano pieces

---

* Performance rights were introduced in Britain in the Dramatic Copyright Acts of 1833 and 1842, but for foreign composers the enforcement of such rights was dependent on bilateral treaties between their countries and Britain.

('bagatelles') and arrangements (such as the British folk songs he arranged for the Edinburgh publisher George Thomson). But the 'tiresome business' of negotiating payment was demeaning. Beethoven yearned for a simpler and more dignified way to sell his work, one that would give him independence and security. 'I call it tiresome,' he wrote to the publisher Friedrich Hofmeister, 'because I should like such matters to be differently ordered . . . There ought to be in the world a *market for art*, where the artist would only have to bring his works and take as much money as he needed. But, as it is, an artist has to be to a certain extent a businessman as well.'[59]

As the market for sheet music developed, composers became more business-minded in their dealings with publishers. They could not expect royalties, except of course in France, but they could hold out for higher fees to reflect the earnings from these arrangements.

Vincenzo Bellini was particularly determined in this respect. Born in Sicily in 1801, and rising as a young man to international fame with *Il Pirata* (1827), *La Sonnambula* and *Norma* (both in 1831), he was, in the words of his biographer, 'a conscious modern artist' who thought he should be paid in accordance with the economic value of his work.[60] Before his death, in 1835, he was earning 16,000 francs for an opera, over three times more than Rossini's highest fee of 5,000 francs only a few years earlier. He justified his monetary demands by claiming that he spent as long on one opera as others did on three or four. Certainly, he could not get away with Rossini's practice of recycling bits of earlier operas because his were published and disseminated internationally. Without effective laws of copyright, Bellini could also argue that he lost much of his deserved income to pirate publications of his works. 'All of Italy, all of Germany, all of Europe is flooded with *Norma*s,' complained his publisher, Giovanni Ricordi. The best copyists were capable of reproducing an entire score after listening to it a few times in the theatre. Bellini became so annoyed by the pirated productions of his operas in his own native Sicily, a lawless state when it came to copyright, that several times he appealed to its government to take measures against them (nothing came of these appeals). Bellini would have liked to find a means of earning royalties on a more regular basis: he would have been a rich man if he had. But piracy prevented that. All he could do with any of his works was to sell the publication rights for the biggest one-time fee that he could get.[61]

From 1840, when the first laws of copyright were introduced in the Kingdom of Piedmont–Sardinia and Austrian-ruled Lombardy and Veneto, Italian composers could start to earn royalties. The development of copyright turned the opera score into a form of capital, whose income was derived from its stage productions and its publication in various arrangements for the home. Gaetano Donizetti, four years older than Bellini and slower to attain his international fame, was the first to spot the potential of his publication rights. Negotiating the contract for his opera *Adelia* in 1840, he wrote to Vincenzo Jacovacci, the impresario for the Teatro Apollo in Rome:

> As to the ownership of the score, I would not ask you for the entire ownership, but *only for the reductions for piano and voice* [Donizetti's emphasis], which would not at all diminish your right to have it performed or to sell it for performance wherever, and if that does not please you, or you think you will lose a lot, I would concede half the price I would expect to earn in Italy . . . provided I could reserve for myself the ownership in France, where, even if you wanted to, you would have no right to prevent me from selling it to whoever wished to publish it.[62]

In Italy, where the laws remained weak until the country's unification in 1861, composers would depend on publishers to enforce their copyright and stamp out piracy – as far as that was possible in places like the Kingdom of Two Sicilies, where pirate publishers were actively protected by the government. The royalty system united the composer and his publisher in a natural economic alliance.

Verdi was the first Italian composer to make substantial profits from the new laws of copyright. The key to his success was his relationship with Giovanni Ricordi, who acted not just as his publisher but as his agent and impresario, promoting his operas, collecting royalties, and using all his powers to protect him against piracy – no easy task. Ricordi was the most important music publisher south of the Alps when he bought the rights to *Oberto*, Verdi's debut opera at La Scala, in 1839. Beginning as a lowly copyist in a small theatre in Milan, he ventured into business, like many copyists, by making his own pirate copies of the scores and selling them to theatres and impresarios. There were no laws against this trade, on which hundreds of small provincial theatres in Italy depended in those years.

The high demand for scores had persuaded Ricordi to set up as a publisher as early as 1808. He also turned to buying scores, building up an important rental library for theatres. His breakthrough came in 1825, when he managed to secure exclusive rights to La Scala's huge archive. It allowed him to rent out scores, sell handmade or printed copies, and publish any number of arrangements from the theatre's complete range of operas. From this base his business grew. He acquired the rights to publish the arrangements of Rossini's operas, the subject of the first real boom in music publishing, and bought new works from composers such as Bellini.

As a young man setting out to make his name and fortune, Verdi was attracted to the charismatic Ricordi by his willingness to be not just his publisher but to manage his affairs. Verdi had a good head for business and always drove a hard bargain. But he did not like to deal directly with the theatre management, fearing that he would get less than he deserved. According to the contract he signed with Ricordi for *Oberto*, Verdi would receive 2,000 Austrian lire (2,290 francs) for rights to the score but no publication royalties. Although the contract was an opportunity for the unknown young composer to stage his work at La Scala, Verdi thought it was 'unjust' that Ricordi could pocket all the earnings from the published score and arrangements. In 1843, with his next major opera, *Nabucco*, Verdi ceded half the rights to Ricordi's junior and most bitter rival, Francesco Lucca, a tactic intended to increase his leverage with the senior publisher. It was a risky strategy – he might have lost Ricordi altogether – but it worked. In November 1843, after the success of *Nabucco*, Ricordi paid Verdi 9,000 Austrian lire (10,300 francs) for the rights to *Ernani* (one third more than the value the composer had given it himself the previous May, when he had offered it to La Fenice in Venice).[63]

From this point, as Verdi's fame increased, publishers competed for his signature. Ricordi paid the most: 9,000 lire for *I due Foscari* in 1844, 18,000 lire for *Giovanna d'Arco* in 1845, and 16,000 lire (18,300 francs) for *Macbeth* in December 1846.[64] All these sums were one-time payments by Ricordi to own all the rights to the score. But starting with *Gerusalemme*, in 1847, there was a fundamental change. Verdi had just been in Paris, where the opera had received its first performance (as *Jérusalem*) in La Salle Peletier. He had been impressed by the *droits d'auteur* system in operation there – it guaranteed a fair reward – and demanded payment from Ricordi on these terms. In the contract for *Gerusalemme* Ricordi lowered the fixed sum (to 8,000 lire) but paid 500 lire (570 francs) every time the score was rented in the first five years, and 200 lire after that.

The publisher was eager to secure monopoly control of Verdi's work – the surest guarantee of profit there could be in the opera industry, as he was quick to recognize. Ricordi had been put out by Verdi's decision to sell the rights to three further operas (*Attila, I masnadieri* and *Il corsaro*) to Lucca since 1846. For his next work, *La battaglia de Legnano*, first performed in Rome in 1849, Ricordi proposed a new type of contract in which Verdi would receive a modest up-front fee (4,000 francs, as opposed to the 24,000 Verdi had been given for *Il corsaro* by Lucca), but agreed to pay 12,000 francs for publication rights for the next ten years in Italy with a further payment of 6,000 francs for publication rights in France and Britain. Crucially, the contract also guaranteed a royalty for Verdi of between 30 and 40 per cent on every sale and rental of the score and a similar amount from the sale of its arrangements, whether in a country that had copyright agreements with Lombardy or not. This became the model of Verdi's future contracts with the Milan publisher, although from 1857 and *Simon Boccanegra* his royalties would rise by 10 per cent.[65]

Once he had acquired the rights to a work, Ricordi made it his business to protect and promote it. This was his attraction for Verdi. From the start of their relationship, Ricordi had been placing warnings in the press against pirate publications of the *Oberto* score. He used his in-house journal, *La gazzetta musicale di Milano*, to publicize his operas, advertising reductions for domestic use and offering copies of them free to subscribers as a supplement to the newspaper.

Ricordi was quick to publish arrangements. He knew how much money could be made from them, and understood their role in the creation of new markets for an opera. As soon as the success of *Oberto* became clear, he brought out arrangements of its winning scenes and arias for piano solo and duet, voice and piano, flute and piano, violin and piano, cello and piano, two violins, mixed combinations of voices, etc. Cheaply priced, they flew off the shelves and into homes across the Continent. The number of arrangements increased steeply with the popularity of each successive Verdi opera: there were seventy for *Oberto*, 253 for *Nabucco* and 267 for *I Lombardi* in the Ricordi catalogue – most of them appearing within a few months of the opera's premiere.[66]

Ricordi could not sell these publications fast enough. The piano-vocal and piano-solo reductions of *I Lombardi* were published barely a few days after the opera's premiere in February 1843. For *Ernani*, Ricordi started advertising the arrangements weeks before the premiere in March 1844. He wrote to La Fenice begging for the swift return of the full score so that the arrangements could be quickly made: 'Any delay would greatly damage me, since the music sells abundantly when hearts are still warm from the successful result produced by the performance in the theatre.' For *Macbeth*, Verdi employed Muzio to make the reductions while he composed the orchestral score. The operation entered a new phase of high-speed production and delivery. 'I am so busy with the arrangements of *Macbeth* that I can hardly keep up with the engravers, and Ricordi is in a fiendish rush,' Muzio wrote on 14 April 1847, shortly after the opera had opened at the Teatro della Pergola in Florence. A week later he wrote: '*Macbeth* is finding enthusiastic supporters in Milan; it's played in all homes, and the numbers are on every piano.'[67]

Pirate editions of these reductions would appear just as fast. On the appearance of each new Verdi opera they would pour out of Naples. So would pirate versions of the orchestral score. Ricordi did his best to combat them by writing to the managers of theatres warning them against their use: they were neither accurate nor authentic. He would shame their publishers by placing notices about their 'thefts' in the local press – a tactic he had used since the early 1830s to defend the works of Bellini.[68] He appealed to the censors in Milan to protect his copyright. After the success of *Nabucco*, when the Lombard market was flooded with reductions by pirate publishers, the censor's office was clogged with complaints by Ricordi. In this chaos, understandably perhaps, the Milan censors took the view that it was not in their authority to guarantee the property rights of authors or their publishers. To defend their copyright, Verdi and Ricordi would need stronger and more international laws.

2

In Berlin, Pauline Viardot met her old friend Clara Schumann. They had become acquainted in 1838, when Pauline gave a concert in Leipzig, the

Clara and Robert Schumann, c. 1850.

home town of Clara Wieck, as the pianist was known before her marriage to the composer Robert Schumann in 1840. The two women, just three years apart in age, had struck up a warm friendship. But it had cooled with Pauline's growing wealth and fame during the 1840s. Clara, who had come to share her husband's serious approach to music, believed her friend had compromised her artistic principles to court popularity. Writing in her journal in 1843, Clara had expressed her disappointment at Pauline's choice of virtuoso songs at a concert she had given in Berlin: 'A pity that such a thoroughly musical creature as Pauline, who certainly has the sense for really good music, completely sacrifices her taste to the public, and thus follows in the footsteps of all the ordinary Italians.'[69]

Now, in February 1847, Clara wanted Pauline to perform in the Berlin premiere of Schumann's oratorio *Das Paradies und die Peri*. Schumann had been having problems with the lead female singer intended for the part and had asked Clara to beg a favour from Pauline, who had come to Berlin to sing in Meyerbeer's *Les Huguenots*. Pauline declined, saying that she did not have the time to learn a new part in the few days left before the premiere. Over-sensitive and distrustful, Clara took the rejection as a personal slight to her husband. Writing in her diary, she accused Pauline of 'lacking feeling' for his 'intimate and German music'. She thought success had gone to her head, that she was motivated by money, and had 'sold her soul' to Meyerbeer, the cosmopolitan embodiment of the new commercialism in music which Robert had been fighting for the past decade.[70]

In 1834, Schumann had founded the *Neue Zeitschrift für Musik* with Clara's father, Friedrich Wieck. The aim of the Leipzig magazine was to renew interest in the music of the past, Mozart and Beethoven in particular, and promote contemporary composers, such as Berlioz and Chopin, who were writing 'serious music' for the ideals of art rather than money. The magazine attacked the commercialism of Grand Opera and its attendant industry of piano arrangements for pandering to the lowest taste. Meyerbeer was the main target – the leader of the 'Philistines' opposed by the righteous 'League of David' (*Davidsbündler*) in Schumann's *Carnaval* (1834–5). His wealth and popularity were obviously galling to Schumann, whose own dramatic works were failures. In a vitriolic review of *Les Huguenots*, Schumann accused Meyerbeer of writing 'vulgar' and 'immoral' music whose sole purpose was 'to flabbergast or titillate': music for 'the circus', Schumann claimed.[71]

Schumann was not alone in his campaign against commercial music. In Britain, France and Germany there were similar reactions against the 'philistine' and 'vulgar' trends of opera, salon and virtuoso music; and similar initiatives by music journals and critics, musical societies and institutions, to develop a new type of concert life for 'serious music'. The inspiration of this movement was the Romantic notion that music, like all art, should elevate the soul; that artists were the spiritual leaders of humanity, prophets and idealists, not businessmen. According to this view, any music with commercial motives could not be considered art. In the journals dedicated to 'serious music' there was moralistic scorn for the 'mercenary speculations' of benefit concerts with crowd-pleasing medleys from familiar operas, for shallow salon music, and for the flashy showmanship of virtuoso soloists, which Turgenev, jumping on the bandwagon, also blamed for the decline of music in St Petersburg in a critical review for the Russian press in 1846.[72] The backlash against the virtuoso was particularly strong. 'Art for him is nothing but gold coin and laurel wreaths,' complained Berlioz.[73] But there was more to it than a reaction against the mercenary egotist. The virtuoso soloist was free to embellish on a piece of music to display his skills. But this was sacrilege in a music culture where value was increasingly attached to the integrity of 'the work' itself. In this culture the performer's role was to play the work as faithfully to the composer's intentions as he could.

By the 1840s, the virtuoso concert was starting to decline as a more serious concert culture developed. Instead of the old miscellanies of a dozen or so pieces – generally a mix of opera numbers, virtuoso instrumental solos, chamber music, overtures, and bits of symphonies and concertos – concert programmes were increasingly devoted to a smaller number of works performed whole. The fall of the miscellany was in part financial: the concert manager had to pay large fees to the soloists. But audiences were also showing signs of tiring of virtuoso potpourris and of wanting something more substantial in their place.[74]

In London the new trend had begun with the foundation of the Philharmonic Society in 1813. Established by professional musicians to assert their independence from noble patronage, the Society was devoted to the promotion of serious music, especially the holy trinity of Mozart, Haydn and Beethoven. Works were performed in their entirety in subscription concerts in the Argyll Rooms. In some ways attendance at such concerts was part of the assertion of a middle-class identity, a way for subscribers to align themselves with the aristocracy as gatekeepers of high culture. Beethoven occupied a dominant position in the Society's repertoire. His Ninth Symphony was commissioned by the Society, which paid £50 for it, although it was performed in Vienna several times before the score arrived in London in 1824.[75]

In Paris the cult of Beethoven was equally strong in the Société des Concerts du Conservatoire established in 1828. Formed by the conductor François-Antoine Habeneck and made up of professors from the Conservatoire and their pupils, its orchestra performed more symphonies by Beethoven than by all other composers combined (360 of the 548 symphonies performed from 1828 to 1871). Its repertoire was dominated by the orchestral works of dead masters, the surest way to guarantee an audience. 'The public accustomed to attending is so used to Beethoven, Mozart, and Haydn that it is almost always cold to the unknown, and especially to the new,' wrote the Paris correspondent of the *Allgemeine Musikalische Zeitung* in 1847.[76] Like the London Phil-harmonic, the Société drew subscribers from the intelligentsia, including many well-known cultural figures, such as Balzac, Hugo, Delacroix and Alfred de Vigny. A devoted follower of Beethoven, Berlioz reviewed the Conservatory concerts in a reverential tone, referring to the public that frequented them as the only group of people capable of appreciat-ing great music and setting them above the merely fashionable bourgeois public that went to the Opéra.[77]

Leipzig had a thriving music culture based on its Conservatory, the leading music college in the whole of Germany, the Leipzig Opera and the Gewandhaus Orchestra. It had more music publishers than any other city in Europe.[78] Many of its citizens belonged to singing clubs and the Bach Society, which kept alive the choral music of the city's famous Cantor of St Thomas's church and director of its Collegium Musicum from 1723 to the composer's death in 1750. The Gewand-haus, or cloth hall, where concerts had been held since the 1780s, was the focus of the city's serious musical life in the nineteenth century. Mendelssohn became the director of the Gewandhaus Orchestra in 1835 and, until he died in 1847, developed a stable repertoire of 'histor-ical' music, focusing on Beethoven and Bach, whose works he rescued from relative obscurity, and reviving interest in Schubert, whose Ninth Symphony he premiered in 1839, ten years after Schubert's death. A growing share of the repertoire was made up of the works of dead mas-ters: 48 per cent in 1837–47 compared to 23 per cent in 1820–25 and just 13 per cent in 1781–5.[79]

Music festivals played an important role in the dissemination of a serious music culture in the 1830s and 1840s. They took off with the coming of the railways, which made it possible for amateur musicians, singing clubs and choirs to travel in large numbers to perform in them. In Germany the male-voice choral movement of the 1840s numbered in excess of 100,000 amateur singers. They were mostly organized into *Liedertafel* (singing clubs) in the Rhineland, Stuttgart and Bavaria, though they were also found in Bohemia and Austria, where the Vienna *Männergesangsverein*, established in 1843, was similar. Proudly civic and middle class in their values, these groups served as a democratic focus for the broader cultural aims of German nationhood. With the coming of the railway the highpoint of their concert life became the Lower Rhine Music Festivals, which since 1817 had rotated between

Aachen, Cologne, Elberfeld and Düsseldorf. All four towns were connected to the railway by the end of the 1840s, enabling them to draw a large and growing public of music lovers and performers for their mainly German repertoire of oratorios, masses and cantatas, overtures and symphonies. Beethoven, Handel and Mozart were consistently the most performed composers at these festivals.[80]

Chamber concerts also played a growing part in the development of a serious music culture at this time. Until the 1800s, there had been no such thing as a professional string quartet playing regular public concerts. Chamber music was for skilled amateur players in a private setting or salon, in contrast to the public music genres of the symphony or opera. The first professional string quartets emerged only in the 1800s. The quartet formed by Ignaz Schuppanzigh was the most important. It put on a series of public subscription concerts in a restaurant in Vienna in 1805. Two years later, the Schuppanzigh Quartet gave the first public performance of Beethoven's Razumovsky Quartets, three long works that took the genre of the string quartet to a new level of technical complexity requiring performance by professionals. As chamber music became harder on the fingers, it moved from the salon to the concert hall.

Societies for chamber music were established throughout Europe during the 1840s. In London the number of chamber concerts increased steeply in the early 1840s, largely due to the establishment of the Beethoven Quartet Society and John Ella's Musical Union, which put on regular concerts of chamber works by the great German composers. The concerts of the Musical Union were characterized by intellectual rigour. Ella was the first to provide detailed programme notes for his audience. He encouraged a purist attitude to music which set itself in opposition to the 'mercenary' motives of virtuoso concerts, miscellanies and benefits. A programme of the Musical Union in 1845 denounced the 'speculations' of commercial concerts which did 'nothing for art' but 'fill the pockets of shopkeepers and Jew speculators'.[81]

In Paris there were several societies promoting chamber works. They were mostly set up by professional musicians, such as the violinist Pierre Baillot, who aspired to the same ideals as the Société des Concerts du Conservatoire. Music publishers became involved as well. In 1838, Schlesinger's *Revue et Gazette musicale* organized a long-running series of concerts for its subscribers to promote the chamber works published by its owner which, the journal feared, were not performed enough because of the popularity of piano pieces and romances in salons.[82]

Piano concerts were changing too. Pianists such as Liszt and Clara Schumann moved away from performing virtuoso pieces in commercial concerts and turned instead to the solo concert, or 'recital' (a term first used by Liszt in 1840). In these recitals they played longer pieces, whole sonatas, from a more serious list of works. Clara Schumann shaped the piano repertoire more than anyone. The programming of her concerts – which would often start with historical ('classical') works by Bach and Beethoven and end with new and more Romantic pieces by Chopin or Schumann – became the model for the modern recital.[83]

It was in the middle decades of the nineteenth century that 'classical music' developed as a concept and a separate category from 'commercial' or 'popular' music. The term 'classical' had been applied to 'ancient music' since the eighteenth century; in the early decades of the nineteenth century it was sometimes used to describe general qualities of excellence. From the 1830s, however, it came to be associated with a more specific corpus of canonic works by dead composers – Beethoven, Mozart and Haydn, in particular – who dominated the performance canon of serious music from the 1830s and 1840s. Although the term was applied to all music, it was most closely linked to chamber works because of their demanding, intellectual character.[84]

In the early nineteenth century there had been no real distinction between 'classical' and 'popular' music. They were played together in miscellanies. But in the mid-century there was a split between the two, expressed in the antagonism felt by Schumann for Meyerbeer: on the one hand, serious classical recitals, chamber and orchestral concerts of whole works; and, on the other, commercial promenade concerts, led by conductor impresarios like Johann Strauss in Vienna, Philippe Musard in Paris, August Manns or Louis-Antoine Jullien in London, in which a mixture of 'popular' orchestral works, dance music, opera arias and virtuoso piano pieces were performed for a much larger audience. The Saturday matinée concerts conducted by Manns at the Crystal Palace (after it was moved to Sydenham in 1854) attracted crowds of 30,000 people, many of them coming down by train from London for the day.*

---

* Pauline Viardot was among them one day in the summer of 1858, when she was performing in London. She came with Henry Chorley, the violinist Joseph Joachim, Anton

Pauline was unusual in singing for both these markets. It was mistaken and unfair of Clara Schumann to accuse her of selling out to commercialism in music. Although she performed in popular concerts, Pauline also sang a demanding repertoire in concerts for connoisseurs. In London, for example, she appeared in several concerts at the Dudley Gallery in the Egyptian Hall, where she joined forces with the soprano Clara Novello and the pianist Charles Hallé to pioneer the cause of chamber works by Beethoven, Schubert, Mendelssohn and Schumann, which at that time were performed rarely because they were thought too avant-garde and difficult. Pauline's performances of Schubert's *Lieder* were particularly important in helping them to become better known. From the start of her career, she also took an active interest in the rediscovery of 'ancient' music, restoring Monteverdi, Lully, Pergolesi, Cimarosa, Gluck and Johann Gottlieb Graun to their place in the concert repertoire, and singing arias from Handel's operas, which at that time were unheard (no Handel opera was performed in full during the entire nineteenth century).[85]

In 1842, on his first tour of Russia, Liszt gave a recital for the Tsar, who arrived late and then talked while the great pianist played. Liszt stopped playing. When the Tsar asked why, Liszt replied: 'Music herself should be silent when Nicholas speaks.'[86] Liszt's sarcasm may have lost him a medal from the Tsar but it struck a mighty blow for the artist's dignity.

By the 1840s, in most of northern Europe if not Russia, the public had become silenced during opera and concert performances. It was a radical departure from the customs of the court, where music was an accompaniment to social intercourse, dinners, balls. Traditionally, from its origins in Italy, the opera house had been a meeting place for the aristocracy. It was not unusual for the audience to move around and talk throughout a performance, only quietening down during the main arias. The French were horrified by the noisiness of Italian audiences.

Rubinstein, Frederick Gye and Charles Hallé, who had just founded the Hallé Orchestra in Manchester. After an alcoholic picnic in the park, they went to the Crystal Palace, where the music competed with various entertainments (jugglers, acrobats, that sort of thing), and then travelled to Greenwich for dinner and more alcohol, where Chorley, drunk, passed out under the table (Héritte-Viardot, *Une famille de grands musiciens*, pp. 146–8).

In his memoirs Berlioz describes a visit to the Cannobiano Theatre in Milan for a performance of Donizetti's *L'elisir d'amore* in 1832:

> I found the theatre full of people talking in normal voices, with their backs to the stage. The singers, undeterred, gesticulated and yelled their lungs out in the strictest spirit of rivalry. At least I presumed they did, from their wide-open mouths; but the noise of the audience was such that no sound penetrated except the bass drum. People were gambling, eating supper in their boxes, etc., etc.[87]

On their honeymoon, in 1840, the Viardots attended a performance of *La Sonnambula* at La Scala in Milan. Pauline was so outraged by the audience's constant talking, eating, getting up, walking around the theatre, calling out to the singers after every aria, that she vowed never to perform on stage in Italy.[88] She never did.

From the 1830s, audience behaviour began to change. Silence gradually became the norm in the major opera houses north of the Alps. Concert audiences became silent as patterns of behaviour came to be dictated by serious music lovers, mostly drawn from the professional classes, rather than by members of the aristocracy. Various explanations have been advanced to account for this shift, from the immersion of the audience in the visual spectacle of Grand Opera to the anonymity and insecurity of the new bourgeois public, for whom the silence was synonymous with respectability and decorum.[89] No doubt all these factors played their part. But at the heart of the phenomenon was the new seriousness towards music: it demanded to be listened to.

The silencing of the concert audience was reflected in the layout of the seating in the public concert hall. In contrast to the informal arrangement of the chairs in the private concert or salon, which left room to move around, the seating in the concert hall was organized in formal rows, so that any movement caused a noisy disturbance. Strict rules of silence were imposed at the London Musical Union, where serious music lovers from the liberal professions were the majority. *'Il piu grand'omaggio alla musica, è nel silenzio'* ('Silence is the greatest homage to music') was the Union's motto. From 1847, programmes for its concerts carried the following notice: 'We entreat members unable to remain throughout the performances, to take advantage of the cessation between each movement of the compositions, to leave WITHOUT DISTURBING ARTISTS AND AUDIENCE.'[90]

At the Leipzig Gewandhaus there was also enforced silence in the concert hall. Above the stage was a motto from Seneca – *Res Severa est Verum Gaudium* (True Joy is a Serious Matter) – reminding listeners that music was an art for stoic contemplation and quiet introspection. Even the layout of the Gewandhaus seemed designed for spiritual reflection: it was closely modelled on St Thomas's church, with the seats parallel to the long aisle walls and facing in towards the nave, so that the listeners were brought together like a congregation; the orchestra was at the far end of the hall, where the altar would be in a church. There was a similar arrangement in the Hanover Square Rooms and the Salle du Conservatoire, where the hall was also darkened by dimming the gas lights before the music started to focus attention on the orchestra and promote inward contemplation by the audience.[91]

Where the centre of medieval cities had been marked by cathedrals, the great bourgeois cities of the nineteenth century were dominated by their concert halls, opera houses, libraries, art galleries and science museums. In contrast to the aristocracy (defined by its leisure) and the labouring classes (by manual work), the bourgeoisie asserted its identity through the idea of culture as a free and independent sphere of

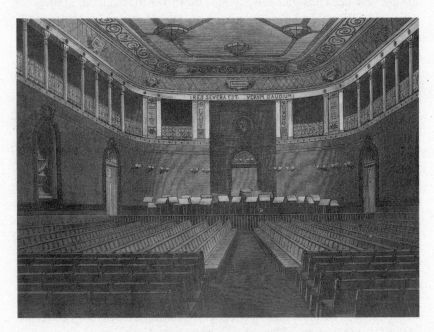

The Leipzig Gewandhaus, engraving, c. 1880.

action for the development of a higher personality. It placed a special value on the artist as a representative of 'genius', the ideal expression of individual enterprise, to whom it looked for spiritual content in its materialist society.

The bourgeoisie identified with the artist's struggle for professional autonomy and independence from the State and aristocracy. There was a concerted effort by composers and musicians to break free from the lowly status of tradesmen and receive recognition as professionals. Liszt was in the forefront of the campaign. In 1835, he wrote a tract on the 'Situation of Artists and Their Place in Society' in which he argued that not much had changed since Mozart's day, when musicians had been forced to eat with the servants. Influenced by the Saint-Simonians and their ideals of music as a morally improving and social form of art, Liszt concluded with a manifesto proposing, among other things, to set up an international association of musicians, develop choirs and music festivals, establish music schools, and publish 'cheap editions of the most important works of old and new composers', which he called the 'Pantheon of Music'.[92]

Most of these ideas were widely shared in the music world of the 1830s and 1840s as the basis for improving the material and social position of composers. They were taken up by Berlioz in his futuristic vision of a whole society organized for music in his tale *Euphonia*, published in the *Revue et Gazette musicale* in 1844. They underpinned the activities of publishers like Schlesinger, who printed cheap editions of the classic works not just for commercial gain but to disseminate a musical canon 'at prices such that any home with a piano may collect the masterpieces of Beethoven, Weber, Hummel and Moscheles'.[93] These aims were the driving force of music festivals and the many singing clubs and choirs in provincial towns – an enormous market for the 'flood of compositions', from oratorios to drinking songs, published for these groups during the 1840s.[94] A musicians' union was established in 1843, with Liszt, Berlioz, Meyerbeer and Schlesinger on its committee, along with a dozen socialists. By 1848, when it came out with a radical manifesto for musicians' rights, it had 2,688 members.[95]

Liszt's ideas were also at the heart of the ever-growing cult of Beethoven. Within a few years of his death, Beethoven was championed as both the first composer to have achieved independence in the marketplace and as the divine creator of a 'heaven-born Art', as the playwright

Franz Grillparzer famously described him at his funeral in 1827. The cult reached its peak at the Beethoven Festival in Bonn, organized by Liszt in 1845. A monument was unveiled to the great composer before a gathering of European dignitaries. Pauline Viardot was the principal attraction in a concert at the Prussian king's nearby Brühl Castle, where, Berlioz recalled, she 'sang three pieces with her usual exquisite skill and poetic expression . . . a dainty cavatina by Charles de Bériot, the infernal scene from [Gluck's] *Orphée*, and a song of Handel's – this last by request of Queen Victoria, who knows how admirably Mme Viardot interprets the old Saxon master'. Chopin was appalled by the merchandising at the Beethoven Festival. There was so much memorabilia on sale, '*véritables cigares à la Beethoven*, who probably smoked nothing but Viennese pipes; and there has already been such a sale of old bureaus and old desks which belonged to Beethoven, that the poor composer *de la Symphonie Pastorale* would have had to drive a huge trade in furniture'.[96]

3

In August 1847, the Viardots returned from London to Courtavenel, their country house south-east of Paris. Turgenev went with them, and stayed on at Courtavenel when they left for Pauline's autumn tour of Germany (Dresden, Hamburg and Berlin). Without a salary or allowance from his mother, he could not afford to travel any more. For two months he lived alone in the château, drafting the first stories of his *Sketches from a Hunter's Album*, and then, in late October, moved to Paris, where he took a small apartment near the boulevard des Italiens.

Desperate for news about Pauline, Turgenev spent a lot of time with her mother, Joaquina, and the Garcia family, who lived nearby. They read to him the daily letters they received from her. Practically a member of the family, Turgenev wrote to Pauline every day:

> I will not let you leave Dresden without greeting you another time, even
> though I do not have much news to give . . . Everything with us is going
> very well. We are getting on quite perfectly, we work, we often see each
> other, we think a lot about those who are absent – we gather every evening at a Spanish brasserie and *speak Spanish*. In four months' time [when

Pauline would return from Germany] I will be speaking only that language. My teacher pays me lots of compliments for my intelligence. But that's only because he doesn't know about my true incentive for learning.[97]

Despite their separation, Pauline and Turgenev were emotionally closer than they had been before. He wrote to her so frequently – and she to him as often as her busy schedule would allow – that their correspondence took on the character of an intimate conversation between two people accustomed to sharing their news every day. They discussed everything – what they were reading, each other's work, the latest opera performances, the smallest details of their lives. 'Ah! Madame,' Turgenev wrote to Pauline on 4 January 1848, 'what a splendid thing long letters are!'

> With what pleasure one begins to read them! It is like entering an avenue of trees, green and cool, in the summer. Ah, it is nice here, you say to yourself, and walk more slowly, listening to the twittering of the birds. You twitter so much better than they do, Madame . . .
>
> *Also, willkommen in Berlin.* I know where you are living; it is not far from the Brandenburg Gate. Forgive me if I allow myself to mention certain details of your apartment, but why are there certain rooms in it which are only named in English . . . and why are they exposed to the elements and rigours of the cold? Please, take care of yourself, and rectify this; it is more dangerous than it seems in this season of influenza and rheumatism.[98]

There was nothing compromising in Turgenev's letters. They could be shown to Louis. But they had a cheerful and flirtatious tone that comes only to a person in love who knows that his feelings are returned.

During the next two and a half years, Turgenev would spend a lot of time at Courtavenel, much of it on his own, writing, reading, walking and hunting with the dogs, while Pauline came and went on tour. Courtavenel was 'the cradle of my literary fame', he explained to the Russian poet Afanasy Fet, who visited him there. 'When I had no means to live in Paris my kind hosts permitted me to spend the winter here alone, fed on chicken broth and omelets which the old housekeeper cooked for me. Here too, in my desire to make some money, I wrote most of the *Sketches*.'[99]

It was at Courtavenel, on 26 June 1849, that Turgenev noted in his diary the 'first time' he was 'with' Pauline – an elusive reference, which could mean anything but does suggest that they were physically intimate. Certainly, around this time, the language in his letters becomes noticeably sensuous.* A few weeks later, when Pauline was in London, he wrote to her from Courtavenel, using for the first time the familiar you ('tu') and once again expressing his most passionate emotions in German (italicized below) to conceal them from Louis Viardot:

> Yesterday evening was unusually still and soft, the air seemed to have taken a bath in milk (Holy Gorgon, what a daring image!), and sounds floated away into the distance over the fields as if they were destined never to die out. I was just about to open the gate, when I suddenly noticed that some living creature was approaching me; it was little Manon, who has been put out to grass. She let me stroke her, and we returned home together. *I can't tell you how often I have thought of you all day; as I was coming home I shouted your name so loudly, I held out my arms to you with such longing! You must have been able to hear it! . . . Beloved! Dearest! God be with you and bless you!* . . . Until tomorrow . . . *What is wrong with V[iardot]? Is he perhaps annoyed that I am living here?* [100]

The Viardots had bought Courtavenel at an auction for 100,000 francs and spent another 30,000 francs restoring it. Courtavenel was a typical château from the reign of Henry IV in the early seventeenth century. Built in grey stone and surrounded by a moat, it had a spacious courtyard, formal gardens, an English park, large trees, orchards, stables and farm buildings, all set amidst the fertile plains of Brie, known as some of the best hunting country in the whole of France. The interior of the house was modernized but filled with antique furniture. The large *salle des gardes* was converted by the Viardots into a theatre where a long tradition of family theatricals began. They called it the *Théâtre des pommes de terre* because the price of entry was a potato picked from the vegetable garden.[101]

Without a railway or important road near by, it was a five-hour journey by diligence from Paris – remote enough to remind Turgenev of his native Orel province, with its poplars, willows, ponds and woods, and

---

* Many of these passages were cut by Pauline from the first publication of Turgenev's letters to her in 1906 (*LI*, pp. xvi–xvii).

The château at Courtavenel drawn by Pauline Viardot in a letter written by her in French and German to Julius Rietz, 5 July 1859. The château was destroyed after its sale by the Viardots in 1864.

to serve as a surrogate for it in his literary imagination. It is ironic that Turgenev's *Sketches from a Hunter's Album*, which are usually perceived as his most 'Russian' work, were written at Courtavenel. Looking at the countryside of France, he felt so much nostalgia for his native Russia that he could see its rural landscape and describe it perfectly. The *Sketches* also bear the influence of the pastoral novels of George Sand, who met Turgenev at Courtavenel in June 1845. They probably discussed their mutual interest in the countryside and the lives of the peasants, for both of them believed in their literary mission to convey to their readers the suffering of the rural poor and their human dignity.[102]

It was George Sand who had suggested the idea of buying a country house. The Viardots had spent two summers at Nohant, Sand's manor in the Berry countryside. Louis had enjoyed the hunting there, and Pauline had been able to relax in the company of friends, including Chopin, Liszt and Delacroix. Nohant had been bought by Sand's grandmother, and Sand herself had grown up there. It was an 'unpretentious house', as Sand described it in *The Story of My Life*. After her first visit to Courtavenel, she had mocked the 'bourgeois pretensions of grandeur' she had detected in her hosts. They had filled their château with expensive furnishings. 'We live here, dear Madame Sand, far more simply here than you down there [at Nohant],' Louis insisted unconvincingly in his reply, 'having no one but a cook and a gardener to serve us all [Nohant has a staff of ten], and living very well off the milk of our cow, the eggs of our chickens and the vegetables from our kitchen garden . . . We go out in our heavy shoes to pick our plums and chat with the shepherds or labourers we meet.'[103]

In Sand's circle of artistic friends there was an attitude to property that Pauline never really shared. Sand's remark about Courtavenel was indicative of a broader disapproval for what she felt increasingly was Pauline's mercenary approach to art. She had sensed it first in 1843, when Pauline had accepted pots of tsarist gold to sing in Russia, a land of tyranny, as far as Sand was concerned, not least because of her intimate relations with Chopin, living in voluntary exile from Poland following the Russian suppression of the Polish uprising in 1831. After Pauline's return from St Petersburg, in 1844, Sand had invited Pauline to visit her and Chopin at Nohant, bringing Chopin's sister Ludwika on her way through Paris from Courtavenel. But Pauline was too busy arranging furnishings at her own château, and kept Ludwika waiting for ten days. Sand was livid. Chopin had not seen his sister in fourteen years, and Ludwika had only a few weeks before her Polish passport would run out. Sand wrote to Pauline accusing her of having lost all sense of decency. Pauline's success had given her delusions of grandeur. She was obsessed with her own celebrity, with 'jewels and roubles', Sand maintained, still reproaching her for her Russian involvement.

It was certainly the case that Pauline made a principle of always pushing for the highest fee. She knew from her family history that her career would be at its height for a small number of years, and she had to make the most of it. By 1855, just ten years after they had reached their peak, her fees were already in decline. It was a typical career pattern for stage actresses and singers of the time; Pauline was not unusual in trying to maximize her earnings when she could. She saw herself as a professional, expected to be highly paid, and refused engagements if the payments offered were not good enough. In 1847, for example, she turned down a contract with Jullien, the impresario, to appear at his promenade concerts in London's Regent's Park. The fee he was proposing was 100 guineas a night for forty performances – promising to earn her £4,200 (106,000 francs) – a sum almost any other singer would have gladly accepted, but she felt he could pay more.[104]

There were many who regarded such behaviour as mercenary, vulgar. Donizetti certainly thought so when he refused her demand for 20,000 francs to sing in *Don Pasquale* in Vienna in 1843, telling Louis that she should wait until she was considered the top singer in Europe before asking for such fees.[105] Gye's diaries show that he too became exasperated by her demands when he tried to engage her for the 1849–50 season at Covent Garden. She wanted £60 (1,500 francs) per night with all expenses paid by the theatre, whereas he could not afford to pay her more than £40 per night. The theatre was in a serious financial crisis; its artists and technicians did not want to work before they were paid but there was no money to pay them. The season was saved only by the chief performers organizing their own company (they called it a 'republic of artists') to share the production costs. Pauline joined the company in 1849 to enable *Le Prophète* to go ahead. But she refused to recommit to it the next season, insisting that she would not come at all 'unless assured her money', and demanding guarantees that she would earn a minimum of £50 per performance. Negotiations rumbled on for several months, until Gye, exhausted, caved in to her main demand and promised she would earn her usual fee of £500 (12,600 francs) per month.[106]

It is hard to say how far she had merited this mercenary reputation – whether it derived from the malicious rumours engineered by Stolz to block her progress in Paris, or whether, perhaps because of this setback, she had grown more pushy than she would have been, had she received the recognition she deserved at the start of her career. The rejection she had suffered at the Opéra had made her tougher as a character. Forced to go abroad to earn a living on the stage, she had become, for a woman in her twenties, unusually resilient, self-assured and strong-minded in her determination to realize her potential. She saw her earnings as a token of her value as a professional artist. This need of validation was certainly part of what made her so determined to maximize her fees. Her credo was a simple one: singers were respected when they were well paid. 'Never sing for nothing!' she would later advise her pupils.[107]

For Sand, money was not a token of respect, but a means of buying independence and freedom to write. Her attitude to money was part of her Bohemian identity. In 1831, she had left her husband and children to start a new life as a writer in Paris. She was one of the thousands of poor students, would-be writers and artists living in the garrets of the Latin Quarter, the cheapest area in Paris at that time. The French called them 'Bohemians' because of their scruffy appearance, which they associated with the gypsies from Central Europe, or Bohemia. The label was adopted by the students as a badge of non-conformity. It was soon taken up by Henri Murger (1822–61), a struggling poet who began writing stories about his poor artistic friends, who in the mid-1840s included the poet Baudelaire, the painter Courbet and the writer Champfleury. Published in a minor magazine, in 1849 the stories were adapted as a play, *La Vie de Bohème*, and two years later were collected in a book, *Scènes de la vie de Bohème*, which became an international bestseller. It fixed the idea of 'Bohemia' and attracted tourists to the Latin Quarter, which Murger soon abandoned for the more expensive streets of the Right Bank. Murger was the son of the concierge in the house where the Garcias lived from 1828 to 1832. Pauline, who had known him as a child, recalled his being ashamed of his origins.[108]

George Sand was the queen of the Bohemians. Her numerous affairs, her dressing in men's clothes and smoking of cigars became part of her Bohemian celebrity, generating interest in her autobiographical writings. In 1847, Sand signed a contract for the serialization of *The Story of My Life* which earned her a staggering advance of 130,000 francs.[109] Sand was not averse to using her own notoriety to increase sales. She made her life a work of art. But the fees she earned did not make her mercenary. Money bought her freedom to pursue her art, it made her independent as a woman and professional writer, but in itself it did not interest her.

Unlike Viardot or Sand, Chopin had no head for money management. In an age when fortunes could be made from piano music for the domestic market, the money that he made from his published works was modest. In 1844, he sold the publication rights in France for his Mazurkas (Op. 55) and Nocturnes (Op. 56) to Schlesinger for just 300 francs apiece. Even smaller payments were made by Breitkopf & Härtel for the rights in Germany. Fees such as this were not enough to support his lavish spending – on luxurious furniture, expensive restaurants and elegantly tailored clothes – nor his generous gifts and loans of money to his needy fellow exiles in Paris. 'You think I am making a fortune?' Chopin wrote to an old schoolfriend, Dominik Dziewanoski, in 1832, when he was still not properly established in Parisian society. 'Carriages and white gloves cost more, and without them one would not be in good taste.' To supplement his income he relied on giving piano lessons to the women of the aristocracy – and in time he made a decent living from teaching. He would try to drive the hardest bargain that he could with publishers and, following the strategy of Beethoven, would attempt to organize the simultaneous publication of his works in different countries to minimize the losses from pirate editions. But he did not succeed. Rarely satisfied by the fees he earned, Chopin developed a strong mistrust of publishers, accusing them of cheating him. With Schlesinger and Pleyel (who were both Jews) he frequently resorted to anti-Semitic diatribes about 'Jewish scoundrels' and their 'Jewish tricks'.[110]

The real problem was Chopin. He did not write the sort of piano music – light and cheerful, easy on the ear, not too difficult for amateurs to play – that publishers would pay high prices for. His works were unconventional in their improvisatory character, intimacy and interiority, and although they were much loved by his circle of admirers, which numbered several thousand in Paris alone, they did not sell in the same quantity as the more popular works of Thalberg, Mozart or Schubert. Schlesinger and Pleyel paid Chopin more than any other publishers. Breitkopf & Härtel thought his prices were too high. Heinrich Probst, their agent in Paris, advised them to let him go because his music was too 'gloomy' and his demands 'exorbitant'.[111]

Chopin would not compromise his principles. 'For the bourgeois class,' he wrote to his old friend Wojciech Grzymała, 'one must do something dazzling, mechanical, of which I am not capable.' Nor could he work quickly. He was a perfectionist and often long delayed the publication of his finest works. Some were published only posthumously, such as the Nocturne in C sharp minor, which he had composed for Ludwika. Sensitive and shy, Chopin was 'not at all fit for giving public concerts', as he explained to Liszt: 'the crowd intimidates me, its breath suffocates me, I feel paralyzed by its curious look, and the unknown faces make me dumb.' He was only comfortable in the relatively intimate environment of the salon, where he would often play to recruit pupils and patrons. When at last, in 1841, Sand got him to agree to give a public concert by subscription, Chopin was so nervous, wanting no publicity at all, that she suggested he might play to 'an empty unlit hall on a dumb piano', as she told Pauline. In the end the concert on 26 April was sold out and Chopin made 6,000 francs. But he would not give another one.[112]

Chopin had asked Pauline to perform at the subscription concert in Paris. It would calm his nerves, Sand explained to her, 'if she sang for him, accompanied by him'.[113] Pauline did not sing on that occasion – Chopin gave a solo recital in the Salle Pleyel packed with his aristocratic supporters on 26 April – but she did take part in a second concert with Chopin in February 1842. Chopin was a keen admirer of Pauline's voice, as he had been of Malibran's before. He went to the opera frequently and loved the music of Bellini in particular. In his piano compositions he tried to emulate the bel canto singing style with its rubato elements and sustained melodies – a *cantabile* effect made possible by Érard's new invention of the double escapement action which helped to make the piano 'sing'. Chopin thought that Pauline's voice was ideal for the piano sound he sought to re-create. At Nohant he would ask her to sing, accompanying her as she sang anything from a Spanish song to a Mozart aria. Sometimes she would follow the piano's lead as he played one of his own pieces, perhaps helping him to shape the long melodic lines with her own vocal improvisation.

Pauline was particularly fond of singing Chopin's Mazurkas. At some point during the mid-1840s she arranged six of them for voice and piano in a manuscript with Chopin's markings, suggesting they had worked on them together at Nohant.* In that milieu of comradeship Chopin had probably approached it as a bit of fun – perhaps also to encourage Pauline as a composer. He was annoyed to discover later on, in 1848, that she had been performing the Mazurkas in a series of concerts in London without due acknowledgement. Pauline had omitted Chopin's name from the programme following her first performance of the arrangements, at Covent Garden on 12 May, when the influential critic J. W. Davison had attacked her in his journal *The Musical World* for

---

* The Mazurkas were: Op. 50, No. 2 in A flat major (which became 'Seize ans'); Op. 33, No. 2 in D major ('Aime-moi'); Op. 6, No. 1 in F sharp minor ('Plainte d'amour'); Op. 7, No. 1 in B flat major ('Coquette'); Op. 68, No. 2 in A minor ('L'Oiselette'); and Op. 24, No. 1 in G minor ('Séparation').

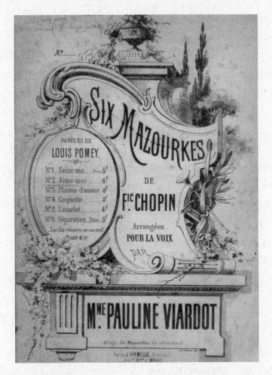

Pauline Viardot's arrangement of six Mazurkas by Chopin with words by
Louis Pomey, 1866 edition by E. Gérard & Cie.

choosing to arrange such 'ugly and affected' mazurkas. From that
point, when she performed the pieces, they were billed as 'Mazurkas,
Madame Viardot, arranged by Madame Viardot'.[114] 'In Viardot's programmes,' Chopin wrote to Marie de Rozières on 24 June, 'there is no
longer the item, "Mazurkas of Chopin" but merely "Mazurkas arranged
by Mme Viardot" – it appears that it looks better.'

> It is all the same to me; but there is a pettiness behind it. She wants to
> have success and is afraid of a certain newspaper which perhaps does not
> like me. It once wrote that she had sung music 'by a certain M. Chopin',
> whom no one knows, and that she ought to sing something else.[115]

The six Mazurkas were frequently performed by Pauline – not always
with acknowledgement to Chopin – in public concerts and private recitals after 1848. They were published, individually and as a collection,
during the 1860s. They were evidently popular because new editions

and arrangements were brought out in 1885 (by Breitkopf & Härtel) and 1899 (by Gebethner and Wolff in Warsaw).[116]

Turgenev's decision to leave Russia cost him dearly in financial terms. In 1847, he received his full allowance of 6,000 roubles from his mother; but the next year she reduced it and then cut it off entirely, leaving Turgenev without any income except what he could earn from his writing or else raise in loans from publishers and friends. In Paris he could barely afford to heat his small apartment on the boulevard des Italiens. As always, he tried to hide his poverty, attending salons smartly dressed but borrowing money for a carriage home. Among his friends he became known for leaving restaurants before the time arrived to pay the bill. According to the literary critic Annenkov, who saw him often in Paris from November 1847, Turgenev 'was a master of concealment, and no one realised how poor he was. We were taken in by the swagger of his speech, so prominent when he told anecdotes, and by his extravagance when it came to expensive adventures and pleasures, for which cleverly he never paid.'[117]

His earnings from his writings were modest. But he lived in expectation that he would inherit a fortune from his mother, which gave him the confidence to continue acting like a gentleman and make generous gestures to his friends. 'He never lost hope of becoming a grand landowner,' recalled Annenkov, 'and, despite his poverty, he once even promised to give Belinsky 100 peasant souls as soon as that was possible. Belinsky took the present as a joke, calling to his wife to "come and thank Ivan Sergeevich: he has made us landowners".'[118]

As the most influential literary critic in Russia, Belinsky was Turgenev's biggest champion. The son of a humble rural doctor, Belinsky was the leading critic at the journal *Annals of the Fatherland*, where many of Turgenev's early stories were published (and several others promised against advances from its editor, Andrei Kraevsky). In 1847, Belinsky was involved in the relaunching of *The Contemporary* (*Sovremennik*), a journal founded by Pushkin that had gone into decline following his death. With its relaunch it was destined to become the leading literary magazine for the socially progressive, Westernizing circles to which Turgenev comfortably belonged. 'We have succeeded in founding a new journal here which will appear from the new year under the most favourable auspices,' Turgenev wrote to Pauline from St Petersburg in November 1846. 'I will be one of its contributors.'[119]

When the first number of the magazine appeared, it contained nine poems by Turgenev, a long theatrical review by him, and 'Khor and Kalinych', the first of what would go on to become his *Sketches from a Hunter's Album*. The *Contemporary*'s new editor, Nikolai Nekrasov, tried to persuade Turgenev to write exclusively for the journal by paying off his debts to Kraevsky. Turgenev rejected the offer, honouring his promise to deliver his promised stories to *Annals of the Fatherland*, although he later used that to beg for further loans from Kraevsky.* Turgenev realized that it was to his advantage to have two journals competing for his work.

'Khor and Kalinych' was glowingly reviewed by the well-known Slavophile writer Konstantin Aksakov in the March 1847 issue of *The Contemporary*. Turgenev's reputation had been launched. The journal published four more of his stories in the May number, along with a series of articles and letters on cultural life in Berlin, Dresden, London and Paris, cities he knew from his travels with the Viardots across Europe. Turgenev was a prolific feuilletonist. It was an easy way to pay his travel costs. Most of all in these feuilletons he wrote about opera. His partisan support of Viardot was sometimes hidden by a pseudonym, sometimes not. He was highly critical of Pauline's rivals Jenny Lind (whom he heard in London) and Fanny Persiani (in Paris). He also wrote a scathing article about the cult of Verdi, knowing that Pauline had never sung in any of his operas. 'Yesterday was the premiere of Mr Verdi's *Lombardi* – given here the title of *Jerusalem* – at the Grand Opera,' Turgenev wrote to Pauline in Berlin on 27 November. 'Mr Verdi has composed some new parts that are perfectly detestable.'[120]

4

On 26 February 1848, Turgenev was in Brussels when he heard the news from Paris. It was early morning and he was in bed in his hotel when someone started shouting, 'France has become a republic!' Two

---

* On 22 October 1849, he wrote to Kraevsky claiming that he 'did not have a penny' and would 'die of hunger' if he did not get a loan of 300 roubles, promising a list of forthcoming works for *Annals of the Fatherland*. Receiving the money on 13 December, he wrote to thank the editor, adding histrionically, 'This money has surely saved me from death by hunger' (*PSS*, vol. 1, pp. 333, 337).

days of street demonstrations by the citizens of Paris had forced the abdication of Louis Philippe, who fled to England with the help of Ary Scheffer, placed at the head of a detachment of the National Guard. A Second Republic had been declared by a provisional government. 'A revolution without me!' Turgenev wrote in his notebook. Within half an hour he was dressed and on his way to the railway station to board a train for the French capital.[121]

He found Paris in turmoil. Omnibuses had been overturned and trees felled to erect barricades in many streets. The provisional government provided little leadership. Dominated by a poet, Alphonse de Lamartine, it called new elections to the National Assembly, introduced universal suffrage for adult men, and promised citizens the 'right to work', establishing National Workshops to relieve the unemployment crisis behind the street protests.

Excitement grew as the revolution spread to other capitals. Railways, telegraphs and newspapers quickly turned the revolution in Paris into a European revolution as other cities followed its example with uprisings of their own. Inspired by the news from Paris, popular revolts broke out from mid-March in Vienna and Berlin, Baden, Dresden, Leipzig, the Palatinate and other German states. Liberal ministers were put in place of the old reactionary governments; political reforms were carried out; and a German national assembly, the Frankfurt Parliament, was elected on a wide male franchise on 1 May. The revolution spread to northern Italy, where the Milanese rose up against the Austrians and the Venetians declared a republic during March; and to Poland, where an uprising against Prussian rule began in Poznán on 20 March. It was soon joined by Polish exiles from Berlin and Paris travelling by rail to join a national independence movement with organized militias to fight the Prussian army and potentially the Russians too, should the Tsar decide to intervene.

The hopes of spring were quickly dashed by violent clashes in Paris during May and June. Disappointed by the moderate government elected to the National Assembly, workers came out on the streets in protests organized by Louis Blanc and other socialists. They fought against the National Guard, loyal to the government. Turgenev witnessed the big street demonstration of 15 May, when workers marched from the place de la Concorde to the Palais Bourbon, where the National Assembly was in session, forced their way into the chamber to read a declaration in support of Poland, and then laid siege to the Hôtel de Ville, proclaiming an 'insurrectionary government' made up of socialists, until they were finally dispersed by the National Guard.[122] To counteract the threat of a socialist uprising, a 'Party of Order' was established and the National Workshops were closed, prompting three days of fighting between workers and the National Guard from 23 June, the June Days. The workers were suppressed and their leaders arrested, and a new government was formed by the Party of Order.

The February Revolution had been greeted with enthusiasm by artists and intellectuals. Socialists from across Europe hastened to Paris to join in the events, among them Herzen, who had emigrated with his family from Russia in 1847 and lived in Italy until the downfall of the July Monarchy. Six years older than Turgenev, Herzen changed his initial opinion of him as a superficial socialite – the young man had matured and become more serious – and the two men became friends, firmly united by their mutual friendship with Belinsky and their commitment to democracy. Turgenev and the Viardots had high hopes for the revolution. Louis was an active member of the radical republican circles which led the revolution from the start. He had played a leading role in the banquet campaign for political reform, beginning in July 1847. At the Banquet de Coulommiers, in October, he proposed the main toast, 'To Reform!' His speech was too inflammatory to be published. He became an energetic propagandist for the revolutionary cause, publishing articles not only in France but in French newspapers in Berlin, where his radical opinions were less likely to attract the attention of the censors.[123] In the April elections to the National Assembly he stood as a candidate in the Seine-et-Marne district, presenting himself to the voters not as a 'man of yesterday' but as a 'man of the day'.[124] Unsuccessful there, Viardot asked George Sand to help him find a seat – she was close to Alexandre Ledru-Rollin, the new Minister of the Interior – but nothing came of her efforts.

Sand was more left-wing than Viardot. She espoused a sort of utopian socialism based on love. In the *Bulletin de la République*, published by the Ministry of the Interior, she wrote a series of 'Letters to the People' in which she declared that the Republic was the 'government of *all* the people, the organization of democracy, the republic of all rights, of all interests, of all intelligences, and all virtues!'. From her sixteenth bulletin, in mid-April, she moved further left, going beyond the calls of

Ledru-Rollin for a parliamentary republic to add her voice to those of Louis Blanc for a workers' revolution to establish a socialist one.[125]

Pauline too was swept along by republican hopes. On 23 March, Sand persuaded Ledru-Rollin to commission Pauline to compose an updated version of the *Marseillaise* (a cantata called 'The Young Republic') for a gala evening in the Salle Le Peletier to mark the renaming of the Paris Opéra as the Théâtre de la République (as the Comédie-Française had been called from 1789 to 1793). Sand was placed in charge of the arrangements for the inaugural ceremony, which the new government would all attend. Her idea was to stake a claim for women artists, to show they could be artists on a par with men. She wanted Pauline to be widely seen, admired by the government, as a symbol of the Republic. She hoped too that Louis might be appointed as the new director of the Opéra to rescue it from its crisis. On the outbreak of the February Revolution the Opéra had been forced to close its doors. Its management was frightened of the mob. The new government set up a commission to support the Opéra financially; but support also meant control. The radicals resented the privileged position of the Opéra, and wanted supervision of its expenses.

On 23 March, in a ceremony presided over by Ledru-Rollin, the Opéra reopened its doors and declared its allegiance to the new Republic by adopting its new name and planting a Liberty Tree in its courtyard. The position of its director, Duponchel, accused of mismanagement, was very weak, and the radicals were calling for his dismissal.[126] There were all sorts of rumours about who might take over, but Sand thought she could secure it for the Viardots. 'I want to see you reign as queen, because I know that you alone are not a bad queen,' she wrote to Pauline towards the end of March. 'Do you get my drift? Let Louis consider it but answer quick. The Opéra will be closed and reconstituted on a grander scale at the expense of the State; Meyerbeer has plans but will not take the lead. Ledru-Rollin is looking for someone else.'[127]

On 31 March, Pauline finished the cantata ('a masterpiece', according to Sand), but migraines prevented her from singing it, so it was performed by the tenor Gustave Roger, accompanied by a choir of fifty girls, all dressed in white with sashes in the tricolour.[128]

Nothing came of Sand's plan to get Louis to become director of the Opéra. He refused to have his name considered, arguing that, if the plans for Pauline to appear in Meyerbeer's new opera were to go ahead, it would represent a conflict of interest. Yet again, he had put her career before his. Under Duponchel the Opéra struggled on. Its director called for extra funds, failed to get them, and again closed the theatre's doors, and, although they were reopened during May, performances were frequently cancelled because people were too scared to venture out onto the streets and the audience was too small. The June Days forced the Opéra to close again.

The chaos of the summer was a disaster for the arts. There was a collapse in the art market. Concert life in Paris came to a standstill. Chopin departed for London. The aristocracy had fled the capital, and Chopin's earnings from giving piano lessons had dried up. One of his devoted followers, Jane Stirling, invited him to England, promising to find him paying pupils and engagements. In London he was helped by Manuel Garcia, Pauline's brother, who had fled Paris, where, having volunteered for the National Guard, he had been horrified by the violence he witnessed during the June Days (at one point he had seen George Sand, standing on the top of a barricade, who, recognizing him, had cried, 'N'est-ce-pas que c'est magnifique, n'est-ce-pas que c'est beau!').[129] Pauline thought that Manuel would hate England, but it became his permanent home. The celebrated singing teacher became a professor at the Royal Academy of Music.

Pauline also called on Chopin when she came to London for the Covent Garden season that summer. Chopin's catastrophic rupture with George Sand in 1847 – the result of ill-feeling, anger, pride and misunderstandings over several years – had brought him closer to Pauline. She pitied him for his broken heart and health – his tuberculosis caused him awful suffering. To help the poor composer she sang in some of the concerts organized for him by Henry Broadwood, the piano manufacturer, beginning with Chopin's recital in Lord Falmouth's mansion in St James's Square on 7 July. Instead of her usual fee of fifteen guineas for a concert, Pauline sang for ten guineas.[130]

On her return to Paris, Pauline moved into a new house she had bought in rue de Douai in the leafy 'New Athens' area in the 9th *arrondissement*. The Viardots had chosen to live there to escape the overcrowded centre, where cholera was rife, and because their dear friend Ary Scheffer had a villa in the neighbouring street. Theirs was a 'pretty little house' on three floors with a large conservatory extending into a garden surrounded by trees at the back, and a courtyard at the front where there were a stable and staff quarters. They bought the house for 75,000 francs and spent at least as much again on converting the conservatory into a gallery for Louis's art collection, where Pauline also had her 'grand salon', a large room decorated with a light-green floral wall-paper, in which she housed an extensive library, her Pleyel piano and an organ made for her by the famous organ-builder Aristide Cavaillé-Coll, for which she had paid 10,000 francs. Ary Scheffer had supplied a portrait of Pauline as a haloed Saint Cecilia on a wooden oval panel, which Cavaillé-Coll attached to the instrument. Pauline justified her lavish spending in a letter to George Sand:

> It is an amusement, which we need – not to spend our lives in earning money only to hoard it. For my part, I am spending quickly all that is possible to spend but trying not to be foolish. [Louis] insists that I should be a *propriétaire* – which is good but not to my profit – and that I should build a nest. I have chosen the frailest branch and stormiest moment to build that nest. We have employed every type of worker, except masons, and our money has been pouring through their hands. I assure you, my Ninounne, that however much amusement I may have in doing up this little house, until it is finished it is just a dream – decidedly, Ninounne, I have no gift for property and Mr Proudhon can be pleased with me. If all property should ever be destroyed, I myself would put the flames to the four corners of my house . . . [131]

Sand replied sarcastically, assuring Pauline that she had done 'good business to buy today when properties are selling for half of what they were worth yesterday, and when those who have the money can double their capital. It is sad for those who are forced to sell! That's what happened to my daughter. Her house was worth 200,000 francs but it is up for sale at 100,000 francs. If you have any more money to spare, I would advise you to buy it.'[132]

The Opéra's financial crisis continued to worsen. In July it needed to be rescued by the government with an 'extraordinary credit' to have any prospect of putting on a season that autumn.[133] All hopes rested with the long-awaited premiere of Meyerbeer's Grand Opera *Le Prophète*. Ledru-Rollin made a point of this, praising Meyerbeer and his forthcoming work, which he believed 'would draw the whole of Europe to Paris'.[134] Negotiations over the contract dragged on for several months.

The Opéra no longer had the money for the lavish set designs and cos-tumes Meyerbeer requested, nor for the high fees Viardot demanded to sing the leading female role. But in the end these were agreed. The Opéra needed the 'celebrity' of Madame Viardot, Meyerbeer explained in a letter to Louis, and the only way to obtain her was to concede to her demands.[135] An extra subsidy was advanced by the government, enabling the contracts to be signed in October, when rehearsals were slated to begin.

Before he arrived in Paris, Meyerbeer had spent the past few months travelling by rail round Germany and Austria checking on productions of his operas. He liked to compose on trains. The final arias for Le Prophète were written in this way, and were then completed in Paris against the noisy background of the revolution in the streets. Marching rhythms and intonations of the Marseillaise crept into the score.[136]

The subject of his opera could not have been more topical. It told the story of the prophet John of Leiden, who led the Anabaptists in an uprising against the Prince-Bishop of Münster in 1534. The Anabaptist revolutionaries took the Westphalian town, established a theocratic community, and held out for a year until they were defeated by the army of the Prince-Bishop. Everybody was aware of the parallels with the revolutionary situation in Europe long before the premiere. 'Meyer-beer has begun rehearsing his Prophète,' Berlioz wrote to Count Wielhorski, 'he is a courageous man to risk launching a work of such dimensions at a time when riots or a change of government can cut him short, however great his eloquence.'[137] Even before it was premiered, there were parodies of the dangerous opera, including one at the Théâtre du Vaudeville whose witty title played on the similarity between the words in French for 'Anabaptist' and 'donkey': L'Âne à Baptiste, ou, Le Berceau du socialisme ('The Baptist Donkey, or the Cradle of Socialism').[138]

Meyerbeer had always been aware of the political dangers in his opera. 'The preaching of revolt that accompanies the destruction of power will cause much trouble,' he had told Scribe when he read the first draft of the libretto in 1836.[139] He took great care to avoid giving Le Prophète a revolutionary message that might get it banned.[140] Whereas Scribe's libretto had ascribed social motives to the Anabaptist uprising, in the final version used by Meyerbeer the popular revolt is manipulated by its dogmatic prophet, who leads it to disaster. Jean

(John of Leiden) is portrayed as a jealous lover inspired by revenge, a religious fanatic deluded into thinking that he is the Messiah by the adulation of his naive followers. It is his mother, Fidès, who makes him see the error of his ways.[141] By making her the moral anchor of the opera (arguably the first to have a mother as the leading female role), Meyerbeer ensured that the only possible conclusion to be drawn was not to trust in false prophets.

As the premiere approached, Meyerbeer became more and more nervous about the reception of the opera, his first for thirteen years. There were over fifty rehearsals in the Salle Le Peletier and Meyerbeer's apartment in rue Richelieu. He made constant changes to the score, called in the leader of the claque to get his opinion, and questioned the musicians of the orchestra on what they thought about the passages that worried him. Above all he depended on the advice of Pauline. She suggested a number of improvements, all of which he accepted.[142] Rarely had a singer played such an important part in the writing of an opera. According to the critic Henry Chorley, who attended the rehearsals, the final version of Le Prophète owed almost as much to her as it did to Meyerbeer. 'She is conductor, stage-manager – in a word, the soul of the opera, which owes at least half its success to her,' concurred Ignaz Moscheles, the composer. Meyerbeer was so pleased with the work of his 'captain', as he called her, that he made it a condition for the performance of the opera in other cities that she sang the role of Fidès, and, in his absence, as in London in 1849, placed her in charge of the rehearsals.[143]

There was also much work to be done with the technical effects, upon which the opera's success would heavily depend. In the third act there would be a dazzling sunrise created by projecting electric light onto a screen from the back of the stage. It was the first time electric light was used in operatic history. The effect was so astonishing that it seemed to Gautier 'to be no longer a painting but reality itself'.[144] Act III would also have a 'skating ballet' performed on roller skates, an unknown invention in Paris at that time which Meyerbeer had seen in a street act. The skater was immediately hired at the Opéra to teach the chorus how to roller-skate. Meyerbeer was keen on introducing new inventions to his operas. It gave them an aura of modernity that appealed to his largely bourgeois audience. For the fourth act of Le Prophète he composed music for an on-stage band of twenty-four brass instruments, including eighteen saxhorns, a new instrument patented in Paris in 1845 by Adolphe Saxe, the inventor of the saxophone.

As the opening night approached, the build-up of excitement was intense. People had been waiting for this opera for years. The newspapers were full of the political parallels (Gautier reported that the dialogue 'could have been drawn from the prose of communist journals'). The first forty performances were sold out immediately. Tickets in the stalls exchanged hands for 250 francs, boxes for 1,200 francs, reported *Le Messager des théâtres*. The production was a windfall for the Opéra, which *Le Crédit* compared to 'all the gold of California'.[145]

Dignitaries arrived from all over Europe for the opening night, 16 April 1849. The recently elected President, Louis-Napoleon, was in the royal box. A large delegation from the National Assembly was in attendance. Turgenev was in the stalls. So was Berlioz. Chopin, back from London and suffering from tuberculosis, dragged himself from his sickbed to the Opéra. Heine could not get a ticket. Nor could Delacroix.

The 'skating ballet' from *Le Prophète* by Meyerbeer: a photograph of hand-painted clay models, 1860s.

The evening was a triumph for Pauline. As the curtain came down on the last explosive scene – in which Jean and Fidès throw themselves into a vast conflagration of electric light engulfing the whole stage – there was a 'long hosannah of bravos, cheers, and foot-stamping', according to the *Journal des théâtres*. There were a dozen calls for Viardot, whose performance, the first of her career at the Paris Opéra, was singled out for praise by Meyerbeer and the critics. None mattered more than Berlioz, who reported in the *Journal des débats* that she had

> displayed a dramatic talent which no one in France had believed her to possess to such a high degree. All her poses, her gestures, her expressions, even her costume, are studied with profound art. As to the perfection of her singing, the extreme skill of her vocalization, her musical assurance – those are things that are now known and appreciated by everyone, even in Paris. Madame Viardot is one of the greatest artists who comes to mind in the past and present history of music.

Returning from the theatre late that night, Pauline wrote a short note to George Sand: 'Victory! VICTORY, my dear Ninounne! and good night!'[146]

The opera was a big commercial hit. The box office took in 10,000 francs a night, enough to rescue it from its financial crisis, until a cholera epidemic in July forced the Opéra to close its doors after only twenty-five performances. The production was brought back in the autumn, however, and ran for two more years at the same high level of receipts.[147] Pauline had been 'rather nervous' on the first night of the revival, Turgenev wrote to Chorley on 6 November, thanks to 'absurd rumours' that were being spread by her enemies 'to punish her for having taken part in a republican banquet in London' (she had even been accused of hiding socialists from the French police); but 'honest people paid no attention to such calumny and insults against people who cannot defend themselves,' Pauline's loyal friend continued, and 'her reception was superb'.[148]

Within three years of its Paris premiere, *Le Prophète* had been produced in fifty cities around the world – from New York and New Orleans to Constantinople and St Petersburg. Pauline toured with the opera, starting out in London, where Thackeray and Dickens were at the opening night on 24 July 1849, and ending in Vienna and Berlin. From Courtavenel, Turgenev read the reports of her progress in the press. He wrote to her incessantly. On the day of her London premiere he followed the action by looking at his watch and imagining the performance. 'Eleven o'clock,' he wrote that night. 'The fourth act has just finished, and they are calling for you; I am applauding too: bravo! bravo! well done! Midnight: I am applauding still with all my might and throwing a bouquet of flowers at your picture. Everything was splendid, wasn't it?'[149]

For the rights to the score Meyerbeer received the highest sum of money ever paid to a composer – 19,000 francs from Brandus for the rights in France, 17,000 francs from Delafield and Beale for the English rights, and 8,000 from Breitkopf & Härtel for the rights in Germany: a total of 44,000 francs. He made a lot more money from the publication of the arrangements, which soon appeared in sheet music for every conceivable instrument and combination of instruments – 'for two and four hands at the piano, one and two violins, two flutes, even for a flageolet!' sneered Berlioz – and at every level of technical difficulty.[150]

Critical opinion was mixed. Berlioz, who had taken a genuine interest in Meyerbeer's music and praised it in the past, was less keen on *Le Prophète*. He thought that it contained good music but went too far in its *coloratura* (ornamentation of the vocal line) and in other musical effects designed to appeal to vulgar tastes. According to the Escudier brothers in their journal *La France musicale*, the music showed much craftsmanship but lacked melodic inspiration. Turgenev too had doubts. Writing in *Annals of the Fatherland*, he recognized the opera's dramatic strength and thought the orchestral writing was extraordinary, but overall the music was eclectic, the work of a composer who had passed his best. Delacroix detested everything about the opera. 'This monstrous work, *Le Prophète*,' he noted in his journal on 23 April, 'is the very abasement of art.'[151]

No one, however, was more critical than Richard Wagner, Meyerbeer's old protégé. He was, he later claimed, so 'filled with rage and despair' when he first heard *Le Prophète* at the Opéra, in February 1850, that, despite being seated in the centre of the stalls, he got up in the middle of the performance, disturbed everybody around him, and left the house.[152]

Wagner had come to Paris as a young man in 1839 to make his name and fortune as an opera composer in the musical capital of Europe. At that time he was composing *Rienzi*, a work modelled on the conventions of Grand Opera (only even longer, at five hours), with ballets, stage effects and huge choral numbers set in Ancient Rome. He wanted *Rienzi* to 'outdo all the previous examples [of Grand Opera] with sumptuous extravagance'. Looking for supporters, Wagner approached Pauline Viardot, who sang some of the music he had written but would not commit herself to perform it publicly. But it was Meyerbeer whose patronage he really sought. On his way to Paris from London he had travelled via Boulogne to meet him and had played him extracts from his opera. Meyerbeer admired Wagner's music and wrote two letters of recommendation to the Paris Opéra, which rejected *Rienzi*. Failure in Paris was normal for a young composer, but Wagner took it as a slight against his genius, and turned against the city, claiming it had lost its soul to commercialism and the love of money, which he rejected for what he claimed to be a higher 'German' form of art. Nonetheless, in 1841 he was grateful to his patron, Meyerbeer, whose letter of support was enough to get *Rienzi* accepted for production in Dresden.[153]

Wagner's artistic debt to Meyerbeer was pointed out by the critics (Hans von Bülow would later joke that *Rienzi* was 'Meyerbeer's best opera'). Liszt believed the scores of *Rienzi* and *Les Huguenots* must have been placed side by side because, he said, some of the pages from Meyerbeer's opera had accidentally made their way into Wagner's. Stung by the plagiarism charge, and still hurting from his failure in Paris, Wagner wrote to Schumann in 1843:

> I don't know what 'Meyerbeerish' signifies, except a cunning angling for shallow popularity . . . But if there really were anything actual, anything consistent that could be called 'Meyerbeerish' . . . then I must confess it would be a marvellous joke on Nature's part if I had drawn anything out of that stream, the mere odour of which is repugnant to me even from a distance.[154]

During his years in Dresden, from 1842 to 1849, Wagner continued to receive support from Meyerbeer. Wagner wrote grovelling letters to him, begging him to get *The Flying Dutchman* (1843) launched at the Paris Opéra. His deference to him continued for as long as Meyerbeer advanced him money and threw banquets for him at his house. 'I weep tears of emotion when I think of the man who is *everything* to me, *everything*,' he wrote. 'My head and heart are no longer mine to give away; they are your property, my master.' But at some point the loans dried up. Wagner's slavish devotion turned to detestation of his generous mentor. 'He disgusts me beyond measure,' Wagner wrote to Liszt. 'This eternally amiable and pleasant man reminds me of the turbid, not to say vicious period of my life when he pretended to be my protector; that was a period of connections and backstairs when we are made fools of by our protectors whom in our hearts we do not like.'[155] Meyerbeer had no idea of Wagner's hatred towards him.

Wagner clothed his poisonous resentment in nationalist ideology. A few years before, in 1837, he had written sycophantically to Meyerbeer: 'I see you fulfilling the mission of the German by taking the virtues of the Italian and French schools as a model so as to make the creations of German genius universal.'[156] But now he attached his cause to a more xenophobic strand of German nationalism in hostile opposition to such cosmopolitanism. In the music world this nationalism had already been expressed by Schumann in his critical assaults on Meyerbeer's *Les Huguenots*. The ideological force of this critique was couched in terms of a contrast between the spiritual qualities of serious 'German' music, which belonged to the higher realm of art, and the frivolity of Italian and French music, which was part of a mere entertainment industry (music 'for the circus', as Schumann had dismissed *Les Huguenots*). This was the polarity by which Wagner now resolved to set himself against Meyerbeer. He wrote to Hanslick in 1847:

> If I were to try to sum up precisely what it is that I find so offensive about the ... opera industry today, I would lump it all together under the heading 'Meyerbeer'. I see in Meyerbeer's music a great skill at achieving superficial effects which prevents his art from attaining a noble maturity ... it denies the essential inwardness of art and strives instead to gratify the listener in every way possible.[157]

This artistic nationalism was sharpened by the German revolutions of 1848–9. Actively involved with Bakunin in the Dresden uprising in 1849, Wagner conceived the revolutions as a national liberation from the bourgeois system of money, and in particular from the domination of international Jewry. It is from this time that his anti-Semitism became a component of his musical philosophy, as articulated in his article 'Jewishness in Music', published in the *Neue Zeitschrift für Musik* in 1850, shortly after he had stormed out in disgust from *Le Prophète*.

Published under a pseudonym ('to prevent the question being dragged down by the Jews to a purely personal level', as he explained to Liszt), Wagner's article was at its heart a personal attack on Mendelssohn and Meyerbeer. Wagner argued that the Jews lacked national character. They were 'disagreeably foreign to whatever European nation they belong'. From this premise he launched an assault on Mendelssohn, who had died only three years previously, claiming that his music was pastiche without true feeling or nationality. The culmination of the article was a veiled attack on Meyerbeer, who, though unnamed, was clearly the target. Associating the Jews with the rule of money and commercialism in the arts, Wagner explained the popular success of this 'famous opera composer' by his 'Jewish' willingness to cater to the lowest tastes for monetary gain. Two years later, in his *Opera and Drama*, published under his own name, Wagner made the object of his attack clear. Describing Meyerbeer as 'a Jew banker to whom it occurred to write some music', he argued that *Le Prophète* was a shallow, incoherent work striving for effects to gratify the audience ('effects without causes', as he famously described the sunrise at the end of the third act).[158]

Meyerbeer was no stranger to attacks. Being rich and successful earned him many enemies. He had even been betrayed by friends before. In 1847, after Meyerbeer had failed to lend him money, Heine wrote an article accusing him of lacking talent and being a 'colossal egotist' who used friends to promote his own celebrity. That was bad enough. But being attacked as a Jew was different. It wounded Meyerbeer, who had always thought of himself as a German, but whose insecurity was rooted in his Jewishness. To be wealthy and successful as a Jew in Germany made him vulnerable, even with the support he received from the Prussian court and the crowned heads of other German states. He suffered Wagner's attack silently, did not defend himself, and gave hints of his feelings only in his diary. He became ill, complaining of stomach pains, which usually appeared when he was stressed, and spent months recovering in spas. How much of his illness was directly caused by Wagner's betrayal is hard to say. But Meyerbeer was changed by it. He did not write another major work for many years. *L'Africaine*, his last Grand Opera, was finished only just before he died.[159]

Meyerbeer was a giant of the nineteenth-century opera world. But in the longer term his reputation fell; his music became a watchword for bad taste and vulgarity, for art's subordination to commerce; in the twentieth century his works lost their place in the opera repertory. Wagnerism's triumph saw to that.

5

After a long struggle with tuberculosis, Chopin died in Paris on 18 October 1849. His sister Ludwika and George Sand's daughter were with him when he died, but not Sand herself. In the last days, as his sickness worsened, Chopin tried to insist that he only be visited by his friends. Pauline saw him several times. But, as she wrote to Sand, she always found a crowd around his deathbed. 'All the grand Parisian ladies considered it *de rigueur* to come and faint in his room, which was congested with artists making sketches, and a man making daguerreotypes wanted to have the bed moved closer to the window so that the dying man should be in the light.'[160]

The funeral took place in the church of the Madeleine on 30 October. A large crowd gathered in front of the church, whose colonnaded façade was draped in black for the occasion. Admission was by ticket only. Around 4,000 people had been invited. Observing the square with its crush of coaches and the guests assembling at the entrance to the church, Berlioz concluded that 'the whole of artistic and aristocratic Paris was there'. On the request of the family, Meyerbeer was one of the pallbearers, along with Delacroix, Prince Adam Czartoryski and Camille Pleyel. Meyerbeer had not known Chopin well, but Chopin had been one of his admirers. Turgenev was in one of the front pews. He had arrived early to be in a good position to hear Pauline sing the contralto part in Mozart's *Requiem*, as Chopin had requested for his funeral, along with the soprano Castellan, the bass Luigi Lablache and the tenor Alexis Dupont, old friends of Chopin. Because women were forbidden from performing in the church, it had taken days of pleading from Chopin's most powerful friends to persuade the Archbishop of Paris to make a special dispensation, allowing Viardot and Castellan to sing on the condition that they remained invisible. They sang their parts from behind a black curtain.[161]

Pauline wanted money to perform at Chopin's funeral. She insisted on a fee of 2,000 francs, almost half the costs for the entire funeral. It was a demand that many would ascribe to mercenary motives. But

Pauline once again saw this as a professional engagement, just like any other, and she had always said that a singer should not sing for nothing. By all accounts, she earned her fee. Turgenev, for one, was very pleased. 'She sang her part magnificently, showing that grandiose but simple church technique of which she has the secret,' he wrote to Chorley.

> The funeral service was very beautiful and moving, too: not a ceremony so much as a genuine goodbye to a beloved friend. There were a lot of women in the church and many of them wept behind their veils. The orchestra played a March by Chopin, sad and plaintive; and one of his little preludes, given on the organ, might have been more moving still had the organist not overdone the 'vox humana' stop . . . By the way, your article on Chopin in the *Athenaeum* pleased me greatly; I think it would be hard to be more understanding or more just: that's the way to speak about the dead.[162]

3

The Arts in the Age of Mechanical Reproduction

In matters of painting and sculpture, the present-day credo of the sophisticated, above all in France, is this: 'I believe in Nature, and I believe only in Nature ... I believe that Art is, and cannot be other than, the exact reproduction of Nature ... Thus an industry that could give us a result identical to Nature would be the absolute of art.' A revengeful God has given ear to the prayers of this multitude. Daguerre is his Messiah.

Charles Baudelaire, 'The Salon of 1859'

I

In January 1850, a man by the name of Charles Gounod called on Pauline Viardot. He had a letter of introduction from the conductor François Seghers, recommending him as a composer. In fact they had met before, in Rome nine years earlier, when Pauline had been on her honeymoon with Louis, and Gounod was a student at the Villa Medici, having just received the Prix de Rome. She had sung an aria from Weber's *Der Freischütz* and he had played the piano part, remarkably, from memory. Pauline had forgotten that meeting, but Gounod had not. He had thought of his connection to Pauline as his entry to the theatre, 'the only place to make his name', as he put it. Until then, composing for the church, he had struggled to establish his career.[1]

Pauline had agreed to give the caller half an hour of her time. But she was so impressed by his music that she spent the whole day in his company and ended up by promising to sing the leading part in any opera he chose to write. She even made it one of the conditions for the renewal of her contract at the Paris Opéra that a work by him should be staged there within a year. Nestor Roqueplan, the Opéra's director, was so anxious to retain his prima donna that he readily agreed to her caprice.

Pauline was keen to find new talent for the stage. She had tired of *Le Prophète*. 'I have sung nothing but the eternal *Prophète* (I have not said immortal),' she wrote to George Sand on 16 February. She was excited by Gounod, whose music promised a renaissance for French opera. 'I have been very happy,' she continued in her letter.

> We have made the acquaintance of a young composer who will be a great man once his music becomes known. He had the Prix de Rome ten years ago, and since then he has worked alone in his study, without seeming to realize that every phrase issuing from his pen is a stroke of genius. In truth, it is a comfort to the art to have before one a great musical future to admire, without always having to give oneself a stiff neck by looking back to the past . . . He will have an opera next winter, if I am on hand, as is probable. Besides his genius, he is a very distinguished man, a noble nature, lofty and simple.[2]

Pauline was infatuated with Gounod. She wrote to all her friends to broadcast her opinion of his genius. He would be the French Mozart. He was handsome, charming, graceful and vivacious, musically connected to her spiritual being in a way that neither Louis nor Turgenev could ever be. Her feelings were returned by the composer.

In the early months of 1850, they spent hours together every day working on his ideas for *Sapho*, the opera based on the Greek myth which he had chosen for Pauline and the Paris Opéra. Gounod was embarrassed that he had been helped by a woman to compose his opera and downplayed Pauline's involvement.[3] Turgenev was consumed with jealousy. He tried to conceal it by sharing Pauline's enthusiasm for the promising composer, and found solace in hunting trips with the mild-mannered Louis, who had long since learned to stifle any jealousy on account of his wife's admirers. But if the husband was not jealous, then Turgenev was. He suffered terribly. According to Herzen, Turgenev took to drinking heavily and visited brothels.[4]

His anguish can be felt in two works written at this time. In *The Diary of a Superfluous Man,* the hero of the story, Chulkaturin, becomes jealous of a prince who wins the heart of his beloved Liza, and challenges him to a duel. Turgenev's play *The Student* (later renamed

Gounod, c. 1850.

A Month in the Country) is even closer to the complicated story of Pauline, Louis, Gounod and himself. The play's married heroine, Natalia Petrovna, spurns her passionate admirer Ryabinin (Rakitin in *A Month in the Country*) when she falls in love with her son's tutor, the student Belyaev (Turgenev later confessed that Rakitin was himself). A note in the margins of the manuscript suggests that Turgenev was unsure how far Pauline was to blame for her affair with Gounod. At the moment when Natalia becomes aware of her love for Belyaev, a heavily reworked passage, Turgenev wrote: 'She herself had not suspected how strong her feeling was.'[5]

Turgenev's torment did not end when Pauline departed for Berlin, where the opera season started with *Le Prophète* in April. A few days after she had left Paris, Gounod's brother died, leaving him to provide for his widow and their baby son. Informed by Gounod of the tragedy, Pauline told him to take them with his mother to Courtavenel, where he could work without disturbance on *Sapho*. As a favour to Pauline, Turgenev went with them to provide moral support, putting off his previous plan to return to Russia when the Viardots had left for Germany. Pauline wrote to Turgenev with specific instructions about which rooms the Gounods were to have. She was treating him as little more than a servant. Turgenev did his best to act as the composer's friend, despite his jealousy of 'that monster Gounod', who received longer letters from Pauline.[6] Gounod and Turgenev went for walks together in the woods. They would sit with each other in the evenings, when Pauline was performing in Berlin, following the probable timing of her arias, applauding her *in absentia* at the end, and even throwing sprays of white lilac at the phantom singer, bits of which Turgenev enclosed in a letter to Pauline. Masochistically, he also told her news about Gounod.[7]

By the start of May, Turgenev could bear it no longer. He wrote to Pauline in despair, telling her in rather formal language that he must return to Russia. He would leave Courtavenel on 10 or 12 May and pass through Berlin on his way. Was Turgenev leaving out of jealousy? He would not say so. But he was depressed, and the sense that he had lost Pauline was at the heart of his sadness. Pauline's response is unknown. She expressed her regret that he was leaving in a letter to Gounod but did not write to him. Turgenev wrote again, insisting he must leave, though saying that it grieved him to do so, after which he added a few bits of news (the activities of the poachers, a change in the weather, Gounod's progress on *Sapho*), before stopping to explain that he could not go on writing with this 'artificial jollity' – nor hide his misery behind a semblance of normality: 'I am dreadfully sad,' he confessed at last.[8]

Perhaps Turgenev was waiting for Pauline to plead with him to stay. He could not bring himself to leave while that was possible. On 12 May, he left for Paris, but two days later he returned, claiming that he had been told by a Russian friend there that the Tsar had ordered the arrest of suspected oppositionists, making it advisable for him to wait a while before returning to St Petersburg. Turgenev was 'as happy as a boy' to be back at Courtavenel, he wrote to Pauline; so much so that he forgave her for having sent in his absence a 'tiny little letter' compared to the 'big, fat, long and compactly written ones' which she had sent to Gounod. If only she would join him at Courtavenel, they could discuss together when he should go back to Russia. Perhaps she could persuade him not to go:

Russia can wait – that vast and sombre figure, motionless and veiled by clouds like the Sphinx of Oedipus. She will swallow me later. I think I can see her great immovable gaze on me, fixed with a gloomy scrutiny befitting her eyes of stone. Do not worry, sphinx, I will return to you, and if I do not solve your riddle, you can devour me at your leisure. Leave me in peace for a little longer! I will come back to your steppes.[9]

Turgenev spent another five weeks at Courtavenel. He was generous towards Gounod, jollying him along as he laboured on *Sapho* and writing to Pauline with praise for his music, which he thought too 'melancholy' and 'lofty' to achieve commercial popularity.[10]

Pauline and Louis returned to Courtavenel in June before departing for London, where Pauline was to sing at Covent Garden as well as in a series of concerts. But she made no effort to discourage Turgenev from returning to Russia. His presence there was now a matter of urgency. In Russia it was rumoured that his connections to French republican circles would soon lead to his being placed on a list of permanent exiles, which would mean his works could not be published in his native land. That was not a risk he could take, because he still depended on the small income from his publications in Russia.[11]

Money, in the end, was the most important factor in Turgenev's decision to return. Deprived of his allowance by his mother since 1848, Turgenev barely scraped a living from his writing. Until the success of his *Sketches from a Hunter's Album* in 1852, he was paid just fifty paper roubles (around sixty francs) per printer's page by the *Contemporary*.* He was frequently reduced to borrowing from his friends or writing begging letters to his publishers in Russia for advances against future plays and stories which he promised to give them. He desperately needed to return to Russia, not just to secure his future as a writer, but to make peace with his mother so that she would resume paying his allowance, without which as a writer he could not survive. He hoped to get a settlement from her that would let him live abroad.

---

* The printer's page in Russia was equivalent to about 5,000 words. It contained several pages of the finished publication, which were then cut for binding in a book. Turgenev's rate of pay was low by European standards – around twelve francs per thousand words, increasing to approximately eighteen francs per thousand words after 1852. At a similar stage of his career, in 1833, Balzac was earning thirty francs per thousand words from the *Revue de Paris* (Honoré de Balzac, *Correspondance*, ed. Roger Pierrot, vol. 2 (Paris, 1962), p. 280).

On 15 June, Turgenev travelled with the Viardots to Paris and saw them off at the Gare du Nord, where they departed on the London train. Although he had not announced his plans, he had brought his bags and favourite hunting dog to Paris, so Pauline was suspicious of his intentions, and their parting was emotional. Four days later, he wrote to her that he was leaving for Russia. She replied, expressing her regret, hoping that he would return, but not asking him to change his mind. He also wrote to Gounod. The next day he received a long reply – the letter of a victor to the vanquished – in which the composer spoke about his hope that they would remain bound by their 'excellent friends, whom we both love very deeply', and asked him 'in her name' to let him know through her about important changes in his life. In a P.S. he also wrote: 'Your laundry bill comes to 8 francs 55 centimes.'[12]

The evening before his departure, Turgenev wrote again to the Viardots. To Pauline he confessed that returning to Russia was like going into the desert. She must promise to remember him and write to him with every trivial detail of her life. When she sat outside her château by the poplars in the courtyard she must think of him at Spasskoe with its old lime trees, gazing back in her direction at Courtavenel. He attached a separate note for Louis, who had consoled Turgenev with the prophecy that his conscience would be clear once he had returned to Russia and made peace with his mother:

> I do not want to leave France, my dear good friend, without expressing my affection and esteem for you, or saying how sorry I am that we must part. I take with me the friendliest remembrance of you; I have come to appreciate the excellence and nobility of your character, and you must believe me when I say that I shall never feel truly happy until I am again able, gun in hand and by your side, to tread the beloved plains of the Brie. I accept your prophecy and will try to believe in it. One's homeland has its rights; but is not the true homeland that place where one has found the most affection, where one's heart and spirit feel the most at ease? There is nowhere on earth that I love so much as Courtavenel.[13]

On 29 June, Turgenev left by steamship from Stettin for St Petersburg, and then went by stagecoach to Moscow, following the course of Russia's first main railway, at that time being built by vast armies of serf labour, finally arriving at his mother's estate at Spasskoe on 5 July.

He found his brother newly married to a German woman, Anna Shvarts, who had been employed by his mother as a paid companion. The tyrannical Varvara Petrovna had refused to give her consent to the marriage, but since she did not give her son enough to live on, he had married Anna without her consent and was now living with her independently. His mother would not allow her within her sight.

Turgenev also found a daughter there, an eight-year-old girl born to one of his mother's household staff, a seamstress called Avdotia, whom he had forgotten while he was abroad. 'I was young,' he explained in a letter to Pauline. 'I was bored in the countryside and took an interest in a pretty seamstress employed by my mother. I whispered some words in her ear – she came to my room – I gave her money – and soon afterwards I went away.'[14] Shortly after his return to Spasskoe he had seen the child being forced to carry a heavy pail of water by a coachman. He complained to his mother, who was entertaining visitors. Varvara Petrovna had the young girl, Pelageya, brought into the drawing-room, and asked her guests to say whom she resembled. 'Why, it is your daughter,' she then told her son.

When she began to show her pregnancy Avdotia had been sent away to Moscow, where she worked in the mansion rented by Varvara Petrovna on Ostozhenka Street, and was later married off to a merchant. The baby was brought back to Spasskoe, where she was brought up by the household serfs. Turgenev was appalled. He felt ashamed. For the next quarter of a century, until her death, he paid a monthly pension to Avdotia. Turgenev felt a sense of duty to his unexpected daughter but no real love or affection. Writing to Pauline, he proposed to give his daughter to a convent or take her with him to St Petersburg and find a boarding school for her. He did not think to bring her up himself. Pauline offered to give the child a home, educating her with her own daughter, who was then nine years old. Turgenev jumped at the offer. No doubt he was happy to have in his daughter (whom he renamed Paulinette) a family connection to Pauline. Turgenev promised to provide an annual income of 1,200 francs to help with the costs of her upbringing. Paulinette was despatched to Paris with a governess. The poor girl did not speak a word of French. The only thing her father told her when she left Spasskoe was to 'worship' Pauline as 'her god'.[15]

Turgenev's hopes of mending his relations with his mother were quickly dashed. She refused to make any sort of financial provision for either of her sons, except to give out small sums when she felt like doing so. 'I have been forced to choose between losing my dignity, my independence – and poverty,' Turgenev wrote to Pauline on 1 August. 'My choice did not take long to make – I have left my mother's house and renounced my inheritance. You will believe me, won't you, my dear friends, when I tell you that it was impossible for me to do otherwise.' The two brothers moved with Anna to Turgenevo, their father's small estate a dozen kilometres from Spasskoe, where Turgenev set up rooms in the abandoned building of a paper factory. Hunting expeditions were his daily consolation. 'I shall spend two months here to arrange my affairs,' he wrote to Pauline, 'and then return to Petersburg to work and live there from my work.'[16]

On 16 November, Varvara Petrovna died. She had been ill for several days. Turgenev was in Petersburg and Nikolai had written to call him back, but the journey then, before the railway, took six to seven days, and Turgenev was too late. 'My mother died without having made any provisions [for her serfs] of any kind,' he wrote a few days later to Pauline:

> she left a multitude of people who depended on her to keep them from the street, so to speak. We shall have to do what she ought to have done. Her last days were really sad – God preserve us from a similar death. Her only desire was to deafen herself. On the eve of her death, even when the agony of the death-rattle had begun, there was – by her orders – an orchestra playing polkas in the neighbouring room.[17]

Her death left Turgenev with a lot of land but also with a lot of debts and obligations to her dependants. There were numerous hangers-on at Spasskoe, favourite servants, doctors, hard-up gentry neighbours looking for a hand-out from Varvara Petrovna – types who fill the pages of Turgenev's works. Capricious to the end, she had added to her will a gift of 50,000 roubles to a serf girl she had chosen to adopt, money which Turgenev had to find from an estate that had been run into the ground by negligent and thieving farm stewards. It would take several years for Turgenev to work out how much money he should make – and how much he had lost – from his estates. With Spasskoe, alone, he possessed a manor with sufficient land and serfs to be able to expect an annual income of at least 6,000 silver roubles, or 24,000 francs. It was certainly enough to live well as a gentleman of leisure, even after he had paid his daughter's allowance. The apartment which he rented in St Petersburg cost 450 silver roubles annually, and when he moved there, in 1855, he paid 1,000 roubles for a live-in cook, one of the best in the capital. But he never got the income which he should have earned from Spasskoe. Preoccupied by literature, he took no interest in the estate's management and turned it over to a series of disastrous managers – beginning with a literary acquaintance from the Belinsky circle, N. N. Tiutchev, who lost him thousands, followed by his uncle, Nikolai Turgenev, a retired cavalry officer, who lost him even more. Naively trusting of people, and careless about money, Turgenev failed to realize the extent of his losses for many years.[18]

Sapho received its premiere in Paris in April 1851. A critical success, it had only six performances, mainly because Pauline could sing only on the first three nights and audiences dropped off steeply after that. George Sand, who had planned a trip to see it at the start of May, arrived to find that *Sapho* had been taken off.[19]

Gounod thought that *Sapho* lacked the theatrical elements that made Grand Opera popular.[20] It was not helped by the censor's heavy pen – wielded in the interests of the popular but increasingly authoritarian Louis-Napoleon – which struck out some dramatic scenes on grounds of immorality and incitement to rebellion.[21]

Before the Paris premiere, Pauline had persuaded Frederick Gye, the manager of Covent Garden, to include *Sapho* in her contract for the 1851 season. She would sing the leading role.[22] Pauline went to London at the start of June. Gounod joined her there a few weeks later. They made some improvements to the opera, removing scenes that dragged, and including a ballet. They had high hopes for London, where *Sapho* would receive its first performance on 9 August. It seemed to have a good chance of appealing to the English, who were in a festive mood for the Great Exhibition, which had opened in Hyde Park on 1 May. But the opera was a failure, receiving only two performances before it was taken off. The London critics were scathing, accusing Gye of putting on the 'monotonous' opera only to please Viardot.[23]

With so many visitors in London for the Great Exhibition, the private concert season was particularly busy that summer, and Pauline was in high demand. But she managed to make several visits to the Crystal Palace, Joseph Paxton's glass and iron exhibition hall, where she was impressed, as she put it in a letter to her mother, by the 'creative similarities between all nations and the sheer inventiveness of humankind'.[24]

The idea of a 'universal exhibition' went back to the Jacobins, who had mounted one to celebrate the industrial achievements of the French Republic in 1798. There had been many others since – in Berne and Madrid in 1845, Brussels and Bordeaux in 1847, St Petersburg in 1848, Lisbon and Paris in 1849. But the Great Exhibition was the first of its kind to be truly international, with over forty countries taking part. It was the original world's fair, a 'global village' under glass.

The decision to internationalize the exhibition was taken by Prince Albert in 1849, following a visit to the Exposition Publique des Produits de l'Industrie Française in Paris. As President of the Royal Society for the Encouragement of Arts, Manufactures and Commerce, the prince was the sponsor of 'The Great Exhibition of the Works of Industry of All Nations' (as the Great Exhibition was officially called), with Henry Cole, a member of the Royal Society who had organized a number of successful exhibitions of industrial art, its chief organizing force. Originally conceived as a means of improving British design standards by comparison with other countries, the exhibition was quickly taken over by free-trade ideologists, who saw the development of international trade as a mechanism for promoting peace and progress, not to mention British interests as the leading manufacturer in the world. Its organizers did not stress the free-trade argument, because foreign governments were still generally opposed to it, but instead turned up the internationalist rhetoric, the old ideals of unity between the nations which had been invoked with the opening of international railways after 1843.

'We are living at a period of most wonderful transition, which tends rapidly to the accomplishment of that great end to which, indeed, all history points – the realization of the unity of mankind,' declared Prince Albert, emphasizing how the 'achievements of modern invention' meant that the 'distances which separated the different nations' were 'gradually vanishing'. The benefits of cultural exchange between nations were at the heart of this discourse. 'The Exposition is calculated to promote and increase the free interchange of raw materials and manufactured commodities between all the nations of the earth,' wrote Charles Babbage, the English polymath best known for his invention of a mechanical computer, whose ideas influenced the layout of the exhibition. 'It is the interest of every people that all other nations should advance in knowledge, in industrial skill, in taste, and in science.'[25]

For Karl Marx, who had been living in exile in London since 1849, the exhibition was 'a striking proof of the concentrated power with which modern large-scale industry is everywhere demolishing national barriers and increasingly blurring local peculiarities of production, society and national character among all peoples'. It was, in other words, a symbol of the globalized economy created by the growth of capitalist networks and international trade. Marx also saw the exhibition as a monument to consumption. It was the foundation of a mass 'consumer culture' – as it would be called today – where a cultural value was assigned to goods over and above their use value. In his view the Crystal Palace – with its tens of thousands of items on display, from railway engines and boilers, electrical devices and machines, telescopes and microscopes, low-cost pianos, furniture of every kind, stuffed birds, umbrellas, pencils, gold and silver objects, porcelain and sculpture, prints and photographs – was a showcase for the fetish of commodities. 'With this exhibition,' Marx and Engels wrote, 'the bourgeoisie of the world has erected in the modern Rome its Pantheon, where, with self-satisfied pride, it exhibits the gods which it has made for itself.'[26]

A spectacle, museum and bazaar, the Great Exhibition blurred the old divisions between art objects, machines and commodities. The idea of the Royal Society was to 'wed high art with mechanical skill', as Prince Albert put it in 1846, and in the exhibition the emphasis was on the productive process of industrial arts ('Art Manufactures', as Cole termed them).[27] Paintings were excluded from the Crystal Palace,* unless they were deemed to demonstrate a new material or technique, but in the Fine Arts Court there were sculptures, ceramics, mosaics and enamels, all exhibited as the precious work of skilled craftsmen.

The narrative created by this curatorial principle represented art as a high-value consumer commodity. The art objects were displayed like merchandise, alongside gold and silver works, clocks and furniture, as

* There had been a plan for a Picture Gallery which the French – the main contributors – had blocked on economic grounds: they did not want to pay the costs of transporting their paintings (Patricia Mainardi, 'The Unbuilt Picture Gallery at the 1851 Great Exhibition', *Journal of the Society of Architectural Historians*, vol. 45, no. 3, Sept. 1986, pp. 294–9).

in a department store.* Glass was the key to this display. The invention of the cast plate-glass method in 1848 allowed the production of the much larger sheets of glass which went into the building of the Crystal Palace, the shopfronts of department stores, and the great iron–glass arcades, the *passages couverts de Paris*.[28]

Much of the art at the Great Exhibition was machine-made – casts and copies of antique statuettes, imitation bronzes, lithographic prints of famous paintings, designed for sale in the mass market. Although the organizers had decided that the objects on display should not have price tags, the decision had been taken only after 'much examination and inquiry', according to Cole. There were many critics of this policy, including Babbage, who argued that the price 'is the most important element in every bargain' and that to omit it was 'not less absurd than to represent a tragedy without a hero, or to paint a portrait without a nose'. Since the main aim of the exhibition was the 'increase of commerce and the exchange of commodities', Babbage suggested that 'sales should be permitted on the premises'. Queen Victoria probably agreed. After visiting the exhibition, she recorded in her diary 'a wish to buy all one saw!'[29]

2

Sketches from a Hunter's Album, the work that would make Turgenev's name, was published in 1852. The book was made up of stories he had previously published, mostly in *The Contemporary*, whose editor, Nekrasov, had wanted to collect them in a single volume since 1847; but it was only three years later, after the success of those that had appeared, that Turgenev began to prepare the publication and wrote the last stories for the book. Hunting stories and sketches were a popular genre, particularly if they doubled up as travelogues or social commentaries. Louis Viardot had achieved a success with his *Souvenirs*

---

* The new department stores, such as the Bazar Bonne-Nouvelle and Au Bon Marché in Paris, Lewis's in Liverpool and Whiteley's in London, would bear a striking resemblance to the exhibition hall. Their architectural grandeur, with glass and iron girders opening up the vast interiors to light, was meant to create spectacle; their layout was designed to direct the movement of their visitors through all the departments, just as the crowds were directed through the exhibition hall.

de chasse (1846), which by 1852 was just about to go into its fifth edition in Hachette's Bibliothèque des Chemins de Fer. Turgenev must have hoped to achieve something similar.

Turgenev had problems with the censors from the start. Any work that set out to expose the conditions of the serfs was bound to run into trouble in Russia, the only country in Europe at that time that had yet to abolish serfdom. After the revolutionary convulsions of 1848, governments across the Continent were wary of the power of the arts, the theatre in particular, to mobilize political emotions. The problem was especially acute in the Austrian Empire, where the counter-revolution had left a legacy of frustrated national sentiment in, among other places, Hungary, the Czech lands and northern Italy. Verdi's opera *Stiffelio* (1850) was butchered by the censors in Trieste because its story-line (a priest forgives his adulterous wife) was seen by the Austrian authorities as an attack on Catholic morals. *Rigoletto* (1851) ran into similar problems before it was first performed at the Teatro La Fenice in Venice. Based on Victor Hugo's play, *Le Roi s'amuse*, the opera's depiction of the French king as an immoral womanizer was deemed unacceptable by the Austrian censors, although after long negotiations they allowed a toned-down version shifted to the extinct Duchy of Mantua under the Gonzaga family.

Nowhere were the censors more active than in Russia. The European revolutions had not spread to Russia in 1848 but there were small groups of revolutionaries and intellectuals committed to democracy, from which the Tsar and his panicky advisers expected trouble any time. To seal off Russia from possible contagion by Western ideas the Tsar established the Buturlin Committee in 1848 to extend his powers of preventive censorship. Any literary activity deemed remotely subversive attracted the attention of the Tsar's police. There was no rhyme or reason to its repressions. In 1849, the Slavophile writer Yury Samarin was imprisoned for an *unpublished* manuscript in which he criticized the nobility in Riga, where he lived. In the same year the so-called Petrashevsky Circle, a group of intellectuals (including the writer Dostoevsky) who met once a week to discuss political ideas, was sentenced to death by a Russian court. Dostoevsky's offence was to have read out Belinsky's by-then famous but forbidden letter to Gogol of 1847 in which the critic had attacked mysticism and called for reform. At the last moment before their execution, the twenty-one 'conspirators' received a pardon from the Tsar, their sentences commuted to various terms of penal labour in Siberia.

Turgenev had already had some trouble with the censors in Russia, who had barred the publication of some of his stories in *The Contemporary* between 1849 and 1851. But these problems were insignificant compared to the storm that erupted on the publication of the *Sketches* as a book in 1852. Aware of the tightening censorship in St Petersburg, Turgenev had let his friend Vasily Botkin give his manuscript to a relatively liberal Moscow censor, Prince V. V. Lvov, who had agreed to advise the writer on what needed to be cut. On the basis of those changes the book was approved for publication by Lvov in March (among the cuts was a dedication to Pauline, whose name had been replaced with asterisks).[30] The censor no doubt thought there was no harm in passing stories that had been mostly published previously. None of them contained a single sentence that could be read as an overt attack on the tsarist system or serfdom (although taken altogether the whole book was suffused with a subtle condemnation of both).

On 28 April, Turgenev was arrested, not apparently for the *Sketches*, but for an obituary of Gogol he had published in the *Moscow Herald* (*Moskovskie Vedomosti*) on 25 March. Turgenev had been deeply shaken by the writer's death in February. 'It is difficult for you as a foreigner to appreciate the huge scale of this loss, so cruel and so complete,' he had written to Pauline. 'Even the most penetrating critics from abroad, a Mérimée for example, saw in Gogol just a humourist in the English mould . . . But you have to be a Russian to understand what we have lost. For us he was more than a writer – he revealed us Russians to ourselves.'[31] Like every Russian writer to emerge in the middle decades of the nineteenth century, Turgenev thought of himself as a 'follower of Gogol'. In an influential article of 1845 Belinsky had described his story 'The Overcoat' as the founding text in a 'new literary school' defined by the critic as the 'reproduction of reality in all its truth'. The term 'realism' was only just beginning to be used, but the idea that the writer ought to show all aspects of society, including its vulgarity and ugliness, as Belinsky argued Gogol had achieved, became the basis of the realist tradition in Russia (as Dostoevsky famously put it, the whole of Russian literature 'came out from underneath Gogol's "Overcoat"').

There was nothing political in Turgenev's article about Gogol. Describing him as a 'great man', it was written, however, in a spirit of exasperation at the general silence in the Russian press about his death, a frustration he expressed in letters to Botkin and Ivan Aksakov, the Slavophile critic, which were intercepted by the Tsar's political police. He also wrote in the same vein to Louis Viardot, who subsequently wrote an article in *Le Siècle*, the French republican newspaper, reporting from an unnamed Russian source that Gogol had been persecuted by the censors in Russia. The article was picked up by a tsarist police agent in Paris who named the source as Turgenev. His report was handed to the Tsar, who was determined to punish Turgenev for his *Sketches*. Ignoring the advice of his police chief simply to place Turgenev under surveillance, Nicholas accused him of 'open insubordination' and ordered him to be imprisoned for a month, followed by a period of house arrest on his estate. The room which served as his prison cell also held the police archives of a whole district, whose secret files he had time to study at leisure. One night he was visited by the chief of police, curious to meet the famous writer, who, after a few glasses of champagne, proposed a toast 'To Robespierre!'[32]

From his cell Turgenev wrote to the Viardots to tell them of his situation: he thought the Gogol article was only a pretext for his arrest, because the authorities had been watching him 'for a long time' – by which he meant the time he had spent in France with them in the company of revolutionary republicans.* It seems likely that he meant to warn the Viardots, who, as he had feared, were being watched by the French police following the coup d'état of 2 December 1851, when Louis-Napoleon dissolved the National Assembly – which had opposed his constitutional reform to allow him to stand as President for a second four-year term – and established his dictatorship. Turgenev was full of gloom and self-pity: 'My health is good but I have aged ridiculously – I could send you a lock of my white hair ... My life is over, all the joy from it has gone – I have eaten all my supply of white bread.'[33]

Turgenev thought that his arrest would stop the publication of his *Sketches*. The Minister of Education gave Lvov a 'severe reprimand' for allowing the book to pass. But it was too late to stop the publication of

---

* Unknown to Turgenev, the Third Section, or political police, had also been compiling a report on his connections to Nikolai Turgenev, a distant relative and one of the main leaders of the Decembrist uprising against autocracy in 1825. Abroad at the time of the uprising, Nikolai remained in exile in Paris, where Turgenev had met him in 1845 (*Turgenevskii sbornik*, p. 212).

the book, which appeared in August and sold out very quickly in both Moscow and St Petersburg – to a large extent because the arrest of its author had made him a celebrity. Prompted by the Minister of Education, the Tsar's chief censor reviewed the published book, decided it was harmful, and concluded that since Turgenev was 'well known to be a wealthy man' his motives for writing it must have been political – to show 'that the peasants are oppressed, that the landowners conduct themselves immorally and against the law, that the priests kow-tow to the landowners, that the local officials take bribes, in sum that the peasants would be better off if they were free'. On the orders of the Tsar the book was now banned and Lvov dismissed from his job.[34]

'I am re-reading your *Sketches from a Hunter's Album*,' Aksakov wrote to Turgenev on 4 October 1852, 'and I cannot understand what Lvov was thinking when he let them pass. The book is a subtle series of attacks, a whole battalion of gunfire against the landed order.'[35] The *Sketches* were a sensation. No book did more to raise the awareness of society about the suffering of the peasantry. For the first time the peasants were portrayed not as simple 'rustic types' with stock expressions and characteristics, as they had been in Romantic literature, but as thinking, feeling, complicated individual human beings. By simple observation of the ways that serfdom shaped their lives, Turgenev had aroused the moral indignation of his readers more effectively than any political manifesto ever could have done. The impact of the *Sketches* was immense. Published in the same year as *Uncle Tom's Cabin*, they had as big an impact in swaying Russian views against serfdom as Harriet Beecher Stowe's book had on the anti-slavery movement in America. It was commonly believed that Tsar Alexander II, who would come to the throne in 1855, had not only read them but was influenced by them in his decision to abolish serfdom in 1861. Turgenev would later claim that the proudest moment in his life came shortly after the Emancipation Decree, when two peasants approached him on a train from Orel to Moscow and bowed down to the ground in the Russian manner to 'thank him in the name of the whole people'.[36]

What struck readers of the *Sketches* most was their visual reality. Strikingly pictorial, they were frequently compared to photographs or daguerreotypes of country life. Turgenev himself said his stories were 'like photographic exposures of what I have seen and heard'.[37] As a writer, he was certainly a realist. He made 'real life' the subject of his writing and always drew his characters from actual people. He aimed to let his readers engage directly with reality – to see it on the page like a transparency without authorial intervention or judgement – through a descriptive prose thick with sensory details. The narrator of the *Sketches* reveals nothing of himself – he acts as a window on to life. But Turgenev thought that realist art should never be reduced to the type of reproduction in a photograph. 'Art is not just a daguerreotype,' he wrote. As he saw it, holding up a mirror to reality should only ever be the starting point for a novelist, whose task was not just to copy but to select and colour what they wanted to be seen, and then let the reader form their own judgement. The observation of reality should never overshadow the writer's own imagination or the search for hidden truths – the motives and ideas that lie beneath the surface of human actions and society. His aim was 'to capture the poetic in reality', as he wrote to the painter Ludwig Pietsch, and this he achieved in the *Sketches*, combining poetry with a photographic vision as few other writers have. After reading them in a French translation, George Sand wrote to Turgenev: 'You are a realist who sees everything, and a poet who makes beauty from reality.'[38]

Turgenev led a quiet life under house arrest at Spasskoe. Kept under constant surveillance, he could not even go hunting on his land without being followed by a policeman. 'Here are my occupations in the day,' he wrote to Pauline in November 1852:

> I get up at 8 o'clock. I breakfast etc. until 9. Then I take an hour's walk. From 10 to 2 pm. I read, or write letters, etc. At 2 I have a bite to eat – or go for a little walk. Then I work 'til half past 4. Dinner at 5 in the house with the Tiutchev family (I live in a wing that looks on to the garden).* I stay with them until 10. We play cards or I read aloud, etc. I go to bed at 10, read until 11, and go to sleep immediately – one day is exactly like the next. It isn't jolly, as you see, but it's not so bad as you might believe.

The worst of it was the isolation from Europe, and those parts of European culture that reached Moscow and St Petersburg. It took fifteen days for a letter from London or Paris to get to Moscow, and another

* The main house had burned down in a fire in 1839.

five or six to reach him at Spasskoe. He was not used to this slow pace
of life and felt the isolation acutely. 'So I am truly stuck here in the
middle of the steppes,' he wrote to Pauline,

> as far from you as possible, far from any news – for we have no journals
> here as you can well imagine. Take an atlas, look on the map of Russia
> for the road that goes from Moscow to Tula and from Tula to Orel – and
> if between these last two towns you find a place called Chern (just before
> you get to another town which has the name of Mtsenk), then you know
> that I am two French leagues (10 versts) from this town.

Missing music more than anything, he begged Pauline to send him an
arrangement of an aria from *Sapho* with 'a little piano accompaniment'
that was not too hard for him to play.[39]

It was not just music that he missed – it was Pauline. On 13 November, the ninth anniversary of their first meeting, Turgenev wrote to
her: 'I am today, as I was nine years ago and will be nine years hence,
all yours, heart and soul. You know this. Nine years! Alas, it will be ten
before I have hope of seeing you again.' Turgenev feared it was too late
to rekindle their romance. He had just turned thirty-four, and she was
thirty-one. After her infatuation with Gounod, Pauline was attempting
to mend her relations with Louis. She had given birth to a second
daughter, Claudie, in May 1852. Turgenev had moved a peasant wife
into his house at Spasskoe. But what he really wanted was a visit by
Pauline.

Her pregnancy had forced her to take a break from the Paris stage.
She had not appeared there in the autumn season of 1851. Her return
was then postponed by Napoleon's coup d'état in December. The
Viardots were personae non gratae with the Imperial regime. Known
for his republican connections, Louis, in particular, was watched by
the police, who followed him on his way to the Sorbonne library and
filed reports on whom he met for lunch. Suspicion also cast its shadow
on Pauline. There was no invitation from the Paris Opéra for the 1852
season. Rumours spread that she had retired from the stage.[40]

Instead, as before, she looked abroad for opportunities. There had
been talk of her appearing for another season in St Petersburg. Now at
the height of her international fame, she could cash in on a trip to Russia before her voice began to fail. The radical connections of the
Viardots were the main problem. The Italian repertoire which Pauline

had proposed to bring with her had been a focal point for the revolutionary sentiment of the Risorgimento in 1848, and as such had come to hold a special interest for Russia's democrats. The Tsar was reluctant to invite Pauline. But there was no denying the popular demand for the return of 'our Viardot', as the Russians had continued calling her, and on the last day of December 1852 a contract with the Imperial Theatre was at last agreed.[41]

Pauline arrived in St Petersburg in January 1853. She sang the parts she had sung in her youth: Rosina in *The Barber of Seville*, Desdemona in Rossini's *Otello*, Amina in *La Sonnambula*, and then sang in private concerts for the court. She received so many jewels that she sold them to a jeweller in St Petersburg and sent the money to her bank in Paris to save herself the trouble (and potential risk) of carrying them back to France.[42] In March she went to Moscow, where the opera was closed because of Lent, so she gave a series of recitals. To the delight of the Muscovites she sang mainly Russian songs – by Glinka, Alexander Dargomyzhsky and Anton Rubinstein – and even wore a *kokoshnik*, the traditional Muscovite headdress.[43] Pauline continued to perform these songs in European concert halls. She did more than anyone in the middle decades of the nineteenth century to make Russian music better known and appreciated in the West.[44]

Turgenev wrote to Pauline in St Petersburg, begging her to visit Orel on her tour. He recommended the serf orchestra of one of his neighbouring landowners for a concert performance. 'They play very well, they have a wide repertoire, and know all the classics,' he assured her. Unless Pauline was accompanied by her husband it would not have been appropriate for her to visit Turgenev at Spasskoe: rumours of an affair would soon spread. Louis did not want to make the trip. Perhaps he was smarting from the gossip about Pauline and Gounod. No doubt too he thought it was unwise for her to visit one of the Tsar's prisoners, given that he was her paymaster. Writing to Turgenev in Spanish – a language he did not think the police would understand – Louis told him that there were too many risks in coming to Orel. Turgenev bowed to his decision gracefully but he was disappointed and felt let down. 'My dear friend,' he wrote to Louis with more than a hint of sarcasm, 'what particularly distinguishes you from others is – your sagacity and common sense. We shall meet only when God wills it, and not before.'[45]

The situation changed when Pauline was in Moscow. News came

that Louis had been taken ill and had left for France. Turgenev was beside himself with frustration. If Pauline would not visit him, he decided he would go to Moscow to see her. A minor relaxation of the conditions of his sentence encouraged him to think this possible. On 1 April, after several petitions on his behalf, including one from the Tsar's own son, Turgenev was officially released from house arrest at Spasskoe and allowed to live in town in Orel under police surveillance. But to go all the way to Moscow was a serious offence and, if caught, he would face a sentence behind bars. He was prepared to take the risk. With a false passport, Turgenev departed on 3 April, spent a week with friends in Moscow, visiting Pauline at the Dresden Hotel, where she was staying, and returned to Spasskoe by 13 April. In his later correspondence with Pauline, Turgenev referred to the secret rendezvous, which, he said, had shown that 'nothing is impossible'.[46] He also used it for a scene in his story 'Enough (Fragment from the Notebook of a Dead Artist)', written between 1862 and 1864, in which the narrator recalls a late-night meeting with his lover in Moscow and writes to her about it after they have parted: 'I have left you, but even here, in this far-off exile, I am filled with you, and as before I am in your power, I still feel your hand on my bowed head.'[47]

3

The *Sketches* were Turgenev's first success financially. Nekrasov sold 3,000 copies to a Moscow bookseller which were all bought in a few weeks. The Tsar's banning of the published book did not prevent it reaching anyone who wanted to read it, because it soon came out in French and other languages, as well as pirate Russian editions reprinted in Berlin, which managed to enter Russia without any obstacles. Technological changes and the ideological diversity of European governments made traditional censorship less effective.

The success of the *Sketches* established Turgenev as a major writer on the European scene. It also meant that he could raise his fees and strike a harder bargain with publishers. If before the publication of the *Sketches* he had earned fifty roubles for every printed page, afterwards he could demand a rate of seventy-five roubles, knowing that if Nekrasov refused to pay, he could find another editor who would do so. The book was not enough to make Turgenev rich or financially secure, even with the income he received from his estate. He was still forced to write to publishers begging them for loans against future works. But he was now a writer who could make a living from his work.[48]

Turgenev was one of a growing number of professional writers living from their literary earnings in Europe. There had long been jobbing writers, lowly hacks and journalists that had been able to support themselves from their writing. Grub Street in London had been full of them since the eighteenth century. But few writers of serious literature earned much from their works before the nineteenth century. For *The Sorrows of Young Werther* (1774), an international bestseller, Goethe received 1,000 thalers (£240)* from his Leipzig publisher. But that was exceptional. The majority of published writers at this time were gentlemen with private incomes, the beneficiaries of patronage, or the holders of a sinecure that enabled them to write. They did not need or even expect to be paid.

In the early decades of the nineteenth century, it became the norm for writers to receive a payment from their publisher. This was normally a one-time payment for the right to print a certain number of their books (usually between 1,000 and 2,000 copies) over a set period of time (no more than a year or two). Once this contract had expired, the writer was free to switch to another publisher. Sometimes writers were persuaded to share in the profits of their publisher instead – a risky strategy because publishers, whose devious reputation was proverbial, could not be relied upon to give accurate figures. Levels of remuneration were not high, as Lucien de Rubempré, the protagonist of Balzac's *Lost Illusions* (1837–43), soon discovered when he came to Paris to launch himself as a writer and received just 400 francs for his novel, a medieval saga in the style of Walter Scott.

The Scottish writer was the first in Europe to make a fortune from his pen – his historical romances were international bestsellers – even if he lost it in the stock market crash of 1825–6. By 1818, Scott was making the fantastic sum of £10,000 a year from his novels, and in 1819, his best financial year, when he published three novels, including *Ivanhoe* and *The Bride of Lammermoor*, he earned £19,000.

* The French franc was not in existence but the silver value was equivalent to 5,500 French livres.

Few writers came close to Scott's earnings. Balzac was among them, but his first ten years in the writing trade were hardly lucrative. He was paid a mere 400 francs – the same amount received by his poor hero Lucien – for his debut novel, *L'Héritière de Birague,* co-written with Auguste Lepoitevin and published in 1821 under two pen names (Balzac's was Lord R'Hoone, an anagram of his name, Honoré). The two friends sold their next novel, *Jean-Louis, ou La Fille trouvée* (1822), for 1,300 francs, which they also divided. For his first novel published under the sole name of R'Hoone, *Clotilde de Lusignan* (1822), Balzac was paid 2,000 francs, a recognition of his pseudonym's success. But for *Les Chouans* (1829), the first under his real name, he earned only half that sum, not enough to clear his massive debts (some 90,000 francs) following the failure of his various business ventures – a publishing house, a printing firm and a type foundry – between 1825 and 1828. By his own calculation, Balzac made just ten francs a day from his work on *Les Chouans* – an amount that could be earned by a skilled craftsman (he referred to himself as a 'poor worker in letters'). He had to spend his whole life writing novels, day and night, to pay off his creditors (his voluminous correspondence is largely taken up with his business affairs). He churned them out at a furious pace, eventually earning handsome fees from his writing (in 1835, the year of his breakthrough novel, *Le Père Goriot,* he earned 67,000 francs), even if his lavish lifestyle meant that he never fully cleared his debts.[49]

Balzac was unusual in managing to live from his writing. Most writers had to supplement their income by doing other jobs: journalism, teaching, working as a civil servant or librarian were common daytime jobs for French and English writers in the first half of the century. As the book market grew, writers pushed for better pay. The structure of the market favoured them, for publishers were plentiful and good writers in demand. In France, in 1832, the ratio of publishers to published fiction writers was just two to one (152 authors were published in that year by no fewer than 73 different publishers). In these conditions the bestselling writers were well placed to push for higher fees or switch to other publishers in their search for better conditions. Victor Hugo knew his worth. He bargained hard with publishers. In 1832, he earned 6,000 francs for his poetry collection *Feuilles d'automne* – six times the sum he had been paid for his *Odes et ballades* in 1828. Balzac was notorious for his aggressive bargaining with publishers, never hesitating to abandon one and take up with another if he felt he had been wronged or could get a better deal. At the height of his fame, in 1844, he sold the serialization of *Modeste Mignon* to *Le Journal des débats* for 9,500 francs; a few months later he resold a revised and expanded version to the publisher Chlenowski for 11,000 francs; and a third variation to Charles Furne, who published it as part of his complete edition of *La Comédie humaine* in 1846. By one calculation, before 1850 the French writer typically had up to thirteen different publishers in the course of his career.[50]

For book as for music publishing the situation was transformed by the introduction of more effective laws of copyright in the middle decades of the nineteenth century. This did more than anything to increase writers' earnings from their work and establish a more stable base for their relations with their publishers. Publishers and writers had a mutual interest in the development of copyright as a form of literary capital in whose exploitation they both shared.

The biggest peril for their business was piracy, the mass reprinting of unauthorized editions, which was a booming industry in the 1830s and 1840s, when new print technologies made this cheap and quick to do. Pirate book publishing was an international business, ultimately uncontrollable without international laws. With its large and porous border France was particularly vulnerable. In Belgium, Holland, Luxembourg, Switzerland and Austria there were scores of publishers whose business was reprinting French books cheaply and sending them back into France.[51] Pirated editions of German books were printed by the Dutch and Austrians for export to the German states (which pirated each other's books as well). English books were reprinted by the Galignani publishing house in Paris and shipped across the Channel for resale at cheap prices. They were pirated on an industrial scale by the Americans, who printed several novels at a time in broadsheets known as 'Mammoths', which sold in great quantities on both sides of the Atlantic.

Belgium and America were the biggest pirate states, feeding as they did off the two largest literary languages. In both states the pirates were protected by their governments, which put the interests of native printers before those of foreign writers and their publishers. Under the newly independent Belgian government, the number of pirate publishers in Belgium rocketed. By 1838, there were 229 pirate presses in

Brussels, and 200 in other Belgian towns, many with the best technology, capable of printing the text in double columns that made their editions so affordable. Three out of four books printed in Belgium were pirated editions for export, most of them transported across the border into France, but some overseas as far as the United States, Brazil, Mexico and Cuba. The international market was so swamped by cheap pirate editions that the publishers of authorized editions were forced to lower their prices to compete with them, which meant increasing print-runs to sustain profits. To squeeze out the pirate Belgian editions of Dumas, for example, Michel Lévy published his complete works in a mass edition of 20,000 copies with each volume priced at just two French francs, instead of the usual 3.5.[52]

Publishers and writers combined forces to campaign for more effective laws of copyright to stamp out this piracy. They advanced new ideas of intellectual property. Throughout Europe the case for more protection was based on the notion of a work of art as a product of the artist's genius and personality, a concept championed by the Romantics. But there was a difference between the French philosophy of *droits d'auteur*, which saw this as a natural right, inalienable and absolute, and the British way of thinking about copyright in which the economic interests of the author, publishers and booksellers needed to be balanced against wider issues of free trade and public access to creative works. Although Britain had passed the first real law of copyright, in 1710, which had given authors fourteen years of protection before their work passed into the public domain, the argument for stronger laws had to overcome the widely held perception that copyright was a 'monopoly' that made books too expensive for the common man.

In 1837, Thomas Talfourd, the writer, judge and politician, introduced a Copyright Bill in the British House of Commons proposing to extend the term of copyright to the author's life plus sixty years. The Bill was opposed by the booksellers' trade, which argued that copyright would cut into its profits, and by a number of MPs, including Thomas Babington Macaulay, the historian, who argued that a longer term would be 'a tax on readers for the purpose of giving a bounty to writers'. Over 30,000 people signed petitions against the Bill, which was defeated several times before eventually being passed in 1842, albeit in a form much watered down (the term of copyright was limited to the author's life plus seven years).[53] The supporters of the Bill, including Wordsworth

1. Ary Scheffer's portrait of Pauline Viardot, oil on canvas, 1840. Scheffer said of her that she was 'dreadfully ugly, but if I were to see her again, I would fall madly in love with her'.

2. The fiery Manuel Garcia in the role of Rossini's Otello. Engraving by Pierre Langlumé, c. 1821.

3. Louis Viardot, c. 1839, during his directorship of the Théâtre Italien.

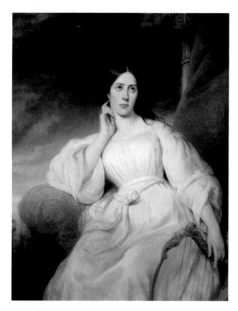

4. Maria Malibran as Desdemona in Rossini's *Otello* (oil on canvas, c. 1830).

5. The earliest known photographic image of Ivan Turgenev, taken at the time of his first acquaintance with Pauline Viardot. Daguerreotype by Josef Weninger, St Petersburg, 1844.

6. No Handel opera was performed in full during the entire nineteenth century, but Pauline Viardot kept alive an interest in his operas' arias by singing them in recitals. This arrangement of her celebrated version of 'Lascio ch'io pianga' from *Rinaldo* was published in London in 1840, shortly after she had sung it there.

7. The cult of Beethoven reached its peak in Europe during the 1840s. In *Franz Liszt Fantasizing at the Piano* by Josef Danhauser (oil on canvas, 1840) George Sand and Rossini (standing over Liszt) are pictured in a group of diverse artists united in their veneration of the German composer.

8. Courbet's large-scale painting *A Burial at Ornans* (oil on canvas, 1849–50) was attacked by critics for its coarsely realist representation of ordinary people, deemed inappropriate for art. Courbet said the painting was 'in reality the burial of Romanticism'.

9. Cézanne, *Girl at the Piano* (oil on canvas, 1868). The piano had a transformative effect on the position of women in the home.

10. Gérôme's *The Duel after a Masked Ball* (oil on canvas, 1857) was one of the most widely copied and engraved pictures in the nineteenth century.

11. *Clair de lune à Valmondois* by Daubigny (1877). An example of the *cliché-verre* method, pioneered by the Barbizon painters and photographers, in which the artist etches on a glass plate coated with collodion and exposes it to light against a sheet of sensitized paper. Its subtle effects had an impact on painting.

12. Daguerreotype of Pauline Viardot, St Petersburg, 1853. Turgenev had it mounted in a wooden case.

13. Louis Viardot (photograph, 1868). One of a series of postcards of European writers sold individually and published in eight volumes between 1855 and 1890.

14. Pauline Viardot's musical salon in Paris (engraving, 1858). Pauline is seated at her Cavaillé-Coll organ.

15. Pauline standing with her daughters Claudie (*left*) and Marianne (*right*) (photograph, Baden-Baden, 1870).

16. The *Konversationshaus* at Baden-Baden (hand-coloured steel engraving, 1858).

17. Degas, *La Chanson du chien* (gouache, pastel and monotype on paper, 1875–77), a marvellous evocation of the singing style of Thérésa (Emma Valladon), the most famous of the café concert singers in the 1860s and 1870s.

and Dickens, based their case for copyright not on the idea of an author's natural rights, but on the protection of his economic property – a cause dear to the British. Dickens's main concern was the industry of pirate publishers who sold cheap reprints of his works, many of them shipped in from America. His tour of the United States in 1842 was noted mainly for his condemnations of this piracy and calls for stronger laws to stamp it out.

In France the campaign for more protection was led by two associations, both involved in the collection of royalties for their members: the Société des Auteurs et Compositeurs Dramatiques, founded in 1829; and the Société des Gens de Lettres, established in 1838 by a committee that included Victor Hugo, Alexandre Dumas and Louis Viardot, with Balzac joining later that year.[54] Balzac was a strident campaigner for the protection of intellectual property (he once smashed a bookshop window in the Palais-Royal when he saw in it a pirated edition of one of his novels). In 1834, he published a *Lettre adressée aux écrivains français du XIXe siècle*, in which he argued for the moral right of authors to their work, demanding that the law protect the products of the mind as it would the merchant's bale of cotton or any other tangible object manufactured by labour.[55] Hugo was less combative in his arguments for copyright, but more effective for having been appointed to the Senate, where, in 1846, he made his maiden speech calling for artistic works to have the same protection as inventions under patent law. The longer that protection the better, he argued, because 'for great artists attempting to create great works, time is what is most important, longevity, the respect and assurance of the law for their thought, their property'.[56]

In 1854, Napoleon III extended copyright to thirty years beyond the death of the author. When this failed to satisfy the publishers and writers, he appointed a commission to look into extending it further. Eventually, in 1863, after much deliberation, the commission recommended that the rights of authors should be limited to fifty years, after which their works should become public property and their heirs stop receiving a royalty for each published copy of their work. The commission's recommendation – loosely based on Hugo's notion of a *'domaine public payant'* – became the basis of a new law in 1866.

In Germany the problem was enforcing copyright in the patchwork of independent states. Although the German Confederation had envisaged a uniform system of copyright legislation, it proved too weak to impose one on its forty-three members, kingdoms, duchies, principalities and free city republics. Saxony and Prussia both passed their own laws, in 1831 and 1837 respectively, but neither could impose its legislation on the other, or any other states. Piracy between them was endemic. None of these issues would be properly resolved until the unification of Germany, when the Empire's laws of copyright would be taken from Prussia, which established copyright for the duration of the author's life and, following their death, for another thirty years to protect their dependants. After a campaign by publishers and writers, the Prussian laws were strengthened in 1856 to benefit the families of those writers who had died before the 1837 law. It meant that the works of authors such as Schiller (1759–1805) and Goethe (1749–1832) could generate an income for their heirs and publishers until 1867, when this extension to the law ended. Schiller's publisher (Cotta in Stuttgart) paid his descendants nearly 300,000 guilders (around 800,000 francs) for the rights to print his works – twelve times the royalties which Schiller himself had received during his lifetime.

A similar reform took place in Russia, where a decree in 1857 extended the duration of copyright protection from twenty-five to fifty years following the author's death. Pushkin's widow had been instrumental in getting the extension through the government connections of her second husband, Lieutenant-General P. P. Lanskoi, whose second cousin was the Minister of the Interior. The copyright on Pushkin's work had been due to expire in 1862.[57]

In Italy, as in Germany, the problem facing writers and their publishers was how to enforce their copyright without national laws and agencies. Until the unification of Italy there was no effective means of protecting literary property in one Italian state from pirate publishers in other parts of the peninsula. 'The Milanese reprint the books of the Florentines; the Florentines will then reprint twice as many books of the Milanese – because they can,' wrote the Italian essayist Niccolò Tommaseo in 1839. 'The book trade is becoming an area for cowardly vendettas . . . fought with arms of ink.' In 1840, a comprehensive law of copyright was passed in all the northern states of Italy under Austrian control. It protected books and music, dramatic works and translations for the duration of their author's life and up to thirty years following the author's death. But the Kingdom of Two Sicilies was not part of this convention and remained a pirate state. Nor did the 1840 law protect works that had been published before it was passed.[58]

A good example of the problems this entailed concerns Alessandro Manzoni's *The Betrothed*, the most-read work of Italian fiction in the nineteenth century. Published in Milan in 1825–7, the book was reprinted by many publishers, none of which consulted Manzoni. By 1839, there were fifty-three unauthorized editions in Italian and fourteen in other languages. Encouraged by discussions of the 1840 law, as well as by an offer of 30,000 Milanese lire (34,000 francs) from a publisher in Paris for a new illustrated version of the book, in 1839 Manzoni brought out a definitive edition of his own with illustrations by his friend the Milanese wood engraver Francesco Gonin, whose work he closely supervised. He revised the text, basing it more firmly on the Tuscan dialect, which would become the standard form of literary Italian. Manzoni spent a fortune on the edition, 80,000 Milanese lire (92,000 francs), hoping that the expense of the illustrations and fine paper would prevent it from being pirated. Ten thousand copies were printed. They sold slowly. Manzoni had underestimated the ability of publishers to reprint illustrations lithographically. A pirate version of Manzoni's new edition with lithographic prints of Gonin's engravings was soon brought out by a publisher in Naples, Gaetano Nobili. It outsold Manzoni's own edition many times. Having suffered a large financial loss, Manzoni wrote to the Minister of the Interior in Naples asking him to put new laws of copyright before the King of the Two Sicilies, Ferdinand II, and compensate him for the money he had lost. His request was not answered.[59]

The Manzoni affair motivated publishers and intellectuals from Milan and Florence, in particular, to organize themselves in a campaign to put pressure on Naples to adopt the 1840 law. Ricordi, who had endless problems with the piracy of Verdi's works, was especially active in calling for new laws and conventions between states. One result of these efforts was a law of 1846 strengthening the legislative framework for the enforcement of copyright in the signatory states of the 1840 law, but it was only after the partial unification of Italy, with a national law of copyright in 1865, that Naples was brought into line.[60]

Backed by stronger laws of copyright, writers across Europe became more assertive in the defence of their economic interests and moral rights in their own work. Longer terms of copyright encouraged publishers to invest in longer contracts with writers. They gave them an incentive to secure the rights to an author's work, not for one edition, as they had done before, but for the duration of its copyright. They would offer higher fees and royalties to keep successful writers for as long as possible.

The royalty system began to appear in the 1850s, gradually replacing the flat-fee system during subsequent decades. Charpentier was its most committed pioneer. Rejecting payments in advance or on delivery, he paid writers only a percentage of the sales, a figure usually equivalent to fifty-five centimes for each copy sold. At first many writers were afraid – they might not sell enough to earn as much as they had done before with the flat fee – but Charpentier's ability to stack high and sell cheap soon convinced them otherwise.[61]

The best-selling writers obviously had the most to gain from royalties. Hugo's contracts with his publisher in France, Pierre-Jules Hetzel, in the 1850s, earned him around 20 per cent of receipts (double the amount of today's standard book contracts). Zola received a royalty of 10 per cent for his first novel, *La Confession de Claude*, in 1865. But the new system had its risks, and many less commercial writers preferred the option of a guaranteed single payment. The two systems co-existed for several decades, often within the same publishing house. Baudelaire's original contract for *Les Fleurs du mal* with Poulet-Malassis and De Broise paid him a royalty of twenty-five centimes per copy, whether sold or not, on a print-run of 1,000 copies priced at two francs each; but for the second edition of 1,500 copies he received a flat fee of 300 francs. Hetzel offered authors the choice of a flat fee or a royalty. He also paid a combination of the two: one sum on the publication of the book, and, once his costs had been paid off, a royalty, whose percentage varied according to sales. For his first book, *Five Weeks in a Balloon*, in 1863, Jules Verne was paid 500 francs on the initial printing of 2,000 copies, and then twenty-five centimes for each copy sold. For his next book, *Expeditions and Adventures of Captain Hatteras*, in 1865, Verne received 3,000 francs and then 6 per cent of the publisher's receipts (a sum equivalent to twelve centimes per copy) on sales over 10,000 copies.[62]

The worst option was to receive a flat fee for a book that went on to become a bestseller. That was Flaubert's misfortune with *Madame Bovary*. Following its serial publication in the *Revue de Paris*, in

December 1856, Flaubert signed a five-year contract with Michel Lévy for rights to the book. An up-and-coming publisher, Lévy paid 800 francs, a reasonable sum for a first novel with a print run of 6,000 copies sold at one franc per volume. A few days later, Flaubert was summoned to the office of the examining magistrate and charged with writing a novel whose 'obscene' story of adultery was said to be an 'outrage to public morals and religion' – a legal prosecution that had been made against other literary works and journals since the introduction of a more restrictive law of censorship to appease the Catholic Church, the main ideological supporter of Louis-Napoleon's dictatorship, in February 1852. Put on trial for immorality in January 1857, Flaubert and his publishers were acquitted. Flaubert's legal expenses were far more than he had earned from the novel. Boosted by the scandal of the trial, *Madame Bovary* sold well over 30,000 copies in the next five years. Feeling he had been cheated, Flaubert demanded 30,000 francs for his next novel, *Salammbô*, in 1862, even insisting that Lévy buy it without reading it. After weeks of haggling with Flaubert's lawyer (there were no literary agents in those days), Lévy agreed to pay 20,000 francs, half in advance, half on its delivery, on condition that Flaubert sign a new and longer lease on *Madame Bovary*. To save Flaubert's pride he proposed to spread the rumour that he had paid 30,000 francs for *Salammbô* and to go to town in publicizing it to reinforce that impression. Flaubert accepted Lévy's terms – to the consternation of many of his friends, such as the Goncourts, who had often heard him say that 'a true man of letters should write books without regard to money or publicity'.[63] By the time Flaubert had finished his next novel, *Sentimental Education*, in 1869, the length of copyrights had been extended by the law of 1866 to fifty years – so Flaubert consequently wanted more from Lévy, and was annoyed to receive only 16,000 francs for the two-volume novel. Eventually, through the intervention of his friend George Sand, one of the publisher's most prized authors, Flaubert got the fee increased to 20,000 francs – a minor but symbolic victory. 'What do you expect? A Jew will always be a Jew. It could have been worse,' Sand reported on the deal to Flaubert on 1 May 1870.[64]

British writers too were becoming more assertive in negotiations with publishers. In 1857, George Eliot had sold her debut novel, *Adam Bede* (1859), to the publisher John Blackwood on a four-year lease for

£800 (20,000 francs), a generous payment for a good first novel in Britain. It became a bestseller. In recognition of the unexpected profits he
had made, Blackwood paid £400 as a voluntary bonus, for which
George Eliot thanked him with a terse note whose tone annoyed the
Edinburgh publisher. On the publication of the book there was speculation about who George Eliot was. Various impostors claimed to be
the author, including one whose publisher attempted to profit from his
claim by advertising a sequel to *Adam Bede*. Eliot was disappointed
that Blackwood had failed to protect her intellectual property by dis-
proving these claims in the press. She was more aggressive in negotiations
with the publisher for her next book, *The Mill on the Floss* (1860).
Claiming that she had a large and ready readership, she asked Blackwood to name his best price. He came back with an offer of £3,000
(75,000 francs) for rights to the serial and the book. He wanted to
retain the pseudonym because public interest about it was guaranteed
to add to sales. This sort of attention was the last thing she needed.
Sensing that Blackwood saw her novel as a form of speculation, she
agreed to sell the copyright only for its first edition. She also talked to
other publishers, including Dickens, who wanted something from her
for his journal *All the Year Round* and let her keep the rights to sell it
as a book. Smith and Elder, the cash-rich London publisher, offered
£4,500 (114,000 francs). By this time, however, she had made her peace
with Blackwood, who paid £2,000 for the book without rights to
serialization.[65]

It was not just money that motivated writers to become more assertive in the defence of their copyright; it was also a concern to protect the
integrity of their work, their intellectual as well as economic property.
This was what the French called *droit moral*, a term that emerged in the
1840s to define an artist's rights to control the form and content of
their published work.[66]

Flaubert, for example, was outraged by the cuts and changes to the
text of *Madame Bovary* proposed by the *Revue de Paris*, where the
novel was serialized in 1856: 'I will not suppress a comma, nothing,
nothing!' Flaubert was famous for the time he took to craft his prose:
he would often spend whole days on a single phrase. 'Every syllable had
its own importance, its own colour, its own music,' Zola wrote of him.
'Naturally, after so much labour, the finished manuscript had a considerable significance for him. It was not vanity but respect for the work

he had put into it, where he had also put his whole being.' Flaubert wrote on thick paper, the most solid he could find, to preserve his original text, with all its punctuation, for posterity. He scrutinized the proofs to make sure that not a word was missed by the printers. To allow unwanted cuts or changes was unworthy of an artist in his view. He was horrified by the attitude of Turgenev, whom he had met in February 1863 at a dinner where the Russian had been introduced to Flaubert's circle by Charles Edmond (his real name was Franciszek Maurycy Chojecki), the Polish writer, translator and librarian of the French Senate. Writing to Edmond in 1864, Flaubert expressed his abhorrence of writing for a newspaper or periodical where the 'mania for correcting ends up by giving all the manuscripts they've bought the same absence of originality'.

> Take for example the style of the *Revue des deux mondes*. Turgenev told me recently that Buloz [the editor] made him take out something from his last novel. For that alone, Turgenev has fallen in my estimation. He should have thrown his manuscript in Buloz's face, and followed it up with a couple of slaps and some spit for dessert . . . When you submit a manuscript, if you are not a rascal, it is because you are content with it. You must have made the greatest effort possible, put in all your soul. A personality cannot be substituted by another one. A book is a complicated organism. Any amputation, any change, takes away from its nature.[67]

Ideas of international copyright were also gaining ground, as publishers and writers across Europe pressed for laws and treaties to protect their works from piracy by foreign publishers in a book market that was fast becoming internationalized.

The Leipzig publisher Bernard Tauchnitz took perhaps the first initiative. He would offer British authors (notably Dickens) a small flat fee to authorize his English-language editions of their works in Germany, and later France. When Tauchnitz started, in 1841, there was no copyright agreement between Britain and either Germany or France. Legally there was nothing to prevent him from publishing his *Collection of British Authors* without paying anything. But he saw the voluntary fee as a step towards the development of international copyright, a cause in which he believed, and thought it was worth paying to market his editions as the 'authorized' or 'copyright' versions, even before copyright existed for foreign writers in Germany or France. His example was soon followed by other publishers, among them Hetzel, who began paying foreign authors for permission to print on the cover of his editions that they had been 'authorized' by them.[68] By winning their goodwill, Tauchnitz put himself in a strong position to publish British authors on the Continent. He bought the rights to many of their works after Britain signed bilateral copyright treaties with European states (beginning with Prussia and Saxony in 1846, and with France in 1851).

Such conventions put in place the founding structures of international copyright. As one might expect, the French took the lead. They suffered most from international piracy. Their biggest publishers (Hachette, Lévy, Charpentier and Édouard Dentu) had a growing export trade through their own networks of booksellers right across the Continent, where the cultural élites all read in French. On 28 March 1852, the National Assembly issued a decree extending copyright to foreign works published in France. The aim of this unilateral declaration was to encourage other states to follow the French example and sign bilateral conventions. A number of treaties were signed by France around this time: with Portugal and Britain in 1851; with Hanover and Brunswick in 1852; with Tuscany and Spain in 1853; importantly with Belgium, the main pirate state in Europe's French book market, in 1854; with the Netherlands in 1855; and with Saxony and Luxembourg in 1856.[69]

These treaties encouraged publishers to expand their business internationally. After 1852, Lévy, for example, developed an extensive network of bookshops across French-speaking Europe and entered into trade agreements with German publishers and booksellers. Hachette was developing a similar network, opening branches in Leipzig and London, by the end of the decade. The German publisher Friedrich Brockhaus had shops in London, Paris and Vienna. Albert Lacroix, the young Belgian publisher, who had bought the rights to publish Victor Hugo's *Les Misérables* in 1862, used part of his profits to establish branches of his company in Livorno and Leipzig.[70]

As a system of international law these bilateral treaties were weak structures. Too many pirate states remained outside the network of bilateral conventions. Eliminating piracy in one country would encourage it to grow elsewhere (the French treaty with Belgium was a massive boost to the pirate trade of French books in Prussia, which had no bilateral agreement with France).[71] The system depended on the willingness of states to enforce the treaties, which made it subject to the ups and downs of international relations. There were many variations in the level of protection, and uncertainties about what was covered by the conventions. Translation, for example, received little protection: in most treaties it was limited to a few years; and in some (e.g. the convention between France and Holland in 1855) there was none at all. Performance rights were left unclarified, leaving it up to the courts to resolve conflicts between artists and theatres.

In October 1856, the Tribunal Civile de la Seine heard a case brought by Verdi against César Ragani and Toribio Calzado, co-directors of the Théâtre Italien. The composer claimed that their productions of *La Traviata*, *Rigoletto* and *Il Trovatore* were infringements of his copyright because he had withdrawn his authorization for them after expressing his dissatisfaction with the leading performers. Verdi's lawyer based his claim on the Code Napoleon and the Decree of 28 March 1852, arguing that while the law remained unclear about the protection of performance rights, the spirit of the legislation suggested that they should be protected. The theatre's lawyer counter-argued that dramatic rights had been excluded from the law deliberately, because the government had used the law to pressure other states to sign bilateral treaties with France. Verdi's rights could only be protected by a treaty between France and those states where the work concerned had been first performed (Veneto in the case of *Rigoletto* and *La Traviata*, the Papal State in the case of *Il Trovatore*). There were no such treaties at the time of the productions at the Théâtre Italien. The lawyer also claimed that the real reason why Verdi had withdrawn his permission was not to do with the quality of the singers, but because he had been offered more money by the Paris Opéra: he was using legal threats to stop a lawful production for his own financial gain. The court found against Verdi, and ordered him to pay 1,000 francs in damages to the Théâtre Italien.[72]

Because of loopholes and uncertainties like this, publishers and artists campaigned for a comprehensive international convention. Ricordi and Hachette were among the most active. Both had foreign investments to protect. In 1858, as a result of their campaign, a Congress on Artistic and Literary Property was organized by the Belgian government in Brussels, an ironic venue given that the city until recently had been the European capital of literary piracy. Attended by 400 delegates, writers, publishers, lawyers, journalists and government officials from a dozen countries, the congress aimed to formulate a multilateral convention protecting copyright for all creative works regardless of national boundaries between the signatory states. Nothing came directly from the congress. Tito Ricordi, who took over his father's company in 1853, was disappointed by its failure to agree on the principle of defending intellectual property as a permanent and inheritable right.[73] Nonetheless, the congress was a start: it had voiced the basic ideas about the need to defend intellectual property on an international basis, and there would be others (in Antwerp in 1861 and 1877, Paris, 1878, London, 1879, Lisbon, 1880, Vienna, 1881, Rome in 1882) to carry on with this objective, culminating in the Berne Convention of 1886, the founding treaty of today's global system of international copyright.

4

Turgenev's *Sketches* soon appeared in foreign translations. A German version of some of the stories appeared first, in 1852, and two years later the full collection was published as a book. It was well received, establishing Turgenev as a major figure on the literary scene in Germany. In 1855, a second volume of his stories appeared there, but the translation was not good. Turgenev was annoyed, though not as much as he was by Ernest Charrière's translation of the *Sketches* into French. The book was published by Hachette in 1854 without Turgenev's name under the misleading title *Mémoires d'un seigneur russe, ou Tableau de la situation actuelle des nobles et des paysans dans les provinces russes* (Memoirs of a Russian Landowner, or a Picture of the Actual Situation of Nobles and Peasants in the Russian Provinces), suggesting that it was a work of non-fiction. The translation was a travesty of the Russian original. Apart from the obvious shortcomings of the translator, the lack of any copyright agreement between France and Russia enabled Charrière to play around as much as he liked with Turgenev's text. 'Monsieur Charrière has made of me the Devil knows what,' Turgenev complained to Sergei Aksakov:

> He has made up whole pages, made up some things and discarded others to an unbelievable degree. Where I, for instance, wrote 'I fled', he

translates these two words in the following manner: *'Je m'enfuis d'une course folle, effarée, échevelée comme si j'eusse eu à mes trousses toute une légion de couleuvres, commandées par des sorciers'* ['I fled on a wild course, frightened and dishevelled, as if I had on my heels a whole legion of snakes, controlled by wizards'].[74]

Eager to assert his moral rights, Turgenev wrote to the French-language newspaper *Journal de St.-Pétersbourg* to warn readers off the Charrière translation. He later authorized a rival one by the Russian literary scholar Henri Delaveau, using it to restore the passages that had been cut by the censor in Russia, although by the time it finally appeared, in 1857, a second edition of the Charrière translation had sold out in France and unfortunately served as the basis for an English translation published in 1855 as *Russian Life in the Interior, or, The Experiences of a Sportsman*. Without international copyright there was no way to prevent its publication as one of Turgenev's works.

The outbreak of the Crimean War (1854–5) had created a large demand in France and Britain for any literature that might illuminate the internal conditions of their Russian enemy, and it was mainly for its social insights that the *Sketches* were so widely read in both countries.* In an article, 'Photographs from Russian Life', in August 1854, *Fraser's Magazine* maintained that Turgenev's *Sketches* were all the more revealing as a social document 'inasmuch as he is not a professed writer' but a nobleman: 'he has not sought "effects" but has transferred to paper, with the vividness of a daguerreotype, the impressions produced upon him by the various personages and scenes he describes.' By the end of the war the *Sketches* had appeared in numerous foreign editions, including Swedish, Hungarian and Danish, most of them translated from the German or the French, though some, like the Polish and the Czech, from the Russian. Four stories had appeared in Dickens's *Household Words*, albeit in a bad translation of the bad Charrière.[75]

---

* Turgenev was not the only Russian writer to be read in Europe in this way. In 1854, Gogol's *Dead Souls* (1842) appeared in a pirate English translation under the extraordinary title, *Home Life in Russia*. The publisher's preface presented the novel as a documentary work whose purpose was 'to throw light upon the domestic life of our ancient allies and present foes' and to give 'an insight into the internal circumstances and relations of Russian society which only a Russian can afford us' (*Home Life in Russia: By a Russian Noble. Revised by the Editor of 'Revelations of Siberia'*, 2 vols. (London, 1854), pp. i–ii).

The *Sketches* not only established Turgenev as a major international writer; they announced the arrival of Russian literature on the European scene. Turgenev was the first of Russia's writers to be widely read in Europe. His stories, in the words of Annenkov, 'lifted the edge of a curtain behind which one could glimpse the mystery of [this] . . . alien people and the work of their consciousness'.[76] In the early decades of the nineteenth century, the Europeans had been largely ignorant of Russian literature. Although there were translations of the works of Pushkin and Gogol, they were clumsy and inaccurate, most of them by Russian émigrés and amateur enthusiasts. Few European universities had Slav or Russian departments, so there was a shortage of competent translators to convey the riches of Russia's literature to a European readership. That began to change in the 1840s with the appearance of two distinguished Russophiles and translators from Russian into French, the base language for translations into other European languages. The first was Xavier Marmier, Professor of Foreign Literature at the University of Rennes and a well-known travel writer, who went to Russia in 1842, met Turgenev, and started learning Russian with his help. In the 1850s, Marmier produced a series of accurate and readable translations of Pushkin, Gogol, Lermontov and Turgenev. The second was the writer Prosper Mérimée, who started learning Russian in 1848, largely to compete with his cousin, Henri Mérimée, who had made his name the year before with a celebrated travel book, *Une année en Russie*, based on the journal of his stay in Russia in 1839–40. Within a year of taking lessons from Madame Lagrené (née Varinka Dubenskaya), a former maid of honour at the Russian court, Mérimée had published a successful French translation of Pushkin's *Queen of Spades* in the *Revue des deux mondes*, followed by translations of other Pushkin stories and poems, which were then translated into other languages (some of his translation of Pushkin's poem *The Gypsies* found its way into Mérimée's *Carmen*, his 1845 novella about Spanish gypsy life). The English version of Mérimée's translation of *Queen of Spades* was reprinted several times between 1850 and 1854. By 1857, when he met Turgenev, who would then become his chief collaborator in translating Russian literature, Mérimée had published a whole series of articles about Pushkin, Gogol and Turgenev in the *Revue des deux mondes*.[77]

Turgenev played a vital role in getting Russia's writers better known in Europe in the 1840s and 1850s – a role he would broaden as a cultural intermediary between Russia and the West over the next thirty years. He was almost certainly the author of an influential but unsigned article on Russian literature in the Paris weekly newspaper *L'Illustration*, in 1845. The publication was organized by Louis Viardot, who at that time was working with Turgenev on translations into French of stories by Krylov, Pushkin, Lermontov and Gogol, the four writers featured in the article. The forthcoming publication of these translations was advertised in the newspaper alongside the article. Published in 1845 as *Nouvelles russes*, the collected stories appeared with the name of Louis Viardot as translator, although he could neither speak nor read Russian. In the preface Louis acknowledged the assistance of his friend Turgenev, 'a celebrated poet and critic', who had provided a basic translation from which Louis then crafted a more finished French version. Through their many connections the Viardots attained a good deal of attention for the *Nouvelles russes* among the Parisian cultural élites. Delacroix, for one, found the stories interesting for their 'extraordinary feeling of reality'.[78]

Paris was the centre of a growing culture of translation in Europe. It was the Continent's most cosmopolitan city, home to more foreign intellectuals than any other city in Europe, so there was no shortage of translators there.[79] It had more foreign booksellers, more publishers with a European reach, more books published in translation and more literary magazines with an international perspective. The most important of these journals was the *Revue des deux mondes*, which specialized in articles on foreign literature (Viardot frequently wrote for it on Spain), often with a view to encouraging translations into French.[80]

French was the language of Europe's cosmopolitan élites. It dominated the translation business. More books were translated from French than from any other language, although by the middle of the century translations from English and German were quickly catching up. French was a medium of exchange between other languages: a book translated from, say, Russian into English, was likely to be translated from Russian into French and then re-translated from the French into English. English books would travel via French into other languages. This explains the dominant position of the French book trade in Europe. French books were sold everywhere. Even in Leipzig, the centre of the German book market, booksellers had more trading links with

Paris than with any other city in the German-speaking lands. The French domination of the continental book trade began to weaken in the middle of the century, however. German became more important as a channel for translation into the developing markets in Slavonic and Scandinavian languages. [81]

Translations made up an increasing share of the fiction published in the middle of the nineteenth century. As the reading public grew, so too did demand for popular fiction of the likes of Dickens's *Pickwick Papers* or Sue's *Mystères de Paris*. Demand ran ahead of the ability of domestic writers in most countries to supply this growing readership, so foreign writers had to fill the gap. Even France and Britain, the dominant literary producers in Europe, saw their markets opened up to a growing number of translated works.

Statistics of book production are problematic and patchy. There is no systematic database for any country in Europe. The best figures come from France, where translated works increased their share of total book production from an estimated 4 per cent in 1831 to 12 per cent by 1859. The sharpest growth was in foreign novels: the number of titles in translation grew from under ten a year in the 1840s to fifty every year in the decade after 1854. [82] Bookshops were flooded with translations into French, particularly in the mass-edition series of foreign literature, such as Gervais Charpentier's Bibliothèque Anglaise, Charles Lahure's Bibliothèque des Meilleurs Romans Étrangers, Lacroix's Librairie Internationale and Hachette's Littérature Étrangère, part of his Bibliothèque des Chemins de Fer, all of which invested heavily in translations in the 1850s and 1860s. Hachette, for example, bought up all the novels of Dickens for an 'authorized translation' in 1856 (a fact which helps to explain the publisher's support of international copyright). [83]

Britain was historically resistant to reading in translation because of the strength of its own literary language and relative cultural isolation from the Continent. Foreign works translated into English remained a small proportion of the British book market – around 3 per cent of total book production in the nineteenth century. But even here the absolute numbers were rising (from a mere 580 translated works per year in the first quarter of the century to over 2,600 by mid-century), and many of the titles were in mass-edition series such as the Routledge Railway Library, which introduced Balzac to an English readership.

The recorded figures of translated books in Britain did not include, moreover, the pirated translations and English adaptations (plagiarizations) of foreign works which filled many pages of the penny press and popular-fiction periodicals such as Dickens's *Household Words*.[84]

With strong literary cultures of their own, France and Britain published fewer translations than countries with a smaller number of domestic writers which were more dependent on translating foreign works. In Austria, for example, the share of total book production made up by translations rose from less than 5 per cent in 1840 to 33 per cent in 1854 – an increase encouraged by the relaxation of censorship after 1848.[85] The Spanish book market was heavily dependent on translations from the French, which made up almost half the country's total book production at the mid-point of the century. French literature was so dominant in Spain that in 1862 Hachette bought Antoine Mezin, the large Spanish publishing house, to facilitate the importation of his books from France.[86]

In the Netherlands translations were even more important in the growing market for fiction. Without bilateral treaties obliging publishers to pay foreign authors royalties,* it was safer and more profitable for them to publish a successful foreign novel in translation than to pay for an original work in Dutch. The costs of translation were lower than the fees demanded for a new novel, especially when writers everywhere were beginning to assert their moral and economic rights. In a small country like the Netherlands, where the reading public was keen to keep abreast of developments in European culture, publishers had a better chance of profit from a famous and successful foreign novel than from an original but untried Dutch work. No wonder there were so few novelists of any note from Holland in the nineteenth century: they could not compete with translations of foreign works.[87]

* The Netherlands had bilateral copyright conventions with Germany (from 1854), France (1855), Belgium (1858) and Spain (1862), but not with Britain, its main source of translated literature. Rights to publish foreign books in translation were handled by a national book trade organization (Vereeniging ter Bevordering van de Belangen des Boekhandels, or VBBB) which registered these titles and protected them from competing publishers in the Netherlands. A Dutch publisher would offer a small fee (usually around £20) to a foreign publisher in order to receive early proofs of a work it wanted to publish in translation in the Netherlands so that it could register its title with the VBBB before its competitors. No other payment was made to the author or the publisher (Van der Weel, 'Nineteenth-Century Literary Translations', p. 33).

One of the results of this translation boom was a growing uniformity of literary subjects, formats, styles and ideas across Europe and the wider world. Writers imitated foreign novels they had read in translation, particularly French and English works, the two most translated literatures. These works became a 'European' standard for the nineteenth-century novel in emerging literary cultures on the Continent's 'periphery', such as Spain and Hungary, or the Scandinavian countries, whose modern literatures would come into existence through their assimilation of French or English writing modes. Predictably, the process caused a good deal of disquiet among those critics who assigned the highest value to national character in their country's literature (the basis of the nationalist reaction against literary cosmopolitanism which developed in these years). They feared that imitation of foreign literatures would undermine their national literature's distinctiveness and originality, eventually leading to an international culture where all literatures would be the same. As one prophetic critic, René Tallandier, put it in the *Revue des deux mondes* in 1846: 'In European literature it will soon no longer be possible to trace the diverse influences, poetic qualities or home-grown varieties of individual nations. One could almost say that foreign literatures do not exist any more. A sad uniformity is enveloping the world.'[88]

In the early decades of the nineteenth century Walter Scott's novels were translated (mostly via French) into nineteen languages and he had his imitators everywhere. In the 1840s and 1850s Dickens had a similar impact on the development of the realist novel in Europe. His works were published in translation in Germany (from 1837); Russia, France, the Netherlands and Denmark (1838); Bohemia, Italy and Poland (1840); Sweden (1842); Belgium, Hungary, Norway (1843); Austria and Moldavia (1844); Finland (1846); Portugal and Spain (1847); Greece (1853); Bulgaria (1859); even Iceland (from 1860). Few of these translations were made directly from English. Most went via other languages with their own dependencies: from French into Spanish and Italian; from German into Scandinavian languages; and from Russian into the Slavonic languages.[89]

Everywhere the influence of Dickens was the same. In France his novels were immediately popular, forcing many critics, who had at first considered his subject matter too vulgar and offensive to qualify as art, to change their views on what was admissible in a novel. The turning point was an influential article by Hippolyte Taine in the *Revue des deux mondes* in 1856 in which the critic and historian praised the dazzling visual realism of Dickens's writing in *David Copperfield*:

> Never did objects remain more visible and present to the memory of a reader than those which he describes. The old house, the parlour, the kitchen, Peggotty's boat, and above all the school playground, are interiors whose relief, energy, and precision are unequalled. Dickens has the passion and patience of the painters of his nation; he reckons his details one by one, notes the various hues of the old tree-trunks; sees the dilapidated cask, the greenish and broken flagstones, the chinks of the damp walls; he distinguishes the strange smells which rise from them; marks the size of the mildewed spots, reads the names of the scholars carved on the door, and dwells on the form of the letters.[90]

In Germany a new breed of realist writers such as Gottfried Keller and Wilhelm Raabe looked to Dickens as a model of the realist writing they espoused. They wanted to move away from the Romantic idealism of Goethe's age, and, as German nationalists, to engage their readers with the real conditions of society, not least of the middle and the lower classes, in order to forge a national identity.[91]

But nowhere was the influence of Dickens so profound as in Russia. 'Your name has enjoyed a wide celebrity,' his translator, Irinarkh Vvedensky, wrote to him in 1849, 'and from the banks of the Neva to the remotest parts of Siberia you are read with avidity'. This was information that so delighted Dickens that when his affairs were going badly he would threaten to pack his bags and leave for Siberia.[92] Dickens's works were all translated into Russian within a year of their appearance in English, and Vvedensky's lively style made them very popular. His literary impact was closely linked to that of Gogol, a follower of Dickens, who, like him, combined realism with melodrama in a manner to inspire later Russian writers such as Dostoevsky and Saltykov-Shchedrin, both keen readers of Dickens. Hailed by Belinsky as the first 'social novel' in Russia, Dostoevsky's *Poor Folk* (1846) was influenced by the author's reading of Dickens, particularly those scenes in which Dostoevsky evokes pathos from the attempts of the poor to preserve their human dignity and care for others even less fortunate than themselves. There are clear Dickensian borrowings in many of Dostoevsky's later works, *The Insulted and the Injured* (1861) in particular.

Turgenev too was a Dickens fan. He read him in English, French and Russian, and considered him to be the leading European novelist. Turgenev would reject comparisons between his realist style and that of Dickens. He did not share the English writer's fondness for caricature, sentimentality or comic distractions. But, like Taine, he prized him for the visual realism of his prose, 'his power of presenting to the eye a vivid, definite figure', as Henry James would later write of Turgenev's admiration for Dickens.[93]

In the preface to his influential book *Le Réalisme* (1857) Champfleury placed Turgenev and Gogol on a par with Dickens, Thackeray, Charlotte Brontë and Berthold Auerbach as leading exponents of the realist novel, whose followers were conquering the literary world: 'Everywhere abroad, in England, Germany, Sweden, Holland, Belgium, America, Russia, Switzerland, I see storytellers charged by the mysterious current of reality.'[94] It is indeed remarkable how writers around Europe were all converging on a similar ideal of their literary art as a true and objective reflection of contemporary social life. The 1850s witnessed the emergence of realist writers right across the Continent: Turgenev in Russia, Auerbach and Fontane in Germany, Flaubert in France, Eliot and Gaskell in Britain.

How should we explain this intellectual convergence? Throughout Europe writers were responding to a new social reality created by the growth of manufacturing industries and the railways; to a new conception of modernity that was all about the here and now ('the transient, the fleeting, the contingent' of Baudelaire); to new ways of looking at the world after the invention of photography. They were writing for a growing market of newly literate urban readers – many from the artisan and working classes – who wanted stories which they could relate to their everyday lives. The novel was the medium par excellence for engaging readers with this contemporary reality. Poetry was caught in the Romantic past, although some poets, such as Elizabeth Barrett Browning in *Aurora Leigh* (1856), called on it to deal with the commonplaces of the present day:

> Nay, if there's room for poets in this world
> A little overgrown, (I think there is)
> Their sole work is to represent the age,

Their age, not Charlemagne's – this live, throbbing age,
That brawls, cheats, maddens, calculates, aspires,
And spends more passion, more heroic heat,
Betwixt the mirrors of its drawing-rooms,
Than Roland with his knights of Roncesvalles.[95]

For Champfleury the task of the artist to focus on the present arose from the new realities highlighted by the revolutions of 1848. He saw the revolutions as a fundamental break in time: the old certainties were swept away, events moved faster, and history appeared, more than ever, to be directed by transient contingencies. The social problems exposed by the popular uprisings had made it all the more important for the arts to reach out to common people and lay bare the real conditions of contemporary society. 'It was only after 1848,' the critic wrote, 'that realism became one of the numerous religions with an "ism" at the end: one could see it every day displayed in advertising posters on the walls, acclaimed in the clubs, worshipped by its followers in small temples [galleries]'.[96]

The issue was not just to fix the attention of society on the sufferings of the labouring poor. That was achieved easily enough – by Dickens in *Hard Times* (1854) or Gaskell in *North and South* (1854–5). It could even be achieved by melodramas such as *Les Misérables* or by *Les Mystères de Paris*. The challenge for realist writers was how to portray the common people without sentimentalizing them or reducing them to types. This was the problem Eliot confronted. She felt that Dickens had successfully portrayed the 'external traits of our town population' but could not 'give us their psychological character – their conception of life, and their emotions – with the same truth as their idiom and manners'. That was what she set out to achieve in her first novel, *Adam Bede*. Turgenev felt the same way about Balzac and George Sand as Eliot felt about Dickens. In his *Sketches from a Hunter's Album* he attempted to convey the thinking and emotions of his peasant characters simply by observing their behaviour, without authorial intervention, so that they would come across as autonomous individuals, whose characteristics and motives were seen to come from within.[97]

Turgenev's approach to the realist novel had a profound influence on the German realist writers who emerged in the 1850s, among them Theodor Storm, August Viedert, Paul Heyse and Theodor Fontane, whose 1853 essay 'Unsere lyrische und epische Poesie seit 1848', a literary survey of the past five years in Germany, advocates a type of realist writing in which the subjects are allowed to generate their own meanings without having the narrator or the author speak on their behalf.[98] This impersonality – the complete removal of the writer's voice from the scientific observation of everyday realities – was the basis of a revolution in the art of the novel.

The international market of translated books underpinned this intellectual convergence. Everyone was reading everybody else. Turgenev was influenced by Dickens and Sand; Flaubert by Balzac; Fontane by Turgenev and Eliot; and Eliot by a whole range of writers: Goethe, Balzac, Dickens, Sand and Keller, whom she read during her extended stay in Germany in 1854. She was also an admirer of the German social historian Wilhelm Heinrich von Riehl, whose study of the peasants, *Land und Leute* (1853), influenced her ideas of the realist literary art, as articulated in her review article about von Riehl, 'The Natural History of German Life' (1856). 'Art is the nearest thing to life,' she wrote, 'it is a mode of amplifying and extending our contact with our fellow-men beyond the bounds of our personal lot.'[99] She had perfectly expressed Turgenev's artistic credo in the *Sketches*.

5

During the first year of his house arrest Turgenev wrote to Pauline with regular requests for her portrait photograph. Reports of her appearance in St Petersburg had claimed that she looked younger than she had done seven years before, when she had last been in the Russian capital. Such reports, he explained to her, 'make me all the keener to see your daguerreotype, and even if I know that it is closer to a caricature than a true likeness, my eyes, nonetheless, will be able to discern the changes in your features'. Weeks went by before Pauline replied to the first request. In the letter that finally arrived there was no daguerreotype but a caricature she had drawn of herself with the caption: 'While you wait for a photograph!'[100]

Turgenev was keen on the new technology. It helped him overcome his isolation in exile. He had his picture taken in Orel and sent it to his friends in Russia and abroad. The fact that a small provincial town in Russia had a photographic studio was evidence of how far the mania for photography had spread in Europe by this time. There was barely any European town where it was not possible to get a cheap portrait done.

New techniques of reproduction had made photography affordable. Most importantly, the invention of the wet-collodion process, in 1851, enabled any number of prints to be made from a single negative. It was a huge advance on the daguerreotype (a complex and expensive process of fixing photographic images on a polished sheet of silver-plated copper preserved under glass) in terms of both quality and economy. Three years later, in 1854, the French inventor André Disdéri developed an ingenious method of mass-producing photographic portraits by using a camera with four lenses and a rotating back to make multiple exposures of an image on one glass-plate negative. Cut from the photographic positive and mounted on a card the size of a calling card, these *cartes de visites* proved so popular that Disdéri was able to reduce his prices to a level that the middle classes could easily afford. Whereas in the 1840s a single photographic portrait had cost between ten and fifty francs, by the later 1850s, a set of twelve from Disdéri cost only twenty francs, and by the 1860s it was just two francs. Photographic studios began to multiply. In Paris the number grew from thirty-nine at the beginning of the 1850s to over 200 at the end of the decade. London saw a similar increase. By the early 1860s, something in the region of 400 million photographic cards were sold in Britain every year.[101]

Mass reproduction began a craze for photographic portraits of celebrities, family groups and the individual self. Writing on the impact of the new technology in 1859, Baudelaire lamented its encouragement of vanity: 'From that moment on, our loathsome society rushed, like Narcissus, to contemplate its trivial image on a metallic plate. A form of lunacy, an extraordinary fanaticism took hold of these new sun-worshippers.'[102]

The photographic portrait put the individual self on an equal footing with celebrities – that was part of its appeal. Photographs of famous people made up a large share of the *cartes de visites* sold by studio photographers, who used them for publicity. Disdéri published a *Galerie des contemporains*, 120 celebrity photographs on mounted cards with a short biographical text and published all together as a deluxe album in 1861.[103] Pauline Viardot was number 69 in Disdéri's gallery. She was regularly photographed for commercial *cartes* and albums, sometimes appearing as herself, sometimes in the costume of one of her famous roles.[104] She was also photographed by Nadar (the pseudonym of Gaspard-Félix Tournachon) who placed his striking portraits of celebrities (Balzac, Delacroix, Baudelaire, George Sand, Berlioz, among others) in the windows of his studio on the boulevard des Capucines. For a modest fee, members of the public could also have their picture taken by Nadar, connecting themselves to such celebrities.

Photographs of famous nobles, military heroes, heads of state and politicians also sold in large numbers. Napoleon III and Queen Victoria were quick to recognize the propaganda power of the new medium. They were the first European heads of state to pose for commercial images. They appeared, not as monarchs in crowns, robes and jewels, but in the universal middle-class attire of suits and crinolines, top hats and bonnets, in family portraits and settings. The photographs were very popular, particularly those of Queen Victoria and Prince Albert, which sold millions of copies each, an essential decoration for countless homes and helping to cement the popularity of the British monarchy.[105]

In its early days photography was generally considered to be a means of record rather than an art. It was admitted to the Great Exhibition in the category of science and technology. But the new technology had a profound influence on the literary and visual arts.

Novelists developed a more visual style of writing, loading their prose with images and external descriptive details, and introducing optical effects, such as open doors and windows, to help visualize their descriptions. The famous opening passage of Dickens's *Bleak House* (1853) is a good example of this photographic realism:[106]

> Fog everywhere. Fog up the river, where it flows among green aits and meadows; fog down the river, where it rolls defiled among the tiers of shipping and the waterside pollutions of a great (and dirty) city. Fog on the Essex marshes, fog on the Kentish heights. Fog creeping into the cabooses of collier-brigs; fog lying out on the yards, and hovering in the rigging of great ships; fog drooping on the gunwales of barges and small boats. Fog in the eyes and throats of ancient Greenwich pensioners, wheezing by the firesides of their wards; fog in the stem and bowl of the afternoon pipe of the wrathful skipper, down in his close cabin; fog cruelly pinching the toes and fingers of his shivering little 'prentice boy on deck. Chance people on the bridges peeping over the parapets into a nether sky of fog, with fog all round them, as if they were up in a balloon, and hanging in the misty clouds.[107]

Flaubert was obsessed with the idea of making his prose visual. He said many times that it was his goal to 'faire voir les choses' (make things visible), to make real objects tangible to the reader.[108] That is why he violently rejected any illustrations for his books: it was his own job to make his readers see. He filled his prose with visual details, accessories to the actions and emotions that 'were almost as alive as the characters', in the words of the Goncourts.[109] Even Emma Bovary is seen by us through the minute features of her physiognomy – the whiteness of her fingernails, the beads of sweat on her bare back, the fine line made by her foot, and so on. A good example of this hyper-visual style is the following passage from *Sentimental Education*, in which Frédéric Moreau, the novel's hero, stops in front of Arnoux's shop-window in the hope of catching sight of Mme Arnoux:

> The high, transparent plate-glass windows presented to one's gaze statuettes, drawings, engravings, catalogues and numbers of *L'Art industriel*, arranged in a skilful fashion; and the amounts of the subscription were repeated on the door, which was decorated in the centre with the publisher's initials. Against the walls could be seen large pictures whose varnish had a shiny look, two chests laden with porcelain, bronze alluring curiosities; a little staircase separated them, shut off at the top by a Wilkton portière; and a lustre of old Saxe, a green carpet on the floor, with a table of marqueterie, gave to this interior the appearance rather of a drawing-room than of a shop.
>
> Frédéric pretended to be examining the drawings . . .[110]

It was the random nature of these details that created their 'reality effect'.[111] This is where the realism of the 1850s differed from previous practices of literary verisimilitude: where writers in the past had selected and arranged the life-like details of their stories in line with their symbolic meaning or importance to the narrative, much as a painter might organize the elements of nature to create a picturesque effect, realists like Flaubert filled their texts with incidental details, appearing as they might in a photograph. The challenge was to capture what was real when reality itself was resistant to structure. As Champfleury wrote,

> Ordinary life is made up of small, insignificant facts as numerous as the twigs of trees – these little facts come together and end in a branch, a branch in a trunk. Any conversation is full of pointless details that cannot

be reproduced without boring the reader . . . A story needs a beginning and a middle and an end. But nature makes no arrangement, no coordination, no framing, no beginning and no end. Does that not make the telling of the shortest story highly difficult? And is it not made easier by a daguerreotype machine?[112]

Painters too were rising to the task of representing the reality of 'ordinary life'. The advent of photography raised the bar of verisimilitude in the visual arts. What people most admired in photography – the clear reflection of unadorned reality, the recording of a precise moment and the visceral sense of 'being there' – was assimilated to the aesthetic of modern art. The impact of photography challenged old ideas of representation.

Critics of photography attacked what they saw as its detrimental impact on the appreciation of beauty and the imagination's role in art. There was a danger, they believed, that painting would become the slavish reproduction of reality. 'If art was just the imitation of nature,' wrote Louis Viardot, 'the most perfect painting would be a well-made diorama, the most perfect statues a wax model.'[113] Baudelaire decried the commercial pressures that were leading, he believed, to the 'daguerreotypization' of visual art:

> Now our public, which is singularly incapable of feeling the happiness of dreaming or of marvelling (a sign of its meanness of soul), wishes to be made to wonder by means which are alien to art, and its obedient artists bow to its taste; they try to strike, to surprise, to stupefy it by means of unworthy tricks . . . In matters of painting and sculpture, the present-day *credo* of the sophisticated, above all in France, is this: 'I believe in Nature, and I believe only in Nature . . . I believe that Art is, and cannot be other than, the exact reproduction of Nature . . . Thus an industry that could give us a result identical to Nature would be the absolute of art.' A revengeful God has given ear to the prayers of this multitude. Daguerre is his Messiah.[114]

Under the impact of photography, artists strived to add pictorial precision to their work, many of them using cameras as an aid to get a better likeness of reality. The hyper-realism of Ernest Meissonier's finely detailed genre pictures was so reminiscent of daguerreotypes that he was accused by several critics of using photographic images as the starting point of his paintings. While cameras could be used as a 'secret tool' in the artist's studio, one critic wrote in 1851, the danger was that its abuse could 'kill real art', which depended rather on imagination than on photographic precision.[115] Public fascination for the latter explained Meissonier's extraordinary success, according to Zola:

> The artistic value of his work has nothing to do with his appeal. The truth is that the public is purely and simply interested in the artist's sleight of hand. It distinguishes the buttons on a waistcoat, the charms on a watchchain. So much detail is rendered that none is lost; that is what arouses this unheard-of admiration. And the best thing is that he paints men four centimetres tall who can be examined with a magnifying glass. This is what excites the crowd ... He is the god of the bourgeoisie that has no feeling for true art.[116]

Artists had used the camera obscura as an aid to drawing since the sixteenth century. But the invention of photography helped them to capture the effects of light and shade in more scientific ways. Nowhere was its impact more important than in landscape painting. Because of the long exposures needed for photography in the early decades of its existence, landscapes were an obvious subject for photographers, especially for those who wanted to establish the new medium as an art form. There was a close relationship between art photography and the landscape painters grouped at Barbizon, a village in the Fontainebleau Forest. Camille Corot had been going there since the 1820s. He was joined by Théodore Rousseau after his rejection by the Salon jury in 1836. By the 1840s, a large group of artists was spending summers there, some, like Diaz, renting peasant cottages, but most, like Millet, Troyon, Daubigny and Courbet, lodging at an inn, the Auberge Ganne, which became a sort of artists' colony. In the 1850s, Rousseau and Millet were permanently based in Barbizon, which, in the words of the art critic Albert de la Fizilière in 1853, had 'given birth to a new science of painting'.[117]

The key to that science was painting in nature itself – setting up an easel *en plein air* and depicting landscapes as they actually appeared: everyday and unpoetic scenes without Romantic idealization or embellishment. *Plein air* painting was relatively new. The outdoor sketch in oils had been done for centuries; it became widespread throughout

Europe in the later eighteenth century. Yet the paintings it produced were not considered 'finished' works, but studies to be finished in a studio. There were problems with oils that limited the time they could be used outdoors. Painters made their paint by grinding pigment powder and mixing it in small amounts with linseed oil, usually storing extra paint in animal bladders; but the oil paint dried so quickly that they could not work for long without mixing more.

Attitudes to *plein-air* painting began to change at the turn of the century, when the landscape painter Pierre-Henri de Valenciennes, who had made oil studies from nature, advocated it in his influential thesis *Éléments de perspective pratique à l'usage des artistes* (1799). The early decades of the nineteenth century saw a gradual shift towards oil painting from nature. Painters could achieve a greater naturalness of colour, light and shade by painting in the open fields. John Constable was the first great landscape artist to do so. From early on in his career, he had sketched in oils, and then used these sketches to work up finished paintings in the studio. In 1815, he painted his first oil painting entirely out of doors, *Boat-Building near Flatford Mill*. The English critics praised the picture for its naturalness and veracity but criticized what they perceived to be its roughness of handling: the picture did not seem 'finished'. Constable did not get the recognition he deserved: in his lifetime he sold only twenty paintings in Britain. But he was well received in France, where three paintings, including *The Haywain*, were displayed at the 1824 Salon and awarded a gold medal. They were subsequently sold by the Parisian dealer John Arrowsmith to French buyers. Géricault was 'stunned' by *The Haywain*. Delacroix was so inspired by its colours that he repainted parts of *The Massacre at Chios* (1824), hoping to achieve the same effect.

The Barbizon painters were deeply influenced by Constable. They would have seen his work in several Paris shows during the 1830s. Their interest in *plein-air* painting was encouraged by the invention of tube paints by John Rand, an American inventor and amateur painter, who took out patents on his 'collapsible tin tubes for colour' in the United States in 1841. Marketed by Winsor & Newton, the London manufacturer of art materials, the tin tubes had the advantage that they could keep the paint from drying out, thus allowing artists to complete a painting *en plein air*. Rand was a smarter inventor than he was a businessman. He earned very little from his invention, which not only transformed painting but later would be used for toothpaste and other creams.[118]

Liberated from the studio, the Barbizon painters took to the forest and the open fields to work directly from nature and capture the effects of light and shade. They would return to the same locations many times, painting them in different seasons, times of day, and weather conditions. They were joined in this endeavour by a group of photographers (Gustave Le Gray, Léandre Grandguillaume, Charles Marville, Constant Dutilleux and Adalbert Cuvelier), whose forest scenes of Fontainebleau were the first photographs to be accepted as artworks in the Salon of 1859. Most of these photographers experimented with *cliché-verre*, a print process in which the artist etches a design on to a glass plate coated with collodion, and then exposes it to sunlight against a sheet of sensitized paper. Fascinated by its subtle contrasts of light and shade, Millet, Corot, Daubigny and Rousseau all worked in the medium, which in turn influenced their own painting. Corot, in particular, found in the effects of photographic light a new visual vocabulary: from the hard-edged architectural realism of his landscape paintings in the 1840s, he moved to a softer and more tonal style of painting with blurred edges and subtle light-and-shade effects.[119]

Turgenev felt a close affinity to the Barbizon painters. He once told the Russian banker and art collector Ivan Tsvetkov that, if he could start his life again, he would choose to be a landscape painter and work in nature, where 'there is so much beauty that the artist never wants for a subject'. Turgenev was the most visual of all the Russian writers of the nineteenth century (Tolstoy thought his descriptions of nature were the best in any literature).[120] This description from the final episode of the *Sketches*, where the narrator sums up all the joys of hunting, is the closest thing in words to a landscape painting by Corot (it might have been the passage Alphonse Daudet had been thinking of when he wrote that Turgenev's nature writing appealed to all the senses, 'smell, sight and sound', at the same time):

And a summer morning in July! Has anyone save a hunter ever experienced the delight of wandering through bushes at dawn? Your feet leave green imprints in grass that is heavy and white with dew. You push aside wet bushes – the warm scent accumulated in the night almost smothers you; the air is impregnated with the fresh bitter-sweet fragrance of worm-wood, the honeyed scent of buckwheat and clover; far off an oak forest rises like a wall, shining purple in the sunshine; the air is still fresh, but the coming heat can already be felt. Your head becomes slightly dizzy from such an excess of sweet scents. And there's no end to the bushes. Away in the distance ripening rye glows yellow and there are narrow strips of rust-red buckwheat. Then there's the sound of a cart; a peasant drives by at walking pace, leaving his horse in the shade before the sun gets hot. You greet him, pass on, and after a while the metallic rasping of a scythe can be heard behind you. The sun is rising higher and higher, and the grass quickly dries out. It's already hot. First one hour, then another passes. The sky darkens at the edges and the motionless air is aflame with the prickly heat.[121]

Turgenev had been introduced to the Barbizon painters by Ary Scheffer, who had been a champion of Rousseau's work since the 1830s. The writer would amass a large collection of landscape paintings by Rousseau, Corot, Daubigny and Courbet, most of which he bought through Paul Durand-Ruel and Alfred Sensier, the Barbizon group's main dealers in the 1850s and 1860s, or at the Hôtel Drouot, the large Paris auction house, which opened up for business in 1852.

The Barbizon painters were quick to take advantage of the new art market serviced by commercial dealers and auction houses in Paris, London, Amsterdam and even Boston, where they sold a lot of pictures in the 1850s through William Morris Hunt, an American painter who had studied with Millet in Barbizon.[122] Despite their rural isolation, the Barbizon painters were sharp-eyed businessmen. Their main buyers were wealthy men from mainly middle-class backgrounds – the opera singer Paul Barroilhet and the haberdasher Paul Collot were among their earliest clients – who identified with them because they too were outside the academic art establishment dominated by the aristocracy. Below these major patrons were the smaller buyers who wanted land-scape paintings for their living rooms and could afford the moderate prices commanded by these painters in their early years. In 1850, Sen-sier organized a sale of fifty-three works by Rousseau. They fetched an average of less than 300 francs per picture.[123]

The railway created a new market for the Barbizon painters. After the opening of the line to Fontainebleau, in 1849, there was an influx of weekend trippers from Paris. The journey took just sixty-five minutes, making it an ideal day out from the city to look at the attractions of the royal palace and the beauty spots of the forest. *Trains de plaisir* began to run the route from 1850. There were eight trains a day in the summer months – twelve by 1857, when 135,000 people passed through the station at Fontainebleau (among them Turgenev and Tolstoy, who made a day-trip together). The artist's colony at Barbizon was one of the attractions for these visitors. They came by the coach-load, many of them taking lunch at Ganne's auberge, where, they were informed by a guide to Fontainebleau in 1853, 'the panels of the cupboards, the wall-divisions are covered with studies and painted sketches which have turned this modest inn into a kind of museum, curious in more ways than one'. The artists objected to this intrusion. In 1852, Rousseau took the extraordinary measure of sending a petition in the name of all the artists to Louis-Napoleon, asking him to protect the forest from the tourist industry. Ten years later, the government established a protected forest area and 'reserve' for the artists.[124] But there was an irony in their plea, because by then it was the tourist trade that had brought them many buyers and made their work much better known.

Of all the Barbizon painters none was more attuned to the workings of the market than Courbet. Not that he was ever really one of them. He was a one-man industry. But he was closer to them than to anybody else, and often spoke for them as the acknowledged leader of the realist movement in painting. Born in 1819 to a landowning family in Ornans near the Swiss border, Courbet was commercially minded from the start of his career. 'If I am making art,' he wrote to Gautier in 1846, 'it is first of all to make a living from it.' When he was a young artist in Paris, his letters home were full of observations on the fluctuating prices of different kinds of art; his decision to concentrate on landscape painting was with an eye to where the money was.

Courbet was the first painter to make his own way as an artist in the developing market. Years of rejection by the Salon early in his career had made him resentful of the academic art establishment and equally determined to succeed as an independent artist in the commercial sphere. He studiously courted private patrons and dealers. From the growing power of the press he came to realize the value of publicity – the only means of marketing his work as an independent artist without patrons or the support of institutions like the Academy. In a letter to the critic Francis Wey in 1850, Courbet set out his credo of self-promotion through scandalous behaviour:

> Yes, dear friend, even in our civilized society, I must lead the life of a savage. I must break free from its very governments . . . I will be so outrageous that I'll give everyone the power to tell me the cruelest truths. You see I am up to it. Do not think this is a whim . . . It is a serious duty, not only to give an example of freedom and character in art, but to publicize the art I undertake.[125]

Courbet sought the company of journalists. He made sure he was always in the press. He gained publicity by painting portraits of celebrities, among them Proudhon and Berlioz, before turning his hand to landscapes. He knew the markets well and tailored his production to their various tastes. 'He realised', in the words of his biographer, 'that the high-society women in Deauville and Trouville, where he went bathing in the summer, did not have the same taste as the bourgeoises who visited his exhibitions in the provinces, and that German collectors were looking for other types of landscape scenes than those favoured by their British counterparts.' His lengthy correspondence with his dealers is filled with observations on this score. 'For London,' he advised, 'the theme is more important than the technique' – a 'snow landscape' and other 'pleasant subjects' would always do well there – whereas in Vienna 'highly coloured, serious paintings' were demanded.[126]

This pandering to commercial tastes was in contrast to the major large-scale works produced by Courbet between 1848 and 1855 when he proclaimed himself a 'realist'. The three large paintings he exhibited at the 1850 Salon (*A Burial at Ornans* (Plate 8), *The Peasants of Flagey Returning from the Fair* and *The Stonebreakers*) were starkly realist images of ordinary people, a visual equivalent of Turgenev's literary depiction of the peasantry in the *Sketches*. There was no attempt to sentimentalize or beautify the people for the purposes of art, as expected in such genre works. His depiction of the mourners in *A Burial at Ornans* – all portraits of the actual people who had been present at his great-uncle's funeral – was unflattering. His critics attacked him for the ugliness of his subjects, which they deemed inappropriate for art. They equated his art with photography. 'In this scene, which could pass for a poorly printed daguerreotype, there is the natural coarseness which one always gets in taking nature at any random moment, and reproducing it exactly as it appears,' wrote the painter and critic Étienne-Jean Delécluze about *A Burial at Ornans*.[127]

Undeterred, Courbet moved outside the art establishment and began to organize his own commercial exhibitions in the provinces, relying on publicity from journalistic friends. In Besançon only 250 people paid the fifty-centime charge to see his works. In Dijon his *exposition payante* was forced to close for lack of interest after only a few days. But Courbet did not give up the idea of making money on his own.

In the autumn of 1853, he was given lunch by the Comte de Nieu-werkerke, the government's Director of Fine Arts, who offered a commission for a painting at the Exposition Universelle des Beaux-Arts, planned by the emperor to coincide with an Exposition Universelle of industrial products in Paris in 1855. The Exposition Universelle was the French response to the Great Exhibition of 1851, and, unlike it, was to showcase painting, in which the French excelled. Courbet was insulted by Nieuwerkerke's proposal, which made it a condition that his sketches for the painting should be submitted for approval first. He told the director that he was 'the only judge' of his own work, that he painted for his 'intellectual freedom', and that while he might send him *A Burial at Ornans*, which had set forth his artistic principles, he hoped instead to mount his own exhibition in competition with the government's. As he explained to his friend and patron, Alfred Bruyas, 'I would make 40,000 francs from it, which I would certainly not get from them.'[128]

Eager for approval by the art establishment on his own terms, Courbet challenged the selection committee by sending not just one, but fourteen canvases, including *A Burial at Ornans* and *The Atelier*, another large-scale work, the size of an academic history painting ('the moral and physical history of my studio', as he described it), representing his rebellion against the Salon (it showed him at work amidst the defeated workers of 1848).[129] The committee accepted eleven works but rejected the rest, including the two large paintings. Stung by the rejection of his most ambitious offerings, Courbet organized a one-man exhibition of his paintings in a temporary structure he had built at his own expense opposite the entrance to the Exposition Universelle in the Palais des Beaux-Arts. He advertised his show, which he called *Du Réalisme*, with posters all around Paris. He published an exhibition catalogue with a statement of his views on realist art and made photographic

Courbet's exhibition was housed in a temporary structure between a
fire station and a sugar refinery, photograph, 1855.

reproductions of his paintings (the first art postcards), which he put on
sale as well. Admission cost one franc, the same price as a ticket to the
Exposition Universelle, where 5,000 works of art, including a major
retrospective of paintings by Delacroix and Ingres, were displayed in
the Palace of Fine Arts.[130]

Five million people visited the Exposition Universelle between May
and November. For six months Paris was the centre of the world. The
vast majority were interested only in the Exhibition of Industrial Products. As Ernest Renan, the historian, remarked, 'all Europe has
bestirred itself to go and stare at merchandise'.[131] Fewer than a million
people visited the Fine Arts exhibition, despite entrance prices being
dropped.

Only a handful came to Courbet's show. On the opening day, according to the artist's friend Champfleury, the sole visitors were Gautier,
Proudhon and 'two old ladies of fashion, haughty and curious, and a
little astonished'. Courbet suffered a large financial loss. But he had
succeeded in presenting himself as an independent artist, the first to
produce, publicize and market his own work. His one-man exhibition

marked the birth of the 'avant-garde' as a market-based attack on the Establishment using shock and publicity techniques. It would inspire many others – Manet, Monet, Gauguin, Rodin, Picasso and every artist afterwards – who sought to make a living from their art.[132]

6

The real money to be made from works of art was not in the sale of the original painting but in its reproduction for a mass market. The new technologies of mass reproduction – lithography and photography – turned artworks into a form of capital, a long-term source of revenue for the owners of their copyright, the artist and the publisher.

The reproduction of a work of art by a major company like Goupil or Gambart not only made possible a good income but gave the artist international fame, because such firms had a growing network of galleries and shops in all the major cities of Europe. These companies were the driving force of the art market's internationalization in the middle decades of the nineteenth century. Their sales of prints opened foreign markets for artists.

They also shaped the type of art that artists made. Goupil and Gambart would tell a painter what sort of works would make good prints or sell well among their clientele; and if he wanted to survive in this market, the artist would adapt his work to these demands. As the imperatives of reproduction came to shape the processes of art production, the nature of the artwork was transformed. In the words of Walter Benjamin in his seminal essay, *The Work of Art in the Age of Mechanical Reproduction* (1935), 'the reproduced work of art is to an ever-increasing extent the reproduction of a work of art designed for reproducibility.'[133]

The copying of art is as old as art itself. Artists and their pupils would make copies of their works to circulate them more widely. Copperplate engravings and etchings had been used to make Old Master prints from the fifteenth century. By the eighteenth century art prints were a thriving industry. Artists such as William Hogarth made good money in the medium, controlling the whole production process and marketing himself. But the nineteenth century was the great age of art in print. The growing spending power of the middle classes created an insatiable demand for inexpensive reproductions for the home. Throughout

Europe the walls of bourgeois homes were filled by framed engravings printed on a scale of mass production made possible by the Industrial Revolution. Many more print engravings were produced in the nineteenth century than in the four previous centuries put together.[134]

This explosion of printed images was underpinned by the invention of lithography, which revolutionized the processes of reproducing graphic art. Liberated from the time-consuming labour of engraving the image onto a copper plate, the printmaker only had to draw it on a lithographic stone, a much speedier process that made it possible for images to be printed in bigger quantities, far more cheaply and quickly than before. The technology was first developed in southern Germany during the 1790s, but was quickly taken up in France, Britain and the Low Countries. Technical improvements in the 1830s, above all the introduction of steel lithographic plates, more durable than copper, made large print-runs possible, which explains the rise of illustrated books and periodicals from that decade.

The demand for print engravings was so high that dealers like Goupil and Gambart were prepared to pay enormous fees for the reproduction rights to paintings by the best-known artists of the day. In 1860, for example, Gambart paid a record British sum of 5,500 guineas (£5,775 or 144,000 francs) for the painting and reproduction rights of *The Finding of the Saviour in the Temple* by Holman Hunt. The painting was a good example of the type of composition that lent itself particularly well to reproduction for the home: filled with people and activity, it had a simple Christian narrative. Hunt was aware of the commercial value of the copyright: he knew that Gambart had done well with the print sales of his 1853 painting *The Light of the World*; and he was encouraged by his friends Wilkie Collins and Dickens to stand firm for the highest price. Even so, Gambart stood to profit more. After he had paid for the engraving and printing, a cost of around £3,000, he cleared a handsome profit of £83,475 (2,103,570 francs) from the shilling entrance fee to see the painting in his Pall Mall Gallery (where it was on show for the next two years), from smaller fees to see the painting on a touring exhibition through Britain, as well as from the sales of engravings.[135]

Gambart's success was connected to his skilful marketing. His Pall Mall Gallery, located in the centre of the fine-art world in London, provided his dealership with the upmarket ambience it needed to gain the confidence of wealthy investors. It attracted a large paying public by retaining the ethos of the Royal Academy in its exhibition practices. To enter the French Gallery, as it became known, Gambart charged a shilling, the same entrance fee as at the Royal Academy, at that time just around the corner in Trafalgar Square, and another sixpence for the catalogue. The paintings in the gallery were selected by a 'visiting committee' of members of the Royal Academy. Behind this emulation of the art establishment was a clever marketing and pricing strategy. The entrance fee made his gallery accessible to the middle classes, yet maintained a certain level of exclusiveness on which the prestige of his print-selling business depended. He was just as skilled in his use of publicity. He advertised his exhibitions in the *Art-Union* magazine, a widely read and influential authority in the Victorian art world, which returned the favour by giving them positive reviews. He cultivated good relationships with journalists to raise press interest in his shows, which were often fronted by 'sensation pictures', panoramic scenes with crowds of people depicted in photographic detail, such as *Life at the Seaside* (1854) or *Derby Day* (1858) by William Frith, which had the potential to attract large crowds (when *Derby Day* was first exhibited it had to be protected by a rail).[136]

Investing in the reproduction rights of a painting involved a range of measures to protect and promote them. Goupil and Gambart were fierce in the defence of copyright for artistic works. Their businesses depended on maintaining the 'authenticity' of their reproductions. At the high end of the market this could mean a limited edition of prints signed by the artists; but at the lower end, where the firm's brand embossed into the paper was the only mark of authenticity, there were the usual risks of piracy encountered by the publishing industry. Both firms used domestic laws and bilateral treaties to enforce their copyright. One of the main reasons why Goupil set up branches outside France – in New York (in 1850), Berlin (1855), London (1857), The Hague (1862) and Brussels (1863) – was to help the Paris office protect its copyright abroad by imposing his brand presence in the major markets of the picture trade.

The Goupil company, Europe's biggest print seller, built its reputation as the publisher of Scheffer, Delaroche and Vernet, the three founding artists of the business. By the 1860s, however, the importance of these artists to the firm was matched by that of Jean-Léon Gérôme, the most popular of Academic painters, who married Goupil's daughter in 1863 (a marriage founded on business interests as much as on love). Goupil purchased the paintings of these artists – often before they were finished – mainly for their reproduction rights. When their paintings were already owned, he bought the rights to reproduce them from copies, reductions or existing engravings, which under French law counted as original works of art if the painting had been sold without the artist retaining the reproduction rights.[137] In 1842, for example, Goupil published Louis Henriquel-Dupont's engraving after Scheffer's *Christus Consolator* (1837), one of the most popular religious paintings in nineteenth-century Europe, which had been purchased at the Paris Salon by the Duc d'Orléans. As a work of art in its own right, the engraving provided Goupil with the legal loophole he needed to profit from this famous work. There were five different versions of the print available in the Goupil catalogue of 1848: from the cheapest at just thirty francs to collectable editions at sixty or eighty francs, according to the quality of the paper, and first proofs, signed by the artist, at 160 francs.[138]

Goupil, like Gambart, worked closely with his artists to ensure that their finished paintings would make for good prints and suit his clients'

Goupil's printing factory outside Paris, engraving, 1873.

tastes. Scheffer owed his huge success in the engravings market to his drawings of poetic figures, a post-1830 aspect of his work that had been encouraged by Goupil.. His first bestselling print, *Francesca da Rimini* (1835), was a reimagining of the scene in *The Divine Comedy* when the narrator Dante and Virgil meet Francesca and her lover Paolo in the Inferno. Equally successful were *Dante and Béatrice* (1846), in which the angelic muse looks up towards Paradise, and *Faust and Marguerite in the Garden* (1846), one of many scenes drawn by Scheffer from Goethe's *Faust*. These were popular subjects, attracting some of the best engravers in Europe, which found a market among those people, mostly from the provinces, 'who wanted to acquire and place before their eyes, in their salon, an image of sentiment and piety', as Henri Béraldi put it in his great chronicle, *Les Graveurs du XIXe siècle* (1885–92).[139]

The market for engravings was more provincial and conventional in its artistic tastes than the market for paintings, which was concentrated in the big cities. The most popular subjects were sentimental scenes from the Bible, literary classics or historical scenes. 'There is not a salon in the provinces,' Zola wrote in his damning essay on Gérôme, 'without an engraving on the wall representing *The Duel after a Marked Ball* (Plate 10) or Louis XIV; and in the bachelor's household you are bound to come across *L'Almée et Phryné devant un tribunal* – such are the piquant subjects permitted between men. More serious people have *Les Gladiateurs* or *La Mort de César*. Monsieur Gérôme works for every taste.'

What Zola deplored most in Gérôme's paintings was the sense that they had been specifically designed 'for the House of Goupil. He makes a painting so that it can be reproduced through photographs and engravings and sold in thousands of copies.'[140]

The invention of photography also transformed the business of reproducing art. Goupil began working in the medium during the mid-1850s, but his first mass edition of photographic reprints – a series of Delaroche's paintings – appeared in 1858. In that year he also launched his 'Galerie photographique' – a series of mounted photographic reproductions of popular paintings designed for framing in the home. By the end of the century the series contained over 1,800 different works, each available in smaller formats as postcards or for collecting in albums. The age of the art postcard and art book had begun.

7

In November 1853, Turgenev was released from house arrest and allowed to return to St Petersburg, under police surveillance, provided that he made a 'full admission' of his guilt. The Tsar agreed to his release on grounds of ill-health – the first signs of the acute gout from which Turgenev suffered for the rest of his life. Turgenev left at once for the capital, taking temporary lodgings and then moving to a spacious apartment by the Anichkov Palace, where he kept a servant and a cook.

Any thought he might have had of leaving Russia to be reunited with the Viardots in France was ruled out by the Crimean War. The conflict had begun in the summer of 1853 with the Russian occupation of the Danubian principalities, Moldavia and Wallachia (nominally under Turkish sovereignty but effectively controlled by the Russians). The occupation aimed to force the Turks to submit to the Tsar's demands in the Holy Lands, where the Orthodox were engaged in a struggle against the Catholics over the right of access to the Holy Places. Russia's aggression prompted France and Britain to send a military expedition to defend the Ottoman Empire and punish Russia by destroying its naval base at Sevastopol in the Crimea. The French and British forces landed on Russian soil in September 1854. Beating the Russians back at the Alma River, for the next eleven months they laid siege to Sevastopol, subjecting it to artillery bombardment on an industrial scale. The invasion stirred the patriotic feelings of even the most Western-oriented Russians such as Turgenev, who wrote to Pauline on 30 October: 'I confess that I would willingly give my right arm to stop any one of our invaders (excuse me!) from escaping, and if there is one thing I regret at this moment, it is not having followed a military career, for then perhaps I might have spilled my blood for the defence of my country.' As long as the war went on, he wrote to Pauline, he could not concentrate on literature, and would gladly exchange his pen for a sword.[141]

One writer who had done just that was Tolstoy, who had joined the army in 1852, the year he had first come to the attention of the literary world with the publication of his memoir *Childhood* in *The Contemporary*. Dissatisfied with his frivolous way of life as an aristocrat in St Petersburg and Moscow, the young count had decided to make a fresh start by following his brother Nikolai to the Caucasus. In 1853, he was transferred to the Russian army on the Danubian Front, and the next year was posted to the Crimea, where he penned his *Sevastopol Sketches*, a masterpiece of realist writing, half fiction and half reportage from the besieged city, which was published in *The Contemporary* in 1855.

Tolstoy and Turgenev met for the first time that autumn in St Petersburg, following the fall of Sevastopol and the defeat of Russia. Turgenev was the older by ten years. The poet Fet, who was at that meeting in Turgenev's apartment, was struck by Tolstoy's 'automatic opposition to all generally accepted opinions'.[142] Living side by side with the ordinary soldiers in the Crimea had opened Tolstoy's eyes to the simple virtues of the peasantry. It had set him on a restless search for a moral way of life that he might live as a Russian nobleman – for a way of life without serfdom – an aspiration shared by Turgenev. Since the death of Nicholas I and the accession to the throne of his son, Alexander II, in March 1855, hopes of liberal reform were increasing. Censorship was loosened. Alexander told the gentry to prepare for the liberation of their serfs. Military defeat had persuaded him that Russia could not compete with the more advanced industrial powers until it swept aside its serf economy and modernized itself on European lines.

Turgenev saw a lot of Tolstoy over the next years. The two men were brought together by their opposition to serfdom. Their estates in Russia were not far apart. Tolstoy's only sister, Maria, lived just a few kilometres from Spasskoe with her unfaithful husband and their three children. Turgenev often called on her, beginning in October 1854, and a brief romance between them developed. 'She is one of the most attractive women I have ever met,' Turgenev wrote to Annenkov on 13 November 1854. 'Lovely, clever, straightforward – I could not take my eyes off her. In my old age (I turned 36 four days ago) I almost fell in love.'[143] Their relationship was the inspiration for Turgenev's *Faust* (1856), an epistolary story of a tragic love affair, whose heroine resembles Maria. Unhappily married, Maria left her husband in 1857, perhaps hoping for a relationship with Turgenev, but by this time he had gone abroad and when he returned, in 1858, he was no longer drawn to her.

With the end of the Crimean War, the way back to Europe for Turgenev was open. The liberal climate in Russia did not detain him for long. In April 1856, less than a month after peace had been restored between Russia and the European powers by the Treaty of Paris,

Turgenev told Pauline that he was applying for an exit visa. He needed some connections in high places to obtain it. 'If I get it – which by the way is far from certain – I count on being at Courtavenel for the beginning of the hunting season on 1 September,' he wrote to Pauline. So many Russians were leaving for Europe that there were no places left on any of the steamships before the end of July. He bought one for the start of August, by which time his passport had come through. On the eve of his departure he wrote to Countess Lambert, a close friend and confidante who would have understood the subtext of his letter to be about Pauline:

> It brings me joy to be allowed to go abroad, yet at the same time I cannot but recognize that it would be better for me not to go. At my age to live abroad – means: to commit oneself to a gypsy existence and discard any thoughts of family life. But what can I do! It is obvious that is my fate. It might be said that people with soft characters depend on 'fate' – which relieves them from the need to exercise their own free will, from the need to take responsibility for themselves. Anyway, the bottle has been opened, so the wine must be drunk.

Turgenev suggested he would stay abroad for at least four years, the term set by his passport from the Russian government.[144]

Travelling by steamship to Stettin, he arrived in Paris in mid-August, and from there set off for London to be reunited with the Viardots, who had been there since June for a season of concerts. Turgenev had not seen them for three and a half years. He returned with them to Courtavenel at the start of September. His relationship with Pauline resumed there, and at once they again became close. Turgenev was accepted as a member of the household, along with his daughter, Paulinette, who was now fourteen, a headstrong and unhappy girl, allowed to speak only French, who did not get on with Pauline or her adopted family at all. There were musical evenings, amateur dramatics and the 'portrait game', in which someone drew a cartoon of a made-up character and everybody wrote down what they thought the character's biography would be. 'How perfectly we spent our time at Courtavenel!' Turgenev wrote to Botkin shortly after their return to Paris on 6 November. 'Each day appeared as a gift – something natural, not at all depending on ourselves, permeated everything.' Botkin was one of the few people in whom he confided about Pauline. He would have understood Turgenev's meaning when he read in the same letter: 'Really, I was very happy all this time – perhaps because "last flowers are sweeter than the sumptuous first-born flowers in the fields".'[145]*

Turgenev took an apartment on the rue de Rivoli. But he spent all his time at the Viardots in the rue de Douai, where Pauline kept an open house with regular Thursday evening musical soirées and smaller, more informal gatherings of friends for music every Sunday afternoon in the 'grand salon' – the large room converted from the old conservatory with the Aristide Cavaillé-Coll organ, recently displayed at the Exposition Universelle in Paris. The centrepiece of the salon was the original manuscript of Mozart's *Don Giovanni*, which Pauline had purchased from a bookseller in London in 1855. The handwritten score had a special personal significance, for Pauline was renowned for her singing of the parts of Donna Anna and Zerlina, while the opera had a long association with her family. Its previous owner, Augustina André, had inherited the document from her father, the composer and music publisher Johann Anton André, who had bought it from Constanze Mozart in 1800. Through her husband, Augustina had offered it for sale to the Imperial Library in Vienna, the Royal Library in Berlin and the British Museum, all of which rejected it for lack of funds. Pauline got it for £180. She kept the precious manuscript in a special wooden box decorated in the neo-Gothic style. Finished in brass, the box had an escutcheon in the shape of an 'M' and an inscription on the lid. It looked more likely to contain the relics of a saint than an orchestral score. Placed on a table by the organ, it turned the room into a sort of shrine, a site dedicated to the cult of Mozart with Pauline as its high priestess.[146]

The list of those who regularly came to the Thursday music evenings reads like a *Who's Who* of the artistic world of Paris in the second half of the 1850s: the composers Berlioz, the young Saint-Saëns and the bon-vivant Rossini, who had known Pauline since she was a child and still held her in the fondest affection; the painters Delacroix, Corot, Doré and Scheffer; writers as diverse as Augier, Renan and Turgenev; and Daniele Manin, the Venetian republican leader of 1848, who lived in exile in Paris. The Viardots involved their own children in the music-making at these receptions. For Louise, the eldest, then a teenager and

---

* A quotation from a Pushkin poem without title of 1825.

already a competent pianist, the concerts were a 'real torture' as she was made to sight-read the accompaniment for top-rate soloists before the distinguished audience. 'It was evidently a good training to become a musician,' she recalls, 'but it felt like a punishment.'[147]

Among the foreign visitors were Liszt and Anton Rubinstein, Chorley, Herzen and Bakunin, and Dickens. Dickens had heard Pauline sing in *Le Prophète* in London in 1849. Although they had mutual friends, he had not called on the Viardots during his trips to Paris in 1850, 1851 or February 1855. It was not until the autumn of 1855, when Dickens came to Paris for the Exposition Universelle, that they finally met. Dickens was in Paris for several months. Within days of his arrival he was visited by Scheffer, who persuaded him to sit for a portrait in his studio in rue Chaptal, just around the corner from the Viardots. Dickens found the lengthy sittings tiresome. They came at a time when he was under intense pressure in his work. 'I can scarcely express how uneasy and unsettled it makes me to sit, sit, sit, with *Little Dorrit* on my mind,' he wrote to his friend John Forster. The painting did not turn out very well. Scheffer was afraid that it resembled a Dutch admiral more than an English novelist, and Dickens, although pleased with the result, did not think it looked like him at all. It was during these sittings that Dickens met Pauline. He gave a reading of *The Cricket on the Hearth* for sixty guests in Scheffer's studio. Pauline was reduced to tears by the reading – the tale of marital fidelity and accusations of betrayal must have struck a chord with her. On a second evening Pauline sang for the English writer, who sent her an instalment of *Little Dorrit* as a token of his gratitude for the 'delight' that her 'great genius' had given him.

From that point Dickens was a regular visitor at the rue de Douai. He was there for what he called 'a very good and remarkably unpretending' dinner with Scheffer and George Sand, who had come up from Nohant for the occasion, in January 1856. 'The Viardots have a house away in the new part of Paris, which looks exactly as if they had moved into it last week, and were going away next,' Dickens wrote to Forster. 'Notwithstanding which, they have lived in it eight years. The opera the very last thing on earth you would associate with the family. Piano not even opened.' The meeting between Dickens and Sand was a mixed success. Sand was bored and unimpressed by Dickens, who did not know her novels, while he found her a 'singularly ordinary woman in appearance and manner' – far, in other words, from his preconception of her as a dangerously immoral free-thinker. 'Chubby, matronly, swarthy, black-eyed. Nothing of the blue-stocking about her,' he wrote to Forster, 'except a little final way of settling all your opinions with hers, which I take to have been acquired in the country, where she lives, and in the domination of a small circle.'[148]

One person missing from the Viardot circle was Gounod. Pauline had fallen out with him in 1852, when he had unexpectedly announced his marriage to Anna Zimmermann, the daughter of a piano professor at the Paris Conservatory. The wedding was to take place at the end of May, the time of the birth of Pauline's daughter Claudie, so there was no question of the Viardots being there. But Pauline was upset that she was not even invited. Several invitations from the Viardots were cancelled by the Zimmermanns at short notice and for no apparent reason. Pauline had sent a wedding gift, a valuable bracelet for the bride, but Gounod had returned it the next day, along with a brief letter in which he explained that he already wished to give his wife a bracelet, so Pauline's gift was not needed.[149] Actually, Gounod had refused the gift on the insistence of the Zimmermanns, who wanted to distance themselves from the Viardots: there had been rumours of the love affair between Pauline and Gounod, and they had received an anonymous letter threatening to reveal it. The fact that Gounod, who owed so much to Pauline, had gone along with this affront outraged Louis, in particular, who wrote to Gounod on his wife's behalf breaking off all relations. Ary Scheffer intervened, pleading with Gounod to make his first social call with his new wife to the Viardots, but when he failed to do so, the Viardots were incensed. They took it as an insult that Gounod would not take the measures needed to defend Pauline's honour. Louis barred him from their home for good. Pauline wrote long letters to George Sand complaining inconsolably about how she had been wronged. Turgenev seized the opportunity to regain favour with Pauline. 'To act as he has done is disgusting,' he wrote to Pauline in August, 'all is finished between me and him. I do not want to think of him again.'[150]

4

Europeans on the Move

Cards like this arrived daily, from Innsbruck, Verona, Vicenza, Padua, and every one started, 'Today we visited the famous local art gallery', or if it wasn't a gallery, it was an arena or a church. Santa Maria something or other.

Theodor Fontane, *Effi Briest*

I

Turgenev travelled constantly between 1857 and 1861. He was incapable of staying still in any place for long. Much of his travel was in search of cures for various ailments but there were emotional torments too. In February 1857, complaining of bladder pains, he left Paris for Dijon to consult a doctor recommended to him by Louis Viardot. 'I plan to spend a week here,' he wrote to Annenkov in St Petersburg, 'return for three weeks to my place of torture, called Paris, visit London, and then come home.'[1]

Restless travel delayed his return to Russia for another eighteen months. Following a brief stay in London to see Herzen, who had settled there in 1852, Turgenev went to Berlin and Dresden; he then took the waters at Sinzig on the Rhine, rushed to Baden-Baden to rescue Tolstoy, who had lost his money in the casino, spent three weeks with him by the seaside at Boulogne, returned to Paris and Courtavenel, where he passed September, travelled for the next six months in Italy, and then took another three to travel back to Russia, passing through Vienna, Prague, Dresden, Leipzig, Paris, London and Berlin on the way.

Turgenev felt unwanted, redundant, in Paris. That was the reason for his restlessness. 'I won't talk about myself – a completely bankrupt person,' he wrote to Botkin before leaving for Dijon. 'I feel as if I am a bit of rubbish they forgot to sweep away – that is my constant mood. Perhaps it will pass when I leave Paris.' Two months later his mood had not improved. Turgenev wrote to Annenkov that he was living through a 'moral and physical crisis' from which he 'would emerge either shattered or repaired! . . . I mean propped up, as a collapsed shed is propped up with logs.'[2]

The cause of his depression was a sudden break in his relations with Pauline. They had been close the previous autumn, following his return from Russia. They had spent a 'blissful' month or so together at Courtavenel, where Turgenev had been 'very happy', as he had written to Botkin, because he had felt close to her. But then there was a sudden change. She became distant, even cold. She rarely answered his letters. To find out news of her he had to write to his daughter, whose own relations with Pauline were poor.[3] The break was a catastrophe for Turgenev. It made him ill. Unable to write, he destroyed all his notes and told his friends that he was finished as a writer. He was then aged thirty-nine. 'Turgenev is pitiful to see,' observed Tolstoy. 'I would not have thought him capable of such a love.'[4]

Pauline's attitude had changed when she became pregnant with her fourth child, Paul, in November 1856. There are two ways this coincidence may be explained. Pauline had a habit of breaking off relations with her male admirers after giving them encouragement. She did it to Gounod, and would do so again to Berlioz. It was as if she enjoyed the flirtation, and the admiration of these famous men, but took fright when they drew too close, threatening her commitment to her marriage, on which she depended more than these admirers realized. Perhaps Turgenev was wounded by the fact that Pauline had conceived a child with Louis at a time when he felt closer to her than at any other time before. He might have even seen it as a betrayal. Feeling rejected, Turgenev went off travelling abroad. 'One cannot live like this,' he wrote to Nekrasov. 'No more sitting on the edge of someone else's nest.' To Tolstoy he confessed in a letter on 20 December: 'I am too old not to have a nest, not to stay at home. In the spring I shall return to Russia – although to leave from here I shall have to say goodbye to the last dreams of so-called happiness.'[5]

An alternative explanation is that Turgenev was Paul's father, or suspected that he might be so, and went away to protect the Viardots from rumours, which were then developing. Perhaps Pauline deliberately withdrew her affections to encourage him to leave. That would certainly explain a curious remark by Pauline in a letter to Rietz, her confidant, in January 1859: 'Love kills, when not allowed to burst into flame. To extinguish it – that is a cruel torture – sad, deadly and terrible.'[6]

There is circumstantial evidence to suggest this explanation may be right, although the most likely source to confirm it, Turgenev's diary, which he had kept since 1851, was destroyed by the writer shortly after Pauline became pregnant, probably because it contained compromising evidence about their relationship, which might have come to light in the event of his death.[7] On Paul's birth, in July 1857, Turgenev wrote an extraordinarily ecstatic letter to Pauline, far more joyous than any of his letters on the birth of her other three children. When Paul was three he fell seriously ill with pneumonia. Pauline asked Turgenev, then in Germany, to come at once to Courtavenel to care for him while she fulfilled a previous commitment to sing in a concert in London. He dropped everything to go. The fact that she had called on him, despite the cooling in their own relations, suggests that she recognized a link between Turgenev and her son. Turgenev always treated Paul with a strong paternal affection – to the extent that Louis once complained that he felt his own position as a father had been usurped by him. The boy played the violin and later became a well-known soloist. It was rumoured that his Stradivarius had been paid for by Turgenev in lieu of an inheritance from the writer's will – it was worth far more than the modest sums Turgenev left to Pauline's daughters. Equally suggestive is a strange aside in Louis's testament, which calls upon his children, 'even my son Paul', to respect their mother following his death.[8]

Paul himself never denied rumours that he was the son of Turgenev. He often told the story of an incident from his boyhood when he had been chided by his mother for being rude to Turgenev. Told to shake hands with his mother's friend, Paul complained that Turgenev had cuffed him on the ear for some earlier misdemeanour and that he would not take punishment from anyone but his father. His comment prompted a 'very meaningful look' between his mother and Turgenev which struck Paul as odd.[9]

If Turgenev was his father, it made sense for him to disappear when

Pauline became pregnant. Distancing himself was the obvious way to minimize the risk of a scandal that could ruin her career. Turgenev's novels are full of restless wanderers, rootless Russians like himself travelling aimlessly around Europe. The unnamed hero and narrator of *Asya* (1857), Lavretsky in *Home of the Gentry* (1859), Sanin in *Spring Torrents* (1871) – these ill-fated, lovesick travellers are his alter egos from the years of separation from Pauline. Like Turgenev, they are all without a nest.

Far from being finished as a writer, Turgenev was productive, completing three of his finest novels* and three minor works, including the novella *Asya*, in his period of wandering, suggesting, in the words of his biographer, 'that this great burst of literary energy was his way of reconciling himself to the personal misery to which he now saw himself condemned'. *Asya* was begun (and is clearly set) in the tranquil spa town of Sinzig, where Turgenev stayed in the Badehaus, nestled on the edge of a pine forest, from which he looked out of his window, as he wrote to Tolstoy, 'across a broad valley of wheat-fields and fruit orchards – and on the horizon a jagged line of hills on the right bank of the Rhine'. The narrator tells the story of his hopeless love for a girl called Asya, who departs the Rhineland spa, leaving him a wistful farewell note, before he finds the courage to propose to her. The tale was a reflection of Turgenev's indecisiveness and feelings of regret about Pauline. Turgenev completed it in Rome, where he also worked on *Home of the Gentry*, another melancholic tale of disappointed love. Its hero, Lavretsky, who is not unlike Turgenev, returns from Paris to his home in Russia after the revelation of his wife's infidelity. He falls in love with Liza, a girl with strong religious feelings, whom he hopes to marry after learning of his wife's death from a report in a French newspaper. The report turns out to be false. Lavretsky's estranged wife appears, asking for his forgiveness, and returns to Paris with a promissory note for a large sum of money from Lavretsky, while Liza enters a convent. The novel might be read as an evocation of Turgenev's feelings of anxiety caused by his relations with Pauline: having tied his happiness to her, which would mean returning to Paris, had he not denied himself the chance of finding a more stable source of love in his homeland?

Turgenev put off his return to Russia because he was 'seduced by the

---

* *Home of the Gentry* (1859), *On the Eve* (1860) and *Fathers and Sons* (1862).

idea of spending a winter in Italy, in Rome in particular, before I turn forty and die', as he explained in a letter to his friends in St Petersburg. He also hoped that he could write well there. 'In Rome it is impossible not to work – and often to work well.'[10] The idea of travelling to Italy had been in his mind from the spring of 1857, when he wrote to Botkin in Moscow suggesting that he join him in Paris to go by train together to London for the Season and then travel to the Rhine, Switzerland and Italy: 'You will be in the most interesting places at the best possible time: Paris in May, England in June, the Rhine and Baden-Baden in July, Switzerland in August' – Italy at that stage planned for the autumn. Botkin was a seasoned traveller. The son of one of Russia's biggest tea merchants, he was a wealthy dilettante, art and music critic, travel writer, and something of an expert on Spanish and Italian art, so he was in many ways an ideal travelling companion. Plans were delayed by Turgenev's trip to Sinzig, but at the end of September they were set. 'So we are going!', Botkin wrote.

> I will be a quiet and patient companion, and ask you only to be patient too. It is very hard for me to travel by night, and in a carriage or wagon. Even from Paris to Marseilles I prefer to stop for a night in Lyons . . . From Marseilles we will have to get somehow to Nice, and then by the corniche to Genoa. Yes! I forgot to say that I do all I can to avoid sea travel . . . We will only go by boat from Genoa to Livorno. And from Florence overland through places where all Christian art has developed.[11]

The journey began easily enough. The final section of the Paris–Marseilles railway had been opened in 1856, enabling passengers to travel the 862 kilometres in just seventeen hours. Crossing into Italy was much slower. The coastal road between Nice and Genoa was notoriously difficult. From 1857 it was further complicated by construction work on the Ligurian railway along the corniche. But the journey was beautiful. 'I have entered Italy from various directions but none with a view as bewitching as this,' Botkin wrote to Fet, who had declined the offer to join them on the trip. 'Palm groves and enormous oleanders and orchards of trees and all nearby the light-blue sea. There are places where you are in ecstasy.' In Genoa, where a lost trunk delayed them for three days, they visited the city's palaces with a guidebook – John Murray's *Handbook for Travellers in Northern Italy* (1854) – and went to the opera in the evenings. 'Genoa is a very pretty town,' Turgenev wrote to Pauline on 27 October, 'but the women are all repulsive, no matter what the guidebook says ... There are some magnificent palaces and some filthy streets (by the way, I found the original of Viardot's Ribera in the Balbi Palace);* Van Dyck's portrait of the Marquis de Brignoles on a large grey horse is "a wonder".'[12]

In Rome they stayed at the Hotel d'Inghilterra, a sixteenth-century aristocratic residence recently converted into a hotel popular with English visitors, partly because Byron and John Keats had both stayed there. Botkin left Turgenev on his own to write, but dined with him and spent the evenings with him at the opera, playing chess or talking about art at the Café Greco near the Spanish Steps, where a group of Russian artists met, including Alexander Ivanov, then completing his great painting, on which he had worked for over twenty years, *The Appearance of Christ before the People*. Turgenev was rejuvenated by his time in Rome. 'Rome is marvellous,' he wrote to Annenkov. 'In no other city do you get that constant feeling that the Great, the Beautiful and Important are always close to hand, constantly surrounding you, so that you, at any time, can enter the sphere of the divine.' To Countess Lambert, his confidante in these years of separation from Pauline, Turgenev confessed that it was 'a city where it is easier to be alone' – an idea he developed in a letter to the Ukrainian writer Maria Markovich when he wrote that 'Rome is a surprising city, which can replace anything – society, happiness and even love.'[13]

Consolation also came from touring around Italy. With Botkin as an expert guide, Turgenev visited the Villa Madama and the Villa Pamphili, picturesque Lake Albano, and Frascati, reachable from Rome by a newly opened railway, one of the first in Italy, which took only half an hour to transport day-trippers from Rome to the pretty hill-town. They also made a longer trip to Naples and Pompei. Separating from Botkin, Turgenev travelled on his own to Florence, where he used his Murray's *Handbook* as a guide to the city's art treasures; and from Florence he went to Pisa, Milan and Venice on his way to Vienna to consult a doctor before returning to Russia. 'Florence is a marvel,' he

---

* Turgenev was mistaken. He must have been confusing one of Ribera's paintings of an *Old Philosopher*, owned by the Balbi family, with his portrait of *Plato*, owned at that time by Louis Viardot. 'My Ribera has no original, because it is an original itself,' an irritated Viardot replied (Zvig., p. 182).

wrote to Botkin on 28 March, continuing with advice from his Murray guide:

> pay attention, by the way, to a painting by Raphael in the Pitti Palace, No. 245 in the 'Education of Jupiter' Room; it is a model for his Madonnas, and the ones in Dresden in particular.
>
> Be healthy and until we meet in Russia, your I. Turgenev
> Ps. Buy yourself a Murray for Florence.[14]

2

Railways made this sort of travel possible. Turgenev used them as often as he could on his travels through Europe. He even learned to write on them.

Less than a year after his return to Russia, in 1859, he was off again to London and Paris, with shorter trips to the spa resorts of Vichy and Ostend on his way back to St Petersburg. He returned to Europe the next spring, travelling by train from the Russian capital to Berlin, Paris, Munich, Bad Soden, along the Rhine to Cologne and Aachen on his way to London, and finally to Ventnor on the Isle of Wight, a seaside resort favoured by the Russian aristocracy and recommended to him by both Botkin and Herzen, where he spent three weeks in August 1860 working on the outline of *Fathers and Sons*.

Dedicated to Belinsky, the short novel is a masterpiece of realist form and narrative technique. More widely read abroad than any of Turgenev's other works, it raised the status of Russian literature to new heights, on a par with English or French fiction, and brought international fame to Turgenev. The main interest of the novel is its tragic hero Bazarov, the original 'nihilist', who rejects every principle or institution that does not serve the social welfare of the people. A medical student, Bazarov is taken by his friend Arkady to stay at his father's estate following their graduation from St Petersburg University. His revolutionary opinions, weakly shared by Arkady, bring the young men into conflict with Arkady's father and uncle, holders of more liberal views. The confrontation between these two generations placed the novel at the centre of political discussions in Russia during the 1860s, when students and young radicals were questioning the tsarist system, rejecting the political quietism of their fathers' generation (the 'men of the forties'), and calling for more action to improve conditions for the peasantry. Caustic, coarse, severely intellectual and self-assured, Bazarov is in many ways a typical example of the student radicals, particularly those from the *raznochintsy*, or non-noble backgrounds, who played a leading role in the revolutionary movement during that decade. But he is more complex than a type. Introduced by Arkady to Anna Odintsova, an elegant widow, he falls in love with her, but is disturbed by his emotions, which militate against his principles. In any case, his feelings are unreturned by Anna, who is cold and self-absorbed. Perhaps, if she had loved him, Bazarov might have softened in his character; he might have given up his angry passion to destroy. The tempering effect of love is revealed in Arkady, whose engagement to Katya, Anna's younger sister, marks the end of his infatuation with Bazarov and his radical ideas. Departing from his friend, Bazarov returns to his humble parents in the countryside and works there as a doctor, dying later from a blood infection after cutting himself while carrying out an autopsy on a victim of typhus.

Turgenev had first conceived Bazarov during his stay at Ventnor. The idea for his hero had come to him from a young provincial doctor, referred to by Turgenev by the letter 'D.' but thought to be a certain Dmitriev, whom he had met on a train, travelling second class, between Moscow and St Petersburg. In his *Literary Reminiscences* (1869) Turgenev describes 'taking sea-baths at Ventnor' when he came to shape his character, who, like all his fictional heroes, had his starting point in a living person, to whom he gradually added suitable invented elements. At the basis of Bazarov 'lay the personality of a young provincial doctor I had been greatly struck by. (He died shortly before 1860.) In that remarkable man I could watch the embodiment of that principle which had scarcely come to life but was just beginning to stir at the time, the principle which later received the name of nihilism.'[15]

It is one of the stranger ironies of literary history that Turgenev's greatest creation – the fictional embodiment of the nineteenth-century Russian revolutionary – should have taken shape in the genteel seaside resort of Ventnor. The Russian circles on the Isle of Wight no doubt had an influence on Turgenev's invention of Bazarov. They were swept up in debates about the imminent Emancipation of the Serfs and the need it would create for social reforms in Russia to raise the peasants out of poverty and ignorance. Much of their discussion would have been informed by the emergence of a new breed of radicals in Russia – young writers grouped around the journal *The Contemporary*, which became a mouthpiece of the revolutionary intelligentsia, alienating liberals like Turgenev, who had been a regular contributor. Turgenev hit on the idea of founding a Society for the Propagation of Literacy and Primary Education, and presented a draft programme to the Russian colony for discussion. According to Annenkov, who visited Turgenev in Ventnor, the programme 'was gone over in detail at evening meetings in Turgenev's cottage, redrafted, and after many arguments, corrections and additions adopted by a committee made up of selected members of the group'. But no practical measures were subsequently taken to set up schools or recruit teachers, and Annenkov was left with the impression 'that the plan was simply based on the idea of demonstrating the necessity, usefulness and patriotic character of the society'.[16]

Turgenev had come to Ventnor for the sea-bathing. He had been hoping for a holiday in the company of Annenkov and the 26-year-old Maria Markovich, who had promised to join him there. Markovich did not arrive, and the other pleasures of a seaside break were soon spoilt by the English weather, which became cold and rainy, ruling out the possibility of sea-bathing. Turgenev described the miserable scene in a letter to Countess Lambert on 18 August:

> The wide and gently sloping strip of yellow-brown sand which forms the sea-shore, not built up in any way and devoid of vegetation, stretches far beyond the limits of the town. With the incoming tide bottle-green waves, cold, northern waves, run right up to the boundary of the uniform houses. When the tide has gone out, straight-backed figures of English people out for a stroll can be seen on the damp, firm, seaweed-striped sand.[17]

Confined to his cottage by the poor weather, Turgenev sat down at the writing table in his room and began his masterpiece. He had nothing else to do.

Turgenev was a seasoned traveller on the railways. With all his touring around Europe and the trips he made to Russia, he must have journeyed more on them than any other writer of his day. By the 1860s it was possible to travel by rail to nearly all of Europe's major cities and to many of its smaller towns. The rate of railway building in the 1850s and 1860s was staggering. Everywhere the railways were seen as the key to economic growth, political stability and national unity. In Germany, where they were viewed as a driving force of unification, connecting all the German states, the length of the completed lines grew from 5,856 kilometres in 1850 to 17,612 kilometres in 1869. Spending on the railways made up a quarter of all investments (government and private) in these years. In France the growth of the railways was no less impressive – from 2,915 to 16,465 kilometres.[18] The railways spread south to Madrid and Rome, north to Copenhagen and Stockholm, east to Moscow and St Petersburg, west to Cornwall and Galway.

By making foreign travel easier and affordable, the railways encouraged people to travel more and further than before. The British led the way. They practically drove the growing tourist industry in Europe. Every major city on the beaten track through France, the Rhineland and Switzerland to Italy boasted grand hotels with names like Hôtel d'Angleterre, Hôtel des Anglais, Hôtel de Londres, Hotel d'Inghilterra, and so on. The Goncourts complained that it was hard for the French to travel in their own country, because the staff in all hotels was interested only in serving tourists from Britain.[19] The British middle classes were the richest in Europe. Living apart from the Continent, they felt a stronger need to travel than their European counterparts. The Grand Tour had been dominated by the British aristocracy. It had set a model of European travel as a means of intellectual betterment.

At the highpoint of the British fashion for the Grand Tour, in the 1780s, the historian Edward Gibbon had estimated that there were up to 40,000 Britons – whole families with their children, tutors and servants – travelling on the Continent in any year. Wealthy young men headed straight for Italy to complete their knowledge of the classics, find out about Continental fashions, and look for sexual adventures. In the early decades of the nineteenth century there was a steady increase in numbers. The travellers were more diverse, with many from the professional classes, who tended to make smaller tours of the Low Countries and the Rhine as far as Switzerland, which had been opened up to easier travel by steamships. But this growth was small compared with the sudden boom in railway travel in the 1850s and 1860s. After the completion of the railway links from London and Paris to the ports on the English Channel, the number of recorded Channel crossings grew from 165,000 in 1850 to 238,000 in 1860 and 345,000 in 1869. By the end of this period passengers could travel from London to Paris in just half a day.[20]

The tourist industry was a creation of the railway age. Even the word 'tourist' was relatively new, entering the French and English languages from the 1810s but gaining widespread currency from the 1840s with the penetration of the Continent by railways, hotels, restaurants, souvenir shops, guidebooks and so on.[21] Whereas foreign travel had previously been the pleasure of a few, the railways made it possible for many more. The cultural élites had their doubts about this revolution in movement. 'The enormous extension of continental travel is one of the great features of the last ten years,' commented the *Edinburgh Review* in 1873:

> During the autumn months the whole of Europe seems to be in a state of perpetual motion. There is a mob at every small railway station. The new hotels (as at Lucerne) are built to receive 5, 6, or 700 guests, and those most frequented turn away daily some 200 applicants, for whom there is no room. Every spot, however difficult of access, is attacked. The remote lake Koenigsee, in Bavaria, to which perhaps a dozen strangers formerly found their way in the course of a month, now supports four boats, while the carriages waiting on the shore may be counted by fifties. The top of the Rigi is worn bare of grass, and is strewn with broken bottles and fragments of *The Daily Telegraph*.

In contrast to the old élites, who could afford to travel for several months and even years, the new railway tourists concentrated all their travel in a few weeks' summer holiday. 'All the world is travelling,' Fontane wrote in *Modern Travel* (1873):

> Just as in the old days people found their entertainment in talking about the weather, so now they find it in travel. 'Where did you go this summer?' is all people say between October and Christmas. 'Where will you be going next summer?' is all they say between Christmas and Easter. Many people spend eleven months of the year preparing for the twelfth [when they travel], as if on the ladder to a higher existence. People live for this twelfth month.[22]

What tourists wanted was a compact version of the Grand Tour. They desired many things: to see the most famous sites of Europe, the culturally important and the picturesque; to focus on those aspects of a place that were nationally 'authentic' and unique to it which they could not see at home; and to return with pride in thinking 'they have seen at any rate as much as their neighbours' – as Trollope put it in his *Travelling Sketches* (1866). The 'true pleasure' of 'the family that goes abroad' begins only when they return home, Trollope continued:

The spirit that instigates them to roam afield is no hankering after fashion . . . The days in which we heard that

> Mrs. Grill is very ill,
> And nothing will improve her,
> Unless she sees the Tuileries,
> And waddles down the Louvre,

are well nigh over, and are certainly over for such sensible people as I am describing. It is not fashion that they seek, nor is it chiefly amusement. Paterfamilias, when he starts, knows that he will not be amused, and already wishes that the journey was over, and that he could be back at his club. Mamma dreads it somewhat, and has more of misgiving than of pleasant anticipation. She has not much of happiness when papa is cross, and he is usually cross when he is uncomfortable. And then the people at the inns are so often uncivil; and she fears the beds! And the girls look for no unalloyed satisfaction. They know that they have hard work before them, and the dread of those slips in their French is not pleasant to them. But it is the thing to do. Not to have seen Florence, Rome, Munich, and Dresden, not to be at home as regards the Rhine, not to have ridden over the Gemini or to have talked to Alpine climbers at Zermatt, is to be behind the world.

'Culture' was the biggest draw. By seeing Europe's greatest works of art and visiting its famous historical places and buildings, tourists sought to cultivate themselves by travelling abroad; they approached culture as acquisitions or commodities they could check off a list of things they had experienced. National galleries and museums were the major reference points for tourists planning their itineraries. International exhibitions – such as those in London (in 1851 and 1862), Paris (1855 and 1867) and Vienna (1873) – equally attracted foreign visitors, although how many is difficult to say with any accuracy.*

---

* At the Great Exhibition in 1851 there were an estimated 50,000 foreign visitors, most of them from France, among 6 million visitors. At the time of the Universal Exposition in Paris, in 1867, there were over 200,000 foreigners registered in the city's hotels but how many more there were among the exhibition's total attendance of between 11 million and 15 million visitors is impossible to tell (Angela Schwartz, '"Come to the Fair": Transgressing Boundaries in World's Fairs Tourism', in Eric Zuelov (ed.), *Touring beyond the Nation: A Transnational Approach to European Tourism History* (Farnham, 2011), pp. 79–102).

In 1857, Turgenev went to the Art Treasures Exhibition in Manchester, one of the biggest of its kind, with 16,000 artworks on display, including many Old Masters. The exhibition drew over 1.3 million visitors from all over Europe to the northern industrial city, many of them travelling, as Turgenev did, with an excursion ticket from London. The Manchester industrial élite, led by George Scharf, the art critic, had organized the show to put their city on the cultural map on a par with London and Paris, whose recent international exhibitions they had contributed to. Turgenev was delighted by its 'many wondrous things', the Raphaels and Rembrandts and Michelangelos, which were arranged in chronological order to show the development of art – at that time a relatively new way of organizing public galleries, pioneered in Berlin's Royal Museum by Gustav Waagen, one of the art scholars behind the Manchester exhibition, but yet to be applied in London's National Gallery.[23]

The nineteenth century was the golden age of the public gallery and museum. Royal collections were opened up in palaces that became themselves more generally accessible – a process that had begun in the final decades of the eighteenth century – or were moved to newly opened national galleries. It is no coincidence that the development of a European tourist trade took place at the same time as the foundation of national collections right across the Continent: London's Victoria and Albert Museum (1852) and National Portrait Gallery (1856); the Hermitage in St Petersburg (1852); the Neue Pinakothek in Munich (1853); the Semper Gallery of Old Masters in Dresden (1854); the Scottish National Gallery in Edinburgh (1859); the National Gallery in Berlin (1876); and the Kunsthistorisches Museum in Vienna (opened in 1891 but planned from the 1850s).[24]

Writers' homes and literary landmarks were also becoming major tourist attractions. Organized excursions to literary shrines account for much of the early tourist traffic within Britain: 'Brontë country' in the Pennines, Wordsworth's Lake District, Shakespeare's birthplace in Stratford – all of these were opened up to tourists by the railways in the 1840s and 1850s. The same was true on the Continent for the homes of writers such as Rousseau, Voltaire, Petrarch, Schiller and Goethe, whose house in Frankfurt was purchased for the public in 1863.[25]

For British tourists on the Continent it was Byron's writings that determined where they went more than any other works of literature. Travellers to the Rhine and Italy were guided by his poetry, which told them what they ought to feel in those places featured in his verse. The Murray guides selected their itineraries to take in as many of the places mentioned by Byron as they could, making sure to cite his poetry at every opportunity (John Murray was also his publisher) and even issuing a pocket edition of his poetry for travellers. If the poet had liked a certain painting or building it would be pointed out to the readers of the guides. With some sites, like the Terni Falls, where the traveller was meant to experience the sublime, Murray's *Handbook* deferred to Byron altogether, merely adding 'such historical and other facts as may be useful' as a supplement to the 'beautiful passage from Lord Byron, in whose judgement, either from above or below, they are worth all the cascades and torrents of Switzerland put together; the Staubach, Reichenbach, Pisse Vache, Falls of Arpenaz &c., are rills in comparative appearance'.

> The roar of waters! – from the headlong height
> Velino cleaves the wave-worn precipice;
> The fall of waters! rapid as the light
> The flashing mass foams shaking the abyss;
> The hell of waters! where they howl and hiss,
> And boil in endless torture; while the sweat
> Of their great agony, wrung out from this
> Their Phlegethon, curls round the rocks of jet
> That guard the gulf around, in pitiless horror set . . .

Childe Harold's Pilgrimage (1816)

The Italian tourist trade was quick to recognize the commercial opportunities of this Byronic trail through Italy. There were Hotel Byrons and Lord Byron restaurants everywhere. In his *Pictures From Italy* (1846) Dickens recounts an episode in Bologna, then 'being very full of tourists', when the waiter at an inn, recognizing that he was from England,* began speaking about 'Milord Beeron' at any opportunity:

> He knew all about him, he said. In proof of it, he connected him with every possible topic, from the Monte Pulciano [sic] wine at dinner which was grown on an estate he had owned, to the big bed itself, which was

---

* The privilege was not reserved for Englishmen. Crossing into Italy in 1831, Berlioz met a Venetian seaman who likewise wanted to tell him about Byron, whom he claimed to have met (Cairns (trans. and ed.), *Memoirs of Hector Berlioz*, pp. 174–5).

the very model of his. When I left the inn, he coupled with his final bow in the yard a parting assurance that the road by which I was going, had been Milord Beeron's favourite ride.[26]

Murray's guidebooks, more than any other, influenced where British tourists went, what they considered 'worth seeing', and how they saw those things. There were other pocket guides for tourists in Europe: Karl Baedeker's, modelled on the Murrays, though geared more to high culture, whose handbooks first appeared in Germany in 1839 (they were translated into English from 1861); the *Guides Joannes*, begun in 1841 by the French travel writer and geographer Adolphe Joanne, a cousin of Louis Viardot, which would later be rebranded by Hachette as the *Guides Bleus*; and the *Satchel Guides* for Americans in Europe, published in New York by Hurd and Houghton from the 1870s.[27] But the Murrays were the most successful. They became the model for all modern tourist guides and were widely used by European travellers, Turgenev among them, in preference to their German and French equivalents.

The first Murray guide, *A Handbook for Travellers on the Continent*, appeared in 1836, sold 10,000 copies in the first five years, and went into its seventeenth edition in 1871. By this time there were separate Murray guides to every country in Europe, from Portugal and Spain to Greece, Turkey, Russia, Poland and Finland, with the most successful, such as those on the Rhine, Switzerland and Italy, selling several tens of thousands of copies each in the 1850s and 1860s. As one reviewer put it in 1855, 'since Napoleon no man's empire has ever been so wide'.[28]

Murray's most important innovation – and one copied by the Baedeker and Joanne guides – was his use of an itinerary. It made his guides more compact and easier to use than previous handbooks. Johann Gottfried Ebel's Swiss guidebook, a mainstay of the Grand Tour, published first in German in 1793, and then translated into English, French and other languages, appeared, for example, in two heavy volumes. The sites of interest were listed in it alphabetically, necessitating the use of a separate map.[29] Murray's books, by contrast, organized the sites into convenient routes, thus dispensing with the need to consult a map. The routes were chosen by the ease and speed of travel between the main sites of interest, thereby channelling the tourist traffic along the major railways, roads and steam shipping lines. In this way the cultural map of Europe was redrawn.

The new guidebooks were essential reading for a public unaccustomed to foreign travel. Most of their readers were travelling abroad for the first time, venturing into foreign countries where they did not speak the languages. They depended on the handbooks to tell them where to go and what to see; to plan their routes so that they could view as much as possible and avoid wasted days in the few weeks they had free for travelling. As Baedeker put it in a letter to Murray in 1852:

> the number of tourists is increasing by the year. Not only rich people set out as soon as the weather improves, the lower classes vie with them in this respect. Students and others belonging to the latter class wish to know in advance more or less what their journey is going to cost them, what they will have to pay at hotels, tips etc. etc.[30]

Like the Baedeker and Joanne guides, the Murrays concentrated on giving practical and descriptive information for the major tourist sites. Murray told his readers what to see. As he wrote in his *Handbook for Travellers on the Continent* in 1858, his guides worked on the principle of limiting themselves 'to matter-of-fact descriptions of what *ought to be seen* at each place', rather than bewildering readers 'with an account of all that *may* be seen'. Intended to appeal to the 'intelligent English traveller', this meant, as one historian has put it, 'outlining possible itineraries, avoiding too many chronological details, judiciously including anecdotes about monuments and other sites, adopting a condensed writing style and extracting pithy quotes from Scott, Byron or other literary figures who had written well and elegantly about particular places'.[31]

The guides helped tourists overcome their insecurities by giving them received opinions with which to respond in a correct fashion to the cultural sites and artefacts they encountered on their travels. Serious tourists followed the advice of their guidebooks religiously, sometimes going without food or sleep to make sure they saw everything. On a tour through Switzerland in 1863, Jemima Morrell, the author of a celebrated *Swiss Journal*, became irritated with her travelling companions when they stopped to admire some fine crockery, seriously telling them they could not spare the time 'when within one hundred yards is that view which Murray says is worth the cost of a journey from London to see'. Heine complained that one could not move in Italy for English tourists 'swarming everywhere; there is no lemon tree without an English lady nearby smelling its perfume, no picture gallery without at least sixty or so Englishmen, each with a guidebook in their hands checking that everything is where it should be'. The Polish philosopher and literary historian Michal Wiszniewski was amused and appalled by the English in Italy, who 'walk everywhere with *Murray's Guide* in hand, wandering open-mouthed through galleries and temples, swallowing everything they hear from the most stupid cicerone'. Watching a group of his countrymen in a church in Italy, James Bryce, an Oxford don, thought these tourists saw 'the sights for no purpose but that of verifying their Murray, which they do with praiseworthy perseverance in front of a crowd of kneeling worshippers'.[32]

By directing tourists on to the beaten track, the Murray guides did more than anything to standardize the experience of foreign travel. Tourists travelled in the expectation of finding those things mentioned in their guidebooks, and those sites became commodities – 'culturally valuable objects' acquired by the tourist in the act of seeing them.[33] Souvenirs enabled tourists to materialize these symbolic acquisitions. Along the tourist routes in Italy, shops sold terracotta replicas of museum sculptures, imitation Murano glass vases, photographic reproductions of Old Masters, models of the Roman temples and countless other souvenirs manufactured specially for the tourist market. In Dickens's *Little Dorrit* (1857) the Meagles home in Twickenham is filled with them:

> There were antiquities from Central Italy, made by the best modern houses in that department of industry; bits of mummy from Egypt (and perhaps from Birmingham); model gondolas from Venice; model villages from Switzerland; morsels of tessellated pavement from Herculaneum and Pompei, like petrified minced veal; ashes out of tombs, and lava out of Vesuvius; Spanish fans, Spezzian straw hats, Moorish slippers; Tuscan hairpins, Carrara sculpture, Trasteverini scarves, Genoese velvets and filigree, Neapolitan coral, Roman cameos, Geneva jewellery, Arab lanterns; rosaries blest all round by the Pope himself, and an infinite variety of lumber.[34]

Travel agencies were equally important in standardizing tourist routes. Many companies responded to the mid-century boom in railway travel on the Continent – Thomas Bennet, who organized excursions to Norway; Henry Gaze, who arranged trips to the battlefield of Waterloo and to Switzerland; the Carl Stangen firm in Germany – but none was as successful as Thomas Cook and Son. An activist in the temperance movement, Cook had started in the early 1840s by organizing day-trips on the Midland railways as a sober entertainment for artisans, mechanics and the working class. His breakthrough came in 1851, when he sold 165,000 return tickets to the Great Exhibition in London on special excursion trains. In 1855, for the Paris Exposition Universelle, he organized and led his first excursions to Europe, two 'grand circular tours' from Harwich to Antwerp, Brussels, Waterloo, Cologne, up the Rhine by steamer to Heidelberg, Baden-Baden and Strasbourg, and then by rail to Paris and London, a two-week journey for £10. Losing money from these tours, it was only six years later, in 1861, that he returned to the Continent, organizing tours to Switzerland and Italy which would become the mainstay of his business for many years.

Cook believed his mission was to facilitate independent travel for as many people as he could. By purchasing in bulk, he was able to obtain discounted rates on railway fares for special tourist routes or 'tours' advertised in *The Excursionist*, his company journal, launched in 1851, which had a monthly circulation of 58,000 by the mid-1860s. A three-week tour to Switzerland in 1863 cost £9 (230 francs) in fares, with hotels and food estimated at a further £6 per person, depending on choice, for neither was provided by the company, although Cook, who went himself on a number of the tours, did make recommendations (from 1868, he introduced a voucher system for travellers at some hotels which became the basis of the modern package holiday). These prices made his tours not only affordable to the middle classes but highly attractive, given their desire to see the most important things in a short amount of time. 'There is a class – a large class who can and do most thankfully appreciate our arrangements,' Cook wrote of his excursionists to Switzerland and Italy in 1865. 'They wish to see something definitely marked out for them, to be assured of its practicability and safety; and they go with all the more encouragement if they can have the personal presence of someone in whom they can confide.' Women were encouraged to travel on their own, knowing it was 'safe and proper' to do so if they were with Cook; the spinster, governess and female schoolteacher became familiar figures on his tours.[35]

In 1865, the novelist Charles Lever, who lived in Italy as the British vice-consul at La Spezia, launched an attack on the 'Cookies'. 'It seems that some enterprising and unscrupulous man has devised the project of conducting some forty or fifty persons, irrespective of age or sex, from London to Naples and back for a fixed sum,' Lever wrote in *Blackwood's Magazine*.

> The thing has 'taken' – the project is a success; and as I write, the cities of Italy are deluged with droves of these creatures, for they never separate, and you see them, forty in number, pouring along a street with their director – now in front, now at the rear – circling around them like a sheep-dog – and really the process is as like herding as may be. I have already met three flocks, and anything so uncouth I never saw before – the men, mostly elderly, dreary, sad-looking, evidently bored and tired – the women, somewhat younger, travel-tossed and crumpled . . . I tell you deliberately it will be all but impossible to live abroad if these outpourings continue; for it is not merely that England swamps us with everything that is low-bred, vulgar, and ridiculous, but that these people, from the hour they set out, regard all foreign countries and their inhabitants as something in which they have a vested right. They have paid for the Continent as they paid for Cremorne [the pleasure gardens in Chelsea] and they *will* have the worth of their money.[36]

Many commentators expressed horror at tourists 'doing Europe', though none with a snobbery to match Lever's. The art critic John Ruskin was scathing in his condemnation of the English touring Europe in a few weeks by rail. 'No changing of place at a hundred miles an hour will make us one whit stronger, happier, or wiser. There was always more in the world than men could see, walked they ever so slowly; they will see it no better for going fast,' he wrote. In 1864, he castigated an audience of Manchester industrialists for building the railways, which he believed were ruining Europe through the tourist industry:

> You have put a railway bridge over the fall of Schaffenhausen. You have tunnelled the cliffs of Lake Lucerne by [William] Tell's chapel; you have destroyed the Clarens shore of the Lake of Geneva; there is not a quiet

valley in England that you have not filled with the bellowing fire, nor any foreign city in which the spread of your presence is not marked by a consuming leprosy of new hotels and perfumers' shops.[37]

The idiocy of tourist travel struck Fontane too. In *Modern Travels* he wrote sarcastically about a group of tourists from 'a small town rifle club' visiting Reinhardsbrunn Castle, once the seat of the Ernestine Saxon dukes near Gotha. They are overawed to learn that the Elector Ernst killed 50,157 head of game over twenty-five years; they write down the imposing figure in their notebooks and gleefully anticipate those future moments when they will have the leisure to calculate how many head per day that works out as.[38]

Turgenev was equally scornful about the tourists he observed in Italy. He ridiculed the English, who, 'having seen a woman with red hair in one town, write in their notebooks that the female population of that town is red-headed'. Watching the Russian tourists, in particular, he maintained that nine out of ten of them were bored, because their tourism was of a superficial kind. They saw only the external features of the city and collected facts about the places they had seen, but did not interact with the people or their culture. They went 'from place to place, never stepping outside their own sphere, or environment, circumscribed by hotels, waiters, bills, bells, servants, hired carriages, hired donkeys and their guides'. To travel 'without entering the life and culture of foreigners' was 'not worth it', he concluded, for there was no point in travelling abroad 'just to breathe the banal air of banal rooms in various Hôtel Vittoria, des Princes, Stadt Berlin, etc'.[39]

Underlying these critiques of tourism was the idea of travel as a higher order of experience abroad. 'Travellers' set themselves apart from vulgar 'tourists' by claiming for themselves a deeper knowledge and appreciation of the life and culture of the foreign places they visited. Whereas 'tourists' went in groups, never mixing with the local population nor staying long enough to try, 'travellers' liked to think they were exploring the 'undiscovered' places of a country, experiencing its 'real', 'authentic' culture in a spiritually enriching way.[40]

Travel writing encouraged this idea. The first great period of railway building coincided with a golden age of travel writing in Europe. There was a boom in the publication of travel books during the 1850s, while new periodicals, like the *Tour du monde*, launched in France in 1860, proved immensely popular, encouraging the appearance of other travel magazines.[41] A number of important and well-known writers contributed to the popularity of the genre, including Stendhal, with his account of travelling through France, Switzerland and Italy, *Mémoires d'un touriste* (1838); Fontane, with his travel writing from England, *Ein Sommer in London* (1854), and five volumes of wanderings through Prussia, *Wanderungen durch die Mark Brandenburg* (1862–89); Dostoevsky with his critical perceptions of Europe from his travels there in 1862, *Winter Notes on Summer Impressions* (1863); and Flaubert and du Camp, with their rich evocation of French peasant life and folklore, *Par les champs et par les grèves,* based on a journey through Brittany in 1847 and published in 1881.

Ruskin's writings on the art of Italy inspired many travellers. Perhaps more than any other nineteenth-century literary work, they embodied the idea of travel as an aesthetic experience of place, setting it apart from tourism. Horrified by the hurried, superficial sightseeing encouraged by the railways and the Murray guides, Ruskin brought out his own books on art and architecture designed to help the serious traveller cultivate an appreciation of the art and culture of a place. In *The Stones of Venice* (1851–3), originally published in three volumes but abridged 'for the use of travellers', and later in his *Mornings in Florence* (1875), Ruskin sought to provide practical advice on what was really worth seeing. He gave scholarly information on the most important buildings and works of art, indicated the best times to see them, and advised how long to spend on each and how long to rest between them to keep the senses fresh. Ruskin's books became essential guides to the cultural experience of Italy. They were cited frequently by the Baedeker and Murray guides, and were often used as supplements to them by travellers. His influence helped to change the tourist cultural map, encouraging the British to travel to the Alps and Venice, for example, in larger numbers than they had done before. *The Stones of Venice*, in particular, raised appreciation for the art and architecture of that city. It did more than any other work to turn Venice from a run-down stop-off on the Grand Tour into an important tourist destination in its own right (it inspired Marcel Proust, whose narrator in *À la recherche du temps perdu* visits Venice with his mother on the back of his enthusiasm for Ruskin).[42]

No less widely used by travellers were the many guides to Europe's art museums by Louis Viardot. Louis had developed his extensive knowledge of the newly opened public art collections of the Continent on his travels with Pauline. Accompanying her on her European tours, he would spend his days in the museums of the major cities cataloguing all their works and writing articles about the collections for the European press. Louis was the first to bring the contents of these new museums to wide public attention. Between 1852 and 1855 he compiled five museum guides, each one published by Hachette in its pocket travel editions under the title, *Guide et memento de l'artiste et du voyageur*, with detailed descriptions of the collections: *Les Musées de France, Les Musées d'Italie, Les Musées d'Espagne, Les Musées d'Allemagne, Les Musées d'Angleterre, de Belgique, de Hollande et de Russie*. The guides were immensely popular. They sold tens of thousands of copies in several French editions, and in many languages. Perhaps only Gautier was better known for his writings on the major art collections of Europe.[43]

Methodical and scholarly, Louis's works had an important influence on the reorganization of Europe's major art collections. He had strong opinions on how paintings should be shown. This was still a time when the newly opened public galleries displayed their paintings without much rhyme or reason, covering walls with motley pictures from waist height to the ceiling. Louis's books helped to establish modern curatorial principles. His guides were organized into national schools and periods in the history of art – a pedagogic scheme adopted by most galleries by the final decades of the nineteenth century. He could not stand to see copies mixed in with originals, or mediocrities with masterpieces, and would fume when paintings were displayed poorly – small works hung too high or detailed paintings placed near windows so that they could not be seen for reflections. He corrected errors of attribution, including some by London's National Gallery, which had mixed up its Zubaráns and Riberas. He indicated gaps in the major collections (there were no Russian paintings at all in the Louvre, for example, and no works by English painters such as Turner, Gainsborough, Hogarth or Reynolds). He pointed out where he believed that an artist or whole school of paintings had been given too much space. He did not hesitate to voice his personal opinions. A fierce defender of artistic liberty, he hated anything that smacked of court or official art. Many of his harshest words were reserved for Charles Le Brun, who had been the favourite court painter of Louis XIV, whose high reputation he thought was undeserved. He was equally dismissive of artistic works of non-European origin (he wanted the entire ethnographic section of the Louvre closed down on the grounds that it contained mere 'bric-à-brac'). But he was a fierce campaigner for painters he believed had been unfairly forgotten or neglected (Vermeer and Rembrandt, for example) and played an important part in the rediscovery of Spanish art in the middle decades of the nineteenth century. He helped the Louvre to organize its Spanish Gallery, opened to the public in 1838, and advised the Prado on the reorganization of its royal collection in the 1840s and 1850s.[44]

How did the railways affect the routes that tourists took on their journeys through Europe? Did they go to the same places visited on the Grand Tour? Or did the widening railway network encourage them to venture off the beaten track?

Before the railways, travellers from northern Europe had a clear and direct aim on the Grand Tour: to get to Italy as fast as possible. For most the Italian peninsula *meant* culture. The majority of British tourists travelled via Paris and Lyons, and then either crossed the Alps or risked the hazards of a rough sea-crossing from Marseilles or Toulon to Livorno or any of the other Italian ports along the Mediterranean coast. They might take a different route on the way home, perhaps going via Venice and Vienna, or taking in the Rhine. But all these places were basically stopoffs on the way to Italy and back. Few tourists deviated from the well-established routes. Towards the end of the eighteenth century there was a growing tourist traffic on its way to Italy through Germany – Hanover, Mannheim, Heidelberg and Dresden became minor destinations on the Grand Tour – but the numbers overall were very small. Hardly anybody went to Spain or Portugal or Scandinavia or Eastern Europe or Russia or the Balkans. The choice of routes was basically determined by cultural preference. Transport had little to do with it. There were few important changes in the transport system before the nineteenth century – some notable improvements in the postal roads through France which cut the journey time from Paris to Marseilles, but otherwise the trip to Italy took as long in the 1780s as it had done a hundred years before.[45]

Options changed from the 1820s, when the introduction of steamboats transformed river travel against the current, opening up the Rhine and the Swiss Lakes for travellers to Italy. Steamboat travel along the Rhine became immensely popular – with a million passengers a year travelling with just the Prussian–Rhenish Steamboat Company by the mid-1830s – not only as an easy route to Basel and across the Alps to Italy but as a scenic tour in its own right. Previously the Rhine route had been shunned by travellers on the Grand Tour. Compared to their French equivalents, the German roads were very poor, the inns uncomfortable, and the cities had a reputation for being smelly and dirty. The poet William Wordsworth complained of all these inconveniences on his journeys through Germany in 1820 and 1828. Even Samuel Taylor Coleridge, an ardent admirer of Germany, could not help but comment on the dirt and stench of Cologne.[46] Steamboat travel on the Rhine cut out some of these problems. But it also catered to a growing Rhineland tourist industry fuelled by several cultural trends.

For English travellers the attractions of the Rhine were its natural beauty, the great river meandering its way between the craggy mountains and overhanging rocks, its medieval castles, Gothic churches, its ancient myths and legends, which they had got to know through the writings of the Romantics. Mary Shelley's *Frankenstein* (1818) was one such text. Mary Godwin (as she was then called) had travelled down the Rhine with her future husband, Percy Bysshe Shelley, on their return from Switzerland in 1814. Running out of money, they had been obliged to travel by the cheaper Rhine route rather than return through France. Viktor Frankenstein, the hero of her novel, is transfixed by the 'blending of all beauties' on that stretch of the river between Mainz and Bonn which would become the centre of the Rhineland tourist industry:

> The course of the Rhine below Mayence [the French name for Mainz] becomes much more picturesque. The river descends rapidly, and winds between hills, not high, but steep, and of beautiful forms. We saw many ruined castles standing on the edges of precipices, surrounded by black woods, high and inaccessible. This part of the Rhine, indeed, presents a singularly variegated landscape. In one spot you view rugged hills, ruined castles overlooking tremendous precipices, with the dark Rhine rushing beneath; and, on the sudden turn of a promontory, flourishing vineyards, with green sloping banks, and a meandering river, and populous towns occupy the scene.

But the biggest influence on English Rhineland tourism was Byron's famous stanzas on the neo-Gothic castle at Drachenfels south of Bonn in *Childe Harold's Pilgrimage*:

> The castled crag of Drachenfels
> Frowns o'er the wide and winding Rhine,
> Whose breast of waters broadly swells
> Between the banks which bear the vine.
> And hills all rich with blossomed trees,
> And fields which promise corn and wine,
> And scattered cities crowning these,
> Whose far white walls along them shine,
> Have strewed a scene, which I should see
> With double joy wert thou with me. [47]

For German travellers, who made up a growing share of this tourist traffic, the Rhine's myths were a vital cultural source of their national identity. The legend of the Lorelei Maiden whose siren song lured sailors to their death beneath her 'murmuring rock', a steep slate hill on the right bank of the river near St Goarshausen, inspired much Romantic poetry, most of it originating from the folk songs and poems compiled by Clemens Brentano and his sister Bettina von Arnim in *Des Knaben Wunderhorn* (1805–8). One by Heine, *Die Lorelei* (1824), was in turn set to music by many composers, among them Liszt and Friedrich Silcher, whose version entered into German popular culture. A site of tourist pilgrimage, the Lorelei rock and its legend provided the inspiration for over twenty German operas between 1840 and 1890. Many of them included the Nibelungen myth, which was intertwined with the Lorelei and the Rhineland in the Romantic nationalist imagination, most famously of course *Der Ring des Nibelungen*, which Wagner began working on in 1848, the highpoint of German patriotic sentiment about the Rhine. Only eight years earlier, the French government had laid claim to the left bank of the river as France's border in the east. The left bank had been conquered by the French Revolutionary Army in 1795 but returned to the Germans, most of it to Prussia, at the Congress of Vienna in 1815. The new French claim gave rise to strong nationalist feelings on the German side. Patriotic marching songs were composed to 'The German Rhine' (1840), a popular poem by the Rhenish jurist Nikolaus Becker, which began:

They shall not have the Rhine,
The free German Rhine. Though like greedy ravens
They hoarsely cry for it. So long as calmly flowing
It wears its garment green. So long as oars resounding
Can beat upon its wave.

To which Musset responded for the French in 1841:

...

Let it flow in peace, your German Rhine –
That our Gothic cathedrals
Be modestly reflected in it;
But be fearful lest your drunken airs
Awaken the dead from their bloody repose.[48]

Steamboats also increased tourist traffic to the Swiss Lakes and the Alps, which, like the Rhine, had been turned into popular destinations by the Romantics and their cult of the sublime. Previously the mountains had been seen as obstacles to be got over on the way to Italy. The decades following the publication of Rousseau's *La Nouvelle Héloïse* (1761), set on the shores of Lake Geneva, saw the arrival of a steady stream of tourists – Shelley and Byron most famously among them in the summer of 1816 – hoping to identify the beauty spots described in the novel. Voltaire's château at Ferney could be visited at the same time. From Geneva, the valley of Chamonix was easily accessible, and it was soon established as a tourist route to see nature at its most divine. Other areas were opened up by the steamboats: the Rhine Falls at Schaffhausen, easily reached by steamer from Basel, where several generations of English tourists gazed in wonder at the wild beauty of the waterfalls; the Bernese Oberland, which had resorts around Lake Thun and Lake Brienz catering to English tourists; and the shores of Lake Lucerne, where many tourists came to climb the heights of Mount Rigi from which they could get a panoramic Alpine view.[49]

The railways built on these developments, bringing tourists to the Rhine and Switzerland in much greater numbers than had travelled there before, and placing these destinations at the centre of the European tourist industry on a par with Italy.

The impact of the railways was complex. The Grand Tour route to Italy remained the preoccupation of Victorian travellers. But the railways gave them more ways to get there, allowing them to visit different cities on the way, and to go at different times throughout the year (trains were less affected by winter conditions than carriages had been). They enabled travellers to plan their journeys to be in the best places at the right time – Venice for the Carnival, Rome for Easter, and so on – as Turgenev and Botkin had done in 1857. The railways also offered special trains and discounts for the major tourist companies, such as Thomas Cook, the main British supplier of railway tickets on the Continent, whose core business was in organizing trips to Switzerland and Italy for the largest public possible. This meant focusing on the most popular and well-established routes – rather than opening new markets by organizing tours to less familiar places in Europe. It was not until 1867 that the company ventured into Austria, and even later when it began to offer tours to Scandinavia (from 1875), Spain (1876) and the Balkans (1889).

The railways did, however, open some new destinations on the Continent. They directed tourist traffic to spas and seaside towns, for example. Spa towns such as Baden-Baden, Wiesbaden and Bad Ems in Germany became busy tourist centres because they were connected to the railway. As summer resorts frequented by the aristocracy and occasional royalty they were able to attract a wealthy clientele from all over Europe by building luxury hotels, restaurants, casinos, concert halls and parks for promenades. The same was true of Ostend in Belgium, Bad Ischl in Austria, and Vichy, Aix-les-Bains and Plombières in France, as it was of seaside towns once made fashionable by emperors and kings but democratized by the railways: Scheveningen on Holland's North Sea coast; Norderney on the coast of Hanover; Heringsdorf on Prussia's Baltic Sea; Trouville, Deauville and Cabourg (immortalized as Balbec in Proust's *À la recherche du temps perdu*) on the coast of Normandy; Cannes, Nice and Biarritz in the south of France; and San Sebastian in Spain. Other summer resorts were creations of the railways and more democratic from the start – the Jewish-dominated spa towns of Karlsbad and Marienbad in Bohemia, for example, which owed their rapid growth to their central position on the continental railway map.[50]

But perhaps the biggest change the railways brought about was in the preferred route to Switzerland and Italy: whereas travellers before the railways had mostly gone through France, where the roads were better than in Germany, the development of the German railways re-directed tourists through the Rhineland on their journey south.

The route from London through Holland, Belgium, the Rhine and Germany to Switzerland was opened up by the railways in the 1850s, the first decade of mass tourism on the Continent. It was soon estab-lished as the most common British route to Italy. Travelling this way, tourists could take in the Rhineland sites celebrated by the Romantics and made famous by Queen Victoria and Prince Albert, who toured the Rhine in 1845; they could then continue through Bavaria, where the British royals were often to be seen, or go more directly to Basel, from where they could visit the Rhine Falls and cross the Alps to Italy. The French route to Italy was less travelled by comparison, even though the Paris–Marseilles line, completed by the mid-fifties, was as efficient as the German route.

It was a turn-around from the days of the Grand Tour, when the French route had been much preferred. British cultural preferences had a lot to do with this. There was a strong anti-French feeling carried over from the wars against Napoleonic France. This was matched by a marked Germanophilia in Victorian society, reinforced by the German background of the royal family, by the pro-German orientation of the Anglican and Nonconformist movements, and by the fashion for the neo-Gothic architectural style, as seen in the building in London of the Albert Memorial (1861), St Pancras Station (1868) and the new Houses of Parliament (between 1840 and 1870). While the British were generally mistrustful of the Papist French, they looked upon the Ger-mans as their Anglo-Saxon brethren.[51] But the rise of German culture on the British tourist map must also be explained by the simple fact that railways made it easier to explore.

3

It is delightful to see, as we travel on, the breaking down of partition walls of prejudice, the subduing of evil passions and unhappy tempers, the expansion of the intellect, the grasping for information, the desire for books and the eagerness of their perusal, the benevolent sympathies excited by a more extended knowledge of the circumstances and suffer-ings of fellow-creatures.

Thus Thomas Cook on the beneficial impact of travelling abroad. The opening up of Europe by the railways gave new meaning to the old idea of travel broadening the mind. People talked of the railroads ending hatreds and divisions by the removal of barriers. 'Travel is fatal to prejudice, bigotry and narrow-mindedness,' Mark Twain wrote in *Innocents Abroad* (1869), his account of a railway journey across Europe to the Holy Land. This idea became a commonplace of nineteenth-century literature.[52]

But there was more at stake than overcoming narrow-mindedness. The sense of being 'European' was itself bound up with the outward-lookingness that came with international travel. The railways enabled people across Europe to see themselves as 'Europeans' in ways they had not done before – some more so, some less so, depending on their history and geography. This feeling of being part of 'Europe' was connected to the possibility of travelling by rail to any part of it. Any small town with a branch-line station could see itself at the centre of a web of railway lines spreading out across the Continent.

'Thirty years ago not one countryman in a hundred had seen the metropolis,' declared *The Times* in 1850. 'There is now scarcely one in the same number who has not spent his day there.'[53] By the end of 1851, 6 million British countrymen and women had travelled into London for the Great Exhibition, where they could see goods and artefacts from fifty different countries and forty colonies from all quarters of the globe. Around the exhibition, in any number of the restaurants that sprang up to feed the crowds, they could also try out different foods from France, Germany and Italy, even Indian curries. The famous chef Alexis Soyer opened a Symposium of All Nations, a gastronomic version of the Exhibition, where 1,500 people could be seated at a gigantic table and inspect the kitchen, where cooks from different countries, even some from China, were at work. For the majority of the exhibition's visitors, it was their first glimpse of life in foreign lands.

At the Paris Exposition Universelle, in 1855, visitors could see not only manufactures but works of art from almost every country in Europe. It was the first time such an international collection of modern paintings had been gathered in a single space, the first time living artists from so many countries had a place to meet and compare their work. At the Palais des Beaux Arts, noted Gautier in his survey of the artworks on display, the public 'would learn more in four hours than in fifteen years' of travelling abroad. The result of this encounter between Europe's artists, concluded Gautier, was a cosmopolitan eclecticism of artistic styles that had its natural centre in Paris, the artistic capital of the world.[54] The art critic Théophile Thoré (best known for his rediscovery of Vermeer's paintings) believed that a 'European school' of art was being formed by this international exchange. 'When the arts of all countries, with their native qualities, have become accustomed to reciprocal exchanges,' he wrote in 1855, 'the character of art will be enriched everywhere to an incalculable extent, without the genius peculiar to each nation being changed. In this way a European school will be formed in place of the national sects which still divide the great family of artists; then, a universal school, familiar with the world, to which nothing human will be foreign.'[55]

This emerging European sensibility was most strongly felt among Europe's cultural élites. For them it was part of a cosmopolitan world-view formed by international travel, the learning of languages, and openness to foreign cultures, without any necessary weakening of their national identity. Turgenev was a living example of this cosmopolitanism. He travelled constantly. His ability to make himself at home in Berlin, Paris, Baden-Baden, London or St Petersburg (and he would live in all of them) was the essence of his Europeanness. The 'Europe' he inhabited was an international civilization, a Republic of Letters based on the Enlightenment ideals of reason, progress and democracy. This is what he meant when he proclaimed: 'I am a European, and I love Europe; I pin my faith to its banner, which I have carried since my youth.' His literary personality was formed by Goethe, Shakespeare and Cervantes before he came to Gogol. His library at Spasskoe contained books in nine European languages. Although he felt himself to be a Russian, and at times such as the Crimean War could be fiercely patriotic, he was opposed to nationalism in all its forms, and refused to believe that the calls of any country should come before those of humanity. His long absence from the country of his birth earned him the reproaches of compatriots who, in the words of Annenkov, writing in his memoirs in 1880, saw it as 'a lack of national beliefs, the cosmopolitanism of a man of means willing to exchange his civil obligations for the comfort and entertainments of foreign life'. Annenkov defended Turgenev:

> It was not the lack of national sympathies in his soul and not haughty disdain for the tenor of Russian life that made Europe a necessity for his

existence, but the fact that intellectual life flowed more generously there, engulfing shallow ambitions, and that in Europe he felt himself simpler, more effective, truer to himself and freer from paltry temptations than when he stood face to face with Russian reality.[56]

Tensions between national feeling and cosmopolitanism shaped not only the identity of Europeans like Turgenev but European politics as well. While the nineteenth century can be seen in terms of the rise of nationalist movements in Europe, there was at the same time a strong counter-current of internationalist sentiment, rooted in the Kantian Enlightenment ideal of a world political community, which gave rise to optimistic hopes for European unification. The dream of a United States of Europe had been articulated by Napoleon, who came close to realizing it through the Confederation of the Rhine, formed in 1806 by sixteen German states under the protection of the French Empire, and later joined by other European client states. According to one of his admirers, the historian Emmanuel de Las Cases, who followed Napoleon into exile on the island of St Helena after his defeat and took down notes of his reflections, the ex-emperor had aimed to found a European legal system and a European currency. 'Europe would be nothing more or less than a single people, and everyone, wherever they went [in Europe], would find themselves in a common fatherland.'[57]

For the next three decades, Europe's revolutionaries and national liberation movements looked for inspiration to the ideas of European unity developed by the Jacobins. An international fraternity was their best means of struggle against the conservative status quo. This internationalism was an important aspect of the 1848 revolutions. Its most influential voice belonged to Giuseppe Mazzini, leader of Young Italy (Giovine Italia), a revolutionary movement aiming to create an Italian republic, whose democratic nationalism was an inspiration for similar societies in Italy, Poland and Germany. In the Mazzinian view, the establishment of democratic nations would strengthen international brotherhood, leading to a European union of democracies to promote peace. National sentiment and cosmopolitanism were complementary, as long as the moral force of internationalism was strong enough to prevent patriotic feelings from becoming aggressive.[58]

Victor Hugo developed this idea at a peace conference in Paris in August 1849. The democratic revolutions of the previous year had led him to believe that the diverse peoples of the European states would form themselves into an international republic, which he called, at various times, 'les États-Unis d'Europe', 'la République d'Europe', 'les Peuples-Unis d'Europe', and 'la Communauté européene'. The foundation of the Second Empire did not change his view, even though it forced him into exile in Brussels, Jersey and then Guernsey. Appalled by the slaughter of the Crimean War – when Europe's 'railways and steamers, instead of carrying the bountiful gifts of nature to and fro, as friendly exchanges of men, were carrying soldiers and engines of destruction' – he reiterated his belief in 'European brotherhood' as an antidote to nationalism and its tendency to lead to wars. Yet here was an irony. For Hugo's vision of this fraternity was one in which the French would dominate. As he saw it, France was destined to become the leader of any European union by virtue of the international standing of its republican principles. In his introduction to a Paris guide for the Universal Exposition in 1867, he looked forward to a time in the twentieth century when there would be 'one extraordinary nation' on the continent called 'Europe' which had Paris as its capital.[59] Paris may not have become the twentieth-century capital of a united Europe, but it was the centre of the European world in which Hugo's generation lived – as Walter Benjamin would put it, the 'capital of the nineteenth century'.[60]

4

During the years of Turgenev's wandering, Pauline herself was on the move around Europe. Because of her husband's opposition to Napoleon III, her chances of appearing at the Paris Opéra had practically disappeared (her one appearance on any Paris stage since the coup d'état of 1851 had been in *Il Trovatore* at the Théâtre Italien in 1855). To maintain her career as an opera singer, she was forced to go on tour. While Turgenev was in Italy, in November 1857, Pauline set off from Paris on a four-month circuit of Berlin, Warsaw and Leipzig, where she first met the conductor Julius Rietz, who would become her confidant in this period of separation from Turgenev. It was a gruelling schedule, not made any easier by the incomplete state of the railways in Poland and problems with the singers (they could only sing in Polish), which meant that Pauline had to retrain them for their parts.[61]

For the first time in her career, Pauline travelled without Louis for the whole duration of the tour. 'Do you know where I am going?' she wrote with excitement to Turgenev on 21 November, in one of the few letters she sent him in these years. 'To Warsaw! And on my own! That is, except for a maid. Is this not courageous for one who has never relinquished her husband's arm?'[62] A decision had been reached that Louis should remain at home to look after the children while the prima donna went on tour: Paul was only six months old, and Marianne (aged three) and Claudie (five) were still too young to be left without both parents. Pauline wrote to Louis every day. Her letters form a sort of journal of her tour.[63] She missed her children terribly. A devoted mother, she wrote to her *petits monstres* every day; she told them how much she loved them, and asked Louis to 'hug them all until they are red'.[64] She told him that she missed him too. But that was not entirely true. In fact she found it liberating to travel on her own, relieved from the burden of her husband's love, which she could not return, as she confided to Rietz in March 1859:

> I will confess in a whisper, a very, very low whisper close to your ear, that these little journeys which I have made alone this winter have been very salutary holidays for me. On the one hand, they have been reposeful for my heart, somewhat fatigued by the expression of a love which it cannot share; and, on the other, absence can only fortify my friendship, my esteem and my great respect for this man who is so noble and devoted, who would give his life to gratify the least of my caprices, if I had any.[65]

Without Louis by her side, Pauline became her own manager. It was an unusual position for a woman at that time, when under the Napoleonic Code women could not sign a contract without the consent of their husband or father. Setting off from Paris without any guarantees of engagements, she made all the travel arrangements, established contacts with the managers of concert halls and theatres, negotiated contracts, and took all decisions on her own, informing Louis of her progress by letter. She did not express the slightest doubt about her management abilities. Having spent her whole life touring as an independent musician, she was more than able to manage without the guidance of a man. But she missed her husband's support and encouragement, as she wrote in this touching letter on 17 December, following a performance of *Norma* in Warsaw:

Yes, I was happy with myself tonight. Dear friend, I believe that you would have been happy too, you, my best judge, whose benevolent severity, whose reliable tastes are so precious to me, you, who I am so happy to please. Oh my good Louis, how I miss your good, encouraging handshake at the moment of stepping onto the stage. How nice it is to hear a friendly voice who says courage, and to see kind eyes that also say all sorts of good things – and then, when back home, to receive a good kiss of satisfaction from a friend.[66]

Pauline's guiding principle on all her tours was to make as much money as she could. She toured with sell-out operas (*Norma*, *Trovatore* and *The Barber of Seville* went with her to Berlin and Warsaw) and added local songs to please her audience, as she had done in Russia by inserting a Russian air into the Act II lesson scene of *The Barber of Seville*. In Warsaw, for example, she introduced her adaptation of Chopin's six Mazurkas into the lesson scene, which was met with wild applause, and then sang his 'Hulanka', which brought the house down. Financial considerations lay behind her decision to delay her departure from Warsaw. Originally scheduled for 16 January, she postponed it for five days because 'the whole of society is organizing a concert for me, guaranteeing me 500 roubles [2,000 francs] in advance,' as she explained to Louis on 15 January.[67] By this time she had already exceeded her initial aim of going back to Paris with 5,000 roubles (20,000 francs) from Warsaw. She had been sure of that since 21 December, when she had written to Louis that she would be back by February: 'I will have achieved more than my goal, and I will be able not to care about all those petty two-sous concerts or even the 300-franc concerts if it so pleases me.'[68]

At this stage of her career, when her voice was showing clear signs of decline, Pauline depended on these tours to maximize her earnings before finally retiring. Six weeks after her return from Warsaw, Pauline set off for another tour of Germany, performing in Berlin, Weimar, Leipzig and Cologne, and then went to London for the 1858 season, appearing in *La Sonnambula* at Drury Lane, before embarking on a two-month tour of the English provinces. The highlight of her tour was the Birmingham Choral Festival, a popular venue for the performance of oratorios by amateur choirs, where she sang in Handel's *Messiah*, Mendelssohn's *Elijah* and *The Creation* by Haydn, works that drew enormous crowds.[69] From London she then went to Budapest, where

Liszt, her former teacher and old friend, had organized a season for her at the National Theatre. The Hungarians were unfriendly. 'We have not set foot in a single Hungarian home, and have not noticed one Hungarian at our receptions,' Pauline wrote to Turgenev on 18 November 1858. But the tour was lucrative, earning some 5,000 francs.[70]

The next spring, Pauline toured the United Kingdom with the Willert Beale opera company, a troupe of almost thirty performers. The schedule was punishing – seventy performances in over thirty towns, among them Brighton, Birmingham, Wolverhampton, Northampton, Sheffield, Leeds and Liverpool by rail, before crossing the Irish Sea by steamboat to Dublin. The company would often travel through the night to arrive in a new town the next morning, leaving time during the day to recruit and rehearse with a choir before a performance in the evening. Beale gave an upbeat account of the tour in his memoirs. 'The company would travel by train and would always put up in the "first hotels". Dinner was at three o'clock, followed by a concert or an opera in the evening, and then supper' – at which they always drank the finest wines. The only downside, according to Beale, was the grey monotony of the English food and the terrible coffee ('not French or even Italian'), which drove the European singers mad. As the only fluent English-speaker, Pauline was often called upon to act as go-between, a role she found exhausting, as she wrote to Rietz from Dublin in April 1859:

> As I generally have to assume the part of stage-manager for the operas in which I sing, being the only one who speaks English well, I serve as interpreter between all my comrades and the costumers, machinists, choristers, supers, etc. It is far more fatiguing than to sing – after four hours' work on the stage I am worn out.

These provincial tours were a demotion for Pauline. Trading on her past fame annoyed her, particularly in England, where the arts were captive to a celebrity culture. 'It delights me to sing when I feel that it gives the audience pleasure,' she wrote to Rietz from London.

> However, it must be admitted that this reciprocal pleasure is never as complete in England as elsewhere. The audience this evening, for instance, knew that I am a 'celebrated singer' – so it applauds everything that I do with equal warmth. Had I sung not quite as well, it would have been no less well satisfied, and had I sung better, it would not have

been better satisfied! And that is what puts a damper on the artist's enthusiasm. Yes, decidedly, in matters of art, the English are great speculators.

This annoyance may explain her scathing comments on English provincial audiences. Attending a concert conducted by Michael Costa in the Leeds Town Hall (which she considered 'the handsomest and the best in all Europe'), Pauline thought he was a 'good musician' but one who was obliged to 'sacrifice the golden calf to English taste':

> he knows that in order to make certain things penetrate the ears of the English public, one has to speak very loud. They require Cayenne pepper in all sorts of aliments, moral as well as physical. That is the reason why Costa has been obliged to add military band instruments to his orchestra for the oratorios in the Crystal Palace. For the rest, they, with the organ, were all that one heard in that immense hall. Costa, transported to Germany, would be a mediocre person; in England he is a man to whom all the public and the musicians ought to feel profoundly obliged.[71]

In fact 1859 turned out to be the pinnacle of Pauline's career. In the early summer of that year she was approached by Léon Carvalho, the director of the Théâtre Lyrique in Paris, to see if she would sing the title part in Gluck's *Orphée*, one of a series of classical revivals around this time, which Berlioz was rearranging for the stage.[72] Carvalho had been impressed by Pauline's voice when he heard her sing at a benefit concert for his wife, the soprano Caroline Miolan. Bold and willing to take risks, he was not the sort of manager to be deterred by the black mark against Pauline's name because of her husband's republican politics: the Théâtre Lyrique received no state subsidy, and relied entirely on ticket sales. Carvalho gambled on her making a successful return to the Paris opera scene – from which she had been almost totally absent since *Sapho* in 1851 – by taking on the role of Orphée, which he believed would be well suited to her contralto voice. Originally written for an alto castrato (in the 1762 Italian version) or high tenor (in Gluck's French adaptation of 1774), the role called for an extraordinary vocal range and versatility, sonorous at the bottom, agile at the top, along with the presence of a tragic actor on the stage – qualities that Pauline had in spades. It must have come as a delight to her to be selected for the role, which Berlioz had previously thought to give to Stolz, her old rival at the Paris Opéra.[73]

The cultural climate of 1859 augured well for the revival. Interest in the Greek myths was at its height in France. The story of the lyre-playing Orpheus and his attempt to bring back his dead wife, Eurydice, from the underworld was widely known and was even studied by schoolchildren as an ancient example of the contemporary bourgeois virtue of marital fidelity. This explains the huge success of Jacques Offenbach's burlesque operetta, *Orpheus in the Underworld*, a parody of the Gluck opera, which opened at the Bouffes-Parisiens on 21 October 1858.

As a dedicated follower of Gluck, a composer he put on a par with Beethoven, Berlioz was keen to take revenge on Offenbach by restoring *Orphée* to the stage. There were also personal reasons for his involvement in the revival. By currying favour with Carvalho, he hoped to get a production of *Les Troyens* at the Théâtre Lyrique. He had finished

Berlioz, 1857.

his masterpiece in April 1858 but was unable to persuade the Paris Opéra to perform it. Then there was his growing passion for Pauline. The two of them had long been friends. Berlioz was a regular visitor at the Viardots' Thursday salon in the rue de Douai, only a few streets away from his own house in the rue de Calais. He encouraged Pauline to compose. She would frequently discuss her compositions with the composer, to whom she had dedicated her lovely song 'En Mer' (1850). By the mid-1850s she was able to count Berlioz as one of her four 'true friends' (the others being Turgenev, Sand and Scheffer). Berlioz was enchanted by the Viardots. In a letter to his sister in January 1859, he described the delight of

> dining at my neighbours M. and Mme Viardot, a charming family in whose company I breathe more easily. They are so intelligent and so good, the two of them, their children are so gracious and well brought up! The flower of art, moreover, fills their house with scent. They love what I love, they admire what I admire in music, literature, and in matters of the soul.[74]

Later that year, at the music festival in Baden-Baden, where they both appeared in August, Pauline sang some pieces from *Les Troyens* with an orchestra. She excelled in the songs of Cassandra and Dido – so much so that Berlioz confessed his spirits had been 'lifted to the skies' and declared that Pauline would be ideal for either of these parts, perhaps even both of them. In September, he spent two days with Pauline at Courtavenel to begin their work together on *Orphée*. Berlioz was ill, suffering acute neuralgic pain, and emotionally tormented by the difficulties of his marital relations with the singer Marie Recio. Pauline took pity on him, encouraging him to pour out his heart to her, as she later wrote to Rietz:

> The sight of this man, a prey to such mental and physical anguish, so unhappy in spirit, so touched by the kind reception we gave him, torn by horrible tortures of the heart, the violence of the efforts which he makes to hide them . . . – all this, I say, wrings my heart. We took a long walk together, in the course of which he became somewhat comforted and quieted. 'All my life,' he said to me, 'has been only one long and ardent aspiration after an ideal which I had conceived for myself. My heart, eager for love, made its choice directly it found one solitary quality, one of the

graces, belonging to this ideal – alas, disillusionment speedily brought the conviction that I had deceived myself. So my life has gone on, and, at the moment when I feel it to be near extinction, this ideal, which I had had to relinquish as if it were the fantastic dream of a heated imagination, appeared all at once to my dying heart! How can you hope that I should not adore it! Let me spend the last days that are left me in blessing you, in thanking you for coming to prove to me that I was not mad.'

Pauline tried to care for him without giving him romantic hope. 'All in all,' she explained to Rietz, 'you will understand that I am labouring under a very painful impression just now, for my heart is full of kindness, and the pain (quite involuntary) which I give him causes me profound grief. Whenever he shall have conquered the violence of this exalted mood (God grant that it come quickly!) I hope to be able to restore some peace to his soul.'[75]

Back in Paris that autumn, their intimacy grew as they collaborated on *Orphée*. Letters were exchanged on a daily basis – sometimes twice a day – between the rue de Calais and the rue de Douai. 'I am ready to advise you to accept all my suggestions, and we will hold counsel on this subject at six o'clock,' Berlioz wrote towards the end of September.

> I did not know that I could be considered such a good counsellor; but I know even less what sort of counsellor I am. Am I a private counsellor, a royal counsellor, an intimate counsellor, a state counsellor or a town counsellor? Am I not an intimate counsellor? Yes, always ready to give intimate advice, the best possible, if not the easiest to follow. And what category of counsellor are you? You are a musical counsellor, and God knows with what joy I accept your advice.[76]

Pauline had a major influence on the revisions of the score, particularly on the shaping and ornamentation of the vocal lines. She also lent a hand to the work of reducing *Les Troyens* for voice and piano, a job that proved beyond a pianist Berlioz had asked to do the job. Pauline volunteered to undertake the 'impossible task', recalled Saint-Saëns, who was then helping with *Orphée*. 'I saw with my own eyes Mme Viardot, pen in hand, eyes alight, the manuscript of *Les Troyens* on her piano, writing the arrangement of the *Chasse royale* [Royal Hunt]' in the second act.[77]

*

Orphée opened on 18 November 1859. It was a personal triumph for Pauline, despite her singing with a throat condition that marred the quality and power of her voice. Chorley thought that 'its unevenness, its occasional harshness and feebleness', was 'turned by her to good account with rare felicity', and that a more 'honeyed voice' might have been unsuitably feminine for the male title role. 'It may be doubted whether such a perfect representative of Orpheus ever trod the stage as Madame Viardot. Her want of regularity of feature, and of prettiness, helped instead of impaired the sadness and solemnity of the mourner's countenance,' the London critic concluded.[78] George Sand was ecstatic: 'This is no doubt the purest and most perfect artistic expression *that we have seen for a half a century, this Orphée of hers – understood, clothed, played, mimed, sung, spoken,* and *wept through* in the way that she interprets it.' Flaubert thought her Orphée was 'one of the greatest things I know'.[79]

Pauline's triumph owed as much to her dramatic skills as to her musicianship. She made herself believable as the embodiment of Orphée, perfectly expressing his emotional development from fear, doubt and disappointed hope while searching for Eurydice to sublime joy on finding her. 'The acting of Mme Viardot surpassed all my expectations,' noted Marie d'Agoult in her diary. 'I have seen nothing ... that came close to this plastic beauty, to this freedom, in its feeling for antiquity. There was no sense that it was planned, contrived, nothing to remind one of the classroom. She made me think constantly of the most beautiful bas-reliefs and Greek vases.'[80]

Part of her success was the costume she designed with Delacroix. She made a detailed study of classical texts in an attempt to reconstruct the ancient hero's dress.[81] Sand, Dickens, Flaubert and Ingres considered the design to be a work of genius. 'How beautiful you are, Madame!', Ingres wrote to her. 'Like a beautiful figure from Antiquity, you wear your Greek costume with the noble grace and familiarity which the painters struggle to achieve in their paintings' – a sculptural conception of the body in performance that inspired many artists (not least Gustave Moreau and Camille Corot) to take up the Orphée theme.[82] Pauline mentioned the costume in her account of the opening night to Rietz on 21 November:

Yes, my friend, *Orphée* has emerged victorious, triumphant, from the profound oblivion in which it was plunged. It was veritably an enormous success. Your friend was acclaimed, recalled with frenzy. My house has not been empty since 9 o'clock Saturday morning. I shall play this evening, then Wednesday, then Friday, then three times a week till the public and I can stand it no longer. The stage-setting is very fine, without attempting, however, to outshine the music. My costume was thought to be very handsome – a white tunic falling to the knees, a white mantle caught up at both shoulders *à l'Apollon*. Flowing tresses, curled, with the crown of laurel. A chain of gold to support the sword, whose sheath is red. A red cord around the waist – buskins white, laced with red. Every phrase, every word was understood by an intelligent audience composed of all that Paris contains in the way of musicians, amateurs, pedants, bald heads, the world of boredom, youthful lions, etc., etc. Well, people embraced each other in the passage-ways during the intermissions, they wept, they laughed for delight, they trampled the floor – in a word, there was a turmoil, a jubilation, such as I never have seen in Paris. The role of Orphée suits me as if it had been written for me.[83]

Pauline Viardot in *Orphée*, photograph by Disdéri, 1859.

Pauline's prediction was correct. She would play Orphée until the public could 'stand it no longer'. By the end of 1859 she had performed it twenty times; by the end of the 1861 spring season, 121 times; and in three years she would sing the part altogether 150 times. This was an extraordinary run for any opera at that time. It was no doubt in part sustained by those who came to the Théâtre Lyrique mistakenly believing they were going to see Offenbach's *Orpheus in the Underworld*, then still running at the Bouffes-Parisiens, and 'were surprised to find that Gluck's opera was not funny'.[84] But, even so, the staying power of *Orphée* was bettered only by Gounod's *Faust*, which had opened at the Théâtre Lyrique in March 1859 and ran alongside *Orphée* on alternate nights until 1862. *Faust* clocked up 314 performances before 1869, when it transferred to the Paris Opéra, where it was performed a thousand times by the end of the century.[85] The two long runs were the first signs of a repertoire that was becoming stabilized.

The fame of *Orphée* spread throughout the Continent, reviving interest in Gluck's music across Europe. Arrangements of the opera and separate numbers of *Orphée*'s main arias were sold in editions bearing Pauline's name. People travelled from all over Europe to Paris to hear her sing. On the opening night of the 1862 season at the Théâtre Lyrique, Dickens made a special trip from London to see *Orphée*. Henry Chorley and the young Arthur Sullivan were in his travelling party. The opera's themes of loss and resurrection – themes that play such a big part in many of his novels – moved Dickens. So did the singing of Pauline. Dickens was seated in the stalls with several members of his family. From a nearby box, where he was sitting with Louis Viardot, Turgenev watched the English novelist, 'his arms folded tightly across his chest and his face drenched with tears'. The curtain fell and Dickens made his way to the exit. On his way he met Turgenev and Viardot with Carvalho. Dickens's face was still visibly wet with tears. Carvalho took him off as a living tribute to Pauline. '*Madame, je vous présente une fontaine!*' he exclaimed. The next day Dickens sent her a letter:

Dear Madame Viardot,

I cannot help it. I *must* thank you for that wonderful performance of last night. When Monsieur Viardot came upon me by accident, I was holding forth about the first act, to my daughter and sister in law, with tears rolling down my face. I came to you in hardly a better condition. I went away when all was done, in a worse. Nothing can be more magnificent, more true, more tender, more beautiful, more profound!

Faithfully yours always
Charles Dickens.[86]

5

Berlioz remained in love with Pauline for about a year. 'If I had the cleverness of a writer, I would be able to articulate the many qualities of heart and spirit that make you a being apart,' he wrote to her on 13 July 1860, 'but I am, as you have said many times, somebody who only feels. I wish I could be with you now, I would summon all the young ones whom you love so much, beg them to take your two hands, put them into mine, and let me adore them in silence for a while . . . what a treasure!'[87]

After that there was a break in their correspondence for eleven months. When it started up again, Berlioz was cooler in his letters to Pauline. Despite everything that she had done for *Les Troyens*, he refused to let her sing the part of Dido or Cassandra in the production scheduled for the autumn of 1861. Berlioz decided, no doubt rightly, that her voice was in decline after hearing her perform the role of Leonore in *Fidelio* at the Théâtre Lyrique, a Carvalho production attempting to capitalize on the commercial success of *Orphée*, in July 1860; and his impression was confirmed when she sang for him in Baden in August. But there was more to Berlioz's cooling-off.

He was angered by developments in the early months of 1861, when Pauline sang to great acclaim some excerpts from Gluck's opera *Alceste* in a concert at the Paris Conservatoire, whereupon the Paris Opéra invited her and Berlioz to stage the work. Pauline asked him to make some alterations to the score to make it easier for her to sing, but Berlioz refused, accusing her of only wanting changes that would help her 'sell the published arrangements for voice and piano later on, as you have done for Orphée's aria'. Outraged by Pauline's mercenary attitude, Berlioz complained to Alphonse Royer, the director of the Opéra, on 31 March 1861:

Absolute fidelity of interpretation is as necessary for the operas of Gluck as it is for the works of great dramatic poets, and it is just as senseless and revolting to pervert his melodies and recitatives by adding notes and changing final cadences as it would be to add words and change rhymes in the verse of Corneille. The only artists to whom one can usefully give advice are those who have a truly moral attitude towards their art, and a sincere respect for great masters . . . As for the others, in spite of any desire they might have to take note of certain opinions, their vulgar vocalist's instincts will always carry the day.

The Opéra set up a committee to look into his complaints, upheld some of them, but ruled that *Alceste* should be staged with Pauline in the title role. Berlioz was eventually persuaded to direct the rehearsals. *Alceste* opened on 21 October 1861; it was a great success; but Berlioz's relations with Pauline had been spoiled.[88]

One last thing had taken place to drive the two apart. At some point in the spring of 1860, Pauline gave a soirée for Wagner at her house in the rue de Douai in honour of his patron Countess Marie Kalergis, niece of the former Russian Foreign Minister Karl Nesselrode, who had recently provided Wagner with 10,000 francs to relieve him of his debts. It was on this occasion that the love duet from Act Two of *Tristan and Isolde* was first performed, with Wagner and Pauline in the vocal parts and the pianist Karl Klindworth accompanying them, before an exclusive audience of Countess Kalergis and Berlioz, invited by Pauline in an attempt to improve his strained relations with Wagner. Berlioz was envious of Wagner's success, of the patronage he enjoyed from the likes of Countess Kalergis that had liberated him from the need to earn a living, as Berlioz did, from music criticism and concert tours.[89] Berlioz believed that Wagner's opera *Tannhäuser*, which had been commissioned at the Paris Opéra by order of the emperor in March, had blocked the way for his masterpiece *Les Troyens* to be staged there. The very manner of the commission – a wager lost by Napoleon III to Princess Metternich obliging him to agree to her demand to put on *Tannhäuser* – underlined the pointlessness of his years of lobbying on behalf of *Les Troyens*. And if *Tannhäuser* succeeded, *Tristan* would come next. Pauline's support for Wagner's cause was thus bound to madden Berlioz, who might have been forgiven for seeing it as a betrayal. Previously she had expressed her dislike of Wagner's music. 'What deadly monotony!' she had pronounced on first hearing *Lohengrin* (1850). Yet now she was warming to the new music, which so divided critical and musical opinion. One can only imagine what Berlioz felt that evening as he listened to her sing the love duet with his greatest enemy. According to Wagner, 'Berlioz merely expressed himself warmly on the *chaleur* of my delivery, which may very well have afforded a strong contrast to that of my partner in the work, who rendered most of her part in low tones.' As for the countess, she 'remained dumb'.[90]

Emotionally, throughout his years of restless wandering, Turgenev never left Pauline. However far apart they were, because of his travelling in Europe, his long trips back to Russia, or her own efforts to keep a distance between them, he remained in love with her. She was the only woman he would ever love, he confessed to Annenkov in March 1857, at the most painful moment of his break from her, when he resolved to run away to Italy.[91]

Sometimes, on his travels, he would write to her, not with the passion he had previously expressed, but giving her his news, making practical arrangements for his daughter, and asking her to write to him. She seldom did. In March 1858, he travelled from Vienna to hear her sing in the Gewandhaus in Leipzig, although he did not meet her then, travelling straight back to Vienna at the end of the concert. He knew that it would lead to dangerous rumours if he was seen in public with Pauline, who had come to Leipzig unaccompanied by her husband.

He did spend some time every year, however, in Courtavenel. Pauline was not always there. She was usually on tour. But they did pass two months there together in the summer of 1859, a period that marks the resumption of their relationship. Turgenev obviously found it hard to be with Pauline and her family – Louis and the children were all there. 'My health is good but my spirit is sad,' he wrote to Countess Lambert. 'I am surrounded by regular family life. What am I here for? And why? Should I really be turning backwards? You will understand what I want to say, and my position.'[92]

'Turning backwards' meant of course returning to his old position of devotion to Pauline, humble and submissive as he had always been. Gradually, he won back her affections. The summer of 1860 was the turning point. Pauline wrote more frequently, and with greater tenderness than she had for many years. It was a mark of her desire to reassert her claim on his emotions that she summoned him from Germany to look after Paul in Courtavenel. 'Madame Viardot wishes me to go, and her will is my law,' Turgenev wrote to Annenkov, explaining his decision to set off at once, at the beginning of July. 'Her son almost died from pneumonia, and she suffered a great deal. She needs to recover in peaceful, friendly company.'[93] The next month she showed signs of jealousy when he told her that he was expecting to be joined on the Isle of Wight by Maria Markovich, the young Ukrainian writer, who did not come in the end.

Was Turgenev happy to be back in Pauline's life? He did not know. As he wrote to Countess Lambert in 1862, he had come to learn that happiness was not something that a person should expect from life.* The idea of happiness was as alien to him as the appearance of his own youthful self. He understood that he had 'missed out on the main prize in life's lottery', by which he meant the sort of love he wanted with Pauline, but recognized that what he had with her would constitute the basis of his well-being for the rest of his existence. His mood was one of resignation, acceptance of his lot (the idea at the root of the word for 'happiness' in Russian, *schast'ye*), acceptance of his destiny. It was in this spirit that he reconciled himself to his position of devotion to Pauline (his 'need to live for someone else', as he put it to Countess Lambert) as the closest he would get to contentment. 'Be approximately satisfied with approximate happiness,' he advised her, 'the only thing on earth which is beyond doubt and clear is unhappiness.'[94]

Pauline and Turgenev reached a new high in their relationship in the autumn of 1862. They spent part of every day together, just the two of them in his apartment in the rue de Rivoli. On one of these occasions, she drew in his notebook the theosophic symbol of a pentagram made up of two triangles. The drawing was important for Turgenev, who

---

* This remained his attitude throughout his life. In 1882, a year before he died, Turgenev wrote to the Russian writer Mikhail Saltykov-Shchedrin, who had complained of being unhappy: 'Let me console you (though it's not much consolation) with the words of Goethe just before he died. Even though his life had been full of all the joys that life can give – he had lived a glorious life – women had loved him – and fools hated him – and his works had been translated in Chinese – and the whole of Europe had been to worship at his feet – and Napoleon himself had said of him: "*C'est un homme!*" . . . – and nonetheless he said, at the age of eighty-two, that in the course of his whole long life he had felt happiness only for *a quarter of an hour!*' (Turg., vol. 11, pp. 89–90).

The symbol drawn by Pauline Viardot in Turgenev's notebook.

marked it with the inscription: 'This figure was done by P[auline] on 6 Nov./25 Oct. 1862 in my room, in the evening, at rue Rivoli, 210.' The same symbol appears on the title page of several of his manuscripts.[95] The figure symbolized the triangular relationship between Pauline, Louis and Turgenev to which Pauline was now pledged.

5

Europe at Play

It has every requisite for a place of listless idleness. There seems nothing to be done (but play), and the people do it. There never was such a mixture of green, gold, sunshine, flowers, dining, dressing, flirting, and promiscuous idleness as in Baden.

Charles Clark, 'Baden-Baden in 1867'

I

In 1863, the Viardots left France and made their home in Baden-Baden, the fashionable German spa town on the edge of the Black Forest. They had spent four months in Baden (as it was generally known) in the summer of 1862, when Pauline was engaged to sing there for the season, and had enjoyed themselves so much that they decided to move there. Towards the end of their stay they had bought a large house with extensive grounds in the Tiergarten area, a wooded hillside on the southern outskirts of Baden, from which there were lovely views across meadows towards the old ruined castle above the town. Ordering major renovations and the building of a gallery-cum-concert hall, the Viardots returned to Paris for the winter, but they came back at the start of May, after Pauline's last performance of *Orphée*.

Turgenev followed them with Paulinette, then aged twenty, and her governess, renting rooms for the three of them in Lichtental, not far from the Viardot villa, although his daughter did not like it there, could not stand the Viardots, and soon returned to Paris, where she lived at first at their old address in the rue de Rivoli, and when the lease on that expired, in a smaller apartment in Passy. Whether Pauline felt guilty for driving her away is hard to say. In her diary, in July 1863, she remarked only that Paulinette was 'a bad girl' whose main fault was not to appreciate her 'adorable father'.[1]

After years of separation, Turgenev and Pauline had become reunited during recent months. Their relationship was calmer and more stable, closer to a marriage than a love affair, and the move to Germany represented a new start for them. 'We are in paradise,' Turgenev wrote to his friend, the poet Louis Pomey, shortly after his arrival in Baden: 'the countryside is delightful, the weather delightful, the atmosphere delightful, and I have found a delightful small apartment where I intend to give you a delightful evening.'[2]

The move was mainly Pauline's decision. Her singing voice had lost its force, worn out after years of stretching over its extraordinary range, and was 'no longer beautiful', in the view of Clara Schumann's daughter, Eugenie. Having been rejected for a major part in *Les Troyens*, Pauline had decided to retire from the Paris Opéra and the other major houses of Europe to concentrate instead on teaching and composing, limiting her stage performances to small provincial theatres, which in her view were of a higher standard in Germany compared to France. 'In Paris it is impossible for me to do anything satisfactory,' she wrote to Rietz. 'I should have to sing bad music prettily (I hate prettiness in art), and do other things that honourable women ought not to do. Ah, dearest friend, you have no idea of the baseness which rules here now in art and in every sphere of public life.'[3]

The seriousness of German music culture was an attraction for the Viardots, but politics was also driving them away from France. For Louis, a convinced republican, the move was rooted in a 'great hatred' of Napoleon III, as Turgenev described it in a letter to Flaubert. Unlike other radicals of 1848, who had made their peace with the Empire's authoritarianism, Louis remained implacably opposed to the imperial regime, whose crackdown against the press and academic freedom continued to offend his democratic principles well into the 1860s, when censorship was loosened and liberal reforms were introduced. Still, as long as Pauline had a chance of singing on a major Paris stage, he remained with her in the capital and refrained from writing anything that might make life more difficult for her. Following her triumph in *Orphée*, she appeared for two more seasons at the Théâtre Lyrique, and even made a comeback at the Paris Opéra, singing in *Alceste*, *Il Trovatore* and *Les Huguenots*, the last in a performance for Napoleon III and the King of Sweden in August 1861. The next year she had a successful run with *La Favorite* at the Opéra.[4] But as soon as Pauline had retired from the Paris stage, Louis's opposition to Napoleon drove them both into self-imposed exile.

As for Turgenev, he had never liked Paris, though how much that was due to his own situation as a foreigner is difficult to judge. 'I cannot tell you how deeply I hate everything French and especially Parisian,' he wrote to his friend Fet in 1860. The French thought that 'everything that is not theirs is wild and stupid', he told Tolstoy; their heads were filled with clichés and received ideas.[5] Germany was more to his liking. He had been a student in Berlin, spoke the language fluently, and felt a close affinity to German culture. But he would have followed Pauline anywhere. He could not live without the Viardots, he told his friends, and would go wherever they went – to Copenhagen or Stockholm, 'the two most boring cities in the world', or even to Australia.[6]

There was another reason for Turgenev's readiness to follow them to Baden, which for him involved a final rupture with Russia. In 1862, his novel *Fathers and Sons* had received a hostile reception in his native land. Everyone attacked the book – the left because they thought Turgenev had sided with the fathers and because they saw in Bazarov a monstrous caricature of the student radicals; the right because they believed on the contrary that he had taken the side of the sons by failing to denounce the novel's radical hero. Turgenev was dismayed by these attacks. For a while he thought of giving up writing. He was particularly upset by the vitriol of the young Russian radicals, who had thrown at him a 'huge amount of mud and filth (and continue to throw it)', as he explained to Pietsch in 1869. They had cursed Turgenev as a 'Judas, fool, and donkey', even as a 'police spy'. These attacks were behind his decision to make a home in Europe in 1863. They were why he would remain there – making only short trips back to Russia – during the next twenty years.

Baden was an excellent choice for all three of them. It was located near the French border, with a good train service to Paris, following the opening of the Rhine Bridge near Strasbourg in 1861; it had an active cultural and social life; and there was excellent hunting in the lovely countryside around the town. 'In effect,' wrote Louis, 'it has all the advantages of nature – a fertile and pretty country with well-kept farms, mountain forests, healthy air and beneficial thermal waters, hunting, fishing and amusements of all sorts – and moreover it is at the centre of Europe, where all the major routes converge, easily reached by visitors who may not have it as their final destination but who willingly would stop there for a while for the pleasures it offered.'[7] As one of Europe's leading spas, famous for its doctors, sulphurous baths and healing waters, Baden was an ideal place to live for Louis, now in his sixties with an ailing liver, as well as for Turgenev, who suffered terribly from gout. With its luxurious hotels, landscaped parks and promenades, casino, opera house and music festival, it was one of the most fashionable watering places in Europe, a playground for the aristocracy, regularly visited by kings and queens, leading statesmen and ambassadors. So many politicians spent their summers there that it became known as 'Europe's summer capital'. According to a French guidebook of 1858, 'When someone wants to know what is Europe's capital city, one must answer: in winter Paris, in summer Baden.'[8]

Baden was an international town, cosmopolitan in its outlook, liberal in its attitudes – in many ways a symbol of European culture before the age of nationalism ushered in by the Franco-Prussian War and Bismarck's unification of Germany.

Baden was part of a European network of continental spas and sea resorts which became the focus of the summer 'season' for an international public. Its winter population was 8,000 inhabitants, three quarters of them German, but in the 'season' between April and October it played host to 50,000 visitors, who came from all around Europe. The most numerous were the French, who arrived by steamers up the Rhine and by trains that took just ten hours from Paris. There was a Franco-German atmosphere in this summer capital. French was spoken in the town; the local newspaper, the *Badenblätter*, was printed both in French and in German; and French food was served in all the restaurants. But Russians also came in large numbers, around 5,000 every year. The Grand Ducal house of Baden had strong connections to the Romanovs going back to the marriage arranged by Catherine the Great between her grandson, the future Tsar Alexander I, and Princess Louise of Baden in 1793. Since then Baden had become one of Europe's major destinations for the Russian aristocracy, who built mansions there, as well as a retreat for writers such as Vasily Zhukovsky and Gogol.[9]

The town existed solely for pleasure. Mornings were given over to the mineral baths, but in the afternoons promenaders strolled along the Lichtentaler Avenue, a tree-lined parkland walk where men would sit at tables playing dominoes or chess, and pass the time in conversation with other passers-by. Conversation was a prized activity – the simple pleasures of sociability being one of the main attractions of spa resorts such as Baden. The art of conversation was so highly valued that the central landmark of the town, the casino, was housed in the *Konversationshaus*, or Salle de Conversation, where all the promenaders would converge to take refreshment in the garden cafés in front of the casino and listen to the orchestra, which played all day in the bandstand. This is the scene that opens *Smoke* (1867), Turgenev's novel set in Baden, when the orchestra performs 'a potpourri from *La Traviata*, then a Strauss waltz, then "Tell Her", a Russian romance set to music by a diligent kapellmeister' – the last to please the many Russians in the crowd. Carriage rides with picnics in the woods, shooting and fishing were also popular activities. Every other afternoon there were horse races at nearby Iffezheim, the 'Goodwood of the Continent', in the estimation of one English visitor, where 'princes, barons, dukes and duchesses' were seated in the stand, there was 'the best music' between races, and 'an excellent restaurant' supplied 'hock, champagne, fruit, and the creature comforts so necessary to refresh the exhaustion of excitement'. In the evenings, the main excitement was to be found in the casino in Baden, but there were also operas and concerts in the Baden Theatre, and sometimes in the Salle de Conversation, when the gambling rooms were closed.[10]

The casino was the key to the development of these cultural attractions. Its profits helped to pay for Baden's parks and walks, grand hotels, pavilions, theatres, music festivals, resident bands and orchestras. Jacques Bénazet, an immigrant from France, had spotted its financial potential during the 1830s. He was following the example of Barbaja, who had used his gambling concessions to finance opera houses in Naples twenty years before. Securing the concession for the Baden casino in 1838, Bénazet invested heavily in the lavish restoration of its gambling rooms. He turned it into a major international attraction, especially for visitors from neighbouring France, where gambling had been outlawed by the July Monarchy. On Bénazet's death, in 1848, the concession was taken over by his son Édouard, an astute businessman and impresario who had studied at the Paris Conservatory and had good connections in the music world. In 1855, he built new rooms in the casino, opulently furnished in a classical French style, and three years later opened the racecourse at Iffezheim. From the profits of his gambling enterprise, Bénazet financed the annual music festival run for him by Berlioz with a budget large enough to attract the top musicians from Europe. He also paid for the building of an opera house. Completed in 1862, the Theater Baden-Baden was inaugurated in August of that year with the premiere of Berlioz's opera *Béatrice et Bénédict*.

Berlioz had first come to Baden for a concert series in 1853, and had been the mainstay of its music festival since 1856. He loved the natural beauty of the place, a 'paradise' he called it, with its 'woods, mountains, streams and fragrant air'. He was in his element in its society, 'intelligent and cultured people who speak French'. But most of all he liked the money he made there, 2,000 francs for organizing just one concert every year. Bénazet was the ideal impresario for Berlioz. His generosity 'has greatly exceeded anything ever done for me by the princes in Europe to whom I am most indebted', Berlioz wrote in his *Memoirs*. What satisfied him most was that he was left alone by Bénazet. As he wrote in 1859,

> everything is organized in favour of the conductor who is in charge; he does not have to put up with penny-pinching and no obstacles of any kind are placed in his way. In the conviction that the best course of action is to let the conductor act with complete freedom, M. Bénazet does not interfere in any way and considers his only function is to pay the bills. 'Do everything in a royal style,' he says, 'I am giving you a free hand.' Three cheers! With music that is the only way to achieve something elevated and beautiful.

No expense was spared on the lavish decoration of the Salle de Conversation when it was 'transformed into a concert hall, adorned with shrubs, flowers, brilliantly lit up, and filled with the most fashionable public in Europe', in the words of Berlioz.[11] The best singers and virtuoso players came to Baden for the festival – among them Clara Schumann and Anton Rubinstein, the violinist Henri Vieuxtemps, and Pauline Viardot, who was the star guest every year from 1859 to 1864.

*

The Viardot villa was soon established as the centre of this musical community. It was a three-storey house designed in the style of a Swiss chalet, large enough to accommodate the entire Viardot household of eleven people, including servants. It had stables and a carriage house, an aviary, and a wooded garden descending to the concert hall and gallery, a long basilica-shaped building, where Louis kept his Old Masters and Pauline hosted musical soirées. The superb Cavaillé-Coll organ was transported from their Paris house and installed in the concert hall flanked by two grand pianos. The score of *Don Giovanni* was also brought to Baden in its special box and placed on a table by the organ, as it had been in the rue de Douai.

The Viardots had spent a fortune on the house. The purchase price of 108,000 francs was almost doubled by the renovation costs, including the building of the concert hall. Then there was the furniture they had to buy, because their Paris home had been rented out furnished. Louis sold some railway stocks and, in an auction at the Hôtel Drouot on 1 April 1863, around fifty of his finest paintings, including landscapes by Poussin, Bruegel, Ruysdael, Wouwerman and Van der Neer, as well as works by Ribera and Zurbarán, and a Velázquez portrait of the infant Maria Theresa (probably the one now in the Metropolitan Museum in New York).[12] He had been slowly selling paintings since the middle of the 1850s, as Pauline's earnings had declined. In 1857, he had sold one of his two Rembrandts, *Slaughtered Ox* (1655), receiving just 5,000 francs from the Louvre, because the painting was damaged.[13] Continued sales could not keep up with the mounting costs of their new house. In 1864, the Viardots put Courtavenel up for sale. Their old country manor was pulled down for materials by its buyer.[14] The Baden house, once it was completed, made quite a statement about Pauline's wealth and status in the fashionable world of Europe's summer capital. Mostly paid for by the money she had earned, the mansion was a symbol of her achievements.

Turgenev, too, was earning money from his work. He had enough to buy a plot of land and build a house. In 1864, the woodland by the Viardot villa came up for sale on the death of its owner. Turgenev bought it for 50,000 francs. He commissioned an architect from Paris to build a mansion in the Louis XIII style – a mixture of the Gothic and Renaissance elements of old French châteaux – favoured by opponents of the Second Empire. A garden was laid out with a 'river' walk

The Turgenev Villa in Baden viewed from the garden. Photograph, 1986, by Nicholas Žekulin. The Viardots' neighbouring house was pulled down long ago.

through the trees leading to the concert hall.* Turgenev was delighted with the building plans. To live so close to the Viardots had been his dream. After years of restless wandering, he now felt that he was putting down his roots, making his own 'nest' at last.[15]

The grandeur of Turgenev's building project marked his arrival as a major writer on the European scene. But the costs of building quickly outstripped his earnings. His daughter's dowry was a further drain on his finances. In February 1865, Paulinette was married to Gaston Bruère, the owner of a glass factory in Rougemont near Besançon in eastern France, where the newly married couple occupied an outbuilding in the courtyard of the factory. Turgenev had promised her a dowry

---

* Turgenev was proud of his 'river' (it was really just a stream) and took offence if visitors did not remark on it (Ostrovskaia, *Vospominaniia o Turgeneve*, p. 9).

of 100,000 francs on her marriage, and another 50,000 francs within a few years. He also paid her an annual allowance of 2,500 francs. To buy the Baden house he had been forced to cash the railway shares he had bought in 1858 as a saving for her dowry. His daughter accused him of putting his own comfort first.[16]

His landed estates did not make enough to meet his mounting costs. They would have earned him more if he had not been quite so generous to his former serfs on their emancipation in 1861. At Spasskoe, Turgenev left his peasants twice as much land as he was obliged to under the terms of the Emancipation Decree. He gave it to them free, relinquishing his rights under the decree to receive payment for the land. It was what one might expect from the author of the *Sketches*, which had done so much to turn opinion against serfdom, but was generous nonetheless. Turgenev's income from the various estates which he retained – 6,000 hectares of fertile land – was never more than 5,000 roubles (20,000 francs) per annum, and in years of harvest failure it was far less (his brother Nikolai, who managed his own estates, earned four times as much from the same amount of land). Turgenev's estates were terribly mismanaged by his uncle, an 'old, dilatory and idle' man, as Botkin described him, who received an annual salary of 2,000 roubles (8,000 francs) but fraudulently earned a good deal more by cheating his absent nephew at every opportunity. Turgenev was naive. Being fond of his uncle, he trusted him. He was himself also careless with money, which did not interest him so long as his needs were met. It took him fifteen years to realize the extent of his uncle's mismanagement, calculating that in one year alone he had lost a staggering 36,500 roubles (146,000 francs) in cash, farm tools and livestock. In 1867, he finally decided to get rid of him. To do so cost him 80,000 francs – the amount his uncle claimed he had been promised by Turgenev in the event of the writer's death and which he now insisted to be paid.[17] A new manager was put in place, a young and energetic local businessman called Kishinsky, who turned out to be even more dishonest.

Turgenev's income from his writing only partly made up for his losses on the land. By the 1860s, he was earning large advances for his works from Russian publishers. Mikhail Katkov paid him 4,300 roubles (17,200 francs) to publish *On the Eve* in the literary journal *Russian Messenger* in 1860; and 5,000 roubles (20,000 francs) for *Smoke*. This was an amount equivalent to 400 roubles (1,600 francs) for every printer's page – five times the rate he had been paid ten years before. The Russians were great readers of literary periodicals, and Turgenev's earnings from the *Russian Messenger* were high by any standards in Europe. As his need for money grew, he pushed hard for even higher fees, demanding 500 roubles per printer's page for his story 'Phantoms' from the *Russian Messenger* in February 1863. Yet there was only so far he could go, so much he could earn from publishers. Other Russian writers wrote long novels for the periodicals, and earned well by doing so because they were paid by the printed sheet. But Turgenev's novels were all short. He simply could not write in any other form.[18]

Turgenev did not earn much more from his novels published in book form, which had a smaller market in Russia than novels in serialized form. Turgenev told the Goncourts that a book in Russia 'brought in very little, 4,000 francs at the most'.[19] He did better with complete editions of his works, of which three were published for the Russian market during the 1860s. For the first, in 1861, he received an advance of 8,000 roubles (32,000 francs), and he succeeded in negotiating higher fees for the later editions. But there were no other sources of income he could count on from his books. He earned almost nothing from abroad. While many of his works had been translated into foreign languages, he was not paid by publishers in countries that did not have a copyright agreement with Russia. Turgenev cursed the 'robber publishers' of these pirated editions of his works, not just because they deprived him of an income, but because they often made such bad translations that his literary reputation was damaged.[20] In the years to come he would become a campaigner for international copyright. But even in those countries, such as France, where bilateral copyright agreements with Russia were already in existence and should have been applied, publishers were slow or even failed completely to pay authors from abroad.

Overall, Turgenev had an annual income of about 10,000 roubles (40,000 francs), roughly half from his estates and half from his writing. It was a substantial sum for any gentleman, practically a fortune for any highbrow writer,* but not enough to keep up with the costs of his

---

* Compare with the estimated earnings of Gautier, of whom the Goncourts wrote in 1868: 'Our good Gautier is one of the richest of those modern starvelings of literature, with his librarian's post, say 6,000 francs, his pension from the Emperor's privy purse, say 3,000, and almost 20,000 a year from the *Moniteur* and the royalties on his books. Who among writers is as rich as that today?' (GJ, vol. 2, p. 187).

Baden house and the payments that he owed to Paulinette. Turgenev was constantly in debt. He sold off bits of land, nearly always cheaply because of his steward's cheating and incompetence; mortgaged parts of his estate; and begged his publishers for loans on promises of delivering a manuscript. Money took a long time to come through from Russia, so he was forced to borrow from his friends to solve his problems of cashflow. Increasingly he borrowed from the Viardots. But still he could not raise enough to pay his daughter's dowry; he even fell behind in paying Paulinette her allowance. Building work on his mansion slowed. Paying out his uncle was the final straw, leaving him so short of cash that he was forced to sell his Baden house to Louis Viardot – at a loss of 60,000 francs. When the building was finally completed, in April 1868, Turgenev moved into the house as a paying tenant of his friend.[21]

A pleasurable routine was established by Turgenev and the Viardots. 'I am happy with my Baden life,' Turgenev wrote to Botkin on 3 October 1863. 'I have never felt as good as this before. I go hunting frequently – and work very little.' He would write in the mornings, and break at lunch to spend the rest of the day with the Viardots, or go hunting with his gun dog Pegasus, who became well known and liked around Baden.[22] There was a steady stream of visitors seeking his advice or help, or just wanting to meet him.

Louis had a peaceful existence. Now well into his sixties, he settled down in Baden to the quiet joys of scholarship. He wrote two books in these years: *Espagne et les beaux-arts* (1866), a collection of essays about art; and *Apologie d'un incrédule* (1867), a statement of his atheist philosophy, which distinguished him from both Turgenev (who was indifferent rather than opposed to religion) and Pauline (who was freethinking but never atheist). The only surviving statement Pauline made was in a letter to Julius Rietz in 1859:

> I cannot propound any formula for my faith, but I have the firm conviction that the soul is immortal, and that all loves shall one day be united – the great loves, whatever their nature, provided that they have made themselves worthy of it . . . Do not laugh at me, dearest friend; I know no more about it than anybody else, and, above all, I cannot give a definite shape to my thoughts on a subject so difficult, so impossible to

explain. All that I know is this – that there is within us all a divine spark which does not perish, and which will end in becoming a part of the great light.[23]

The *Apologie* was written in the context of a Europe-wide debate about the divinity of Christ sparked in France by the publication of Renan's *Vie de Jésus* (1863), in which the philosopher had portrayed Jesus as a human and historical figure, whose godly status was created by his followers. Renan was a friend of Louis Viardot. In 1856, he had married Cornélie Scheffer, the niece of Ary Scheffer, which had brought him even closer to the Viardot circles. Written in a lively and accessible prose, his *Vie de Jésus* became a *succès de scandale*. It sold 168,000 copies in France by the end of 1864, and was soon translated into all the major European languages. The book's success, according to Sainte-Beuve, was its appeal to what he called the 'large and indecisive floating mass of minds' – the religious disposition of most people in the nineteenth century who were 'neither believing nor disbelieving' in the Bible but accepted it as a source of moral values while they got on with the pursuit of their worldly happiness. Catholics attacked the book. Some Church leaders tried to get it banned. Others condemned its appearance as a mark of the decadent immorality of the Empire's liberal culture and called for stricter censorship.[24]

Viardot's book was written largely to defend Renan, whose endorsement appears as a footnote to the text. 'My dear friend,' Renan wrote to him on 17 April 1867, 'I have read your *Apologie*, which should not be called that, because the wise man has nothing to defend. It is an account of your own beliefs written not for others but yourself, and it strikes me as exact and rigorous.' Like Renan, Viardot saw the divinity of Christ as a human invention. From the earliest times, mankind had needed divine myths to explain the universe, but science was now answering the questions of creation, argued Viardot, who maintained that Darwin's theory of 'auto-creation' could equally apply to the cosmos: planets were not formed by God, but by the heat of their suns, which could also destroy them.[25]

At the heart of Louis's atheism was his belief in human agency. 'It is not God that directs me, but my own liberty, my conscience,' he concluded. This was the real message of his book, which, like Renan's *Vie de Jésus*, was as much a statement of freedom – the liberty to question and reject religious orthodoxy – as an examination of the Bible's claims. It was a defence of freedom of expression against Church and State.

Louis spent most of the day in his study, appearing only with the family at meals or sometimes to join Turgenev on hunting trips. Pauline was the busiest of the three. She filled the house with her various activities. Up by dawn, she would spend two hours with the children, teaching them Italian, music and drawing, before seeing her pupils.[26] Singers came from all around the world to study with the famous soprano, who charged twenty francs per hour for lessons. Pauline's reputation as a teacher was consolidated by the publication of her *L'École classique du chant*, recommended by the Paris Conservatory, in 1863, which became a standard work.[27] Pauline's pupils found her to be strict and demanding but generous with her time and always ready to help launch their careers by giving them advice and writing to her contacts in the music world. 'She has something of the hussar in her character,' noted the soprano Aglaja Orgeni, who started lessons with Pauline in May 1863. 'She is dashing, strong-willed, frank in character, sometimes even blunt, and devoid of any sentimentality, but she has a good heart.'[28]

In the afternoons Pauline received visitors, wrote letters, practised or composed music. Evenings belonged to family and friends. They were taken up with music-making, amateur theatricals, spoofs, charades and the portrait game, much as they had been at home in the rue de Douai and Courtavenel, only now such entertainments could take place every evening, because Pauline was no longer absent at the theatre. The Viardot household was almost wholly given over to the pursuit of pleasure and frivolity, according to the serious-minded Clara Schumann, who had bought a cottage near the Viardots in Lichtental to spend the summers with her seven children resting from her winter concert tours.[29]

On Sunday afternoons Pauline hosted a musical salon in the concert hall to which she invited Baden's high society. The Prussian queen, Augusta, an old friend of Pauline's, was a regular at these concerts, often with her tone-deaf husband, King Wilhelm, later to become the German emperor, although their friendship with the Viardots, convinced republicans, was treated with discretion in the German press on instructions from the court.[30] The Queen of Holland, the Grand Duke and Duchess of Baden, the Russian Grand Duchess, Elena Pavlovna, even the French empress, Eugénie, came along to hear their host perform with Clara Schumann, Johannes Brahms, and Nikolai and Anton

Rubinstein, among other musicians, including some of Pauline's pupils, who were thus exposed to the experience of performing. Clara Schumann thought these concerts showed Pauline to be a snob. Reporting on the opening concert, in 1864, she complained to Brahms, who had just spent the first of several summers in a boarding house in Lichtental so as to be close to her:

> Madame Viardot consecrated her Palace of Arts (as she calls it) the other day, and to the first ceremony she invited high society (the Queen of Prussia etc.), but she naturally did not want me; and afterwards she had a reception for the populace, for which I was considered good enough. The whole thing was not very dignified . . . [31]

Clara Schumann did not move in the same high circles as Pauline. Too poor to afford a house in Baden, she felt excluded from this society, and became resentful and jealous. Others saw the Viardot salon in more idealistic terms. Ludwig Pietsch, for one, believed it was a bold attempt 'to realize the concept of a cosmopolitan society, uniting people of different national origins around the ideals of Art'.[32]

The German writer Adelheid von Schorn recalls one of Pauline's more informal musical salons where 'everybody in her artistic circle was gathered'. In the middle of them all was Turgenev, suffering from gout and 'lying in a big armchair, his bandaged leg stretched on a foot-rest . . . The striking white-haired figure of the writer was the focal point of this whole society.'[33]

The move to Baden had allowed Turgenev to become a member of the Viardot household – practically a member of the family – in ways that had not been possible before. In Paris he could be no more than a visitor. People gossiped about his relations with Pauline, and few thought they were platonic. To avoid a scandal they had needed to maintain respectable appearances – probably the reason why Turgenev had gone away during her last pregnancy. But in Baden attitudes were more relaxed. Pauline was accepted in the highest circles there, despite her stage background, and was not subjected to the social snubs and insults endured by many singers in Paris. People came to Baden for pleasure. Great men were seen there with their mistresses. Courtesans like Cora Pearl, the famous English beauty, mistress to Charles de Morny, the half-brother of the emperor, lived in Baden in an opulent lifestyle. In this live-and-let-live town it was easier for Pauline and

Turgenev to maintain their unconventional relationship. There was less gossip about them than there had been in Paris. The only sign of awkwardness, if that is what it is, comes from Pauline's diary, in an entry for 23 July 1863, where she writes of being with Turgenev at a reception in the old castle given by the Grand Duke and Duchess of Baden. Pauline notes that Turgenev appears nervous, and that 'there is always a certain discomfort with him [*il y a toujours un certain gêne avec lui*]' at social gatherings – an observation she marked for deletion in the last years of her life, when she prepared her papers for posterity.[34]

Turgenev and Pauline now lived more freely together, practically as man and wife, in a domestic setting with Louis. They were both in their forties, Turgenev forty-five and Pauline forty-two, when they settled in Baden, an age when they might expect an active sexual life, whereas Louis, at the age of sixty-three, was, as far as one can tell, happier with the pleasures of the mind than with those of the body. Turgenev made no effort to conceal his feelings for Pauline, nor the nature of their relationship from his visitors. Natalia Ostrovskaya, the wife of an old acquaintance of Turgenev, recalls visiting the writer at his house in 1863. Shown into a sparsely furnished room by his housekeeper, she waited for Turgenev, who had been called away by Madame Viardot. Seated by his writing desk, Ostrovskaya looked around the room: there were a painting on the wall, a portrait drawing just above his desk, a framed photograph and bronze bust on it – all of Pauline Viardot.[35]

Pauline's children were not all aware of Turgenev's true relationship with their mother, who confessed her feelings for him only to her diary.* Paul, the youngest, who was only six years old when the family moved to Baden, thought of him as his mother's friend. But the eldest, Louise, in her early twenties, was bitterly resentful of his constant presence in her family. Headstrong and judgemental, she had felt neglected by her mother since childhood and argued with her frequently. Soon after their arrival in Baden, Louise married Ernest Héritte, a French diplomat in Berne, and departed with him for the Cape Colony in southern Africa, where he took up a new post.[36]

Turgenev was particularly fond of Pauline's second daughter, Claudie,

---

* There are several entries in her diaries expressing fear and longing for him when he travelled abroad, especially to Russia, where he went in 1864 and 1868. See e.g. HL, MUS 264 (365), Pauline Viardot Journal, 13 Jan. 1864, 23 June 1868.

or 'Didie', who at that time was entering her teenage years. A vivacious beauty with a striking resemblance to her mother, she was affectionate, even flirtatious with Turgenev, who lavished her with feelings of paternal affection he had never shown to his own daughter. Whereas Claudie had a talent for painting and spoke several languages, Paulinette was an ordinary girl. 'I have nothing in common with my daughter,' he wrote to Countess Lambert; 'she likes neither music nor poetry nor nature – not even dogs – and these are the only things I love.'[37]

Louis took a benevolent view of Turgenev's involvement with his children. He had always played an unassuming part in the household. But there were moments when he suffered from a sense that his own role as a father and a husband had been usurped by his friend. In November 1865, Louis wrote a letter to Pauline assuring her that he had never once suspected her of anything unworthy of herself, but warning nonetheless that gossip had arisen from certain 'appearances'. A little prudence was thus necessary. Without naming Turgenev, Louis then expressed his own regret at feeling far too often – when it came to conversations about music, for example, or even to relations with the children – that the role he ought to occupy had been occupied by someone else.[38]

2

The 1860s were the heyday of the Continental spa. Only twenty years before, Europe's best-known mineral spas – Vichy, Plombières, Aix-les-Bains, Bad Ems, Davos – had been simple rural places frequented only by the aristocracy and Europe's royals, whose need for cures was reinforced by their tendency to eat and drink too much. The railways opened up the spas to the bourgeoisie and professional classes, fattened by prosperity. Their new money fuelled the growth of luxury hotels, casinos, theatres, restaurants, high-class brothels and other entertainments in these health resorts. Connection to a railway was the surest guarantee of popularity: new spa towns such as Karlsbad and Semmering were made by their location on a major line, while old ones such as Plombières and Vichy were revived by the arrival of branch lines. By the 1870s, the railways had connected the great spas of Europe in a network of resorts with the same type of pleasure culture in each place.[39]

Light music was everywhere. It was played by the spa orchestra, morning, noon and night, in bandstands and pavilions; by chamber groups and ensembles in concert rooms; by pianists and singers in cafés and restaurants. There was no escaping it.

Strauss II was omnipresent in spa towns. His dance music was the soundtrack of society at play. Johann Strauss I had conquered Europe with his waltzes, beginning in Vienna during the 1820s. His orchestra would pack the Sperl, the city's biggest dance hall. Because the waltz required body contact between the dancers, it was attacked by defenders of morality, but it was its sexual danger (memorably described by Flaubert in the waltz scene of *Madame Bovary*) that gave the dance its popularity. All the Strauss family were involved in this music business – Johann and his wife Anna, as well as their three sons, Johann, Josef and Eduard. They exported the 'waltz craze' into Germany, the Low Countries, France and Britain through their tours in the 1830s and 1840s. After the death of Johann Strauss I, in 1849, the family business was taken over by his eldest son, Johann Strauss II, then aged twenty-four, who led it to new heights of international fame. His orchestra was wanted everywhere – in dance halls and casinos, cafés, restaurants, and pleasure gardens like the Vienna *Volksgarten*. By the 1850s, the Strauss business had 200 employees, including music copyists, coach drivers and bookkeepers. It was a sophisticated company with clever strategies of marketing and publicity. Strauss II, for example, who composed only waltzes until the age of forty-four, would give them topical names and themes or add gimmicks to help them 'catch on' with a public always keen for novelty. New technologies inspired many of his tunes: 'Telegraphische Depeschen' (1858) mimicked the sounds of the telegraph machine; while 'Accelerationen' (1860), composed for the Engineering Students Ball, had its waltz theme speed up like a train. Strauss assumed control of every aspect of the family business. Having fallen out with his music publisher, Carl Haslinger, for instance, he set up as a publisher himself.[40]

In 1853, Strauss broke down from exhaustion. Handing over control of the business to his brothers, he went to the spa at Bad Gastein to recover. While he was there he was approached by a Russian businessman, the new director of the Tsarskoe Selo Railway Company, who offered him a lucrative contract at the summer resort of Pavlovsk, near St Petersburg. The company hoped to boost its traffic by offering daytrippers the attraction of Strauss concerts in the 'Vauxhall Pavilion', named after the Vauxhall Gardens in London, a public entertainment space dating back to the seventeenth century, on which many nineteenth-century spa towns would be based (Spa in Belgium had its own *Waux-hall* for concerts and balls). In Pavlovsk the Vauxhall Pavilion served both as the railway station and as the entrance to the park (hence the derivation of the Russian word '*vokzal*' for a station). The concerts took place every evening between May and September, and went on for many years. They proved extremely popular, producing a booming trade for the railway. Strauss would bring the concerts to an abrupt halt when the last train to St Petersburg sounded its whistle, although there were some occasions when the audience refused to leave and urged the band to play on.[41]

Strauss toured widely in Europe. He made good use of the railways to circulate around the spa resorts of the German-speaking lands, which were an important market for his orchestra. For many years he

Strauss and Brahms in the spa town of Ischl, Austria, 1894.

did a summer season at Baden, where he had a grand villa. A compulsive gambler, he was frequently seen in the casino, often losing badly yet undeterred. Brahms was a great admirer of Strauss's music. The two men met in Baden in 1862 when they were introduced by Richard Pohl, the music critic and editor of the *Badenblätter*, the town's newspaper. Strauss's presence in Baden was, along with Clara Schumann, a major draw for Brahms, who spent several summers there, renting rooms in a boarding house in Lichtental. In the evenings he would walk to the spa's park to hear Strauss's orchestra.[42] His own interest in dance music was influenced by Strauss. The sixteen Waltzes Op. 39 were composed in 1865, the Liebeslieder waltzes (Op. 59) in 1868, while the Hungarian Dances date from 1869.

Strauss's influence was ubiquitous. His waltzes were the main attraction in the dance fever that swept Europe. In Paris dancers flocked to the Jardin Mabille, which reached the height of its popularity in the 1860s. It was a place for tourists to meet prostitutes and watch the high kicks of the cancan dancers, who in those days did not wear underskirts.[43] Dance music was also dominant at venues like the Jardin Turc, a café in the Marais district with a music garden decorated in the Chinese style, confusingly, where the dashing young conductor Louis-Antoine Jullien (he wore white gloves and used a jewelled baton) had established a tradition of popular orchestral concerts of polkas and quadrilles accompanied by fireworks, cannon fire, light shows, and so on. It was a winning combination, largely copied from his friend Philippe Musard, which Jullien then exported to London as the basis of his promenade concerts – visually spectacular events with huge orchestras, military bands and choirs that attracted thousands from the 'one-shilling public' (the lower-middle and artisan classes) to pleasure parks and gardens such as Vauxhall and Cremorne or the Surrey Zoological Gardens.

Jullien's concerts were part of a revolution in the middle decades of the nineteenth century: the appearance of a popular-music industry. Throughout Europe a new breed of entrepreneur-conductors and composers were responding to a growing demand for entertainment music. Jullien and Musard in Paris and London, Strauss in Vienna, Josef Gung'l in Berlin and Munich, Hans-Christian Lumbye (the 'Strauss of the North') in Copenhagen, Joseph Labitzky in Karlsbad – all churned out waltzes, polkas and quadrilles.[44] There were commercial openings for light music everywhere. Paris had the *concerts populaires*, cheap Sunday concerts in the vast rotunda of the Cirque d'Hiver given by the orchestra of Jules Pasdeloup from 1861, where a new audience was introduced to the popular classics. A more eclectic mix of music – from *chansons* to opera medleys – could be heard at the *café-concerts*, which became popular in the 1850s and 1860s, when the development of the great boulevards by Baron Haussmann attracted crowds in search of entertainment in the evenings. Cafés opened on all the main boulevards. They drew the most varied crowd, from gentlemen in top hats with their wives in crinolines to foreign visitors and a new class of prostitutes, according to the Goncourts, who noted in their journal in 1864 that Paris whores were 'now seated underneath the gas-lights at the tables in the boulevard cafés'.[45] The main attraction of the *café-concert* was that members of the audience were allowed to smoke and drink. There was no entry charge, but prices were raised on concert nights and waiters went round the tables pressing customers to order more. The singers and musicians were paid a performance royalty (5–6 per cent of earnings) regulated and collected by their union, the Syndicat des Auteurs, Compositeurs et Éditeurs de Musique. Most were street musicians but some came from the opera and operetta houses – they were either out of work or moonlighting – for high fees could be earned by star performers capable of bringing in a crowd.[46]

No star was bigger than Thérésa – the stage name adopted by Emma Valladon sometime around 1863 when she emerged from the popular theatres and cafés of the boulevard du Temple and started singing *chansons* at the newly opened Café Eldorado for 200 francs a month. She was soon lured away by Arsène Goubert, the owner of the rival Café Alcazar, who paid her 300 francs a month. Soon the whole of Paris was coming to see her. 'She is a big woman with a good-natured air, completely natural, with an incisive voice that allows her to express clearly the meaning of the words she is singing,' wrote Henri Dabot, who heard her sing at the Alcazar in 1865. Her repertoire was not obscene but some of her comic songs – most famously her 'Rien n'est sacré pour un sapeur!' (Nothing's Sacred for a Sapper) – were full of sexual innuendoes which she communicated through her body language, acting and expression in her voice (a performance captured by Degas in a series of paintings in the 1870s (see Plate 17)).[47]

Until 1867, *café-concerts* were forbidden by French law to imitate theatres. They could not have a stage, or singers dressed as actors, and they had to start at an earlier time than the theatres. But from 1864, when theatres were released from state control, the rules for *café-concerts* were liberalized, allowing them to become more like theatres, vaudevilles or music halls. The Goncourt brothers described the El-dorado at this time:

> A large circular auditorium with two rows of boxes, decorated with gilt and imitation marble; dazzling chandeliers; a café inside, black with men's hats; bonnets of women from the *barrières* [outlying districts]; soldiers, children with caps; a few hats of prostitutes accompanied by shop assis-tants; a few pink ribbons in the boxes; the visible breath of all these people, a cloud of dust and tobacco smoke.
>
> At the back a stage with footlights: on it a comedian in evening dress. He sang ditties interspersed with farmyard noises, the sounds of animals on heat, and with epileptic gesticulations – a Saint Vitus's dance of idiocy. The audience was delirious with excitement.[48]

Another well-known vaudeville, the Bataclan (1864), began as a *café-concert* in the chinoiserie style made popular by the French campaign in Indochina between 1858 and 1862, but with acrobats and jugglers it gradually moved from concerts into vaudevilles. The Folies Bergère (1869) took a different route. It charged an admission fee, as in a the-atre, but allowed customers to drink inside (hence Manet's *A Bar at the Folies-Bergère*), and to come and go at any time, as they might at a *café-concert*, where there was no entrance fee. The offering at the Folies Bergère was a mix of comic operettas, popular songs, dancing girls and acrobats. Although it catered to a mainly bourgeois public, it offered them a taste for the demi-monde of the music hall. Widely imi-tated in the 1870s, this hybrid form of entertainment, known as '*théâtre promenoirs*', marked the start of the sex industry around Pigalle, a few streets away from the Viardots' house in the rue de Douai. The bar-girls at the Folies Bergère were also prostitutes, who would openly approach the men and haggle with them over their prices.[49]

The commercial-music industry developed just as quickly in Britain. The London music halls evolved in a similar manner to the Parisian vaudevilles, although most had started out as saloon bars or entertain-ment rooms at the back of a pub so that drinking could be carried on. For a small admission fee or higher price for drinks, customers were entertained with songs, comedy and a wide variety of 'speciality acts', from sword-swallowing to drag artists. The Canterbury Hall (1852), the first tavern music hall with 700 seats, was converted by its owner, Charles Morton, from a skittle alley. Resembling a *café-concert* with seating around tables, it specialized in operetta numbers and ballads. It was so successful that it was replaced by a hall twice its size in 1856 with a grand entrance and staircase ascending to a bar on the upper floor. Encouraged by his success, Morton opened the Oxford Music Hall, a huge entertainment complex with a combined music hall and tavern on the site of a demolished public house on Oxford Street. 'The great gay glaring hall and balconies were crammed in every part,' noted Arthur Munby, who visited the newly opened music hall in 1862; 'there was barely standing room in the crowd, which was chiefly made up of men; business men, clerks, & others, of no very refined aspect.'

> Socially speaking, the audience were a good deal higher than those I have seen in similar Halls at Islington and elsewhere. One result of this was that the women present were whores, instead of respectable wives & sweethearts. Therefore another result was that there was nothing wholesome or genial in the folks' enjoyment: they drank their grog staring gloomily or lewdly grimacing; and the worthless dread of your neighbour which half-educated respectability creates kept them silent and selfish.

Such grim excitements counted as pleasure in Britain, where 400 music halls were opened in provincial towns during the 1860s.[50]

Music publishers played an important part in the development of this entertainment industry. The 1860s saw the introduction of faster mechanical lithographic presses able for the first time to combine words and music in one printing. It was a breakthrough for the sheet music business, enabling publishers to produce cheap but quality editions of classic works and popular arrangements of songs and ballads in print-runs of tens and hundreds of thousands. Most of the biggest publishers organized or sponsored concerts to promote their sheet music. Novello was among the first. Inspired by its success at the Handel Festival in 1859, Novello launched a series of one-shilling choral and orchestral concerts, where its popular editions and arrangements could be cheaply bought. The publishers Chappell and Cramer co-financed the building of the St James Concert Hall in Piccadilly (1858), where they sold sheet music and instruments at 'Pops' concerts. Boosey launched its Ballad

Concerts in the St James Hall. The company had realized that its biggest profits came from the sale of sheet music for the sort of ballads sung in music halls, and had begun to focus its activities on these ballads. To promote its songs Boosey engaged famous singers for such concerts. Large amounts of money could be made on the ballad concert circuit, especially by women, for female-voice arrangements were by far the largest market for ballads.

One of the most successful performers was Antoinette Sterling, an American who studied with both Pauline Viardot in Baden and with her brother, Manuel Garcia, in London during the 1860s. Sterling made a fortune by opting for a royalty on sales of the sheet music she had promoted instead of a flat fee for her concert appearance, as most other singers had been paid. Boosey was the first to encourage the royalty system as a way of sharing publication risks with the singers, as well as giving them an interest in promoting its music by performing in as many concerts as they could. Sterling's earnings from her royalties were modest to begin with, but she struck gold when she promoted 'The Lost Chord' (1877), the sentimental and pious ballad by Arthur Sullivan, which sold half a million copies in its first quarter of a century. With a royalty of 6d (sixty-two centimes) for each sale, Sterling earned £12,500 (315,000 francs), or £500 per year, from this one song alone.[51]

3

The move to Baden allowed Pauline to spend more time composing. She had been writing songs and chamber music since the 1830s but she now turned her hand to other forms, writing operettas with Turgenev for her pupils to perform in the theatre they were building in the garden of his house. Turgenev had been sketching the libretto of an operetta, *Le Dernier Sorcier*, since 1859. The plot is very silly, even by the standards of an *opéra bouffe*. It involves Krakamiche, an old and once-powerful sorcerer now deprived of his magic, whose presence in the forest has upset the woodland elves; there is a romance between his daughter, Stella, and Prince Stelio, whose marriage comes about through the intervention of the Queen of the Elves. Full of humour and satire, the operetta followed in a long tradition of home entertainment

The first performance of *Le Dernier Sorcier*, in Turgenev's villa in Baden, 20 September 1867. Drawing by Ludwig Pietsch.

at the Viardots' – amateur theatricals, charades and spoofs – where Pauline and Turgenev indulged their love of childish fun (Louis was too stiff and serious to participate and usually retreated to his study).*

The first performance of *Le Dernier Sorcier* took place on 20 September 1867 before invited friends in the completed but still unoccupied Villa Turgenev. Lanterns in the driveway guided guests towards the brightly illuminated entrance-hall, from which they entered the salon, where, as Ludwig Pietsch described it, 'a plain green curtain pinned against the wall and surmounted by oleander branches' defined the stage area. Around the stage the thirty guests were seated in chairs and armchairs, informally arranged, and there was a piano, where Pauline took her place. As she played the overture, the curtains parted to reveal the set: 'flower-pots and oleander trees represent a forest and the win- dowed cardboard wall in the corner represents the [sorcerer's] ruined

---

* Turgenev was the life and soul of these domestic parties, when he was not suffering from gout, keeping everybody entertained with his funny stories, silly dances and animal impersonations (his favourite party trick to entertain the children at the dinner table was to eat his soup like a chicken).

hut.' Louis Pomey played the role of Krakamiche, although for a gala performance in October, when the Prussian king attended, the sorcerer was played by Turgenev. 'I did not sing, I hasten to say, but only acted, and not as badly as might have been expected,' he explained to Annenkov. 'The guests enjoyed the speech of Krakamiche and understood it as a parody of His Imperial Highness Napoleon III, which brought forth heavy laughter from King William.' Pauline's pupil Marie Hasselmans sang the part of Stella – one of the aims of the operettas being to provide her students with the experience of performing for an audience. But the stars of the production were the three youngest children of Pauline – the fifteen-year-old Claudie as the Queen of the Elves, Marianne (thirteen) as the main elf, and Paul (ten) as Krakamiche's servant, Prelimpinpin. Their involvement gave the operetta the informal atmosphere of a family theatrical, from which its charm derived. At the centre was Pauline, not just the composer, but piano-orchestra, conductor and stage manager. 'My mother,' recalled Paul, 'accompanied on the piano, supervised everything, ran into the wings in the intermissions to re-attach a fairy wing or fasten a pin.'

> After the performance a supper invariably consisting of cold meats and potato salad was offered to the performers. The supper took place in our house and the entire length of the two gardens had to be crossed; these nocturnal processions, with everyone still in costume, were not the least picturesque aspect of those memorable evenings.[52]

There were other Viardot–Turgenev operettas – *Trop de Femmes*, *L'Ogre* (with Turgenev in the title role) and *Le Miroir* – all performed in the Thiergarten Theatre in Turgenev's garden in 1868–9. But none was as successful as *Le Dernier Sorcier*, which had two seasons of performances before receiving its public premiere at the Weimar Court Theatre on 8 April 1869, the birthday of Princess Sophie, the Grand Duchess consort of Saxe-Weimar-Eisenach (in Weimar there was a long tradition of celebrating the birthdays of the Grand Ducal couple with festival performances of operas and plays in the Court Theatre).[53] The European press had picked up on its success. One of the invited guests at a performance in the Thiergarten Theatre was Sextius Durand, a correspondent of *La France musicale*, who told its readers that the operetta was 'worth a hundred times more than those you see in our

Paris theatres'. Turgenev was delighted. His starting point had been his admiration for Jacques Offenbach, whose *opéras bouffes* he had seen many times. He adored their humour and satire. Since his first trip to Paris, in 1845, Turgenev had been a devotee of the boulevard theatres. He was often to be seen at the Variety or the Théâtre de la Porte Saint-Martin. Pauline shared his enthusiasm for Offenbach. She had been going to the Théâtre des Bouffes-Parisiens, the composer's own theatre, since the 1850s, many times accompanied by Turgenev. Louis did not go with them. The *bouffes* were not his sort of thing. So this was an interest that Turgenev could embrace, knowing that it would unite him with Pauline in an artistic marriage of their own. '"Vive Offenbach!",' he had written to Pauline after a performance of *La Grande-Duchesse de Gérolstein* at the Variety Theatre in Paris. 'Viardot will crush me with contempt but I must confess that I was enormously amused . . . The humour and high spirits are stunning.'[54]

Offenbach was a regular visitor to the spas of Bad Ems and Baden, only 250 kilometres apart, where he cut a dandyish figure in yellow trousers and waistcoat, light-blue velvet coat, grey gloves and grey hat.

Jacques Offenbach, c. 1870.

He spent most of his spare time in the casino, but came at least on two occasions to the Viardot villa, once for a performance of *Le Dernier Sorcier*, which he enjoyed.[55] He had started going to Bad Ems for his rheumatism in 1858, but liked it there so much, apart from his wife and family, free to work and visit the casino and his mistresses, that he spent in all ten seasons there (he once quipped in the curious Franco-German jargon he had made his own that he would have been as rich as Meyerbeer had it not been for his three passions: 'le cigare, la femme, *und dann noch* un peu le jeu!'). Offenbach's operettas were the cultural highlight of the summer season at Bad Ems, and many people went there because of them alone. In 1863, a bonanza year, he had ten operettas playing at Bad Ems, including *Lischen et Fritzchen*, which became a big commercial hit with its best-loved tune, 'Je suis Alsacienne, je suis Alsacien', being sung by everyone. The story goes that Offenbach composed the whole operetta in a week to win a bet.[56]

The cosmopolitan atmosphere of the spa towns attracted Offenbach. A Jew from Cologne, born in 1819, the year of the last great pogrom in nineteenth-century Germany, Offenbach had made his home in France. His composition style was an eclectic mix of influences from Mozart and Rossini, French comic opera, the cancan and dance music of many nationalities. The course of Offenbach's career had zig-zagged to avoid obstacles posed by anti-Semitism, which he encountered even at the height of his success. Cartoons emphasized his Jewishness by giving him an elongated crooked nose, and many critics followed Wagner's lead in characterizing his 'commercial' music as 'Jewish'.[57] According to the Goncourts, the journalist Ernest Daudet liked to say that Offenbach was 'the worst type of Jew' because he kept his wife on 'the small change that tumbled from his pockets' while he lived the life of a *bon vivant*.[58]

The young Jakob (as he was known in Germany) had been drawn to France because of its greater liberties for Jews. Trained at the Conservatory, Offenbach had soon made a name for himself in the salons, dance venues and *comédie en vaudeville* theatres of Paris with his light dance music and burlesque skits during the 1840s. But what he really wanted was to write for the Opéra-Comique, the stage on which the works of Auber, Adam and Donizetti had been premiered. For several years, he lobbied its director, but no commission came, so he worked as a composer at the Comédie-Française. In desperate financial straits, in

1854 he considered emigrating to America. But then he thought 'of starting a musical theatre myself':

> I said to myself that the Opéra-Comique was no longer the home of comic opera, and that the idea of really gay, cheerful, witty music – in short the idea of music with life in it – was gradually being forgotten. The composers who wrote for the Opéra-Comique wrote little grand operas. I felt sure that there was something that could be done by the young musicians who, like myself, were being kept waiting in idleness outside the portals of the lyrical theatre.[59]

A precedent had been set already by Hervé (the theatre name of Florimond Ronger). Hervé had established his own theatre on the boulevard du Temple in 1854, where he staged his one-act comic operettas (he called them *Folies concertantes*).* He commissioned one by Offenbach, a nonsense piece, *Oyayaye, ou La Reine des îles,* about a double-bass player (played by Hervé), shipwrecked on a cannibal island, who escapes from the cannibals by sailing off on his double bass. Encouraged by this success, Offenbach secured the lease on the Salle Lacaze, an abandoned theatre on the Champs Élysées opposite the entrance to the Exposition Universelle, which had only just opened when the theatre began business on 5 July 1855. The Salle Lacaze was tiny but sumptuously furnished with velvet chairs, which made it appear rather princely to the bourgeois public that frequented it. The theatre was largely financed by the editor of *Le Figaro*, Hippolyte de Villemessant, who had taken over the newspaper in 1854, the year he befriended Offenbach, filling it with lively stories, anecdotes and gossip to attract the same public Offenbach was entertaining with his *opéras bouffes*. Villemessant invested in the theatre and promoted it in *Le Figaro*.[60]

The Théâtre des Bouffes-Parisiens opened with Offenbach conducting four of his own *opéras bouffes*, one-act satirical farces. The Salle Lacaze was packed to the rafters. A significant proportion of the audience was made up of foreign tourists and visitors to the Exposition who wanted entertainment in the evenings. But many others came from the

---

* The strict French laws of theatre licensing allowed Hervé to stage only one-act operas with no more than two characters. He found various ingenious ways around these restrictions. In one work, for example, he has a singing corpse for a character.

banlieues: they could travel into Paris for an evening on the new suburban trains to join the promenaders on the boulevards.

Offenbach appealed to the subversive humour of the boulevard. He poked fun at pomposity, hypocrisy and false sanctity – all easy targets in Second Empire France. He had no shortage of subjects. In a society where money could be quickly made and quickly lost through speculations on the stock market there were ample opportunities for satire, and Offenbach exploited most of them. Many of his plots revolve around fortunes being made, only to be lost again. They show people spending money without care, losing themselves in luxury and pleasure, living for today because they know that what they gained from speculation might disappear tomorrow as easily as it had come yesterday.

Offenbach himself was on the run from creditors when he wrote his first full-length operetta, *Orpheus in the Underworld* (1858). A subversive parody of Greek mythology, it used the Orpheus story to show the gods behaving badly, subject to the same lusts, jealousies and intrigues as humans. Orpheus and Eurydice are not star-crossed lovers but a nagging married couple. Jupiter is shown making love to girls in the presence of his jealous wife. The other gods all follow his example, putting on a semblance of correct behaviour when Public Opinion, a character-narrator introduced by Offenbach to represent the Greek chorus, appears in the interests of Morality. In the end Public Opinion is dismissed by Jupiter, and the gods descend to Hell in a Bacchanalian orgy dancing the 'Infernal Gallop' or music hall cancan.

The plot suggests that Offenbach intended *Orpheus in the Underworld* as a satire on Napoleon III (Jupiter) and his cronies (all the other gods), but this passed unnoticed on the opening night. Although the reviews were good, early ticket sales were disappointing. Offenbach was afraid he would have to close after only eighty performances. But fortune struck in the form of Jules Janin, the emperor of the critics, who six weeks after its first night reviewed *Orpheus* in the *Journal des débats*. Normally in favour of Offenbach, he was mildly critical of it. Offenbach saw his chance to stir up controversy: he published a provocative letter to Janin in *Le Figaro* in which he defended his play. Janin took the bait, responding with a tirade against *Orpheus* as the profanation of 'holy and glorious antiquity', and denouncing it as 'blasphemous'. That was just what Offenbach had needed to revive his struggling show. To be denounced by the pedantic Janin was the best possible publicity. Attendance rose at once, the Théâtre des Bouffes-Parisiens was packed out every night, takings increased to 60,000 francs a month, and, instead of closing after eighty, *Orpheus* went on playing for 228 consecutive performances. Its dance music was heard everywhere, from the Jardin Mabille to suburban taverns, even by the barrel-organ players in the street. Finally the production closed, but in April 1860 it was staged again at a gala evening at the Théâtre-Italien. Ironically, Napoleon III had agreed to be present on the sole condition that *Orpheus* was performed. For this one performance Offenbach received 22,000 francs, a bronze sculpture from the Tuileries as a gift from the emperor, and a note of thanks from His Imperial Majesty for an 'unforgettable evening'.[61]

Orpheus in the Underworld proved so successful, touring all over Europe, that it became a model for all the fifty operettas composed subsequently by Offenbach. Money, sex and war are the constant subjects of his parodies. In *La Belle Hélène* (1864), performed 700 times in Paris alone, he retold the story of Helen of Troy's elopement with Paris in a contemporary setting. Helen is presented as a fashionable woman of society who runs off with the handsome Paris because she is bored; she does not care what people think, nor about the consequences of her behaviour, as long as she enjoys herself. As the chorus sings when the lovers are together,

> Il faut bien que l'on s'amuse,
> Qu'on se donne du bon temps,
> Et que de la vie on use
> Jusqu'à trente ou soixante ans!
> La la la la la la la la . . .[62]
>
> [We must have fun,
> Have a good time,
> And in life spend on it
> Up to thirty, sixty years!
> La la la la la la la la]

In *La Vie parisienne* (1866) the object of his satire shifted to the present, and in a sense to the audience itself, in so far as he made fun of tourists in Paris. The operetta starts in the Gare du Nord (only just completed in 1864) and follows the adventures of the Goldremarcks, a Swedish baron and his wife, who, like other tourists from around the world, have come to taste the pleasures of 'gay Paree'. The Baron longs to drink champagne with courtesans, the Baroness to see the star singers of the city's opera houses and cafés:

> Je veux, moi, dans la capitale
> Voir les divas qui font fureur,
> Voir la Patti dans *Don Pasquale*,
> Et Thérésa dans *Le Sapeur*!

> [As for me, in the capital
> I want to see the divas who are all the rage,
> To see Patti in *Don Pasquale*,
> And Thérésa in *The Sapper*!]

And throughout the chorus sings:

> Du plaisir à perdre haleine
> Oui voilà la vie parisienne![63]

> [To let pleasure take your breath away
> Yes that is the Paris life!]

By 1867, when the world came to Paris for the Exposition Universelle, the *opéras bouffes* of Offenbach had not only become one of the city's main attractions for foreign visitors; they were among its biggest exports to Europe and beyond. London, Brussels, Frankfurt, Vienna and Budapest – all were swept up by the craze for Offenbach. The composer was on constant tour, delivering the scores, collecting royalties, helping with productions of his works. In 1867, *La Belle Hélène* played across the Continent, from Constantinople to St Petersburg; it made its debut in the United States, Japan, Indochina and Australia. The age of global entertainment had begun.

4

Paris, hôtel Byron,
Saturday, 15 June 1867, 8 a.m.
My Dear Madame Viardot, at 5 o'clock precisely we pulled into the station; at 6 I was installed in a room where I can hardly move about; and at 7 I took a bath ... for it has to be admitted, only Paris can afford you such comforts.[64]

Turgenev came to Paris for the Exposition Universelle on the Champ de Mars. He set off there after finishing his bath. The gigantic exhibition hall, an oval-shaped complex of six concentric galleries, the outer almost two kilometres in length, was filled with machines of every kind and dimension, their noise drowning out the hubbub of the crowd, steam from their engines billowing to the glass ceiling. After a few hours of walking through the galleries, Turgenev was worn out. 'My feet could not go any farther,' he reported to Pauline, 'I was utterly bewildered by this chaos [*tohu-bohu*] of machines, furniture, diamonds, emeralds as big as melons, drapery of every colour, crystals, weapons, palaces, kiosks, pottery, porcelain, horses, dogs, paintings, statues, Chinese men and women, signs, waterclosets (I entered them four times) . . . etc. etc.'[65]

Turgenev was only really interested in the paintings, which he returned to inspect the next day. He was full of praise for the fourteen pictures by Meissonier ('certainly at present the finest painter in the world'), a view we may now ridicule (Meissonier has been out of fashion for at least a hundred years) but one shared by the crowds that swarmed in front of them. He was also disappointed that he did not have the money to buy a 'lovely landscape' by the Bavarian painter Karl von Piloty (another artist seen as staggeringly bad today).[66] He did not even visit Édouard Manet's one-man show. More than fifty of his paintings were displayed in a pavilion he had had constructed in the avenue d'Alma, opposite one of the entrances to the Exposition Universelle, just as Courbet had done in 1855. Although Turgenev was a friend and literary ally of the young Émile Zola, a champion of Manet's art, Turgenev's tastes in painting were more conservative.

For Napoleon III the Exposition was an opportunity to display to the world the splendour of his newly renovated capital. Baron Haussmann had been given extra funds to make sure his main building projects – a network of grand boulevards, railway termini, blocks of uniform apartment buildings, squares, parks and gardens, a sewage system and underground pipes for street gaslights – were ready for the Exposition's opening on 1 April. The old Paris of narrow streets was largely demolished; the labouring classes who had lived there were priced out of the centre by new property development. The city was barely recognizable to those who had been away for a few years. Turgenev, who was one of them, thought Paris had become bigger, grander, so that even with a million visitors for the Exposition Universelle, it 'felt no more crowded' than he remembered it.[67]

Haussmann's Paris became a model for renovation projects in other capitals during the 1860s: the Ringstrasse in Vienna, Hobrecht's plan for the rebuilding of Berlin, Cerdà's Barcelona Plan, the Lindhagen project in Stockholm, the 'Radial road' and boulevards in Budapest, the redesign of Brussels, Cairo with its boulevards and parks constructed under Ismail Pasha – all were inspired, more or less, by the example set by the French capital.[68] Haussmann's Paris gave them the idea of what a city ought to be.

Haussmann often emphasized that the city he was building did not belong to Parisians, alone: it was to be an international capital, belonging equally to the people of the French Empire and to foreign visitors, who could get to it by rail from every corner of the Continent. 'Paris is a capital of consumption, a huge workshop, an arena for ambitions, a rendezvous for pleasure,' Haussmann told a banquet of financiers.[69]

The idea of Paris as a market-place for pleasure had long been part of its identity. But it became central to the city's image from the 1860s, when Haussmann's engineering created new commercial spaces on the boulevards – restaurants, cafés, shops and galleries, vaudevilles and theatres – specifically for enjoyment. Cherished and promoted by Parisians, the cult of Paris as a capital of pleasure was a valuable propaganda tool for its tourist industry. There were books to guide visitors to the city's grand hotels, department stores and shopping galleries, theatres, racecourses, even night clubs and brothels; they all assured their readers that it was the greatest pleasure city in the world. As Alfred Delvau wrote in his guide for tourists, *Les Plaisirs de Paris*, published just in time for the Exposition Universelle in 1867,

> People can say anything about Paris, but not that it is a dull town. It is, on the contrary, a capital of pleasure and with greater pleasures than in any other town; nowhere else can a man enjoy himself as much and in so many varied ways, and whoever cannot find amusement is a man who does not know how to look for it.

This was the Paris of the *flâneur* – the idle stroller and anonymous spectator on the crowded boulevard, for whom, in the words of Baudelaire, it was 'an immense joy to set up house in the heart of the multitude, amid the ebb and flow of movement . . . the fugitive and the infinite'.[70] To sit in a café and watch the passers-by was a pleasure in itself.

Paris was a flurry of parties, balls and receptions for dignitaries, who came from all around the world for the opening of the Exposition Universelle. The hotels were overfilled, and many, like Turgenev, were installed in tiny rooms. Cafés, restaurants, night clubs, brothels worked around the clock and theatres doubled their performances to keep the tourists entertained: the Vaudeville revived its biggest recent hit, *La Dame aux camélias*; the Opéra gave the premiere of Verdi's *Don Carlos*; the Théâtre Lyrique offered Gounod's *Romeo and Juliet*. Meanwhile, on 12 April, Offenbach's *La Grande-Duchesse de Gérolstein* received its premiere at the Variety Theatre with the star Hortense Schneider in its title role.

On his first evening in Paris, Turgenev went to see the operetta with some friends. He loved its energy and comic satire against war. *La Grande-Duchesse de Gérolstein* was the biggest theatrical attraction during the Exposition Universelle, earning over 5,000 francs per night in ticket sales (by the time its first run ended on 30 November, it had received 200 performances and earned 870,000 francs).[71] As a parody of petty royal power, the operetta had run into trouble with the French censors, who saw in its libretto references to Bismarck, the Romanovs and the Spanish queen, Isabella, and, not least, a satiric portrait of Napoleon III and his court; but once the action was removed to the relatively distant eighteenth century, it was free to go ahead. All the royal heads of state visiting the Paris Exposition went to see the *opéra bouffe*. The French emperor saw it on 24 April, and was seen to 'laugh and smile, but also to wind the tips of his mustache – ever the sign of his perplexity'. Tsar Alexander II, informed that the court of Gerolstein was a parody of Catherine the Great, telegraphed ahead from Germany to his ambassador in Paris to reserve a seat for him so that he could check on it himself. Bismarck saw the operetta shortly afterwards, understood it as a parody of petty German kings, and found it very amusing. 'That is right! That is exactly how it is,' he was reported as saying. 'We are getting rid of the Gerolsteins, there will soon be none left. I am grateful to your Parisian artistes for showing the world how ridiculous they were.'[72]

The sharpest edge of Offenbach's satire was pointed at the stupidity of military generals pushing kings to needless wars. The message was timely. Tensions between France and Prussia were rising steadily. Prussia's military defeat of Austria in 1866 had destabilized the European balance of power, according to the French, who feared the rise of a united Germany under Prussian leadership. In April 1867, the constitution of a North German Confederation was adopted by twenty-two previously independent states, some of which had been annexed by the Prussians following their victory against the Austrians. Bismarck, the Minister President of Prussia, became the Confederation's Chancellor. The arrival of the Prussian king in Paris ('without his army', as Mérimée observed sarcastically in a letter to Turgenev) suggested that the threat of war had receded for the time being. But it had not gone away. 'If war breaks out, it will be terrible – and no one knows where or how it will end,' Turgenev wrote to Pauline from St Petersburg, where he had made a short trip in April. 'Let us hope that we shall not hear the cannon in Baden.'[73]

Along with *La Grande-Duchesse de Gérolstein*, the biggest cultural event at the Paris Exposition was the instant hit of Strauss's 'Blue Danube' ('An der schönen blauen Donau', to give the waltz its proper Geman name). When it had been first performed in Vienna in February, the waltz had flopped, receiving only one encore. The problem had been the chorus, which Strauss had included in this original version: its song about the river protecting the Austrians was too close to the bone after their defeat by Prussia. But the melody was good, and Strauss was persuaded to rewrite it in a purely orchestral version for Paris, where Emperor Franz Joseph would host a ball at the Austrian Embassy. The Austrians were interested in closer relations with the French to secure their influence in the southern German states and stop the progress of their common Prussian enemy. They were also keen to restore something of their national pride by promoting Strauss at this glittering international ball. The embassy ballroom and adjoining garden were decked out in white and gold satin, the candelabras filled with flowers in red, white and blue; and a giant waterfall cascaded over roses in the grand reception hall. The 'Blue Danube' was a sensation.

Villemessant, who was at the ball, recognized an opportunity to advance his political influence by helping to foster closer relations between France and Austria. Over the next weeks he filled the pages of *Le Figaro* with articles in praise of Strauss. He gave a dinner for him in the editorial rooms to which both Turgenev and Flaubert were invited, along with Alexandre Dumas fils, Gautier and the painter

James Tissot, who praised Strauss's music in *Le Figaro* as 'a delicate embroidery, full of good cheer, releasing suppressed laughter, punctuated with little arias, pirouettes . . . Strauss! What magic there is in the name!' Villemessant's publicity helped turn the 'Blue Danube' into a hit tune played in cafés and dance venues everywhere. Strauss's publisher received so many orders for the piano arrangement that his copper plates were soon worn out – they only printed 10,000 copies at a time. He had 100 new plates made to produce a million copies – the biggest ever printing of a piano score until that time – which went on sale around the world.[74]

5

Clara Schumann wrote to Brahms on 3 October 1867:

> *I have a little item of musical gossip to tell you.*
>
> *Mme Viardot has composed some small operettas, two of which she has had played by her children and pupils. I heard each of them three times, always with the same pleasure. What skill, what finesse, what grace, what wit! They are marvellous.*[75]

Pauline's compositions numbered several hundred by the time she died. They never entered the musical canon, but were highly thought of during her lifetime.[76] Reviewing her *Ten Songs*, in 1850, Henry Chorley, Pauline's friend, thought that they were 'better than much which passes for good in music: they are individual in style – not assuredly Italian – not strictly German – not precisely French. Their originality does not reside in their "melodies" so much as in their entire structure.'[77] Chopin praised her Spanish songs. Like George Sand, he took an interest in folk music, and liked how Pauline had adapted it to the art music form. Liszt thought she was the first 'female composer of genius'. In 1859, he wrote in the *Neue Zeitschrift für Musik*:

> Her works contain so much tender and delicate feeling, so much skill in harmonic subtleties (which would be envied by many famous composers), that we must regret that Mme Viardot has not invested more effort in her talent as a composer; it is our hope that these sparks of genius so close to the inspiration of Chopin turn into a flame.[78]

Turgenev encouraged Pauline to compose. Battling against her lack of confidence, he was lavish with his praise of her music and did all he could to promote it. With his help as a translator, Pauline composed an album of twelve songs to Russian poems by Pushkin, Fet and Turgenev himself; it was published by August Johansen in St Petersburg in 1864. Five further albums of Pauline's Russian songs were published by Johansen in the next few years, all of them with the close involvement of Turgenev, who arranged favourable publicity, paid for the later albums to be published, and even got his friends to buy up the unsold stock, without Pauline ever finding out.[79]

In 1865, Pauline's old friend Julius Rietz stayed with her and Louis in Baden. During his stay he heard her sing her Russian songs. On his return to Dresden, Rietz wrote to Pauline, suggesting that she write a piano sonata and urging her to compose in a larger form, to try a symphony for example, which he would be pleased to conduct in a concert in Dresden, where he was Hofkapellmeister. Turgenev was delighted with Rietz's letter. He wrote to Pauline from his estate at Spasskoe, where he had gone for a short visit, to encourage her:

> That should give you wings – it is so much more than any one of us dilettantes could have said to you – and if you do not finish your sonata, if I return to find not even a lovely adagio almost completed – it will be necessary to scold you. I imagine that a musical idea is easier to develop broadly when its form is not determined in advance . . . And so, to work! I encourage you as someone who has hardly written anything of late. But no! I give you my word of honour that if you set out to write your sonata, I will renew my literary work [he had not written anything substantial since *Fathers and Sons*] . . . A novel for a sonata. How does that suit you?[80]

Pauline did write a sonata – a set of three for violin and piano which have all survived. But she never wrote a symphony or concerto. Nor did she ever try her hand at larger operatic forms, although this too was a possibility proposed to her more than once. After the success of *Le Dernier Sorcier* at the Weimar Court Theatre, Pauline was invited by the Grand Duke of Weimar to write a Grand Opera. But this never came about. There were also plans for her to write a full-length opera based on George Sand's novel *La Mare au diable*. Pauline had received the libretto from Sand in 1859. By 1862, she had completed two of the three projected acts. But then work stopped. Finally, in a long letter dated 7 June 1869, Louis, not Pauline, gave an explanation to their friend:

> Pauline has never imagined herself to be a composer, she has written a fairly large number of small pieces of music, always in accordance with the circumstances that presented themselves ... In her operettas, for example, one finds a chorus of elves teasing the sorcerer, a song of the rain, a lullaby to put the ogre to sleep; Pauline finds the musical equivalent for the character of these easily. But she is not enough of a composer, she cannot find to a sufficient extent within herself and without the aid of a particular circumstance the musical ideas that are necessary to succeed in all topics. However charming a comedy *La Mare au diable* may be, it offers only two such circumstances ... The other scenes belong to the category of those where the composer must draw from within himself [sic] the melodic ideas and harmonic resources. Pauline has tried to do this on several occasions, at different times; she has never been satisfied with what she has done and has torn up these futile efforts.

Louis suggested giving the libretto to 'someone who is more of a composer, for example Bizet'.[81]

Whether it reflected Pauline's judgement of her own music or Louis's personal opinions, the letter points to many of the obstacles preventing women from composing major works and entering the canon on a par with men.

Pauline had received no formal training in a musical academy. Her mother had sent her to study composition with Anton Reicha in her teenage years, but her lessons had stopped short of counterpoint and orchestration, basic skills for composing music on a larger scale. Women were excluded from composition classes in most conservatories. Even when they were admitted to a musical academy, they were taught separately from men, trained for the most part as singers or pianists to prepare them for a career as performers or teachers. If they were taught harmony at all, it was at a lower level than the men. In the Paris Conservatory, for example, women were allowed to take lessons in keyboard harmony for performers from 1859, but it was another twenty years before they received instruction in composition harmony. Until then, only two conservatories in Europe – Brussels and Leipzig – offered composition classes for women.[82]

Private composition lessons could be organized by supportive families, but such families were very rare. Musically talented daughters might well be encouraged to play the piano or sing well as an accomplishment but few were given the support to compose music, which was seen as a profession exclusively for men.

The young Fanny Mendelssohn (1805–47) was perhaps not as gifted as her younger brother, Felix, in his teenage years, when he composed his early masterpieces, the Octet and the Overture to *A Midsummer Night's Dream*, but she had precocious talent, which received less encouragement than his. Their father, Abraham, paid for only Felix to be educated musically. 'Music will perhaps become his profession,' he wrote to Fanny when she was fifteen, 'while for you it can and must be only an ornament.' She married the painter Wilhelm Hensel, who encouraged her composing and found her texts to set to songs. Felix too was supportive. But he thought that women should be wives and mothers first, and did not think she was serious enough to embark on a career in cómposing music for publication, which required full-time work. As he put it in a letter to their mother in 1837:

> From my knowledge of Fanny I should say that she has neither inclination nor vocation for authorship. She is too much that a woman ought to be for this. She regulates her house, and neither thinks of the public nor of the musical world, nor even of music at all, until her first duties are fulfilled. Publishing would only disturb her in these, and I cannot say that I approve of it.[83]

Faced with all these obstacles, Fanny felt compelled to conceal her identity on the publication of her first pieces – three Lieder published in the name of Felix Mendelssohn (Opus 8 and 9).* Perhaps, as Pauline thought, she simply lacked the confidence to compete with her brother as a composer.[84]

Clara Schumann published some of her first Lieder in a joint collection with her husband, Robert. They were arranged in such a way that critics could not tell which songs were hers and which were his. Living in the shadow of her husband's genius, Clara did not have much faith in her own abilities as a composer. In 1839, two years after her

---

* Her authorship was revealed only in 1842, when Queen Victoria received Felix Mendelssohn at Buckingham Palace and expressed her desire to sing for him her favourite of his songs, 'Italien', which he confessed was by Fanny.

engagement to Robert, she had written in her diary that she ought to give up her belief, which had been encouraged by her father, that she had the talent to compose ('a woman must not wish to compose – there was never one able to do it'). By that time she had written several piano compositions and a Piano Concerto. Reviews of the works she published in her own name were polite but patronizing. They always pointed out her status as a 'woman composer' and usually recommended that she focus on the smaller music forms (piano and chamber pieces) because women were not capable of composing large-scale works (symphonies and concertos). Even Robert shared this view. Writing of her G Minor Piano Trio (Op. 17) in 1846, Schumann praised some passages but added: 'naturally it is still women's work, which always lacks force and occasionally invention.' Damned with faint praise by her own husband, Clara lost all confidence. One year later, when Robert published his first Piano Trio (Op. 63), she compared her own piano trio unfavourably to his, deciding that it 'sounded quite effeminate and sentimental' (inferior female qualities). From that point, she wrote about her music as if she were ashamed of it; she composed almost nothing more. After Robert's death, in 1856, when she was left with seven children, she was too busy performing even to consider composing. Pauline certainly discouraged her from doing so, warning her that there was little to be earned from writing music, and that 'even the biggest talents would die of hunger if they had only their small income from their composing'.[85]

Lack of confidence held back Pauline too. According to the singer Anna Eugénie Schoen-René, who studied with her in Baden, Pauline hid her compositions 'like a fault'.[86] She would sing an aria she had composed and let her guests suppose, as she told them, that it was a newly discovered composition by Mozart. It was not until the 1880s that she even thought to enforce her copyright and collect royalties from her published works.[87] Her insecurity would certainly explain why Turgenev went to such great lengths to encourage her. It would account for the problems she encountered in trying to compose a full-scale opera, and why she left it to Louis to announce her 'failure'. Pauline had been 'scared and paralysed' by the 'necessity of equalling or nearly equalling the creative level of her illustrious partner', Louis explained to George Sand, the librettist whom he had in mind. Pauline felt out of her depth.[88] She was more comfortable composing small-scale works:

songs and piano pieces, the violin sonatas and the salon operettas which she wrote with Turgenev in Baden.

Salon music was certainly the music most composed by women in the nineteenth century. It was a sphere of creativity accessible to 'amateurs' without formal training in the composition skills necessary to compose larger works (just as women artists, excluded from the art academies where men were instructed in the human nude and history painting, were active mainly in the 'lower' painting genres such as landscapes and portraits). In the view of serious music critics the term 'salon music' was virtually synonymous with 'woman's music' – a 'lesser form' of music for the home. Most of the salon music composed by women remained unpublished, its composers long forgotten. Loïsa Puget wrote several hundred romances, which she sang to great acclaim in the salons of Paris during the 1840s. Josephine Martin performed many of her piano works alongside works by Liszt, Thalberg and others. But only a small fraction of these compositions were published.

Music for the home was a big market, and some women managed to break through. Charlotte Barnard ('Claribel') was a prolific hymn and ballad composer whose works were immensely popular, occupying a commercial space between operetta and the music hall. Her best-known song, 'Come Back to Erin', became so well known that it assumed the status of an Irish folk song in New York vaudevilles, where sentimental Irish tunes were popular. The Polish pianist and composer Tekla Bądarzewska-Baranowska also struck gold with her 'A Maiden's Prayer', originally published in Warsaw and reissued as a supplement to Schlesinger's *Revue et Gazette musicale de Paris*. Pianistically trite with brilliant effects that were not hard to play, the piece remained a bestseller until the beginning of the twentieth century, when it became a symbol of provincial mediocrity ('And tomorrow morning I won't have to listen to that "Maiden's Prayer" any more,' says Irina, bound for Moscow, in the final act of Anton Chekhov's *Three Sisters*, as its saccharine melody wafts into the garden from a drawing-room).[89]

Louise Farrenc (1804–75) and Louise Bertin (1805–77) were exceptional in overcoming the obstacles preventing women from composing music in larger forms – Farrenc wrote orchestral works, Bertin operas – but they had considerable advantages. Both were encouraged by their families: Farrenc was born into a dynasty of distinguished artists, the Dumonts, and she married an amateur composer turned music publisher who championed her work; while Bertin's father was the editor of the influential *Journal des débats*. Both Farrenc and Bertin had composition lessons from an early age (Farrenc studied with Reicha, who also taught Pauline; Bertin with the Belgian critic and composer François-Joseph Fétis). Farrenc's early compositions were reviewed favourably by no less a critic than Schumann; her first Overture was praised by Berlioz. She was made a full professor of piano at the Paris Conservatory in 1842, and even won her battle to be paid the same amount as her colleague Henri Herz. But her orchestral works were infrequently performed – a fact attributed by Fétis, writing three years after Farrenc's death, to the problems women faced in acquiring the recognition needed for a concert manager to justify the costs of a concert. And without regular performances it was practically impossible to get a large-scale work published:

> Unfortunately, the genre of large scale instrumental music to which Madame Farrenc, by nature and formation, felt herself called involves performance resources which a composer can acquire for herself or himself only with enormous effort. Another factor here is the public, as a rule not a very knowledgeable one, whose only standard for measuring the quality of a work is the name of its author. If the composer is unknown, the audience remains unreceptive, and the publishers, especially in France, close their ears when someone offers them a halfway decent work.[90]

6

From 1863, Turgenev made short trips from Baden to Paris, where he kept his apartment in the rue de Rivoli. He went to see his daughter, to buy and look at art, and to meet his literary friends, Mérimée, Flaubert, Sainte-Beuve and the Goncourts, who regularly convened for long dinners at Magny's restaurant on the left bank of the Seine. Turgenev was introduced to the Magny circle by Charles-Edmond Chojecki, the Polish émigré writer, translator and librarian of the French Senate, on 28 February 1863. A brilliant conversationalist, the Russian writer made a strong impression on the Goncourt brothers, who noted in their diary:

> He is a delightful colossus, a gentle, white-haired giant; he has the appearance of an old and gentle forest or mountain wizard; he looks like a druid

or the kindly old monk in *Romeo and Juliet*. He is handsome, but in a strange and venerable way, grandly handsome like Nieuwerkerke. But Nieuwerkerke's eyes are a silky blue, whereas Turgenev has the blue of the heavens in his eyes. The kindness of his gaze is matched by the caress and little singing sounds of his Russian accent, something like the humming of a child.[91]

It was at that dinner that Turgenev first met Flaubert, who would become a close and lasting friend. Turgenev took an instant liking to the French novelist, whose writing he had read and admired perhaps more than any other writer's at that time. The next day, he sent him two translations of his books, the *Sketches from a Hunter's Album* and *Rudin*, promising to send him Mérimée's translation of *Fathers and Sons* and *First Love*, both out in French in 1863. He invited him to dinner with Pauline, who was keen to meet him too, at his apartment in the rue de Rivoli. Flaubert could not come, but he wrote a warm reply full of praise for Turgenev's writing, which 'delighted' him: 'I have considered you a master for a long time. But the more I study you, the more your

Flaubert, c. 1870.

skill leaves me gaping. I admire the forceful yet restrained quality of your writing, the sympathy that extends down to the lowest human creatures and brings landscape to life. One sees and one dreams.'[92] Soon afterwards Turgenev left for Baden. He invited Flaubert to visit him, but the Frenchman was famously reclusive and seldom ventured beyond Rouen or Paris, so the invitation was not taken up. But on his trips to Paris Turgenev made a point of seeing him.

Turgenev and Flaubert were drawn together by a profound mutual affinity. They shared a similar view of art, admired the same writers, and approached their literary craft in a like manner, setting out to show reality rather than expound on it. 'How many things have I found in your work that I have felt and experienced myself!' Flaubert wrote to Turgenev in March 1863. Both men were pessimistic in outlook: they had given up all hope of finding rational solutions to the problems of the world through politics (the lesson each had learned from the failure of 1848) or finding happiness through married love (a theme that runs through both their writings).* They both found consolation in their work, the main thing that united them. Their correspondence contained more than mutual flattery. They helped each other as writers. Flaubert was particularly indebted to Turgenev, who could read his works in French (Flaubert could not read Russian). Between 1868 and 1870 Turgenev made several trips to Flaubert's house in Croisset to help with his problematic novel *The Temptation of St Anthony*. 'What a listener, and what a critic!' Flaubert reported to George Sand:

> He staggered me with the depth and crispness of his judgements. If only all those who mess about with books could have heard him, what a lesson! He misses nothing. At the end of a section of a hundred lines, he can remember a weak adjective; he made two or three exquisite suggestions on points of detail for *Saint Anthony*.[93]

Isolated intellectually, Flaubert was increasingly dependent on the friendship of Turgenev. 'You are, I think, the only man with whom I can have a conversation,' he wrote to him. 'I no longer see anybody

---

* 'Don't you think,' Flaubert once wrote to a friend, 'that life would be more tolerable if the idea of Happiness did not exist? We expect things that life can't give' (Flaubert, *Correspondance*, vol. 5, p. 419).

who is interested in art or poetry.' The feeling of connection between
them was mutual. Turgenev wrote to Flaubert in 1868:

> From the first time I saw you (you know, in a sort of inn on the other
> bank of the Seine) I have felt a great liking for you, – there are few men,
> especially Frenchmen, with whom I feel so relaxed and at ease and yet at
> the same time so stimulated. It seems to me that I could talk to you for
> weeks on end, but then we are a pair of moles burrowing away in the
> same direction.[94]

Turgenev was one of the few literary people to understand the value
of Flaubert's later works. When *Sentimental Education* came out in
1869 to poor reviews in France, Turgenev tried to boost his friend's
morale by sending him copies of more favourable pieces in the German
press, most of which he had himself arranged. 'Yes, certainly, people
have been unfair to you, but this is a time to brace yourself and hurl a
masterpiece at your readers,' he wrote to him encouragingly, reminding
him of his earlier successes with *Madame Bovary* and *Salammbô*.
'Don't forget that people judge you by the standards you yourself have
set, and you're bearing the weight of your past.'[95]

Turgenev campaigned to get Flaubert's novels published in Russia.
He acted in effect as his literary agent, publicist and translator. The
liberal climate of reform in Russia during the 1860s encouraged publishers to translate books from Western Europe. Russian readers had
been starved of them during the repressive reign of Nicholas I. In 1866,
Mikhail Stasiulevich, a liberal history professor, began publishing *The
Messenger of Europe* (Vestnik Evropy), named in honour of the Russian writer and historian Nikolai Karamzin, who in 1802 had
established a literary journal by the same name, which had brought to
Russians the latest European ideas. Stasiulevich's aim was to publish
works from Europe in translation alongside new Russian works. He
also published articles on politics and literature from correspondents in
Germany, France, Italy and Switzerland. Because reports from abroad
were not subject to tsarist censorship, these articles were an effective
channel for promoting ideas of European progress in Russia, where the
journal sold 8,000 copies every month, a high number in itself, though
the actual number of readers was likely to be three or four times more
as copies passed from hand to hand. Stasiulevich insisted on paying for
translation rights, even though there was no legal obligation for him to

do so, as there was no copyright protection for foreign works in Russia, and other publishers regularly published pirate translations. But he only paid for advance proofs, insisting on his need to publish first in Russia, because once a book appeared in print there was nothing to protect his investment. 'You can assert your rights on every page, but that will not stop anyone in Russia from publishing their own translation, if only your original is for sale in a bookshop,' he explained to the German writer Berthold Auerbach, whose *The House on the Rhine* (published in Germany in 1869) was serialized in *The Messenger of Europe* between 1868 and 1870.[96]

Turgenev soon became an important intermediary between the journal in St Petersburg and the European literary scene. He took an active part in selecting works for translation (sometimes on the basis of their likely impact on social attitudes in Russia rather than their literary worth). It was Turgenev who had organized the translation of *The House on the Rhine*, and who wrote a preface to the novel, which, though rather dull as a story, was of moral interest to Russian readers as an exploration of the legacies of slave-owning (its hero, Sonnenkamp, whose real name is Banfield, is a retired slave-owner from Louisiana with a dark past). As an agent for Stasiulevich, Turgenev introduced a number of the most important European writers to a Russian readership. Flaubert was one of the first. Through Turgenev's efforts, a long article on *Sentimental Education* appeared in the January 1870 issue of the *Messenger*, followed the next month by a review of all Flaubert's works. Meanwhile Turgenev set about translating *The Temptation of St Anthony* for publication by Stasiulevich.

As well as introducing European writers to Russia, Turgenev acted as an ambassador for Russian literature in Europe. He collaborated with translators, advised his foreign publishers on what books they should translate, and wrote articles about the latest Russian works in French and German periodicals (in 1868, he announced the arrival of a masterpiece called *War and Peace*). As the first of the great nineteenth-century Russian writers to attain a popular appeal in other languages, Turgenev had a major influence on the translation of Russian writers in Europe – both in terms of the language used by translators to communicate a sense of 'Russian-ness' and in terms of the types of books considered suitable for a Western audience. Turgenev's views were taken seriously by European publishers, who were eager to exploit this new source of literary talent. Pierre-Jules Hetzel, his French publisher, was particularly keen, publishing *The Cossacks* (1863) by Tolstoy, *Prince Serebrenni* (1862) by Aleksei Tolstoy, and the *Folk Tales* by Maria Markovich, which Turgenev had translated from Ukrainian into Russian in 1859. Most of these translations were by Mérimée, who, like Turgenev, was committed to promoting Russian literature in France. Both men saw it as a means of healing rifts between the two countries after the Crimean War, and as a means of promoting their cosmopolitan ideals against the rise of nationalism in Europe.[97]

Turgenev was considered an important writer in Germany, to some degree because he lived there (and even came to think of himself as a German) during the 1860s. Through translations of his work and articles about him in the press he became well known and popular – perhaps more so than many of the best-known German novelists, such as Raabe and Keller. Even Theodor Storm, who revered Turgenev, found himself in his shadow.[98] The critic Viktor Hehn talked with irritation about a 'cult of Turgenev' in Germany. Turgenev used his influence to get other Russians published in German: Gogol, Dostoevsky and Tolstoy. He had excellent relations with German publishers and translators, including Friedrich Bodenstedt, a well-known lyricist and travel writer, who was also Professor of Slavic Languages at Munich University. Turgenev was delighted with Bodenstedt's translation of his story *Faust* (1862), considering him to be a 'great stylist', and offering to pay him to translate his other works so that they would attract publishers and become better known in Germany. Two large volumes of Turgenev's works were published in translation by Bodenstedt during the 1860s. *Fathers and Sons* appeared in German translations by Wilhelm Wolfsohn and Claire von Glümer in 1865 and 1868, respectively. And in 1869 Turgenev's collected works began to be published in twelve volumes by Eric Behre, a German-language publisher in Mitau, Latvia.[99]

Turgenev earned nothing from these translations. Though France and Russia had a bilateral agreement, it was still difficult to enforce copyright. The most a writer could hope for (but not expect) was a small payment as a gesture of good will on the publication of their work by a foreign publisher. Turgenev often warned his fellow Russian writers not to expect any earnings from their works in translation. In 1868, when his friend Mikhail Avdeev asked for his advice on how to find a publisher in France for his recent novels, Turgenev replied:

In Paris translations from foreign languages are published badly and reluctantly, because they do not pay well. Dickens is exceptional – and not even one of his novels has come out in a second edition, whereas the likes of *Monsieur, Madame et Bébé* by G[ustave] Droz has already come out in 20 editions. My books have been translated – but I personally have never received a kopeck – while the translator, as an act of great kindness, is paid no more than 300 or 400 francs, and not always anything at all.[100]

It was not the money that mattered to Turgenev so much as becoming known abroad. Although he complained about the loss of income to foreign publishers who printed pirate versions of his works, what really bothered him was the poor quality of most of these translations, something he also could not control. He was more interested in his moral rights – the preservation of his work's integrity – than in the protection of his economic property through copyright. The struggle of the artist for moral rights – a campaign pioneered by Verdi from the 1840s – was carried on by writers like Turgenev with greater urgency in the 1860s and 1870s when the development of an international book trade made it even more important to have a good translation for a writer's reputation in foreign markets. Turgenev did not hesitate to complain when his prose was mangled in translation by pirate publishers. On 1 December 1868, for example, he wrote to the *Pall Mall Gazette*, protesting that their translator's mutilation of his novel *Smoke* was bound to damage him 'in the eyes of the English public, whose good opinion cannot be valued too highly by any man who holds a pen'. He demanded that the London journal publish his protest. Two days later, the full letter was printed under the title, 'M. Tourgueneff and his English Traducer'.[101]

By the end of the 1860s, all Turgenev's books had been translated into French and German (the English were slower to translate from foreign languages). He liked to joke with Russians that his literary stock was worth more in Europe than in Russia.

Turgenev and Pauline were also instrumental in getting Russian music better known in Europe. Their closest contact in the Russian music world was Anton Rubinstein, who regularly came to Baden in the summer, partly to visit his powerful patron, the Russian Grand Duchess, Elena Pavlovna, who held court in her mansion there, but mainly to indulge his weakness for gambling. 'He constantly plays roulette and has squandered everything, even some of his clothes, so that the next day he had to put on an old frockcoat and go gloveless,' wrote Mily Balakirev to his fellow Russian composer César Cui in 1863. During that summer Rubinstein came almost every day to the Villa Viardot. He helped Pauline with the composition of her Russian songs, and started making sketches for an opera based on Turgenev's novel *Rudin* – until Turgenev, who had agreed to write the libretto, gave up on the task. The following January, in St Petersburg, Turgenev saw Rubinstein again. The two of them promoted Pauline's songs. Turgenev attended one of his recitals in the Philharmonia, the new concert hall of the Conservatory, which Rubinstein had established in 1862 with the support of the Grand Duchess. Turgenev was not a fan of the pianist's virtuoso style. 'He performs as he always does,' he wrote to Pauline after the concert, 'he starts by giving you vertigo and ends by boring you, or at least exhausting you.'[102] But he applauded Rubinstein's campaign to raise music standards in Russia.

In 1859, with that aim in mind, Rubinstein had founded the Russian Musical Society. It put on concerts of mainly German music and gave classes to aspiring musicians at the Mikhailovsky Palace, home to Grand Duchess Elena Pavlovna, who was German and a proselytizer of her nation's cause. From these beginnings the idea of a conservatory had taken shape. It was conceived as a European music school dominated by the conventions of composition developed in the music of Bach, Haydn, Mozart and Beethoven. Its German academic orientation was fiercely criticized by a group of nationalist composers, the so-called 'Mighty Five' (Balakirev, Cui, Mussorgsky, Borodin and Rimsky-Korsakov), all young men and self-taught amateurs, mostly from the minor gentry, who bitterly resented the 'foreign' court connections of conservatory composers such as Tchaikovsky (one of its first graduates) and saw themselves as pioneers of a more 'authentically Russian' music style. Where Rubinstein was scornful of the amateurism of Russian composers (he called Glinka a dilettante), they retaliated by accusing him of denigrating Russia from the heights of what they called his 'European conservatorial grandeur'. There was a strong element of personal animosity, even anti-Semitism, in their battles against Rubinstein. They called him 'Tupinstein' ('dull'), 'Dubinstein' ('dumb-headed') and Grubinstein ('crude'). They railed against his cosmopolitanism (a synonym for 'Jewish rootlessness' in Russian nationalist discourse), which they

feared would stifle 'authentic' Russian forms. In 1862, in direct opposition to Rubinstein's Conservatory, the nationalist composers founded
the Free Music School, setting it the task of cultivating native talent on
the 'purely Russian' principles established by their hero, Glinka (whose
music is in fact steeped in Italian and German influences). In the words
of Vladimir Stasov, the influential critic who acted as their champion, it
was time for the 'hoopskirts and tailcoats' of the Europeanized St Petersburg élites to make way for the 'long Russian coats' of the provinces.[103]

Turgenev sympathized with their artistic desire to break free from
academic conventions, but he could not agree with their attacks on the
Conservatory, which he thought was essential for the education of professional musicians in Russia. He was critical of the amateurism which
he believed characterized the arts in Russia, and even more so of the
Slavophiles who dressed it up as Russian 'genius' and 'spontaneity'. He
believed that Russia's artists needed to be brought up to the level of
their European counterparts, to immerse themselves in European civilization, in order to transcend its influence and stamp a national
character on their own art: it was not enough for them to draw from
folk culture, as the Slavophiles argued. Turgenev was equally impatient
with the way the nationalists depicted Glinka as a genius 'greater than
any other composer after Beethoven', as Cui put it in 1864. Glinka was
a talented composer, Turgenev conceded, but such inflated claims were
dangerous, encouraging delusions about Russian greatness which could
not help its integration into Europe. Turgenev's view is voiced by the
character Potugin in his novel *Smoke* when he declares that Russia has
no great artists and dismisses the example of Glinka:

> Exceptions, you know, merely confirm the rule, but even in this case we
> could not refrain from boasting. If you were to say, for example, that
> Glinka was a really remarkable musician whom circumstances, both
> external and internal, prevented from becoming the founder of Russian
> opera, there would be no argument. But no, that's not good enough. He
> must immediately be promoted to full general and made Master of the
> Royal Music. Other nations will be cut down to size; they've got nothing
> like this, it will be said, while some colossal self-taught genius, whose
> work is nothing but a pitiful imitation of second-rate foreign practition-
> ers, is immediately pointed out. Genuinely second-rate. They are easier
> to imitate.[104]

Turgenev had first heard the music of Mussorgsky and Balakirev at a concert in St Petersburg in 1867. To begin with he was sceptical, reporting to Pauline:

> This evening I went to a grand concert of the music of the future – Russian – because there is one of those as well.* But it is absolutely pitiful, devoid of ideas, or originality: it is simply a bad copy of what is done in Germany. And such insolence is reinforced by a total absence of the civilization that distinguishes us. Everyone is thrown into the same bag – from Rossini and Mozart to Beethoven. Come now, it is pitiful.[105]

In the 1870s Turgenev would come round to the Mighty Five. He was introduced to them by Stasov, whom he knew as a prolific writer about the arts in Russia and as the director of the Public Library in St Petersburg. Turgenev often argued with Stasov, whose dogmatic promotion of the nationalist school conflicted with his liberal Westernist opinions, but he respected him for bringing Russian culture to the attention of the West. As Turgenev became more acquainted with the music of the Mighty Five, he recognized its originality, and with Pauline campaigned for their works to be included in the European repertoire. He could not agree with their nationalist agenda, nor with any nationalism in the arts, but he admired their vitality.

It was not only in Russia that musical nationalism began to take hold during the 1860s. A similar phenomenon was taking place in the Austro-Hungarian Empire. Austria's military defeat by France and the loss of most of its remaining Italian possessions in 1859 brought about a relaxation of government controls on the cultural activities of other subject nationalities in the hope that this would prevent them from developing independence movements of their own. In this newly opened cultural space the Czechs were especially active. They published collections of Bohemian folk songs, established choral groups, and organized subscriptions to finance the construction of a national theatre where more Czech plays and operas could be performed than had been licensed by the Austrian authorities in the Estates Theatre, where the repertoire was dominated by German and other foreign works.

---

* A reference to Wagner's self-promoting essay 'The Music of the Future' ('La Musique de l'avenir') published originally in a French translation in 1860 and in German ('Zukunftsmusik') in 1861.

A temporary national theatre was completed in 1862, and the first stone of the future National Theatre was laid six years later in a ceremony attended by 60,000 provincial subscribers and visitors brought to Prague by special trains. The opening of the Provisional Theatre prompted the Czech patriot Count Jan Harrach to announce a competition for a national opera – one that would be sung in the Czech language and use folk song and dance to create a feeling of 'Czechness'. The eventual winner was *The Brandenburgers in Bohemia* by Bedřich Smetana (1824–84). It told the story of the country's liberation from German occupation in the thirteenth century. Like most members of the Prague intelligentsia, Smetana had been educated in German: he wrote his diary and letters in German, and when, in 1860, he first switched to Czech he made numerous mistakes. Encouraged by the removal of restrictions on Czech cultural expression, he transformed himself from a composer mainly known for his Lisztian piano works into a composer of Czech music. His comic opera *The Bartered Bride* (1866) became the most frequently performed in the Czech operatic repertoire. Its folk-like music and dances, colourful costumes and stage designs made it far more than an opera: it was a popular entertainment, attracting a national audience from all social classes, and a cultural symbol of Czech nationhood.

The popularity of *The Bartered Bride* – not just in Prague but across Europe – rested largely on the notion of its 'authenticity' – the fanciful idea that its folk-like elements were deeply rooted in the ancient peasant culture of Bohemia. In fact many of the folk songs in the opera were as much German as Bohemian, and most of them were relatively new, while 'Czech dances' like the polka or beseda, which Smetana used to give *The Bartered Bride* a national character, were performed widely in Europe.[106] Nineteenth-century nationalisms depended on 'invented traditions' – on the unifying force of national myths and the popular belief in old ('authentic') cultural traditions, which in reality were mostly recent creations.[107]

The invention of 'Hungarian music' was similar in this respect. The '*style hongrois*' was a stylized evocation of Gypsy and Turkish music created by composers such as Haydn in the eighteenth century. Liszt developed it in his *Hungarian Rhapsodies*, nineteen piano pieces composed between 1846 and 1885, as did Brahms in his *Hungarian Dances*. Both composers recognized the gypsies as the main carriers of Hungarian folk music. They thought the gypsy scale (with two augmented seconds), gypsy tunes and rhythms were the fundamental basis of the folk songs performed by the Hungarian peasantry. In its art-music form the *'style hongrois'* became popular throughout Europe, played by bands at spa resorts like Baden, where the exotic gypsy element was appreciated by the cosmopolitan public. Liszt had never learned Hungarian. Born in Austria, he spoke and wrote in French and German, the languages of the countries in which he lived the best part of his life. But he identified himself as a Magyar, and he was a prominent supporter of the Hungarian national cause, whose political leaders saw the ancient Magyar tribes as the ethnic basis of Hungarians. Liszt's 'Hungarian' music was recruited by the nationalists, music critics and composers, who denied its gypsy content and claimed instead that it was rooted in the folk songs of the Magyar peasantry. On this invented tradition Hungarian music would be built.[108]

7

In the summer of 1867, Dostoevsky came to Baden in a desperate attempt to turn around his fortunes at the roulette wheels. Heavily indebted and pressed by creditors, he had left St Petersburg with his new wife, Anna Grigorievna, previously employed by him as a stenographer to speed up work on his novella *The Gambler* (1866), written in a hurry to repay his gambling debts. Anna raised the money for the trip herself, hoping a few months abroad would help her husband recover from the stress of his financial worries, which had begun to make him ill. His epileptic fits were becoming more frequent.

The Dostoevskys travelled by rail to Dresden, but after three weeks Dostoevsky became bored and persuaded Anna to let him go off on his own for a few days to Homburg to try his luck in the casino. Two of his many creditors in Russia had filed charges against him, so he justified his gambling passion (the real reason why he had wanted to come to Europe in the first place) by the urgent need to clear his debts to avoid the danger of imprisonment on returning home. In a ten-day gambling frenzy he lost heavily. Anna sent him money which he lost again. Dostoevsky pawned his watch and lost that too. He returned to Dresden filled with remorse, furious with himself for losing self-control and spoiling everything for his new wife, and yet still, like all gambling addicts, convinced he could win it back. Securing a loan from Katkov, whose *Russian Messenger* was serializing his successful novel *Crime and Punishment*, Dostoevsky set off with Anna for Baden, having now persuaded her that, with more time together there, he would avoid the mistakes he had made in Homburg by placing his bets hurriedly. Arriving in Baden, they took two small rooms above a blacksmith, where noisy work began at 4 a.m. They could not afford anything better. Dostoevsky began gambling immediately. Anna recalled the next five weeks as 'some kind of nightmare which took complete possession of my husband'.[109]

In his novel *Smoke* Turgenev describes the gaming rooms where Dostoevsky joined

the same well-known figures crowded round the green tables with the same dull, avaricious, partly puzzled, partly embittered, essentially predatory expression which gambling fever imparts to even the most aristocratic features; the same plumpish, exceedingly foppishly attired Tambov landowner, with the same incomprehensible convulsive haste, eyes on stalks, chest leaning on the table, ignoring the cold sneers of the croupiers, scattered with his sweaty hand to all four corners of the table the golden discs of louis d'or at the very moment when they announce '*rien ne va plus*', thus depriving himself of all possibility of winning anything, even when luck was with him.[110]

Dostoevsky had no luck. He lost all their money in a week and then started pawning possessions. He would get down to his last thaler, and then win, and then lose again, and return to the pawnshop. They fell into debt with their landlady. Anna wrote to her parents begging them for money. She pawned the diamond ring and ruby brooch and earrings, her wedding gift from Dostoevsky, who lost those too. He would go down on his knees, sob and beg forgiveness for the shame he had brought on them – and then go back to the gaming rooms. He was acting like a character from one of his novels.

A few days after their arrival in Baden the Dostoevskys ran into the writer Ivan Goncharov, who told them that Dostoevksy had been spotted by Turgenev, who had not approached him because he knew 'how gamblers do not like to be spoken to'. Turgenev was the last person Dostoevsky wanted to see. He had borrowed fifty roubles (200 francs) from him after losing heavily at Wiesbaden (the setting of *The Gambler*) and had not repaid the debt. Now he was obliged to call on him to avoid giving the impression that he was afraid of being asked for the money.[111]

Dostoevsky and Turgenev had a long relationship of ups and downs, going back to the 1840s, when they emerged together on the literary scene in St Petersburg. In the early 1860s they had got on relatively well. Dostoevsky had been one of the few people to understand Turgenev's *Fathers and Sons*. Turgenev had been grateful and agreed to write a story ('Phantoms') for Dostoevsky's journal *Time* (*Vremia*) and, when the journal was closed down by the tsarist government, he gave it to its successor, *Epoch* (*Epokha*), where it appeared in 1864. Dostoevsky's growing problems with money (exacerbated by his brother's death in 1864, which left him with his debts and his wife and children to support) made him resentful of the better-off Turgenev, a landed aristocrat who, he thought, could write at his leisure rather than being forced to rush things out.

Dostoevsky made his visit to Turgenev on 28 June. As he recounted to the Russian poet Apollon Maikov, 'even before that I disliked the man personally'. The embarrassment of his unpaid debt played its part in that, he admitted, but 'I also dislike the aristocratically farcical embrace of his with which he starts to kiss you but offers his cheek. The horrible airs of a general.' The conversation started on the critical reception of Turgenev's *Smoke* but soon became an argument about Russia and Europe, the old debate between Slavophiles and Westerners and a central theme of the novel. According to Dostoevksy, whose sympathies were with the Slavophiles, Turgenev stated that his views were expressed by the character Potugin, an extreme Westerner who thought that Russia had contributed nothing to European civilization. Turgenev had abused Russia and the Russians 'monstrously' and had 'said that we ought to crawl before the Germans', Dostoevsky continued. When Turgenev said that he was writing an article against the Slavophiles, Dostoevsky told him to buy a telescope, because Russia was a long way off from Baden and Paris: 'Train your telescope on Russia and examine us, because otherwise it is really hard to make us out.' The implication of this sarcastic insult was obvious: by choosing to live abroad, Turgenev had lost touch with Russia, and that had showed in his last novel. Now the gloves came off. Dostoevsky lost control – the humiliations he had suffered in the past three months in Germany swelled up inside him as he attacked the German people as 'thieves and swindlers . . . much worse and more dishonest than ours'. What had European civilization done for them? These words maddened Turgenev, Dostoevsky reported. 'He turned pale (literally: I'm not exaggerating a bit, not a bit!) and said to me: "In talking like that you offend me *personally*. You should know that I have settled here permanently, that I consider myself a German, not a Russian, and I'm proud of it!" ' Dostoevsky apologized, saying that, although he had read *Smoke*, he had no idea he felt that way. He then took his leave, vowing to himself never again to visit Turgenev.[112]

At ten o'clock the next morning, when Dostoevsky was still asleep, Turgenev called at the house where they were staying and left a card with the maid. As Dostoevsky had told him that he never rose from bed before eleven o'clock, he took the call to mean that Turgenev did not want to see him either but had repaid his visit as a gentleman. The two men saw each other once again, at the Baden railway station on 13 August, when the Dostoevskys were departing for Switzerland, but they did not even exchange bows.

The feud between them did not end in Baden. Dostoevsky's letter to Maikov was sent on to the journal *Russian Archive* (*Russkii Arkhiv*) with a request to preserve it for posterity but not to publish it until 1890. Told of this by Annenkov, Turgenev wrote to the journal's editor denying he had said what Dostoevsky claimed he had said about Russia, and claiming he would never have divulged his 'intimate convictions' to a man like Dostoevsky, whom he considered 'a person, who as a consequence of morbid seizures and other causes, is not in full control of his own rational capacities'.[113] Dostoevsky brooded on his hatred of Turgenev and took revenge by satirizing him in *The Devils* (a work on which he started in 1869) in the character of Karmazinov, a vain, pompous, 'statesmanlike' writer, whose 'shrill voice' gave him the affected air of a 'born gentleman'. Karmazinov 'sneers contemptuously at Russia', says he is 'going abroad for good' because the 'climate is better and the houses are of stone and everything much stronger', and claims that the laying down of a new water pipe in Karlsruhe, where he has been for the last seven years, is 'much dearer to me than all the questions of my beloved mother-country – during the whole period of these so-called reforms [after 1861]'. The cruellest part of the parody was

Karmazinov's long-awaited reading of his latest story to a bored provincial audience:

> Imagine over thirty printed pages of the most pretentious and useless chatter; and, besides, this gentleman read it in a sort of mournfully condescending tone of voice, as though he were doing us a favour, so that it sounded rather like an insult to our public. The subject . . . But who could make it out – that subject of his? It was a sort of account of certain impressions and reminiscences. But of what? And what about? However much we knit our provincial brows during the first half of the reading, we could not make head or tail of it, and we listened to the second part simply out of politeness. It is true, there was a lot of talk about love – the love of the genius for some lady – but, I confess, it produced rather an awkward impression on the audience. For the great genius to tell us about his first kiss, seemed to my mind somehow inconsistent with this short, little fat figure.[114]

Turgenev was wounded to the quick. He felt betrayed by Dostoevsky, who had praised 'Phantoms' (the story parodied) when he published it in *Epoch* (he did not know that Dostoevsky had written to his brother that it 'contained a lot of rubbish: there is something sordid, morbid and senile about it; it evidences *lack of faith* due to impotence – in a word, the whole of Turgenev and his convictions'). Turgenev added that before defaming him, Dostoevsky might have paid him back the money he had borrowed years before.[115]

The novel at the centre of this long dispute marked a new lowpoint in Turgenev's relations with his critics in Russia. He had worked on *Smoke* for several years. Intermingled with its love story and satire of the Russians in Baden is a discourse about Russia's place in Europe which for Turgenev had its roots in the hostile Russian reception to his previous novel, *Fathers and Sons*. He had been stung, in particular, by the criticisms he received in left-wing student circles, where he was attacked for drawing in Bazarov a travesty of their kind.

Smoke was Turgenev's answer to the radicals, especially to those, like his old friend Herzen, living still in exile, who believed in the populist idea that the home-grown egalitarianism of the peasant commune showed a way for Russia to become a socialist democracy without following Europe's bourgeois path. Turgenev thought this was nonsense.

The peasants he had seen on his trip to Russia in 1862 were too worn down by poverty to become agents of democratic change. Police repression of the student demonstrations in St Petersburg that year had persuaded him that nothing basically had changed in Russia – or could change – with the new reforms. This was the pessimism that informed the speeches of Potugin decrying Russia's backwardness as well as the delusions of the Slavophiles that Russia could be something other than a copy of Europe. As he put it to Herzen: 'We Russians belong in language and in nature to the European family, "*genus Europeum*", and consequently, in accordance with the unalterable laws of physiology, must travel the same road.'[116]

On its publication in the *Russian Messenger,* in April 1867, the novel was attacked in Russia from all sides. The fact that it appeared at a time when Moscow was the host to a Pan-Slav Congress that whipped up Russian nationalist feeling did not help. Annenkov reported that the reading public was outraged by a novel 'inviting them to believe that all of the Russian aristocracy, indeed all of Russian life, is an abomination'. Critics accused Turgenev of abandoning Russia – of even hating it – and blamed the Viardots for his betrayal. Newspapers printed letters from provincial readers claiming that the book was an 'attack on Russia by the West'. The members of Moscow's exclusive English Club passed a motion to send a letter to Turgenev banning him from their midst in perpetuity (he had never been inside their precious club). In Baden he was snubbed by the Russian community. 'Judging from the reviews and letters,' Turgenev wrote to Annenkov, 'I am cursed by everyone from one end to the other of our great fatherland. "I have insulted our nation – I am a liar and a slanderer – I don't know Russia in the least." ' But Turgenev was defiant, adding in another letter to his friend that he was happy with his 'persecuted Potugin, who believed only in European civilization'.[117]

In 1864, Countess Lambert had written to Turgenev reproaching him for not living in Russia. She accused him of abandoning his Christian duty as a Russian writer to serve his people, preferring the comforts and pleasures of the West. Turgenev replied that he was not a Christian, at least not in her sense, or any for that matter, and that the only way he had to serve his country was 'as a writer, an artist':

There is no necessity for a writer to live continuously in his own country and write about the changes in its life – at least there is no need to do this all the time . . . Who knows, maybe one day I will want to write a work that has no particular significance for Russia – to set myself a broader task . . . I see no reason why I should not settle in Baden. I do this not out of any desire for pleasure (that is the lot of youth) but simply so as to weave a little nest for myself in which to await the approach of the inevitable end.[118]

8

In November 1868, the Viardot family moved to Karlsruhe for the winter. Baden was a sleepy town at this time of the year, and they wanted to be somewhere bigger with an art school Claudie could attend. There were no art teachers good enough in Baden, according to Pauline.[119] An hour's train ride to the north, Karlsruhe had a population of 30,000 residents, four times as many as Baden, with a ducal palace at the centre of the town, a court theatre, gallery and a large array of cultural societies, including six glee clubs, a Philharmonic Society, a Museum Association, a literary society and an arts club. Three weeks later, Turgenev joined them there, lodging in a hotel by the railway station, a short walk from the Viardots' spacious apartment in Lange Strasse. Pauline kept a lively salon attended by the leading cultural figures of the town, including the painters Karl Lessing, the director of the gallery, and the Norwegian landscape artist Hans Gude, who taught at the School of Art.

On 29 January, Turgenev organized a party of Russians to see Wagner's latest opera, *Die Meistersinger von Nürnberg*, at the Karlsruhe Court Theatre. Pauline also went along. She had meant to be in Munich for the *Meistersinger*'s premiere the previous June but had been unable to travel because of illness. The opera delighted her. In February she made it to Munich and heard it once again, noting in her diary that the music pleased her more and more.[120] She wrote to Wagner full of praise for it, receiving in reply a copy of the score inscribed by him with the words: '*An der Meistersängerin Mme Viardot* [To the Meistersinger Mme Viardot]'. Pauline had been so intent on listening to the music in the National Theatre in Munich that when some people in a neighbouring box had started talking during the performance she had sternly told them off. The incident had been related to the composer, who wrote to Pauline with his customary arrogance: 'That gave me almost as much pleasure as *Die Meistersinger* gave to you.'[121]

Overcoming her earlier reservations about Wagner's music, Pauline had become a committed 'Wagnerian' during recent years. She maintained close relations with the composer, who sent his niece to study singing with her in Baden, advised other singers to do the same, and often asked Pauline to send her pupils to perform in his operas.* In February 1869, Pauline wrote to Turgenev from Weimar, where she had gone to see a performance of *Lohengrin*, an opera she had previously detested: 'Decidedly, yes, decidedly, Wagner is the only composer whose works have any interest for me. Oh, I will not deny it, I am a Wagnerian to my fingertips, my poor friend! It is a pull I can't resist.'[122]

Turgenev was slower to come round to this 'music of the future'. His musical tastes were, like Louis's, instinctively conservative. Wagner was the 'founder of the school of groaning' in music, he teased Pauline. After attending a rehearsal of *Das Rheingold* in Munich, he reported to a Russian friend: 'The music and the text are equally unbearable, but you know among the Germans there are people for whom Wagner is practically Christ.' Turgenev was hostile to the cult of Wagner. He liked only small parts of his operas (he was 'mad keen' on the 'Ride of the Valkyries', for example, which he had heard in a concert performance in 1863). But Pauline's musical opinions were laws to him, and he tried to accept them on Wagner too. 'I sense that the music could be very beautiful,' he wrote to her, 'but it is unlike anything I've ever liked before, and still like, so I need a certain effort to change my *Standpunkt*. I am not at all like Viardot – I can still do that – but an effort is needed.'[123]

The point at which Pauline had become converted to Wagner was ironically his lowest ebb – the fiasco of *Tannhäuser*'s Paris premiere back in March 1861. Pauline liked the opera, but it had been hissed in

---

* The great Wagnerian singer Marianne Brandt studied with Viardot in Baden-Baden during the 1860s. She shared the role of Kundry with Amalie Matema and Therese Malten at the Bayreuth premiere of *Parsifal* in 1882.

a protest by the young men of the Jockey Club. It was the custom of these Parisian aristocrats to dine before the opera and arrive at the theatre in time for the ballet in the Second Act (many of them kept a mistress in the corps de ballet); they would usually leave immediately afterwards. Wagner had not wanted a ballet scene at all in *Tannhäuser* but agreed to one (the unballetic 'Bacchanal of Venusberg') when told by the Opéra's director, Alphonse Royer, that a dance scene was compulsory. Insisting that the only place where dancing would make sense was at the start of the First Act, Wagner inserted the scene there, refusing Royer's pleas to postpone it to the Second Act to accommodate the Jockey Club. To get his way Wagner appealed to his Austrian patron, Princess Metternich, who had got the opera commissioned by Napoleon III. She intervened on his behalf. The members of the Jockey Club were angered by the change, which obliged them to arrive at the start. They saw it as an act of German arrogance by the composer and Princess Metternich. After three nights of disruptive protest, Wagner withdrew *Tannhäuser*. 'It was the man, above all, who was hissed, far more than the composition,' Pauline wrote to Rietz:

> Wagner made himself so detested in advance, by artists and public, that he was treated unjustly, in a revolting manner. They did not wish to hear the music. If they had heard it, they might have hissed just the same! Wagner will not have profited by the lesson, but he can always boast that he was the victim of a cabal.[124]

This was Wagner's second setback at the Paris Opéra, following his failure to get *Rienzi* performed there in 1841. It put an end to his long-held ambition to become a major player on Europe's most important operatic stage, and turned his attentions towards Germany. He now sought to promote his 'music of the future' as a higher form of art, whose lofty mission was to give expression to the German national spirit and liberate its culture from French civilization and other foreign influences. In his essay 'The Artwork of the Future' (1849), written in exile in Zurich following the failure of the Dresden Uprising, Wagner used the term *Gesamtkunstwerk* – a unity of the arts in a single music drama – to define his artistic principles and set his work apart from French Grand Opera with its 'monstrosities' of virtuoso singing, sensational effects and entertainments posing as art.[125]

Finally pardoned for his role in the Dresden Uprising, Wagner returned to Germany in 1862 and set about the task of finding for himself a wealthy German patron for his nationalist cause. His luck turned in 1864, when the young Bavarian king, Ludwig II, a passionate admirer of Wagner's music, invited him to Munich, where all Wagner's debts were cleared by his royal admirer, and *Tristan and Isolde* received its premiere in June 1865. Wagner's ability to extract large amounts of money from Ludwig and his scandalous affair with Liszt's daughter, Cosima, at that time married to the conductor Hans von Bülow, caused so much unrest at the Bavarian court that Wagner was forced to leave Munich. Maintained by Ludwig in a villa in Tribschen on Lake Lucerne, he finished *Die Meistersinger* there.

Wagner first conceived of this opera in the spa town of Marienbad, where he had gone to take the waters in 1845. He read about the mastersingers and Hans Sachs (1494–1576), the poet, songwriter, shoemaker and Lutheran reformer, in Georg Gottfried Gervinus's history of German poetry (1835–42). Wagner made a prose draft at that time for what he then envisaged as a comic opera revolving around the singing contest held by the city's mastersingers, poets and musicians who practised various trades. But he did the main work on the opera during the 1860s, when his conception of it changed in two main ways: first, the Hans Sachs character became more heroic and noble, partly under the influence of Schopenhauer's concept of the renunciation of the will in *The World as Will and Representation*, a work Wagner read in 1854; and secondly, a nationalistic meaning to the opera was now imposed, as set out in Wagner's essays 'What is German?' (1865) and 'German Art and German Politics' (1867), in which the mastersingers are meant to represent the traditional values and creative spirit of the German folk. Hans Sachs's appeal to the people at the end warned against the dangers of foreign influence in Germany:

> Beware! Evil tricks threaten us; if the German people and kingdom should one day decay, under a false, foreign rule, soon no prince would understand his people; and foreign mists with foreign vanities they would plant in our German land; what is German and true none would know, if it did not live in the honour of German Masters.

Within a year of its Munich premiere, *Die Meistersinger* was performed at Dresden, Dessau, Karlsruhe, Mannheim, Hanover and Weimar, with Vienna, Königsberg, Berlin and Leipzig following in 1870. The opera would become a focal point of the German nationalist movement in the Franco-Prussian War and the unification of Germany.

Wagner saw his music dramas as the start of a new German art. 'I am the most German of all of them, I am the German spirit,' he noted in his diary in September 1865. To grasp their nationality the Germans had to see themselves, their national drama, on the stage. Wagner filled his operas with German myths, folk legends (some genuine, some appropriated), landscapes and historical figures. Through his propagandists he marketed his music as a purely 'German' art – spiritually higher than the commercial forms of operatic art in France and Italy. There was an irony in this campaign: the Wagner movement deployed all the methods of the modern 'culture industry' – artistic manifestos, self-promotion and publicity, the cult of the pioneering artist as prophet and celebrity – to promote his 'music of the future' as a brand.[126]

The focus of the movement was the founding of a theatre for Wagner's operas. In 1848, Wagner had made plans for a 'German national theatre of the kingdom of Saxony' – state-sponsored but separate from the court – in Dresden and Leipzig. From the 1860s, his preference was to have a theatre where German music dramas would be performed without charge for the people – an idea close to the music festivals that had sprung up in Germany in the early decades of the nineteenth century but also copied from the Greek ideal of theatre in the service of community. He envisaged a festival in a small German town, 'entirely free from the influence of the repertory system in vogue in our permanent theatres', where a simple amphitheatre would be built 'only for artistic purposes', as he put it in his Preface to the poem of *Der Ring des Nibelungen* in 1862. He was partly influenced by the modern bourgeois type of theatre he had known in Riga, where he had been musical director from 1837 to 1839, in which there were no tiered boxes, as in the European opera houses for the aristocracy, but a wide auditorium with steeply rising stalls and unbroken sight lines to the stage, a sunken pit to make the orchestra invisible, and lights that were lowered during the performance to focus the attention of the audience. In 1864, he went to Munich with a promise from Ludwig to build such a theatre for the *Ring*, on which he began to work. Gottfried Semper, who had designed the Dresden Opera House, was brought to Munich to work on plans for a monumental amphitheatre to meet his requirements. But after he was forced to leave Munich, Wagner looked for a smaller German town to build a theatre of his own. The place chosen was Bayreuth. As Wagner explained, he had wanted a location in Bavaria, to benefit from Ludwig's patronage. He also wanted it to be roughly in the centre of Germany, not in a fashionable spa, which might attract the wrong type of urban crowd, nor somewhere with a commercial theatre of its own.[127] Bayreuth was to be a site of pilgrimage to his 'new art'.

On 28 January 1870, the first of two performances of *Der letzte Zauberer* – the German version of *Le Dernier Sorcier* – took place in the Karlsruhe Court Theatre. The production had been commissioned by the Grand Duke Friedrich and Grand Duchess Louise of Baden, who had seen the operetta in Baden and heard of its triumph in the Weimar Court Theatre. They wanted it to have a similar success on the Karlsruhe stage.

Eduard Devrient, the director of the Karlsruhe Court Theatre, then aged sixty-nine, was at the end of his career, and neither Pauline nor Turgenev had thought enough of his abilities to have much to do with his company since their arrival in the town a year or so previously.[128] Musically conservative, Devrient was an enemy of Wagner and known to be opposed to the Grand Duke's insistence that his operas be included in the theatre's repertoire. They were expensive to produce and demanding on his singers, and postponements of the opening night were often necessary. Although *Die Meistersinger* had been performed in Karlsruhe (Turgenev had seen it there in January 1869), Devrient thought it was 'a tormented, self-contradictory and boring monster, palmed off and forced upon the stupidity of the world with dazzling effrontery. The fact that it has achieved dissemination is a question of fashion, like chignons or Chinese dresses; nobody considers them beautiful, but everybody wears them.'[129]

The animosity between Devrient and Wagner became public in March 1869, when Wagner published a revised edition, this time in his own name, of his notorious essay of 1850, 'Jewishness in Music'. Devrient denounced it as poisonous lies, and countered it by publishing his own memoirs about Mendelssohn. Pauline too had been disgusted by the reissuing of the anti-Semitic article. Her great patron Meyerbeer, its main target, had died in Paris only five years earlier – his body taken by train from the Gare du Nord to Berlin for burial in the Jewish cemetery with vast crowds lining the streets in both cities to pay their last respects

to the composer, who, in the words of Émile Ollivier, the French statesman, had done so much to establish a 'harmonic bond' between France
and Germany.[130] Now, more than ever, his death symbolized the passing of the cosmopolitan idea of European culture which his life and
work had embodied. Pauline was outraged by Wagner's racist diatribe.
She might be a fan of Wagner's art, but she detested his politics and did
not much like the man. She wrote in protest to Wagner, a fact that
became known to the public. Wagner replied by claiming that her sympathy for Mendelssohn and Meyerbeer made Pauline 'a Jew' herself.[131]

Der letzte Zauberer was received coldly by the Karlsruhe audience,
and there was some hissing at the end. The applause was 'scanty',
according to Devrient, and none of the performers received a curtain
call. Turgenev put a brave face on the failure, insisting in a letter to
Pietsch that it had been 'far from a fiasco'. But the German press was
merciless. 'A total failure,' reported a Leipzig music weekly. 'The high
expectations were in no respect satisfied. The applause, which was
weak from the beginning, gradually diminished and ended in a percep-
tible hissing.' In the influential Leipzig music paper, the *Allgemeine
Musikalische Zeitung*, on 9 February, an anonymous reviewer was
scathing about Pauline, who had sung the leading female role: 'Nothing but silence is appropriate not only for the impression that this artist,
who was justly feted decades ago, now makes, but also for the text and
music of the entire work.' The public reaction was menacing. Turgenev
was accosted in the street by a German army officer indignant at the
high fees rumoured to have been paid to Viardot and Turgenev, which
he said had deprived him of hearing the best tenors of the day.[132]

There was little doubt that the operetta had been sabotaged in a
well-orchestrated campaign – a fact confirmed by a later article in the
Allgemeine Musikalische Zeitung, on 23 February, which reported
that there had been 'certain circles' spreading 'dark rumours' about the
operetta during the rehearsals, circles which had also organized the
cold reception and hissing of the performance. Elsewhere in the press
there were heavy hints that the people who had been responsible for
this were Wagner and his nationalist supporters in Karlsruhe. They had
interpreted the comic satire about the sorcerer and the forest elves as
an attack on Wagner's opera *Das Rheingold* and sought revenge on
Viardot and Turgenev. But nationalism was at the bottom of it all. The
German nationalists who followed Wagner were violently opposed to

the cosmopolitanism represented by the Viardots' presence in Baden. As Turgenev wrote to Pietsch, of all the factors behind the hostility they met, the most important of them was the 'deep disparagement of foreigners and their presumptuousness' in putting on an opera in Germany.[133]

9

In February 1870, Turgenev and the Viardots moved to Weimar. For the next three months they lived in the Hôtel de Russie. The Karlsruhe art school had been a disappointment to Claudie, who now pursued her studies at the Grand Ducal Art School in Weimar, where the Belgian painter Charles Verlat, an old friend of Ary Scheffer, took an interest in her work.[134] Supported by Liszt, a former *Kapellmeister* at the Weimar court and a frequent presence there, Pauline was invited by the Grand Duke, a musical enthusiast, to reproduce her roles in *Orphée* and *Le Prophète* at the Weimar Court Theatre. She decided that these were to be her last appearances on the public stage. She also sang in a number of concerts in the Weimar area, including one in Jena, on 3 March, where she gave the first performance of Brahms's *Alto Rhapsody*.

In May they returned to Baden, and from there Turgenev soon departed for St Petersburg, where he met Stasiulevich, before travelling to Spasskoe, where he set about the task of 'making money' by selling off a large chunk of his land and completing his new story, 'A King Lear of the Steppes'.[135] On 12 July, Turgenev began the journey back from Russia to Baden. Stopping in Berlin, he found himself in the hotel dining room eating 'directly opposite General Moltke', Chief of the Prussian General Staff.[136] It was the evening of 15 July. Earlier that day the German army had been mobilized for war with France. Famous for his view that no war could be planned beyond the first encounter with the enemy, Moltke had a lot to think about, but with his calm exterior, refined manners and evident intelligence, he seemed to Turgenev the personification of power.

The immediate cause of the Franco-Prussian War was the Ems Despatch, Bismarck's craftily edited press-release version of a telegram he received from King Wilhelm's secretary on 13 July. The telegram informed him of the king's meeting with Count Benedetti, the French

ambassador to Prussia, during his morning stroll in the Kurpark of Bad
Ems. Relations between France and Prussia had been strained by the
question of the Spanish succession: fearful of the growth of Prussian
power and afraid of encirclement by an alliance of Germany and Spain,
France had protested against Spain's offer of the Spanish throne to
Prince Leopold of the Prussian Hohenzollern-Sigmaringen lands. On
2 July, Leopold had withdrawn his acceptance of the crown, but the
French now wanted more from the Prussian king: a guarantee that no
member of the Hohenzollern dynasty would ever reign in Spain. That
was the assurance Benedetti sought in what was in fact a polite and
friendly meeting with Wilhelm on the promenade of the Kurpark. The
king rejected the request in decisive but diplomatic terms, conveyed in
the telegram to Bismarck from his secretary. Bismarck, though, was
eager to provoke a war with France, which he thought was necessary
for the Prussian takeover of the southern German states. The Chancellor released the king's answer to Benedetti in a form designed to make
it seem like a cold refusal, an insult to the French. Mistranslated into
French by a news agency in a way that made it even worse, the despatch
was published in France the following day, 14 July, or Bastille Day, to
an outcry from excited crowds in Paris demanding war. The emperor's
declaration of war duly followed on 19 July.

By the time Turgenev left Berlin, on 16 July, Prussian troops were on
the move, destroying bridges and cutting communication lines across
the Rhine. Turgenev arrived in Baden just before civilian railway travel
to the town became impossible. A few days later, Brahms was unable to
get through from Vienna via Bad Wildbad to come to the relief of Clara
Schumann, terrified of the 'barbaric Turkish' soldiers rumoured to be
in the French army. She wrote to him from Baden:

> Everybody who has a house (the Rosenhayns, the Viardots, the Guaitas)
> is advising me to stay quietly here, for if they can't get enough soldiers
> billeted on inhabited houses they will open closed ones and use them,
> and then everything will be ruined. So I am staying on though still feeling
> very anxious, as we have no man to protect us.[137]

Turgenev and the Viardots were also staying put. 'Baden is completely
deserted,' Turgenev wrote to his brother Nikolai on 27 July, 'but I am
staying here and will stay even if the French break through – what can
they do to me?' Life went on in an atmosphere of unreality. Turgenev

was determined to take part in a chess tournament scheduled to be held in Baden in the first week of August. He played the game at a high level, was a member of the Baden club, and had been appointed the vice-president of the tournament committee. The competition went ahead in the Salle de Conversation to the distant sound of the French and Prussian guns. 'It was strange and sad to see in this peaceful and beautiful plain, under the gentle glow of a half-covered sun, the shameful smoke of war,' Turgenev wrote.[138]

When the war began, Turgenev and the Viardots were hoping for a Prussian victory. Their friends in France, and most in Russia, were on the side of France. But they saw the conflict as a fight for liberty against Napoleon's imperialism, and, as residents in Germany who counted Bismarck and the Prussian king and queen among their friends, they felt a certain loyalty towards Prussia. Their main thought was that a defeat for France would bring about the end of Napoleon III's regime. 'I don't need to tell you,' Turgenev wrote to Ludwig Friedländer, 'that I am wholeheartedly on the German side. This is truly a war of civilization against barbarism – but not in the sense that the French think. Bonapartism *must* be defeated, whatever the cost, if public morality, liberty and independence are to have a future in Europe.' France had to be taught a lesson 'as we were taught a lesson at Sevastopol [in the Crimean War],' Turgenev wrote in his fictional 'Letters from the Franco-Prussian War', which were published in Russia.[139]

In the early stages of the war, Turgenev and the Viardots feared an invasion by the French, who had amassed their troops in Strasbourg to advance east to Baden, hoping that they would be joined by Austria–Hungary in occupying the south German states. Pauline and her daughters knitted garments and blankets for the Prussian soldiers in Baden, and sang in concerts to keep them entertained. The French breakthrough never came. Instead the Prussians quickly advanced towards Metz, an important fortress town deep in France where Napoleon III assumed command of the newly titled Army of the Rhine, which was soon forced to retreat by the more effective Prussian troops. The Prussians laid siege to Strasbourg, using trains to bring 200 heavy guns that began a month-long bombardment of the town on 23 August. From the heights of the Old Castle in Baden, Clara Schumann and her children could see the spire of Strasbourg Cathedral and hear the cannonades, which 'made our cottage tremble', recalled Eugenie.[140] By 2 September, the French had been defeated at Sedan, resulting in the capture of Napoleon III and his army, the formation of a Government of National Defence and a Third Republic in Paris. Bizet, Fauré and Saint-Saëns signed up for the National Guard, which carried on the fight against the Prussian troops attacking the capital.

Turgenev was delighted by the Prussian victory. 'The whole Viardot family is healthy and happy,' he wrote to Pietsch on 9 September.

> We are organizing concerts and readings for the benefit of the wounded – and that is how we pass our days. The downfall of the Empire was a source of great satisfaction for poor Viardot, whose heart bleeds nonetheless – although he realises that all this was the punishment deserved by France. As for me, I ought to be a German completely, because a French victory would have been a defeat for Liberty – but you really did not need to destroy Strasbourg. That was clumsy and inexpedient. What will now happen in Paris?

For four months, beginning on 19 September, the Prussians laid siege to Paris. They attacked the French at Orléans, Le Mans and Amiens, and took Rouen (Flaubert's house at Croisset was occupied by ten invading troops, forcing the writer to move with his elderly mother into lodgings in Rouen). The prolongation of the war turned Turgenev and the Viardots against the Prussians. 'The fall of the empire brought great joy,' Turgenev wrote to a Russian friend on 18 September, 'but the aggressive greed for conquest that has overtaken Germany is not a consoling sight.' Four weeks later he wrote to his German friend, the writer and translator Paul Heyse: 'Are you satisfied with Alsace or do you also have your hearts set on Lorraine? I am beginning not to understand nor to recognize the Germans I once loved.'[141] It seemed to him that the Germans had become the military aggressors, and were intending to destroy the new republic in which Turgenev and the Viardots had invested all their hopes.

Meanwhile, in Baden, they began to feel the full force of German nationalism as victory gave way to triumphalism among the local populace. 'We no longer hear the cannon from Strasbourg,' Turgenev wrote to William Ralston on 9 October, 'but we do see Germans in their hundreds of thousands travelling there in pilgrimage to see their new conquest.' German flags began to appear on buildings in Baden. Clara Schumann put one out and prayed for German unity. Brahms was overjoyed by the Prussian victory. A German patriot who idolized Bismarck, he composed a thunderous *Triumphlied* for orchestra and chorus to celebrate the victory. Nationalist parades were held in Baden. Extremists made life difficult for the French inhabitants in an attempt to force them out. Every night a crowd would gather by the entrance to the Villa Viardot and make *Katzenmusik*, a threatening din with drums and horns.[142]

The war had given rise to strong nationalist feelings on both sides of the Rhine. The loss of Alsace to the Germans was bitterly resented by the French. Germans were expelled from France, and the French from Germany. The Prussian victory was a turning point in European history. Politically it reinforced the growing nationalist currents that worked against the cultural cosmopolitanism developing across the Continent – eventually leading in the longer term to the disintegration of this European culture in the First World War. More immediately, the foundation of the German Empire was a catastrophe for the cosmopolitan culture of Franco-German spa towns like Baden, which joined the empire in 1871. No longer favoured by the French, who turned instead to their own spa resorts, they lost their international atmosphere, and with it much of their cultural excitement and significance.

It was also a disaster for those artists who had thrived in their cosmopolitan culture. None suffered more than Offenbach, who was attacked by nationalists on both sides. In Germany he was accused of treason for writing anti-German songs, while in France he was denounced for siding with the country of his birth. Neither charge was justified. Although born in Germany, Offenbach had chosen France. He was a French citizen. He did not recognize the German claim of blood and soil on his nationality. To clarify his position and protect his kin from possible attack in Germany he wrote an open letter to Villemessant for publication in *Le Figaro*:

> Certain German journalists have spread the calumny that I have composed many songs against Germany. The most terrible insults have accompanied these assertions. I have family and friends in Germany I still hold dear – and it is for them that I beg you to print this: From the age of fourteen I have lived in France; I have received letters of naturalization; I have been made a *Chevalier de la Légion d'honneur*; I owe everything to France and believe that I merit the title of a Frenchman, which I have earned by

my work and honour, but I plead guilty to a weakness for my first country.[143]

In September, Offenbach and his family fled from France to San Sebastian, the royal seaside town in northern Spain.

In France, meanwhile, anti-German feeling was at boiling point. 'They want us to hate the Germans, whom we love,' George Sand wrote to Louis on 8 September. 'What a test for European civilization!'[144] The nationalist mood made life impossible for the Viardots. They were attacked by the French press for choosing to live in Baden, for being friends of the Prussian king and queen, and for not returning to France on the outbreak of the war. They received letters accusing them of treachery. One addressed to Louis from Adolphe Crémieux, the republican Minister of Justice, made Pauline so angry that she felt obliged to defend her husband, as he had more than once defended her against unjustified attacks. Following the rules of social etiquette, she wrote not to the minister, but to his wife, Madame Crémieux:

> Is it because of my friendship with the Queen of Prussia for almost thirty years that the patriotism of my husband has fallen under suspicion? A man who sacrificed his whole career to help mine as an artist? A man who out of love for France, because of his hatred for the Imperial government, lived with me in exile in the Duchy of Baden, on the frontier of our beloved country? And for that you think what? That we chose to be Germans? Oh, that is a bad joke [*oh la mauvaise plaisanterie*]![145]

The war was a disaster for Pauline financially. Concert life in Baden had come to an end, and she had lost her pupils, who returned to their families. On 18 October, with Paris under siege, she left with her children for Ostend, from where they sailed to England. As it was for many others, London became a refuge for the Viardots. Manuel had been living there since 1848, and had many influential contacts in the music world. Pauline could count on students, concerts and engagements in the capital.

Louis stayed behind in Baden, having fallen ill in the last week, so Turgenev accompanied Pauline and the children to Ostend. They travelled by coach to Mannheim and by steamship down the Rhine as far as Cologne – the railways being in the hands of the Prussian military, which blocked civilian passengers – and then went by train to Antwerp and Ostend. From there the Viardots sailed to Dover, where they were met by Manuel, who took them to their temporary lodgings in Seymour Street near Portman Square. The next day Pauline went to the Union Bank, where she had left £100 in an account, and deposited the money she had salvaged from Baden: 970 francs (£38). It was enough to live on for a few months.[146]

From Ostend, Turgenev returned at once by the same route to Baden to look after Louis and oversee the packing up of their houses. Three weeks later, the Villa Viardot was boarded up. Turgenev's house was also closed – as far as that was possible, for a chimney blown down by a storm had 'crashed right through the roof and practically destroyed the whole building', as Turgenev wrote to Annenkov on 28 October. 'When I had it built I had told my architect, a French scoundrel, that with the winds we get here such tall chimneys could be dangerous: "Monsieur" – he replied – "these chimneys are as solid as France."' By early November, Turgenev was ready to depart from Baden with Louis. 'I am leaving in a few days' time and plan to stay in London until the New Year,' he wrote to Annenkov. 'From London I will send you my address. The rest of the Viardot family is already in London: the war has ruined them and Madame Viardot must try to earn a living in England, the only country where that commodity can still be found.'[147]

6

The Land without Music

The English are the only cultured race without a music of their own (music-hall ditties excepted). I say music of their own, for perhaps more foreign music is performed in England than in any other country.

Oscar Schmitz, 1904

I

Louis and Turgenev arrived in London on 13 November 1870. Pauline and the children were still in lodgings in Seymour Street but after Louis's arrival they moved together to a handsome Georgian house in Devonshire Place in Marylebone. Turgenev rented rooms just around the corner from the Viardots in Devonshire Street, but could not bear the cold and damp, nor the smoke from the coal fires, and soon moved to what he hoped were better rooms in Bentinck Street, a short walk away. He was no more comfortable there. He complained bitterly about the English cooking of his landlady. 'It's a country where they can't make anything from a potato or an egg,' he wrote to Henry James, who had moved to London in 1869.[1]

Turgenev spent little time at Bentinck Street. From morning until night he was at the Viardots. Theirs was a five-storey house with spacious rooms on the lower floors. They had a governess, a cook and two live-in housemaids, according to the census of 1871. Yet compared to their living arrangements in Paris and Baden, they thought of this as roughing it – a view shared by Clara Schumann, who wrote to Brahms after visiting them at Devonshire Place in February:

329

30 Devonshire Place, where the Viardots lived.

Madame Viardot made a very sad impression upon me here. I saw her the other day in a most uncomfortable and dirty residence and she told me about the appalling pupils she has here. What an indignity for such an artist, and how sad that she should be forced to do it . . . I had tears in my eyes when I was at her house but fortunately she did not realise it for she would have laughed at me.

Paul Viardot – at that time aged thirteen – recalls the 'gloomy house' in his memoirs: 'the yellow fog and gas street-lamps lit up in the middle of the day when it was dark as night; the cold and damp, the silent meals punctuated by the hurried steps and cries of the newspaper sellers announcing German victories.'[2]

The Viardots were living in straitened circumstances in London. Most of their money had been invested in their Baden villa. They had not tried to sell the house in case they returned to Germany after the war was over – a possibility that became ever less desirable during their time in London. Meanwhile they were forced to make ends meet. Louis sold some more of his Old Masters, including his second Rembrandt, *An Old Man in Military Costume* (1631), for which Turgenev found a buyer in Grand Duchess Maria Nikolaevna, sister of Tsar Alexander II, in January 1871.[3]

London was expensive. Paul's school fees and the cost of keeping servants were higher than they had been in Baden, and Pauline would not give up entertaining in the lavish way to which she was accustomed. The Viardot tradition of musical soirées continued at Devonshire Place. There were informal recitals of chamber music, evenings of Spanish songs and Pauline's famous operatic scenes, and a number of performances of *Le Dernier Sorcier* for a new circle of artistic friends and politicians, the cream of London society, including Charles Hallé, Arthur Sullivan, Frederic Leighton, Anthony Trollope, Robert Browning, George Eliot and her 'husband', George Lewes,* Richard Monckton Milnes (Lord Houghton) and, on at least one occasion, the then Prime Minister, William Gladstone.[4] They were soon joined by their friend Saint-Saëns, who had fled Paris in April 1871. Charles Gounod, who had come to London the previous September, was another frequent visitor. He and the Viardots had been reconciled after they had fallen out over his rejection of Pauline's wedding gift in 1852. Pauline had contacted him in 1864, and since then they had kept up a friendly correspondence.[5] Now, in London, they were brought together by their common misfortune.

The Viardots depended on Pauline's income from teaching. She attracted students not only by her fame as a singer and teacher but also by the presence of her brother, himself one of Europe's most sought-after teachers of bel canto. In 1854, Manuel Garcia had invented the laryngoscope – a device using mirrors to view the larynx and glottis – which brought him worldwide recognition in the scientific and the music worlds. The instrument enabled him to add science to his training of the voice. Among the stars who studied under him were Jenny Lind, Giulia Grisi, Antoinette Sterling and the tenor Julius Stockhausen. When Pauline arrived in London, he referred many of his younger students on to her. Pauline complained that they were not as good as her pupils in Baden, but they were many in number, and they helped to pay the bills.[6]

Pauline supplemented her income by performing in concerts, and,

---

* Pauline Viardot was probably the model for the prima donna in George Eliot's dramatic poem *Armgart* (1870).

despite her earlier decision to retire from the stage, in provincial theatres, her voice now deemed not strong enough for the operatic stage in London. She resumed her touring career with the Willert Beale opera company, spending whole weeks on the road to places such as Derby, Northampton, Manchester and Newcastle. When she was away, Turgenev felt her absence as a 'physical malaise', as he explained on 5 December 1870, when she was in Edinburgh:

> It is as if I had too little air, I have a secret, nagging anxiety that I can't escape from and which nothing will distract. When you are here, I have a quiet joy – I feel 'at home' [written in English] – and I want nothing else. Ah, *theuere Freundin* [beloved friend], I have the whole of my beautiful and dear past of 27 years to treasure and respect. And things will be the same for us as for Burns' 'Joe Anderson, My Jo' – we will go down hill together.*[7]

The idea that they were over the hill was hardly justified numerically (Turgenev was only fifty-two, and Pauline forty-nine, while Louis had turned seventy), but, having lost their happy life in Baden, it must have felt that way to them.

Pauline's earnings were not enough to meet their living costs, even with the money from the sale of Louis's Old Masters. The Viardots depended on Turgenev for financial help, as he had relied on them in previous years. Their faithful friend was forever going down to Coutts'

---

* Turgenev is referring to Robert Burns's poem 'John Anderson, My Jo' (1789):

> John Anderson, my jo, John,
> When we were first acquent;
> Your locks were like the raven,
> Your bonie brow was brent;
> But now your brow is beld, John,
> Your locks are like the snaw;
> But blessings on your frosty pow,
> John Anderson, my jo.

> John Anderson, my jo, John,
> We clamb the hill thegither;
> And mony a cantie day, John,
> We've had wi' ane anither:
> Now we maun totter down, John,
> And hand in hand we'll go,
> And sleep thegither at the foot,
> John Anderson, my jo.

Bank in the Strand to arrange money transfers to Louis. On his trip to Russia, in the early months of 1871, he even sold a plot of land to raise the 80,000 francs in cash for Claudie's dowry in railway shares. The investment was 'enough to provide an annual income of 5½ or even 6,000 francs', as he explained to Pauline.[8]

On his return from Russia, Turgenev moved into new lodgings in Beaumont Street, just behind the mews of the Viardots in Devonshire Place. He was re-creating the arrangement of their *ménage à trois* in Baden – next door to each other but detached. Living in a separate house was mainly for appearances. He suffered in the cold and damp and soon fell ill with flu and gout. From Beaumont Street he wrote to Flaubert on 6 May:

> I am in England – not for the pleasure of being here – but because my friends, almost ruined by the war, have come here to try to earn a little money. The English have some good qualities – but they all – even the most intelligent – lead a very hard life. It takes some getting used to – like their climate. But then where else can one go?[9]

London had a large community of French exiles. They had come in several waves, beginning with the mass arrival of royalists fleeing from the revolutionary terror after 1793; then again in 1848, when Napoleon, as president, had clamped down on the socialists and radical republicans. An even larger number, around 4,000 of Napoleon's political enemies, had fled to England following his coup to overthrow the Second Republic in December 1851. Victor Hugo was among them, arriving first in Jersey, from which he was expelled for supporting a newspaper that had been critical of Queen Victoria, and then settling with his family in Guernsey, where he lived from 1855 to 1870. Most of his fellow countrymen did not stay long in Britain, but by the middle of the 1850s there were around a thousand exiles in London, mostly concentrated in Soho and Fitzrovia. Leicester Square was the cosmopolitan centre of French London, with the Sablonière Hotel acting as headquarters and reception centre for the latest arrivals. A 'dingy modern France', Thackeray called the area. 'There are French cafés, billiards, estaminets, waiters, markets, poor Frenchmen, and rich Frenchmen . . .' The third and biggest wave of émigrés arrived after the outbreak of the Franco-Prussian War. By the mid-1870s, there were an estimated 8,000 Frenchmen living in London. Cash-strapped exiles, including many artists, settled in

Soho, but the better-off, deterred by Soho's prostitutes, moved into the fashionable districts of Fitzrovia and Marylebone.[10]

Britain altogether was a haven for political exiles from Europe. There were no laws to prevent immigrants from coming into the country, regardless of their nationality or beliefs, nor any legal means to stop them from continuing with their political activities once they were living in Britain. The Alien Act of 1848 did allow the government to deport individuals if a court accepted that they were a threat to state security, but the Act lapsed in 1850, never having once been used. The British sense of liberty extended to the protection of revolutionaries against foreign governments. Mazzini, Marx and Engels, Louis Blanc, Ledru-Rollin and Herzen all used London as their propaganda base. In 1858, after an attempt by the Italian revolutionary Felice Orsini to assassinate Napoleon III, the French government demanded measures against Orsini's collaborators in Britain, where the bombs he had thrown at the emperor's carriage had been made. Palmerston's government duly introduced a bill to make conspiracies to murder outside Britain a felony in British law. But the bill was defeated in the House of Commons, which passed a vote of censure against the government for caving in to Napoleon's demands, forcing Palmerston to resign.[11]

Britain's strong economy also made it a magnet for economic migrants from the Continent. Most settled in London, where their trades were in demand: French dressmakers, jewellers, engineers, found for the most part in Soho; German bakers, watchmakers and musicians, mostly in Fitzrovia; Italian food importers, ice-cream makers and barrel-organ players in the Little Italy of Clerkenwell.[12]

No one came to Britain for the weather or the food. Foreigners complained about them both. They saw the country through the prism of anglophobic clichés widely distributed on the Continent: London's melancholic fog, the coldness of the English temperament, its materialism, hypocrisy, 'perfidious Albion', and so on.[13] Flora Tristan's *Promenades dans Londres* (1840) probably did more than any other book to popularize these stereotypes, certainly among the French:

> In London you breathe melancholy in the air, it enters you through all
> your pores. There is nothing more lugubrious . . . than the appearance of
> this city on a foggy day or in the rain and dark . . . It makes you feel

profound despair . . . disgust for everything, and an irresistible desire to end your life by suicide . . . On such noxious days, the Englishman is under the spell of his climate and behaves like a brute.[14]

It was a European commonplace to connect the English climate to the English temperament. Victor Schoelcher, the French anti-slavery campaigner, thought that England was 'the coldest country on the earth in every sense'. Fontane, who spent four years in London in the 1850s, concluded that hospitality had 'become extinct' in English hearts: 'their country is open, but the houses are closed.'[15]

The stuffiness of the English upper class was observed by visitors of every nationality, especially the Russians, whose aristocracy was noted for its liveliness and private informality. On his first day in London, Turgenev was taken to one of the Pall Mall clubs for lunch by his Russian friend Nikolai Zhemchuzhnikov. Irritated by the over-stiff waiters, who served each cutlet in turn on a separate silver plate, Turgenev could not stop himself from banging on the table and growling Russian words – 'Radishes! Pumpkin! Turnips! Kasha!' – to express his mirth. 'He poked fun at me, at the English and at England', once the waiters had retreated, Zhemchuzhnikov recalled.[16]

Turgenev's friend Herzen, who had lived in London since 1852, became acquainted with an Englishman who had been employed as a servant in the Paris household of the Viardots. Shocked by their informal ways, he had soon left them. Asked what had offended him, the Englishman replied: 'They are not the sort of people who are *comme il faut*: it was not just the wife who spoke to me at dinner but the husband too.'[17]

English eccentricities were another commonplace. Europeans explained them by Britain's separation from the Continent. The *Guide Joanne* to London warned its readers:

> Long deprived of contact with the peoples of the Continent, or accustomed by their pride to consider them barbarians, the English have created their own peculiar code of etiquette, stiff and stilted like themselves, whose absolutely rigid laws are observed with servility . . . A foreigner is expected to know and observe them on pain of not being recognized as a *gentleman*.[18]

The Viardots were accustomed to the English and their eccentricities. They had been coming to their country for thirty years. Louis thought the English were bizarre. In his *Souvenirs de chasse* he compared their country to a 'vast convent', such was their conformity to absurd rules of etiquette. A 'foreigner who failed to doff his hat when greeting someone in the street, or dared to use a knife to eat his fish, was considered badly born'. Invited for a weekend's hunting on a great estate in Gloucestershire, he found that even in the wet and cold of an English May the women dressed for dinner 'as if they were going to a ball', in white muslin dresses that left their shivering arms and necks exposed. Thinking they had dressed up so absurdly on account of her presence, Pauline said they really needn't have, but one of them replied that it was not for her – they dressed like that every night: if their father was at home alone he would still appear for dinner in white tie.[19]

Even after thirty years, the Viardots found it hard to sympathize with the English. Like many Europeans of their social class and cosmopolitan outlook, they found the English stuffy, cold and conceited. Pauline was exasperated by their lack of musicality, their following of fashion and celebrity, and by the constant need to flatter them for their 'bad taste'. At an after-concert dinner with Queen Victoria at Buckingham Palace, in 1850, Pauline had complained to Turgenev that the English royals knew neither how to dress nor hold a conversation about music properly:

> The queen was dressed like a sugar-barley stick (*bâton de sucre de pomme de Rouen*) wrapped in blue and silver, tight around the body and quite stiff. With all that on, it could not have been comfortable for her to eat. When she came to the artists, she had no idea about what to say, but said the same kind of thing to them all – so to me she said, for example, 'I much admired you recently in *The Prophet* – it must have been tiring – but it was lovely, especially the church scene.' Then she moved on.[20]

The French, of course, were predisposed to be critical of the English, having as they did an inborn sense of cultural superiority over them, as Herzen noted, tongue in cheek, in *My Past and Thoughts* (1870):

> The Frenchman cannot forgive the English, in the first place, for not speaking French; in the second, for not understanding him when he calls Charing Cross Sharan-Kro, or Leicester Square Lesesstair-Skooar. Then his stomach cannot digest the English dinners consisting of two huge pieces of meat and fish, instead of five little helpings of various ragouts,

fritures, salmis and so on. Then he can never resign himself to the 'slavery' of restaurants being closed on Sundays, and people being bored to the glory of God, though the whole of France is bored to the glory of Bonaparte for seven days in the week.[21]

Herzen sided with the French on this last point in fact. 'Life here is about as boring as that of worms in a cheese,' he wrote from London to a Russian friend. Most Europeans shared his view. 'The evenings in London for a foreigner are very depressing,' wrote Edmondo de Amicis on his first visit to the city in the early 1870s:

A ferocious melancholy would descend on me. I'd grown used to the splendour of Parisian boulevards and the festive crowds which throng them; the streets of London seemed dark and gloomy by comparison. I missed the packed cafés, the sumptuous shops, and even the strange magic-lantern shows on the boulevard Montmartre, conveniently forgetting the indignation I also felt at the sight of the brazen and ostentatious prostitution which is rife all over Paris.

For the French socialist leader, Jules Vallès, who had fled to London in 1871, the domination of the Protestant religion killed all joy in London life. 'Adultery is impossible here. Religion is virtually compulsory and highly disagreeable. The English god is ugly, unsympathetic, and yellow with age ... Catholic ecstasies pose a danger to the chastity of women. The reformed religion is therefore not something blondes are likely to go wild over.'[22] The tyranny of inactivity that ruled English Sundays maddened Louis Viardot:

Sunday is the day of rest and festivity throughout the Continent, from Cadiz to Arkhangelsk; but in England Sunday is the day of nothingness. It is erased from the calendar, removed from life. Sunday, it does not exist. Do you want to eat as usual? You had better buy your provisions the day before because nothing is on sale. Do you want to call on friends? The houses are all closed, only churches open at prayer times. Do you want to write or receive letters? The postal service does not work. What stupidity! What hypocrisy! The English rail against the papists who eat fish or prefer frogs on Fridays rather than roast beef, yet they permit this fetishism of Sundays to the point that every week Parliament receives a petition signed by thousands demanding imperiously the prohibition of all railway and steamship services as an abominable profanation of the holy day.[23]

For Louis, as for many European visitors, the Protestantism of the English was connected to their practical, prosaic, passionless and business-minded character. 'The inside of an Englishman's head can be fairly compared to a Murray's *Guide*,' Hippolyte Taine, the French critic and historian, wrote in *Notes on England* (1872): 'a great many facts but few ideas; a great deal of exact and useful information, statistics, figures, reliable and detailed maps, short and dry historical notes, useful and moral tips by way of a preface, but no all-inclusive vision, and no relish of good writing.'[24]

It was a commonplace of European thought, especially among the Romantics, that the English were a commercial people but not an artistic one. Heine hated England, the 'seriousness of everything, the colossal uniformity, the machine-like movement' – you could send a philosopher to London, he wrote, 'but on pain of your life not a poet'. Clara Schumann wrote to Brahms from a concert tour in London in 1865 that 'all artistic interest, in fact all idealism of every kind is sacrificed here to "business"'.[25] Still, she would come to England nineteen times.

Chopin similarly thought the English had a better sense for money than music. During his visit to London in 1848 he gave his friends in Paris an account of a typical conversation with an English society lady:

THE LADY: Mr. Chopin, how much do you cost?

CHOPIN: My fee is 20 guineas, madam.

THE LADY: Oh! I only want you to play a little piece.

CHOPIN: My fee is the same, madam.

THE LADY: Then you will play a lot of pieces?

CHOPIN: For two hours, if you wish, madam.

THE LADY: Then that is settled. Are the 20 guineas to be paid in advance?

CHOPIN: No, madam. Afterwards.

THE LADY: Very reasonable, I'm sure.[26]

2

The British were sympathetic to the French exiles of 1870. They had mostly sided with the French in the Franco-Prussian War. They saw them as the underdog, as Clara Schumann explained to Brahms in a letter from London in February 1871:

It is when I live here that I realize how deeply I am attached to Germany. What makes it stronger this time is the anti-German feeling of the English, who express their sympathy for the weaker side, that is to say, for the French. At first I thought that this was the English being jealous of the Germans, who have just proved their greatness, but certain Germans who live here assure me that the English are motivated by pity.[27]

To help the French exiles, the British formed a National Society for Aid to the Sick and Wounded, which became the British Red Cross. For the émigrés in London a Mansion House Relief Fund was set up by musicians, among them the composers William Sterndale Bennet and Arthur Sullivan, which organized a number of benefit concerts, including one with Pauline for a packed audience in the Exeter Hall.

British attitudes to Germany were permanently altered by the war. Previously, the Victorians had seen the Germans as the European nation closest to themselves: they shared their Saxon origins, their Protestant religion, in the north of Germany at least, and their moralizing seriousness. They also had a monarchy with German ties. All these connections made for a strong Victorian Germanophilia. Views changed after 1870. The German victory against France – until then the greatest power on the Continent – gave rise to British fears of military aggression by Germany. It was expressed in the bestselling novel by George Chesney, *The Battle of Dorking* (1871), the first in a genre of 'invasion literature', which told the story of Britain's conquest by a German-speaking country, referred to only as 'The Enemy'.[28]

The British were reluctant to become involved in European politics. Confident that their free-trade values would spread through Europe, and concerned with keeping taxes down, Queen Victoria's governments pursued a consistent policy of non-intervention on the Continent, unless of course the interests of the British Empire were at stake, as in the Crimean War, the only European war fought by Britain in this period. The idea that, as Europe's greatest power, Britain had a moral or religious duty to champion righteous causes on the Continent seldom mustered much support from the public or the press.[29]

When they took an interest in a foreign cause – the national-liberation movements of the Poles, Italians and Hungarians all received a sympathetic hearing in Britain – it was because they saw the nationality involved as the underdog, fighting against bullies and tyrants, and projected their own liberal values onto them. On a visit to Britain in 1864, Garibaldi was welcomed as a hero of the anti-Papist movement, credited with all the virtues of an English gentleman, and compared to Sir Walter Raleigh and Sir Francis Drake. The unification of Italy – completed with the capture of Rome in 1870 – was seen by the British as a victory for their own constitutional principles against the authoritarianism of the Austrians and the Papacy.[30]

British insularity was not just political. Culturally the British held aloof from Europeans on the Continent. They toured in groups, their Murray guides in hand, rarely interacting with the local population, and criticizing anything that struck them as too 'foreign' (i.e. different from how things were organized at home). Ignorant of European languages, they expected to be understood by tradesmen, waiters, porters and everybody else they had to deal with, provided they spoke to them loudly and slowly enough in English.

Guidebooks encouraged British travellers to adopt a colonial attitude towards the natives of the European countries they were visiting. 'In general a firm, courteous and somewhat reserved manner is the most effective,' advised Richard Ford in his popular *Handbook for Travellers in Spain* (1855). 'Whenever duties are to be performed, let them see that you are not to be trifled with. The coolness of an Englishman's manner, when in earnest, is what few foreigners can withstand.'[31] No European country was exempt from criticism, and no area of European life more subject to such reprimands than the sewage system and plumbing, which, in fairness, did lag behind the standards achieved in Britain by the middle decades of the nineteenth century. Murray's guide to Switzerland, in 1846, mentioned recent improvements to the Swiss roads, accommodation and general conditions of travel, but noted that

> even in the first-class inns the houses are deficient in proper drainage and want of ventilation, and the passages and staircases are unwholesome and offensive from bad smells. Care should be taken to impress on the landlords how disgusting and intolerable to English ideas such a nuisance is. There is no excuse for it.[32]

The British had a firm belief in their superiority to the Europeans, indeed to all foreigners. They believed that Britain was the envy of the world because of its ancient liberties and traditions of parliamentary government and the rule of law. These ideas were central to their national identity. Their confidence was rooted in their country's military victories against the continental powers, especially the French, in the conquests of the British Empire, and in Britain's status as the first industrial society. Isolated from the Continent by their geography, the British had a strong sense of their special character, based upon their history as a long-unconquered island and, above all, on their Protestant religion, setting them apart from 'Catholic Europe', which in this myth was backward morally.[33] It was a narrative encouraged by the great Whig historians of the Victorian age, such as Lord Macaulay in his *History of England* (1848–61), who presented the country's history as a march of progress from the Magna Carta to the modern constitutional monarchy – the highest possible form of social and political evolution.

European travel confirmed Britons in their view of Europe's moral backwardness. 'It has long appeared to the author,' Henry Mayhew wrote in *German Life and Manners* (1864),

that travelling southward from England is like going backward in time – every ten degrees of latitude corresponding to about a hundred years in our own history; for, as in France we see society in the same corrupt and comfortless state as prevailed in our nation at the beginning of the present century, so in Germany we find the people, at the very least, a century behind us in all the refinements of civilization and the social and domestic improvements of progress; whilst in Spain the denizen lives a positive medieval life, among the same dirt and intellectual darkness, the same beggary and bigotry as preceded the Reformation in our land. In Russia, too, we observe the state of villeinage and serfdom existing almost at this day, as it did with us in the feudal time of the Conquest; whilst, in Central Africa, we reach the primitive condition of nature – the very zero of the civilized scale – absolute barbarism itself.[34]

3

At the end of June 1871, Turgenev went with William Ralston, the British Russian scholar and Turgenev's English translator, to visit Alfred Tennyson, the Poet Laureate. They spent two days at his house, a mock-Tudor mansion at Blackdown, on the Sussex and Surrey border. After a long walk, a game of chess and dinner, the two great men got down to talking literature. Turgenev did not much like the poetry of Tennyson – it smacked too much of the British Empire and Progress – but at least he had read it. He was also able to converse at length about Byron, Shelley, Scott, Swinburne, Dickens and Eliot, all of whom he had read in English. Tennyson, by contrast, showed little familiarity with European literature, and, to his guests' surprise, had not the slightest contact with his Continental colleagues, despite his extensive travels in Europe. Tennyson admitted that he had not read a single work by Hugo, Sand or Musset, although on Turgenev's recommendation he later read *Consuelo* and *La Petite Fadette*, books written by George Sand almost thirty years before. As for the Russians, Tennyson had not read a single one of them, not even Turgenev himself.[35]

Tennyson was not unusual. Turgenev found that British writers were generally unfamiliar with contemporary European literature. The two main exceptions, with whom he was acquainted from his time in London, were Thomas Carlyle, who had a good knowledge of French and German literature, and George Eliot, who had lived in Germany, was a distinguished translator, and had read extensively the major modern European writers, including Goethe, Balzac, Keller and Sand.

In literary terms the British were the most insular nation in Europe. The English language was so dominant, its literature so rich and global reach so wide, that its readers barely took an interest in foreign works. Compared to other European countries, Britain was a tiny importer of foreign literature. It had a thriving book trade of its own; more titles were published in English than in any other language on the Continent, so there was not much demand for literature in foreign languages. As the book trade grew, though, the number of translations into English steadily increased. From the mid-century mark of 2,600 foreign titles translated into English every year, the number published annually rose to almost 4,000 by the 1870s, when popular editions of classic foreign fiction became a stock in trade of the Standard and Railway libraries. But overall this was a tiny share of the book trade in English compared to the number of translations in other European markets. Translated works made up only 2.88 per cent of the books published in English in 1870 – even less than the 3.78 per cent in 1800 – whereas in the biggest book-importing countries (Scandinavia, Germany, the Netherlands,

Spain and Italy) foreign literature made up almost half the total book production in the 1870s. Even France – the only other country with a literary language as dominant as English – had a larger appetite for foreign literature: translations represented around 12 per cent of French book production in 1870.[36]

If the British did not read much foreign literature, they imported European art, opera and music on a larger scale than any other country on the Continent. Culturally, they were more dependent on the Europeans than they liked to admit to themselves. Britain's wealth enabled it to buy in the best of the arts from Europe rather than produce its own.

In 1870, Britain was the largest trading nation in the world. The London docks, where over 40,000 ships would annually unload their cargo from around the globe, were bigger than a city in themselves. Foreign trade was the basis of the country's wealth. Britain had a bigger and richer middle class than any other country in Europe. Salaries in the liberal professions were far higher than on the Continent. According to Taine, writing in the early 1870s, a visit from a doctor cost from five to ten francs in Paris but a guinea (around twenty-seven francs) in London; a professor at the Sorbonne earned 12,000 francs a year, but an Oxford professor had an annual salary of up to £3,000 (75,000 francs); a journalist received 200 francs for a page of copy in the *Revue des deux mondes* but 500 in equivalent English publications, while *The Times* paid as much as £100 (2,500 francs) for a single article. Taine did not mention the industrialists and noblemen, whose annual revenues were in the order of £200,000 (5 million francs), nor the wealthy families with substantial houses in and around London who earned several thousand pounds a year. 'To earn a lot, consume a lot – such is the rule,' he concluded. 'The Englishman does not save money, does not think of the future, at most he will insure his life. He is the reverse of the Frenchman, who is frugal and abstemious.'[37]

London's wealth had acted as a magnet to foreign composers and musicians from the early eighteenth century, when Handel settled there as a young man. They could earn more from a single London season than from many years of working on the Continent. Handel had his ups and downs but in most years received handsome profits from his operas and oratorios. In the 1760s, Mozart's father, Leopold, made 'a good catch of guineas'. Haydn earned a fortune during his two visits in the 1790s, netting around 15,000 gulden (40,000 francs), a dozen times his annual salary from Prince Esterházy.[38]

'Here they pursue music like a business, calculating, paying, bargaining,' noted Mendelssohn on his first visit to London in 1829. The city offered profitable opportunities. Berlioz was brought to London in 1847 on promises of huge performance fees by Jullien (who had also tried unsuccessfully to recruit Pauline Viardot). Jullien failed financially and Berlioz was never paid. But the French composer went on thinking of the English capital as the monied Mecca for music. He wrote in 1853:

> After the French Season, 'the London Season! the London Season!' is the rejoicing cry of every Italian, French, Belgian, German, Bohemian, Hungarian, Swedish and English singer; and the virtuosos of the nations reiterate it with enthusiasm as they step on to the steam-boat, like Aeneas' soldiers repeating 'Italie! Italie!' as they boarded their vessels.[39]

Foreign-born musicians played a vital role in the musical life of Victorian Britain. However much the British liked to think about themselves as apart and different from the Europeans, they were culturally dependent upon them. Three immigrants did more to put the islands on the map of European music than any British musicians in the nineteenth century. The Italian-born conductor Michael Costa (1808–84) came to London in 1830 and worked there for over fifty years, raising standards of performance through a series of reforms, including changes to the layout of the orchestra, the rigid disciplining of its musicians, and the introduction of the modern system of a sole conductor with baton (instead of the older system practised by the British in which control was divided between the first violin, a musical director and a *Maestro al Cembalo*). The German-born conductor August Manns (1825–1907) had worked as a bandmaster for the Prussian army in Berlin before taking over the direction of the Crystal Palace concerts from 1855 to 1901, during which he introduced a large range of new works to the English concert repertoire and championed the music of young British composers, including Charles Stanford, Edward Elgar and Arthur Sullivan. The third important immigrant was Charles Hallé (1819–95), or Karl Halle, as he was called before he came to London. Born in Hagen in Westphalia, Hallé became known as a conductor in Paris, where he moved in the circles of Chopin, Liszt, Sand, and Pauline and Louis Viardot during the 1840s. The revolution of 1848 drove him to London, where he performed as a concert pianist, introducing many new works to the concert repertoire (he was the first pianist to perform the complete Beethoven sonatas in Britain). In 1853, Hallé moved to Manchester, where he set up the Hallé Orchestra and put on concerts at the Free Trade Hall which would raise the British standard of orchestral playing to new heights.

When Verdi came to London with his opera *Masnadieri*, in June 1847, he was impressed by the enormous fees he could earn there. Instead of getting 20,000 francs for a new opera, as he did in Italy, he could make as much as 80,000 or even 100,000 francs. 'Oh, if I could just stay here for a couple of years, I would carry off a sackful of these holy coins,' Verdi wrote to a friend in Milan.[40] The wealth of London made it one of Europe's most important cities for the opera industry. The finest singers all went there, lured by higher rates of pay than they could earn in almost any other city in Europe.[41]

By 1847, London boasted three main opera venues: Her Majesty's Theatre (where *Masnadieri* was put on), previously known as the King's Theatre; the Royal Italian Opera at Covent Garden; and the Theatre Royal in Drury Lane. There were also smaller opera houses such as the Lyceum, where mainly English operas were performed. The large size of London's solid middle classes was the basis of this buoyant market: there were at least 200,000 households with an annual income of £300 or more living within easy reach of the city's theatres by the early 1860s, when the opening of the London Underground and new suburban railways created an even larger catchment area for the opera business.

Unlike the majority of opera companies in continental Europe, where monarchs, states or wealthy patrons subsidized productions until the 1860s, London's opera houses, although licensed by the state, had long been forced to manage on their own as private businesses. Revenues from subscriptions and box office sales constituted 85 per cent of Covent Garden's annual income between 1861 and 1867.[42] These commercial pressures were intensified by the rivalry between the two main opera houses – Her Majesty's and Covent Garden – which competed with each other for the top singers. James Mapleson and Frederick Gye, the managers of the two respective theatres, were astute businessmen. They selected their repertoire on solely economic grounds (the costs of production and likely profits from the box office), which meant choosing operas, tried and tested on the Continent, whose popularity was guaranteed. The London opera repertoire, as a result, was made up entirely of foreign works.[43]

The foreign domination of the London music scene made life hard for British composers. Not one British opera was performed during the main season at Her Majesty's or Covent Garden before the 1870s. The two attempts to establish an English national opera in the off season at Covent Garden – one by the Pyne-Harrison Company from 1858 to 1864 and the other by the Royal English Opera Company in 1864–6 – were both commercial failures. None of the operas performed by these two companies made it into the canon. Vincent Wallace's *The Desert Flower* lasted just two weeks in 1863, and Michael Balfe's *Blanche de Nevers* was equally a flop.[44]

It was just as difficult for a British composer to break into the concert music repertoire. There were too few commissions for new works, too few orchestras to perform them, and too many works by better-known composers from abroad. Excluded from the serious music scene, the leading British composers focused on more popular forms, particularly ballads for the music hall or home, where good money could be made. Two of the best-selling British ballads of the Victorian era were composed for operas: 'I Dreamt I Dwelt in Marble Halls' from Michael Balfe's *The Bohemian Girl* (1843); and 'Scenes That are Brightest' from Vincent Wallace's *Maritana* (1845). Even Arthur Sullivan, the great young hope of British music in the 1870s, could not earn a living from writing serious music and turned his hand instead to composing hymns, parlour songs and operettas in the style of Offenbach. His first surviving effort, *Cox and Box* (1866), became a staple of the Victorian repertoire, with catchy songs like 'Rataplan', which were easy for an amateur to sing, selling tens of thousands of copies. His collaboration with the playwright William Gilbert began in 1871 with a two-act burlesque called *Thespis, or The Gods Grown Old*, commissioned as a Christmas entertainment by the Gaiety Theatre. Its resemblance to *Orpheus in the Underworld* was noted by reviewers, although more than that is hard to say, because the score is lost.[45]

The British were acutely conscious of their musical inferiority. There were frequently discussions in the music press about why there was no native composer of any note. Foreigners had less difficulty explaining it. Fontane doubted if the English had an 'ear for harmony' at all, so much 'mediocre music' did they not only tolerate but actively seek out in taverns and music halls. The French critic Henri Moulin thought the English had their strengths in literature, but they were 'the only people in Europe who were unmusical – they have not produced a single great musician, neither composer nor performer'.[46] Until Elgar burst onto the international music scene at the turn of the twentieth century, this remained the European view of the English. The most famous statement of it was by the German writer Oscar Schmitz, a frequent visitor to London, in *The Land without Music* (*Das Land ohne Musik*, 1904). Schmitz argued that among the many English virtues – commercial practicality and common sense, kindness, humour and so on – the one thing that they lacked was musicality. 'The English,' he wrote, 'are the only cultured race without a music of their own (music-hall ditties excepted). I say music of their own, for perhaps more foreign music is performed in England than in any other country. This means not only that their ears are less discerning, but that their whole inward life must be poorer.'[47]

The same imbalance was evident in the world of fine arts. Along with Paris, London was the centre of the international art market. The major London galleries had dealerships and buyers in all the European capitals. London was awash with artworks from the Continent. According to the import duty figures at Customs House in London, the number of foreign paintings imported into Britain grew from an average of 11,585 per year in the 1840s to over 50,000 per year in the 1870s. The import boom was almost wholly due to the growing spending power of the British middle class (the average value of imported paintings was under £10 in the 1870s).[48] The taste for foreign art was shaped increasingly by the development of public and commercial galleries, international exhibitions, foreign travel, art journals and influential critics such as Ruskin focusing attention on European art.

By the 1860s, the size and wealth of the London art market was able to attract a growing number of artists. James McNeill Whistler moved to London in 1859. 'You can earn far more here in a month (don't say a word of this) than you can there [in Paris] in a year,' he wrote to the painter Henri Fantin-Latour. For years he tried to convince him to move to England.[49] Fantin-Latour did not come, but four years later Whistler did persuade his friend Alphonse Legros to settle in London. Legros had achieved only moderate success as a young artist in Paris during the 1850s, but his etchings and paintings received wide acclaim in England, winning medals at the Royal Academy. He married an English woman and taught at the National Art Training School (as the Royal College of Art was named at that time) before becoming the Slade Professor of Fine Art at University College London in 1876.

Gustave Doré made his fortune in the London galleries. Already known for his illustrations, he scored a huge success with an exhibition of his works in London in 1867, prompting him to move there and open his own gallery in Bond Street the following year. His large religious paintings found a lucrative market in a public starved of art in Protestant churches. From 1868 to 1892, two and a half million visitors would pay a shilling each to see the preachy paintings in the Doré Gallery. Doré's popularity earned him an enormous contract – worth £10,000 per year – to engrave 200 city scenes for *London: A Pilgrimage* (1872), a book which proved such a success that Doré received commissions from other British publishers and became a regular contributor to the *Illustrated London News*.

Manet also thought of trying his luck in London, where the success of Doré and his friend Whistler stood in contrast to his own failing fortunes in Paris. 'I believe there is something to be done over there,' Manet wrote to Fantin-Latour following a visit to London in 1869. 'The feel of the place, the atmosphere, I liked it all and I'm going to try and show my work there next year.' Manet's plans were interrupted by the Franco-Prussian War, when instead he joined the National Guard.[50]

The war brought many other artists to London. James Tissot, another friend of Whistler, arrived in June 1871, having fought in the defence of Paris against the Prussians in the autumn of 1870. Tissot was a wealthy artist of European fame whose many contacts in the London art market enabled him to find buyers there quickly. He spent eleven successful years in London, churning out the sort of paintings that appealed to English high society: portraits of well-dressed ladies, gentlemen in white tie at receptions, and so on. Goncourt reported a rumour that his London studio had 'an antechamber where one could always find iced champagne at the disposition of his visitors and, outside his workshop, a garden where a servant in silk stockings spent all day brushing and polishing the leaves of the trees'.[51]

Gérôme arrived in 1870 with an equally lucrative brand of art tailored for the English market. His highly finished paintings had sold well at Gambart's French Gallery in Pall Mall during the 1860s. On his arrival in London, Gérôme turned out a series of paintings in the moralizing English realist style, which earned him wide acclaim at the Royal Academy exhibitions of 1870 and 1871.

The Barbizon painter Daubigny had also come to London with a reputation well established by two previous visits to the city, and with a wide range of artistic contacts, including Whistler, Legros and Leighton. Daubigny sold a large number of paintings in London, mainly through Durand-Ruel, who had fled to London with the bulk of his collection from Paris in September, catching the last train from the besieged city before the Prussians cut the railway link. Durand-Ruel was the biggest Paris dealer of the Barbizon painters. His father's gallery had dealt in them since the 1840s, and when he took over, in 1865, he bought almost no one else. In London, Durand-Ruel took out a lease on a gallery in New Bond Street – unfortunately already named the 'German Gallery' – and organized an exhibition of 144 French works he had brought from Paris. Because he was unknown in London, he formed an imaginary committee of the Society of French Artists (most of whom were unaware of their membership of it) and used its name to advertise his gallery.[52]

Durand-Ruel opened up the London market for the Barbizon painters. But the Impressionists, whose early work he championed, made no headway in England.

When the Franco-Prussian War began, Monet had been on his honeymoon with his wife and their young son at the seaside resort of Trouville in Normandy. They fled to London, where Monet gave *The Beach at Trouville* to an exhibition organized by Daubigny for the Distressed Peasantry of France. It was admired by Durand-Ruel, who had been following Monet's work. Another of his Trouville paintings (*The Harbour at Trouville*) was included by Durand-Ruel in the first annual exhibition of the Society of French Artists in December 1870. There would be eleven exhibitions in the next five years, as Durand-Ruel built up his connections to the French painters and developed a network of clients in London. Through Monet he became acquainted with Camille Pissaro, who on the outbreak of the Franco-Prussian War had fled with his family to Norwood, then a village on the outskirts of London, where he started painting *plein-air* scenes in an Impressionist style. Durand-Ruel included at least two of Pissaro's Norwood paintings in his second exhibition in March 1871, and from then became his main dealer and promoter, buying up a large stock of his work. Neither Monet nor Pissaro sold many paintings in London. British taste was too conservative – too restricted by the conventions of the Royal Academy – to appreciate these avant-garde experimentalists in painted light. Durand-Ruel later claimed that he did not sell a single work by the Impressionists during his year in London.[53]

For their part, the French artist refugees did not think a lot of their British counterparts. 'How awful modern English painting is!' declared Daubigny. 'They certainly have need of our influence ... When they paint fruit or flowers, they appear to be made of glass or sugar. Land-scapes seem to be made of chenille or seem to have been brushed in with hair. Figures are as rigid as iron.' The sculptor Jules Dalou, who arrived in London in July 1871, complained that the British public did not like nudes, unless they were sanitized and scented like 'English soaps'. Pissaro was scathing about British art, an attitude informed largely by his commercial failure in Britain. 'My painting doesn't catch on,' he wrote from London to the art critic Théodore Duret in June 1871. 'Here, one is only met with disdain, indifference, and even rudeness; one experiences the jealousy and most selfish defiance of colleagues – here, there is no art: everything is a business matter.'[54]

The idea that the British were no good at art was, like their hopeless-ness with music, a European commonplace. Moulin put it down to the fact that the English school of painting was only a century old (he dated it from Reynolds and Gainsborough). There was no sense of the sublime, no transcendental wonderment, in British art, he claimed; the dull grey skies were limiting; the English aristocracy favoured genre paintings of their horses and hunting dogs, which, the critic thought, 'gave the measure of the true industrial genius of this people'.[55]

Louis Viardot was scornful about British art, its public sculptures in particular, having spent the best part of his year in London visiting its collections. He ridiculed the marble statues by Sir Richard Westma-cott, the 'most celebrated sculptor of England', on the pediment of the British Museum. The figures were meant to represent the 'progress of civilization' but they were 'wanting in harmony, grace, and dignity', Viardot thought, and would have been better placed at 'the chief entrance of the docks of London, the naval arsenal at Woolwich, the observatory of Greenwich, or the northern railway'. In *Les Merveilles*

'The English should never meddle in painting.' Extract of Turgenev's letter to Pauline Viardot with a sketch of the figures described from a painting at Grosvenor House.

de la sculpture (1869), translated into English as *The Wonders of Sculpture* (1872), Viardot concluded that there was no English sculpture worthy of inclusion in his book:

> I have met with no single work worth mentioning by a native sculptor in any public or private collection or drawing-room. It is the same in the public gardens, parks, and squares. Could I write a description of the bronze equestrian statue of the Duke of Wellington, erected in Piccadilly in front of his residence, and opposite that other grotesque statue representing this illustrious statesman and warrior on foot as a Fighting Achilles, which is perfectly nude and perfectly black? The equestrian statue . . . most resembles Punch mounted on Balaam's ass – at least so it has been caricatured by the witty Charivari of London, to whose pages it properly belongs.[56]

Turgenev was just as unimpressed by an exhibition of contemporary English painting at Grosvenor House – a 'frightful, dreadful chamber of horrors!' as he described it to Pauline Viardot:

> Miserable colours, infantile drawing; these gentlemen think to fall back on expression, which, aiming to be profound and poetic, is merely ill-defined, idiotic and sickly. There is a medieval demoiselle with leggings who is picking [sic] apricots on a vine – all in the sky – (from the front Mlle Spartalis)* – which would make you laugh – or cry like a baby! And what ridiculous subjects! For example: a painting two metres long by half

* Turgenev means the Pre-Raphaelite artist Marie Spartali Stillman (1844–1927).

a metre wide: at the top an angel with bizarre wings who holds below
her a knight in armour – who in his turn holds beneath him a woman
dressed in lilac gauze: all three figures dangle in the sky as I have drawn
them here [a sketch is attached]. The picture is entitled Rosamunda!! No!
The English should never meddle in painting.[57]

4

London was never going to be more than a temporary refuge for the
Viardots. Once the war was over and it was safe to return to the Continent, they would go back to Baden or Paris.

In the early months of 1871, the Prussian siege had brought Paris to
its knees. People lived in the ruins of buildings which had been destroyed
by the daily bombardment. Food stocks became dangerously low.
Rationing was introduced – 400 grammes of bread per day per citizen,
though how much of it was bread was hard to say. Parisians grew
accustomed to horsemeat. 'As for the two staple items of the diet of the
poorer classes, potatoes and cheese,' Edmond de Goncourt noted in his
diary on 7 January, 'cheese is just a memory, and you have to have
friends in high places to obtain potatoes at twenty francs a bushel.'[58]
Authority collapsed. The left-wing leaders of the National Guard took
power, forcing the Thiers government and its armed forces to evacuate
the capital and retreat to Versailles; there was an uprising by the Paris
workers, an urban revolution to reclaim their city from Haussmann's
bourgeoisie; and a Commune was established to introduce their revolutionary demands, including workers' control of their workplaces. The
government rallied its troops and attacked Paris from Versailles. As the
troops approached the city, the Communards erected barricades and
launched a campaign of terror against 'counter-revolutionaries'. By the
end of May, following a week of street fighting, government troops had
reoccupied the capital. There were summary trials and executions of
the Communards; over 40,000 were taken prisoner, many of them later
deported by military tribunals.

At this point the Viardots were still thinking of returning to Baden.
Turgenev was keen on the plan. He had been back to their house in
February to check that it was in order, and recalled the 'happy years'
they had spent there.[59] Back in London, on 6 May, he wrote to Flaubert

that he would remain there until 1 August, when he would return to Baden, stopping off in Paris to see him. 'Perhaps you will come to Baden, where we shall live for a while like moles, hiding in their holes and you could hide there with us.'[60] News of the defeat of the Commune did not make them change their minds, even though they were concerned for the safety of their house in the rue de Douai, an area affected by the fighting. On 29 July, the Viardots vacated their house in Devonshire Place and left with Turgenev for Boulogne, where they spent a few days by the sea. They then continued on their journey to Baden, while Turgenev travelled back to London to wind up all their affairs there.

As they crossed the English Channel, the Viardots must have been relieved to be leaving, despite their nervousness about the risks that lay ahead. Pauline did not like the English much. She found them too provincial, too cold and stiff – too uncontinental, in a word. They were not really Europeans after all. Louis was unhappy in London. He could not speak English. He was in poor health, suffering from rheumatism, and the English weather did not help. He was worried about money, about their property in Baden and Paris, both affected by the fighting, and was depressed about the news from France.[61]

Turgenev was only slightly happier. In the ten months he spent in England he had done very little work. He needed to feel settled before he could write. The only thing he managed to do much work on, his novella *Spring Torrents*, remained unfinished in Britain – 'My cursed story is becoming as drawn out as a rubber band; the devil knows when I will finish it!' he complained to Annenkov[62] – and bore no trace of his stay there. Loosely based on the events of his own youth in Germany, the love story is filled rather with nostalgia for his carefree former existence in that country.* Yet in London Turgenev had an active social life, found new literary and artistic friends, and even joined the Athenaeum and Garrick clubs. The lifestyle of the English landed gentry suited him – their love of country sports especially. In August he enjoyed

---

* The novella could be read as an evocation of Turgenev's longing for innocent romance – something he had sacrificed to his devotion to Pauline. Sanin, its narrator, recalls his engagement to a German girl he had met in Frankfurt on his European travels thirty years before. To raise money for their marriage he meets the wife of a Russian acquaintance in Wiesbaden, hoping that she might buy his estate in Russia. Seduced by her beauty and alluring power, he follows her to Paris and lives there as her 'slave' until she casts him aside.

a hunting trip to Pitlochry in Scotland, where he was a guest of the industrialist Ernst Benzon at Allean House, though he did not form a high opinion of the poet Robert Browning, who was there with his son, a keen hunter. 'Browning is extremely vain and not at all amusing,' he reported to Pauline. 'His son gives the impression of a very nice boy with a large red wart on the end of his nose.'[63]

Turgenev was also drawn to the liberalism of the English. He was closer in his views to their evolutionary politics than to Louis Viardot, whose sympathies were radically republican, bordering on socialist. At the end of May, Turgenev went with Ralston to Cambridge, where they stayed at Trinity. After dinner at High Table in the college hall, they forsook the port in the Master's Lodge and went instead to the Cambridge Union to listen to a debate by the students, at that time in the middle of their post-exam festivities. The motion was: 'In the opinion of this House, the Parisian Commune is deserving of sympathy and respect.' The proposition was defeated by 102 votes to 14, prompting Turgenev to remark to Ralston as they left: 'Now at last I understand why you English are not afraid of a revolution.'[64]

While Turgenev was in Scotland, the Viardots returned to Baden. They found their house in a ruinous condition, with many of its windows smashed – no doubt by German nationalists who knew its owners to be French. The war and the absorption of the Grand Duchy of Baden into the German Empire had changed the character of the spa town. Gone was the cosmopolitanism of its pre-war days, and in its place was a more uniformly German atmosphere. Feeling they were unwelcome, the Viardots decided to sell their Baden home and return to Paris, where the newly proclaimed republic was more in line with their beliefs. The Baden aristocracy was 'furious' with their decision, claiming they had 'insulted' the newly proclaimed Emperor Wilhelm and the Empress Augusta, their former friends and patrons in Baden.

Although he did not like Paris, Turgenev accepted their decision to return to France. 'I am happy and think it is a good idea to go back to the rue de Douai,' he wrote to Pauline from Edinburgh, where he attended the centenary celebrations for Walter Scott on 12 August and gave a speech which, though cheered and reported in the press, had left him with the impression that 'no one had the slightest idea' who he was, nor 'any interest' in his subject. 'And while we're on the matter [of the rue de Douai], why don't you install me there, since you have some rooms to let? It would cost me less than a hotel. It's an idea that came to me just now. Think about it and let's talk.'[65]

By the end of August, Turgenev had rejoined the Viardots in Baden. It took a while to find a buyer for their properties. The Viardot villa was eventually sold to Moritz Karo, the Hungarian Consul, for 123,000 francs – a big loss on the money spent on it by the Viardots. Turgenev's house (which he had sold to the Viardots) was purchased by a German businessman from Moscow, Hermann Achenbach. Louis and Pauline returned to Paris in October to move back into the house in the rue de Douai and prepare it for the family – the house was in need of repairs – while Turgenev remained with their children in Baden. Builders in Paris were difficult to find – so many buildings had been damaged in the fighting – and it was only at the end of November that the works were sufficiently completed for Turgenev and the children to rejoin Pauline and Louis. During these last weeks in Baden, Turgenev oversaw the moving out of all the furniture from his mansion – the only home he had really loved. 'I am feeling sorry to have lost my nest,' he wrote to Annenkov, 'but then it is not without reason that I have nomadic Tatar blood.* The sense of settlement is not in me – and any house I have is like a tent.'[66]

---

* The Turgenevs were indeed descendants of the Tatar tribes, which invaded Russia in the thirteenth century. By the fifteenth century they had taken up positions in the military and civil service of Muscovy.

7

Culture Without Borders

Living in Paris for personal reasons, he served his country in Europe. We nicknamed him the ambassador of the Russian intelligentsia. There was not a Russian man or woman in any way connected to writing, art or music, on whose behalf Turgenev did not intervene.

Maksim Kovalevsky, 'Memories of Turgenev' (1908)

I

The Viardots returned to Paris at the end of October 1871. They were shocked by the damage to the city by the Prussian bombardment and the fighting between Thiers's troops and the Communards. There had been running battles in the area leading up to Montmartre, where they found the houses pitted by bullet holes and the streets still cluttered by the remains of barricades. Thiers's mansion in the nearby place Saint-Georges had been torched by the Communards, leaving nothing but a burned-out shell. Their own house in the rue de Douai was unscathed but dilapidated after years of being rented out to a family with many children, who had left during the siege. Returning with the Viardot children from Baden, Turgenev found the house in a chaotic state, as he wrote to Annenkov on 24 November. 'It is full of labourers decorating, cleaning, scraping, moving furniture – none of it conducive to my work.'[1]

The household was gradually restored to the luxury and splendour of ten years before, when the Viardots had last lived there. Pauline's Cavaillé-Coll organ was brought back from Baden and reinstalled in the *Grand Salon*, where Louis had his picture gallery. Despite his sale of many paintings to cover the expenses in Baden, he still had important works, including several by Velázquez and Ribera. The ground floor rooms, where they entertained, were richly furnished with oriental carpets, heavy cashmere curtains and hangings, and large vases of flowers. They had an 'exotic eastern feel', according to the writer Hjalmar Boyesen. Pauline saw her students in the first-floor drawing room, where she kept her Pleyel grand piano. On the coffee-coloured walls there were portraits of George Sand, Gounod, Saint-Saëns and Turgenev, and a full-length picture of Pauline's sister, the great singer Malibran.[2]

To begin with Turgenev had two rooms in the attic. It was the first time he had lived in the same house as the Viardots – the point when his relationship with Pauline and Louis became more or less open. In 1874, when their daughter Claudie married, he was given four small rooms she had vacated on the second floor. Turgenev had a study, a 'cramped and airless room' with two little windows and a ceiling far too low for his tall frame; there were a desk covered with his papers, an ottoman, a stool, and paintings covering the walls. Next door, in the library, was a boudoir piano, its lid covered with a thick layer of dust, and, off a narrow corridor, there were a salon and a bedroom, where the jurist Anatoly Koni, who visited Turgenev, noticed through an open door that 'everything was in disorder', the bed unmade, a curtain falling from its rail. Turgenev was dressed shabbily at home: his clothes had missing buttons, according to Elena Repchanskaya, one of Pauline's Russian students, who often called on him. She took it as an indication of his sad existence, without a wife to care for him. Yet, despite this shabbiness, he had 'impeccable comportment', recalled Louise, who sensed his presence in the house from the smell of his eau de Cologne.[3]

Visitors were shocked by the humble quarters of the great writer, who lived like a lodger in his old friends' house. Russians took offence on his behalf. 'The apartment resembled a modest set of furnished rooms – the same small passages and corridors, the same doors, stoves and furniture. It was unworthy of a wealthy nobleman,' thought Petr Boborykin, the Russian journalist and memoirist. 'Who else, with gout, would climb so many stairs to the upper floors and live there with the sound, from ten o'clock each morning, of loud and piercing roulades and solfeggios sung by Mme Viardot's pupils in the drawing-room below? I cannot imagine how he worked.'* It seemed tragic to Boborykin that Turgenev lived in 'bivouacs and temporary quarters', as if he were a 'nomad'.[4]

Turgenev only lodged upstairs. Most of the time he spent down-stairs, reading, playing chess with Louis, listening to Pauline making music, taking meals with the family, in whose daily life he played a central part. In many ways he acted as a second father to the Viardot children, especially to Claudie and her younger sister, Marianne. Turgenev and the Viardots no longer kept up the appearance of living separately, as they had done in Baden and London. They did nothing to conceal their relationship, which became a source of malicious and misleading public gossip, some of it finding its way to the police, who kept the Viardots under regular surveillance because of their left-wing sympathies and alleged immorality. Turgenev, the authorities believed, had been 'expelled from Russia' as a 'revolutionary' after the appear-ance of his 'nihilist tract', *Fathers and Sons*. The agents they assigned to read his mail and follow him around Paris reported to the Prefect of Police that he was 'considered by the nihilists to be one of their lead-ers'.[5] They also followed Louis Viardot, whom they suspected of disseminating socialist ideas at the Sorbonne, where in fact he just went to use the library. The following report on Turgenev and the Viardots was typical of police intelligence:

> Madame Viardot lives most of the time alone with Monsieur Tourguéneff in the house at rue de Douai. Monsieur Viardot, who has cold relations with his wife, lives almost permanently with his son at their property in Bougival. He comes to Paris for a few days only during holidays, mainly out of habit rather than to spend the holidays in the circle of his family. Why he allows the presence of Tourguéneff in his house remains unknown: despite the rumours that his wife and Tourguéneff are lovers, Monsieur Viardot remains on the friendliest terms with him: none of their neigh-bours knows what goes on between them and there is nothing else on which to base conclusions about the character of the relations between these three persons.[6]

---

* Turgenev had an acoustic tube installed so that he could hear the singing lessons while he wrote.

18. Tissot, *London Visitors* (oil on canvas, 1874). Armed with a guidebook, the well-dressed tourists are standing at the entrance of the National Gallery contemplating which site they should visit next. The two youths are 'bluecoat boys', students of Christ's Hospital School who served as tour guides.

19. Repin's portrait of Turgenev (oil on canvas, 1874), commissioned by Tretiakov for his museum of Russian art in Moscow. The Viardots did not like the portrait, and Repin was obliged to make changes, souring his relations with Turgenev.

20–21 (*below*). Khalarmov's portrait (oil on canvas, 1875) was favoured by Turgenev and the Viardots, who displayed it with the artist's portraits of Pauline and Louis Viardot (plate 21, oil on canvas, 1875) in their picture gallery at the rue de Douai.

22. Corot, *Peasant Woman Collecting Wood* (oil on canvas, Italy, c. 1870). Turgenev was the owner of several Corot landscapes. He loved the sensory 'impression' they created of actually being in nature.

23. Rousseau's *Le Givre* ('Hoar frost', oil on canvas, 1845), one of Europe's most expensive paintings when it was sold for 60,000 francs in 1873.

24. Renoir, *La Grenouillère* (oil on canvas, 1869). Painted by Monet as well as Renoir, the Grenouillère riverside restaurant near Bougival was 'the birthplace of Impressionism', according to Kenneth Clark.

25. Manet's portrait of *Zola* (oil on canvas, 1868). On the wall above the desk is a reproduction of Manet's *Olympia* (1863), and on it Zola's pamphlet on Manet, which helped to promote the artist's work.

26. Degas, *The Orchestra at the Opéra* (oil on canvas, 1870). The composer Chabrier, a friend and early patron of the Impressionists, is depicted in the box, the sole member of the audience to be seen.

27. Renoir, *Madame Georges Charpentier et ses enfants* (oil on canvas, 1878). The publisher and his wife, Marguérite, were key supporters of the Impressionists, helping them to get established through their salon.

28. Monet, *Gare St.-Lazare* (oil on canvas, 1877), one of several paintings of the station included by Monet in the Third Exhibition of the Impressionists, where it was praised by Zola: 'You can hear the rumbling of the trains, their smoke billowing under the vast glass interior. Our artists must find the poetry in these stations, as their fathers found it in the forests and rivers.'

29. 'The Pirate Publisher – An International Burlesque That Has Had the Longest Run on Record', cartoon, *Puck*, 24 February 1886. Authors from Europe and America (among them Wilkie Collins, Tennyson, Browning, Verne, Daudet, Zola, Björnsen, Freitag and Mark Twain) accuse the publisher of reprinting their works abroad without paying them, while the publisher insists that he is supported by the law. The Berne Convention, adopted by ten states in September 1886, was the first effective law of international copyright.

30. Villa Viardot at Bougival (photograph c. 1900).

31. Turgenev's dacha ('Les Frênes') at Bougival (photograph, 2018).

32. Detail of the stained-glass panels in the front door at 'Les Frênes'. The scenes depict Turgenev hunting in the Russian countryside (photograph, 2018).

33. Portrait medallion of Pauline Viardot worn by Turgenev, with his initials on the back. Musée Tourguéniev, Bougival (photograph, 2018).

34. Turgenev's bedroom at 'Les Frênes' (photograph, 2018).

35. Claudie Viardot's pencil drawing of Turgenev moments after he had died, 3 September 1883.

36. Pauline Viardot in old age (photograph, c. 1900).

Rumours of this sort – and worse – continued to dog the Viardots, especially Louis, who had political ambitions on their return to France.[7] In October 1874, he stood for election as an independent Radical candidate in municipal elections in the Madeleine district in Paris. His campaign was undermined by malicious gossip – spread sufficiently widely for the inept police to be aware of it – that he was an 'old pimp (*macq*) living from the earnings of his wife', a 'prostitute and lesbian', who had sexual relations with her students. Louis lost the election. The next year he was asked to stand for the Sorbonne but declined the nomination, citing his old age as the reason (he was seventy-five), although in truth he was afraid of exposing Pauline and himself to such rumours once again (he went on to stand again for election at the age of eighty-one in 1881, but did not win).[8]

When they returned to Paris, Pauline was aged fifty, Turgenev fifty-three. Neither was too old for a sexual relationship, but one does not seem likely. Turgenev claimed that he was impotent, or so he told his friends over a long and alcoholic dinner at Flaubert's apartment shortly after his return to Paris. He had said many times in recent years that his relations with Pauline had become easier because their sexual passions had declined. With his white hair and beard Turgenev looked considerably older than his years (when he was out in public with Louis, strangers often thought they were brothers). He suffered terribly from gout and bladder pains (probably the effect of venereal disease contracted many years before). He was not in a condition to be Pauline's ardent lover. He was her devoted friend, admirer, artistic soulmate, financier, supporter and adviser, errand-runner, helper to her children – in short, her 'slave', according to his friends. Among them was Flaubert, who wondered 'how a man could degrade himself to that extent'.[9] He called Turgenev a 'soft pear' (*poire molle*) – cruel perhaps in the light of his declared impotence – which became the Russian's nickname at the Viardots.[10] According to Henry James, a resident in Paris in 1875–6, Turgenev was constantly at Pauline's bidding, even leaving dinners early to be home by 9.30 p.m. to say goodnight to her before she went to bed.[11]

James thought Turgenev was a man 'with something pressing upon him and making him unhappy, more than he knows'. It was an impression some of his friends shared, among them Flaubert, although others, like George Sand, took a slightly different view. Sand had struck up a warm friendship with Turgenev when he came with the Viardots to stay with her – now an old recluse at Nohant – in October 1872. She had not read Turgenev when she met him at Courtavenel during the 1840s, but now she recognized him as a 'great poet' and, in the three days that they spent together, came to adore him for his lively conversation and childish love of games.[12] Following a later visit by Turgenev with Flaubert, in April 1873, Sand wrote to the latter, who had complained of not seeing enough of the Russian because Pauline kept him on too tight a rein: 'No, that giant does not do as he likes, I have noticed that. But he is one of the class that finds its happiness in being ruled, and I can understand it, on the whole. Provided one is in good hands – and he is.'[13]

Turgenev himself would frequently complain of feeling lonely in these years. 'I have close friends whom I love, people who love me,' he told a Russian visitor, 'but not everything that is dear and near to me is as near or dear to them; not everything that interests me is of interest to them; and there are long periods when I feel isolated and alone.'[14] This was the price Turgenev paid for living on the edge of Pauline's nest. The intensity of his devotion was not shared by her, and so his love for her declined, or rather changed in nature over time, becoming closer to a deep friendship. It was from this loneliness, the desperation of old age, that Turgenev fell in love with a series of much younger women – all Russians – in the 1870s.

The Viardots resumed their custom of hosting a salon. On Thursday evenings they held a musical soirée in the *Grand Salon*, where the Parisian cultural élite would meet, and on Sunday afternoons a more informal gathering, where there were games, theatricals, charades, comic songs and music-making among family and friends. Saint-Saëns once appeared as a ballerina in a lampoon mime of the diabolic temptations offered to Robert in *Robert le diable*, the Grand Opera by Meyerbeer. The famous 'Dance of the Nuns' was then performed by all the guests dressed in white sheets, beating the rhythm on saucepans while Pauline played the piano arrangement of the score.[15]

Writing to his brother, Henry James gave this account of a Thursday musical soirée at Madame Viardot's, 'a most fascinating woman', he remarked, 'as ugly as eyes in the sides of her head and an interminable upper lip can make her, and yet also very handsome or, at least in the French sense, *très belle*'.

Her musical parties are rigidly musical and to me, therefore, rigidly bore-some, especially as she herself sings very little. I stood the other night on my legs for three hours (from 11 to 2) in a suffocating room, listening to an interminable fiddling, with the only consolation that Gustave Doré, standing beside me, seemed as bored as myself. But when Mme. Viardot does sing, it is superb.[16]

Caroline Commanville, Flaubert's niece, recalls 'Madame Viardot, wear-ing a simple but elegant black dress, moving graciously around the room, greeting each group of her guests in turn, leaning in to speak to certain individuals . . . Standing by a doorway on his own, Turgenev watched her all the time, and when she passed by him, they exchanged smiles.'[17]

These Thursday evenings were an important fixture of the Paris music scene. They were attended by the leading French composers of the day, among them Gounod, Saint-Saëns, Fauré, Lalo, Bizet (a neigh-bour in the rue de Douai), Massenet and Franck (employed as a music teacher to Paul Viardot in the 1870s). Many of their chamber works were first performed at the Viardots' before an invited audience of influ-ential guests: patrons of the arts, concert managers and impresarios, politicians, writers and their publishers, critics and the owners of their newspapers. Most of these figures reappeared at Saint-Saëns's Monday musical parties at his mother's house in the Faubourg Saint Honoré and at Lalo's parties on Fridays. In this way they began to form a stable network of personal connections that shaped artistic tastes and made things happen in the cultural world of Paris in the 1870s and later.[18]

Turgenev and the Viardots were at the heart of this network. They promoted young composers, artists, writers through their connections in the music world, the art establishment, journalism and publishing, in effect performing a role that would become the business of an agent in the modern sense.* As influential figures with an international reach, they also served as intermediaries between different cultures in Europe, intro-ducing Russian music, art and literature to France, Britain, Germany,

---

* Agents had existed in an informal sense, as middlemen, since at least the early nine-teenth century, but the modern professional agent began to appear in the 1870s, at first mainly in the English-speaking world. The Glaswegian A. P. Watt was probably the first, his agency dating from the later 1870s, when he set up in London, advertised himself as a literary agent, and charged a 10 per cent commission on the income earned for his clients.

Spanish art and music to the French, French and German writers to Russia, and so on. Through their international connections they were helping to advance the cultural integration of the Continent.

There were many Russians in Paris. Most were temporary residents, idle noble travellers and tourists; but there were also long-term émigrés, political exiles and revolutionaries, students, writers and artists. In this community Turgenev was a crucial intermediary. 'We nicknamed him the ambassador of the Russian intelligentsia,' recalled Maksim Kovalevsky, the sociologist, who was a student at the Collège de France during the mid-1870s. 'There was not a Russian man or woman in any way connected to writing, art or music, on whose behalf Turgenev did not intervene.'

> He took an interest in the Russian students of Mme Viardot, brought Russian musicians to her attention, acted as the Secretary of the Paris club of Russian artists, made arrangements for the exhibition of their works, sent publicity about them to the Paris press, wrote letters of intro-duction to those who approached him, gave money to those he considered needed it, usually without return, and petitioned on his own or through acquaintances on behalf of [Russian] foreign correspondents, even at the risk of endangering his own relations with the authorities, which could have stopped him from returning to Russia.[19]

The club of Russian artists (formally entitled the Society for the Mutual Aid and Patronage of Russian Artists in Paris) was founded by Turgenev and the landscape painter Aleksei Bogoliubov, who settled in Paris because of poor health in 1872. The club met on Tuesday evenings at the mansion of the Russian Jewish banker and philanthropist Baron Günzburg in rue de Tilsitt. Russian artists auctioned their artworks and Turgenev gave readings (a pince-nez balanced on his nose) to attract the expat crowd. Turgenev also played a leading role in the Russian Reading Room, which he established with German Lopatin, the exiled Russian revolutionary, and which held concerts and readings to raise money for political émigrés and students in Paris. Turgenev gave a large part of his library to the Reading Room, and Pauline hosted several private concerts to raise money for it, delighting the Russian audience by singing mainly Russian songs.[20] Tsarist secret-police agents kept a watchful eye on these evenings.[21]

Pauline's singing career was effectively over. The Jena premiere of

Brahms's *Alto Rhapsody*, in 1870, was her last significant performance in public. She did sing in several private concerts in the 1870s, although her voice retained only traces of its former power and intensity.[22] Her central importance in the music world now continued in her role as a teacher and promoter of young musicians and composers in whose talent she believed. On her return to Paris, in 1871, she was appointed Professor of Singing at the Conservatoire, a post she held until 1875, when she resigned in frustration with the rigid pedagogic policies of her colleagues. But her teaching manual, *L'École classique du chant* (1864), a guide to the bel canto style with annotations on 300 arias and songs, continued to be used by the Conservatoire until the twentieth century.

The Viardot household became an informal headquarters for a group of French composers, all members of the Société Nationale de Musique, founded at the time of the defeat by Prussia in February 1871 to promote the cause of 'serious' French music, chamber music in particular, and liberate it from the domination of the German tradition.[23] As the co-founder and president of the society, Saint-Saëns was the intermediary between these composers and Pauline, who was by this time an old and dear friend (he dedicated *Samson and Delilah* to Pauline, who sang the leading part in a concert performance with the composer at the piano in 1874, although by the time the opera was finally premiered in Weimar, three years later, she was too old to star in it).[24]

It was Saint-Saëns who first brought Fauré to the Viardots in 1872. The unknown young composer, then aged twenty-seven, had been taught piano by Saint-Saëns at the École Niedermeyer, the austere Paris boarding school for religious music which Fauré had attended from the age of nine, and he was presented to the Viardots as Saint-Saëns's favourite protégé. Fauré became a frequent visitor at the rue de Douai. Naturally shy, he grew in confidence in the warm family atmosphere and took comfort from the maternal attentions of Pauline, who encouraged Fauré to compose. His songs Op. 4 and Op. 7 are dedicated to Pauline, the songs of Op. 8 and Op. 10 to Marianne and Claudie, and his Violin Sonata (Op. 13) to Paul Viardot – all works dating from this time. Fauré fell in love with Marianne, eight years younger than himself, and the two became engaged.[25] But Marianne broke their engagement. She could not be the maternal wife he wanted her to be. Shortly afterwards, she married the composer Victor-Alphonse Duvernoy. Fauré took a long time to recover. It is often said that his *Requiem* was written in response to this lost love. But musically perhaps the break from Marianne was a blessing in disguise, as Fauré himself later acknowledged: Pauline would have steered him towards opera and choral music (as she did with Duvernoy), whereas Fauré's strengths were as a composer of piano and chamber works.

Of the young composers encouraged by Pauline, Massenet was the best-known for his opera and choral works. In 1872, he was introduced by Saint-Saëns to Pauline, who invited him to dinner in the rue de Douai and asked to hear some of his music. The unknown composer, then aged thirty, played some extracts from his three-part oratorio *Marie-Magdaleine*. Pauline was impressed. Based on Renan's *Vie de Jésus*, the oratorio was musically modern, eschewing the classical conventions, such as fugues, in favour of an operatic form with oriental colour that captured well the dramatic effect of Renan's story of Jesus, not as God but as a living human being. Pauline took it on herself to get the work performed, offering herself for the main female part. *Marie-Magdaleine* was premiered in Paris in April 1873 at one of the 'national' concerts organized by the Société. It was an instant sensation, launching Massenet's career and winning him the highest praise of Gounod, Bizet and Tchaikovsky, who heard it on a trip to Paris that summer. Massenet would later write that he owed his 'entire career' to Pauline Viardot.[26]

For these young French composers, the chance to hear Spanish music was one of the main attractions of the Viardot salon. Pauline had established herself as one of the principal exponents of Spanish song in France, a country where Hispanic music had been little known before she began her career during the 1830s. She had added Spanish songs to her concert repertoire, researched, transcribed and published them, and made them known to composers, Berlioz and Gounod among them, who took a growing interest in the music of 'exotic Spain'.[27] The young French composers of the Société, who regularly heard her sing these songs at her salon, were drawn to Spanish music partly by its popular appeal (in the 1860s the country's dance and folk music had become established features of *opéras comiques*, vaudevilles and *café-concerts* in Paris),[28] and partly by their search for an 'authentic' folk tradition that had links to southern France and could specifically draw the French away from the influence of the Germans. Ideas of Pan-Latinism were becoming influential in France at this time, partly as a reaction to the rise of Pan-Germanism and Pan-Slavism.[29] Saint-Saëns,

Bizet, Massenet and Lalo all wrote works with French-styled borrowings from Spanish dances and folk songs.

Inspired by the Spanish music he heard at the Viardots, Saint-Saëns wrote 'El desdichado' (1871), a duet dedicated to Marianne and Claudie which was set to a Spanish verse and composed in the form of a Boléro, a dance that became widely known in European capitals around this time. Lalo's *Symphonie espagnole* (1875), less a symphony than a violin concerto, was composed for the Spanish violinist and composer Pablo Sarasate, a regular at Pauline's musical parties, as indeed was Saint-Saëns's earlier work in a Spanish style for violin and orchestra, *Introduction and Rondo Capriccioso* (1863).

Bizet too was drawn towards the Spanish music he learned from Pauline, especially the Habanera, the syncopated 2/4 rhythm dance which came to Spain from Cuba in the nineteenth century. The Habanera was made popular by the Basque composer Sebastián Iradier (1809–65), whose 'La Paloma' (1860), his version of the dance in a folk style, was performed everywhere in the Hispanic world. Pauline had been adding his songs to her repertoire since the 1850s. She corresponded with Iradier, often asking for his latest scores so that she could introduce them to the concert hall.[30] It was through Pauline that Bizet first became acquainted with Iradier. His music library contained many of Iradier's scores.[31] Bizet borrowed from his composition 'El Arreglito' (1864) for 'L'amour est un oiseau rebelle', the famous aria in his opera *Carmen* (1875), mistakenly assuming that it was an original folk song (warned about his plagiarism, Bizet added an acknowledgement to Iradier to the later versions of his score). The Habanera was not the only contribution by the Viardot circle to Bizet's opera. It was Turgenev who had directed the opera's librettists, Ludovic Halévy and Henri Meilhac, to Mérimée's *Carmen* (1845) and persuaded them, against their initial reservations, that the novella would make a good story for an opera. Louis Viardot had advised Bizet about Spanish literature, particularly Guillén de Castro's sixteenth-century play *Las mocedades del Cid* (based on the medieval legend of 'El Cid'), which Bizet used for his unfinished opera by that name.* And it was Pauline who acquainted

---

* Massenet would reuse parts of the libretto for his 'Spanish' opera *Le Cid* (1885). See Hugh Macdonald's 'Bizet Catalogue' (http://digital.wustl.edu/bizet/works/Don_Rodrigue.html).

him with her father's Spanish operas. She had dozens of Garcia's unpublished scores. One of the songs in his comic opera *The Man in Servant's Disguise* (1804), an Andalusian *palo*, 'Cuerpo bueno, alma divina', was the inspiration for the famous entracte to Act IV of Bizet's opera. A heavily edited version of the song had been published in an album, *Échos d'Espagne* (1872), which Bizet owned, but Pauline introduced him to the original and helped him to re-create its Spanish character.[32]

Bizet's *Carmen* was the ultimate expression of the French nineteenth-century cult of exotic Andalusian Spain, a cult that had begun in the 1820s when Louis Viardot had published his first book, *Lettres d'un Espagnol*. It contained all the stereotypical elements of 'Spanishness' – gypsies, smugglers, bullfighters, flamenco dancers, guitarists, castanets – that had since become established as popular components of the dramatic arts in France. There was a vogue for plays with Spanish themes in the boulevard theatres. Spanish dance was regularly featured in French *opéras comiques*, vaudevilles and *café-concerts*. Flamenco dancers, singers and guitarists performed in the salons of Paris. The mid-1870s were the highpoint of French cultural interest in Spain (at the Exposition Universelle in Paris in 1878 the biggest crowds were to be found at the Spanish exhibits). Beyond the exotic stereotypes, there was a growing appetite for realistic views of Spain, as demonstrated by the huge success of Baron Charles Davillier's account of his travels in *L'Espagne* (1874), illustrated by Gustave Doré, whom he took, as he explained, so that he 'could make us acquainted not with the Spain of the *opéra comique* and keepsakes, but the real Spain'.[33]

Bizet's researches into Spanish culture were in keeping with this new French interest in 'authentic' Spain. But the elements of Spanish music, subject, style and colour he put into *Carmen* were tailored by the Frenchman to fit in with the *opéra comique* form, in which the old stereotypes of Spain were expected. Only part of Mérimée's novella went into the libretto, a more compact tragic drama about the downfall of the soldier Don José, who abandons his childhood sweetheart and his military duties for the fiery gypsy Carmen, whose subsequent attraction to the *Toreador* Escamillo provokes him to murder her.

The first performance took place at the Opéra-Comique on 3 March 1875. The Viardots and Turgenev were in the audience, along with Gounod, Offenbach and Massenet. Initially there was a cold reception for the work. Critics expressed outrage at the 'immoral' nature of the characters, at the sordid realism of the opera's depiction of the lower classes, and (at a time when anti-German feeling was still running high in France) at what was thought to be the 'Wagnerism' of the score.[34] Ticket sales were poor. Half-empty houses saw the first performances. Bizet was distraught, even suicidal, according to his friend Gounod. Having always struggled to achieve success, he saw this latest setback as a fatal blow to his career. He withdrew to Bougival, became ill from swimming in the cold river, and died from a heart attack, no doubt brought on by the stress of his failed opera, on 3 June. He was aged just thirty-six. Sympathy for the composer brought a change of fortune to his opera. Ticket sales improved. It was brought back in the autumn and had a successful run (among those who saw it then was Tchaikovsky, who declared it to be 'a masterpiece in every sense of the word'). Not seen again in Paris until 1883, *Carmen* meanwhile triumphed in Vienna, Brussels, London, Dublin, New York and St Petersburg. It became immensely popular in Germany (Bismarck saw it twenty-seven times).[35]

In Spain its reception was complex. First performed in a Spanish translation at the Teatro de la Zarzuela in Madrid in 1887, many critics attacked it for pedalling the old Romantic stereotypes – bullfighters, gypsies, smugglers and so on – portraying 'oriental' Spain as a primitive and violent society. They felt that modern Spain – which was becoming more connected to the rest of Europe by mass communications and travel – deserved to be better known by foreigners. But others were delighted by what they saw as the opera's veracity; they praised its music and dances, its realistic staging and costumes as true reflections of 'authentic' Spain. Indeed the Habanera from *Carmen* would be rearranged in many different versions and circulated around the Iberian peninsula as a quintessentially 'Spanish' work.[36] It was no longer possible, or even meaningful, to distinguish between what was nationally 'authentic' and what foreign or international – so much cultural exchange was there across national borders in the modern world.

2

Russian music too found new popularity in Europe. Turgenev and Pauline acted as the go-betweens, connecting people in the European music world with the new generation of composers then emerging in Russia.

Throughout the 1870s, he made short trips to Russia. Improvements in the railways had made this possible. During the previous decade there had been a boom in railway-building in Russia– a development encouraged by the country's defeat in the Crimean War, which had exposed Russia's military weakness against the industrial powers, and by the need to improve its transport system for food exports to the West, the main means of raising capital for the country's industrialization. Turgenev had invested heavily in the newly floated Russian railway shares. He also had a personal vested interest in them. The time it took for him to travel to his estate from Paris was drastically reduced by the opening of a line from Warsaw through Smolensk and Vilnius, completed in 1871. It enabled him to travel to Orel without going via Moscow or St Petersburg. From Paris to his Spasskoe estate – a journey that had taken up to three weeks in the 1850s – now took just five days.[37]

On his trips to Russia he resumed his acquaintance with Stasov and the 'Mighty Five', as well as other Russian composers, such as Dargomyzhsky, championed by the nationalist critic. He had been told by Stasov that the circle often met to perform works in progress among themselves. At first the five were reluctant to let Turgenev join their group. While they recognized his literary genius, they were suspicious of his previous attitude towards their school and his support for their arch-rival Anton Rubinstein. But Stasov persuaded them to change their minds, and on Turgenev's visit to St Petersburg, in May 1874, they put on a private concert for him at the critic's house. With four hands at the piano, they performed the final act of Cui's uncompleted opera *Angelo* (1876), which Turgenev liked, and Dargomyzhsky's *The Stone Guest* (1872), which he did not. On that trip Turgenev got to know Mussorgsky. He met him at a dinner, found him sympathetic ('his nose is completely red, he is a drunkard, and his manners completely natural') and heard him 'sing, or rather groan, several extracts of his opera [*Boris Godunov*] and another that he is composing now [*Khovanshchina*], which struck me as characterful and interesting, on my word of honour', he reported to Pauline. '*Allons, allons, messieurs les Russes*!!'[38]

Excited by the promise of these Russian composers, Turgenev bought a load of scores and sent them to Pauline, urging her to give them to her musical connections in Paris. The Mighty Five were only just beginning to be known outside Russia, partly through the activities of Liszt, a keen supporter of their music, and partly through their championing by Jules de Brayer, the organist at Chartres Cathedral, who made tran-scriptions of their works. Twenty-seven of the imported scores went to the Conservatoire – works by Tchaikovsky, Rimsky-Korsakov, Cui and Mussorgsky, including *Boris Godunov*, which had only just received its first performance in St Petersburg in January 1874. It is highly probable that Claude Debussy, a long-time student at the Conservatoire, knew these scores by the time of his graduation, in 1879, when he joined the household of Nadezhda von Meck, the wealthy widow of a Russian rail-way magnate and patron of Tchaikovsky, as a piano teacher for her eleven children and as her musical companion. Through von Meck, with whom he spent the next year in Russia, Debussy became well acquainted with the music of Tchaikovsky, Rimsky-Korsakov and Borodin.[39]

Turgenev was most excited by the young Tchaikovsky, and made a point of seeking out his music during visits to Russia. He was partic-ularly impressed by the *Six Romances*, Op. 6, which he had heard performed at an all-Tchaikovsky concert in Moscow in 1871. He had the music sent to Pauline in London, who liked them so much, esp-ecially the last, 'None But the Lonely Heart', that she at once performed them at her musical parties at Devonshire Place.[40] Later, in Paris, she introduced the *Romances* to the concert repertoire and made them popular. During the summer of 1874, when he was again in Russia, Turgenev sent Pauline a piano arrangement of Tchaikovsky's sym-phonic poem, *Romeo and Juliet* (1871), which she played at the public piano recitals for which she was mainly known in Paris at that time.

Tchaikovsky was aware of Pauline's role as a promoter of his work. He was engaged to her former pupil, the Belgian singer Désirée Artôt, before she broke it off in 1869. Tchaikovsky was a frequent visitor to Paris in the 1870s but did not meet Pauline then. At the end of 1876, he began to think of putting on a concert in Paris the following March. He wrote to the Russian composer Sergei Taneyev, who was then staying in Paris: 'Would it be seen as madness on my part if I were to ask Viardot, through Turgenev, to take part in my concert? After all, she has performed my songs, hasn't she? If it is a mad idea, then just throw away the enclosed letter. But if you think it is all right, then please go to Turgenev and hand him this letter.' The concert did not take place because Tchaikovsky was unable to raise the funds. But Taneyev was at a concert at Pauline's house that spring and accompanied her at the piano while she sang 'None But the Lonely Heart', with what one guest that evening described as 'her characteristic passion, expressiveness, and impeccable diction'. Lopatin, who heard her sing the song at one of her parties, recalled: 'She was an old woman. But when she sang, "Ia strazhdu" ['I am suffering'] it made my flesh creep. How much expression she put into it. Her eyes, her pale and hollow cheeks! You should have seen the audience!'[41]

The French were receptive to Russian culture in the 1870s. Defeat by Prussia moved France closer to Russia as a diplomatic ally against Germany. It was a rapprochement that continued, on and off, culminating in the Franco-Russian Alliance of 1894. The French invested heavily in the Russian economy, the railways in particular, and as Russia opened to the West, Western interest in it grew. There was a boom of travel-writing about Russia, including the bestselling *Voyage en Russie* by Gautier. British writers shared the enthusiasm. Lewis Carroll had gone to Moscow and described it as a wonderland ('you see as in a looking glass distorted pictures of the city') in his travel diary, which became an inspiration for his *Through the Looking Glass* (1871). Two extensive travellers in Russia – Donald Mackenzie Wallace and Anatole Leroy-Beaulieu – produced what were arguably the first objective foreign histories of the country in the 1870s, and both sold in large numbers.[42] In sum, Russia was no longer simply seen as an 'Asiatic barbarism' – an oriental 'other' to contrast with 'European Civilization' – as it had been thirty years before, in the days of the Marquis de Custine. It was coming to be understood as part of Europe itself.

European interest in Russia grew with the international exhibitions of these years – in London (annually between 1871 and 1874), Vienna (1873) and Paris (1878) – where Russian arts and crafts drew some of the largest crowds. At the Paris Exposition in 1878 there was also a well-attended series of Russian music concerts conducted by Nikolai Rubinstein, which featured works by Tchaikovsky, Glinka, Anton Rubinstein and Dargomyzhsky, though not the music of the Mighty Five, which was a source of puzzlement and disappointment to many. The Paris press was united in its critical response: it thought the music interesting but unoriginal, too German or Italian in style. They had expected to hear something more exotically 'Russian' in its national character. There had been a similar reponse to Tchaikovsky's *Romeo and Juliet*, which was hissed at the *concerts populaires*.[43]

Expectations of a distinctive national style were central to the growing receptivity of Western audiences to those cultures placed on the 'periphery' of the European continent (Russia, Spain, Scandinavia, the Czech lands, Hungary, etc.). They wanted Russian music to sound 'Russian', Spanish music 'Spanish', Hungarian 'Hungarian' (even if it was composed by Brahms) in a way that they did not of, say, German, Italian or even French music (which only needed to sound *not* German). They wanted music from these countries to seem exotically different, full of folk motifs, with gypsy and bohemian dances. Such expectations encouraged the production of a 'national style for export' from these lands. Nationalists, in turn, promoted myths of folk-based authenticity in their arts and music, not just for the purposes of their own nation-building but to assert their country's distinctiveness among the other nations of Europe. That was the programme of Stasov and his followers. Cui's book *La Musique en Russie* (1880) was written to promote awareness of their nationalist music in Europe, where it had a lasting influence on public expectations of what Russian music should sound like.

Turgenev was horrified by the exoticization of Russian culture in the West. He wanted Russian artists to become a part of 'European Civilization', and believed that the expression of their national character ought to be subordinate to that – internalized within their art, not worn on their sleeve. That was why he saw great art in Pushkin, Tolstoy and Tchaikovsky: their Russianness did not militate against their Europeanness.

Turgenev's views were equally opposed to Stasov's when it came to the promotion of Russian artists in Europe. There were many Russian painters in Paris. The younger ones were mostly from the Academy of Arts with prize scholarships to study in the studios of established artists (e.g. Bonnat, Gérôme or Lefebvre) under the direction of Bogoliubov, the Russian émigré painter appointed to supervise their work. Most of them were influenced by French genre and landscape art, especially the Barbizon painters, although they were also introduced to the broader trends of European painting in Paris: Bogoliubov steered them to the Spanish painter Marià Fortuny as a counterbalance to the French.

Turgenev was impressed by the young painter Alexei Kharlamov, the most Western-oriented of the Russian students in Paris, who painted mainly genre works and portraits. He went overboard in praising him, comparing him to Rembrandt, whose technique Kharlamov had studied at the Hermitage. He commissioned Kharlamov to paint portraits of Pauline, Louis and himself (Plates 20 and 21), which were indeed exceptionally good from a technical standpoint. They were hung together in the picture gallery at the rue de Douai, and Turgenev made a point of inviting friends to inspect the three paintings (even Victor Hugo was asked to come along). The portraits of the Viardots were displayed in excellent positions at the 1875 Salon (Louis was a member of the jury there) and the picture of Turgenev prominently hung at the Salon of the following year, when Zola, in his annual review, singled out Kharlamov for the highest praise, although he thought his study of Turgenev had given to his friend 'a hard and sad expression' that was 'not at all his usual look'.[44]

Through his many connections in Paris, Turgenev launched Kharlamov on the art market. Goupil sold a number of his paintings at his most luxurious gallery, opposite the vast, newly opened Paris Opéra, the Palais Garnier, and sent many to his London branch, where English dealers snapped up Kharlamov's 'pretty pictures', according to an envious friend, the Estonian painter Ernst Liphart, who thought he was corrupted by Turgenev's definition of success. 'When a picture dealer comes to your studio and offers you good money for one of your paintings in the conviction that he can immediately resell it with an enormous profit to some collector that he has in mind already, that is the meaning of success,' Liphart heard Turgenev say. If true, it was a long way from Turgenev's earlier views; perhaps it was a reflection of his own evolution as a writer in the commercial world of publishing. 'Poor Kharlamov,' Liphart wrote, 'he became the victim of this theory of his protector. The craze for small Italianate paintings which the English dealers encouraged him to churn out killed the Kharlamov promised by his portraits of the Viardots.'[45]

Turgenev promoted other Russian artists in Paris. He wrote articles about them in the press, put them into contact with dealers, and helped them to find buyers for their work. He arranged the sale of four paintings by Arkhip Kuindhzi to Charles Sedelmeyer, the Austrian dealer in Paris. With the help of Louis Viardot, who praised them in the French and Belgian press, he got two sculptures by Marc Antokolsky displayed at the 1878 Exposition Universelle in Paris, where they were awarded a gold medal, earning Antokolsky many foreign commissions.[46]

He was particularly active on behalf of Vasily Vereshchagin, whose large battle paintings and Central Asian landscapes he had first seen on a visit to Moscow in 1876. Two years later he visited the artist's studio at Maisons Laffitte, near Paris, and was so struck by Vereshchagin's originality that he thought of writing a biography of him. Turgenev organized a large-scale exhibition of his work, the first one-man show for a Russian artist in Paris, placing adverts in the newspapers, writings articles to promote it, and getting over thirty critics to review the show, all of them extremely favourable, in the French and international press. The exhibition was a huge success, with 50,000 visitors and long queues at the *Cercle artistique de la rue Volney* to see the outsized canvases, whose impact came from their brilliant light and colour and from their unusual scenes of the Central Asian steppe. Vereshchagin went on to similar successes in Vienna, where an estimated 130,000 people, one sixth of the city's adult population, visited the show at the Künstlerhaus in just three weeks during the autumn of 1881; in Berlin the following spring, when the exhibition was seen by 134,000 paying visitors (and by many others free); and in Hamburg, Dresden, Budapest and Brussels during 1882.[47]

Turgenev's relations with the painter Ilia Repin were more problematic, because of the artist's close connections to Stasov. The nationalist critic had adopted him as the brightest star of the Wanderers (*peredvizhniki*) – painters who had broken from the Academy of Arts in the early 1860s and, like the Mighty Five in music, set out to create works in a 'Russian style'. Recognizing Repin's talent, Turgenev disapproved of the nationalist and politically committed art he was encouraged to develop by Stasov. He criticized his *Slavic Composers* (1872), commissioned for the concert hall of Moscow's Slav Bazar Hotel, because he thought it 'false and artificial' to represent both dead and living composers together in a single scene. He also took against Repin for writing to Stasov (in a letter published by the critic) that he 'renounced' Raphael.[48] For Turgenev, who worshipped at the altar of European Civilization, this was equivalent to saying that he renounced Christ.

Repin came to Paris as a prize scholar of the Academy in 1873 and remained there for the next three years. Exposed to Western art, he began to break free from the Russian national school and to paint in a manner influenced by the Impressionists, whose first exhibition, in 1874, took place while he was working on *A Parisian Café* (1875), one of his most impressionistic works. Repin was commissioned by the Moscow textile manufacturer and art patron Pavel Tretiakov to paint Turgenev's portrait in Paris (Plate 19). It was meant to be displayed in the gallery of famous Russians that Tretiakov was planning to add to his museum of national art. The painting did not go well – the Viardots did not like it – and Repin was forced to make changes, which he thought made the portrait worse. Not convinced by Repin's talent as a portraitist, Turgenev turned to Kharlamov instead and always made his preference for the latter's portrait of him clear.[49]

The prominent position given to Kharlamov at the Salon enraged Repin, whose *Parisian Café* was hung so high that it went completely unnoticed (when, after three weeks, he exercised his right to ask for the picture to be rehung in a lower position, the committee placed it higher still). 'Here you need protection and connections,' he wrote to the painter Ivan Kramskoi in Russia. Unlike Kharlamov, Repin found it difficult to sell his paintings in Europe. 'The Russians don't buy them, and nor do the French,' he complained to Stasov. Turgenev was not encouraging. He wrote to Stasov telling him that it would be better for Repin 'to return under your wing, even better to Moscow. This is where he comes from, his milieu.' Repin's failure to break into the Paris art market – the capital of the art world – became a source of bitter disappointment to the painter, who later blamed his failure on Turgenev's dislike of the Russian nationalist school: 'we were all idealists with a social tinge and Turgenev, after all, was an aesthete.'[50] It was a resentful recognition of the writer's crucial role as an intermediary between Russian artists and the Paris art establishment.

3

Turgenev was a keen art buyer in the 1870s. He was a frequent presence at the Hôtel Drouot, the vast Paris auction house, a *bourse* of art and bric-à-brac, where his tall and graceful figure, usually seated on the front benches, where he could see the paintings best with his lorgnette, was well known to the auctioneers. He also bought from private galleries, particularly from Durand-Ruel, and sometimes from the artists' studios themselves. Flaubert was amused by Turgenev's 'picture-buying mania', as he described it to George Sand in May 1874: 'Our friend

Exhibition Room at the Hôtel Drouot. Engraving after Daumier, 1862.

now spends all his time in the auction rooms. He is a man of passions: so much the better for him.'[51]

Turgenev was flush with cash at the time of this buying spree. In a letter to Claudie in August 1874, he joked that he had the Midas touch ('I am overwhelmed by gout and gold') and drew a cartoon of himself weighed down by bags of money. His books were selling well. He was receiving high advances for the serial rights to his new works. For his novel *Virgin Soil* he was paid 9,000 roubles (36,000 francs) by *The Messenger of Europe*, making him the best-paid novelist in Russia. He earned well from his collected works in eight volumes, whose third edition was published in Moscow in 1874–5.[52]

In his art purchases Turgenev was heavily dependent on the expertise of Louis Viardot. The art market was a risky place. There were many forgeries and mistaken attributions, even in the most reputable galleries.

375

Turgenev got his fingers burned on more than one occasion – as, for example, when he bought a painting passed off as the work of Jules Dupré from the dealer Oudrat, who had sold it on behalf of the banker Alphonse de Rothschild, but would not take it back when the forgery was exposed.[53] If Turgenev liked a painting he would ask Louis what he thought of it. Bogoliubov said that he deferred to Louis on all matters about art and had no opinions of his own – an idea repeated by Repin, who described Viardot as a 'great expert' on paintings, albeit one 'exclusively concerned with the virtuosity of the brushwork', which he would examine in microscopic detail, 'holding a pince-nez in front of his eyes'. This assessment of Turgenev's judgement is not entirely fair. Louis's taste was for the Old Masters, especially the Spanish school, on which he was a great authority, whereas Turgenev had a more eclectic collection, a mix of old and contemporary works, typical of many amateur collections at that time. Émile Bergerat, the essayist, described it as 'the ideal poet's collection', with some good works and some not so good, 'like all collections put together hastily (a collection of quality is the work of a lifetime) ... He collected pictures randomly, without financial motive, solely for the pleasure of having lovely and familiar things around himself.'[54]

The core of his collection was French landscape art, including many by the leading Barbizon painters. He had landscapes by Corot, Rousseau, Millet, Diaz, Dupré, Daubigny, Courbet, Boudin, Chintreuil. Yet perhaps suprisingly he did not have a single work by the Impressionists. It was not unusual for Barbizon collectors to move on to buying the Impressionists, if not sooner then later. The two schools were displayed side by side at Durand-Ruel's gallery. They were close artistically and similar in their approach to landscape art, a field where Corot, admired by Turgenev in particular, was the closest thing there was to a forerunner of the Impressionists (as late as 1896 the painter Henri Matisse considered Corot to be an Impressionist). Turgenev championed the painter's duty to capture what he himself called the 'impressions made by nature' rather than to copy it with photographic precision. That was what he aimed to do in his own prose descriptions of landscape. He once explained to a Russian friend, the poet Yakov Polonsky, that Corot's paintings worked as realism if they were viewed, not close up for their literal reproduction of reality, but rather from a distance of a few metres for the sensory 'impression' which they re-created of actually being amidst nature through effects of colour, light and shade.[55] This was what the Impressionists were essentially attempting to achieve.

The absence of their pictures is even more surprising given that, in 1874, Turgenev had bought a house with the Viardots at Bougival, a village on the Seine just outside Paris, where Renoir, Monet, Sisley and Morisot (a friend of the Viardots) were not only residents but painted summer river scenes. Bougival was one of the *banlieues*, or suburbs, of Paris where the countryside was being taken over by the summer houses of the city's middle class; it was a haven for artists looking to escape the bustle of Paris; and at weekends it was invaded by day-trippers coming in by train to enjoy the pleasures of the riverbank, with its picnic spots, boats for hire, restaurants and cafés. The Goncourt brothers described walking by the river on a Sunday afternoon in Bougival in June 1862. The grass areas were filled with people, painters, picnickers, couples 'reading aloud from *Le Figaro*', but at last they 'found a corner where there was no landscape painter sitting at his easel and no slice of melon left behind . . .'[56]

That whole stretch of the River Seine, from Bougival to Argenteuil, was a magnet for the *plein-air* painters of Paris. Many of the struggling Impressionists chose to live in these *banlieues* because the rent was cheaper than in Paris, which they could reach easily by train. In the early 1870s, Monet lived at Argenteuil, Pissarro at Pontoise, Sisley and Renoir in Louveciennes-Voisins near Bougival. The Goncourt brothers called this bit of river 'the landscape studio of the modern French school' (Kenneth Clark located 'the birthplace of Impressionism' at the riverside café of La Grenouillère near Bougival, where in 1869 both Monet and Renoir painted river scenes (see ill. 24) with bathers, boaters, women promenading in luminous white dresses, the whole scene softened by the warm glow of late-afternoon sunlight and the rippling reflections of the trees and sky in the waters of the Seine).[57]

Turgenev and the Viardots had rented a summer house in Bougival in 1873 and liked it there so much that they decided to buy their own place. The house they chose the following year – a typical example of the neo-classical pavilion ('*pavillon de plaisance*') built in the 1830s – was on a large plot of wooded land that had once been part of the estate of the Empress Josephine but now belonged to a doctor. They bought it for 180,000 francs, two thirds paid by Turgenev, and spent another 15,000 francs on improvements. Pauline did not like the house. She thought it was too 'bourgeois' and 'banal', the house of a 'grocer' without any 'sentiment of art or taste' – and she said it was too small. But Turgenev liked its rustic feel. He thought about the hunting he could do with Louis, and planned to build a chalet in the woods where he could write. 'Les Frênes' (ash trees), as he named the house, was partly Swiss in style but closer in character to a dacha, and everything inside it, from the simple wooden furniture to the stained-glass panels in the doors with scenes of Russian country life (Plate 32), was meant to remind him of his home. This was the place where Turgenev would do all his writing, the place where he felt happiest in his last years. 'Bougival,' he wrote, 'is for me what Mecca is for the Muslims.'[58]

The popularity of the Barbizon painters was reflected in the high prices their works commanded. Durand-Ruel, who owned most of their stocks, knew how to raise their value. 'The brave Durand knows no obstacles and affirms that your paintings must increase to the prices of Meissonier,' Sensier wrote to Millet in 1873. Millet's prices would exceed those of Meissonier. Sums over 20,000 francs were regularly paid for his paintings in the early 1870s (*The Shepherd* sold for 40,000 francs in 1872), making him one of the most expensive painters of that time, although some of the prices for Rousseau were even higher still (*Le Givre* (Plate 23) fetched 60,000 francs in 1873).[59]

Meanwhile the Impressionists were struggling to sell their work at all. There were many art collectors, like Turgenev, who shied away from buying them. They were too avant-garde, and not safe investments like the Barbizon painters. The Impressionists were ridiculed at their First Exhibition at Nadar's photographic studio on the boulevard des Capucines in the spring of 1874. 'Public opinion against these dangerous innovators was whipped up so intensely [by the press],' recalled Durand-Ruel, 'that visitors arrived with the firm intention of laughing and did not even bother to look.'[60] An auction of their works at the Hôtel Drouot the next year occasioned such riotous commotion, with people shouting insults at the works, that Charles Pillet, the auctioneer, had to call in the police to protect the paintings, most of which were sold for trifling sums, many for less than 100 francs. According to the *procès verbal* of the sale, seventy-three works came under the hammer, fetching a total of 11,496 francs, an average for each painting of 157 francs, with many bought back by Durand-Ruel at higher prices just to support their stock value. At their Second Exhibition, at Durand-Ruel's gallery in April 1876, the Impressionists were scorned again. 'There has just been opened at Mr Durand-Ruel's an exhibition of what is said to be painting,' wrote the critic of *Le Figaro*. 'Five or six lunatics, of whom one is a woman, have chosen to exhibit their works. There are people who burst into laughter in front of these objects. Personally I am saddened by them. These so-called artists style themselves Intransigents, Impressionists.' Durand-Ruel was berated by the art establishment for backing them. 'I was treated as a madman and a person of bad faith,' he wrote. 'Little by little the trust I had succeeded in inspiring disappeared and my best clients began to question me. "How can you," they would say, "after being one of the first to have loved the 1830 school [the Barbizon painters], now praise these pictures in which there is not a shred of quality?"'[61]

The Impressionists explained their failure in terms of the public's inability to recognize their worth. The scandal of their first two exhibitions became part of their mythology of unacknowledged genius (in the

Les peintres impressionnistes pouvant doubler l'effet de leur exposition sur le public, en y faisant exécuter de la musique de Wagner.

'The Impressionist painters can double the effect of their exhibition on the public by having Wagner's music played at it.' Cartoon by Cham (Amédée de Noé) in *Le Charivari*, 1877.

twentieth century this idea was central to their brand). As Monet put it to Durand-Ruel in 1881, 'There are scarcely fifteen amateur collectors in Paris capable of liking a painting without the imprimateur of the Salon. There are 80,000 buyers who won't buy a thing if it has not been in the Salon.' The problem faced by the Impressionists was less to do with their landscapes than with their portrayal of human figures which seemed an affront to established concepts of beauty (Courbet had also fallen foul of these artistic conventions). It took time for sensibilities to accept the new aesthetic principles of the Impressionists. Henry James, for example, failed completely to appreciate what the Impressionists were attempting to achieve when he visited their Second Exhibition. He thought they were trying to be realists, that they treated 'unadorned reality' in a loose way, and that none of them showed 'any signs of possessing first-rate talent'. The effect, he said, was 'to make me think better than ever of all the good old rules which decree that beauty is beauty and ugliness ugliness, and warn us off the sophistications of satiety'. But eight years later, in *The Art of Fiction*, James began to embrace their aesthetic enterprise, famously declaring that a 'novel is in its broadest definition a personal impression of life'. And later he would change his mind completely about the Impressionists. In his 1905 essay 'New England: An Autumn Impression', he praised the 'wondrous' Manet, Degas and Monet for offering the 'momentary effect of a large slippery sweet inserted, without a warning, between the compressed lips of half-conscious inanition'.[62]

Taste does not develop on its own. It is shaped by intermediaries – by influential patrons, critics, dealers and collectors – who take the lead in buying and promoting works that are new and difficult for the establishment and the general public to accept. Such intermediaries would play the decisive role in changing attitudes to the Impressionists. The first signs of this change were discernible in the critical reaction to their Third Exhibition in 1877, but the real transformation began only in the next decade, when Durand-Ruel found a market for them in America.

The role of the critic was vitally important in this transformation in artistic tastes. One of the earliest to champion the cause of the Impressionists was Théodore Duret, a friend and promoter of Manet from 1865, who started buying Pissarros and Monets in 1873. Duret did not write a great amount about their works until his booklet *Les Peintres impressionnistes*, in 1878, but he spent a lot of time persuading friends and contacts to buy them, including Étienne Baudry, the writer and dandy, and Charles Ephrussi, the art critic and collector from a family of bankers in Odessa who was one of the models for Proust's Swann in *À la recherche du temps perdu*. Duret advised Sisley and Pissarro on what subjects would attract buyers, on how much they could ask for their paintings, and sometimes acted as a sales agent (later he would act as a buyer and adviser to Louisine and Henry Havemeyer, the American sugar baron, whose large collection of Impressionist paintings was bequeathed to the Metropolitan Museum of Art on Louisine's death in 1929).[63]

In terms of his influence Zola was the most important critic to champion the Impressionists in the 1870s. It was Zola who would bring Turgenev round to them in the later 1870s, although by then the Russian writer was no longer buying art.[64] Zola had promoted Manet and his artistic followers as far back as 1863, when Manet's paintings, including *Le Déjeuner sur l'herbe*, had been rejected by the Salon but famously displayed in the so-called 'Salon des Refusés' allowed by Napoleon III. Zola identified with Manet and the other rejected painters (among them Courbet, Pissarro, Cézanne, Whistler and Fantin-Latour) as the pioneers of a truly modern form of art, breaking free from the conventions of 'boudoir painting' and the conservative establishment of the Academy. He saw them as allies of his own campaign for a modern literature. His support for Manet, in particular, was vigorous and loud. 'Manet will be one of the masters of tomorrow,' he wrote in *L'Évènement* in May 1866, 'and if I had a fortune, I would do good business by buying up all his paintings. In fifty years, they will be worth twenty times the price they reach today, while certain paintings valued now at 40,000 francs won't then fetch even 400.' The article, republished with a second study of Manet as a pamphlet in 1867, laid the basis for a long friendship, cemented when the two men at last met through the artistic circle at the Café Guerbois, where Zola was brought by Cézanne, his friend since boyhood. Pissarro, Monet, Renoir, Degas, Fantin-Latour and the Belgian Alfred Stevens were regulars at the café, which served as a sort of headquarters where these artists courted journalists.[65] Manet's gratitude for Zola's articles was expressed in his celebrated portrait of the writer at his desk (ill. 25). Pinned on the wall behind him is a print of Manet's *Olympia* (1863), and on the desk, clearly visible, is Zola's pamphlet on Manet.

Zola was consistent in his championing of the Impressionists throughout the 1870s. He defended them as realists in portrait art – where they had been ridiculed – using the same argument Turgenev had advanced for Corot's landscapes. 'At twenty steps,' he wrote in a review of the Third Exhibition of the Impressionists, 'one cannot make out clearly the nose or the eyes of a person's face. To replicate a face as one sees it, you do not need to paint the wrinkles on the skin but its living expression.' Praising all the painters in the exhibition, Zola was especially enthusiastic about Monet and his seven canvases of the Gare Saint-Lazare (Plate 28): 'You can hear the rumbling of the trains, their smoke billowing under the vast glass interior. Our artists must find the poetry in these stations, as their fathers found it in the forests and rivers.'[66]

The place where Zola met the Impressionists most often was at the salon of his publisher, Georges Charpentier, a keen early patron of the Impressionists. On Friday evenings at the Charpentiers they rubbed shoulders with writers, actors, journalists and politicians, including on occasion Léon Gambetta, Jules Ferry and Jules Grévy, three of the Republic's most senior political leaders. Charpentier had taken over the family business, famous for its standard pocket library, the Bibliothèque Charpentier, when his father, Gervais, died in 1871, and at once had taken it in a modern direction by signing Zola and Flaubert. He was the publisher Zola had been looking for – one who could pay 500 francs a month to give him the security he needed, as he had put it in 1868, to 'do something big' (i.e. write his Rougon-Macquart series of twenty novels, which would begin three years later with *La Fortune des Rougons*). Such was Zola's gratitude that some people thought he championed the Impressionists to ingratiate himself with Charpentier.[67]

The publisher had bought his first Impressionist painting at the Hôtel Drouot in 1875, paying 180 francs for Renoir's *Le Pêcheur à la ligne* (The Fisherman). Renoir soon became a regular visitor to the Charpentiers' house in the rue de Grenelle, where he painted the celebrated portrait *Madame Georges Charpentier et ses enfants* (Plate 27), a picture Proust, who went as a young man to their Friday salon, would invoke as a reminder of 'the poetry of an elegant home and beautifully dressed women' in *À la recherche*.[68] Through Renoir the Charpentiers began to buy from other Impressionist painters, who often wrote to them for loans against future sales. In 1879, Charpentier established the weekly journal *La Vie moderne* to promote their ideas and help them along financially by paying them for articles. At the instigation of his wife, whose artistic views were often sought by the Impressionists, he opened a gallery for them in the Passage des Princes, one of the arcades built by Haussmann, near the boulevard des Italiens. At the first exhibition, for Manet, in 1880, a free catalogue was given out to passers-by in the street, but no paintings sold.[69]

Charpentier's salon was critical in getting other patrons to invest in the Impressionists. Many of their earliest collectors were regulars at his salon (Duret and the opera singer Jean-Baptiste Faure, for instance) or part of the broader Parisian élite that mixed with that crowd. Still, the number of people buying the Impressionists in the 1870s was no more than fifty in Paris. Some were friends of the artists, such as the composer Emmanuel Chabrier, a friend of Manet and Degas, who depicted him, the only member of the audience to be seen, in his painting *The Orchestra at the Opéra* (1870; Plate 26). Others were artists themselves, notably the Impressionist painter Gustave Caillebotte, who had inherited a private income of 100,000 francs a year from his father's business in military supplies. He not only bought a lot of the Impressionists' paintings but lent money to them too. Most of the early buyers, however, were self-made men – manufacturers, financiers, professionals, who identified with modern art (it showed the world in which they lived, right-bank Paris in particular). They had diverse motives for their purchases: to furnish their mansions with paintings which they liked; to buy art for speculative purposes; and to make a statement about their status as major patrons of the arts. Their support contributed to the social construction of a more bourgeois image for the Impressionists.

Among these early Impressionist collectors was Ernest Hoschedé, the owner of a large department store. He was the original buyer of Monet's *Impression, Sunrise*, the work that gave its name to the movement, paying what was then a high price for its paintings, 800 francs, in a transaction handled by Durand-Ruel. Henri Rouart, another early buyer, was an engineer and manufacturer of the metal tubes for paint used by the Impressionists. Rouart was an old friend of Degas, who painted him in front of his factory in a portrait dated circa 1875. Rouart was a regular buyer at the Hôtel Drouot sales, beginning with the

Barbizon painters but gradually amassing a large collection of Impressionists. Another buyer at the Drouot auctions was Victor Choquet, a civil servant at the Ministry of Finance, where he had an annual salary of 4,000 francs, although he also had an income from his father's textile factory. Choquet was a friend of Monet, Renoir and Cézanne, whose work he defended with passion (at the Third Exhibition, to which he lent many paintings, he stood in the gallery and 'accosted those who laughed, making them ashamed of their unkind comments, lashing them with ironic remarks', according to Georges Rivières, the art critic). A fourth collector, Paul Gachet, was the son of a mill owner, who practised as a doctor in Auvers-sur-Oise, something of an artists' colony, where he often hosted the Impressionists and sometimes treated them medically (on Pissarro's recommendation Vincent Van Gogh came to him for medical advice in the last weeks of his life). Gachet purchased many of their paintings (he also had thirty by the Post-Impressionist Cézanne) and frequently appeared in their portraits. A fifth and more unusual collector was Eugène Murer, a pastry cook with a shop in Paris, where he met the Impressionists through Gachet and the painter Armand Guillaumin, a childhood friend. Murer bought a hundred paintings, often taking art in lieu of money owed to him by the Impressionists, and was well known to haggle over prices, never wanting to pay more than 200 francs for any work.[70]

More than anybody else, it was Durand-Ruel who enabled the Impressionists to break into the market. Without him, in all probability, they would not have become widely known and the history of modern art would have been entirely different. In the early 1870s, Durand-Ruel was the only Paris dealer to back the Impressionists. He saw their work as a development of the Barbizon painters, and believed that he could repeat the success he had achieved with them by using the same strategies. The basic idea of his business plan (which would become common practice in the modern dealer system) was to buy a large amount of an artist's work and raise its value by promoting it. He was the first of a new breed of art dealers who changed public taste by stimulating interest in an unknown brand of art, as opposed to the more established practice of dealing in those works of art which were already known and in demand.

Durand-Ruel bought up works by the Impressionists wholesale, borrowing from bankers, and, if necessary to corner the market, entering into partnership with other dealers, such as Hector Brame, with whom he had acquired a virtual monopoly in the works of Corot and Rousseau after 1865. As a long-term investor in their work, Durand-Ruel was as much a patron as a dealer to the Impressionists. He gave them loans and encouragement when they most needed them. There were times when he came close to bankruptcy because their paintings did not sell. To raise their value on the market Durand-Ruel employed a number of innovative strategies borrowed from investors on the stock exchange. He pushed up the bidding for his own artists to increase their perceived worth (just as Saccard, the speculator in Zola's novel *Money,* buys shares in his own bank to raise their value). As he had done with the Barbizon painters, he founded an art review to promote the Impressionists. He specialized in one-man shows, a practice that became more common from the 1880s as other dealers learned from his success, and, instead of hanging paintings in the crowded manner usual at that time, gave each picture lots of space to emphasize its importance. He campaigned hard to get their works into public galleries and museums, recognizing these as 'our best publicity'. He loaned their works to international exhibitions, and built links with agencies and dealers to develop foreign sales. The art market was internationalized at an ever growing rate from the 1870s, as cheaper photographic reproductions, the telegraph and a faster postal system enabled information about new paintings to cross national frontiers more easily. Durand-Ruel was one of the first dealers to exploit fully these developments with agencies in Europe and America. It was in the United States and Russia that through him the Impressionists would find their biggest markets in the last two decades of the century.[71]

Financial problems forced Turgenev to sell his art collection in 1878. His money problems had begun two years earlier. The Balkan Crisis, leading to the outbreak of the Russo-Turkish War in 1877, depressed the value of the rouble, which became harder to exchange for francs. 'My finances have been paralysed completely,' Turgenev complained to Flaubert. Meanwhile, his estates were also yielding less. They were even more mismanaged by his steward, Kishinsky, than they had been by his uncle before him – a fact Turgenev took nine years to recognize before eventually sacking him in August 1876, by which point he had been robbed of 130,000 francs, 'a large part of my fortune', as he explained to Flaubert. 'From a man of substantial means ("rich" I never was) I have been turned into a person barely able to make ends meet.' Louis advised Turgenev to let his brother manage his estates, or to sell them off and live like any bourgeois from the capital: 'No more stewards, no more farms, no more delays, no worries, and no accounts.' But Turgenev could not bring himself to let go of his ancestral home, and leased out his lands instead, from which he received a modest annual income of 5,000 roubles (approximately 20,000 francs once the exchange rate improved). This, together with his literary earnings, would have been enough for his own needs, had it not been for the problem of his daughter Paulinette. Her husband had proved to be a disastrous businessman and was losing money heavily at his glass factory. He had already squandered the capital Turgenev had sent with instructions that it should be set aside for his grandchildren, George and Jeanne, as French law allowed him to do. Turgenev tried to borrow money from his brother – Nikolai refused – and then took a loan of 15,000 francs from Baron Günzburg against his Russian railway shares. But even that was not enough to save his daughter from ruin. So, reluctantly, he put his pictures up for sale.[72]

The auction took place at the Hôtel Drouot on 20 April. Turgenev was stuck in bed with gout, so he asked Antokolsky to go for him and try to push up the bidding. The sale catalogue details forty-six paintings, mostly landscapes by the Barbizon artists with a dozen older Dutch works. It was a bad time for the sale. The recent deaths of several Barbizon painters had flooded the art market with their works, as their studios were cleared, and prices fell accordingly. Hoschedé and Faure had both sold their collections at the Hôtel Drouot earlier in the year, and both had suffered big losses – Faure withdrawing most of them when reserve prices were not reached, while Hoschedé, who had been forced to sell by bankruptcy, sold his collection for a song (117 paintings, including five Manets, nine Pissarros, thirteen Sisleys and sixteen Monets, had gone for just 70,000 francs). Monet's *Impression, Sunrise*, went to Georges de Bellio, a Romanian living in Paris, for 210 francs, a quarter the amount Hoschedé had paid for it four years before, while a Sisley landscape, *Aqueduct at Marly*, was snapped up by the pastry cook Murer for just twenty-one francs.[73]

Turgenev had an equal disaster. The paintings in the sale had cost him 50,000 francs. They went for only 37,000 francs. Eleven of the paintings were bought by the Paris dealer Jules Féral, most of the rest by dealers from abroad. Turgenev compared his losses to the French defeat at the battle of Sedan.[74]

4

On his return to Paris from London, Turgenev had resumed his friendships with the writers of the Magny circle, Flaubert, Zola, Renan and Goncourt, who no longer met at Magny's, but at Le Brébant and other restaurants. They were joined by younger writers, Alphonse Daudet and, from 1873, Guy de Maupassant, barely out of college, a protégé of Flaubert, who had known his mother since childhood. George Sand, who came on notable occasions, called them 'Flaubert's school'.[75]

Once a month the friends would meet at the Café Riche for what they called the 'Dinner of the Hissed Authors' (*'dîner des auteurs sifflés'*), or 'dinner of the five', places at the table limited to those who had experienced a literary catastrophe: Flaubert, Zola, Goncourt, Turgenev and Daudet. Once a week, on Sunday afternoons, the broader group would meet in the apartment of Flaubert, three small rooms on the top floor of a house on rue Murillo with a superb view over Parc Monceau, and from 1875, when straitened means forced him to move to cheaper accommodation, a set of spartan attic rooms overlooking roofs and chimneys at the unfashionable end of the Faubourg Saint-Honoré. Dressed 'like a Turk' in a tunic, red-and-white-striped trousers and *calotte*, Flaubert would warmly greet each guest, recalls Zola, and take them to his drawing-room, where he smoked constantly from small clay pipes he had made himself and arranged in a rack; 'when he really liked you, he would even give you one.' The conversation would last for many hours and range over every subject – sex, love, death, adventures in brothels – returning always to the latest books and general themes of literature; it was often coarse in language, and 'neither men nor things were spared'.[76]

Henry James, who had come to Paris as a columnist for the *New York Tribune*, sometimes joined the Flaubert circle, but he thought that none of them was comparable to Turgenev, his idol as a writer and as an embodiment of the European cosmopolitanism with which James identified.* James accused the French writers of being narrow-minded and ignorant of anything that was not French. Turgenev was certainly regarded as the most international of the group. He often introduced his friends to foreign literature, and impressed them with his ad hoc translations of Goethe into French.[77]

Flaubert was at a low ebb. He had frequent bouts of depression in the 1870s. Several of his closest friends had died in recent years, including Louis Bouilhet, his childhood friend, and Gautier. 'For the last three years,' he wrote to Turgenev on Gautier's death in October 1872, 'all my friends have been dying one after the other, without a break! There's only one man left in the world now with whom I can talk, and that's you. So you must look after yourself, so that I shan't miss you, along with the others.' Flaubert's literary stock was in decline. Following the failure of *Sentimental Education*, he had lost confidence. Always looking for literary perfection, he took five years to finish his next book, *The Temptation of St Anthony*, an idea he had worked on since the 1840s, whose third and final version was eventually published in 1874. It too received terrible reviews. Flaubert became reclusive, spending whole months at his country house in Croisset with just a servant, Émile, and his greyhound, Julio, for company, coming into Paris only on occasion to see his close circle of literary friends.[78] He was repulsed by contemporary society, by the modern world of railways and commerce, by the bourgeoisie and its 'philistine' values, by the 'stupidity' of the public and the 'Barbarism rising from beneath the ground' – all things he would rant about. As he wrote to Turgenev: 'I have always tried to live in an ivory tower; but a sea of shit is beating up against its walls, it's enough to bring it down.'[79]

From the mid-1870s Flaubert was beset by growing financial problems, as his literary earnings went into decline and he spent what remained of his inheritance to support his beloved niece, Caroline Commanville, his only close surviving relative, whose husband's saw-mill business

---

* Something close to his outlook was expressed in the scene from *The Europeans* (1878), his most Turgenevian novel, in which Gertrude interrogates her distant cousin Felix on meeting him for the first time after his arrival in Boston from Europe:

'You are a foreigner of some sort,' said Gertrude.

'Of some sort – yes; I suppose so. But who can say of what sort? I don't think we have ever had the occasion to settle the question. You know there are people like that. About their country, their religion, their profession, they can't tell.'

had failed. There was a danger they would have to sell the Croisset house, which his mother had bequeathed to Caroline. 'Poor Flaubert,' Turgenev wrote to Zola. 'Fate is abominably brutal to strike at the one man in the world least capable of making a living from his work.'[80]

Flaubert's friends tried to arrange a sinecure for him at the Bibliothèque Mazarine in the Institut de France, where the librarian was retiring, having fallen ill. Several writers held such positions.* At first Flaubert was too proud to accept help, but Turgenev persuaded him to take the post if he was offered it. Encouraged by Madame Charpentier, who had spoken to Gambetta on the matter and received a vague promise that he 'wanted to do something' for Flaubert, Turgenev made a number of attempts to lobby the great republican leader, who, as President of the Chamber of Deputies, had the power to make the appointment.[81] After finding all doors closed, by chance Turgenev came across Gambetta at the house of Juliette Adam, the writer, founding editor of *La Nouvelle Revue* and hostess of one of the leading republican salons in Paris. 'I explain the matter to her,' Turgenev recounted in a letter to Flaubert.

'But Gambetta is here – he's having an after-dinner smoke – we shall know all directly.' She comes back two minutes later: 'Impossible my dear sir! Gambetta has already got people in mind.'† The dictator arrives with measured step: I've never seen trained dogs dance around their master like the ministers and senators etc. surrounding him. He starts to talk to one of them. Mme. Adam takes me by the hand and leads me to him: but the great man declines the honour of making my acquaintance, and repeats – loud enough for me to hear: 'I don't want it – it's been said – it's impossible.'

---

* Jules Troubat was the librarian at Compiègne Palace, Louis Ulbach at the Arsenal, while Leconte de Lisle and Anatole France were employed at the Senate Library.
† Flaubert's old friend Frédéric Baudry, the deputy director of the Mazarine and a distinguished scholar with political connections, had been nominated for the job, which he had been coveting for twenty years. Flaubert felt humiliated by the incident, whose outcome was reported in *Le Figaro*. According to Maupassant, who visited Baudry to find out what had happened for Flaubert, Turgenev was to blame for lobbying Gambetta before trying to find out what the situation was (Kerandoux (ed.), *Gustave Flaubert, Guy de Maupassant*, p. 167). Flaubert later accepted a supernumerary post at the Mazarine created for him by Baudry. He did not go there once.

'Come, my good fellow,' Turgenev consoled Flaubert, 'we must throw all that overboard – and get back to work, literary work, the only thing worthy of a man such as you.'[82]

If Turgenev was unable to do much for Flaubert in France, he did a lot to help him become better known abroad. He acted in effect as his international agent, securing publishing contracts, supervising translations, sending his works to literary contacts, and finding friendly critics to write about his publications in Russia, Germany and other countries on the Continent.* When Flaubert finally completed his *Temptation of St Anthony*, towards the end of 1873, Turgenev campaigned tirelessly to ensure that copies of the proofs were put into the hands of publishers and critics in Vienna, Munich, Berlin, London, Strasbourg and St Petersburg. Translations of it immediately appeared in German in Strasbourg and in Russian in St Petersburg, albeit in the latter with major cuts by the censors, who saw it as an attack on religion (Flaubert complained to Sand that the cuts had cost him 2,000 francs because his contract with *The Messenger of Europe* had, as normal, stipulated payment according to the number of printed pages). The Russian translation was a 'terrible fiasco', Turgenev reported to Pauline on 25 May 1874. 'The Russian public has not been tempted by his *Anthony*,' he added in a letter to Zola, 'and this fact must be kept from him.' The German publication, by contrast, was favourably reviewed in several major periodicals, all the reviews by friends of Turgenev, including Julian Schmidt, 'the Sainte-Beuve of Germany', as Flaubert informed Charpentier, no doubt repeating what Turgenev had told him. 'The good Turgenev . . . has sent from Berlin a favourable article about *St Anthony*,' Flaubert wrote to Sand. 'It is not the article that pleases me, but him. I have seen a lot of him . . . and like him more and more.'[83]

Apart from promoting Flaubert's works abroad, Turgenev translated them. He was a prolific translator, both of French works into Russian and, with the help of Louis Viardot and Mérimée, of Russian into French, although it is hard to say how many works he translated, because only

---

* The British took longer to appreciate Flaubert. The first translation of *Madame Bovary*, by Eleanor Marx-Aveling, the daughter of Karl Marx, appeared only in 1887, thirty years after its original publication in France. The novel was too scandalous for the prudish Victorians. A tame adaption of it, *The Doctor's Wife* by Mary Braddon, was published in 1864.

one appeared in his collected works, and because the names of translators seldom appeared on the title page of books. Following the failure of *St Anthony* in Russia, Turgenev took it on himself to translate Flaubert's next work into Russian, the *Three Tales* (1877), made up of the the short stories 'The Legend of St Julian', 'A Simple Heart' and 'Herodias'. Turgenev's idea was to get the stories published in *The Messenger of Europe* before they came out in France, allowing Flaubert to earn twice as much from them (Stasiulevich, the editor of the *Messenger*, would only pay for works in translation if they had not yet appeared in their original language, because, once they were in print, other publishers could freely translate and publish them in Russia, where there was no copyright protection of foreign works). Turgenev negotiated a good deal for Flaubert with Stasiulevich, who agreed to pay 750 silver roubles (around 3,000 francs) for the three stories, on the condition that Turgenev promised to give his next novel to the *Messenger*. Flaubert approved Turgenev's plan, and in 1876 the Russian spent three days with him at Croisset to discuss the work (twice Flaubert wrote to his niece from Paris ahead of the visit asking her to check the length of the beds because of the Russian's 'gigantic size').[84]

Desperate for money, Flaubert was impatient for the translation to be done quickly. But Turgenev (who gave his payment to Flaubert) proved too slow for his liking. He took great care over the translation, successfully conveying the subtlety of Flaubert's style in Russian, and counted it as one of his own finest literary achievements (this was the translation he included in the 1880 edition of his collected works). It then transpired that Stasiulevich would not print Turgenev's translations until after the appearance of his novel *Virgin Soil*, which began to be serialized in *The Messenger of Europe* in January 1877. Two of the stories were eventually published in the April and May issues of the *Messenger* that year. 'A Simple Heart' was rejected by Stasiulevich, who found the story of an old servant devoted to her stuffed parrot 'less successful' than the other two; like Turgenev, he foresaw problems with the scene where she confuses the parrot with 'the dove of the holy ghost'. Religious sensibilities were likely to be offended. 'You can well imagine the cries of the censors!!' Turgenev agreed.[85]

Zola was another writer promoted by Turgenev in Russia. Many of his books were published in translation in *The Messenger of Europe* before they appeared in French – this unusual arrangement insulated him from the Paris critics at the time of his writing and made him all the more audacious in his 'experimental novels' of the 1870s.[86] There was much in Zola's personality that Turgenev did not much care for. He thought he was too self-regarding, too much in a hurry for success; but he recognized his talent none the less, and gladly helped him become famous in Russia at a time when he was only starting out in France.[87]

Aged just twenty-eight when he was introduced to the Flaubert circle in 1868, Zola was not only ambitious but practically shameless in his self-promotion through journalism and publicity. He had started out as an advertising agent for Hachette in 1862, and had mastered the technique of selling books through notices and articles in newspapers and provincial journals, using his contacts in the book-world and the press to launch himself as a writer. When Lacroix bought his first book, *Tales for Ninon*, in 1864, the publisher made it a condition that Zola handled the publicity; the print-run of 500 copies (not bad for a first-time writer) was as much a vote of confidence in his ability to sell the book through his tried-and-tested methods of publicity as it was in his literary talent. From 1866, when he left Hachette, Zola wrote a books page (mainly gossip) for *L'Évènement*, the literary supplement to *Le Figaro*, where his articles on the controversial paintings of Manet brought him notoriety, which he courted to promote himself. When he joined the Magny group, he had just achieved a big success with his darkly brilliant murder thriller *Thérèse Raquin* (1867). In Charpentier he found the publisher he had been looking for – one who would pay him 30,000 francs for ten novels in five years, 500 francs in monthly payments, in exchange for his copyright, including sales to foreign publishers. The deal was quite good, but not enough to cover Zola's living costs, so he had to supplement his income by journalism, which meant that he fell behind on delivering two novels every year. His situation worsened after 1872, when one of his articles, a left-wing polemic on the unemployment crisis, led to the suppression of the Parisian daily *Le Corsaire*, causing all the Paris newspapers to shun Zola. By the time Turgenev rescued him by getting him a contract with Stasiulevich, Zola was so destitute that he was obliged to sell his only mattress in a flea market.[88]

The contract was for Zola to write a monthly 'Letter from Paris' for *The Messenger of Europe* at a rate of fifteen francs per printed page. It would earn him between 400 and 500 francs a month. He could write on any theme he chose, although many of his articles were on topics suggested by Turgenev, who had a 'good nose' for which themes would most appeal to a Russian readership. From the first letter, about the election of Alexandre Dumas to the French Academy in April 1875, to the last, on the Paris art scene in 1880, Zola wrote a total of sixty-four letters on a range of topics, from light and humorous sketches of the French clergy and different types of marriage around France to a long and controversial article about George Sand's romantic idealism, following her death from a painful intestinal blockage in June 1876. Flaubert and Turgenev were shattered by Sand's death. The latter was in Russia but Flaubert rushed to Nohant for the funeral, a religious service in the village church organized, against Sand's wishes, by her daughter, Solange Clésinger, and attended by the great and good. The Viardots refused to go, not because they had fallen out with their old friend in any way, but because Louis was an atheist: as a man of strong, unbending convictions, he thought it was hypocritical for her to receive a Christian burial, considering the life that she had lived, and would not have anything to do with it.

Zola's vivid letters from Paris proved immensely popular in Russia. The democratic intelligentsia recognized in them an echo of their own radical tradition of literary and social criticism going back to Belinsky. Their success attracted the attention of other editors, who tried to recruit Zola. In 1876, on the advice of Turgenev, he rejected an advance from Saltykov-Shchedrin, the editor of *Notes from the Fatherland*, to write four articles a year for 100 roubles (around 380 francs) per printed page; but he used the generous offer to increase his fee from the *Messenger*, albeit only to one fifth of the sum he had turned down. Having proved his loyalty, Zola, in return, always asked Stasiulevich to send back the manuscripts of his letters so that he could resell them, and forty-seven of the sixty-four would reappear in French journals.[89]

The popularity of Zola's letters in turn made his novels commercially attractive to Stasiulevich, who offered him a contract very similar to the one he gave Flaubert, which meant paying for an early copy of the manuscript in instalments so that he could get them translated and serialize them in *The Messenger of Europe* before they appeared in France. Everything depended on the timely despatch of the instalments, because, if they were delayed and the book was printed first in France, it would be published in a quick (and error-ridden) translation by other Russian periodicals, who legally were not obliged to pay a kopeck for the copyright. It was a risk Stasiulevich was prepared to take, because of Zola's popularity, and he invested happily. Zola was a bestseller in Russia long before he became one in France. The third novel of the Rougon-Macquart series, *Le Ventre de Paris* (The Belly of Paris), was published in translation by six different journals in St Petersburg alone, and then appeared in two book editions within months of its French publication in 1873 (before his agreement with Stasiulevich). Its sales were higher in Russian than they were in French in the 1870s. Overall, between 1871 and 1881, the literary journals of St Petersburg published fifty-one separate translations of Zola's novels, making him the most translated foreign writer in Russia. For the fifth novel in the Rougon-Macquart series, *The Sin of Abbé Mouret*, Stasiulevich agreed to pay thirty roubles (120 francs) per printed page for advance copies of the three instalments. The novel was 80,000 words, or sixteen print-er's pages (Zola had the skill of a journalist in writing precisely to length), earning the writer 480 roubles, or 1,920 francs. The instalments appeared in the first three issues of *The Messenger of Europe* in 1875, months before the book appeared in any form in France. The same deal was agreed for the sixth novel, *Son Excellence Eugène Rougon* (1876), which ran as a serial in the *Messenger* before its publication in France.[90]

L'Assommoir (1877), the seventh in the Rougon-Macquart series, was turned down by Stasiulevich because the novel had been sold already to the weekly journal *Le Bien public** – Zola having been unable to resist an advance payment of 10,000 francs – which meant that it would be published before *The Messenger of Europe* would have time to translate it. By the time of the novel's appearance in the *Messenger's* pages, other Russian journals would be running it. On Turgenev's advice, Zola offered extracts of the novel to Stasiulevich, and these were printed in *The Messenger of Europe* before the book appeared in France. *L'Assommoir* was such a huge success in France – its sales sent soaring by the scandal it had caused through its depiction of alcoholism, sex and violence among the Parisian working class – that Zola

---

* *Le Bien public* later dropped the serial following complaints from its subscribers, who took offence at Zola's shocking portrait of the working class.

quickly became rich. He no longer needed to write journalism, nor to be published in Russia, where his relations with Stasiulevich were becoming strained by what the latter wrongly saw as the declining quality of Zola's work. The editor disliked his frequent use of slang and the sexually explicit scenes of *Nana* (1880), the ninth novel in the Rougon-Macquart series, which made it too much of a risk to publish in Russia, given tsarist censorship, although he published extracts of the runaway bestseller, which in France sold in fifty editions, or 55,000 copies, within a year.[91]

By this stage, Turgenev too was falling out of sympathy with Zola's brand of Naturalism, whose graphic details about working-class conditions bordered on 'indecency'. 'I've dipped into *L'Assommoir*,' the Russian wrote to Flaubert; 'I am not very taken with it (this strictly between the two of us). There is much talent in it, but it is heavy-going, and there is too much stirring of the chamber pots.' In a letter to Stasiulevich, Turgenev reported that 'the words "fuck", "piss", "shit" and "buttocks" (*foutre, pisser, merde, fesses*) have been counted in the novel by someone – they appear 720 times.'[92]

As for Flaubert, he thought the novel was 'superb' in parts and contained many 'incontestable truths', but that Zola had gone too far in it to court controversy for self-promotion and publicity – methods alien to Flaubert, who believed in writing as an art rather than a business. He could not stand Zola's weekly columns in *Le Bien public* in which he proselytized the ideas of his Naturalist school. As an independent writer, Flaubert had no truck with any movement in the arts, and accused Zola of using his as a form of marketing. One night at Brébant's, after Flaubert had attacked his journalistic promotion of the Naturalist school, Zola replied, according to Goncourt, with his own attack on Flaubert's social class:

> This evening Flaubert, while paying tribute to his colleague's genius, attacked the prefaces, the doctrines, the naturalist professions of faith, in a word all the rather flamboyant humbug with which Zola helps along the sales of his books. Zola replied roughly to this effect: 'You, you had private means which allowed you to remain independent of a good many things. But I had to earn my living with nothing but my pen; I had to go through the mill of journalism and write all sorts of shameful stuff; and it has left me with – how shall I put it? – a certain

taste for charlatanism . . . I consider the word *Naturalism* as ridiculous as you do, but I shall go on repeating it over and over again, because you have to give things new names for the public to think that they are new . . . You know, I divide what I write into two parts. On the one hand there are my novels, on which I shall be judged and on which I wish to be judged; and on the other there are my articles for the *Bien public*, for Russia and Marseilles, which are just so much charlatanism to puff my books.[93]

Turgenev was responsible for getting other writers published in Russia. He set up Daudet as the Paris correspondent of the Russian daily *New Times* (*Novoe Vremia*), from 1878 to 1879. The conservative newspaper published twenty-seven of Daudet's articles, several of his stories and extracts from his autobiographical novel *Le Petit Chose* (1868). Turgenev had discovered the story about Daudet's childhood at a railway bookstore in the Russian provinces shortly after it came out in French (a perfect illustration of the way the railways were internationalizing the book trade) and had been praising it to friends in Russia ever since. It was Turgenev who also established Jules Vallès as the London correspondent for the Russian journal *Word* (*Slovo*), from its establishment in 1878, although the name of the exiled Communard could not be printed because it would 'frighten the censors', as Turgenev explained to Zola (the populist journal was closed down by the tsarist government in 1881). Otherwise the Russians were delighted by Vallès's articles, which were 'hostile to the English, to their arrogance and rudeness', as the Frenchman described them.[94] The articles appeared at a time of mutual hostility between Russia and Britain because of the Russo-Turkish War. Turgenev followed the war closely. He was enraged by Britain's backing of the Turks, despite the Turkish massacre of the Ottoman Bulgarians, and in his satiric poem 'A Game of Croquet at Windsor' had blamed Queen Victoria for the bloodshed.

As an agent for *The Messenger of Europe*, Turgenev also introduced the writings of Maupassant, Goncourt, Taine, Auerbach and Storm to its pages. He negotiated the contracts for each writer and usually oversaw the translation of their work. He acted as a sort of manager for the union of translators in Russia, mostly students on miserable pay, whose work he saw as essential to the ideal of bringing European civilization to the Russians. When no one could be found to translate well enough the works he considered most important (a collection of Heine's poems, Markovich's short stories, the poetry of Walt Whitman) he translated them himself.[95]

As the best-known Russian writer in the West, Turgenev also served as an ambassador for his country's literature. He negotiated book contracts for many Russian writers, not just in France but in Germany and Britain too. Ostrovsky, Goncharov, Aleksei Tolstoy and Saltykov-Shchedrin – all owed their entry into Europe's literary market to Turgenev's agency.[96] The most important service he performed, however, was to bring to the attention of a European readership Tolstoy's novel *War and Peace*.

Turgenev had fallen out with Tolstoy in 1861. A clash of personalities was at the heart of it. Ten years older than Tolstoy, Turgenev felt paternal towards him but, because he admired him so much, and perhaps from envy, looked for faults in his writing, which the younger Russian found wounding (he later wrote that he thought Turgenev was 'laughing' at his work, which had made him 'afraid and ashamed'). The two men quarrelled constantly, patched things up, and then broke completely as a consequence of a violent argument about Turgenev's daughter, Paulinette, in which Tolstoy mocked Turgenev's patronizing attitude towards his serfs and – despite the fact that he himself had fathered several children with serf girls on his estate – insulted him by drawing attention to her illegitimacy.[97]

For the next seventeen years they did not talk to each other. But Turgenev recognized the magnitude of Tolstoy's achievement in *War and Peace*, which he read for the first time in 1868, a year after it came out (he read the book six times in the next ten years). He wrote about the masterpiece to all his European friends, declaring it to be the greatest novel of the nineteenth century, and urging them to get it published in their own countries. Because of its immense length, Turgenev first arranged the translation of a much shorter work, *The Two Hussars*, and got it published in *Le Temps* in 1875 with an introduction by himself to inspire interest in *War and Peace*. The novella created little interest among the French, and no requests to translate *War and Peace* were forthcoming, neither into French nor into any other language (British readers had been equally unimpressed by a translation of *Childhood and Youth*, prompting Turgenev to complain that they were unable to appreciate such fine psychological writing and merely thought of Tolstoy as 'an imitation of Dickens'). Turgenev wanted to translate *War and Peace* himself, cutting all the philosophical digressions which he thought would alienate a European readership, but since his relations with Tolstoy were so frosty he gave up on the idea.[98]

All that changed in April 1878 when Turgenev, in Paris, received a letter from Tolstoy. Remembering their old friendship, Tolstoy no longer felt any hostility, and hoped Turgenev felt the same. He recalled all the good in him, claimed that he owed his 'literary celebrity' to him, and proposed, 'if you could pardon me', to 'offer all the friendship I can give'. Turgenev replied expressing his delight that the 'misunderstandings between us are a thing of the past', and declaring his goodwill towards Tolstoy, 'both as a person to whom I was sincerely devoted, and as a writer whose first steps I welcomed earlier than others, and in whose new works I have always taken the liveliest interest'.[99] Two months later, on his return to Russia, he went at once to see Tolstoy.

The next year a French translation of *War and Peace* was printed in St Petersburg. Bearing the editorial brand of Hachette in Paris, the title page did not give the name of the translator, Princess Irène Paskévitch, but stated only 'Traduit par une russe'. Turgenev asked Annenkov to send him ten copies – more requests would soon follow and 500 copies would eventually be sent – which he gave to his most influential literary friends, publishers and critics in Paris, advising them that the translation did not do justice to the original, from which there were many cuts. He was uncertain if it would appeal to French readers. 'The import of it all is a long way from what the French like and look for in books,' he wrote to Tolstoy, 'but truth, in the end, is its own master. I am counting, if not on a brilliant triumph, then on a solid, if gradual, victory.'[100]

Turgenev's influence gave the book a vital push on the way to that victory. At every opportunity he spoke about the book to people he encountered at soirées, at dinners, in salons, and many heard of it for the first time through him. 'None of us had known of Tolstoy until then,' recalled the journalist V. P. Semenov, 'but Turgenev talked of nothing else.' Renan, Taine, Anatole France were all turned into Tolstoy fans by Turgenev's urging that they read his masterpiece. It was Flaubert's opinion that mattered most to Turgenev. 'Thank you for making me read Tolstoy's novel,' Flaubert wrote at last in January 1880.

It's first rate. What a painter and what a psychologist! The first two [volumes] are sublime; but the third goes terribly to pieces. He repeats himself and he philosophises! In fact the man, the author, the Russian are visible, whereas up until then one had only seen Nature and Humanity. It seems to me that in places he has some elements of Shakespeare. I uttered cries of admiration during my reading of it ... and it's long! Tell me about the author. Is it his first book?

Turgenev replied at once:

My good old fellow,
You cannot imagine the pleasure your letter gave me and what you say about Tolstoy's novel. Your approval confirms my own ideas about him. Yes, he is a man of great talent, and yet you put your finger on the weak spot: he also has built himself a philosophical system, which is at one and the same time mystical, childish and presumptuous, and which has spoilt his third volume dreadfully ... I don't know what the critics will say. (I have sent 'War and Peace' to Daudet and Zola as well.) But for me the matter is settled: *Flaubertus dixit*. The rest is of no significance.[101]

5

Turgenev's own works were translated into other European languages with increasing frequency in the 1870s. During the previous decade he was already widely read in Germany, partly because he lived there and was seen by the reading public as an important writer in their midst. A German edition of his collected works appeared in twelve volumes between 1869 and 1883. In France and Britain, where only a handful of his books had previously been translated, there was a boom in Turgenev translations. In Britain, by the end of the century, his works would appear in over sixty translations in book form or in journals, in addition to a fifteen-volume edition of his novels translated by Constance Garnett, and in France his rise was similar.[102]

Publishers were quicker to translate his books, usually within a year, and his shorter works would appear in translation within weeks of their being published in Russia. His story 'The End of Chertopkhanov', first published in the November 1872 issue of *The Messenger of Europe*, appeared in a French translation (as '*Le Gentilhomme de la steppe*') in the *Revue des deux mondes* on 1 December. Because of the limited protection against pirate translations, Turgenev felt it was important to get an early copy of the manuscript to those foreign publishers he trusted so that he could oversee the translation to ensure its quality. By publishing an 'authorized' translation first, the market for unauthorized translations would be drastically reduced, for even pirate publishers would be more inclined to steal the former than pay a new translator. This was the strategy Turgenev adopted with his novel *Virgin Soil* (1877), which went with his own corrections into German, French, English, Italian, even Swedish, directly from his manuscript; they appeared in these translations almost at the same time as the novel's publication in Russia. Within the year, it had been translated into nine foreign languages, including Polish, Czech, Serbian and Hungarian, with additional translations in Croatian, Romanian and Danish on the way.[103]

What Turgenev saw in the growth of foreign sales was part of a general expansion in the European market for translations from the 1870s. The main factor driving this was a steep rise in the number of new readers, as the system of compulsory education was extended by most European states (in Britain the Education Act was passed in 1870, in Germany the key laws were introduced after the foundation of the Empire in 1871, and in France the 'Ferry Laws' were enacted in 1881–2). Demand for books outstripped supply in most European languages, especially in small but highly literate countries such as Holland and Scandinavia, which depended heavily on translating foreign works, though even dominant literary cultures, such as Britain, France and Germany, were opening their markets to more imports from abroad.

Nation-building was another force behind this growing traffic in translations. In Russia, for example, where more foreign works were published in translation than in any other European country, the dissemination of Western literature was viewed as a means of overcoming Russia's cultural backwardness and implanting democratic values in its society by all those who looked to Europe as a source of progress and enlightenment – the Westernizing intelligentsia and liberal nobility. Elsewhere the opening of literary markets helped new nations to liberate themselves from the cultural domination of imperial rulers. In the Habsburg Empire the nascent literary cultures of the Czechs, Croatians, Hungarians and Serbs were extremely receptive to works translated from French, English or Russian as a means of breaking free from the domination of the German language and its literature. Statistics show that in the final decades of the century the empire's Slavs were far more active than its Germans in translating foreign literatures. They were also increasingly translating from each other's literatures – the Czechs from the Hungarians and Poles, Hungarians from the Czechs, Croatians from the Serbs, and so on – all as an alternative to reading German literature.[104]

The market for translations took off in a wide variety of literary forms. Translations were a lucrative addition to the 'standard' and 'railway' libraries, the pocket mass editions established by Routledge, Hachette, Charpentier and other publishers in the middle decades of the century. They were also attractive to newly founded publishers without a backlist of domestic authors, nor the capital to invest in copyrights. A large share of the market in translations was for popular fiction, detective and crime stories, children's literature and science fiction, especially the *voyages extraordinaires* of Jules Verne, the most translated author of the nineteenth century and the first genuinely 'international bestseller'. *Around the World in Eighty Days* (1873) really did go round the world – in fifty-seven different languages by the end of the century.

Literary periodicals were increasingly important as a medium for translations. The 1870s witnessed the beginning of a steep rise in the number of journals across Europe, as new publishing technologies, mechanization and the railway network reduced printing and distribution costs. Established journals like the *Revue des deux mondes*, a major outlet for translations, increased sales substantially; imitations of the *grande revue* were found in other countries (e.g. the *Deutsche Rundschau* in Berlin and *España moderna* in Madrid). There was a proliferation of smaller cultural reviews, the *petites revues*, which as startup businesses depended heavily on translations as a cheap alternative to paying for original writing, although many of these journals were committed to a cosmopolitan agenda in which translations played a vital part. Belgium was a case in point. The number of new literary journals published there rose from under twenty every year in the 1850s to as many as sixty every year during the 1890s. Many of these new journals carried translations between Flemish, French and German, the country's three main languages, with the aim of promoting what was termed the 'Belgian spirit', defined by the journal *L'Art moderne* as a cultural space for the cross-fertilization of Latin and Germanic sensibilities.[105]

These reviews became a focus for literary and artistic groups, which linked them to journals with a similar philosophy on the European scene. In this way they came to provide an important network for the development of international cultural movements, such as Naturalism, Symbolism, Impressionism, and so on. The *Revue des deux mondes*, for example, had a commitment to socially progressive literature which it shared with *España moderna* and *The Messenger of Europe*, both modelled on the *grande revue*, which naturally increased the traffic of translations between them. *España moderna* regularly published works by Zola and Daudet in translation, not least because its founder, the financier and art patron José Lázaro Galdiano, was guided by his mentor, the novelist Emilia Pardo Bazán, a pioneer of Zola's Naturalist movement in Spain. It was through Zola that she had discovered Russian literature, first Turgenev, later Dostoevsky and Chekhov, whose works often appeared in translation in *España moderna*.[106]

Periodicals were important as a platform for critics to promote the cause of writers from abroad. Turgenev owed a great deal of his success in the West to the support of influential critics. In Germany he was heavily promoted by the writer Julian Schmidt, who in 1870, in one of the earliest biographical portraits of Turgenev published outside Russia, portrayed him as the equal of Dickens and Schiller.[107] His other great promoter in the German-speaking lands was Friedrich Bodenstedt, whom he had first met in Baden in 1863. Bodenstedt not only served as Turgenev's translator but acted as his agent, or intermediary, by selecting works for translation most likely to appeal to a German readership. Bodenstedt's own reputation as a writer and Professor of Slavic Languages at Munich University guaranted the widest review coverage for Turgenev in the German press.[108]

In France this role was played by Mérimée, Turgenev's main translator in the 1860s, and by Lamartine, the poet and statesman, whose entry on Turgenev in his multi-volume *Cours familier de littérature*, written at the end of the 1860s, was in effect the first biography of the Russian writer to appear in France. In the English-speaking world Turgenev owed his fame to the tireless efforts of William Ralston, his translator, who used his wide connections in London's literary circles to get his works reviewed in leading journals like *The British Quarterly*

Review, The Athenaeum and *The Contemporary Review*. It was also thanks to Ralston that Turgenev was awarded an Honorary Degree by Oxford University in 1879.[109]

Meanwhile, in America, Turgenev was promoted by the critics William Dean Howells (editor of *The Atlantic Monthly*), Thomas Sergeant Perry (the foreign books reviewer for *The Atlantic Monthly* and *The Nation*) and Henry James (who wrote about the European literary scene in *The North American Review, The Atlantic Monthly* and *The Nation*). Turgenev was already known in the United States. His *Sketches from a Hunter's Album*, with its subtle condemnation of serfdom, had an obvious significance for a country in which slavery was still such a contentious issue. James had been reading Turgenev since his teenage years, when his family had travelled in Europe, and his novels became an important part of his cosmopolitan education. But it was at Harvard, where James met Howells and Perry, that he came to see in Turgenev's writing a new literary philosophy. The three men took a lively interest in continental European literature. They read the *Revue des deux mondes*, whose literary aesthetic they absorbed. Perry, in particular, was influenced by the essays of Julian Schmidt, co-editor of the Vienna journal *Grenzboten*. Through Schmidt they discovered the German village writers such as Auerbach and the Norwegian tales of Bjørnson, which they embraced as a more realist alternative to the English melodramas of Dickens and Trollope. They also found in Schmidt an argument for holding up Turgenev as 'the greatest living novelist' – a claim Perry made on the basis of an article by the German critic favourably comparing the *Sketches* to *Uncle's Tom's Cabin* by pointing out the superior affective impact of Turgenev's dispassionate rendering of selected details to Beecher Stowe's 'authorial rhapsodizing and sentimentality'. In Turgenev they had found their model for a new type of poetic realism which they promoted in America.[110]

Through such international networks literary periodicals played a vital role in the cultural integration of Europe, bringing writers from the Continent's periphery closer to its major capitals, and provincial writers closer to the metropolitan centres. They also were important in getting writers from the other Francophone countries (Belgium and Switzerland) and German-speaking cultures outside Germany (Austria, Bohemia and the Baltic lands) better known in the main literary markets for those languages.

The boom in Russian novels in French translation took off in this way during the 1880s. Zola and Turgenev had prepared the ground, but the sudden spurt of French interest in Russian literature was mainly due to the influence of Eugène-Melchior de Vogüé's bestselling book, *Le Roman russe* (1886), which had appeared as a series of essays about Russian writers in the *Revue des deux mondes* and the *Revue bleu* around 1883. As the French ambassador to Russia from 1875 to 1882, de Vogüé had travelled widely in the country, and became absorbed in its culture. He wrote on Russia in the *Revue des deux mondes* over a period of many years, and was personally acquainted with Turgenev, Dostoevsky and Tolstoy, whose characters he vividly portrayed. The main impact of *Le Roman russe* came from its idea that the Russians could revive the realist tradition, which, de Vogüé argued, had lost its way in France: Russian novels had a spiritual aspect lacking in the materialist realism of Zola or Flaubert. The message struck a chord with a public that had begun to grow tired of naturalism and wanted something new and different, and the effect was immediate. The French translation of *War and Peace*, which had sold fewer than a thousand copies since its publication six years earlier, became a bestseller, with 20,000 copies sold between 1886 and 1889. Over the same period there was a steep rise in the number of translations of other Russian novels into French.[111]

Networks of supporters in the European journals were equally important in the breakthrough of the three great Scandinavian playwrights, Ibsen, Bjørnson and Strindberg. Their most important promoter was a Russian diplomat in Sweden, Count Maurice Prozor, a writer and translator from Russian and Norwegian into French. He was so impressed by the European premiere of Ibsen's *Ghosts* at the Helsingborg State Theatre in southern Sweden, in 1882, that he translated it himself and got extracts of it published in *La Revue indépendante*, a newly established Paris journal (not to be confused with the long-defunct periodical of the same name founded by George Sand and Louis Viardot) which became a tribune of the Naturalists and Symbolists. That publication put him into contact with another diplomat, Edouard Rod, the French ambassador in Switzerland and an Ibsen fan, who had written articles about the Norwegian playwright in *Le Temps*. With Rod's help Prozor got the play produced in Paris, in 1890, in a production based on his complete translation in *La Revue indépendante* the previous year. *Ghosts* was soon produced in all the major theatres of the Continent. It was translated from Prozor's French into many languages. Ibsen had been launched on an international scale. In the future all his plays would be published in translation simultaneously with their appearance in Danish, allowing them to receive their first performance simultaneously in the European capitals. Literature had become internationalized.[112]

The acceleration of translations did not lead to more diversity of national cultures, as one might expect, but to quite the opposite: a growing uniformity or standardization of literary forms, with 'all of Europe reading the same books'.[113]

Commentators had long seen this happening. Writing in the *Revue des deux mondes* in 1846, the French critic Saint-René Taillandier had lamented the disappearance of diversity in the national literary cultures of Europe. 'One could almost say that foreign literatures do not exist any more,' he wrote, 'as if the world was enveloped by a sad uniformity.' Jean-Jacques Ampère, the French philologist, writing in the *Revue* in 1853, diagnosed the causes of this uniformity in a typically French manner. It had begun, he argued, as the 'servile copying' of France by the other nations of Europe. 'To start with, the literatures of Europe's nations were entirely different, but through imitation they became similar, and today, without imitation, they are all alike.'[114]

Ampère overlooked the British novel, which had its imitators in Denmark and Holland, even Germany and France. But the French model became dominant in southern and central Europe, from Spain and Italy to Hungary and Bohemia, where the book market was flooded with translations from the French. Native writers imitated successful imports.[115] National cultures in these countries thus developed, not by their own home-grown means, as nationalist myths would have it, but through the borrowing of foreign means. The 'Spanish' novel was not Spanish, the 'Italian' not Italian, the 'Hungarian' not Hungarian: they were all imitations of the French.

No French writer was more imitated than Zola. He had a truly global literary reach. The influence of Zola differed in each country, according to social conditions, but everywhere his novels were perceived as an agency of progress and modernity. In Italy, where '*Zolaismo*' was embraced by liberal progressives as an ally in their cause against the

Church's influence, there were 'thousands of greenhorn Zolaists [*zolistes de lendemain*]', as Felice Cameroni, one of the critics who had been promoting him, wrote to Zola with some exaggeration in 1879. Giovanni Verga and Luigi Capuana, both Sicilians, were conscious imitators of Zola, seeing in his documentary style a modern way to write about the real lives of the poor. In Spain the impact of Zola was almost equal to a cultural revolution, as radical intellectuals embraced his movement as a way to overturn the conservatism of Catholic society. One group founded a journal, *Germinal*, named after Zola's masterpiece about a miners' strike. His style of social realism was adopted by many of the country's leading writers, including Benito Pérez Galdós and Bazán.[116]

Zola's writings had a radical impact on the small and provincial literary cultures of Sweden, Norway and Denmark. Championed by the critic Georg Brandes, whose lectures at Copenhagen University began the 'modern breakthrough' in Scandinavian literature, Zola's works were widely talked about during the 1880s. Young writers, in the words of Strindberg, who counted himself one of them, 'adored Zola' and all tried to write like him. [117]

In the Netherlands the upcoming writers of that time, Frans Netscher and Lodewijk van Deyssel (the pseudonym of Karel Thijm), were inspired by Zola's frank approach to sexuality – a far cry from the oppressive Calvinism of Dutch society – and by his attempts to apply science to his writing. They saw his scientific approach as the key to a modern literature in the service of society and progress. In Germany, where Zola's novels were the most widely read of any foreign writer in the 1880s, they appealed to a public looking for a new type of realist literature. They were widely read by the German working class, who saw in them a truthful reflection of their own lives.[118] It was a type of social novel they would soon find in their own German emulators of the Zola style. Among them was Gerhart Hauptmann, whose first work, *Bahnwärter Thiel* (1888), the story of a railway signalman who kills his wife, could not have been more Zolaesque.

Britain was the only European country where Zola had almost no following, with just George Moore, the 'Irish Zola', acknowledging his influence. The reasons are not hard to find. Britain had in Thomas Hardy its own version of Zola, and in Dickens and Eliot a well-established realist tradition that made it independent of influences from the Continent.

6

Paris played host to the world again with the opening of the Exposition Universelle, the largest exhibition of its kind so far, on 1 May 1878. Thirteen million people paid to enter it, around half a million from abroad (Flaubert complained that the city's prostitutes would be worn out). There were two enormous sites, the main building, in the Champ de Mars, and, connected to it by the Pont d'Iéna on the other bank of the Seine, the Trocadéro Palace, specially constructed in a half-Byzantine and half-Moorish style for the great event.[119] Among the new inventions on display, visitors could see an aluminium flying machine by Félix du Temple, a telephone by Alexander Graham Bell, and a phonograph by Thomas Edison, the first mechanism capable of recording and reproducing sound.

The exhibition was a symbol of France's resurrection after the defeat of 1871. In contrast to the previous Exposition, in 1867, which had brought prestige to the French Empire, this one was perceived as a celebration of the French people and republican values – a victory symbolized by France's gift to the United States of the Statue of Liberty, whose completed head was unveiled in the gardens of the Trocadéro Palace on 30 June.

The frieze above the main entrance showed France summoning the nations of the world. The Avenue of Nations in the Champ de Mars was lined by buildings representing typical examples of the architectural style of nearly every country in Europe, and quite a few from Asia, America and Africa. The public, noted Zola, 'mostly came in search of amusement': they wanted 'curiosities, tropical bazaars and cafés, restaurants where they could try extraodinary drinks and listen to strange music'. Large crowds were drawn to the Chinese, Japanese and Persian exhibits, and there was a lot of interest in the log huts made by Russian peasants without a single nail. Zola himself was so smitten by the Norwegian Pavilion that he bought it, had it dismantled at the Exposition's end, and rebuilt it in the garden of his mansion at Médan, newly purchased with the fortune he had made from *L'Assommoir*.[120]

Six weeks after the opening of the Exposition, an International Writers' Congress met in Paris to discuss proposals for an international treaty to protect literary copyright. Attended by 200 writers from countries all around the world, the congress elected Victor Hugo as its chairman for the ceremonial sessions and Turgenev for the working ones. The idea of the congress went back to the Brussels conference of 1858, the first attempt to draw up international laws of copyright. After Brussels there had been a second congress in Antwerp, in 1861, and then one in Manchester, in 1866, but a conference planned in Paris to coincide with the 1867 exhibition did not materialize, so the organizing council of the Société des Gens de Lettres called another one to take place at the time of the next world fair, thinking it would bring a lot of writers to Paris. Turgenev helped to draw up the lists of invited writers from abroad. But the foreign delegations were not large, and for every foreigner there were two French delegates. Most of the latter were jobbing writers for the *feuilletons*, the workers of an industry in popular fiction to help sell newspapers, according to the leader of the Russian delegation, Petr Boborykin. One of them had no idea who Flaubert was. Goncourt, Zola, Maupassant and Flaubert were all absent from the conference.[121]

The congress began with a public session in the Théâtre du Châtelet on 11 June. After the opening formalities, Hugo gave a long and lofty speech in praise of literature as the legislator of civilization and setting up the congress as its international parliament. Declaiming in a strong impassioned voice with long pauses for effect, he reminded Boborykin of an old actor. The delegates, seated in the stalls, listened with religious awe. The cult of Victor Hugo was at its height in France. The writer – who had returned from exile only on the fall of Napoleon III – was hailed as the moral conscience of the Republic. With his white hair and beard he assumed the role of national sage. He would hold court at his salon in rue de Clichy, where admirers would come to hear his views, which he gave on anything and everything, and his words of wisdom would later appear in the press.[122]

Turgenev did not care much for Hugo – he thought *Les Misérables* was 'false from start to end' – and was irritated by this universal reverence for him. Among friends, like Flaubert and Zola, who shared to some extent his annoyance with this cult, he poked fun at Hugo's pomposity (he invented a special word for it, '*hyperbombifocasse*' – 'hyperbombification').[123] He liked to tell the story of a visit to his salon, probably in 1875:

Once, when I was at his home, we were chatting about German poetry. Victor Hugo, who does not like people talking in his presence, cut me short and began to give a portrait of Goethe.

'His best work,' he said in an Olympian tone, 'is *Wallenstein*.'

'Forgive me, dear master [Turgenev interjected]. '*Wallenstein* is not by Goethe. It is by Schiller.'

'It matters not. I have read neither Goethe nor Schiller, but I know them better than those who have learnt their works by heart.'

He also liked to tell how once at Hugo's house a group of young French writers were talking of the possibility of a local street being named after Hugo. They all agreed that the street was too small to do him honour and began to compete by listing bigger streets. Finally, one of them suggested that the whole of Paris should be renamed Hugo. Hugo paused in thought and then said to the young man, '*Ça viendra, mon cher, ça viendra!* ['That will come, my dear fellow, that will come!']'[124]

Turgenev's own speech was modest. In five minutes he outlined to the congress how the great French writers of the past 200 years had helped Russian literature to emerge on the European scene, naming Pushkin, Lermontov and Gogol as no longer disciples of the French but as their colleagues (whereupon there were cries of 'Turgenev! Add Turgenev!').[125]

Turgenev was a poor public speaker. His voice was too high-pitched and weak to command a hall. As the chairman of the working sessions, which took place in the Masonic Lodge of the Grand Orient of France, he struggled to maintain control of the delegates, and often had to be helped out by Edmond About, the French novelist, who was the real organizing force of the congress.

The French stood firmly by the position they had long held: that authors' rights were a form of natural property, unrestricted by national boundaries. The purpose of the congress, as About defined it, was 'to draw up an international law by which the foreign writer shall enjoy in every country the same advantages as that nation's own writers – that without his consent he may neither be reprinted, nor translated, nor performed on the stage'.[126] Most of the foreign delegations agreed with the French, but some of the smaller countries, which depended heavily on imported literature, wanted greater freedom for translations; so it was resolved to divide the delegations into national groups, which would advance their proposals to the congress for a vote (where the French would win as they had the majority of delegates). The Slav group (Russians, Poles and Czechs) met at the Viardot house in the rue de Douai.

Turgenev was in a difficult position. The Russian delegation was flatly opposed to the French proposal: they wanted to protect the livelihood of Russian translators, and since fewer Russian writers were translated into foreign languages than foreign writers into Russian, they could not see a benefit to Russia in accepting the protections suggested by the French. A similar position was adopted by the other Slavs. Turgenev's own views, however, were on the French side. He had long complained of 'thieving publishers' and their pirated translations of his work abroad. It was not just that they deprived him of the foreign royalties which he would have earned with international protection, but that these unauthorized translations were so poor that they might damage his literary reputation where they appeared. Many times he wrote to foreign periodicals to complain and warn their readers about them. He was most outraged by those that falsely claimed to be translated with his authority. One pirate publisher in Germany brought out a translation of his novel *On the Eve* with a fabricated preface 'From the Author'. Even more infuriating was an incident in 1877, when a French translation of 'A Strange Story', originally published in *The Messenger of Europe*, was retranslated into Russian and published as an 'original Turgenev story' with a different title ('A Priest's Son') in *New Times*. There were numerous mistakes in the new version and the whole tone of the story had been lost. Turgenev complained to Stasiulevich, asking him to join him in a letter of complaint to Aleksei Suvorin, the editor of *Novoe Vremia*, although in the absence of any Russian laws of international copyright he recognized that there was nothing more that they could do: 'The law is on the side of such gentlemen, but decent people would not take advantage of such laws.'[127]

Turgenev was a firm believer in the need for international laws: honourable behaviour was not enough to protect authors' rights when printed texts crossed national frontiers. In May 1878, the Swedish-Finnish architect and writer Jac Ahrenberg, a delegate at the writers' congress, visited Turgenev at Bougival, where he recorded his frank views on copyright:

Turgenev said that he had been exploited in a shameful way by Swedish publishers. Without consulting him, they had translated his works, mostly from the German and French editions. A few days ago, he himself had seen in Mr Nilsson's window a copy of his *Spring Torrents* with no indication of the translator's name and without any Swedish publisher having even asked him about the matter. Well, one publisher had asked, and asked in such a way that Turgenev had not even replied to the letter. The letter supposedly began with 'although he, the publisher, had a legal right in the case of translations to do as he wanted . . . he nevertheless offered the author' – what Turgenev called *'un pourboire'* [a tip], presumably a few hundred crowns. Nilsson was sorry for his grievance, said that the Swedish editions were small, that it was not worth while to publish a book, if the author had to be paid a fee, that the Russians had the same right vis à vis the Swedish writers, though Sweden, regrettably, did not have and never had had Turgenev's like; that he, Nilsson, had no part in this *bellum omnium inter omnes* [war of all against all], he was but a commission agent and sold what others sent him. The conversation lasted a long time, and in the end the *causa mali* was brought forward, a letter from Turgenev's Russian publisher, which claimed (surely erroneously) that Turgenev's works were printed, sold and read in Sweden more than even any Swedish writer's, and ended with the petition that Turgenev, with the support of his great reputation, should take measures to curb this mischief and obtain, at least for himself, compensation for his work. The whole thing gave me the impression that, as surely as the old man was right in his claims for compensation, he just as much needed his money.

Turgenev spoke heatedly and with justified indignation about these translations into foreign languages. His sharp criticisms of this 'new Varangian trading and plundering' were, however, humorous rather than satirical or ironic. He made one remark, among others, that struck me: 'If this right to translate without compensation is not revoked, small nations shall be stifled in competition on the literary market. It will always be better business for a publisher to choose a masterpiece for nothing (I'm not talking about my own works now) than to pick from among the few domestic original works that might be good enough. But foreign masterpieces are less necessary for a nation's spiritual life than domestic works of lower rank. The consequence is that publishers get fatter while authors die out, and so the nation's literature suffers a heavy blow. Small nations are, more than others, forced to protect themselves against foreign influences. Better to have a few poor publishers and a small but viable literature. Look at Italy and Spain! Their literatures are dead. Why? Well, before the last edition of a French novel has left the printing presses, it has been exploited by a publisher in these countries.'[128]

Turgenev had hoped that the Russian delegation would 'silently approve the French proposals', as he had written to Stasiulevich. The danger that he had seen for small nations could equally apply to Russia, where he feared that young writers might find it hard to publish because of the influx of foreign translations. He had also been concerned that 'the Russians should not give the French cause to accuse us of illiberal views in not wanting equal rights [between nations] – an accusation fully justified.' At their meeting in the rue de Douai he managed to persuade the Slav group that, since the French would reject out of hand any proposal for freedom of translations, they should propose a compromise of copyright protection for a limited period (between two and five years depending on the category of work).[129]

This was the proposal he advanced on their behalf at the congress. Turgenev underlined that for young literary nations such as Russia, especially in those where there was censorship, it was important to maintain freedom of access to foreign literary and scientific works: this was the surest guarantee for the spread of European civilization to these less fortunate societies. He also argued for permissiveness on grounds of equity: 'We Russians cannot yet afford to pay authors money for translations from the French. You, the French, do not translate us, and practically ignore us, but we translate all your latest works. And who are our translators? Poor students, for whom this work is their only means of livelihood.' One of the French delegates shouted at this point: 'Let them pay me just two sous! The important thing is the recognition of my rights!' – a sentiment applauded by the French majority. Turgenev was supported by several of the smaller delegations – the Romanians, the Dutch and the Portuguese – who claimed that in their countries it was impossible to earn a living from writing, there were no native writers, and that those from the richer nations should look on the translation of their works as an advertisement in these markets. Turgenev made a final plea: 'These translators are not brigands. They are to some extent the pioneers of civilization in our country. You may say that what they introduce they take from you. That is true, but there are precedents. If Peter the Great had not been an illustrious brigand, I would not be talking to you here today.' There was laughter and applause. But in the vote his proposal was rejected by all but twenty of the delegates.[130]

The congress passed a series of proposals advanced by the French for copyright protection of authors' rights, including translations and adaptations, in all countries equally. It then closed with a banquet and more speeches calling on national governments to draw up the necessary international laws. Turgenev did not go to the banquet but went instead to the Folies Bergère with the Viardots. He was tired and fed up with the congress, a 'comedy' he called it, which had produced 'some general phrases' but no results of any real significance (*'patati et patata'*). 'I've had enough of it,' he wrote to Flaubert, 'and I'm leaving for Karlsbad.'[131]

Turgenev allowed his name to be included on the honorary committee of the International Literary and Arts Association (ALAI), which organized a series of conferences in London (in 1879), Lisbon (1880) and Vienna (1881) to draft proposals for international laws of copyright. But he attended none of these. He thought his role in London would be 'miserable', and even in Vienna, where he was declared an Honorary President, he saw no purpose in his being there: the Russians were showing every sign of backing out of any agreements on international copyright.[132]

Turgenev had been wrong when he had told Flaubert that the congress 'won't and can't produce any result'. The resolutions it had passed were enshrined in a draft convention of international copyright at the ALAI Conference in Berne in 1883, discussed by governments at diplomatic conferences in the same city in 1884 and 1885, and formally adopted by ten states (France, Belgium, Britain, Germany, Haiti, Italy, Liberia, Spain, Switzerland and Tunis) as the Berne Convention for the Protection of Literary and Artistic Works (the founding document of a copyright union which today incorporates 172 countries) on 9 September 1886. Most of Europe's smaller states, those predominantly book-importing, remained outside the convention, although many joined it later on: Norway (in 1896), Denmark (1903), Sweden (1904), Portugal (1911) and the Netherlands (in 1912). The Austro-Hungarian Empire was kept out by its non-German parts, the main importers of foreign translations, which held the majority in the Reichsrat. The Russians too refused to join the convention. But there was an irony. They had based their opposition to the French proposals on the reasoning that they translated more works from the other European languages than the other way around, but their decision not to join the convention went a long way to reverse this imbalance. After 1886, there was a steep and sustained rise in the number of translations of Russian books in Europe. It was partly the result of increased Western interest in Russian literature, but mainly because Russian books were unprotected by the convention and thus cheaper to translate and publish than works under international copyright.

The Berne Convention was one of the towering achievements of international law in the nineteenth century. It came at a highpoint of internationalism – a time when the International Red Cross was established in all the major countries of Europe, when Socialists were organized through the Second International, and the women's international movement took substantial form. The force of international law was increasing, and European states were signing up to international norms and conventions: an International Telegraphic Union (1865); a Union for the Metric System (1875); a Universal Postal Union (1875); an International Meridian Conference to establish standard time (1884); and an Agreement on Goods Transport by Rail (1890), which coordinated the timetables and technical requirements for the railway companies of nine continental European states.[133]

The Berne Convention was not yet sufficient to eradicate the problem of international piracy. States outside the convention – notably the USA and Russia – continued to provide a legal loophole for pirate publishers.* The wording of the convention was ambiguous in certain areas – performance rights, for example – which gave rise to legal fights between the creators of music or dramatic works and concert or theatre managers. But overall the treaty was a crucial piece of legislation, whose guiding principles remain in force today. It encouraged publishers of music, literature and art to expand their business internationally, and enabled artists to collect an income from their work around the world.

* The USA joined a less protective Universal Copyright Convention in Geneva in 1952. It did not accede to the Berne Convention until 1988. The Soviet Union signed the Berne Convention in 1975, Russia reaffirming its adherence in 1995.

8

Death and the Canon

There have never been living great men. It is posterity that has made them.

Flaubert, 1870

I

Turgenev returned every year to Russia in the later 1870s, usually in order to attend to his estate and business affairs, which lurched from one disaster to the next. His short stays attracted little interest from the Russians, who had come to regard him as an émigré, if not a total foreigner. On the publication of his novel *Virgin Soil*, in 1877, he had been attacked by Russian critics from all sides who claimed that he had lost touch with Russia, where the novel – a complicated story about a group of populists who leave their noble households to 'simplify' their lives and spread socialist propaganda to the peasants – is set. Its chararacters, it must be said, lack the life-like qualities of those in his earlier novels; they feel like types to carry his political message – that however good and honest these young revolutionaries may be as people, their cause itself is false and bound to fail. Turgenev had accepted the charges. 'There is no doubt that *Virgin Soil* has failed,' he wrote to his brother Nikolai;

> and I am beginning to think that its fate is merited. One cannot suggest that all the journals have entered into some kind of league against me; rather it must be admitted that I made a mistake: I took upon myself a labour that was beyond my powers and I fell down under its weight. In fact, it's impossible to write about Russia without living there.

Because he could not write of any other place he talked of giving up fiction.[1]

But that all changed on his visit to the country in the early months of 1879, following the unexpected death of Nikolai, who left a small part of his large fortune, around 250,000 francs, to his cash-strapped sibling in his will. Turgenev was given a returning hero's welcome at a series of banquets in the writer's honour organized by prominent representatives of science, education and the arts in both Moscow and St Petersburg. Now his absence from the country was seen as his protest against autocracy. Students thronged outside the houses where he stayed in the hope of catching sight of the white-haired giant they now hailed as the embodiment of their democratic hopes. Turgenev had returned to a society in a ferment of expectations of reform: pressure for a constitution was mounting, and, in spite of terrorist attacks by the revolutionaries, Tsar Alexander II was coming round to granting one.

Turgenev understood why he was welcomed so ecstatically. On 4 March, he gave a reading of one of his *Sketches* at a benefit concert for poor students in the Assembly Hall of the Moscow Nobility. It became a political demonstration. 'Imagine more than a thousand students in this colossal hall,' he wrote to Pauline the next day.

> When I enter there is an uproar loud enough to bring the building down, shouts of 'hurrah!', hats are flying in the air. Then two enormous wreaths are presented, then a young student representative shouts a speech into my ear – every sentence prompts another outburst; in the front row the rector of the university is pale from fear; and I, while trying not to pour oil on the fire, answer in the hope of saying more than platitudes. Later, after the reading, I am escorted from the hall by a huge crowd. From the adjacent rooms I am called out twenty times. Young women try to grab hold of my hands in order to kiss them! It was a mad scene. If a colonel of the gendarmerie had not escorted me out, in the most polite manner, and got me into my carriage, I would still be there. The reason for this frenzy I well understand: on the eve of reforms which are always promised and postponed, these young people are all charged with electricity like a Leyden jar; I served as a machine to discharge it. In doing so my liberal views were as important as any of my writings. If these poor young people did not demonstrate, they would burst![2]

Such demonstrations were not welcomed by the Russian government. Police spies reported to the Tsar on the writer's every move. Reactionaries accused him of inciting revolution. Soon Turgenev was approached by one of the Tsar's courtiers, who said His Highness was interested to know when he planned to return abroad. Concerned not to fall foul of the Tsar and jeopardize his chances of future visits to Russia, and perhaps fearful of his possible arrest, Turgenev packed his bags and left without delay. At the border he was told by the tsarist official, 'We have been expecting you.'[3]

Although it had been cut short, Turgenev was delighted with his visit to Russia. He felt he had been reconciled with Russian youth and the progressive sections of society. Time had softened the controversies stirred by his novels of the 1860s, *Fathers and Sons* and *Smoke*; a new generation of Russians had grown up with ideas close to his liberal views; and he was now fondly remembered as the author of the *Sketches from a Hunter's Album*, which had done so much to end serfdom. For the first time, he felt this was a Russia in which he might find a home. Pauline sensed that she could end up losing him. 'My good, dear Tourgline,' she wrote to him on 25 March,

> I have just received your letter with the photograph. Thank you. I am replying to it with the certainty that my letter will find you settled happily still in Petersburg, where your latest triumphs may encourage you to put down roots. That is very well, provided you do not develop 'Heimweh' [homesickness] when you will be in Paris. Are you planning to abandon us? I fear you will get bored of Paris, where you are not surrounded by this frenzy of admirers – where you only have the same old people, who are getting older by the day, who look at you with a more quiet joy . . . God, what happiness it will be to see you here again. I am afraid you will not have the strength to tear yourself away from all that youth that prowls and bounces around you![4]

The one prowling youth that Pauline really feared was Maria Savina, an actress whom Turgenev had met earlier that March, after her sensational performance in his long-neglected play *A Month in the Country* at the Alexandrine Theatre in St Petersburg. Young and beautiful, Savina was the most exciting talent of the Russian stage. Turgenev at once fell in love with her. He saw her constantly. After his return to

Paris, he sent her passionate letters, declaring his love for her. The letters expressed an old man's sexual yearning for a young woman (he was sixty-one and she twenty-five) but contained nothing to suggest that they were lovers.

His infatuation stemmed no doubt from the growing sense of loneliness he felt, both as an exile from Russia and as an old bachelor. Before his relationship with Savina, there had been other young women, all Russians, in whose affections he had found solace when he felt isolated or neglected by Pauline. From 1873, there had been a long flirtation with the young widow of a Russian general, Baroness Julia Vrevskaia, which had only broken off on the outbreak of the Russo-Turkish War in 1877, when she left for the front to volunteer as a nurse. She died in a military hospital from typhus fever in January 1878.

The foolishness of an old man who fails in his conquest of a young woman is the stuff of comedy. But there was a sadness in Turgenev's longing for a younger woman's love. Perhaps it was nostalgia for his youth, for its romantic possibilities, which he had sacrificed to his devotion to Pauline. His ardent love for Pauline had weakened – changed in form – as the two became older. It had become an intimate friendship in which his emotional existence was contained. He was incapable of breaking this relationship. He was dependent on Pauline, even though he knew his passion for her was reciprocated only by her 'quiet joy'. Emotionally he needed her, in spite (and perhaps because) of the torment she caused him.

According to Anatoly Koni, the jurist in whom he confided about affairs of the heart, Turgenev was unsuited to marriage: he would have become bored with a loving wife (or perhaps with the everyday banalities of married life). 'For him to love for a long time, and to become accustomed to love, he needed the sort of person who would make him suffer, doubt, waver, be secretly jealous and dejected – one who, in a word, would torment him.'[5] Pauline was this tormenter. He was devoted to her like a slave.

Koni recalls a conversation with Turgenev in the autumn of 1879, when the jurist, then aged thirty-five, visited him in Paris. Turgenev advised him to get married. It was impossible to imagine, Turgenev explained, 'how lonely and wearisome old age can be when you have to cling to the edge of a stranger's nest, accept kindness as if it were charity and be in the position of an old dog, which is not driven out because people have got used to it and pity it'. According to Savina, Turgenev felt a profound disappointment, even resentment, about the sacrifices he had made for his unofficial marriage to Pauline. He expressed his feelings in a poem which he read to her, his voice shaking with emotion, from a 'large book bound in green leather' that he kept locked up in a drawer in his desk at Spasskoe. The poem, which has not survived, told the story of an 'overmastering love for a woman to whom a whole life had been given and who would not bring one little flower or shed a single tear on the writer's grave'. When Savina asked him what he meant to do with this poem, Turgenev replied that he would burn it to prevent it being published after he had died: 'It might hurt her.'[6]

Turgenev returned to Russia in February 1880. He wanted to resume his relationship with Savina. He saw her frequently during the five months he spent in Russia, from February to July, the longest he had stayed for almost twenty years. There were fleeting encounters, stolen moments in her changing room at the theatre, and exchanges of flirtatious notes. On one famous occasion he even travelled to the railway station at Mtsensk, twenty kilometres from his estate at Spasskoe, so that he could join her in her compartment for the hour's journey to Orel. From the letter which he wrote to her after he had left the train to spend the night in a hotel, it would seem that they had kissed ('If I live for a hundred years I shall never forget those kisses') but she had rejected his further advances, resulting in Turgenev, no doubt realizing that he had made a fool of himself, distancing himself from her ('If the bolt must remain closed, you had better not write to me, but I kiss your hands, your feet, and everything you'll allow me to kiss – and even what you won't allow').[7] The cooling off was temporary. His infatuation started up again. The next summer Savina spent five days with him at Spasskoe – a place Pauline never visited – though by that time she was about to marry someone else.

One of the reasons for Turgenev's long stay in Russia was his involvement in a Pushkin festival culminating in the unveiling of a monument to the Russian poet in Moscow on 6 June. The idea of a public statue had been promoted since the 1840s, when Belinsky had concluded his series of articles on Pushkin by looking forward to a time when Russia's 'classical' poet would be recognized with a monument. From the 1860s, when the campaign was taken up, first by Pushkin's old schoolfriends at the Lycée in Tsarskoe Selo and then by the Society of Lovers of Russian Literature (OLRS), which specialized in literary commemorations, the call for a statue of Pushkin began to assume a national symbolic importance. There were no public monuments to literary or artistic heroes in Moscow or St Petersburg: only statesmen and military figures shared that honour with the tsars. The unveiling of a Pushkin monument was seen by many as a new beginning for Russia. It would mark the moment when it was reborn as a nation in the European sense, a society independent of the State, on a par with the Germany of Goethe or the England of Shakespeare. Coming at a time of liberal reform, it was also seen as a turning point in the state's relations with society, a chance for the country to be reunited by the values of its literature.[8]

Turgenev played a leading role in the preparations for the festival. Acting as ambassador-at-large for the OLRS, he helped to acquire Pushkin memorabilia for the main exhibition, wrote to writers all around the world to invite them to attend (not many came, but Hugo, Tennyson and Auerbach sent congratulatory telegrams), and accepted a commission from Stasiulevich to write a pamphlet on Pushkin 'for the people' to be read aloud and distributed free in Moscow's public reading rooms on the day of the unveiling of the monument. The pamphlet turned out to be pitched too high. 'I don't know how to write for the common people, who don't read Pushkin anyway, only for the cultured few,' Turgenev admitted to Stasiulevich. Just before the start of the festivities, on hearing that Tolstoy would not attend, he travelled down to his estate at Yasnaya Polyana in a last attempt to change his mind. Tolstoy would not listen to Turgenev's arguments. He had declared his intention to give up literature and live a simpler Christian life with the peasants. He refused to have anything to do with the 'comedy' of honouring a man of easy morals, like Pushkin, whose poetry meant nothing to the peasantry.[9]

Huge crowds turned out for the unveiling of Alexander Opekushin's statue in Moscow on 6 June 1880. Pushkin souvenirs of every type were available from sellers in the streets: portraits, clay busts and statues, cheap editions of his poetry, song albums and musical arrangements of his verse. To the orchestral sound of the 'Coronation March' from Meyerbeer's *Le Prophète* (Pushkin had composed a poem by the same name as the opera) delegations from all over Russia approached in turn to lay wreaths by the monument. There were banquets, public readings, ceremonial meetings and eulogies by dignitaries.

Turgenev's speech at the opening session of the OLRS was eagerly awaited by a public keen to hear what he would have to say about the country's great poet. As a famous exponent of the Westernist philosophy, he had given much offence to the Slavophiles and nationalists by cutting Russia's cultural achievements down to size. Turgenev's eulogy was a disappointment to his audience. While acknowledging that Pushkin was the first and finest national poet, he stopped short of ranking him with the greatest European poets – Shakespeare, Goethe and Homer – who had higher universal qualities. It was a measured, nuanced argument, which paid homage to the great leap Pushkin had made in the creation of a Russian literature, but it did not satisfy the nationalist, euphoric mood, which demanded Pushkin's elevation to a higher world significance.

Dostoevsky stole the show by satisfying this demand in his explosive panegyric at the closing session of the OLRS, the next day, on 8 June. The speech was the starting point of Dostoevsky's fame as a national prophet. He hailed Pushkin as a world-historic genius, greater even than Shakespeare, Cervantes or Schiller, because he possessed that uniquely 'Russian' quality of embodying the spirit of all humanity: 'The greatest of European poets could never so powerfully embody in themselves the genius of a foreign, even a neighbouring, people . . . Even Shakespeare's Italians, for instance, are almost always Englishmen. Pushkin alone of all world poets possessed the capacity of fully identifying himself with another nationality.' His universal spirit, Dostoevsky claimed at the messianic climax of his speech, was a revelation of Russia's destiny to unite all the peoples of Europe in a Christian brotherhood. 'The hall was in hysterics,' Dostoevsky reported to his wife, 'and when I finished I can't tell you the roar, the wail of rapture . . . For half an hour they called me back, waved handkerchiefs . . . "Prophet! Prophet!" they shouted in the crowd. Turgenev, about whom I put in a good word in my speech, rushed up and hugged me with tears.' In his own report on Dostoevsky's speech, Turgenev described it to Stasiulevich as 'false from start to end, but extremely pleasing for Russian self-esteem'.[10]

2

When Turgenev was at Spasskoe preparing his Pushkin speech he received the devastating news of Flaubert's death. 'I took the blow in a most brutal fashion,' he wrote to Zola on 23 May, 'by reading the obituary notice in *Golos* [a Petersburg daily]. I need not tell you how deeply grieved I am: Flaubert was the man I loved most in the world. It is not only a great talent that has passed away but a rare spirit, and a centre for us all.' The details of his death came a few days later in a long letter from Maupassant, who had received a telegram from Flaubert's niece on 8 May, telling him to come quickly after Flaubert had collapsed from an epileptic fit. He was dead by the time Maupassant arrived on the train from Paris to Rouen.[11]

The funeral took place three days later at Croisset. After a perfunctory mass in the parish church, the mourners followed Flaubert's coffin to the Rouen Monumental Cemetery, a journey of a few kilometres. Zola was shocked by the small turnout of literary people from Paris (aside from himself, just Goncourt, Daudet, Maupassant, Théodore de Banville, Huysmans and a few others, but not Hugo or Dumas) and above all by the small size of the congregation from Rouen – no more than a hundred mourners in total. 'What seems inexplicable, unforgivable, is that Rouen, the whole of Rouen did not walk behind the body of one of its most illustrious sons,' Zola wrote. 'You could say that the Rouen people are all in commerce and don't take literature seriously. But this big city must have schoolteachers, lawyers, doctors, a population that reads books, who at least have heard of *Madame Bovary*.'[12] The burial itself could have come straight from the pages of that masterpiece. The hole prepared by the gravediggers was not long enough for the coffin of Flaubert, who was almost six feet tall (1.81 metres). Lowered into the ground, the coffin became stuck at an angle, the feet higher than the head, and was left in that position for the final rituals.

When Turgenev returned from Russia, he got together a committee of writers to raise the funds for a monument to Flaubert in Rouen. Goncourt, Daudet, Maupassant and Zola joined it along with Charles Lapierre, the editor of the daily newspaper *La Nouvelliste de Rouen* and an old friend of Flaubert, but Victor Hugo was too proud to sit on the same committee as Zola, who had criticized his work. Of the

12,000 francs demanded by the sculptor, Henri Chapu, only 9,000 was collected from the public in five years. They had to scrape the rest together from their own pockets. The monument was finally unveiled on 23 November 1890. The weather was miserable. Goncourt, Zola and Maupassant were among the tiny crowd of Parisian dignitaries sheltered from the wind and rain in a marquee while the statue was unveiled to the oompahs of a fairground band – another scene that could have come straight out of *Madame Bovary*.[13] Goncourt gave the main address:

> Now that he is dead, poor Flaubert is starting to be given the status of a genius, as his memory deserves. But do you know that when he was alive the critics were reluctant to admit that he even had talent? What did all his masterpieces earn for him? Rejection, insult, moral crucifixion. One could write a good book on all the errors and injustices committed by the critics against writers from Balzac to Flaubert. I recall an article by a political journalist arguing that Flaubert's prose was a disgrace to the reign of Napoleon III, and another in a literary journal where he was reproached for writing in an *epileptic style* – only now you understand how much poison that epithet contained for the man to whom it was addressed . . .
>
> At a time when money is transforming literature and art into commerce, Flaubert stands as one of the last of an old generation of artists never motivated by money, resisting its temptations even at the cost of his own fortunes, and writing only books that satisfied his taste in art, books which paid him badly in his own lifetime but which earned him posthumous glory.[14]

Flaubert had to wait a long time to get the recognition he deserved. It was not until the centenary of his birth, in 1921, that the French state acknowledged his significance by unveiling a monument to him in the Luxembourg Gardens. But the death of other writers would be marked by large-scale state and civic funerals during the 1880s.

Dostoevsky died from a pulmonary haemorrhage in January 1881. If his Pushkin speech had been the origin of Dostoevsky's status as a national prophet, his funeral was the start of a national cult. It was the closest any writer had yet come to a state funeral in Russia, with both the Church and government taking on responsibility for the arrangements and sending representatives. Huge crowds turned out for the procession through St Petersburg. Tearful students left their lecture halls to line the streets from Dostoevsky's home in Kuznechny Lane to the Alexander Nevsky Monastery. The representatives of sixty-seven delegations carried wreaths as they walked behind the coffin. Fifteen different choirs sang at various points along the way. As the cortège approached its destination, the gates of the monastery opened and its monks filed out in procession to honour the deceased – a ceremony normally reserved for the interment of a tsar.[15]

'Nothing like it had been seen before in Russia,' Stasov wrote. Only a few decades previously, Pushkin's funeral had been closed to the public, his body taken from St Petersburg by the police to prevent crowds from gathering. But now the state was claiming Dostoevsky as its own. The Tsar ordered the Ministry of Finance to grant a lifetime pension of 2,000 roubles (8,000 francs) a year to Dostoevsky's widow, the first time such a pension had been given in Russia, and places were reserved for Dostoevsky's children in the Corps des Pages and the Smolny Institute, though neither place was taken up. A public fund was established for the publication of a first complete edition of Dostoevsky's works, and another for a monument to the writer. Turgenev contributed fifty roubles (200 francs), a modest sum. He had not forgotten Dostoevsky's unpaid debt and cruel baiting of him over many years.[16]

Victor Hugo's funeral, on 1 June 1885, was on an even larger scale. It was one of the biggest state occasions the French capital has ever seen. From the moment it was known that he was dying, large crowds gathered outside Hugo's house in the avenue d'Eylau. A young Romain Rolland was among the many students who missed school to join the crowd of Hugo fans, many of them workers, waiting for announcements from the balcony. Ever since the writer's birthday celebrations in 1881, it had become a tradition for his admirers to gather on the street outside his house and wait for Hugo to appear. Hugo took five days to die. He played the part of the Romantic death to perfection, making sure to issue statements to family and friends around his bed ('I am ready!', 'It is a dead man who speaks to you!', 'If death must come it is welcome!', etc.), which he knew would find their way to the newspapers. The international press published daily updates on his condition.[17]

By the time Hugo died it had been decided by the government to honour him with a state funeral and 'pantheonization'. Hugo had requested to be buried in a poor man's coffin. Even in death he was conscious of the need to cultivate his image as a man of the people. For the lying in state Hugo's simple coffin was put on top of a monumental catafalque bearing his initials and placed underneath the Arc de Triomphe, which was draped in a black mourning veil, surrounded by a dozen burning torches, and illuminated with electric light. Maurice Barrès compared the dramatic *mise-en-scène* to the funeral arrangements of the Roman emperors. Nietzsche thought it was an 'orgy of bad taste'. On the night before the funeral, monster crowds assembled at the Arc de Triomphe and lined the Champs Elysées, taking up positions for a better view of the funeral processsion to the Panthéon. The area began to take on the appearance of a huge fairground as pedlars sold cheap souvenirs – pictures of the deathbed scene, Hugo silhouettes, songsheets, pamphlets of his poems, wooden models of his characters. By the morning there were two million people on the procession's route, more than the entire population of Paris, and perhaps another million would join them later on. The government was worried that the funeral could become a workers' uprising and put more police and soldiers on the streets. The thickest crowds were in the rue Soufflot

For Hugo's lying in state, before his funeral on 1 June 1885, his coffin was placed on a monumental catafalque underneath the Arc de Triomphe in Paris.

leading to the Panthéon. At its colonnaded entrance the representatives of nineteen delegations gave their eulogies and placed their wreaths on the steps in turn before Hugo's body was laid to rest in the necropolis.[18]

His placement in the Panthéon was a symbolic victory for the secular tradition of honouring the 'great men' of the nation. The tradition had been inaugurated by the revolutionaries in 1791, when the National Assembly had ordered the creation of the Panthéon in the church of Sainte-Geneviève. Designated as a civic burial place, the Panthéon was named in imitation of the Roman model. The remains of Descartes, Voltaire and Rousseau were transferred to the Panthéon's crypt. Over the course of the nineteenth century the building had become a battleground between Church and State. Under the Bourbon Restoration it was returned to the Church; the 'infidel remains' of Voltaire and Rousseau were removed from the crypt and hidden behind an unmarked door under the portico. After the July Revolution the Panthéon was restored, its 'infidels' brought out again, but no other bodies were buried there. Louis Philippe added to the building the pediment *'Aux grands hommes, la patrie reconnaissante'* with its depiction of France distributing laurels to the nation's famous men (the first woman to be buried there was Marie Curie as late as 1995). Napoleon III restored the building to the Church, which became a site of pilgrimage. It remained a religious shrine until 1885, when Hugo was the first man to be interred in the crypt since Jacques-Germain Soufflot (1713–80), the architect of the Panthéon, in 1829. Hugo's death had provided the impetus for the Republican government to take over the building and reconvert it to the Panthéon so that the freethinking poet could be buried in a suitably secular place.

Hugo was the first of many writers to be buried in the Panthéon. He was later joined by Zola (who became his crypt-mate in 1908) and by Dumas *père* (in 2002). Of the eighty people given a state funeral in the Third Republic between 1878 and 1940 a quarter were major figures in the arts. Hugo's death marked the moment when the secular values of the Republic were properly established as a force for national unity. The Republican victory in the elections of October 1877 had ended the hopes of conservatives for a restoration of the monarchy. Moderate republicanism could now build its intellectual infrastructure – founded on the Enlightenment ideals of the Revolution – as a national ideology. The cult of artists and philosophers represented an essential part of this campaign. It had taken off with the celebrations for Voltaire and Rousseau on the centenary of their deaths in 1878. Louis Viardot was on the organizing committee for the celebrations of both.[19] There were banquets for the civic leaders in all the major towns, statues of the two men were unveiled, and their works published in jubilee editions and pamphlets. For the Voltaire centennial (organized, ironically, by the Menier chocolate company) there was a ceremonial event in the Théâtre de la Gaieté on 30 May. Hugo gave a legendary speech, widely published in the press and issued as a pamphlet, in which he presented the great writer and philosopher as the embodiment of his faith in progress, revolution and democracy. To cement the symbolic link between the Revolution and Rousseau, the main event to mark his centenary, a grand ceremony attended by 6,000 people in the Cirque Américain in Paris, was held, not on the day of Rousseau's death, 2 July, but twelve days later, on 14 July, the anniversary of the storming of the Bastille, which would be commemorated from this time on (it became a national holiday in 1880).[20]

The official cult of Hugo reinforced this connection between the nation's great writers and the Revolution's intellectual principles, of which, it was said in the eulogies that appeared on his death, Hugo had been the main champion in the many tests they had faced in the nineteenth century. His pantheonization was proclaimed as a victory for the Republic's secular ideals against the old 'Moral Order' of the clergy and the monarchists. But it was a bitterly contested one. The Church attacked the 'pagan' cult of worshipping a man instead of God.

To consolidate that victory the Ministry of Fine Arts inaugurated a large programme of monumental sculptures for the Panthéon in 1889, the centenary year of the Revolution, marked too by the opening of the Eiffel Tower at the Exposition Universelle in Paris. The centrepiece of the Panthéon commission was a sculptural ensemble of the revolutionaries with a figure representing the National Convention, but there were also individual sculptures of the great philosophers who had laid the intellectual foundations of the Revolution (Descartes, Voltaire and Rousseau), of the statesmen who had enacted it (such as Mirabeau), and one was planned for Hugo, who had embodied its republican values in the nineteenth century. Auguste Rodin was awarded the commission for a statue of Hugo. The sculptor chose to depict the poet in exile, seated with the Tragic Muse on the rocks of Guernsey, one

Rodin and his statue of Hugo in the garden of the Palais-Royal, 1902.

hand to his head, lost in contemplation, the other stretched out to the sea, a gesture of defiance against the dictatorship of Napoleon III. The project was rejected by the ministry, which found another site for Rodin's bronze in the gardens of the Palais-Royal, so Rodin worked on two alternatives – a seated Victor Hugo, shown in plaster at the Salon of 1897, and a standing one for the Panthéon which he never completed.[21]

Hugo's name was everywhere. Death had raised him to the status of a national saint. Mass editions of his works were found in every local bookshop and public library. Schoolchildren were made to learn his poetry by heart; textbooks told his story of exile and resistance to the Second Empire as a moral instruction in republican principles. There were various initiatives to establish a Victor Hugo Museum. The mayor of the 16th *arrondissement*, where Hugo had lived in the avenue d'Eylau, petitioned the Paris government to protect his house as a 'sacred' site, and many people wrote with the same request. In 1889, a group of businessmen rented Hugo's former home to set up business as a 'National and Universal Pilgrimage at the Victor Hugo House and Museum' (*Pélerinage national et universel à la Maison et au Musée*

Victor Hugo), intended mainly as an attraction for visitors to the Exposition Universelle.[22] The house was not protected by the city of Paris. Nor was it later used as a museum (today it stands above a boutique selling underwear).* But on Hugo's birthday in 1881 the avenue d'Eylau was renamed after him.

Before the middle of the nineteenth century it was rare for a figure in the arts to be commemorated by a public body or the state. Monuments to monarchs and military heroes filled the streets and squares of Europe's cities, but statues of the nation's cultural heroes were few and far between. It was only from the 1860s that states began to give more weight to the commemoration of national heroes of culture.

Across Europe there was a steady increase in the public celebration of artistic anniversaries: the Schiller centenary (1859), the Shakespeare tercentenary (1864), the six-hundredth anniversary of Dante's birth (1865), the celebrations for the Walter Scott centenary (at which Turgenev had spoken in 1871), the fifth centenary of Petrarch's death (1874), the centenaries for Voltaire and Rousseau (1878), for the Irish poet Thomas Moore (1879) and the third centenary for Luís de Camões, the great Portuguese poet of the sixteenth century (1880). Monuments to writers, artists and composers appeared with growing frequency, almost equalling the number built for statesmen and soldiers, which in the first half of the century had heavily outnumbered them. Between 1800 and 1840, the states of Europe erected seventy-five monuments to monarchs, politicians and military heroes – three times the number they unveiled for figures in the spheres of culture, science and philosophy (twenty-three). In the last four decades of the century, when the craze for public statues reached its peak, the numbers were more equal: 512 for the men of power against 401 for those of ideas, science and the arts.[23]

Streets and squares, libraries, halls and theatres were named after famous men from the cultural and scientific fields. Commemorative plaques were placed on buildings where they had lived. London's blue-plaque scheme, the oldest in the world, began with the unveiling of a sign for Byron at his birthplace in Holles Street (the building was later

---

* A Victor Hugo Museum was later opened in the house in the place des Vosges where Hugo lived between 1832 and 1848.

demolished). House museums became part of a booming tourist trade in pilgrimages to literary and artistic shrines. By 1900, over 30,000 tourists travelled every year by rail to Shakespeare's birthplace in Stratford. The train timetables coincided with the start and end of the performances at the Shakespeare Memorial Theatre, opened in 1879, so that Londoners could make it a day-trip and take in a matinée before returning to the capital.[24] The railways also drove the growing tourist traffic to destinations sacralized by their association with creative 'geniuses' ('Brontë Country', Wordsworth's Lake District, the shores of Lake Geneva connected with Rousseau, Weimar as the crucible of Goethe and Schiller, etc.). These monuments and sites were both nationalist and European in their cultural significance: much of the national pride in these figures was based on the idea of their 'universalism' – as the country's 'gift' to other countries and the world.

The house museum was the focus of this cult. The Schiller House Museum was one of the earliest to open, in 1847. On his visit to Weimar, in 1869, Turgenev made 'the obligatory pilgrimage' to it, noting the smallness of the room in which Schiller died ('any well-off craftsman would now refuse to live in it'). He was disappointed that the Goethe house remained closed.[25] The poet's grandson was stubbornly refusing to sell it. But on his death, in 1885, the house was taken over by the Duchy of Saxony-Weimar and opened up to the public. By this time, writers' house museums were being set up everywhere – the Musée Pierre Corneille near Rouen, Dante's house in Florence, Cervantes' in Madrid – and many more were opened by the time the First World War broke out.

Why was there such a marked increase in the commemoration of artistic figures at this time? The Romantic cult of the artistic genius had been a part of European culture since the eighteenth century. But in the final decades of the nineteenth century it became part of the marketing of art in a culture where successful writers, artists and musicians were treated as celebrities, their biographies examined in the media in an effort to explain their creativity. This preoccupation with the artist's private life and personality was easily transferred to the canonic figures of the past. Biographies of the great artists, writers and composers multiplied, becoming one of the biggest literary genres by the end of the century.

States and national movements claimed these geniuses for their own ends. Goethe was the 'German' genius, Dante the 'Italian' poet – their creativity interpreted as an expression of the national character, their poetry the basis of the national language. This was an age of nation-building and nationalist movements across Europe. New nations came into existence (Italy, Romania, Germany) or struggled for their liberation from multi-national empires (Hungary, the Czech lands, Serbia, Croatia, Poland, Ukraine, Ireland, and so on). All the European states increasingly depended on culture – above all on the broad dissemination of a national literature – to unify society.

The spread of mass communications made this use of culture possible: writers, artists and composers became known to a wider public than had been conceivable before the railways or lithography; they were national heroes and celebrities. When Hugo died the whole of France came to a stop. When Verdi died, on 27 January 1901, shops and theatres closed their doors in a sign of national mourning. Three days later, in what is said to be the largest showing of the Italian people in their country's history, 300,000 mourners lined the streets in freezing early-morning temperatures to watch the funeral procession in Milan, and at points along the way, or so the story goes, the crowds

Verdi's funeral, Milan, 30 January 1901.

431

spontaneously broke into singing the 'Va pensiero' chorus from Verdi's *Nabucco*, a sort of informal national anthem.[26]

The cult of Verdi was central to the national identity fostered by the new Italian state. Although *Nabucco* had been first performed in 1842, it was only after the unification of Italy that the famous chorus of the Hebrew slaves – a lament for the loss of their homeland with symbolic parallels for Italians under foreign rule – attained its national significance and popularity. From the 1860s the Italian state promoted the idea of the Risorgimento as a popular uprising and rebirth of the nation. It championed Verdi's operas, particularly those with patriotic themes such as *Nabucco*, *I Lombardi* and *Ernani*, which could be used to cultivate a national consciousness. Verdi's music was promoted as the inspiration and expression of the nation's unity – Verdi as 'the bard of the Risorgimento' became part of the Italian national myth.[27]

Public commemorations of important artists played a vital role in the nation-building projects of the European states. In Italy, in 1865, the sixth centenary of Dante's birth was commemorated in Florence, the new capital of King Victor Emmanuel II. It was billed as a celebration of the country's 'national poet', whose *Divine Comedy* (1320), written not in Latin but in the Tuscan vernacular, was said to be the start of Italy's protracted cultural unification. In Germany the centenary of Schiller's birth was an important moment in the development of a liberal nationalist sentiment. It was celebrated in ninety-three German towns and cities, and in more than twenty outside Germany. Schiller statues were unveiled in Weimar (in 1857), Jena and Marbach (1859), Mannheim and Mainz (1862), Hanover and Munich (1863), Frankfurt-am-Main (in 1864 and 1880), Hamburg (1864), Marbach-am-Neckar (1867), Berlin (1871), Vienna (1876), Ludwigsburg (1883), Wiesbaden (1905), Nüremberg (1909), Königsberg (1910), Stuttgart (1913) and Dresden (1914).[28]

In Belgium the death of Hendrik Conscience, in 1883, gave birth to a full-blown cult of the popular and prolific Flemish writer, 'the man who taught his people to read', as the elaborate memorial monument to him in his native Antwerp was inscribed. For Flemish-speakers, who had long been dominated by the francophone culture of Belgium, Conscience was a source of national pride. He was given two state funerals, one in Brussels, the other in Antwerp. In many Flemish towns statues of Conscience were unveiled, streets and squares named after him.[29]

In other countries under foreign rule the commemoration of a 'national poet' brought together national liberation movements. In Slovenia the nationalist cult of Valentin Vodnik (1758–1819), the 'first Slovenian poet', culminated in the opening of a monument to him in Ljubljana's Vodnik Square in 1889. In Hungary the nationalist movement was united in a long campaign to commemorate the revolutionary and patriotic poet Sándor Petőfi (1823–49), which finally succeeded with the erection of a monument in Budapest in 1882. In Poland, under Russian rule, statues of the 'national poet' Adam Mickiewicz (1798–1855) began to be erected only during the centenary celebrations of his birth.

If the 1880s were a highpoint in the public celebration of national heroes in the arts, it was also at this time that the notion of a 'canon' of great works and artists worthy of commemoration took root in societies throughout Europe.

The word 'canon' was not yet used in this secular manner. It applied only to saints and scriptural texts approved by the Church. But the idea of a canon in its modern sense – a stable list of classic works enshrined in the value-system of societies – began to find expression from the middle decades of the nineteenth century. For many years it was articulated by the term 'world literature', which Goethe had first used in 1827 to describe, not a set canon, but the international circulation of literary works in Europe, including works of non-European origin. Cultural exchanges between nations would enrich their literatures and lead to the creation of a hybrid fusion between them – what he termed 'world literature'. Goethe came to his idea from the observation of contemporary reality. He was impressed by the growth of international trade, and saw a parallel between the development of a global market in material goods and one in literature: the first would lead to the second. Influenced by Goethe, Marx and Engels reached the same conclusion in *The Communist Manifesto* (1848). The globalization of the capitalist market was giving 'a cosmopolitan character to the production and consumption' of intellectual creations as well as material goods in every country, they maintained:

> In place of the old local and national seclusion and self-sufficiency, we have intercourse in every direction, universal inter-dependence of nations. And as in material, so also in intellectual production. The intellectual

creations of individual nations become common property. National one-sidedness and narrow-mindedness become more and more impossible, and from the numerous national and local literatures, there arises a world literature.[30]

By this time the idea of a world literature was being widely used for a collection of literary masterpieces from all over Europe and the world. Lists of such works were beginning to appear. In 1849, Auguste Comte published his *Positivist Calendar*, an almanac of 558 'great men' from all historic ages and nations, which he proposed as an alternative to the calendar of saints. Two years later, in his *Catéchisme positiviste*, he compiled a list of 150 books that he believed should constitute a basic reading course for all educated citizens. The list proved influential throughout northern Europe, especially in Britain, where it appeared in translation and inspired other registers, including one, in 1886, by John Lubbock, the head of the Working Men's College. His directory of the world's best hundred books (including several in Arabic, Chinese, Persian, Sanskrit and other languages) was widely circulated in the press. It had an enormous impact on the reading culture of the self-improving working class, generating a new mass market for the 'classics'.

The idea of compiling an agreed list of the world's greatest books gained ground more broadly on the Continent around this time. It had been discussed by the International Writers' Congress in 1878. The Polish writer Wacław Szymanowski had campaigned for one in the hope of getting recognition and quotas on the list for the smaller literary nations like his own. Turgenev had been drawn to the idea. It appealed to his European cosmopolitanism, to his belief in cultural enrichment through translation and exchange between nations. And it was true to the Goethian ideal of a world literature which he had followed all his life. Much of his translation work and activities as an intermediary between cultures had been carried out with the aim of helping to create, if not a world literature, then at least a European one. He wanted to promote an international corpus of literary works around which the nations of Europe could unite. By advancing mutual understanding between different nationalities, literature could play a role in the creation of a European cultural identity.

Turgenev gave much thought in his last years to the idea of publishing a library of classic works, not just for Russia but for Europe. On his visit to St Petersburg, in 1879, he announced that he would like to organize a group of Russian artists to illustrate a series of publications of the Russian classics for the widest readership. He cited as his model the illustrated editions of Goethe and Schiller that had recently been published in Germany. In November 1880, he recruited Maupassant to a literary project he had long been planning and was hoping to extend to all the major countries of Europe. He wanted him

> to write a series of articles in *Gaulois* [a Paris newspaper] about the great writers of Europe – a project I strongly approve and for which I shall put myself entirely at your disposal for directions and advice. For Russia, for example, begin with Pushkin or Gogol; for England Dickens, for Germany Goethe, and from there, once you get the hang of it, proceed to the gods of small nations. I am sure that you will do a splendid job.[31]

For the next six months, Maupassant immersed himself in research for a 'Gallery of European Writers', as he outlined it to Turgenev, but the project fizzled out, and in *Gaulois* all he published was a series of sketches of a few important writers, mostly after they had died.[32]

3

In addition to state commemorations and published lists of the best books, a European canon was being formed by economic forces in the final decades of the nineteenth century. The movement of people, money and commodities across national boundaries, the new technologies of print and photographic reproduction, mass communication and transport, and the establishment of more effective laws of international copyright combined to produce by the 1880s a relatively stable repertoire of 'classic' works in music, opera, the ballet, drama, art and literature right across the Continent.

This canon first developed in the concert repertoire, where as early as the 1840s the serious-music movement championed by Schumann, Berlioz and other critics and composers had established a programme of chamber and orchestral classics dominated by the three most venerated dead masters, Beethoven, Haydn and Mozart. This was a new development. In 1800, the concert repertoire had mainly consisted of music by living composers – 80 per cent of all the music performed in the concert halls of Vienna, Leipzig, Paris and London; but in these four cities, by 1870, the same proportion of the repertory was music by composers who were dead.[33] The concert hall became a museum where the same familiar music was endlessly repeated. It became increasingly difficult for young or even living composers to get their works performed, especially if their works were difficult or experimental, or required large orchestras and choruses – a concern voiced by Liszt and Berlioz, who both suffered on this score. One music critic reported on a visit to Paris in 1863:

> Works more recent [than Beethoven's] are heard here extremely seldom, and it has been only a few years since even Mendelssohn was first accepted on the programmes of the Conservatoire concerts. Schumann and Schubert are but little known as instrumental composers; . . . a few cautious attempts have been made, in concerts established especially for this purpose, to present works of living composers to the public . . . but the attempts met with no real sympathy, and the public, quite content not to compromise itself, would rather be allowed to admire pretty much the same pieces by famous masters every year; the musicians, for their part, find this so convenient that they do not feel impelled to challenge this routine.[34]

Convenience and familiarity were certainly a large part of the explanation for this growing musical conservatism. But it did not come about from a general rejection of new music (an attitude that appeared only in the twentieth century). Rather, it developed from the economics of the concert hall. Well-known works were cheaper to produce – they required less rehearsal by the orchestra and soloists; and the oldest scores were free of copyright. They also gave a better guarantee of filling seats, for the entirely legitimate reasons that they were popular. As cities grew in size and became accessible to more people because of improvements in suburban railways, bigger concert halls were built, adding to the risk of untried music and further reinforcing the dominance of classic works: concert managers could turn an easy profit by providing a familiar repertoire for this larger audience, a good part of it drawn from the lower-middle and artisan classes, who, being new to serious music, were interested mostly in the famous works.

The railways once again were instrumental in opening the market by allowing more extensive concert tours. Soloists and orchestras could introduce the classics to a provincial public or pay their way around the world by playing the familiar works. In 1885–6, Anton Rubinstein toured through Europe, starting from St Petersburg and Moscow and travelling to Vienna, Berlin, Leipzig, Prague, Dresden, Paris, Brussels, Utrecht, London, Liverpool and Manchester, performing in more than a hundred concerts, 'historical recitals', in which he aimed to cover the development of the classical canon for piano. In the same decade, Albert Gutman, the music agent, impresario and publisher, brought whole orchestras to Vienna. 'A touring orchestra, playing not dance music but the greatest works of the symphonic repertoire, is a novelty reserved for our railway age,' marvelled Eduard Hanslick, the city's leading music critic, thereby helping Gutman fill the Philharmonic Hall.[35]

Publishing was a key factor in the popular dissemination of the classical canon. Technical improvements in lithographic printing in the 1870s enabled music publishers to print mass editions of the now standard works at affordable prices. The classic music library of Edition Peters was launched in Leipzig in 1867, an important 'classic year' in the history of German publishing when, in line with earlier legislation by the Prussian parliament, copyright protection was removed from works by authors dead for more than thirty years. The market was flooded by cheap mass editions of the works of Mozart, Haydn, Schubert and Beethoven, all of whom had died before 1837. Edition Peters was the most successful venture of this kind, although it was closely rivalled by Breitkopf & Härtel's Volksaugabe series (People's Edition), which also dates from the 'classic year' of 1867, and by Novello's Cheap Classics and Octavo editions, which had been established earlier.[36] The distinctive covers of Edition Peters (green for works of dead composers not in copyright, pink for newer works in copyright) were found in every piano-owning home. The idea that the classics should be readily accessible to everyone was taken very seriously by Max Abraham, who took over the directorship of Peters from 1880. He considered it, by his own description, his 'holy duty to make sure that the works of the great masters are available in an easily legible style'. He employed expert editors to produce definitive editions of the standard works, and made sure to have them ready for release as soon as their copyright ran out and they entered into public ownership. In 1894, on the death of Abraham, the Peters Music Library was left to the city of Leipzig.[37]

*

Economics also underlay the entrenchment of a stable opera repertoire. Between 1860 and 1885, a small group of the most profitable operas emerged from the many hundreds produced over the past century to dominate the repertory of music theatres in Europe. Over the same period the production of new operas fell, as programmes focused more and more on proven hits. At London's Covent Garden, for example, the share of first-season productions declined from 23 per cent of all performances in the 1850s to only 8 per cent between 1861 and 1878. A similar decline occurred at Her Majesty's Theatre, where the business-minded manager, James Mapleson, was forced to compete with Covent Garden by offering the most popular works – 'the inevitable Trovatore, the always welcome Lucrezia, the universally popular Martha, the stately Norma, the magnificent Huguenots, and the unequalled Don Giovanni', as James Davison, the music critic of *The Times*, described the programme in 1861.[38]

The same thing was happening all across the Continent. By the 1860s, La Scala in Milan was producing only one or two new works every year instead of the five or six that had been customary in the 1820s and 1830s. At the San Carlo Theatre in Naples the number of premieres declined from six per year in the 1820s to just one in the 1870s. At Madrid's Teatro Real the number fell from eight per year in the early 1850s to only one or two in the 1870s. The story was the same at the Vienna Hofoper, where there were eight premieres per year in the 1830s and 1840s, but only two by the 1870s.[39]

The emergence of a standard repertoire can be seen most clearly at the Théâtre Italien in Paris, where the number of new operas declined to an average of less than one per year in the 1870s. The range of different operas was dramatically reduced – from seventy-two in the repertoire of the 1810s to only twenty-eight for the entire decade of the 1870s. Operas tended to stay longer in the repertory. Only 10 per cent of those produced in the 1810s continued to be part of the theatre's active stock in the 1840s; but of those performed in the 1870s, two thirds remained in the repertoire for over thirty years. The theatre's repertory was dominated by the great workhorses of Italian opera: Rossini's *Barber of Seville*, Bellini's *Norma* and *Sonnambula*, Donizetti's *Lucia*, Verdi's *Rigoletto*, *Traviata*, *Trovatore* and *Aida*.[40]

A standard operatic repertoire was emerging globally. By the final quarter of the century, a visitor to Paris was likely to be offered the same choice of operas as he or she might find in London, Milan, Naples, Madrid, Berlin, Vienna or St Petersburg – or, for that matter, in Buenos Aires or New York. With a few exceptions, such as the now long-forgotten masterworks of Meyerbeer, the operas on offer across Europe in the final decades of the nineteenth century are still at the core of the repertoire today.[41]

The laws of the market were the key to this development. No longer able to rely on state or royal subsidies, the great opera houses of Europe had to make their way on ticket sales, an unreliable source of income for their managers. London's theatres were ahead in this respect. They had never really had large subsidies and were more used to operating as commercial businesses than theatres on the Continent, where state grants were either ended or reduced only in the 1850s and 1860s. In Italy the declining wealth and power of the Habsburgs and Bourbons led to cuts in subsidies before 1861. But after the unification of Italy the idea of supporting opera houses from the state budget was deemed incompatible with the free-trade ideology of the country's parliament, which abolished them altogether in 1867. Theatres might continue to be subsidized by their city governments, but these grants were small and unreliable, resulting in a crisis for those houses which had once been backed by wealthy courts, such as the theatres of Naples, Modena and Parma.[42]

In France a reform of 1864 ended all state subsidies except for the national theatres in Paris: the Opéra, the Opéra-Comique and the Théâtre Lyrique. It was left to the *communes* (municipalities) to decide whether they would subsidize their own theatres. The reform led to a period of uncertainty and financial crisis for many regional theatres, which were now forced to compete with more commercial forms of entertainment such as operetta and *café-concerts*. In this competitive environment it made no sense for them to run the risk of producing untried operas. Where their licence obliged them to put on a set number of new works every year, they found ways to get around the rules. At the Lyrique, for example, where two new operas were meant to be presented every year, Carvalho used a loophole in the licence to include translations into French of old and well-established works.[43]

Meanwhile the mounting costs of staging opera, especially Grand Opera, discouraged the commissioning of new and risky works. Singers were becoming more expensive as the international demand for their services increased. With steamships and railways it was possible for the big stars to do extensive tours (the great soprano Adelina Patti had her own train), so opera managers were forced to pay more to keep them.[44] Italian singers, in particular, were in high demand abroad, especially America, where they could earn higher fees. 'The best Italian singers are rarely heard or seen in their native land,' lamented the British impresario Walter Maynard in the 1860s. 'As soon as they have means to do so, they seek their fortunes in other countries, where they receive better pay.'[45] It was an ironic consequence of its own international success that the birthplace of opera was relegated to the lower division of the global market once big money called the tune.

There was another reason for the falling number of new works in the opera repertoire: the supply was running out. As Gye observed in his prospectus for the 1867 Covent Garden season, it was becoming increasingly difficult for the director of an opera house to buy new works, because the composers who had been responsible for the expansion of the repertoire in the 1830s and 1840s – Rossini, Donizetti, Bellini, Auber, Meyerbeer and Verdi – were either dead, no longer writing, or composing fewer operas.[46] The development of copyright protection was a major reason for this falling off in production. Once they were able to earn a living from their royalties, composers could simply work less than they had done from necessity when they earned a single fee from each opera. The best illustration is Verdi, arguably the first composer to make his fortune out of royalties, who had long declared his intention to liberate himself from what he called the years of 'the galleys' when he was forced to write an opera every year. His chance came after 1860, when new laws of copyright were introduced in Italy. Between 1839 and 1859 Verdi composed twenty-four operas; but between 1860 and 1893 he wrote only five.

Underpinning these commercial pressures was the growing size of the public able to attend the opera. It allowed theatres to survive from ticket sales by programming popular operas. The population of the major opera cities expanded rapidly between 1860 and 1900: London's grew from 2.5 million to 6.8 million, Paris's from 1.8 to 3.3 million, and Milan's from a quarter to half a million. The railways opened up the cities to day and weekend trippers from the provinces and suburban areas, enabling theatres to put on longer runs of the most successful operas by drawing from a larger catchment area. Bigger theatres could be built, with more public seating in the stalls, where tickets could be purchased for a single performance, as opposed to private boxes, owned or rented for a whole season, where the capacity was limited. Tickets could be ordered and sent out by post, and agencies began to operate, offering discounts to the big hotels for purchases in large numbers.

Mapleson was the first opera manager to gear his programme to this larger public in Britain. From 1862, he extended the season at Her Majesty's well into the summer months, when London's élites traditionally left for the country and the theatre closed. He lowered prices to attract the middle classes, put on matinée performances, allowing the suburban public to catch an evening train home, started earlier in the evenings, and ended the requirement of formal dress. One of his aims had been to attract 'the numerous foreign and country visitors' who had come to London for the International Exhibition in 1862. But profits were so good that he expanded on this policy. From 1863, Mapleson replaced a row of private boxes with cheaper public seats, advertised productions in the regional press, and started ticket sales by post and telegraph. The musical taste of this suburban public was decidedly conservative: it would come by rail for an evening at the opera to hear familiar classics but would not make the journey for an unknown work.

For all these reasons theatres across Europe became more cautious, increasingly relying on a programme of well-loved operas to make a profit from their ticket sales. The repertoire became so standardized that it formed a 'canon' in effect, although critics and historians would define it in such terms only in the twentieth century. The 'canonic' operas – *Don Giovanni*, *The Barber of Seville*, *Robert le diable*, *Lucia di Lammermoor*, *Norma*, *Rigoletto*, *Traviata*, *Faust* – were an institution in themselves – a badge of European Civilization that every national opera house in Europe and beyond adopted as a marker of its Europeanness.

Music publishers had a powerful influence on the opera repertoire. The biggest firms were able to determine which works were performed as well as set the standards of how they were produced. As the owner of an opera's score, the publisher was able to control the terms on which it was leased to a theatre. It was not uncommon for Ricordi or Edoardo Sonzogno, the two big Milan publishers, to make the loan of a money-making score dependent on the theatre undertaking not to perform an opera published by a rival company in the same season – a practice possible because so many theatres were dependent on a big 'hit' to break even. In this way they aimed to raise their market share. Ricordi, for example, had a near monopoly on the operas staged at La Scala during the 1880s (one in four was by Verdi, a Ricordi composer). His hold was broken only in the 1890s, when Sonzogno had successes at La Scala with *Le Cid* by Massenet and *Cavalleria Rusticana* by Mascagni.[47]

In the contract for the leasing of a score the publisher could set strict conditions on the production (the choice of singers for the major parts, the size of the orchestra, the staging, costumes, props and set designs, even detailed instructions on the singers' gestures and expressions). These were usually the terms demanded by the composer as part of his moral right to protect the work's integrity. They were often detailed in a staging manual, known in Italian as the *'disposizioni sceniche'* and in French as a *'livret de la mise-en-scène'*. The publisher's enforcement of these conditions played a vital part in fixing the canonic form of operatic works. Previously, in the early decades of the century, an opera could be tampered with in any way the theatre chose: whole scenes could be cut or songs inserted for popular effect; while singers like the young Viardot or Malibran would embellish their vocal lines and sometimes even improvise. An extreme example of this tampering was in 1834, when the Paris Opéra put on Mozart's *Don Giovanni* as a Grand Opera in five acts, including a ballet with a medley of Mozart tunes from all his best-known works in the first act and a dance at the end for the funeral of Donna Anna, who was made to fall in love with Don Giovanni before committing suicide.[48] Less dramatic adaptions continued to be common over the next fifty years. It was only when the publisher enforced a composer's moral rights that this malpractice stopped and a standard version of an operatic work was established in the repertoire.

Publishers were able to control productions internationally. That was certainly the expectation of Verdi, who constantly reminded Ricordi of his duty to ensure that his operas were faithfully translated and produced around the world as he had specified in the score, the libretto and *disposizioni sceniche*. There was a clause in all Ricordi's contracts that legally obliged the theatres borrowing or purchasing his scores to be accurate and faithful to the composer's wishes, with substantial

The Ricordi shop in London, c. 1900.

fines for their failure on various accounts.[49] The publisher enforced these moral rights through a network of agencies, which distributed scores, collected royalties, checked on the progress of productions, and took measures to prevent unlicensed productions, if necessary by legal means. The Milan company had offices in Naples, Rome and London by the middle of the 1870s, in Palermo and Paris (from 1888), Leipzig (1901) and New York (from 1911).[50] With the transatlantic telegraph, Ricordi in Milan could readily oversee the running of his global empire.

Milan was the centre of an opera industry stretching across Europe and into the world beyond. The presence of Ricordi and La Scala was the key to the city's international influence. Theatre agents and impresarios travelled to Milan from far and wide to negotiate performance rights, purchase scores, and hire singers, who gravitated there in large numbers, as did the best singing teachers, dancers and designers, because of its importance as a hiring market. In 1890, there were 4,500 singers living in Milan (a city with a total population of around 400,000). Only a small fraction found employment in the major European opera houses. Many of the rest formed companies and toured by rail to the smaller cities of Europe, while others crossed the Atlantic by steamship to tour in North and South America, where all the major capitals had opera houses by the 1870s. There were even touring companies of Italian singers from Milan in India, New Zealand and Australia.[51]

Opera singers had been touring round the world since the age of Rossini, when Manuel Garcia and his family had left Europe for New York and Mexico. In those days the touring groups consisted of a few singers. They would take what they could pack in a few trunks, the costumes and the props, and perform in halls or theatres with simple makeshift sets, hiring an orchestra in the town when they arrived or playing all the parts on a keyboard. With the advent of the railways and steamships the nature of the touring opera was changed completely. A whole company could now go on tour, not just the lead singers but an orchestra and chorus, with all the sets, just as they were specified in the production manual by the composer and his publisher. In this way the railways helped to spread the standard repertoire, so that when an opera was produced in a small provincial town, a Lecce, Graz or Baden, it looked the same as it did on stage in Milan, Vienna or Berlin: the sets, decorations and effects, props and costumes were identical.

Angelo Neumann's international touring Richard Wagner Theatre was arguably the first to make extensive use of the railways. It played an important role in the dissemination of the Wagner canon across Europe during the 1880s. Formerly a singer who had taken part in Wagner's own productions of *Tannhäuser* and *Lohengrin*, Neumann formed his touring company in 1882, when he was managing the Leipzig Opera House. Taking advantage of a financial crisis that had kept the Bayreuth Theatre closed since 1876, Neumann bought the performance rights, costumes, sets and props of the *Ring* cycle from Wagner, and chartered his own special train with five wagons, in which the scenery, a complete orchestra and the singers, including many of the leading artists from the Bayreuth Festival, went on several summer tours. The impresario took *Der Ring des Nibelungen* to London, Russia, Austria and Italy, where his company gave the first Italian performance of the *Ring* in the Teatro La Fenice in Venice in 1883. From 1885, when he became its director, Neumann turned the German Theatre in Prague into a Wagnerian stronghold, not least because a brilliant young conductor by the name of Gustav Mahler, a passionate disciple of the 'music of the future', performed several Wagner operas during his brief tenure as its principal conductor from the same year. Before he died, in 1883, Wagner was begrudgingly forced to admit that Neumann, a Jew, had done more than anyone to enhance his reputation in Europe.

In the world of opera, as in other cultural spheres, the railways strengthened international networks between cities. These inter-city connections were at times more important in the creation of a standard repertoire than nation states. Operatic scores, production styles, singers and conductors moved on lines from Milan to Palermo and Cairo; from Berlin via Leipzig, Dresden and Vienna to Prague and Budapest; from Prague to Ljubljana, Zagreb, Lemberg and Kiev; and from St Petersburg to Odessa and Tbilisi. Through these networks of musical communication and exchange a European style of opera developed that transcended national boundaries.[52]

Opera houses became more alike in their design. The basic architectural elements – the colonnaded entrance with the portico, the grand foyer and sweeping staircase to the loggia and auditorium, the classic-baroque style and general effect of opulence and grandeur – were adopted everywhere as a badge of Europeanness. The Viennese architects Ferdinand Fellner and Hermann Helmer built some forty theatres with these same elements in the Habsburg Empire and the German-speaking lands between 1881 and 1913. The geographic distribution of their theatres could be used to map the spread of German culture in Europe.

Size and safety were the key criteria. Gas lighting had caused a series of devastating theatre fires in the 1870s, culminating in 1881 when the Théâtre Municipal in Nice burned down after a gas explosion and the Ringstrasse Theatre in Vienna caught fire, burning to death 450 people in the audience. Better safety regulations were introduced across Europe. Theatres were rebuilt with an iron stage instead of wood, a safety curtain, more exits, electric lighting and power (the Savoy Theatre in London, home to the D'Oyly Carte Opera Company, was the first to be fully lit by electricity when it opened in 1881). The growing wealth and civic pride of Europe's cities involved building theatres on the largest scale. They were meant to be a symbol of the city's status as a 'European' capital. Sometimes the effect was grandiose. The Graz

State Theatre (1899), built by the ubiquitous Fellner and Helmer, was designed on the proportions of a national rather than municipal theatre (its 1,800-seat capacity was much too big for the city's modest population).[53] The Teatro Massimo in Palermo (1897), the biggest opera house in Italy and third largest in the whole of Europe, was a thumping statement of Sicily's arrival on the European scene.

Opera was the first European cultural medium to be truly globalized. The nineteenth-century canon of operatic works was conveyed to every quarter of the globe by touring companies, colonial rulers and opera enthusiasts, from the Khedive of Egypt, a fan of Offenbach, to Italian expatriates in North and South America. Verdi's opera *Il Trovatore* was arguably the first to have a global reach. Within three years of its premiere in Rome, in 1853, it had been performed in sixty cities, including Constantinople, Alexandria, Rio de Janeiro, Puerto Rico, Buenos Aires, Montevideo, Havana and New York; in 1860, it had arrived in Mexico, Peru, Chile, Venezuela, Colombia, Guatemala, Canada and Australia; by 1870, it had been performed in India, China, the Dutch East Indies, the Philippines and the Cape Colony in southern Africa. Verdi was delighted by his worldwide fame. 'Were you to go to India, or to the depths of Africa, you can hear *Il Trovatore*,' he boasted to a friend in 1862.[54]

Opera houses in the European style opened all around the world – from Algiers to Cairo, where one was built to mark the opening of the Suez Canal in 1869 and Verdi's *Aida* was first performed; from Calcutta, where the British had an opera house from 1867, to Shanghai, Hong Kong and Hanoi, where the French had a theatre modelled on the Palais Garnier from 1901. Even in the middle of the Amazonian jungle, in Manaus in Brazil, there was an opera theatre, a distant outpost of European civilization, built with Tuscan marble, Glaswegian steel and cast iron from Paris, all paid for by Brazil's rubber barons between 1884 and 1896. It was said that the theatre had been built to lure the world's most famous tenor, Enrico Caruso, to Manaus. For its opening, in 1897, Caruso came to sing the part of Enzo in Amilcare Ponchielli's *La Gioconda* (1876), a Ricordi opera first performed at La Scala. The story of the Teatro Amazonas (the starting point of Werner Herzog's movie *Fitzcarraldo*) is a fitting symbol of the opera's global reach.

4

The dissemination of a comparable art canon was also taking place across Europe. Louis Viardot played a small but notable part in it.

The popular museum guides which he had published with Hachette became standard works, used by thousands of visitors to the great art collections of Europe, and reissued many times in the later decades of the nineteenth century. His judgements on the most important works of art were cited frequently in the handbooks – the Murrays and Baedekers and *Guides Joannes* – that directed tourists to the major galleries in ever-growing numbers. Visitor numbers were not commonly recorded by museums in the nineteenth century, but from the fragmentary data that we have it is clear that by the final decades of the century visiting museums and art galleries had become a mass activity, with several hundred thousand people passing through the doors of Europe's most visited collections – the Louvre, the National Gallery, the Rijksmuseum and the Old Masters Gallery in Dresden – every year. The best figures were collected at the Rijksmuseum, where the annual number of visitors increased from an average of 37,000 in the second half of the 1870s, when the national collection was still housed in the Trippenhuis in Amsterdam, to an average of 427,000 between 1885 and 1889, when it was housed in its new building.[55]

The success of his guides led to further books by Viardot, *Les Merveilles de la peinture* (1869) and *Les Merveilles de la sculpture* (1872), both translated into English and German, which provided a historical compendium of the great artworks in every European country from ancient Greece and Rome to the Renaissance in Italy, including the Spanish, German, Flemish, French and English schools. Reprinted many times, they probably did more than any previous history of art to define a canon of European artworks and make it widely known. In 1877, a second and expanded English version of *Les Merveilles de la peinture* appeared as *A Brief History of the Painters of All Schools* with Woodburytype reproductions, a recently invented mechanical technology (patented by the English photographer Walter Woodbury in 1864) for printing photographic images with a much higher tonal quality than previously achieved.[56]

The organizing principle of Viardot's guides – the chronological division of artworks into different national schools – was adopted by museums too. In the early nineteenth century public galleries had displayed their paintings in a mixed-up way – Watteaus next to Tintorettos, and so on – without guiding principles. But from the middle of the century the pedagogic ideas of museum guides like Viardot's were increasingly reflected in the layout of such galleries, with the rooms arranged in historical order, from antiquity to the modern era, to display the history of art. Gautier, a great connoisseur, noted the beginning of this transformation at the Louvre in 1849. 'Now, a walk through the Museum is a complete course in the history of art,' he wrote. 'The long wall is a lesson, and every step along it teaches something new: you see the birth, development and maturation of the great schools of Italy, Flanders and Holland, replaced slowly by the French, the only school alive today.'[57]

Illustrated books and museum guides played a vital role in the definition and dissemination of an art canon at this time. They began to appear for a mass market from the 1860s, when the introduction of new photomechanical techniques, such as Woodburytype, collotype, photogravure and photolithography, dramatically reduced the cost of printing reproductions in art books compared to the luxury editions of the early nineteenth century with their print engravings of artworks. In the days of black-and-white photography, the best way to reproduce a painting photographically was not directly from the painting, whose colours would create a blurred effect, but from an etching of the work. Photographic albums of engravings sold very well in the 1870s, helping in particular to make the works of Dürer and Rembrandt achieve a canonic status they had not enjoyed before.[58]

Photographic reproductions of the Old Masters appeared in a wide variety of commercial formats – from large prints mounted on card and framed for wall display to postcards, *cartes de visites*, and small photographs for collecting in albums. Picture dealers such as Goupil and Gambart had photographic prints of the great artworks for all budgets. Launched in 1858, Goupil's 'Galerie photographique' offered reproductions of 1,802 paintings in three different editions each by the end of the century. Photographs of the great works of art were popularly sold by subscription. The Russian artist Alexander Benois recalls from his boyhood in the 1870s that 'twice or three times a year' a new Raphael issue would arrive at his home in St Petersburg, where it would be 'greedily perused by the whole family'.[59]

Art periodicals began to appear with photographic illustrations from the 1870s. They quickly found a mass market. *The Picture Gallery* (1872–80), a monthly publication, was said to be 'so much appreciated by the artisan classes in the North of England that there is quite a rush for it on the day that it arrives in one or two of the principal manufacturing towns'.[60]

In France the most popular publication of this sort was the bi-weekly magazine *Galerie contemporaine* (1876–86), published in Paris by Ludovic Baschet, a gallery-owner and artist. It combined photographs and short biographies of literary celebrities with Woodburytypes of artworks exhibited at the Salon. The popularity of the Salon exhibition, which in 1876 had attracted half a million visitors, alerted Baschet to the business potential of cheaply reproducing works from it. Printed by the Goupil company, the photographic reproductions were luxuriously mounted on a board that could be detached from the magazine for collecting and framing. Readers were encouraged to assemble their own private gallery of artworks in their home. The circulation of the *Galerie contemporaine* is not precisely known, but its modest price (1.5 francs per issue) and the fact that up to 50,000 prints could be obtained from a Woodburytype mould suggest that it was sold in tens of thousands of copies. Encouraged by the magazine's success, Baschet launched a cheaper weekly version, *Musée pour tous: Album de l'art contemporain* (1877–9), which usually consisted of four large prints of contemporary works accompanied by a short text about the artist on the facing page. He also published more expensive books with photographic reproductions of the country's most important works of art – those exhibited at the Exposition Universelle in Paris, for example, or the paintings on permanent display in the Musée du Luxembourg, the national collection of contemporary art. By advertising them in his magazine, Baschet's aim was to encourage readers of the *Galerie contemporaine* to graduate to these *éditions-de-luxe*, which offered them a digest of the art canon being formed in museums.[61]

In 1880, Baschet founded his own publishing house, Librairie d'Art Ludovic Baschet, entirely dedicated to art books with photographic illustrations of canonic works of art. He later moved into illustrated guides and catalogues for art museums, galleries and the annual Salon, whose popularity continued to increase. He was one of the first publishers to exploit this new market (the origins of the museum-shop economy of art books and postcards that we know today). He understood the urge of the museum visitor not just to see a masterpiece but, in the later words of Walter Benjamin, to 'get hold' of it and possess it as an object 'by way of its likeness' in a photographic print. Mass reproduction transformed artworks into consumer products or commodities.

The reproduction of artworks began to influence the art canon. Having seen a painting in a museum, people were more likely to buy its reproduction as a souvenir, and if they knew an artwork through a reproduction, they were far more likely to visit a museum to see the original. The layout of museums increasingly reflected this relationship: the best-known works were placed in prime positions and reproductions of them put on sale in the entrance or museum shop. By selecting works of art for reproduction and channelling the flow of readers to museums, publishers like Baschet helped to shape the art canon.

When Turgenev announced his idea of an illustrated library of the Russian classics, he knew that it would mean competing in a crowded market of cheap books for the widest readership. Five years previously, in 1874, Stasiulevich had launched his 'Russian Library' of classic works, including volumes by Pushkin, Lermontov, Gogol, Turgenev and Tolstoy, each priced at seventy-five kopecks, regardless of length or how much it had cost to produce them. It meant that the series was affordable to the newly literate masses of Russia's artisan and working class. The first volume in the series, a collection of Pushkin's stories, appeared in 10,000 copies (all profits from it went to famine relief in the Samara countryside, where there was a harvest failure in 1874). Five years later, at the time of Turgenev's visit to St Petersburg, the publisher Suvorin launched his 'Inexpensive Library' of pocket-sized editions of the Russian and foreign classics, each costing only forty kopecks, which he sold in huge print-runs of up to 100,000 copies through his network of bookshops.[62]

Across Europe publishers were launching mass editions of classic literary works in collectable libraries and series. Cheaply priced, these popular editions became standard items in millions of homes, effectively establishing a European literary canon by the end of the nineteenth century.

This was a competitive market. To keep prices down publishers were forced to concentrate on reprints of classic works, no longer in copyright, which they knew were popular. The pattern had been set by the railway libraries of the 1850s and the cheap mass editions of Routledge, Hachette, Charpentier and Lévy, who explained the business model of his Collection Michel Lévy when he launched the series of one-franc novels in 1856. 'The main interest of the public is the price,' the publisher announced, 'so this is why we have decided to publish only successful works in order to sell more and reduce the price.'[63] From the 1860s a wide range of publishing initiatives aimed to make available the classic works of literature as cheaply as possible. The fiercest rivalry was in Britain, where by the turn of the century five major series (Cassell's National Library, Chandos Classics, Routledge's World Library, Heinemann's International Library and Joseph Dent's Everyman Library) competed for the sixpenny market of paperback classics.

Not all these initiatives were motivated solely by commercial gain. In 1863, for example, a group of printers in Paris formed a non-profit cooperative group to launch the Bibliothèque Nationale, a series of selected classic novels that sold widely until the First World War. The collection's idealistic aim, stated on the back of every cover, was to bring 'the greatest works of literature into the most modest homes'. Its editors selected books for their 'undisputed literary quality' and for their ability to 'form the minds of citizens' – classic works by Molière or Montesquieu but also, and increasingly, books by more modern authors such as Chateaubriand, Michelet and Lamartine.[64]

The Catholic Church was also instrumental in the development of an international book trade, whose main aim was not so much profit as the dissemination of a morally instructive literature, to the young especially, through parochial libraries, religious schools and institutions, and bookshops supported by the Church. The leading Catholic publishers in France and Germany published mass editions of books in series approved by the Church, exporting them in translation to Austria, Croatia, Spain and other Catholic communities with less competitive publishing industries.[65]

In Germany the most successful series of secular canonic literature was the Universal-Bibliothek launched by Anton Reclam in 1867. Its 'classics for the people' with their yellow covers remain popular today. Reclam came from a family of booksellers in Leipzig which had been active in the liberal movement for a united Germany during the 1840s. The publication of improving works at prices which the masses could

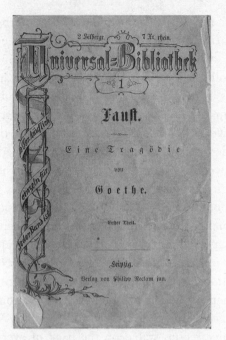

Reclam's edition of Goethe's *Faust*, 1867.

afford was an important part of their political ideals. Reclam's first big series, the Wohlfeile Unterhaltungsbibliothek für die gebildete Lesewelt (Inexpensive Entertainment Library for the Educated Reading World), published sixty volumes between 1844 and 1847. Ten years later the company brought out a German translation of Shakespeare's plays in twelve volumes. But the turning point for the publication of the German classics came in 1867, the so-called 'classic year' when copyright protection was removed from works by authors dead for more than thirty years. The masterpieces of writers such as Schiller, Goethe and Lessing became public property. The market was soon flooded with popular editions of the German classics. But the dominant position of the Universal-Bibliothek was quickly established.

Reclam was able to keep the price of his volumes down to just twenty pfennigs each by saving costs. He reduced the size of the format and printed in a smaller font on thin and cheaper paper. He economized on marketing by advertising the collection as a whole, rather than its individual titles, and by offering discounts to booksellers who took the complete series and displayed it prominently in their shops. Stereotypes

Universal-Bibliothek stock-room, 1930.

were also important. By allowing multiple and quick reprints, they enabled Reclam to reduce wastage by testing out the market with a safe print-run and reprinting if there was a high demand for the title. The first work in the series, Goethe's *Faust*, for example, appeared in two volumes in November 1867 with an initial printing of 5,000 copies. It sold out in four weeks. A reprint of the same size was released in December, followed by a third, of 10,000 copies, in February 1868. The Universal-Bibliothek was so successful that eighty titles were added every year in the 1870s, rising to 140 a year in the next decade. By 1896, the year of Reclam's death, the series had 3,470 titles. No other publisher had done more to make the literary canon so accessible, nor to modernize the publishing and marketing of books. By the First World War the Universal-Bibliothek was selling 1.5 million copies every year in automatic vending machines (similar to modern drink and snack machines) situated in more than a thousand railway stations, hospitals, schools, parks and squares.[66]

In the Habsburg lands and countries such as Italy and Spain, where literacy levels were lower than in Britain, France or Germany, popular editions of the classics were important in extending readership, especially among the young. In Budapest the Universal Novel Library and Illustrated Library of Master Authors published dozens of standard works during the 1880s. In Prague the Zlata Library brought out fifty-seven volumes of translated classics, including novels by Dickens, Twain, Kipling, Flaubert and Balzac, between 1892 and 1911. In Madrid the Biblioteca Universal had over seventy volumes, half of them translations, in 1881. Children's books were the best sellers. The literate population was young in countries such as Spain and Italy, where many publishers were kept in profit by children's libraries. The most popular translations were classics such as *Robinson Crusoe*, *The Last of the Mohicans*, *Journey to the Centre of the Earth* and *Around the World in Eighty Days*.[67]

Literacy rates were rising fast across Europe. This was the underlying base of the boom in cheap book publishing during the last decades of the nineteenth century. In Italy the literate proportion of the population grew from 25 per cent to 50 per cent between 1861 and 1901, largely as a result of free and compulsory primary education, introduced from 1877, though a large gap remained between the north and south (82 per cent were literate in Piedmont but only 21 per cent in Calabria in 1901). In Spain the rate of literacy increased from 20 per cent in 1857 to 46 per cent in 1913, with the highest rates of growth in Barcelona and Madrid. In Britain, France and Germany more than four fifths of the population was considered literate by the 1880s. Among the young the rate was even higher after the introduction of free and universal primary schooling.[68]

Schools played a key role in establishing a canon of literary works. The idea that children should be made to read a list of classic books was taken up by teachers' groups, educators and governments across Europe. It was widely held that reading the exemplary works of a nation's literature would instil patriotic values in schoolchildren, encouraging them to take pride in its language and heroes. Literary anthologies were carefully selected to promote these principles. In Germany, where books for schools were regulated by the state, publishers were issued a mandatory list of German poems to be included in anthologies (Goethe, Schiller, Lessing and Uhland were at the top of it) for pupils to learn by heart. The list of writers appearing in these school anthologies was remarkably stable between the 1890s and the 1910s, with only one or two relatively recent authors (such as Storm and Fontane) allowed to enter it in the years before the First World War.[69]

In France the Ferry laws established state control of the school curriculum. Schools were instructed to teach a list of classic works, which appeared in all the government-approved school manuals and anthologies. There were around a hundred authors on this list in 1882, but only thirty on the literature curriculum, and just thirteen on the programme of the *baccalauréat*. In Britain, too, there was a growing emphasis on teaching children the classics of English literature. School editions of these works appeared, along with anthologies, such as *The First Sketch of English Literature*, which was almost ubiquitous in schools. Although the British state was less interventionist than the French, the Mundella Code, issued by the government Committee on Education, obliged school inspectors to listen to all pupils reading individually from children's classics, such as *Robinson Crusoe* (1719) by Daniel Defoe and *Tales From Shakespeare* (1807) by Charles and Mary Lamb.[70]

The growth of public libraries was equally important in disseminating the canon, especially in smaller towns and rural settlements, where libraries were more likely to carry only the classics: the smaller the collection the more canonical it was.[71] The 1880s were a turning point in the development of the public library movement throughout Europe. In the middle decades of the nineteenth century, European states had taken little interest in libraries. It was left to philanthropic bodies to raise the funds for public reading rooms and libraries, which grew in number slowly and sporadically. Even in Britain, where the Public Libraries Act of 1850 had allowed municipal authorities to collect a penny rate for libraries, only a handful of the country's boroughs had established one in the Act's first twenty years. Attitudes were changed by the introduction of compulsory primary schooling: once it became clear that a whole new generation of the lower classes would be literate, governments and public bodies became more involved in the establishment of libraries, mainly out of concern to influence what people read.

Britain took the lead. After the passing of the Education Act in 1870 – the first legislative step towards compulsory primary schooling – the public-library movement grew with the support of local government, public bodies and philanthropists, such as Andrew Carnegie, who endowed many of the country's smaller libraries. Between 1870 and

1890 there was an almost eightfold increase in the number of free libraries in England (from fifty-two to 408), most of the growth in the 1880s in small county libraries, and by the eve of the First World War 62 per cent of the population lived within a library authority.[72]

In France there was a threefold rise in the number of public libraries (from 773 to 2,991) between 1874 and 1902. The greatest increase took place in small and medium-sized towns, where most of the country's population lived. Places such as Firminy (with 17,000 inhabitants), Rive-de-Gier (15,000) and Beaune (12,000) got their first free public library after 1885, though none had more than 1,500 books.[73] Much of the initiative came from philanthropic organizations such as the Bibliothèques des Amis de l'Instruction, established in 1861 by the printer Jean-Baptiste Girard, whose declared, rather hopeful aim was to wean the labouring classes off the cabaret by opening libraries for them.

The public-library movement was slower to develop in the rest of Europe. But everywhere it gathered pace from the 1880s, as public groups became more active in pushing for the opening of libraries. In Germany there was the Verein für Förderung der Volksbildung (Society for the Promotion of Popular Education), which opened some 200 rural libraries; in Transylvania the *Kulturvereine*, which organized a hundred libraries in the German-speaking towns; in Holland the Vereeniging voor Volksbibliotheken; and in Italy the Società Promotrice delle Biblioteche Popolari, which opened 540 public libraries between 1867 and 1893. The socialist movement was also very active in promoting workers' libraries, especially in Germany, where the Social Democrats built a vast network of 1,147 *Arbeiterbibliotheken* with a total stock of 833,857 books before 1914.[74]

Public libraries were concerned to ensure that their readers had 'good' books. They were mostly organized by philanthropic groups that believed in wholesome reading as a means of popular enlightenment. Many published lists of recommended books to guide librarians. The Société Franklin, for example, a close ally of the Bibliothèques des Amis de l'Instruction, released annual catalogues of morally improving literature, which it believed should form the core collection of every public library. Its catalogues of the 1860s were seriously classical: Corneille, Molière, Racine, Cervantes, Shakespeare and Schiller, but no contemporary novelists, not even Hugo or Balzac. By 1883, the catalogue had become more permissive, including 'modern classics' such as

Scott, Dickens, Balzac, Hugo, Sand, Dumas (*père* and *fils*) and Gogol. A similar change was noted in the catalogues of other library societies: the Bibliothèque du Cercle Girondin and the Ligue de l'Enseignement, whose catalogues of 1892 included for the first time works by Stendhal, Hugo, Flaubert, Zola and Maupassant.[75] Public libraries were clearly being forced to think in terms of the market, to select books that were not only classic but also popular. They were recognizing that a nineteenth-century canon had been formed.

5

On his return to Russia, in 1879, Turgenev had negotiated a new contract for his collected works. Three editions had been published previously by the Salaev company in Moscow – the first (in five volumes) in 1865, the second (in eight) in 1868–71, and the third (in nine) in 1874–5. They had earned Turgenev a good income, around 6,000 roubles (24,000 francs) annually, enough to overcome the losses he made on his estates and help to provide a comfortable existence for himself and the Viardots. As a writer Turgenev had attained canonic status in Russia, and there was a large and growing market for complete editions of his works. The sudden death of Turgenev's brother, which had prompted his return to Russia, made Turgenev think more carefully about the need to put his affairs in order. The contract with Salaev was due to expire when the printed copies of the third edition had sold out. He was anxious to negotiate a new edition, either with Salaev or another publisher, that would yield a long-term income for Pauline and his daughter after his own death.

The contract he proposed to Salaev shows how businesslike he had become in his literary affairs. Setting out his terms to the Moscow publisher, Turgenev acted like a modern agent, using offers from other publishers to negotiate a higher advance against future royalties. He demanded to be paid a royalty of 25 per cent of the sale price (between fifteen and eighteen roubles for the nine volumes, according to the paper quality).* From a first print-run of 5,500 copies, he stood to earn between 20,000 and 23,000 roubles (80,000–92,000 francs), one third

---

* A higher royalty than earned today by most writers.

paid on his signature of the contract, the remainder two years after-wards. He excluded from the contract any rights to *Sketches from a Hunter's Album*, Turgenev's highest-earning work, which he published separately in a popular edition the next year, although it had been included in the previous editions of his collected works.[76]

Turgenev was not satisfied with Salaev. There were too many errors in the third edition of his works. On 13 May 1882, he wrote to his old friend Annenkov appointing him his literary executor and instructing him to find a publisher willing to pay a large capital sum in advance for the outright purchase of his copyright.[77]

Turgenev needed money to support his daughter and her two small children, who were now his dependants. Paulinette had fled from her husband, Gaston, whose factory in Rougement had gone bankrupt, after he had started drinking heavily and had threatened to kill her. 'Every day I am expecting her to arrive here with her children,' Turgenev wrote to Annenkov from Paris on 25 February. 'I will need to keep her hidden until I can organize the séparation de corps et de biens – and so once again I need to get my hands on cash. I have sold my beloved Rousseau [painting], I will sell my horse, my carriage, and so on.' Paulinette arrived a fortnight later. She was terrified of being tracked down by Gaston, who by law could take the children. For their safety, Turgenev sent them with a chaperone to Solothurn in Switzerland, where he paid their board at the Hotel La Couronne and sent them a monthly allowance, which Paulinette complained was not enough.[78]

Turgenev's main concern – and the real reason why he needed to negotiate a large advance – was to leave Pauline with an inheritance when he died. He was sixty-four. His health had been poor for several years. Gout, rheumatic pains, problems with his bladder, stomach and liver – these had aged him terribly in the 1870s. His illness became more acute in the spring of 1882, around the time when he appointed Annenkov his literary executor. His back, chest and shoulders were in constant pain (a symptom of the undetected cancer of the spine that would kill him) and the gout became so painful that he could barely stand without crutches. Confined to bed for days on end, he had hallucinations. At times he would talk in a fevered state of half-madness, perhaps an effect of the morphine he took to relieve the pain. Convinced that he was about to die, Turgenev added an amendment to his will on 15 May: he left all his property in France and his literary earnings to the Viardots, stipulating only that his manuscripts and letters were to go to Annenkov.[79]

Turgenev's will was to be one of the main reasons why his friends and admirers in Russia became so hostile to Pauline. The Russians were resentful that their great writer lived abroad, and blamed her for his absence. Rumours spread that she was keeping him from returning, that he was her prisoner. Such malicious gossip was reinforced by the reports of those Russians who had called on Turgenev in Bougival or Paris, only to be turned away by Pauline because he was too sick to receive them. Even some who did see him were determined to believe that he was mistreated by the Viardots ('It was painful and offensive to see this great man dying in a foreign land among foreign people indifferent to his suffering,' wrote Princess Tenisheva on visiting Turgenev at Bougival in the spring of 1882).[80] It was put about that Pauline was trying to kill him, or have him declared mad, so that she could get her hands on his inheritance. Turgenev's failure to visit Russia in the summer of 1882, as he had planned, was seen as further evidence of his being kept in France against his will.

Disappointed not to see his estate one last time, Turgenev wrote a farewell letter to the Spasskoe peasants which serves as a testament to the benevolent paternalism of his liberal gentry class:

> Rumours have reached me that for some time much less vodka is being drunk in your village; I am very glad of it and I hope that you will keep on abstaining from drink: drunkenness spells ruin for the peasant. But I am sorry to hear that your children do not go to school regularly. Remember that today an illiterate person is worse than a blind or an armless one. As in former years, I am presenting you with an acre of woodland. I am confident that you will do no harm to my house or to my park or, generally, to my estate, and I rely on you to see to it. And now, peasants of Spasskoe, let me say goodbye to you all and wish you every prosperity. Your former landlord.

Gloomy and depressed, Turgenev began a journal of his illness and treatment. He called it 'My Death Roll'. The doctors were unable to decide what his illness was. The famous Paris surgeon and neurologist Jean-Martin Charcot diagnosed a heart disease, angina pectoris, brought on by his gout. He thought there was not much he could do, but prescribed a lengthy stay in bed with a course of cauterization with a Paquelin machine (used for electroshock therapy). A second doctor, Paul Segond, advised country air and encouraged the sick man to wear a Pulvermacher chain – a copper-and-zinc belt run by a voltaic battery that was widely advertised in magazines and newspapers to help relieve rheumatic pain by electrotherapy.* In addition to the Pulvermacher chain Turgenev used a Baunscheidts Lebenswecker, or 'Life-Awakener', the invention of a German specialist in nervous disorders, which was said to ease rheumatic pain by shooting needles into the affected area by a pump action. The celebrated Swiss physician François-Sigismond Jaccoud, who came to see Turgenev in July, put him on a strict milk diet, which Turgenev ignored, until a month later, when the prescription was confirmed by L. G. Bertenson, a distinguished Russian physician, who saw him on a visit to Paris. None of these quack remedies had much effect. Only morphine brought relief from the cancer pain.

In January 1883, Turgenev was subjected to an operation to remove a lump from his lower abdomen misdiagnosed by seven doctors as a neuroma requiring urgent removal. To avoid risking what they also wrongly thought was a weak heart, they carried out the operation without a general anaesthetic. Turgenev's abdomen was frozen with ether before the knife cut into it and a cyst, the size of a walnut, was excised. 'During the operation,' Turgenev later wrote to Daudet, 'I thought about our dinners and looked for words to give you an accurate impression of the sensation of the steel cutting through my flesh – just as a knife would cut through a banana.' The operation brought no improvement to Turgenev's condition. It was not even clear if the tumour had been malignant. It took weeks for the wound to heal. His pain got worse. He became dependent on morphine, began to over-dose, and had frequent paranoid delusions and thoughts of suicide, probably the effect of too many drugs. In one of his fits in the middle of the night he demanded to be given poison, accused those closest to him of plotting to kill him, and said that Pauline, who had heard his screams and hurried to his room, was a monster worse than Lady Macbeth. Perhaps in his fevered state he thought that he was seeing her in the sleepwalking scene of Verdi's opera, one of her most celebrated roles.

---

* At the end of *Madame Bovary*, the pharmacist, Monsieur Homais, a keen follower of new discoveries, takes to wearing the galvanic chain, stunning Madame Homais when he undresses to reveal 'the golden spiral' underneath his flannel vest.

In one of his saner moments, around 20 April, Turgenev asked to be transferred to Bougival. He wanted to die in his dacha there. On 28 April, he was fit to travel. Carried on a stretcher from his rooms on the second floor, he was greeted on the first-floor landing by Louis, partly paralysed from a recent stroke, who was brought out in a wheelchair to say farewell. The two men embraced.[81]

A week later, on 5 May, Louis died from a second stroke.[82] He was eighty-two years old. 'His final moments were those of a sage,' Pauline wrote to her brother-in-law, Léon Viardot, on 21 May. 'He sensed death approach and welcomed it as if to smile at those around him whom he loved. He died without suffering, adored by his family and friends, respected by everyone.' Louis was buried in the Montmartre cemetery. There was no religious ceremony, as Louis had insisted from his atheist convictions, and there were few obituaries in the Paris press. The republican activist, editor, opera director, Spanish scholar, critic, writer and literary translator, art expert and collector – perhaps the closest thing to a nineteenth-century 'Renaissance Man' – was already a forgotten man.

Louis's death made Turgenev even more determined to secure a legacy for Pauline and the Viardot children. He had become increasingly impatient with Annenkov's efforts to negotiate an outright sale of his copyright for a lump sum. He was keen to have a contract for a posthumous edition of his works to be published on his death, and wanted an advance of 60,000 roubles (240,000 francs) for this edition – enough to guarantee Pauline's financial security. Turgenev must have calculated that a lump sum would be easier for her – both financially and legally – than an income from his royalties. Frustrated with Annenkov, Turgenev reassigned the task to Alexander Toporov, his amanuensis in St Petersburg, whom Savina described as 'like an icon-lamp ever burning before Turgenev'. Stasiulevich, who visited Turgenev in July, noted with surprise how seriously he was taking the issue, for he had known him as a man who had always looked on his literary rights with careless indifference and naivety. Eventually, in August 1883, Toporov struck a deal with the publisher I. I. Glazunov in the Russian capital. Turgenev's copyright was sold outright to Glazunov for 80,000 roubles (320,000 francs) – a sum equivalent to his literary earnings for eleven years, according to the writer's calculations in 1882. Turgenev was delighted. In one of his final letters (number 6,173 of the 6,175 published in the

Soviet edition of his works) he wrote in gratitude to Glazunov, expressing his relief that he had found a publisher to secure his literary inheritance.

By this stage Turgenev was too weak to hold a pen. Most of his letters were dictated to Pauline or Louise Arnholt, the Viardots' housekeeper, who nursed him in these final weeks. But there were days when he felt well enough to get up from his deathbed, go outside a little, and even scratch a few lines in his own hand. On one such day, 11 July, he wrote in pencil to Tolstoy to tell him he was dying, that he was happy to have lived at the same time as him, and 'to express to you my last request. My friend, return to literary activity. After all, this is your gift, from which everything else comes. Oh, how happy I would be, if I were able to believe that my request had some influence on you.'[83]

Turgenev's literary activities consisted of one more short story, 'Un fin' (An End), written just two weeks before he died. The story had been germinating in his head for a long time but he was too weak to write it down, so he asked Pauline to help him. She proposed that he dictate the story to her in Russian, a language she could write, if he was prepared to be patient. But Turgenev was afraid that, if it was in Russian, he would want to stop at every phrase to give it better shape, at every word to search for a better expression. He was too weak for that, the work would be exhausting, and he needed his ideas recorded more quickly. On Turgenev's suggestion the story was dictated in the various languages they both knew – French, German, Spanish, English and Italian with bits of Russian in between – and then turned by Pauline into French for Turgenev to review.[84] Its composition was a fitting symbol of the cosmopolitan culture they had both promoted all their lives.

In these final days and nights Pauline and her daughters, Marianne and Claudie, were at Turgenev's bedside constantly. Even Paul and Louise arrived in Bougival to help. There was a steady trail of Russian visitors who came to say farewell – Bogoliubov, Prince Meshchersky, Vereshchagin, who found Turgenev looking like a ghost, pale and withered, his eyes sunken in a face he barely recognized.

The end came on Monday 3 September. The Viardots were grouped around Turgenev's bed. His daughter was not there. She could not arrive in time from Switzerland. She had been warned of the possibility that he might die 'at any moment' by telegram only on the morning of his death. Given morphine to relieve the pain, Turgenev started talking in various languages, French, German, English, but mainly in Russian. The time, he said, had come to 'say farewell like the Russian Tsars'. In his delirium he kept repeating the name of Tsar Aleksei and then, as if trying to correct himself, said 'the second', possibly his effort to say the name of Alexander II, the emancipator of the serfs. Pauline bent down to kiss the dying man. Recognizing her, he became animated and said: 'There is the Tsarina of Tsarinas, how much good she has done!' He then began to mutter senselessly in Russian, imagining himself to be a dying peasant saying farewell to his family. According to Meshchersky, who was there, his last words in Russian were: 'Farewell my dear ones, my whitish ones!' He then slipped away into unconsciousness. He died at 2 p.m. on the next day.[85]

As soon as the body had been washed and dressed in clean linen, photographers and artists were summoned to make images of the dead man's face for release to the newspapers. By 5 p.m. the photographer, Morel, had arrived from the Paris studio Photographie Anonyme. He took several portraits from various angles, which soon began to circulate for sale as postcards both in Paris and in St Petersburg. The sculptor Pierre-Nicolas Tourgueneff, a distant relative of the writer, made a death mask of the head as well a model of his left, non-writing, hand (the fingers of his right hand had become too twisted in his agony to be usable). Pauline and Claudie both made sketches of Turgenev's face. Contorted with pain at the moment of his death, the face gradually relaxed into a more peaceful expression. According to Stasiulevich, 'he had never looked so beautiful nor so great in his lifetime'. Once the signs of suffering had passed, his face took on the heroic 'image of a deep thinker with unusual energy, which, when he was alive, had not been apparent because of the dominating kindness in his face and his readiness to smile at any time'. Stasiulevich was so impressed by one of Claudie's sketches, which had captured this expression, that he begged her to allow him to publish it in Russia as a gift from those Turgenev loved in France.[86]

Pauline was devastated by Turgenev's death. In a matter of a few months she had lost the two men in her life. 'Ah, my friend,' she wrote to Pietsch on 8 September, 'it is too much, too much suffering for one heart. I don't understand why mine has not broken.' To the composer Ambroise Thomas she wrote on the same day: 'I have lost my dearest friend. We awaited with terror the approaching end, but at the same time we took it as deliverance because the sick man's suffering was intolerable . . . His death resembled that of my dearly beloved husband, and as a result I have experienced a double agony.'[87]

There was a funeral service at the Russian Orthodox church in the rue Daru on 7 September. Placed before the altar, the coffin was covered with wreaths and surrounded by foliage. The candlelit church was packed. Among the mourners were many of the leading figures in French cultural life – Renan, Saint-Saëns, Daudet, Massenet, About, Goncourt – as well as Russians of every social class, from Prince Orlov, conspicuous in full court uniform with a ribbon and star on his chest, to poor Russian students and artists, 'many of them nihilists and revolutionaries', according to the French police, which had its secret agents in the church. Goncourt noted how the ceremony had 'brought out from the houses of Paris a whole little world of flat-faced giants with beards like the Almighty'.[88]

Turgenev had made it clear that he wanted to be buried in Russia. A week before his death he told Meshchersky and Stasiulevich that his ideal would be to rest at the feet of his 'teacher' Pushkin, whose grave was in the cemetery of the Svyatogorsk Monastery near Pskov, but since he felt unworthy of that honour he would like to be buried near his friend Belinsky in the Volkovo Cemetery in St Petersburg.[89] It was a surprising choice. Belinsky had championed Turgenev's early work and influenced his realist approach to literature, but Turgenev had not been the best or closest friend to him, and at times had sacrificed their friendship to his obsession with Pauline. In 1847, when Belinsky was dying from tuberculosis in Paris, Turgenev reneged on his promise to help him back to Russia, and even failed to drag himself away from the Viardots in Courtavenel to make the short journey to Paris to say farewell. Perhaps he was tormented by remorse over the way he had treated Belinsky, who died without Turgenev seeing him again. But this hardly seems a likely reason for his decison, more than thirty years later, to be buried near the famous critic, who had defined the realist principles of Russian literature. Pushkin, after all, was his first choice. By asking to be buried near Belinsky, he was surely thinking of his place in Russia's literary pantheon.

Stasiulevich was placed in charge of the arrangements for Turgenev's burial. There were endless obstacles: long delays in getting permission to remove the body, which required a passport to leave France;

drawn-out exchanges with the city *duma* in St Petersburg, which could not decide whether they would pay for the funeral of a man who was alleged to have had leftist sympathies, a controversy ignited by the Russian publication of an interview with Lavrov, the exiled revolutionary, who told a Paris newspaper that Turgenev had subsidized his paper *Forward* (*Vpered*);* more hold-ups when Pushkin's ring, which was supposed to be worn by Turgenev on his journey back to Russia, was withdrawn by its donor, Pavel Zhukovsky, who had suddenly decided to hold on to it, necessitating delicate approaches by Pauline to persuade him to honour his promise. There were even problems finding space for Turgenev's grave in the Volkovo Cemetery, all the places near Belinsky having been already occupied. The tsarist authorities proposed exhuming Belinsky's remains and reburying them in a new location with Turgenev's, but Belinsky's widow objected, so more time was lost until an alternative was found. All this while, Turgenev's body was held in the basement of the Russian church.[90]

Pauline decided not to travel with Turgenev's body to Russia. Her daughter Claudie went instead with her husband, George. In a letter to Stasiulevich Pauline explained her decision by citing unspecific 'business problems' which she said had forced her to remain in Paris: 'otherwise I would have gone with my children to see dear Russia once again and bring back the precious remains of my best friend, the great man we are all mourning.' Perhaps she took Turgenev's own advice to her, a few years earlier, in one of his *Poems in Prose*, 'When I am No More' (December 1878), which began:

> When I am no more, when everything I once was has crumbled into dust – oh you, my only friend, you, whom I loved so deeply and so tenderly, you who will surely survive me – do not go to my grave . . . There will be nothing for you to do there.[91]

On the other hand, Pauline's failure to return with his body to Russia could be seen to justify the disappointment Turgenev had expressed in the poem he had read to Savina – the poem that had told the story of a great love for a woman 'who would not bring one little flower or shed a single tear on the writer's grave'.

---

* The city duma voted 3,000 roubles towards the costs of the funeral, but the city mayor lodged a protest, and the question was disputed for the best part of the next ten years.

His return to Russia started at the Gare du Nord on 3 October. Turgenev would make his last journey across Europe on a passenger train. His coffin had a wagon of its own. The floor was strewn with flowers, its inside walls were covered with black cloth on which were hung many wreaths. A white sash with 'Les Frênes' – the name of the dacha he had built in Bougival – inscribed in gold was draped over the coffin. At its head was a large green wreath from 'La famille Viardot'. On the platform by the carriage a temporary chapel was constructed where a farewell service, organized by Pauline, was attended by 400 guests, including Renan, Zola, Daudet, Jules Simon and Pierre-Jules Hetzel, Turgenev's publisher, as well as the Viardots. A choir performed Russian sacred music, which made a deep impression on the congregation, especially the French, according to Prince Obolensky, who was among the Russians there. Renan led the eulogies, paying homage to Turgenev as a man and writer, the moral conscience of his nation, and as a citizen of Europe too. When all was said and done, the mourners stepped back, Stasiulevich, who would travel with the coffin, climbed into a first-class carriage, and the train set off.[92]

At every station on its journey across Europe crowds turned out to honour Turgenev. In Berlin, where his entry into Europe had begun, a large congregation of passengers assembled spontaneously around the funeral carriage, where a priest appeared to bless the coffin before it left on its way to Vilnius and St Petersburg. The German train went as far as the small town of Verzhbolovo, on the border with Russia, where it arrived in the early morning of 6 October. All night in the wind and rain huge crowds had been waiting at the station to greet the writer back on Russian soil. The local priest performed a service with thanksgiving prayers, and wreaths were laid by a dozen delegations, including one from the Tsar's customs officers. The authorities were worried about the possibility of Turgenev's funeral train giving rise to protests on its passage through Russia. The assassination of Alexander II by revolutionaries, in 1881, had made them wary of any public gathering. Police repressions were being carried out on the orders of the new Tsar, Alexander III, who had insisted that a demonstration of respect for Turgenev should be taken as a sign of opposition to the government – an idea encouraged by his reactionary advisers, who exploited Lavrov's revelations to reinforce the regime's anti-liberal policies. At every station between Verzhbolovo and St Petersburg they stopped the train for inspection (God knows what they were expecting to find) and put on guards to accompany the coffin as far as the next station. There was a frantic exchange of telegrams between stationmasters, local governors and the Ministry of the Interior, as the train progressed towards the capital. The Russian press was forbidden by the Tsar to publish details about where the train would stop, or what time it would arrive.[93]

Even so, the crowds turned out. At Kovno they waited all night in the station hall, where they were confined by the police. But, when the train arrived in the early morning, they broke through the cordon and ran towards the funeral carriage, where wreaths were placed in the wagon and a service carried out by priests. At Vilnius the platform was already packed with people – many holding wreaths and portraits of Turgenev – when the passenger train pulled in. At Dinaburg there was such a throng of mourners by Turgenev's carriage that Stasiulevich became concerned that people would be pushed onto the tracks beneath the train. Delegations had arrived with wreaths from every section of the town's population – from a girls' high school, a musical society, the *zemstvo* board, firefighters and librarians. At Pskov, where the train arrived in the pouring rain at 2 a.m. on 9 October, there was a massive crowd headed by a delegation of the city's leaders with a wreath 'From the people of Pskov', which they laid by the coffin in a funeral service led by priests. 'Nowhere else was Turgenev's body honoured with such passion,' Stasiulevich observed in a letter to his wife, 'if you think about the time of our arrival, the miserable weather, and the distance from the town to the station [over two kilometres].' At Gatchina, seven hours later, the entire town appeared to have turned out in the morning sun. The platform was filled by a dense mass of humanity. At the spot where the funeral carriage stopped there were waiting a delegation of schoolchildren, a church choir and some priests, who tried to climb into the wagon and perform the liturgy in the brief time before the train continued on its journey to St Petersburg. They did not succeed.[94]

In St Petersburg, where the train arrived on time, at 10.20 a.m., at the Warsaw Station, the authorities had better control of the demonstrations of mourning. The public had been cleared from the platforms. Only a small delegation of priests and officials from the funeral commission was allowed to meet the train. Following a solemn mass, the wooden coffin was carried from the station and placed on a hearse draped in white and golden cloth. The coffin was covered with wreaths, and a portrait of Turgenev placed on top of it along with a silver cross. The procession then began. The hearse was followed by 178 delegations from literary, theatrical, artistic, academic, professional, national, civic and many other bodies, each bearing wreaths with suitable inscriptions and many also carrying portraits of the dead writer. Behind them a long line of priests and monks completed the procession, which took three hours to finish its progress through St Petersburg to the Volkovo Cemetery. Despite a heavy police presence, there was an enormous crowd, around 400,000 people, who lined the streets along the route. Claudie walked behind the hearse. She wrote to Pauline later on that day:

> George and three venerable old gentlemen walked at the four corners of the hearse. I was placed directly behind it with the grand wreath of Les Frênes carried by four young men, then the literary groups, the delegates, committee members, people bearing tickets allowing them to enter the church, then a very colourful tail of people. Mounted police and armed Cossacks rode alongside the procession. The size of the crowd along the streets, on balconies, at windows, right up to the roof of every house from the station to the church, was too great to say; several hundred thousand Russians bowed their heads and crossed themselves as the body passed. It was truly grandiose.

At the Volkovo Cemetery access to the funeral service was severely limited. The place was teeming with police agents. But the service ran its course with due solemnity and dignity. Poems were composed for the occasion and read out in the church. Speeches were given by the writer Dimitry Grigorovich, an old friend of Turgenev, and by the rector of the university. Then, at the graveside, as Pauline read in Claudie's letter,

> The coffin was gently lowered onto a bed of flowers at the bottom of the grave. Around it stood the numerous delegations with their offerings, a student choir sang, then the priests arrived to say a final prayer, and three short eulogies were given. Someone pointed out to us a group of peasants from Spasskoe who had come to say a last farewell to their liberator.[95]

Epilogue

'The rest of my life will be without happiness,' Pauline wrote to Ludwig Pietsch on the death of Turgenev. 'I will abandon myself to the bitter joy of memories.' She was in a desperate state, according to Louise, who explained this by the death of her father, omitting any mention of her mother's other loss. Pauline tried to kill herself by jumping from a window. For several weeks her children kept her under watch and put a lock on the windows. She said her life was now over (she was sixty-two), that what remained of it was no more than an epilogue.[1]

Pauline lived for another twenty-seven years. She led a full and busy life. In 1884, she sold the house in the rue de Douai and moved into an apartment near the National Assembly, at 243 boulevard Saint Germain, which she filled with the antique furniture and ornaments she had collected all her life.* The top-floor flat was light and spacious with a marvellous view across the place de la Concorde towards the Champs-Elysées.

Pauline's singing days were long over but she continued to compose,

* Much of the collection was sold by auction at the Hôtel Drouot on 28–29 January 1890 – perhaps a sign that Pauline needed cash, or perhaps that she decided to live without the memories these items meant for her. The sale catalogue included: a Louis XIV sofa and four chairs in blue velvet with ivory; a large Louis XIV wooden table with marble; Louis XIV-style consoles; candelabras in the Louis XIV style; tables, armchairs, sofas in the Louis XVI style; mirrors in the Louis XIII style; heavy window drapes in blue velvet; silk curtains in red and white stripes; bedroom furniture in a Chinese style; oriental carpets; Belgian tapestries; Venetian glass; Delft vases; an English billiard table; bronze sculptures representing hunting scenes; bronze and wooden busts; stained-glass windows; a screen of wood and glass made by Pauline; a Pleyel upright piano and an Érard grand piano; and a vintage wine collection with a thousand bottles, dating back to the 1870s (BMO, LA-VIARDOT PAULINE-5).

Pauline Viardot on her balcony in Boulevard Saint-Germain, Paris, c. 1900.

mainly for her own amusement and the pleasure of her friends, although some works, notably *Le Rêve de Jésus* (1892), a music drama, were publicly performed.[2] She also went on teaching until the end of her life. Among the hundreds of pupils she had taught were the great contralto Marianne Brandt (1842–1921), celebrated for her interpretation of Wagnerian roles; the French contralto Jeanne Gerville-Riache (1882–1915), who in her short but brilliant career sang the part of Geneviève in the first performance of Debussy's *Pelléas* et *Mélisande* (1902); the Hungarian soprano Aglaja Orgeni (1841–1926), who after a long career of singing mainly in Italian opera became a renowned teacher at the Dresden Royal Conservatory; and the soprano Margarethe Siems (1879–1952), a student of Orgeni as well as of Viardot, who was best known for her creation of three leading roles in the first performances of three operas by Richard Strauss: Chrysothemis in *Elektra* (1909), the Marschallin in *Der Rosenkavalier* (1911) and Zerbinetta in *Ariadne auf Naxos* (1912).

Pauline's apartment was an active centre of music life in Paris. She kept up her tradition of hosting concerts on Thursday evenings where her pupils could perform. Massenet, Saint-Saëns, Fauré, Franck, Chabrier and Delibes were regular visitors. In 1886, Saint-Saëns arranged for an ensemble of his friends to give a private concert of *Le Carnaval des animaux* for Liszt, then with just a few months left to live, who made a rare appearance at Pauline's house. The next year, a visitor from Norway, Edvard Grieg, played an arrangement of his Piano Concerto. It was the first time the piece was performed in France.

Tchaikovsky also visited. He had been aware of Pauline's role as a promoter of his works in France since the 1870s, but it was not until his stay in Paris in the summer of 1886 that he finally decided to call on her. He appeared on 12 June with the cellist Anatoly Brandukov. Caught in a storm on their way, they arrived drenched, but, as Tchaikovsky noted in his diary, 'the circumstances made it easier for us to become acquainted'. He was enchanted by the 'little mother [mamasha] Viardot', as he described her in a letter to his brother: 'during the three hours I spent at her house I must have kissed her hand about a dozen times.' She was 'such a wonderful and interesting woman', he reported to his sister-in-law. 'In spite of her seventy years, she comes across as a woman of forty. She is so full of energy, takes an interest in everything, knows about everything, and is extremely kind,' he enthused. Tchaikovsky was excited to have seen the *Don Giovanni* manuscript, which Pauline kept in its presentation box on a table in her living room (in 1892 she donated the score to the Paris Conservatory). Tchaikovsky noted in his diary: 'Saw the orchestra score of Mozart's *Don Giovanni*, written IN HIS OWN HAND ! ! ! ! ! ! ! ! !' The composer was enthralled by Pauline's talk of Turgenev, a writer he had always loved but never met. Asked by his patron Nadezhda von Meck whether Pauline recalled Turgenev, Tchaikovsky replied: 'I can assure you that not only does she remember him, but we spent almost all the time talking about him, and she told me in detail how together they wrote [the story] *The Song of Triumphant Love*.' Shortly afterwards, Tchaikovsky read the story and made some sketches for a vocal composition based on it, though he never completed the work.[3]

There was a steady stream of visitors from Russia. They wanted information about Turgenev, asked for his possessions, wanted interviews about his private life. For them Pauline was important only as the 'mistress' of 'their' writer. The Russians were hostile to Pauline, despite her considerable efforts to promote Russian music in Europe (which she would continue long after Turgenev's death) and her generous decision to return to Russia a number of his possessions – including a case and ring that had belonged to Pushkin and Kharlamov's portrait of Turgenev – which he had bequeathed to her.[4] They accused her of depriving Russia of its great writer, of corrupting him by keeping him in Europe through her malign influence. Even Russians in Paris who had once been her friends would turn against Viardot. Among them was Lopatin, who had set up the Russian Reading Room with Turgenev and been many times in Pauline's house, where she gave concerts to raise funds for them. 'For the Russians,' Lopatin later claimed, 'there is a marked difference between Turgenev's works before he met her and those afterwards. Before they contained the people – after they did not. She took the Russian out of him.'[5]

Bogoliubov was one of the few Russians to defend Pauline. Writing on Turgenev's death, he reminded his compatriots that it was she, not they, who had sat by his bed during the last months of his terrible illness, and warned that they were not to judge: 'Turgenev and Viardot did not lead the lives of ordinary people. They were united by their spiritual qualities . . . in ways that are not our business.' As one might expect, Pauline was spirited in her own defence. She told Bogoliubov:

> By what right do the so-called friends of Turgenev take it on themselves to condemn him and me for our relationship? Every person is born free, and their actions, provided they do not cause harm, are not subject to the judgement of anybody else. Our feelings and actions were based on rules accepted by ourselves, not understood by the crowd, nor indeed by many people considered by themselves to be decent and intelligent . . . We understood each other much too well to care what other people said of us, for those who really knew and loved us both recognized the rules that bound us.[6]

Part of this resentment of Pauline was based on the assumption that she was the sole inheritor of Turgenev's property and literary estate, thus depriving Russia of its due. The idea went back to the writer's final illness, when he had made an amendment to his will bequeathing his property in France and his literary earnings to Pauline. Reports circulated in Russia that Viardot had made him change his will, that she was keeping him a prisoner in France so that she could further pressure him to sell his lands at Spasskoe and leave her the cash from those as well. The rumour gained in currency as old friends of Turgenev complained on his death that they had not been left anything: the writer Polonsky made a fuss on this account, claming that his wife had been held in affection by Turgenev but forgotten in his will.

In fact the situation was confused. Never good with money or practical matters, Turgenev had left his affairs in a mess. The amendment leaving Pauline his literary rights was negated by his deal with Glazunov which had sold them to the publisher for fifty years. Adding to this inconsistency, a year before his death Turgenev had given full control of his literary estate to Annenkov. There were, moreover, different wills, one in French and one in Russian, which said different things about his literary property (Turgenev had forgotten to destroy the first when he made the second will). As for his landed property, there was no more clarity. One of the wills had seemingly bequeathed his estates in Russia to his daughter Paulinette. Although she had fled her violent husband in 1882, she now returned to Gaston to support her claim in the French courts, where he represented her. But Pauline also had a claim to Spasskoe. She had kept a legal document from 1864 showing that Turgenev still owed her 30,000 roubles (120,000 francs) – the loan he had received from the Viardots that year to buy his plot of land in Baden and pay for his daughter's dowry. The debt was set against his property at Spasskoe, worth around 165,000 roubles at the time of Turgenev's death. It is inconceivable that Turgenev had not repaid this debt (the sale of his house to the Viardots in 1868 would have been the obvious time to cancel it). The retention of this bill of debt – which should have been annulled when Turgenev repaid the 30,000 roubles – would thus suggest that he had wanted Pauline to keep it as protection of her claim to Spasskoe, or at least a part of it.

Under Russian law Turgenev had no right to leave his land to Viardot: ancestral estates like Spasskoe were not subject to wills and could not be given away if there was a legally recognized family member to inherit it. Apart from Gaston's claim on Paulinette's behalf, which was rejected by the Russian courts, a case was made by two distant cousins of Turgenev on his mother's side, Kleopatra Sukhotina and Olga Galakhova, both from Orel, who had never met the writer (Turgenev had not even been aware of their existence). After years of legal argument, much of it conducted through the Russian consulate in Paris, the matter was finally resolved in 1887 when the Orel District Court awarded Spasskoe to Sukhotina and Galakhova but ordered them to repay Turgenev's debt to Viardot, who accepted the sum of 46,020 roubles (184,000 francs), allowing for interest, in renunciation of her claim based on the bill of debt from 1864. Turgenev left a generous gift to each one of Pauline's four children (Paul was left the Stradivarius violin), but his own daughter and grandchildren received nothing from his will.[7]

On 30 September 1883, the *Berliner Tageblatt* published its obituary of Turgenev. 'For twenty years now we Germans have become more accustomed to regard Turgenev as one of our own,' wrote the literary critic Bruno Steuben. 'In no other country have his works been so often translated, eagerly read, admired as enthusiastically as in ours.' Over the next thirty years, however, Turgenev's international standing as a writer went into a slow decline. In 1914, Thomas Mann complained that the Russian novelist had been unfairly disregarded for too long. He himself adored his works and read them many times throughout his life. In 1949, he said that, if he was banished to a desert island, *Fathers and Sons* would be among the six books he would take.[8]

The waning of Turgenev's popularity was largely due to the rise of other Russian writers, such as Dostoevsky and Tolstoy, whose works appeared in translation with increasing frequency after 1886. The publication in that year of de Vogüé's bestselling survey of Russian literature, *Le Roman russe*, which soon appeared in many languages, led to something of a 'Russian craze' across Europe and America. Publishers responded by bringing out translations, which were cheap to publish because Russian writers remained unprotected by the Berne Convention on international copyright. In France the number of Russian novels published in translation averaged around two a year in the early 1880s, but soared to a peak of twenty-five in 1888. In the United States, twenty-seven different editions of Tolstoy's works were published in 1889 alone.[9]

Until then, Turgenev had been by far the best-known Russian writer in the West. His elegant prose style had previously fixed the boundaries of 'Russianness'. The discovery of Dostoevsky and Tolstoy – seemingly more 'Russian' than the Europeanized Turgenev – altered Western expectations of Russian literature. Now their readers in the West wanted Russian writers to be roughly primitive and spiritual, motivated by the big ideas about human existence, exotically original, to write at greater length – in sum, unlike anything in the rest of European literature. The change in attitudes could be abrupt. On 7 October 1887, Goncourt wrote in his diary of his late friend:

> Turgenev – it is incontestable – was an outstanding conversationalist but as a writer he was overestimated . . . Yes, he was a remarkable landscapist, could describe hunting in the woods like no one else, but he was a minor painter of humanity, lacking grandeur of vision. In effect, there was an absence in his work of the primitive roughness [*rudesse primitive*] of his country, the roughness of old Moscow, of the Cossacks, and in his books his own countrymen seem to me to have the air of Russians painted by a Russian who could have spent his whole existence at the court of Louis XIV.[10]

Despite his declining readership, Turgenev remained a major influence on European and American writers, perhaps more so than any other Russian, with the possible exception of Chekhov. He cast his subtle spell on writers as diverse as Thomas Mann, Guy de Maupassant, John Goldsworthy, Thomas Hardy, George Moore, and, above all, Henry James, who read him all his life, loved him as a man, and shared his basic attitudes to literature and life. 'Turgenev is in a peculiar degree what I may call the novelist's novelist,' James wrote in *The House of Fiction*, 'an artistic influence extraordinarily valuable, and ineradicably established.'[11]

The 'invasion' of the Russians, as the flood of translated Russian novels became known, was soon followed by the coming of the Scandinavians (Ibsen, Bjørnson and Strindberg), whose dramas played in theatres across Europe during the 1890s. This was the highpoint of literary cosmopolitanism on the European continent.

There was a widening range of literatures that came to be translated into English, French and German, the dominant literary languages. Books in Polish, Italian and Spanish broke into the European market alongside those translated from the Russian and Scandinavian languages, and an ever larger number of translations ran in periodicals, which appeared in astonishing profusion at the turn of the twentieth century.

The influx of foreign books led in many countries to protests by those who feared that it would undermine the distinctive nature of their domestic literatures. Such concerns had long been voiced by critics who assigned the highest literary value to national character. As early as 1846, Saint-René Taillandier had warned in the *Revue des deux mondes* that the growing number of foreign translations risked creating uniformity between the literatures of separate countries. As the book trade became internationalized, nationalist defenders of individual literary languages and traditions grew in strength. Across Europe, from the 1870s, they expressed their growing opposition to the cosmopolitanism that had defined European culture from the early decades of the nineteenth century. This reaction fuelled the growth of political nationalism on the European continent, a development that led to the outbreak of the First World War.

Anti-cosmopolitanism was particularly strong in France, where the Dreyfus scandal* was indicative of a growing anti-Semitism in the French Catholic establishment. 'We have really been invaded, and from every side at once,' wrote Henry Bordeaux, a Catholic traditionalist, lawyer and writer, in *Le Correspondant* in 1901. 'If we do not keep our guard, soon there will be no French literature.'[12] Similar reactions could be found across the continent. The opening of countries to international currents was accompanied in most of them by a reactive nationalism in the arts and politics.

The issue was most acute in literature, the carrier of the national language and ideas. This was where defenders of tradition made their stand against the universal avant-garde. In the visual arts, where by the end of the century an Impressionist aesthetic had become assimilated into national traditions across Europe, there was a stronger tendency to regard the emergence of this international idiom as a positive development. As André Hallays put it in 1895, for the first time in history a genuinely European style of art was beginning to emerge:

> It is not only writers who are converging into a European school; even more than them, artists are accelerating the advance of cosmopolitanism.

---

* In 1894, a Jewish army captain, Alfred Dreyfus, was unjustly convicted of espionage, sentenced to life imprisonment, and held on Devil's Island until 1899, when he was brought back to France and put on trial again after the appearance of new evidence – some of which confirmed his innocence, while other documents were fabricated by the army to frame him. The court found Dreyfus guilty, once more sentenced him to ten years of imprisonment, but pardoned him. In 1906, he was exonerated and reinstated in the French army, where he served in the First World War.

Already now it is practically impossible to class painters by national schools. A few months ago, visiting the Munich galleries, I was struck by how far the nomadic spirit of the painters, the accidents of their artistic formation, and their conformity to the same aesthetic, most often literary, made it hard to tell where they came from. Their styles are so scrambled and confused that an art critic, even well-informed, would always hesitate and often be mistaken in attributing the paintings: there are Italians painting in the English way; Scandinavians who could be taken for southern Italians.[13]

It was at this point that the idea of a 'European culture' – as a synthesis of artistic styles and works from across the continent and as an identity based on common values and ideas – began to emerge in the discourse. The term itself was seldom used before this time. People rarely spoke of a 'European culture' in the first three quarters of the nineteenth century. They spoke most commonly of 'European Civilization', a Eurocentric term inherited from the Enlightenment, by which they meant Western reason, liberty, the classical artistic heritage and science, held up as universal values on which human progress was founded. This was a European ideology but not itself a marker of a distinct European *cultural* identity. You could believe in it wherever you came from.

Notions of Europe as a cultural space – shared by 'Europeans' and uniting them – first appeared in the early decades of the nineteenth century. Saint-Simon conceived of Europe as having a 'civilizing mission' defined by its secular spirit, in which the arts would take the place of religion, race or nation in uniting peoples on the Continent.[14] Goethe thought that a hybrid type of European culture would be formed through the growth of cultural traffic and exchange between nations. But it was only in the final quarter of the century that such ideas gave way to the notion of a distinct European sensibility, or cultural identity: a sense of 'Europeanness' shared by Europe's citizens regardless of their nationality.

Nietzsche was a pioneer of this notion. In *Human, All Too Human* (1878) he presented the idea that European nations would be weakened, and one day extinguished, by international 'trade and industry', and that the 'circulation of books and letters' would bring about a 'common high culture'. As a result of 'this unceasing hybridization', Nietzsche argued, a 'mixed breed' would emerge, that of 'European man'. An enemy of nationalism, which he called the 'sickness of the century',

Nietzsche advanced his ideal of 'the good European' – the 'homeless' citizen of Europe – as an antidote to it. In his view, *Homo Europaeus* was already being formed:

> Whether that which now distinguishes the European be called 'civilization' or 'humanization' or 'progress'; whether one calls it simply, without implying any praise or blame, the *democratic* movement in Europe: behind all the moral and political foregrounds indicated by such formulas a great *physiological* process is taking place and gathering greater and ever greater impetus – the process of the assimilation of all Europeans, their growing detachment from the conditions under which races dependent on climate and class originate, their increasing independence of any *definite* milieu which, through making the same demands for centuries, would like to inscribe itself on soul and body – that is to say, the slow emergence of an essentially supra-national and nomadic type of man which, physiologically speaking, possesses as its typical distinction a maximum of the art and power of adaptation. This process of *becoming European*, the tempo of which can be retarded by . . . the still-raging storm and stress of 'national feeling' . . . will probably lead to results which its naive propagators and panegyrists, the apostles of 'modern ideas', would be least inclined to anticipate [emphasis as in original].[15]

The arts played a central role in this evolving concept of a European cultural identity. More than religion or political beliefs, they were seen as uniting people across the continent. The Danish critic Georg Brandes argued, for example, that advances in transportation, communication and printing, and the growth of translations, had opened up the various literatures of Europe to a 'modern European sensibility'.[16] The process did not have to mean the loss of nationality. But it did entail a greater openness on the part of each country, a recognition that any national culture is the result of a constant dialogue across state boundaries and of the assimilation of separate artistic traditions into a larger European world.

In his essay 'The Crisis of the Mind' (1919) Paul Valéry, the French poet, reflected on the nature of this European culture on the eve of the First World War:

> In a book of that era – and not one of the most mediocre – we should have no trouble in finding: the influence of the Russian ballet, a touch of

Pascal's gloom, numerous impressions of the Goncourt type, something of Nietzsche, something of Rimbaud, certain effects due to a familiarity with painters, and sometimes the tone of a scientific publication . . . the whole flavoured with an indefinably British quality difficult to assess!

Valéry thought this complex fusion was 'characteristic of the modern epoch', by which he meant a 'way of life' as well as a time. Europe, he maintained, had reached the apogee of this 'modernism' in 1914, just before 'the illusion of a European culture' was then lost on the battle-fields of Flanders and Poland.[17]

Paradoxically, it was in the post-war years – after that illusion had been shattered – that the ideal of a coherent European cultural identity really came into its own. For Europe's intellectuals, the war was a catastrophe, unravelling the densely interwoven connections built up among Europe's nations and threatening to destroy its cultural suprem-acy. Oswald Spengler's *The Decline of the West* (1918) was only one of many books predicting the demise of European civilization. To reverse its decline the 'European project' (as it then came into existence) needed an idea of Europe that upheld its special character and position in the world. There was a growing emphasis on European high culture as the source of this identity. Animated by nostalgic yearning for the inter-nationalism of fin-de-siècle Europe, liberal thinkers recast Europe and its culture as a 'shared inheritance' based on 'a desire for understand-ing and exchange' between nations, in the words of Valéry; as a 'spiritual unity', as the sociologist Georg Simmel put it; and as a 'supra-national realm of humanism', as Stefan Zweig, the Austrian Jewish writer, wrote in *The World of Yesterday* (1942). Zweig's work was suf-fused with this nostalgic longing for the certainties of nineteenth-century Europe, not least because it was finished on the eve of the writer's suicide, as the 'illusion of a European culture' collapsed once again.

'How many changes you have witnessed in your life,' Saint-Saëns wrote to Pauline Viardot on 19 December 1909:

The railways, steamships, telegraphs, gaslights, electric telegrams and lighting – you have seen them all come into existence; and now there are cars that move on their own, speaking telegraphs and aeroplanes . . . And how many changes in the field of art! You made your debut when Rossini, Bellini and others were at the height of their glory; you saw, after the brilliant reign of Meyerbeer, how – and from what fogs? – the art of Richard Wagner rose ... and now the rise of Richard Strauss's art, the precursor of the world's end: it is the Antichrist in music. When Elektra* recognizes her brother, Orestes, *three tonalities* are heard simultaneously! The technique has been baptised, and named *heterophony*. There was no need for a new word: *cacophony* would have sufficed.[18]

Pauline did not altogether share Saint-Saëns's mistrust of the modern movement in music. She had always been receptive to new forms of art. But she was, as he implied, a figure firmly rooted in the glorious achievements of the previous century. That is certainly how she was seen in the final years of her long life. She received many visitors – scholars, writers, composers and musicians – who asked her questions about all the people she had known. What could she tell them of Rossini, Gounod, Berlioz, Liszt or Meyerbeer – of Sand or Delacroix – all now long since dead? What had Chopin's piano-playing sounded like? What was she prepared to say about Turgenev as a friend? Did she have letters they could see? What to her were memories of friendship, emotions, love, had become to a younger generation the documentary material of music, art and literary history.

There is no surviving evidence of Pauline's art. We can never know what her singing sounded like. The phonograph arrived too late to record it. The earliest recording of the great bass Feodor Chaliapin dates from 1901; the tenor Ernest Caruso made his first recording in 1902. Perhaps the closest we can get to Pauline's style of singing are the crackly recordings made in 1905 by Pauline's former pupil Marianne Brandt, then aged sixty-three, whose young voice had reminded Turgenev of Viardot's. The three songs she recorded on Pathé cylinders – Schumann's 'Frühlingsnacht' (Spring Night), the drinking song from *Lucrezia Borgia* and Fidès's aria 'Ah mon fils' from *Le Prophète* – had all been sung by Pauline many times.[19]

The phonograph was one of the many new inventions – along with talking films and the telegraphone (the first magnetic audio recorder) – displayed at the 1900 Exposition Universelle in Paris, whose main entrance on the place de la Concorde, a three-arched dome topped by a giant female figure representing Paris with her open arms, could be

---

* Saint-Saëns is referring to the opera *Elektra*, first performed in Dresden in 1909.

Entrance to the Exposition Universelle, Paris, 1900.

seen from the windows of Pauline's apartment. The Exposition was the last of the great nineteenth-century exhibitions in Paris and was meant to be a synthesis of the achievements of the past one hundred years as well as an opening of the twentieth century. Modernity was the key theme. The first line of the Paris Metro was completed for the fair. Moving pavements carried visitors around the site at different speeds. People came with portable cameras. And inside the Grand Palais, the main exhibition hall in the Art Nouveau style, there were modern works of art – one by Gauguin, three by Cézanne, eight by Pissarro, twelve by Manet and fourteen by Monet – alongside those by David, Delacroix, Ingres and Meissonier to represent the glories of nineteenth-century French painting. Rodin had his own pavilion just outside the Exposition grounds, but unlike Courbet or Manet before him he also had the blessing of the city of Paris, which financed his exhibition of sculptures.

Pauline's career had spanned a crucial period in the history of the music business. Cheap mass printing had permitted the dissemination of the music canon through sheet music. People came to concerts or the opera house with a detailed knowledge of the music, which they had learned by playing it themselves, either in arrangements or in the original. With the arrival of recorded music the canon of familiar classics became far more widely known, enjoyed by people who could not afford a piano. But those who went to public concerts were less likely to read music, to know these pieces from a score, or understand them in a way that had made the experience of listening to live music so precious and intense in the nineteenth century.

During the last years of her life, Pauline was increasingly confined to her apartment, where she was looked after by her former pupil Mathilde de Nogueiras. She was active to the end, composing music, teaching pupils, helping them to launch their singing careers by writing letters to her many contacts in the music world, despite the pain it must have caused her just to hold a pen, judging from her awkward handwriting.[20] She had terrible rheumatic pains in her fingers, hands and arms; she was practically blind, with cataracts in both her eyes; and her hearing became poor. 'I have become frightened to go out,' she confided to her diary in 1907.

> I dare not cross the street. I have lost physical confidence. If I am asked a question, I take a long time to respond, as if I want it to pass through a filter first; often the question is repeated, because they think I have not understood. That troubles me. I have grown indifferent to many things. I rarely give my opinion, it does not seem worth the trouble. In general, I speak little, particularly with the family, I don't know why. I often think they listen only from respect, but pay no heed to what I say.[21]

One thing she was not indifferent to was the arrival of Sergei Diaghilev and his *saison russe* in Paris that year. Diaghilev's idea – to bring the arts of Russia to Europe – was one dear to Pauline's heart. She had been promoting Russian music for the previous sixty years. The first season featured music by Tchaikovsky, Rimsky-Korsakov, Glinka, Borodin, Scriabin, Mussorgsky and Rachmaninov; it culminated in the sensation of Chaliapin's performance in the title role of *Boris Godunov*, the first time Mussorgsky's masterpiece had been performed outside Russia, at the Paris Opéra on 19 May 1908. The next year the Ballets Russes were launched with an opening production of Nikolai Tcherepnin's *Le Pavillon d'Armide* at the Théâtre du Châtelet, followed by *The Firebird* (1910), *Petrushka* (1911) and *The Rite of Spring* (1913) by Stravinsky. This was the point when Russia took its place right at the heart of Europe's cosmopolitan culture, the moment when the influence of the Russian ballet became part of the complex fusion that defined any European work of art in the years before the First World War. Despite their Russian folk tale narratives, exotic stage-sets and costumes, all designed to appeal to the French, the Stravinsky ballets were in fact a synthesis of European elements, the music drawn as much from Debussy, Ravel and Fauré as from Russian folk song and its champions in the nationalist school. If the French saw the ballets as authentically 'Russian', the Russians thought they sounded French.[22]

Diaghilev had close connections to Pauline. His father and stepmother had met her when they had visited Turgenev in Paris in the 1870s, while his aunt, the opera singer Alexandra Panaeva-Kartseva, had studied with Pauline on the advice of Turgenev. Diaghilev was keen to meet Pauline when he came to Paris in 1906 to launch an exhibition of modern Russian art. She had known Tchaikovsky, whom he idolized, and had good contacts among the city's cultural élites, whose support he needed for his *saisons russes*. The meeting did not take place.[23] Diaghilev was soon immersed in the fashionable salons of Madame Melanie de Pourtalès, Countess Greffulhe and Misia Sert, who financed both his Russian concert seasons and the Ballets Russes. With such backing the ambitious impresario had no need to visit an old lady like Pauline. But everything he would achieve with the Ballets Russes in Paris was the fulfilment of the cultural ideals she had embodied all her life.

Pauline died on 18 May 1910. She fell asleep in an armchair and died, without waking, at three o'clock in the morning. According to Louise, who was with her, as Pauline slipped away she made a movement with her hands and appeared to be talking to people in her head. 'Norma' was the only word she said – the name of one of her most famous roles. The funeral took place two days later in the Basilica of Sainte-Clotilde in Paris. Saint-Saëns gave the main address. Fauré's 'Pie Jesu' was sung by a soprano accompanied by César Franck on the Cavaillé-Coll organ, for which the church is famous.[24] It was a religious ceremony, conducted according to the rites of the Roman Catholic Church, a fact which would have shocked Pauline's husband, a diehard atheist. But the gravestone over their two bodies, lying side by side in the cemetery at Montmartre, is devoid of any Christian sign.

References

LIST OF ABBREVIATIONS
Archives

ANF	Archives Nationales, Paris
APP	Archive de la Préfecture de Police, Paris
ASR	Archivo Storico Ricordi, Milan
BL	British Library Manuscripts Division, London
BMD	Bibliothèque Marguerite Durand, Paris
BMO	Bibliothèque-Musée de l'Opéra (BNF), Paris
BNF	Bibliothèque Nationale de France, Paris
DR	Durand-Ruel Archive, Paris
FM	Fitzwilliam Museum, Department of Manuscripts, Cambridge
GARF	State Archive of the Russian Federation
GK	Generallandesarchiv Karlsruhe, Karlsruhe
HL	Houghton Library, Harvard
IRL	Institute of Russian Literature (Pushkin House), St Petersburg
JMA	John Murray Archive, Edinburgh
NYPL	New York Public Library, Manuscripts Division, New York
OR	Manuscript Division, Russian National Library, St Petersburg
RGALI	Russian State Archive of Literature and Art, Moscow
ROH	Royal Opera House Archives, London
SBB	Stadtarchiv Baden-Baden, Baden-Baden
SHM	State Historical Museum, Moscow
SP	St Petersburg Public Library, Manuscripts Division, St Petersburg
TCA	Thomas Cook Archive, Peterborough
TCL	Trinity College Library, Cambridge
TMS-L	Turgenev Museum Spasskoe-Lutovinovo, Orel

Published Primary Sources

Cahiers	*Cahiers Ivan Tourguéniev, Pauline Viardot, Maria Malibran*
GJ	Jules and Edmond Goncourt, *Journal-Mémoires de la Vie Littéraire. Texte intégrale établi et annoté par Robert Ricatte*, 3 vols. (Monaco, 1956)
IPA	*Iz parizhskogo arkhiva I. S. Turgeneva*, 2 vols. *Literarturnoe nasledstvo*, vol. 73 (Moscow, 1964)
LI	*Lettres inédites de Tourguénev à Pauline Viardot et à sa famille*, ed. Henri Granjard and Alexandre Zviguilsky (Lausanne, 1972)

NCI   Ivan Tourguénev, *Nouvelle correspondance inédite*, ed. A. Zviguilsky, 2 vols. (Paris, 1971–2)

NPG   N. P. Generalova (ed.), *I. S. Turgenev: Novye issledovaniia i materialy*, 4 vols. (Moscow–St Petersburg, 2009–11)

PSS   I. S. Turgenev, *Polnoe sobranie sochinenii i pisem: v tridtsati tomakh: Pis'ma v vosemnadtsati tomakh, Pis'ma*, 16 vols. (Moscow, 1982–2014)

Soch.   I. S. Turgenev, *Polnoe sobranie sochinenii i pisem v tridtsati tomakh. Sochineniia v dvenadtsati tomakh* (Moscow, 1978–86)

TMS   Thérèse Marix-Spire (ed.), *Lettres inédites de George Sand et de Pauline Viardot, 1839–1849* (Paris, 1959)

Turg.   I. S. Turgenev, *Polnoe sobranie sochinenii i pisem v dvadtsati vos'mi tomakh. Pis'ma v trinadtsati tomakh* (Moscow, 1961–8)

Vosp.   *I. S. Turgenev v vospominaniiakh sovremennikov. Perepiska I. S. Turgeneva s Polinoi Viardo i ee sem'ei* (Moscow, 1988)

Zvig.   Alexandre Zviguilsky, *Correspondance Ivan Tourguéniev–Louis Viardot: Sous le sceau de la fraternité* (Paris, 2010)

INTRODUCTION

1. *Rapport fait à la commission sur le tracé des embranchements dirigés du chemin de fer de Paris à Lille* (Paris, 1844), p. 7.
2. *Le Messager du Nord*, 17 June 1846.
3. *L'Écho du Nord*, 18 June 1846.
4. Guy Gosselin, *La Symphonie dans la cité: Lille au XIXe siècle* (Paris, 2011), pp. 165–6.
5. Berlioz, *Correspondance générale*, eds. Pierre Citron, Frédéric Robert and Hugh Macdonald, 8 vols. (Paris, 1972–2003), vol. 3, no. 1045.
6. *Le National*, 15 June 1846, p. 2.
7. The study of international cultural transfers has a well-established bibliography in French and German but not in English. See e.g. Michel Espagne and Michael Werner (eds.), *Transferts: Les Relations interculturelles dans l'espace Franco-Allemand (XVIIIe–XIXe siècles)* (Paris, 1988); Frédéric Barbier (ed.), *Est–ouest: Transferts et réceptions dans le monde du livre en Europe (XVIIe–XXe siècles)* (Leipzig, 2005); Béatrice Joyeux-Prunel, *Nul n'est prophète en son pays? L'internationalisation de la peinture des avant-gardes parisiennes, 1855–1914* (Paris, 2009); Philipp Ther and Peter Sachel (eds.), *Wie europäisch ist die Oper? Die Geschichte des Musiktheaters als Zugang zu einer kulturellen Topographie Europas* (Vienna, 2009); Christophe Charle, 'Comparaisons et transferts en histoire culturelle de l'Europe: Quelques réflexions à propos de recherches récentes', *Les Cahiers Irice*, no. 5, 2010/11, pp. 51–73; Sylvain Briens, *Paris: Laboratoire de la littérature scandinave moderne, 1880–1905* (Paris, 2010); Sven Müller et al., *Oper im Wandel der Gesellschaft: Kulturtransfers und Netzwerke des Musiktheaters im modernen Europa* (Vienna, 2010).
8. Kenneth Clark, *Civilisation: A Personal View* (London, 1969), p. 160.
9. Edmund Burke, 'First Letter on a Regicide Peace' (1796), *Writings and Speeches*, ed. Paul Langford, 9 vols. (Oxford, 1981–2000), vol. 9, pp. 242–3.

1 EUROPE IN 1843

1. *Severnaia pchela*, no. 244, 30 Oct. 1843, no. 248, 4 Nov. 1843, no. 268, 27 Nov. 1843.

2. *Lettres et papiers du Chancelier Comte de Nesselrode, 1760–1856*, 11 vols. (Paris, 1908–12), vol. 8, p. 220; Heinrich Heine, *Lutèce: Lettres sur la vie politique, artistique et sociale de la France* (Paris, 1855), p. 412.

3. *Camille Saint-Saëns on Music and Musicians*, ed. R. Nicholls (Oxford, 2008), p. 167.

4. Gerd Nauhaus (ed.), *The Marriage Diaries of Robert and Clara Schumann*, trans. Peter Ostwald (Boston, Mass., 1993), p. 200.

5. *Severnaia pchela*, no. 247, 3 Nov. 1843.

6. HL, MUS 264 (365), Pauline Viardot Journal, memoir dated 1887.

7. HL, MUS 264 (365), Pauline Viardot Journal, memoir dated 1887.

8. Julie Buckler, *The Literary Lorgnette: Attending Opera in Imperial Russia* (Stanford, 2000), pp. 42–4.

9. Rutger Helmers, '"It just reeks of italianism": Traces of Italian Opera in "A Life for the Tsar"', *Music & Letters*, vol. 91, no. 3, Aug. 2010, p. 387.

10. Alexander Pushkin, *Eugene Onegin: A Novel in Verse*, trans. James Falen (Oxford, 2009), p. 226.

11. BNF, NA Fr. 162778, Papiers Viardot, vol. 7, Varia, f. 1, 'Engagement de Pauline Viardot avec le théâtre de St Petersbourg'.

12. Richard Taruskin, 'Ital'yanshchina', in *Defining Russia Musically: Historical and Hermeneutical Essays* (Princeton, 1997), pp. 196–8; Buckler, *Literary Lorgnette*, p. 60.

13. Carlotta Sorba, 'Teatro d'opera e società nell'Italia ottocentesca', in *Bollettino del diciannovesimo secolo*, vol. 4, no. 5, 1996, p. 38.

14. Jutta Toelle, 'Opera as Business? From Impresari to the Publishing Industry', *Journal of Modern Italian Studies*, vol. 17, no. 4, 2012, pp. 448–59.

15. Stendhal, *Life of Rossini*, trans. Richard N. Coe (New York, 1957), p. 1.

16. Bruno Cagli and Sergio Ragni (eds.), *Gioachino Rossini: Lettere e documenti*, 3 vols. (Pesaro, 1992–2000), vol. 1, pp. 65–86. See also Philip Eisenbeiss, *Bel Canto Bully: The Life and Times of the Legendary Opera Impresario Domenico Barbaja* (London, 2013), pp. 51–2.

17. Alan Kendall, *Gioacchino Rossini: The Reluctant Hero* (London, 1992), p. 123.

18. ANF, AJ/13/1161, I, *Nominations et engagements de Rossini comme compositeur puis comme directeur du Théâtre-Italien*.

19. Patrick Barbier, *Opera in Paris 1800–1850* (Portland, 1995), pp. 188–91; Hervé Lacombe, *The Keys to French Opera in the Nineteenth Century*, trans. Edward Schneider (Berkeley, Calif., 2001), p. 50; David Cairns (trans. and ed.), *The Memoirs of Hector Berlioz, Member of the French Institute, Including His Travels in Italy, Germany, Russia and England, 1803–1865* (New York, 1969), p. 90.

20. Arthur Loesser, *Men, Women and Pianos: A Social History* (London, 1955), p. 344.

21. William Ashbrook, *Donizetti and His Operas* (Cambridge, 1982), pp. 209–10.

22. Herbert Weinstock, *Donizetti and the World of Opera in Italy, Paris and Vienna in the First Half of the Nineteenth Century* (London, 1963), p. 55.

23. Catherine Menciassi-Authier, 'La profession de chanteuse d'opéra dans le premier xixᵉ siècle', *Annales historiques de la Révolution française*, no. 379, 2015, pp. 183–201.

24. 'Madame Malibran à Naples', *Revue et Gazette de Paris*, no. 16, 20 Apr. 1834, p. 130; Gabriella Dideriksen, 'Repertory and Rivalry: Opera and the Second Covent Garden Theatre, 1830–56', Ph.D. diss., King's College London, 1997, p. 31; M. Sterling Mackinlay, *Garcia the Centenarian and His Times* (London, 1908), pp. 111–12.

25. Donald Sassoon, *The Culture of the Europeans: From 1800 to the Present* (London, 2006), p. 531; Mai Kawabata, *Paganini: 'Demonic' Virtuoso* (Woodbridge, 1988),

pp. 78–83. On the element of spectacle: Gillen Wood, *Romanticism and Music Culture in Britain* (Cambridge, 2010), pp. 9, 105–23, 169.

26. Serge Gut and Jacqueline Bellas (eds.), *Correspondance de Liszt et de la comtesse d'Agoult*, 2 vols. (Paris, 1933–4), vol. 2, p. 377.

27. Alan Walker, *Franz Liszt: The Virtuoso Years, 1811–47* (Ithaca, NY, 1988), pp. 130, 289; Nauhaus (ed.), *Marriage Diaries of Robert and Clara Schumann*, p. 233.

28. Patrick Barbier, *Pauline Viardot* (Paris, 2009), p. 14.

29. See John Rosselli, 'From Princely Service to the Open Market: Singers of Italian Opera and Their Patrons, 1600–1850', *Cambridge Opera Journal*, vol. 1, no. 1, Mar. 1989, pp. 1–32.

30. James Radomski, *Manuel Garcia (1775–1832): Chronicle of the Life of a Bel Canto Tenor at the Dawn of Romanticism* (Oxford, 2000), pp. 34–5.

31. BNF, NA 16274, Papiers de Pauline Viardot, vol. 3, Lettres adressées à Louis Viardot, Pauline Viardot to Louis Viardot.

32. Benjamin Walton, 'Italian Operatic Fantasies in Latin America', *Journal of Modern Italian Studies*, vol. 17, no. 4, 2012, pp. 460–71.

33. BNF, NA Fr. 16278, Papiers Viardot, vol. VII, Varia, f. 120.

34. April Fitzlyon, *Maria Malibran: Diva of the Romantic Age* (London, 1987), p. 44.

35. See e.g. NYPL, JOE 82-1, 14, Letter from Pauline Viardot to Julius Rietz, 21 Jan. 1859; HL, MUS 264 (365), Pauline Viardot Journal, memoir dated 1887.

36. Michèle Friang, *Pauline Viardot* (Paris, 2008), p. 15.

37. Radomski, *Manuel Garcia*, p. 286.

38. BNF, NA Fr. 16278, Papiers Viardot, vol. 4, IV, *Lettres*, p. 472 (Letter from Maria Malibran to Joaquina Briones, July 1827).

39. HL, MUS 264 (365), Pauline Viardot Journal, entry July 1879, memoir dated 1887.

40. BNF, NA Fr. 16278, Papiers Viardot, vol. VII, Varia, f. 175; HL, MUS 264 (365), Pauline Viardot Journal, memoir dated 1887.

41. *Gazette musicale de Paris*, 4 Sept. 1836.

42. HL, MUS 264 (365), Pauline Viardot Journal, memoir dated 1887; *Gazette musicale de Paris*, 24 Dec. 1837; 3 June 1838.

43. Ernest Legouvé, 'Concerts de M. de Bériot et de Mlle Garcia', *Revue et Gazette musicale de Paris*, no. 51, 23 Dec. 1838; Alfred de Musset, 'Concert de Mlle Garcia', *Revue des deux mondes*, 1 Jan. 1839.

44. Cited in April Fitzlyon, *The Price of Genius: A Life of Pauline Viardot* (London, 1964), p. 52.

45. TMS, p. 21.

46. HL, MUS 264 (365), Pauline Viardot Journal, memoir dated 1887 (where she claims the fee was 6,000 francs for each performance, but this cannot be correct).

47. Pauline Garcia to Celeste Nathan, 13 May 1839. Private collection.

48. Cited in Barbara Kendall-Davies, *The Life and Work of Pauline Viardot-Garcia*, vol. 1: *The Years of Fame, 1836–1863* (Amersham, 2004), p. 87.

49. BNF, NA 16274, Papiers de Pauline Viardot, vol. 3, Lettres adressées à Louis Viardot, f. 17, Charles de Bériot to Louis Viardot, 26 July 1838.

50. BNF, NA 16274, Papiers de Pauline Viardot, vol. 3, Lettres adressées à Louis Viardot, f. 157, Malibran to Louis Viardot, 15 Dec. 1833; Louis Viardot, *Espagne et beaux-arts: Mélanges* (Paris, 1866), pp. 443–4; A. Pougin, *Maria Malibran: Histoire d'une cantatrice* (Paris, 1911), p. 97.

51. Louis Viardot, *Souvenirs de chasse* (Paris, 1849), p. 9.

52. Louis Viardot, *Lettres d'un Espagnol*, 2 vols. (Paris, 1826); Viardot, *Espagne et beaux-arts*, p. 79.

53. See further, Daniel L. Rader, *The Journalists and the July Revolution in France: The Role of the Political Press in the Overthrow of the Bourbon Restoration 1827–1830* (The Hague, 1973).

54. Ibid., pp. 459–61.

55. BNF, Aux Électeurs . . . de Seine-et-Marne. Louis Viardot [20 Mar. 1848].

56. The best account of the fire is Jean-Louis Tamvaco, *Les Cancans de l'Opéra: Chroniques de l'Académie royale de musique et du théâtre, à Paris sous les deux Restaurations: Première édition critique intégrale du manuscrit Les cancans de l'Opéra, ou, Le Journal d'une habilleuse, de 1836 à 1848*, 2 vols. (Paris, 2000), vol. 1, pp. 384–6.

57. BMO, LAS Viardot 1, Lettre de Louis Viardot à Robert, London, 20 June 1838.

58. ANF, AJ/13/1160, 1, Contract between Robert and Viardot for the management of the Théâtre-Italien (1838).

59. Armando Rubén Puente, *Alejandro Aguado: Militar, banquero, mecenas* (Madrid, 2007), pp. 19–21; Jean-Philippe Luis, *L'Ivresse de la fortune: A. M. Aguado, un génie des affaires* (Paris, 2009).

60. Louis Véron, *Mémoires d'un bourgeois de Paris*, 6 vols. (Paris, 1853–5), vol. 2, p. 253; Louis Viardot, *Galerie Aguado, choix des principaux tableaux* (Paris, 1839); Ilse Hempel Lipschutz, *Spanish Painting and the French Romantics* (Cambridge, Mass., 1972), pp. 123–8.

61. ANF, AJ/13/1160, II, Rossini Archives. Letter from Aguado to Rossini, 28 Dec. 1831 (giving him 100,000 francs); Cagli and Ragni, *Gioachino Rossini*, p. 265.

62. Anne-Sophie Cras-Kleiber, 'L'Exploitation de l'Académie royale de Musique sous la monarchie de Juillet', diss., École de Chartres, 1996, p. 145; Cagli and Ragni, *Gioachino Rossini*, pp. 522–9.

63. ANF, AJ/13/180, II, Cahier des charges et supplément (1831).

64. Cras-Kleiber, 'L'Exploitation', p. 141; ANF, AJ/13/1160, 1, Contract between Robert and Viardot for the management of the Théâtre Italien (1838).

65. Tamvaco, *Les Cancans*, vol. 1, pp. 183–4, 242–4, 251, 429, 503.

66. Ibid., pp. 435–9.

67. Duc de Montmorency, *Lettres sur l'Opéra (1840–1842)* (Paris, 1921), pp. 176–8.

68. See her correspondence with the Philharmonic Society in London: BL MUS, RPS 328, f. 129.

69. Montmorency, *Lettres sur l'Opéra*, p. 172.

70. Letter from Pauline Garcia to Joaquina Briones, Sept. 1839, private collection.

71. Alfred de Musset, 'Les Débuts de Mademoiselle Pauline Garcia', in *Oeuvres complètes*, 11 vols. (Paris, 1866), vol. 9, pp. 123, 125–6; Gustave Dulong, *Pauline Viardot, tragédienne lyrique*, Cahiers, no. 8, 1984, p. 78; Théophile Gautier, *Historie de l'art dramatique en France depuis vingt-cinq ans*, 6 vols. (Paris, 1858–9), vol. 2, p. 92.

72. George Sand, *Journal intime* (Paris, 1926), p. 104.

73. *La Revue indépendante*, vol. 1, 1841, pp. v–xx.

74. HL, MUS 264 (365), Pauline Viardot Journal, memoir dated 1887.

75. BNF, NA Fr. 16272, Papiers Viardot, vol. 1, Lettres adressées à Pauline Viardot, f. 304, Jaubert to Pauline Viardot, 17 June 1840.

76. HL, MUS 264 (365), Pauline Viardot Journal, memoir dated 1887.

77. *Allgemeine Musikalische Zeitung*, no. 41, Oct. 1838, p. 677.

78. NYPL, JOE 82-1, 27, Letter from Pauline Viardot to Julius Rietz, Paris, 17 Mar. 1859

79. Ibid., 4, Letter from Pauline Viardot to Julius Rietz, Weimar, Dec. 1858.

80. TMS, p. 24.

81. TMS, p. 217.

82. As her mother and former manager, Joaquina continued to advise her on her singing engagements (BNF, NA Fr. 16272, Papiers de Pauline Viardot, vol. 1, Joaquina Garcia to Pauline Viardot, Brussels, 23 Mar. 1847, ff. 128–9).

83. BNF, NA Fr. 162778, Papiers Viardot, vol. 7, Varia, ff. 1–32.

84. John Rosselli, *Singers of Italian Opera: The History of a Profession* (Cambridge, 1995), pp. 66–7.

85. ANF, AJ/13/180, IV, Dissolution of the Duponchel and Las Marismas company and its replacement by a company formed by Léon Pillet; Montmorency, *Lettres sur l'Opéra*, p. 157.

86. On Stolz, see Karin Pendle, 'A Night at the Opera: The Parisian Prima Donna', *The Opera Quarterly*, vol. 4, no. 1, 1986, pp. 82–3.

87. 'Critique théatrale', *La Revue indépendante*, vol. 1, 8 Dec. 1841, p. 524.

88. BNF, Aux Électeurs . . . de Seine-et-Marne. Louis Viardot [20 Mar. 1848].

89. TMS, p. 57. See further, Tom Kaufman, 'The Grisi–Viardot Controversy, 1848–1852', *The Opera Quarterly*, vol. 14, no. 2, 1997, pp. 7–22.

90. TMS, p. 101.

91. Ibid., pp. 47–8.

92. HL, MUS 264 (365), Pauline Viardot Journal, memoir dated 1887.

93. TMS, pp. 159–61.

94. Ibid., pp. 60, 159, 181; Patrick Waddington, 'Some Gleanings on Turgenev and His International Connections, with Notes on Pauline Viardot and Her Family', *New Zealand Slavonic Journal*, 1983, p. 209.

95. TMS, p. 181.

96. Ibid., pp. 187–8.

97. Gerhard Stahr, 'Kommerzielle Interessen und provinzielles Selbstbewusstsein: Die Eröffnungsfeiern d. Rhein. Eisenbahn 1841 u. 1843', in Manfred Hettling (ed.), *Bürgerliche Feste: Symbolische Formen politischen Handelns im 19. Jh.* (Göttingen, 1993), p. 49.

98. Willim Makepeace Thackeray, *The Roundabout Papers: The Biographical Edition of the Works of William Makepeace Thackeray*, vol. 12 (London, 1914), p. 233.

99. Cited in Wolfgang Schivelbusch, *The Railway Journey: The Industrialization of Time and Space in the Nineteenth Century* (Berkeley, Calif., 1986), p. 38.

100. Jules Michelet, cited in Nicholas Faith, *The World the Railways Made* (London, 1990), p. 58.

101. Waltraud Linder-Beroud, 'Das Eisenbahnzeitalter in Lied und populärer Kultur: Zur Mentalitätsgeschichte der Mobilität am Beispiel der Eisenbahn', in Nils Grosch (ed.), *Fremdheit, Migration, Musik: Kulturwissenschaftliche Essays für Max Matter* (Münster, 2010), p. 312.

102. Camillo Cavour, *Le strade ferrate in Italia*, ed. A. Salvestrini (Florence, 1976), pp. 61–3.

103. Remo Ceserani, *Treni di carta. L'immaginario in ferrovia: L'irruzione del treno nella letteratura moderna* (Genoa, 1993), pp. 50, 53.

104. Schivelbusch, *Railway Journey*, pp. 70–71.

105. Karl Marx, *Grundrisse: Foundations of the Critique of Political Economy*, trans. Martin Nicolaus (London, 1993), p. 524; Linder-Beroud, 'Eisenbahnzeitalter', p. 311; Jürgen Osterhammel, *The Transformation of the World: A Global History of the Nineteenth Century* (Princeton, 2014), p. 726.

106. W. F. Rae, *The Business of Travel: A Fifty Years' Record of Progress* (London, 1891), p. 5.

107. Stefano Maggi, *Le ferrovie* (Bologna, 2017), p. 70.

108. Schivelbusch, *Railway Journey*, p. 233.

109. TMS, pp. 121, 184.

110. Henryk Opieńsky (ed.), *Chopin's Letters*, trans. E. Voynich (New York, 1988), p. 363.

111. For an excellent survey of this transformation, see Tim Blanning, *The Culture of Power and the Power of Culture: Old Regime Europe, 1660–1789* (Oxford, 2003).

112. Frédéric Barbier, 'Les marchés étrangers de la librairie française', in Roger Chartier and Henri-Jean Martin (eds.), *Histoire de l'édition française*, 4 vols. (Paris, 1983–7), vol. 3: *Le Temps des éditeurs: Du Romanticisme à la Belle Époque*, pp. 279–80. On the importance of the German market for French book exports, see Frédéric Barbier, 'Les Échanges de librairie entre la France et l'Allemagne 1850–1914', in Espagne and Werner (eds.), *Transferts*, pp. 236–52.

113. Frédéric Barbier, *L'Empire du livre: Le livre imprimé et la construction de l'Allemagne contemporaine (1815–1914)* (Paris, 1995), pp. 213–15.

114. W. E. Yates, 'Internationalization of European Theatre: French Influence in Vienna between 1830 and 1860', *Austrian Studies*, vol. 13, 2005, Austria and France, p. 45.

115. Gosselin, *La Symphonie dans la cité*, p. 170.

116. Sophie de Schaepdrijver, *Elites for the Capital? Foreign Migration to Mid-Nineteenth-Century Brussels* (Amsterdam, 1990), p. 16.

117. Carlo Gatti, *Il Teatro alla Scala nella storia e nell'arte, 1778–1963*, 2 vols. (Milan, 1964), vol. 2, pp. 11–27.

118. Viardot, *Souvenirs de chasse*, p. 58.

119. Peter Kemp, *The Strauss Family: Portrait of a Musical Dynasty* (London, 1985), pp. 31–2.

120. Cairns (trans. and ed.), *Memoirs of Hector Berlioz*, p. 420.

121. Cited in Richard Osborne, *Rossini: His Life and Works* (Oxford, 2007), p. 116.

122. John Mayne (trans. and ed.), *The Painter of Modern Life and Other Essays* (New York, 1964), p. 13.

123. F. M. Scherer, *Quarter Notes and Bank Notes: The Economics of Music Composition in the Eighteenth and Nineteenth Centuries* (Princeton, 2004), p. 147; Tim Blanning, *The Romantic Revolution* (London, 2010), p. 176.

124. Christopher Prendergast, *For the People by the People? Eugène Sue's 'Les Mystères de Paris': A Hypothesis in the Sociology of Literature* (Oxford, 2003), p. 66; B. P. Chevasco, *Mysterymania: The Reception of Eugène Sue in Britain, 1838–1860* (Berne, 2003), p. 40; James Allen, *In the Public Eye: A History of Reading in Modern France, 1800–1940* (Princeton, 1991), p. 55.

125. Martyn Lyons, *Le Triomphe du livre: Une histoire sociologique de la lecture dans la France du XIXe siècle* (Paris, 1987), p. 50; Henri Loustalan, *La Publicité dans la presse française* (Paris, 1933), p. 20; Pierre Pellissier, *Émile de Girardin: Prince de la presse* (Paris, 1985), pp. 98ff.

126. Jean-Louis Bory, *Eugène Sue* (Paris, 1962), p. 296.

127. Nora Atkinson, *Eugène Sue et le roman feuilleton* (Paris, 1929), p. 38.

128. Brynja Svane, *Les Lecteurs d'Eugène Sue: Le Monde d'Eugène Sue II, Textes: Cultures & Société*, 3-86 (Copenhagen, 1986), p. 347; Atkinson, *Eugène Sue*, p. 28; F. W. J. Hemmings, *The King of Romance: A Portrait of Alexandre Dumas*, p. 117.

129. Ibid., pp. 118, 138.

130. 'Notes from Paris', *Punch*, no. 5, 1843, p. 12; Charles Augustin Sainte-Beuve, 'Vérités sur la situation en littérature', *Portraits contemporains*, 5 vols. (Paris, 1888), vol. 3, p. 431.

131. Simon Eliot and Jonathan Rose, *A Companion to the History of the Book* (Chichester, 2009), pp. 273–4, 291–2.

132. Alexis Weedon, *Victorian Publishing: The Economics of Book Production for a Mass Market 1836–1916* (The Nineteenth Century Series; Farnham, 2003), p. 66;

Jean-Yves Mollier, *Louis Hachette* (Paris, 1999), p. 301; Barbier, *L'Empire du livre*, p. 454; Ronald Fullerton, *The Foundation of Marketing Practice: A History of Book Marketing in Germany* (London, 2016), p. 54.

133. Allen, *In the Public Eye*, table A.7.

134. Frédéric Barbier, 'Une production multipliée', in Chartier and Martin (eds.), *Histoire de l'édition française*, vol. 3, p. 105.

135. Allen, *In the Public Eye*, table 1.1; Eliot and Rose, *Companion*, p. 304.

136. Dietrich Bode, *Reclam: Daten, Bilder und Dokumente zur Verlagsgeschichte 1828–2003* (Stuttgart, 2003), p. 14.

137. J.-Y. Mollier, *Michel & Calman Lévy ou la naissance de l'édition moderne 1836–1891* (Paris, 1984), p. 264.

138. Anik Devriès, 'La "Musique à bon marché" en France dans les années 1830', in Peter Bloom (ed.), *Music in Paris in the Eighteen-Thirties* (Stuyvesant, 1982), p. 245.

139. Yves Chevrel, Lieven D'hulst and Christine Lombez (eds.), *Histoire des traductions en langue française: XIXe siècle (1815–1914)* (Paris, 2012), pp. 290–91; Isavelle Olivero, 'The Paperback Revolution in France, 1850–1950', in John Spiers (ed.), *The Culture of the Publisher's Series*, 2 vols. (London, 2011), vol. 1: *Authors, Publishers and the Shaping of Taste*, pp. 76–8.

140. Olivero, 'Paperback Revolution', pp. 83–4.

141. Frédéric Barbier, 'Libraires et colporteurs', in Chartier and Martin, *Histoire de l'édition française*, vol. 3, pp. 237–40; Frédéric Barbier, 'La diffusion en Eure-et-Loire au XIXe siècle', in Jean-Yves Mollier (ed.), *Le Commerce de la librairie en France au XIX siècle 1789–1914* (Paris, 1998), pp. 162–3; Lyons, *Le Triomphe du livre*, pp. 152, 159; Martyn Lyons, *Reading Culture and Writing Practices in Nineteenth-Century France* (Toronto, 2008), pp. 50, 53–4.

142. Olivero, 'Paperback Revolution', p. 167.

143. [Carlo Collodi,] *Un romanzo in vapore: Da Firenze a Livorno. Guida storica-umoristica di Carlo Lornezini* (Florence, 1856).

144. Christine Haug, 'Ein Buchladen auf Stationen, wo sich zwei Linien kreuzen, müsste gute Geschäfte machen': Der deutsche Bahnhofs- und Verkehrsbuchhandel von 1850 bis zum Ende der Weimarer Republik im internationalen Vergleich', in Monika Burri, Kilian T. Elsasser and David Gugerli (eds.), *Die Internationalität der Eisenbahn 1830–1970* (Zurich, 2003), pp. 71–89.

145. Barbier, 'Libraires et colporteurs', pp. 246–7; Jean Mistler, *La Librairie Hachette de 1826 à nos jours* (Paris, 1964), pp. 81, 131.

146. Viardot, *Espagne et beaux-arts*, pp. 360, 368; Anne Marie de Brem, *L'Atelier d'Ary Scheffer* (Paris, 1992), p. 18; Mrs Grote, *Memoir of the Life of Ary Scheffer* (London, 1860), pp. 26–8, 49.

147. NYPL, JOE 82-1, 7, Letter from Pauline Viardot to Julius Rietz, Weimar, 24 Dec. 1858; Camille Saint-Saëns, *Musical Memories* (London, 1921), pp. 145–6.

148. See Peter Burke, 'Art, Market and Collecting in Early Modern Europe', in *Artwork through the Market* (Bratislava, 2004), pp. 71–7.

149. Nicholas Green, 'Circuits of Production, Circuits of Consumption: The Case of Mid-Nineteenth-Century French Art Dealing', *Art Journal*, vol. 48, no. 1, 1989 (Spring), p. 30.

150. Ibid., p. 98.

151. André Joubin (ed.), *Correspondance générale d'Eugène Delacroix*, 5 vols. (Paris, 1936–8), vol. 2, pp. 191–2. The critic Ludovic Vitet attacked the painting in 'Exposition des tableaux en bénéfice des Grecs; II. M. Delacroix', *Le Globe*, 3 June 1826, pp. 372–4.

152. Michèle Beaulieu, 'Louis-Claude Viardot, collectionneur et critique d'art', Société d'Histoire de l'Art Français, séance du 4 février 1984, in *Bulletin de la Société d'Histoire de l'Art Français*, 1984, pp. 243–62.

153. Pamela Fletcher and Anne Helmreich (eds.), *The Rise of the Modern Art Market in London: 1850–1939* (Manchester, 2013), pp. 27–9; Dianne Macleod, *Art and the Victorian Middle Class: Money and the Making of Cultural Identity* (Cambridge, 1996), pp. 24, 49–55, 93, 393–4, 420, 447, 473–4. See also James Hamilton, *A Strange Business: Making Art and Money in Nineteenth-Century Britain* (London, 2014).

154. Thomas M. Bayer and John R. Page, *The Development of the Art Market in England: Money as Muse, 1730–1900* (London, 2011), p. 96; Marie-Clause Chaudonneret, 'Collectionner l'art contemporain (1820–1840): L'Exemple des banquiers', in Monica Preti-Hamard and Philippe Sénechal (eds.), *Collections et marchés de l'art en France 1789–1848* (Rennes, 2005), pp. 274–6; GJ, vol. 1, p. 877.

155. Antoine Étex, *Essai d'une revue synthétique sur l'Exposition Universelle de 1855* (Paris, 1856), p. 56.

156. Constance Cain Hungerford, *Ernest Meissonier: Master in His Genre* (Cambridge, 1999), pp. 106–9.

157. Samuel Hall, *Retrospect of a Long Life from 1815 to 1883*, 2 vols. (London, 1883), vol. 1, pp. 346–7.

158. Brem, *L'Atelier d'Ary Scheffer*, pp. 45–6, 50–55.

159. On this practice, see Patricia Mainardi, 'The 19th-Century Art Trade: Copies, Variations, Replicas', *The Van Gogh Museum Journal* (2000), pp. 61–73.

160. Vincent Pomarède, 'Eugène Delacroix: The State, Collectors and Dealers', in Arlette Sérullaz and Vincent Pomarède, *Delacroix: The Late Work* (London, 1999), p. 59.

161. Hubert Wellington (ed.), *The Journal of Eugène Delacroix*, trans. Lucy Norton (London, 2010), p. 181. See further, Sérullaz and Pomarède, *Delacroix*; Stephen Pinson, 'Reproducing Delacroix', *Visual Resources*, vol. 14, no. 2, 1998, pp. 155–87.

162. Maxime du Camp, *Le Salon de 1857* (Paris, 1857), p. 51.

163. Malcolm Warner, 'Millais in the Marketplace: The Crisis of the Late 1850s', in Fletcher and Helmreich (eds.), *Rise of the Modern Art Market*, p. 222.

164. Kisiel Marine, 'La peinture impressionniste et la décoration, 1870–1895', *Sociétés & Représentations*, no. 39, 2015/1 (Spring), pp. 257–88.

165. Marquis de Custine, *L'Espagne sous Ferdinand VII*, 2 vols. (Paris, 1838), vol. 2, pp. 234–6.

166. Louis Viardot, 'Une nuit du Pâques au Kremlin du Moscou', *L'Illustration*, 11 April 1846, p. 86.

167. Marquis de Custine, *Russia*, 3 vols. (London, 1844), vol. 3, p. 353.

168. TMS, pp. 207–9.

169. See the classic account by Edward Said, *Orientalism* (New York, 1978). For a longer perspective on the idea of Europe, Federico Chabod, *Storia dell'idea d'Europa* (Milan, 2007).

170. See Roberto Dainotto, *Europe (In Theory)* (Durham, 2007), and Maria Todorova, *Imagining the Balkans* (Oxford, 1997).

171. Ibid., p. 73.

172. A. Hugo, 'Ce que nous entendons par l'Orient', *Revue de l'Orient. Bulletin de la Société Orientale*, vol. 1, nos. 1–4, 1843, p. 7.

173. Katarina Gephardt, *The Idea of Europe in British Travel Narratives, 1789–1914* (Farnham, 2014), pp. 65–75.

174. Théophile Gautier, *Voyage en Espagne* (Paris, 1981), pp. 236–7. On the Romantic myth of Spain, Luis Méndez Rodriguez, *La imagen de Andalucía en el arte del siglo*

XIX (Seville, 2008); Calvo Serraller, *La imagen romántica de España: Arte y arquitectura del siglo XIX* (Madrid, 1995); James Parakilas, 'How Spain Got a Soul', in Jonathan Bellman (ed.), *The Exotic in Western Music* (Boston, Mass., 1998), pp. 137–93.

175. Viardot, *Lettres d'un Espagnol*, vol. 1, pp. 28–9.
176. Albert Bensoussan, 'Traducir el *Quijote*', *Mélanges de la casa de Velázquez: Cervantès et la France*, vol. 37, no. 2, 2007, pp. 11–31; Chevrel, D'hulst and Lombez (eds.), *Histoire des traductions*, pp. 569–71; Marta Giné-Janer, 'Voyages des textes: Les récits fantastiques de Mérimée en Espagne', *Cahiers*, no. 27, 2003, pp. 119–38; *NCI*, vol. 2, p. xv.
177. Viardot, *Lettres d'un Espagnol*, vol. 1, pp. 28–9; Heine, *Lutèce*, p. 412.
178. J. G. Kohl, *Russia* (London, 1844), p. 506.
179. Françoise Genevray, *George Sand et ses contemporains Russes* (Paris, 2000), p. 31.
180. TMS, pp. 81–2.
181. *Turgenevskii sbornik*, vol. 5, p. 352; N. S. Nikitina (ed.), *Letopis zhizni i tvorchestva I. S. Turgeneva: 1818–1858* (St Petersburg, 1995), p. 88.
182. *PSS*, vol. 13, p. 248.
183. Tamara Zviguilsky, 'Varvara Pétrovna Loutovinova (1788–1850): Mère d'Ivan Tourguéniev', *Cahiers*, no. 4, 1980, p. 50; *M. M. Stasiulevich i ero sovremenniki v ikh perepiskakh*, 5 vols. (St Petersburg, 1911–13), vol. 3, p. 222; N. A. Ostrovskaia, *Vospominaniia o Turgeneve* (Petrograd, 1915), p. 27; GJ, vol. 2, p. 541; Leonard Schapiro, *Turgenev: His Life and Times* (Oxford, 1978), p. 56.
184. Maksim Kovalevskii, 'Vospominaniia ob I. S. Turgeneve', *Minuvshie gody*, vol. 1, August 1908, p. 10.
185. I. B. Toman, 'I. S. Turgenev i nemetskaia kul'tura', *Turgenevskii sbornik* (Moscow, 1988), p. 31.
186. James L. Rice, 'Varvara Petrovna Turgeneva in Unpublished Letters to Her Son Ivan (1838–1844)', *Slavic Review*, vol. 56, no. 1, 1997 (Spring), p. 6.
187. Anton Seljak, *Ivan Turgenevs Ökonomien: Eine Schriftstellerexistenz zwischen Aristokratie, Künstlertum und Kommerz* (Basel, 2004), pp. 89–90; Schapiro, *Turgenev*, p. 31.
188. The knout was deemed so dreadful that it was abolished by the tsarist government in 1845, although it was soon replaced by the gauntlet. See Daniel Beer, *The House of the Dead: Siberian Exile under the Tsars* (London, 2016), pp. 272–3.
189. Ivan Turgenev, 'Avtobiografiia', *PSS*, vol. 15, p. 207; Seljak, *Ivan Turgenevs Ökonomien*, pp. 66, 81; Zviguilsky, 'Varvara Pétrovna Loutovinova', p. 64.
190. *Turgenevskii sbornik*, vol. 5, p. 352.
191. Fitzlyon, *Price of Genius*, p. 164.
192. Nauhaus (ed.), *Marriage Diaries of Robert and Clara Schumann*, pp. 248, 266; Nancy Reich, *Clara Schumann: The Artist and the Woman* (London, 1985), p. 96.
193. BNF, NA Fr. 16278, Papiers Viardot, vol. 7, Varia, f. 1, 'Engagement de Pauline Viardot avec le théâtre de St Petersbourg. Codicil, 26 Jan. 1844'.
194. Fitzlyon, *Price of Genius*, p. 180.
195. T. N. Livanova, *Opernaia kritika v Rossii*, vol. 1, vyp. 2 (Moscow, 1967), p. 66.
196. TMS, p. 218.
197. Patrick Waddington, 'The Role of Courtavenel in the Life and Work of Turgenev', in *Issues in Russian Literature before 1917: Selected Papers for the Third World Congress for Soviet and East European Studies* (Columbus, Ohio, 1989), p. 109.
198. HL, MUS 232/10, Meyerbeer to Louis Viardot, 1 Feb. 1846; Viardot, *Souvenirs de chasse*, p. 154; BNF, NA 16274, Papiers de Pauline Viardot, vol. 3, Lettres adressées à Louis Viardot, f. 259, Lettre d'Eugène Scribe, Aug. 1845.
199. Livanova, *Opernaia kritika*, p. 45.

200. Louise Héritte-Viardot, *Une famille de grands musiciens* (Paris, 1923), p. 68; Viardot, *Souvenirs de Chasse*, p. 215; Zvig., p. 69.
201. HL, MUS 264 (365), Pauline Viardot Journal, memoir dated 1887.

2 A REVOLUTION ON THE STAGE

1. Ute Lange-Brachmann and Joachim Draheim (eds.), *Pauline Viardot in Baden-Baden und Karlsruhe* (Baden-Baden, 1999), p. 148; Zvig., p. 220.
2. *PSS*, vol. 1, pp. 208–9.
3. Ibid., p. 210.
4. Eduard Hanslick, *Hanslick's Music Criticism* (New York, 1963), p. 34.
5. BNF, NA Fr. 16274, Papiers Viardot, vol. 7, Lettres adressées à Louis Viardot, Meyerbeer to Louis Viardot, f. 169; HL, MUS 232/10, Meyerbeer to Pauline Viardot, 8 May 1851.
6. BNF, NA Fr. 16272, Papiers Viardot, vol. 1, Lettres adressées à Pauline Viardot, Meyerbeer to Pauline Viardot, 1 July 1845; Meyerbeer to Pauline Viardot, 20 July 1846; HL, MUS 232/10, Meyerbeer to Pauline Viardot, 14 July 1845; Meyerbeer to Louis Viardot, 13 May 1846.
7. TMS, p. 232.
8. BMO, LA-VIARDOT PAULINE-65, Louis Viardot to George Sand, 22 Feb. 1847.
9. *PSS*, vol. 1, pp. 213–14.
10. *I. S. Turgenev v vospominaniiakh sovremennikov*, 2 vols. (Moscow, 1988), vol. 2, pp. 259–60.
11. BNF, NA Fr. 162778, Papiers Viardot, vol. 7, Varia: f. 3, Contract with Beale, 27 Mar. 1847; p. 16, Contract with Gye, 27 Feb. 1852; p. 18, Contract with Gye, 19 Mar. 1855; TMS, p. 240.
12. Reiner Zimmermann, *Giacomo Meyerbeer: Eine Biografie nach Dokumenten* (Berlin, 2014), p. 336; Jean-Claude Yon, 'Le Prophète, un opéra dans la tourmente politique', in Brzoska and Strohmann (eds.), *Meyerbeer: Le Prophète*, p. 152.
13. A. J. Meindre, *Histoire de Paris et de son influence en Europe depuis les temps les plus reculés jusqu'à nos jours*, 5 vols., (Paris, 1855), vol. 5, p. 332; P. Mansel, *Paris Between Empires* (London, 2001), p. 354.
14. Robert Letellier, *Giacomo Meyerbeer: A Reader* (Newcastle, 2007), p. 128. See also Jane Fulcher, 'Meyerbeer and the Music of Society', *The Musical Quarterly*, vol. 67, no. 2, Apr. 1981, pp. 213–29.
15. Jennifer Jackson, *Giacomo Meyerbeer: Reputation Without Cause? A Composer and His Critic* (London, 2011), p. 83.
16. John Rosselli, *The Life of Bellini* (Cambridge, 1996), p. 119.
17. Anselm Gerhard, *The Urbanization of Opera: Music Theater in Paris in the Nineteenth Century*, trans. Mary Whittall (Chicago, 1998), pp. 318–41; Fabien Guilloux, 'Le Livret du *Prophète*: Notes en marge d'une édition critique', in Brzoska and Strohmann (eds.), *Meyerbeer: Le Prophète*, pp. 41–2.
18. David Charlton (ed.), *The Cambridge Companion to Grand Opera* (Cambridge, 2003), part IV: 'On the Italian Assimilation of Grand Opera'; Gloria Staffieri, 'Grand Opera in Preunified Italy: Metamorphoses of a Political Genre', *The Opera Quarterly*, vol. 25, nos. 3–4, July–Oct. 1939, pp. 203–29.
19. See further, Jane Fulcher, *The Nation's Image: French Grand Opera as Politics and Politicized Art* (Cambridge, 1987).
20. Véron, *Mémoires*, vol. 3, p. 104.
21. Steven Huebner, 'Opera Audiences in Paris 1830–1870', *Music & Letters*, vol. 70, no. 2, May 1989, pp. 206–25.

22. BMO, Série FO 143, 'Académie royale de musique Direction-entreprise Véron, journal des recettes et des dépenses commencé le 1er juin 1831'.
23. Gerhard, *Urbanization of Opera*, pp. 25–33; William Crosten, *French Grand Opera: An Art and a Business* (New York, 1948), pp. 27–31; Tamvaco, *Les Cancans*, pp. 215–16; Véron, *Mémoires*, vol. 3, p. 115.
24. Véron, *Mémoires*, vol. 3, p. 182.
25. ANF, AJ/13/187/V, Direction Véron, Représentation de Robert le Diable (1831).
26. Jackson, *Giacomo Meyerbeer*, p. 104.
27. Henri Blaze de Bury, *Meyerbeer et son temps* (Paris, 1856), pp. 61–2; Letellier, *Meyerbeer: A Reader*, p. 368; Robert Letellier, *Meyerbeer Studies: A Series of Lectures, Essays and Articles on the Life and Work of Giacomo Meyerbeer* (Madison, 2005), p. 23.
28. *The Diaries of Giacomo Meyerbeer*, trans. Robert Letellier, 4 vols. (Madison, 1999–2004), vol. 1: *1791–1839*, p. 16.
29. See Murray Pittock (ed.), *The Reception of Sir Walter Scott in Europe* (London, 2006).
30. Opieński (ed.), *Chopin's Letters*, p. 157.
31. Cited in Crosten, *French Grand Opera*, pp. 62–3.
32. See A. Randier-Glenison, 'Maurice Schlesinger, éditeur de musique et fondateur de la *Gazette musicale de Paris, 1834–1846*', *Fontis artis musicae*, vol. 38:1, 1991, pp. 37–48; Katharine Ellis, *Music Criticism in Nineteenth-Century France: 'La Revue et Gazette Musicale de Paris' 1834–1880* (Cambridge, 1995); Katharine Ellis, 'The Uses of Fiction: *Contes* and *nouvelles* in the *Revue et Gazette musicale de Paris*, 1843–1844', vol. 90, no. 2, 2004, pp. 253–81; Emily Dolan and John Tresch, 'A Sublime Invasion: Meyerbeer, Balzac and the Opera Machine', *The Opera Quarterly*, vol. 27, no. 1, 2011, pp. 4–31.
33. Rémy Campos, 'Le commerce de la critique: Journalisme musical et corruption au milieu du xixᵉ siècle', *Sociétés & Représentations*, no. 40, 2015/2 (Autumn), pp. 221–45.
34. John Rosselli, *The Opera Industry in Italy from Cimarosa to Verdi: The Role of the Impresario* (Cambridge, 1984), p. 144.
35. Crosten, *French Grand Opera*, pp. 24–5.
36. Kerry Murphy, *Hector Berlioz and the Development of French Music Criticism* (Ann Arbor, 1988), pp. 53, 70–71; Henry Raynor, *Music and Society since 1815* (New York, 1976).
37. Tamvaco, *Les Cancans*, vol. 1, pp. 285–6.
38. Véron, *Mémoires*, vol. 3, pp. 232–41; Crosten, *French Grand Opera*, pp. 41–5; Théophile Gautier, *Histoire de l'art dramatique en France*, vol. 1, p. 192.
39. Heinrich Heine, 'Über die französische Bühne: Vertraute Briefe an August Lewald', in *Sämtliche Schriften*, ed. Klaus Briegleb, 6 vols. (Munich, 1968), vol. 3, p. 339.
40. Cited in Carlotta Sorba, 'To Please the Public: Composers and Audiences in Nineteenth-Century Italy', *The Journal of Interdisciplinary History*, vol. 36, no. 4, *Opera and Society: Part II* (Spring 2006), p. 609.
41. Stendhal, *Life of Rossini*, p. 207 (Stendhal's emphasis).
42. Robert Letellier, *Meyerbeer's Robert le diable: The Premier Opéra Romantique* (Newcastle, 2012), p. 108.
43. Arthur Loesser, *Men, Women and Pianos: A Social History* (London 1955), pp. 156–7.
44. Ibid, p. 362
45. Ibid., p. 235.

46. Mary Burgan, 'Heroines at the Piano: Women and Music in Nineteenth-Century Fiction', in Nicholas Temperley (ed.), *The Lost Chord: Essays on Victorian Music* (Bloomington, 1989), p. 43.

47. Cyril Ehrlich, *The Piano: A History* (Oxford, 1976), pp. 10, 27–34, 37, 109–10.

48. Loesser, *Men, Women and Pianos*, p. 386; Andreas Ballstaedt and Tobias Widmaier, *Salonmusik: Zur Geschichte und Funktion einer bürgerlichen Musikpraxis* (Wiesbaden, 1989), p. 32.

49. Benjamin Vogel, 'The Piano as a Symbol of Burgher Culture in Nineteenth-Century Warsaw', *The Galpin Society Journal*, vol. 46, Mar. 1993, pp. 137–46.

50. Anne Swartz, 'Technological Muses: Piano Builders in Russia, 1810–1881', *Cahiers du monde russe*, vol. 43, no. 1, Jan.–Mar. 2002, p. 122.

51. Ivan Turgenev, *Home of the Gentry*, trans. Richard Freeborn (London, 1970), pp. 169–70.

52. Ballstaedt and Widmaier, *Salonmusik*, p. 194.

53. Leon Botstein, 'Listening Through Reading: Musical Literacy and the Concert Audience', *19th-Century Music*, vol. 16, no. 2, 1992 (Fall), p. 135.

54. Thomas Christensen, 'Four-Hand Piano Transcription and Geographies of Nineteenth-Century Musical Reception', *Journal of the American Musicological Society*, vol. 52, no. 2, 1999 (Summer), pp. 255–98 (statistics on p. 257).

55. Richard Wagner, *My Life*, trans. Andrew Gray (Cambridge, 1983), p. 155.

56. H. C. Robbins Landon (ed.), *Haydn: Chronicle and Works*, 5 vols. (London, 1976–80), vol. 1, pp. 350–51; Blanning, *Culture of Power*, pp. 166–8.

57. Jan Swafford, *Johannes Brahms: A Biography* (New York, 1997), p. 153.

58. Jan Swafford, *Beethoven: Triumph and Anguish* (New York, 2014), pp. 453–4, 477.

59. Ibid., p. 263. See further, Staffan Albinsson, 'Early Music Copyrights: Did They Matter for Beethoven and Schumann?', *International Review of the Aesthetics and Sociology of Music*, vol. 43, no. 2, 2012, pp. 265–302.

60. Rosselli, *Life of Bellini*, p. 64.

61. Ibid., pp. 75–7; Timothy King, 'Patronage and Market in the Creation of Opera before the Institution of Intellectual Property', *Journal of Cultural Economics*, vol. 25, no. 1, Feb. 2001, p. 40; John Rosselli, 'Verdi e la storia della retribuzione del compositore italiano', *Studi Verdiani*, vol. 2, 1983, p. 17.

62. Guido Zavani (ed.), *Donizetti: Vita, musiche, epistolario* (Bergamo, 1948), p. 515.

63. Stefano Baia Curioni, *Mercanti dell'opera: Storie di Casa Ricordi* (Milan, 2011), p. 103; Luke Jensen, *Giuseppe Verdi and Giovanni Ricordi with Notes on Francesco Lucca* (New York, 1989), p. 40.

64. Curioni, *Mercanti dell'opera*, p. 107.

65. Ibid., pp. 151–3; Rosselli, 'Verdi e la storia', pp. 22–3.

66. Jensen, *Giuseppe Verdi*, Appendix to ch. 2.

67. Ibid., pp. 35, 41, 73.

68. Curioni, *Mercanti dell'opera*, pp. 77, 244.

69. Nauhaus (ed.), *Marriage Diaries of Robert and Clara Schumann*, p. 200.

70. Beatrix Borchard, '"Ma chère petite Clara – Pauline de mon coeur": Clara Schumann et Pauline Viardot, une amitié d'artistes franco-allemande', *Cahiers*, no. 20, 1996, p. 138; Fitzlyon, *Price of Genius*, pp. 210–11.

71. Jackson, *Giacomo Meyerbeer*, pp. 128–9. See further, Leon Plantinga, *Schumann as Critic* (New Haven, 1967).

72. *PSS*, vol. 1, p. 286.

73. Hector Berlioz, *Evenings with the Orchestra*, ed. and trans. Jacques Barzun (New York, 1956), p. 68.

74. William Weber, 'The Origins of the Concert Agent in the Social Structure of Concert Life', in Hans Bödeker, Patrice Veit and Michael Werner (eds.), *Le Concert et son*

public: Mutations de la vie musicale en Europe de 1780 à 1914 (Paris, 2002), p. 134; Jeffrey Cooper, *The Rise of Instrumental Music and Concert Series in Paris 1828–1871* (Ann Arbor, 1983), pp. 102–3.

75. Cyril Ehrlich, *First Philharmonic: A History of the Royal Philharmonic Society* (Oxford, 1995), pp. 33–44.

76. William Weber, 'Wagner, Wagnerism and Musical Idealism', in David Large and William Weber (eds.), *Wagnerism in European Culture and Politics* (Ithaca, NY, 1984), p. 50.

77. Murphy, *Hector Berlioz*, pp. 137–8.

78. Peter Schmitz, *Johannes Brahms und der Leipziger Musikverlag Breitkopf & Härtel* (Göttingen, 2009), p. 71.

79. Weber, 'Wagner, Wagnerism and Musical Idealism', p. 38.

80. James Garratt, *Music, Culture and Social Reform in the Age of Wagner* (Cambridge, 2010), p. 117; Botstein, 'Listening Through Reading', p. 133; Cecelia Hopkins Porter, 'The New Public and the Reordering of the Musical Establishment: The Lower Rhine Music Festivals, 1818–67', *19th-Century Music*, vol. 3, no. 3, Mar. 1980, pp. 219–23.

81. William Weber, *Music and the Middle Class: The Social Structure of Concert Life in London, Paris and Vienna* (London, 1975, new edn 2004), p. 24.

82. Cooper, *Rise of Instrumental Music*, pp. 69–70.

83. William Weber, *The Great Transformation of Musical Taste: Concert Programming from Haydn to Brahms* (Cambridge, 2008), pp. 162–4.

84. 'What is the Meaning of the Word "Classical" in a Musical Sense?', *Musical Library Monthly Supplement*, no. 25, Apr. 1836, pp. 64–5; Weber, *Great Transformation*, pp. 122–4.

85. Melanie Stier, *Pauline Viardot-Garcia in Grossbritannien und Irland* (Hildesheim, 2012), pp. 175–9, 213–16; FM, Gen/G/Gounod/3, Charles Gounod to Henry Chorley, 21 Feb. 1851. See also Nikolai Žekulin, 'Pauline Viardot et la "Musique ancienne"', *Cahiers,* no. 34, 2010, pp. 47–77. The first performance of a full Handel opera after the composer's death in 1759 was Oskar Hagen's production of *Rodelinda* in Göttingen in 1920 (communication by Barbara Diana).

86. Walker, *Franz Liszt: The Virtuoso Years*, p. 289.

87. Cairns (trans. and ed.), *Memoirs of Hector Berlioz*, p. 250.

88. HL, MUS 264 (365), Pauline Viardot Journal, memoir dated 1887.

89. See James Hudson, *Listening in Paris: A Cultural History* (Berkeley, Calif., 1995); Richard Sennett, *The Fall of Public Man: On the Social Psychology of Capitalism* (New York, 1974). See also Weber, *Music and the Middle Class*, p. xxix.

90. Christina Bashford, 'Public Chamber-Music Concerts in London, 1835–50: Aspects of History, Repertory and Reception', Ph.D. diss., King's College London, 1996, p. 173.

91. Antje Pieper, *Music and the Making of Middle-Class Culture: A Comparative History of Nineteenth-Century Leipzig and Birmingham* (London, 2008), pp. 99–103.

92. Christopher Gibbs and Dana Gooley (eds.), *Franz Liszt and His World* (Princeton, 2006), pp. 153–60.

93. Devriès, 'La "Musique à bon marché"', p. 231.

94. Garratt, *Music, Culture and Social Reform*, pp. 117–21.

95. Joel-Marie Fauquet, 'L'Association des artistes musiciens et l'organisation du travail de 1843 à 1853', in Hughes Dufourt and J.-M. Fauquet, *La Musique et le pouvoir* (Paris, 1987), pp. 103–11.

96. Swafford, *Beethoven*, pp. 934–5; Berlioz, *Evenings with the Orchestra*, p. 343; Opieński (ed.), *Chopin's Letters*, p. 295.

97. *PSS*, vol. 1, pp. 231–2.

98. Ibid., p. 248.

99. Afanasy Fet, *Moi vospominaniia*, 2 vols. (Moscow, 1890–91), vol. 1, p. 113.

100. *PSS*, vol. 1, pp. 307–8.

101. Héritte-Viardot, *Une famille de grands musiciens*, p. 118.

102. See Waddington, 'Role of Courtavenel'.

103. TMS, pp. 204–8.

104. Michael Steen, *Enchantress of Nations. Pauline Viardot: Soprano, Muse and Lover* (Cambridge, 2007), p. 153.

105. Zavani (ed.), *Donizetti*, p. 641.

106. ROH, Collections, SC 1/1/10-11, Frederick Gye Diaries and Correspondence, 18–20 July 1849, 27 Oct. 1850.

107. HL, MUS 264 (365), Pauline Viardot Journal, memoir dated 1887.

108. Mackinlay, *Garcia the Centenarian*, pp. 96–7.

109. Belinda Jack, *George Sand: A Woman's Life Writ Large* (London, 2001), p. 304.

110. Jeffrey Kallberg, 'Chopin in the Marketplace: Aspects of the International Music Publishing Industry', *Notes*, vol. 39, no. 3, Mar. 1983, p. 549; Opieńsky (ed.), *Chopin's Letters*, p. 169; Tad Szulc, *Chopin in Paris: The Life and Times of the Romantic Composer* (New York, 1998), p. 223.

111. *Breitkopf und Härtel in Paris: The Letters of Their Agent Heinrich Probst between 1833 and 1840*, trans. Hans Lenneberg (Stuyvesant, 1990), pp. 25, 61.

112. Kallberg, 'Chopin in the Marketplace', p. 550; Opieńsky (ed.), *Chopin's Letters*, vol. 1, pp. 334, 358, 648–9.

113. TMS, p. 105.

114. Alan Walker, *Fryderyk Chopin: A Life and Times* (London, 2018), pp. 564–5.

115. Jean-Jacques Eigeldinger, *Chopin vu par ses élèves* (Neuchâtel, 1979), p. 264.

116. Carolyn Shuster, 'Six Mazurkas de Frédéric Chopin transcrites pour chant et piano par Pauline Viardot', *Revue de Musicologie*, vol. 75, no. 2, 1989, pp. 265–83. See further Magdalena Chylińska, John Comber and Artur Szklener (eds.), *Chopin's Musical Worlds: The 1840s*, trans. John Comber (Warsaw, 2007), pp. 126–37.

117. Cited in Seljak, *Ivan Turgenevs Ökonomien*, p. 89.

118. Ibid., p. 92.

119. *PSS*, vol. 1, p. 215.

120. *PSS*, vol. 1, p. 232.

121. Nikitina (ed.), *Letopis zhizni i tvorchestva I. S. Turgeneva*, p. 135.

122. *PSS*, vol. 1, p. 267.

123. BNF, NA Fr. 16274, Papiers Viardot, vol. 7, Lettres adressées à Louis Viardot, f. 23.

124. BNF, Aux Électeurs . . . de Seine-et-Marne. Louis Viardot [20 Mar. 1848].

125. Jean Larnac, *George Sand révolutionnaire* (Paris, 1947), p. 163.

126. ANF, AJ/13/180, 2, AJ 13/1160, 9, Correspondence between Ledru-Rollin and Duclot, 1848; ANF, AJ/13/180, 2, Fermeture, 'Au nom du peuple', April 1848.

127. TMS, p. 248.

128. Ibid., pp. 249–50.

129. BNF, NA 16274, Papiers de Pauline Viardot, vol. 1, f. 130, Manuel Garcia to Pauline Viardot.

130. Shuster, 'Six Mazurkas', p. 270; Mackinlay, *Garcia the Centenarian*, p. 170; BL MUS 329, f. 129, 31 May 1848; Letter from Paulin Viardot to Lord Falmouth, June 1848, private collection.

131. NYPL, JOE 82-1, 14, Letter from Pauline Viardot to Julius Rietz, 7 June 1839; TMS, p. 256.

132. TMS, p. 259.

133. Brzoska and Strohmann (eds.), *Meyerbeer: Le Prophète*, pp. 152–6.

134. *Diaries of Giacomo Meyerbeer*, vol. 2: *1840–1849*, p. 296.

135. BNF, NA 16274, Papiers de Pauline Viardot, vol. 3, Lettres adressées à Louis Viardot, ff. 177–8, Meyerbeer to Louis Viardot, 24 June 1848.

136. Zimmermann, *Giacomo Meyerbeer*, p. 339; *Diaries of Giacomo Meyerbeer*, vol. 2, pp. 295–8.137. Letellier, *Meyerbeer Studies*, p. 196.

138. *L'Âne à Baptiste, ou, Le Berceau du socialisme, grande folie lyrique en quatre actes et douze tableaux* (Paris, 1849).

139. Zimmermann, *Giacomo Meyerbeer*, p. 326.

140. Gerhard, *Urbanization of Opera*, pp. 254 ff.

141. Karin Pendle, *Eugène Scribe and French Opera of the Nineteenth Century* (Ann Arbor, 1979), pp. 502–4.

142. Frederic Coubes, 'Pauline Viardot dans *Le Prophète*', *Cahiers*, no. 2, 1978, pp. 109–16.

143. Stier, *Pauline Viardot-Garcia in Grossbritannien*, pp. 44–6, 50.

144. Gautier, *Histoire de l'art dramatique*, p. 86.

145. Marie-Hélène Coudroy, *La Critique parisienne des 'grands opéras' de Meyerbeer* (Paris, 1988), p. 11.

146. Brzoska and Strohmann (eds.), *Meyerbeer: Le Prophète*, p. 158; Giacomo Meyerbeer, *Briefwechsel und Tagebücher*, ed. Heinz Becker, 8 vols. (Berlin, 1959, 2006), vol. 4, pp. 487–8; Fitzlyon, *Price of Genius*, p. 245; TMS, p. 273.

147. BMD, 091 VIA, Letter from Pauline Viardot to Mme Puzzi (1849); Meyerbeer, *Briefwechsel und Tagebücher*, vol. 2, pp. 372–3.

148. FM, GEN/T/Turgenev, Turgenev to Henry Chorley, 6 November 1849.

149. *PSS*, vol. 1, p. 300.

150. Ibid.; Brzoska and Strohmann (eds.), *Meyerbeer: Le Prophète*, p. 465; Robert Letellier, *The Operas of Giacomo Meyerbeer* (Cranbury, NJ, 2006), pp. 197–8; Johannes Weber, *Meyerbeer: Notes et souvenirs d'un de ses secrétaires* (Paris, 1898), p. 90; *Le Journal des débats*, 20 and 29 April, 27 October 1849.

151. Murphy, *Hector Berlioz*, p. 134; *La France musicale*, 29 Apr. 1849, p. 3; A. Gozenpud, *I. S. Turgenev* (St Petersburg, 1994), p. 46; Wellington (ed.), *Journal of Eugène Delacroix*, p. 102.

152. Wagner, *My Life*, p. 436.

153. Ibid., pp. 129–42.

154. Tom Kaufman, 'Wagner v Meyerbeer', *The Opera Quarterly*, vol. 19, no. 4, 2003, pp. 648–9.

155. Ibid.

156. Meyerbeer, *Briefwechsel und Tagebücher*, vol. 3, p. 28.

157. Letellier, *Meyerbeer: A Reader*, p. 306; Kaufman, 'Wagner v Meyerbeer', p. 649.

158. Paul Rose, *Wagner: Race and Revolution* (London, 1996), pp. 80–82.

159. Hans Becker, *Der Fall Heine–Meyerbeer* (Berlin, 1958), p. 101; Henri Blaze de Bury, *Meyerbeer et son temps*, p. 217.

160. Jim Samson, *Chopin* (Oxford, 1996), p. 260.

161. Benita Eisler, *Chopin's Funeral* (London, 2003), p. 3; *PSS*, vol. 1, p. 332.

162. FM, GEN/T/Turgenev, Turgenev to Henry Chorley, 6 Nov. 1849.

3 THE ARTS IN THE AGE OF MECHANICAL REPRODUCTION

1. 'La Villa Medicis en 1840: Souvenirs d'un pensionnaire', *Gazette des beaux-arts*, 1 April 1901, p. 272; Charles Gounod, *Mémoires d'un artiste* (Paris, 1896), p. 175.

2. Thérèse Marix-Spire, 'Gounod and His First Interpreter, Pauline Viardot – Part 1', *The Musical Quarterly*, vol. 31, no. 2, Apr. 1945, pp. 195–6.

3. See his letter to Henry Chorley, in which he writes about her input into the first act in which she helped him change the 'ode of Sapho', but asks the music critic to keep this to himself: FM, Gen/G/Gounod/1, Charles Gounod to Henry Chorley, 11 Oct. 1850.

4. A. I. Gertsen, *Sobranie sochinenii v tridtsati tomakh* (Moscow, 1954–64), vol. 24, p. 17.5. Patrick Waddington, 'Turgenev and Gounod: Rival Strangers in the Viardots' Country Nest', *New Zealand Slavonic Journal*, no. 2, 1976, p. 14.

6. *NCI*, vol. 1, p. 41.

7. *PSS*, vol. 2, p. 21.

8. *NCI*, vol. 1, pp. 36–9.

9. Ibid., vol. 2, p. 20; Waddington, 'Turgenev and Gounod', pp. 18–20.

10. *NCI*, vol. 1, p. 41.

11. Waddington, 'Turgenev and Gounod', p. 25.

12. BNF, NA 16278, Papiers Viardot, IV, Lettres, ff. 368–9, Pauline Viardot to Ivan Turgenev, June 1850; Waddington, 'Turgenev and Gounod', pp. 25–7.

13. Ibid., p. 28.

14. I. S. Turgenev, *Moskovskoe Vremia* (Moscow, 2018), p. 89.15. A. Ostrovskii, *Turgenev v zapiskakh sovremennikov* (Leningrad, 1929), pp. 91–2; *Turgenevskii sbornik: materialy k polnomu sobranii sochinenii i pisem I. S. Turgeneva*, 5 vols. (Moscow, 1964–9), vol. 2, p. 326.

16. *PSS*, vol. 2, pp. 40–41.

17. Ibid., pp. 71–3.18. Ibid., pp. 74, 82; Seljak, *Ivan Turgenevs Ökonomien*, p. 110.

19. BNF, NA Fr. 16274, Papiers Viardot, vol. 7, Lettres adressées à Louis Viardot, George Sand to Louis Viardot, 28 Apr. 1858.

20. Gounod, *Mémoires*, p. 187.

21. See Steven Huebner, *The Operas of Charles Gounod* (Oxford, 1990), p. 31.

22. BNF, NA Fr. 16278, Papiers Viardot, vol. 7, Varia, f. 15, 28 Feb. 1851.

23. *The Times*, 11 Aug. 1851, p. 3. See Stier, *Pauline Viardot-Garcia in Grossbritannien*, pp. 112 ff.

24. Pauline Viardot to Joaquina Garcia, July 1851, private collection.

25. Paul Young, *Globalization and the Great Exhibition: The Victorian New World Order* (Basingstoke, 2009), pp. 51–2; Charles Babbage, *The Exposition of 1851* (London, 1851), pp. 42–3.

26. Karl Marx and Friedrich Engels, 'Review: May–October 1850', *Neue Rheinische Zeitung*, cited from Marxist-org Internet Archive.

27. Clare Pettitt, *Patent Inventions: Intellectual Property and the Victorian Novel* (Oxford, 2004), p. 86.

28. Walter Benjamin, *The Arcades Project*, ed. Rolf Tiedemann, trans. Howard Eiland and Kevin McLaughlin (New York, 2002).

29. Pettitt, *Patent Inventions*, pp. 145–6; Charles Fay, *The Palace of Industry 1851* (Cambridge, 1951), p. 53.

30. Valentin Kovalev, 'Zapiski okhotnika', *I. S. Turgeneva: voprosy genezisa* (Moscow, 1980), pp. 54–8; V. P. Botkin and I. Turgenev, *Neizdannaia perepiska, 1851–1869* (Moscow–Leningrad, 1930), p. 12.

31. W. Rowe, *Through Gogol's Looking Glass* (New York, 1976), p. 113; *PSS*, vol. 2, p. 122.

32. *GJ*, vol. 2, p. 499.

33. A. Dunin, 'Ssylka I. S. Turgeneva v Orlovskuiu gub.', *Minuvshchie gody*, no. 8, 1908, pp. 34–6; *Vsemirnyi vestnik*, no. 1, 1901, Prilozhenie (Appendix), p. 31; Waddington, 'Some Gleanings on Turgenev', p. 211; *PSS*, vol. 2, pp. 134–5.

34. *PSS*, vol. 2, p. 135; Kovalev, 'Zapiski okhotnika', p. 196; Yulian Oksman, *I. S. Turgenev. Issledovaniia i materialy* (Odessa, 1921), pp. 18–20, 31–42.

35. *Russkoe bogatstvo*, no. 8, August 1894, p. 476.

36. B. Sokolov, 'Muzhik v izobrazhenii Turgeneva', in I. N. Rozanov and Iu. M. Sokolov (eds.), *Tvorchestvo Turgeneva: svornik statei* (Moscow, 1920), p. 203.

37. See e.g. 'Photographs from Russian Life', *Fraser's Magazine*, Aug. 1854, p. 210; Alphonse de Lamartine, 'Littérature Russe: Ivan Tourgueneff: CXXXI Entretien', in *Cours familier de littérature par mois* (Paris, 1866); N.M., 'Cherty iz parizhskoi zhizni I. S. Turgeneva', *Russkaia mysl'*, no. 11, 1883, p. 325.

38. Kovalev, 'Zapiski okhotnika', p. 120; Patrick Waddington, *Turgenev and George Sand: An Improbable Entente* (London, 1981), p. 66.

39. Dunin, 'Ssylka', p. 38; *PSS*, vol. 2, pp. 34, 40, 42–3, 165, 197.

40. HL, MUS 232/10, Meyerbeer to Pauline Viardot, 14 May 1852.

41. *PSS*, vol. 2, 159; T. N. Livanova, *Opernaia kritika v Rossii*, vol. 1, vyp. 2 (Moscow, 1967), pp. 11, 34.

42. HL, MUS 264 (76), Pauline Viardot to Louis Viardot, 17 Mar., 22 Apr. 1853; Pauline Viardot to Louis Viardot, 25 Apr. 1853, private collection.

43. HL, MUS 264 (76), Pauline Viardot to Louis Viardot, 27 Mar. 1853.

44. Philip Taylor, *Anton Rubinstein: A Life in Music* (Bloomington, 2007), p. 41; V. T. Sokolov, 'A. S. Dargomyzhskii v 1856–1869 gg.', *Russkaia Starina*, vol. 46, no. 5, 1885, p. 345.

45. *PSS*, vol. 2, p. 200; Fitzlyon, *Price of Genius*, pp. 291–2.

46. 'Turgenev v dnevnike P. A. Vasil'chikova', in *I. S. Turgenev. Novye materialy i issledovaniia: Literaturnoe Nasledstvo* (Moscow, 1967), p. 349; Dunin, 'Ssylka', p. 37; *PSS*, vol. 2, p. 244.

47. *Soch.*, vol. 7, pp. 220–29.

48. Seljak, *Ivan Turgenevs Ökonomien*, pp. 114–16, 491; *PSS*, vol. 3, pp. 62, 77, 143.

49. René Bouvier and Édouard Maynial, *Les Comptes dramatiques de Balzac* (Paris, 1938), p. 85. Honoré de Balzac, *Correspondance*, ed. Roger Pierrot (Paris, 1962), vol. 2, pp. 621, 740.

50. Pettitt, *Patent Inventions*, p. 65; Christophe Charle, 'Le Champ de la production littéraire', in Chartier and Martin (eds.), *Le Temps des éditeurs* (Paris, 1985), vol. 3, pp. 148–50.

51. Frédéric Barbier, 'Le commerce international de la librairie française au XIXe siècle (1815–1913)', *Revue d'histoire moderne et contemporaine*, vol. 28, no. 1, 1981, pp. 94–117.

52. Christine Haynes, *Lost Illusions: The Politics of Publishing in Nineteenth-Century France* (Cambridge, Mass., 2010), p. 76; Herman Dopp, *La Contrefaçon des livres français en Belgique 1815–1852* (Louvain, 1932), pp. 74–6, 81, 94.

53. Catherine Seville, *The Internationalisation of Copyright Law: Books, Buccaneers, and the Black Flag in the Nineteenth Century* (Cambridge, 2006), p. 16; Peter Baldwin, *The Copyright Laws: Three Centuries of Trans-Atlantic Battle* (Princeton, 2014), p. 110; Richard Swartz, 'Wordsworth, Copyright, and the Commodities of Genius', *Modern Philology*, vol. 89, no. 4, 1992, pp. 482–509; T. B. Macaulay, *Speeches by Lord Macaulay: With His Minute on Indian Education*, ed. G. M. Young, Oxford, 1935, p. 164.

54. Isabelle Diu and Élisabeth Parinet, *Histoire des auteurs* (Paris, 2013), pp. 344–7.

55. Graham Robb, *Balzac: A Biography* (London, 1994), p. 239; Honoré de Balzac, 'Lettre adressée aux écrivains français du XIXe siècle', in *Oeuvres diverses*, ed. Pierre-George Castex, vol. 2 (Paris, 1990), p. 1250.

56. Victor Hugo, *Oeuvres complètes de Victor Hugo: Actes et paroles*, 3 vols. (Paris, 1937–40), vol. 1, pp. 306–8.

57. Stephan Füssel, *Schiller und seine Verleger* (Frankfurt, 2005), p. 311; Michael Westren, 'Development and Debate over Copyright in Imperial Russia, 1828–1917', *Russian History*, vol. 38, nos. 1–2, Spring–Summer 2003, p. 160.

58. Maria Iolanda Palazzolo, 'I tre occhi dell'editore: Cultura meridionale e mercato librario tra Otto e Novecento', *Meridiana*, no. 5, 'Città', 1989, pp. 169–98.

59. Alessandro Manzoni, *Epistolario di Alessandro Manzoni*, ed. Giovanni Sforza, 2 vols. (Milan, 1883), vol. 2, pp. 49–53.

60. Laura Forti, 'Alle origini dell'industria musicale italiana: Casa Ricordi e il diritto d'autore (1808–1892)', diss., Università Commerciale Luigi Bocconi, 2006, pp. 29–50; Curioni, *Mercanti dell'opera*, p. 80.

61. Olivero, 'Paperback Revolution', in Spiers (ed.), *Culture of the Publisher's Series*, vol. 1, p. 83.

62. Chartier and Martin (eds.), *Histoire de l'édition française*, vol. 3, pp. 138–9, 197–202; Diu and Parinet, *Histoire des auteurs*, p. 171; Ernest Vizetelly, *Emile Zola: Novelist and Reformer* (London, 1904), p. 114.

63. *GJ*, vol. 2, p. 867; George Sand, *Correspondance*, ed. Georges Lubin, 26 vols. (Paris, 1964–91), vol. 22, pp. 32, 45.

64. Haynes, 'The Politics of Authorship', p. 106; Frederick Brown, *Flaubert: A Biography* (London, 2007), pp. 429–30.

65. Kathryn Hughes, *George Eliot: The Last Victorian* (London, 1998), pp. 210–11.

66. Diu and Parinet, *Histoire des auteurs*, p. 369.

67. Émile Zola, 'Gustave Flaubert', *Oeuvres complètes,* 21 vols., ed. Henri Mitterand (Paris, 2002–10), vol. 10, p. 151; Francis Steegmuller (ed. and trans.), *The Letters of Gustave Flaubert, 1857–1880* (London, 1982), p. 78.

68. Simon Nowell-Smith, *International Copyright Law and the Publisher in the Reign of Queen Victoria* (Oxford, 1968), pp. 43–4; A. Parménie and C. Bonnier de la Chapelle, *Histoire d'un éditeur et de ses auteurs: P.-J. Hetzel* (Paris, 1953), pp. 233–4.

69. Barbier, 'Le commerce international de la librairie française', pp. 97–9.

70. Jean-Yves Mollier, 'Les Réseaux des libraires européens au milieu du XIXe siècle: L'Exemple des correspondants de la maison d'édition Michel Lévy frères, de Paris', in Barbier (ed.), *Est–ouest*, pp. 126–31. For more on Lacroix and *Les Misérables*, see David Bellos, *The Novel of the Century: The Extraordinary Adventure of 'Les Misérables'* (London, 2017).

71. Jules Hetzel, *La Propriété littéraire et le domaine public payant* (Brussels, 1860), p. 48.

72. ANF, AJ 13/1178, Le Droit, Journal des Tribunaux, 16 Oct. 1856, ff. 1–2.

73. Forti, 'Alle origini dell'industria musicale italiana', p. 40.

74. Nicholas Žekulin, 'Early Translations of Turgenev's "Zapiski okhotnika" into German, French and English', *New Zealand Slavonic Journal*, Festschrift in honour of Patrick Waddington (1994), pp. 229–34.

75. 'Photographs from Russian Life', p. 210; '*Zapiski okhotnika*', I. S. Turgeneva (1852–1952): *sbornik statei i materialov* (Orel, 1955), pp. 45–7, 112–16.

76. Pavel Annenkov, *The Extraordinary Decade: Literary Memoirs*, ed. Arthur P. Mendel, trans. Irwin R. Titunik (Ann Arbor, 1968), p. 201.

77. Xavier Darcos, 'Mérimée slavophile', *Cahiers*, no. 27, 2003, p. 15; Gilbert Phelps, *The Russian Novel in English Fiction* (London, 1956), p. 16; John L. Chamberlain, 'Notes on Russian Influences on the Nineteenth-Century French Novel', *The Modern Language Journal*, vol. 33, no. 5, 1949, pp. 374–6.

78. M. Cadot, *La Russie dans la vie intellectuelle française (1839–1856)* (Paris, 1967), p. 428; Wellington (ed.), *Journal of Eugène Delacroix*, p. 218.

79. Christophe Charle, *Les Intellectuels en Europe au xixe siècle: Essai d'histoire comparée* (Paris, 1996), pp. 123–7.

80. Michel Espagne, *Le Paradigme de l'étranger: Les Chaires de littérature étrangère au xixe siècle* (Paris, 1993), pp. 156–7, 195, 275; Thomas Loué, 'La *Revue des deux mondes* et ses libraires étrangers dans la lutte contre la contrefaçon belge (1848–52)', in Mollier (ed.), *Le Commerce de la librairie*, p. 327.

81. Sassoon, *The Culture of the Europeans*, pp. 33, 51.

82. Chevrel, D'hulst and Lombez (eds.), *Histoire des traductions*, pp. 266 ff.

83. Lieven D'hulst, 'Traduire L'Europe en France entre 1810 et 1840', in Michel Ballard (ed.), *Europe et traduction* (Ottawa, 1998), pp. 137–55; Chevrel, D'hulst and Lombez (eds.), *Histoire des traductions*, pp. 286, 293–4; Michael Hollington (ed.), *The Reception of Charles Dickens in Europe*, 2 vols. (London, 2013), vol. 1, pp. 20, 169.

84. Sassoon, *Culture of the Europeans*, p. 39; Peter France and Kenneth Haynes (eds.), *The Oxford History of Literary Translation in English*, vol. 4: *1790–1900* (Oxford, 2006), p. 34.

85. Norbert Bachleitner, 'Produktion, Tausch und Übersetzung im österreichischen Buchhandel im 19. Jahrhundert', in Barbier (ed.), *Est–ouest*, pp. 115, 122.

86. Isabelle Olivero, *L'Invention de la collection: De la diffusion de la littérature et des savoirs à la formation du citoyen au XIXe siècle* (Paris, 1999), p. 106; Jean-François Botrel, 'L'Exportation des livres et modèles éditoriaux français en Espagne et en Amérique latine (1814–1914)', in Jacques Michon and Jean-Yves Mollier (eds.), *Les Mutations du livre et de l'édition dans le monde du XVIIIe siècle à l'an 2000* (Paris, 2001), p. 224.

87. Sassoon, *Culture of the Europeans*, p. 51; Adriaan van der Weel, 'Nineteenth-Century Literary Translations from English in a Book Historical Context', in Martine de Clercq, Tom Toremans and Walter Verschueren (eds.), *Textual Mobility and Cultural Transmission* (Leuven, 2006), pp. 27–40.

88. Philippe Régnier, 'Littérature nationale, littérature étrangère au XIXe siècle: La Fonction de la *Revue des deux mondes* entre 1829 et 1870', in Michel Espagne and Michael Werner (eds.), *Philologiques. III. Qu'est-ce qu'une littérature nationale? Approches pour une théorie interculturelle du champ littéraire* (Paris, 1994), p. 300.

89. Hollington (ed.), *Reception of Charles Dickens in Europe*, vol. 1, pp. xxv–xxviii, 6–7, which incorrectly dates the first Russian translation of a work by Dickens, *Dombey and Son*, in 1847. *The Pickwick Papers* was translated into Russian in an abridged edition in 1838, and in a complete edition in 1840.

90. Cited in Stephen Regan (ed.), *The Nineteenth-Century Novel: A Reader* (London, 2001), p. 23. See further, Joseph T. Flibbert, 'Dickens and the French Debate over Realism: 1838–1856', *Comparative Literature*, vol. 23, no. 1, 1971 (Winter), pp. 18–31.

91. Hollington, *Reception of Charles Dickens in Europe*, pp. 20 ff.

92. Patrick Waddington, 'Dickens, Pauline Viardot, Turgenev: A Study in Mutual Admiration', *New Zealand Slavonic Journal*, no. 1, 1974, pp. 59–60.

93. Ibid., p. 60.

94. Champfleury, *Le Réalisme* (Paris, 1857), p. 6.

95. Elizabeth Barrett Browning, *Aurora Leigh* (New York, 1996), p. 149.

96. Champfleury, *Réalisme*, p. 2.

97. George Eliot, 'The Natural History of German Life', *The Essays of 'George Eliot' Complete*, ed. Nathan Sheppard (New York, 1883), p. 143; Aleksandr Zviguil'skii, *Ivan Turgenev i Frantsiia: Sbornik statei* (Moscow, 2010), p. 92.

98. Peter James Bowman, 'Fontane and the Programmatic Realists: Contrasting Theories of the Novel', *The Modern Language Review*, vol. 103, no. 1, Jan. 2008, pp. 130–31. On Turgenev and Viedert, see Vladimir Viedert and Nicholas Žekulin, 'The Viedert–Turgenev Correspondence', *New Zealand Slavonic Journal*, 1991, pp. 1–50.

99. Eliot, 'Natural History of German Life', p. 271. See further, John Rignall, *George Eliot, European Novelist* (Farnham, 2011).

100. *PSS*, vol. 2, pp. 191, 201, 205, 306; Zvig., p. 168.

101. Elizabeth McCauley, *Industrial Madness: Commercial Photography in Paris, 1848–1871* (New Haven, 1994), pp. 39, 73; Elizabeth McCauley, *A. A. E. Disdéri and the Carte de Visite Portrait Photograph* (London, 1985); Peter Hamilton and Roger Hargreaves, *The Beautiful and the Damned: The Creation of Identity in Nineteenth-Century Photography* (London, 2001); Quentin Bajac, '"Une branche d'industrie assez importante": L'Économie de daguerréotype à Paris , 1839–1850', in *Le Daguerréotype français: Un objet photographique* (Paris, 2003), pp. 47–8.

102. Charles Baudelaire, 'Le Public moderne et la photographie: Lettre à M. le Directeur de la *Revue française* sur le Salon de 1859', *Revue française*, vol. XVII, 20 June 1859, p. 263.

103. *Galerie des contemporains. Texte biographie par Dollingen. Portraits en pied, photographés par Disdéri* (Paris, 1861).

104. NYPL, JOE 82-1, 32, Letter from Pauline Viardot to Julius Rietz, 23 Apr. 1859; TMS, p. 286.

105. Theodore Zeldin, *France, 1848–1945*, 2 vols. (Oxford, 1973–7), vol. 2: *Intellect, Taste and Anxiety*, pp. 435–6; Dominique de Font-Réaulx, *Painting and Photography: 1839–1914* (Paris, 2012), pp. 144 ff; Hamilton and Hargreaves, *Beautiful and the Damned*, p. 45.

106. There is an extensive literature on Dickens, English realist literature and the impact of photography in the mid-Victorian era. For a good introduction, see Nancy Armstrong, *Fiction in the Age of Photography: The Legacy of British Realism* (Cambridge, Mass., 1999).

107. Charles Dickens, *Bleak House* (1853).

108. See e.g. Gustave Flaubert, *Correspondance*, 5 vols., eds. Jean Bruneau and Yvan Leclerc (Paris, 1973–2007), vol. 2, p. 35 (letter to Louise Colet, 16 Jan. 1852).

109. *GJ*, vol. 1, p. 642.

110. Flaubert, *Sentimental Education*, p. 25. 111. Roland Barthes, 'The Reality Effect', *The Rustle of Language*, trans. Richard Howard (New York, 1986), pp. 141–8.

112. Champfleury, *Réalisme*, p. 96.

113. Viardot, *Espagne et beaux-arts*, p. 353.

114. Charles Baudelaire, 'The Salon of 1859', in *The Mirror of Art: Critical Studies* (London, 1955), pp. 228–9.

115. Roubert Paul-Louis, 'La critique de la photographie, ou la genèse du discours photographique dans la critique d'art, 1839–1859', *Sociétés & Représentations*, no. 40, 2015/2 (Autumn), pp. 213–14.

116. Émile Zola, 'L'École française de peinture à l'exposition de 1878', *Oeuvres complètes*, pp. 992–3.

117. Albert de la Fizilière, 'Les Auberges illustrées', *L'Illustration*, vol. 22, 24 Dec. 1853, p. 425.

118. See the John Rand Collection at the Smithsonian Institution: http://www.aaa.si.edu/collections/john-goffe-rand-papers-6737/more.

119. On the impact of photography on the Barbizon landscape painters, see: Kermit Champa, *The Rise of Landscape Painting in France: Corot to Manet* (Manchester, NH, 1991), pp. 82 ff; André Jammes and Eugenia Janis, *The Art of French Calotype* (Princeton, 1983), pp. 82–91; Kimberly Jones et al., *In the Forest of Fontainebleau: Painters and Photographers from Corot to Monet* (New Haven, 2008), pp. 154–63; Malcolm Daniel, *Eugène Cuvelier: Photographer in the Circle of Corot* (New York, 1996), pp. 13–15; Aaron Scharf, *Art and Photography* (London, 1979), pp. 77–9, 89–92.

120. I. S. Zil'bershtein, 'Vospomonaniia I. E. Tsvetkova, 1874', in *I. S. Turgenev. Novye materialy i issledovaniia: Literaturnoe Nasledstvo*, p. 417.

121. I. S. Turgenev, *Sketches from a Hunter's Album* (1852), p. 247; Alphonse Daudet, *Quarante ans de Paris, 1857–1897* (Geneva, 1946), p. 268. See also Cynthia Marsh, 'Turgenev and Corot: An Analysis of the Comparison', *The Slavonic and East European Review*, vol. 61, no. 1, Kiev Congress Papers, Jan. 1983, pp. 107–17.

122. René Brimo, *L'Évolution du goût aux États-Unis d'après l'histoire des collections* (Paris, 1938), p. 51.

123. Simon Kelly, 'Early Patrons of the Barbizon School: The 1840s', *Journal of the History of Collections*, vol. 16, no. 2, 2004, pp. 161–72; Rolande Miquel and Pierre Miquel, *Théodore Rousseau: 1812–1867* (Paris, 2010), p. 110.

124. Nicholas Green, *The Spectacle of Nature: Landscape and Bourgeois Culture in Nineteenth-Century France* (Manchester, 1990), pp. 118–19; Jones et al., *In the Forest of Fontainebleau*, pp. 21–3.

125. Petra ten-Doesschate Chu (ed. and trans.), *The Letters of Gustave Courbet* (Chicago, 1992), pp. 60, 98–9.

126. Petra ten-Doesschate Chu, *The Most Arrogant Man in France: Gustave Courbet and the Nineteenth-Century Media Culture* (Princeton, 2007), pp. 50–52, 148.

127. Cited in Font-Réaulx, *Painting and Photography*, p. 60.

128. BNF, Yb3 1739 (1)-4, Gustave Courbet to Champfleury, Nov. 1854.

129. Ibid., Courbet to Champfleury, Nov. 1854. For this interpretation of *L'Atelier*: Béatrice Joyeux-Prunel, *Les Avant-gardes artistiques 1848–1918* (Paris, 2015), p. 53.

130. *Paris Universal Exhibition, 1855. Catalogue of the Works Exhibited in the British Section of the Exhibition, in French and English; Together with Exhibitors' Prospectuses, Prices Current, &c.* (London, 1855), p. 2.

131. Pierre Assouline, *Discovering Impressionism: The Life of Paul Durand-Ruel* (New York, 2004), p. 58.

132. Gerstle Mack, *Gustave Courbet* (New York, 1951), p. 137. See further, Oskar Bätschmann, *The Artist in the Modern World: The Conflict between Market and Self-Expression* (Cologne, 1997), pp. 122–30.

133. Walter Benjamin, *The Work of Art in the Age of Mechanical Reproduction*, trans. J. A. Underwood (London, 2008), p. 12.

134. Bayer and Page, *Development of the Art Market in England*, pp. 86, 247.

135. Ibid., p. 120; Jeremy Maas, *Gambart: Prince of the Victorian Art World* (London, 1975), pp. 115–16. Gambart outlined the business plan in a letter to his fellow print dealer George Pennell on 12 Nov. 1860. It is reproduced in Robert Verhoogt, *Art in Reproduction: Nineteenth-Century Prints after Lawrence Alma-Tadema, Jozef Israëls and Ary Scheffer* (Amsterdam, 2007), pp. 185–6.

136. Pamela Fletcher, 'Creating the French Gallery: Ernest Gambart and the Rise of the Commercial Art Gallery in Mid-Victorian London', *Nineteenth-Century Art Worldwide*, vol. 6, no. 1, 2007 (Spring).

137. Goupil's exploitation of this legal loophole led to a lawsuit brought by the descendants of Scheffer, Delaroche and Vernet against his company. See Agnès Penot, *La Maison Goupil: Galerie d'art internationale au XIXe siècle* (Paris, 2017), pp. 56–7.

138. Verhoogt, *Art in Reproduction*, pp. 292–4, 304.

139. Henri Béraldi, *Les Graveurs du XIXe siècle*, 12 vols. (Paris, 1885–92), vol. 12, p. 17.

140. Émile Zola, 'Nos peintres au Champ-de-Mars', *Écrits sur l'art* (Paris, 1991), p. 184.

141. *PSS*, vol. 2, pp. 279, 283, 305, 315; vol. 3, p. 11.

142. Aileen Kelly, *Toward Another Shore: Russian Thinkers between Necessity and Chance* (New Haven, 1998). p. 41.

143. *PSS*, vol. 2, p. 320.

144. *PSS*, vol. 3, pp. 85, 106, 117.

145. Ibid., pp. 132, 134.

146. Mark Everist, 'Enshrining Mozart: Don Giovanni and the Viardot Circle', *19th-Century Music*, vol. 25, nos. 2–3, 2001–2 (Fall/Spring), pp. 165–72; Catherine Vallet-Collot, 'Don Giovanni: Un manuscrit légendaire', *Revue de la BNF*, no. 54, 2017/1, pp. 108–19.

147. NYPL, JOE 82-1, 12, 7, Letter from Pauline Viardot to Julius Rietz, 7 Jan. 1859; Saint-Saëns, *Musical Memories*, p. 148; Héritte-Viardot, *Une famille de grand musiciens*, p. 93.

148. John Forster, *The Life of Charles Dickens*, ed. B. W. Matz, 2 vols. (London, 1911), vol. 2, p. 185; Waddington, 'Dickens, Pauline Viardot, Turgenev', pp. 56–8.

149. BNF, NA 16274, Papiers de Pauline Viardot, vol. 1, f. 255, Gounod to Pauline Viardot.

150. Thérèse Marix-Spire, 'Gounod and His First Interpreter, Pauline Viardot – Part II', *The Musical Quarterly*, vol. 31, no. 3, July 1945, pp. 299–317; *PSS*, vol. 2, p. 141.

4 EUROPEANS ON THE MOVE

1. *PSS*, vol. 3, p. 201.

2. Ibid., pp. 195, 219.

3. *LI*, pp. xvi, 83–4, 89.

4. I. S. Zil'bershtein, 'Poslednii dnevnik Turgeneva', *IPA*, vol. 1, p. 366.

5. *PSS*, vol. 3, pp. 161–2, 251.

6. NYPL, JOE 82-1, 10, Letter from Pauline Viardot to Julius Rietz, 1 Jan. 1859.

7. Zil'bershtein, 'Poslednii dnevnik Turgeneva', p. 366.

8. BNF, NA Fr. 16278, Papiers Viardot, vol. 7, Varia, ff. 74–6, Testament de Louis Viardot.

9. *PSS*, vol. 4, p. 211; Zvig., p. 28; Kendall-Davies, *The Life and Work of Pauline Viardot-Garcia*, vol. 1, p. 416.

10. Schapiro, *Turgenev*, p. 163; *PSS*, vol. 3, pp. 236, 257.

11. Botkin and Turgenev, *Neizdannaia perepiska, 1851–1869*, pp. 116–17, 138–9.

12. Fet, *Moi vospominaniia*, vol. 1, p. 212; *PSS*, vol. 3, p. 264.

13. IRL RAN, f. 365 (Botkin), op. 1, d. 68, l. 107; I. M. Grevs, *Turgenev i Italia* (Leningrad, 1925), pp. 33–41; *PSS*, vol. 3, pp. 269, 278.

14. Ivan Turgenev, 'Poezdka v Al'bano i Frascati', in *Soch.*, vol. 11, p. 81; *PSS*, vol. 3, p. 307.

15. Ivan Turgenev, *Literary Reminiscences*, trans. David Magarshack (Chicago, 1958), p. 193; Richard Freeborn, 'Turgenev at Ventnor', *Slavonic and East European Review*, vol. 51, no. 124, July 1973, pp. 387–8.

16. P. V. Annenkov, *Literaturnye vospominaniia* (Moscow, 1960), p. 452.

17. Freeborn, 'Turgenev at Ventnor', p. 389.

18. Allan Mitchell, *The Great Train Race* (New York, 2000), p. 70; James M. Brophy, *Capitalism, Politics and Railroads in Prussia, 1830–1870* (Columbus, 1998), p. 70.

19. GJ, vol. 2, p. 2.

20. Jeremy Black, The *British Abroad: The Grand Tour in the Eighteenth Century* (New York, 1992), pp. 7–12, 57–9; John Towner, 'The Grand Tour: A Key Phase in the History of Tourism', *Annals of Tourism Research*, vol. 12, no. 3, 1985, pp. 310–12; Jozsef Borocz, 'Travel-Capitalism: The Structure of Europe and the Advent of the Tourist Source', *Comparative Studies in Society and History*, vol. 34, no. 4, Oct. 1992, pp. 710–12; Jan Palmowski, 'Travels With Baedeker – The

Guidebook and the Middle Classes in Victorian and Edwardian Britain', in Rudy Koshar (ed.), *Histories of Leisure* (Oxford, 2002), p. 107; 'A Flight', *Household Words*, 30 August 1851.

21. Borocz, 'Travel-Capitalism', p. 721.
22. *The Edinburgh Review*, vol. 138, no. 282, Oct. 1873, p. 497; Theodor Fontane, 'Modernes Reisen: Eine Plauderei' (1873), in *Von, vor und nach der Reise: Plaudereien und kleine Geschichten* (Berlin, 1999), p. 5.
23. *PSS*, vol. 3, pp. 216, 231; *Exhibition of Art Treasures of the United Kingdom, Held at Manchester in 1857: Report of the Executive Committee* (Manchester, 1859). Elizabeth A. Pergram, *The Manchester Art Treasures Exhibition of 1857: Entrepreneurs, Connoisseurs and the Public* (Farnham, 2011), p. 63.
24. Nick Prior, *Museums and Modernity* (Oxford, 2002), pp. 37 ff; James J. Sheehan, *Museums in the German Art World: From the End of the Old Regime to the Rise of Modernism* (Oxford, 2000), pp. 83–4.
25. Ian Ousby, *The Englishman's England: Taste, Travel and the Rise of Tourism* (London, 1990), pp. 38–9; Gail Marshall, 'Women Re-Read Shakespeare Country', in Nicola Watson (ed.), *Literary Tourism and Nineteenth-Century Culture* (Basingstoke, 2009), p. 95; Bodo Plachta, 'Remembrance and Revision: Goethe's Houses in Weimar and Frankfurt', in Herald Hendrix (ed.), *Writers' Houses and the Making of Memory* (London, 2007), p. 55.
26. Barbara Schaff, 'John Murray's *Handbooks* to Italy: Making Tourism Literary', in Watson (ed.), *Literary Tourism*, pp. 106 ff; *Handbook for Travellers in Central Italy*, 5th edn (London, 1858), p. 270; *The Complete Works of Charles Dickens: Pictures from Italy and American Notes* (New York, 2009), pp. 65–6.
27. On Joanne and the Viardots: TMS, p. 174; Daniel Nordman, 'Les Guides-Joanne: Ancêtres des Guides-Bleus', in Pierre Nora (ed.), *Les Lieux de mémoire*, II: *La Nation*, 3 vols. (Paris, 1986), vol. 1, pp. 530–35.
28. John Mackenzie, 'Empires of Travel: British Guidebooks and Cultural Imperialism in the Nineteenth and Twentieth Centuries', in John Walton (ed.), *Histories of Tourism: Representation, Identity and Conflict* (Clevedon, 2005), p. 22; Nicholas Parsons, *Worth the Detour: A History of the Guidebook* (Thrupp, 2007), p. 182; John R. Gretton, Introduction in W. B. C. Lister (ed.), *A Bibliography of Murray's Handbooks for Travellers* (Dereham, 1993), p. ii.
29. Johann Ebel, *Anleitung auf die nützlichste und genussvollste Art die Schweiz zu bereisen*, 2 vols. (Zurich, 1793).
30. JMA, MS.40035, Karl Baedeker to John Murray, 20 Oct. 1852.
31. Rudy Koshar, 'What Ought to be Seen: Tourist Guidebooks and National Identities in Modern Germany and Europe', *Journal of Contemporary History*, vol. 33, no. 3, 1998, p. 323.
32. Jemima Morrell, *Miss Jemima's Swiss Journal* (London, 1963), p. 23; Henri Heine, *Reisebilder: Tableaux de voyages*, 2 vols. (Paris, 1856), vol. 2, p. 171; Michal Wiszniewski, *Podrdz do Wioch, Sycylii i Malty*, ed. H. Barycz (Warsaw, 1982), p. 110; John Pemble, *The Mediterranean Passion: Victorians and Edwardians in the South* (Oxford, 1987), p. 72.
33. James Buzard, *The Beaten Track: European Tourism, Literature, and the Ways to 'Culture' 1800–1918* (Oxford, 1993), p. 77.
34. Charles Dickens, *The Complete Works of Charles Dickens (in 30 volumes, Illustrated)*, vol. 1: *Little Dorrit* (London, 2009), p. 201.
35. Jill Steward, '"How and Where to Go": The Role of Travel Journalism in Britain and the Evolution of Foreign Tourism, 1840–1914', in Walton (ed.), *Histories of Tourism*, p. 46; TCA, *Cook's Excursionist and International Tourist Advertiser*, 28 August

1863, p. 5; *Guide to Cook's Tours in France, Switzerland and Italy* (London, 1865), p. 32.

36. 'Continental Excursionists', *Blackwood's Magazine*, vol. 97, Jan.–June 1865, pp. 231–2.37. Edward Cook and Alexander Wedderburn (eds.), *The Works of John Ruskin*, 39 vols. (London, 1903–12), vol. 5, pp. 380–81; vol. 18, p. 89.

38. Fontane, *Modernes Reisen*, p. 5.39. Ivan Turgenev, 'Iz-za granitsy: pis'mo pervoe', in *Soch.*, vol. 11, pp. 303–7.

40. See Buzard, *Beaten Track*, chs. 1 and 2.

41. Mollier, *Louis Hachette*, p. 343; Chartier and Martin, *Histoire de l'édition française*, vol. 3, p. 39.

42. Elsa Damien. 'Ruskin vs. Murray: Battles for Tourist Guidance in Italy', *Nineteenth-Century Contexts*, vol. 32, no. 1, 2010, pp.19–30; Keith Hanley and John Walton, *Constructing Cultural Tourism: John Ruskin and the Tourist Gaze* (Bristol, 2010), pp. 78, 133–4, 144–5.

43. See Maxence Mosseron, 'Du "grand musée européen" au musée intérieur: Frontières de l'art et de la création chez Théophile Gautier', *Romantisme*, no. 173, Mar. 2016, pp. 79–87.

44. Beaulieu, 'Louis-Claude Viardot', pp. 243–62.

45. J. Towner, *An Historical Geography of Recreation and Tourism in the Western World, 1540–1940* (New York, 1996), pp. 106–11; Black, *British Abroad*, pp. 10, 23, 59.

46. Parsons, *Worth the Detour*, p. 203; Rolf Lessenich, 'Literary Views of English Rhine Romanticism, 1760–1860', *European Romantic Review*, vol. 10, nos. 1–4, 1999, p. 497.

47. Mary Shelley, *Frankenstein, or The Modern Prometheus* (Oxford, 1969), p. 155; George Byron, *Childe Harold's Pilgrimage*, in *The Poetical Works of Lord Byron* (London, 1837), p. 34.

48. Cecelia Hopkins Porter, *The Rhine as Musical Metaphor: Cultural Identity in German Romantic Music* (Boston, 1996), pp. 46–53, 61, 112, 120–22.

49. Michael Heafford, 'Between Grand Tour and Tourism: British Travellers to Switzerland in a Period of Transition, 1814–1860', *Journal of Transport History*, 3rd Series, vol. 27, no. 1, March 2006, pp. 25–47.

50. Catherine Lavenir, *La Roue et le Stylo: Comment nous sommes devenus touristes* (Paris, 1999), pp. 299 ff; Alain Corbin, *The Lure of the Sea: The Discovery of the Seaside in the Western World, 1750–1840* (Los Angeles, 1994), pp. 270–77; Peter Borsay and John K. Walton (eds), *Resorts and Ports: European Seaside Towns since 1700* (Buffalo, 2011), pp. 39–40; Gabriel Désert, *La Vie quotidienne sur les plages normandes du Second Empire aux Années folles* (Paris, 1883), pp. 59–60. On the Bohemian spa towns: Mirjam Zadoff, *Next Year in Marienbad: The Lost Worlds of Jewish Spa Culture*, trans. William Templer (Philadelphia, 2007).

51. See John Davis, *The Victorians and Germany* (Oxford, 2007).

52. John Pudney, *The Thomas Cook Story* (London, 1953), p. 74; Mark Twain, *Innocents Abroad* (Oxford, 1996), p. 427.

53. *The Times*, 12 Jan. 1850.

54. Théophile Gautier, *Les Beaux-Arts en Europe, 1855* (Paris, 1855), pp. 1–2; Patricia Mainardi, *Art and Politics of the Second Empire: The Universal Expositions of 1855 and 1867* (New Haven, 1989), p. 70.

55. Théophile Thoré, 'Des tendances de l'art au xixᵉ siècle', *Revue universelle des arts*, vol. 1, 1855, p. 83.

56. 'Tourguéniev et la France: Actes du Congrès International de Bougival, 8–9 Mai 1981', *Cahiers*, no. 5, 1981, p. 35; Phelps, *Russian Novel in English Fiction*, p. 54; *PSS*, vol. 1, p. 284, and vol. 2, p. 27; Annenkov, *Extraordinary Decade*, p. 203.

57. Emmanuel de Las Cases, *Mémorial de Saint-Hélène*, 2 vols. (Paris, 1842), vol. 2, pp. 144–5.

58. Giuseppe Mazzini, *A Cosmopolitanism of Nations: Giuseppe Mazzini's Writings on Democracy, Nation Building, and International Relations*, ed. Stefano Recchia and Nadia Urbinati (Princeton, 2009), p. 2.

59. Victor Hugo, *Oeuvres complètes*, eds. Jacques Seebacher and Guy Rosa, 15 vols. (Paris, 1985–90), vol. 10, pp. 6, 302.

60. Walter Benjamin, 'Paris, the Capital of the Nineteenth Century', in *The Writer of Modern Life: Essays on Charles Baudelaire* (Cambridge, Mass., 2006), pp. 30–45.

61. HL, MUS 264 (76), f. 88–9, Pauline Viardot to Louis Viardot, 9 Dec. 1857.

62. *LI*, p. 318.

63. See Hilary Poriss, 'Pauline Viardot, Travelling Virtuosa', *Music and Letters*, vol. 96, no. 2, 2015, pp. 185–208

64. HL, MUS 262 (76), Pauline Viardot to Louis Viardot, undated.

65. NYPL, JOE 82-1, 29, Letter from Pauline Viardot to Julius Rietz, 26 Mar. 1859 (trans. from 'Pauline Viardot-Garcia to Julius Rietz, Letters of Friendship', *The Musical Quarterly*, vol. 1, no. 4, Oct. 1915, pp. 549, 552).

66. HL, MUS 264 (76), Pauline Viardot to Louis Viardot, 17 Dec. 1857 (trans. Poriss, 'Pauline Viardot', p. 205).

67. HL, MUS 264 (76), Pauline Viardot to Louis Viardot, 15 Jan. 1858 (trans. Poriss, 'Pauline Viardot', p. 199).

68. HL, MUS 264 (76), Pauline Viardot to Louis Viardot, 21 Dec. 1857.

69. *Revue et Gazette musicale de Paris*, 15 Aug. 1858.

70. BNF, NA Fr. 16275, Papiers Viardot, vol. IV, Lettres adressées à Claudie et George Chamerot, Ivan Tourgenev et divers, ff. 342–3, Pauline Viatrdot to Ivan Turgenev, 18 Nov. 1858.

71. NYPL, JOE 82-1, 29, Letters from Pauline Viardot to Julius Rietz, 26 Jan., 13 Feb. 1859 (trans. from 'Pauline Viardot-Garcia to Julius Rietz, Letters of Friendship', *The Musical Quarterly*, vol. 1, no. 4, Oct. 1915, pp. 532, 538).

72. See William Gibbons, *Building the Operatic Museum: Eighteenth-Century Opera in Fin-de-Siècle Paris* (Rochester, NY, 2013).

73. Joël-Marie Fauquet, 'Berlioz's Version of Gluck's *Orphée*', in Peter Bloom (ed.), *Berlioz Studies* (Cambridge, 2006), p. 195.

74. Berlioz, *Correspondance générale*, vol. 5, p. 645.

75. Ibid., pp. 713–14; 'Pauline Viardot-Garcia to Julius Rietz, Letters of Friendship', *The Musical Quarterly*, vol. 2, no. 1, Jan. 1916, p. 42.

76. BNF, NA Fr. 16272, Papiers Viardot, vol. 1, Lettres adressées à Pauline Viardot, f. 35.

77. Berlioz, *Correspondance générale*, vol. 6, pp. 36, 41n.

78. Henry Chorley, *Thirty Years' Musical Recollections*, 2 vols. (London, 1862), vol. 2, pp. 55–60.

79. Patrick Waddington, 'Pauline Viardot-Garcia as Berlioz's Counselor and Physician', *The Musical Quarterly*, vol. 59, no. 3, July 1973, p. 395; Flaubert, *Correspondance*, vol. 3, p. 83.

80. Charles Dupêchez, *Marie d'Agoult, 1805–1876* (Paris, 1994), p. 264.

81. HL, MUS 264 (360), Pauline Viardot-Garcia Papers, 'Costumi', 1858 and undated; BMO, LAS Delacroix (Eugène) 1, Delacroix to Pauline Viardot, 18 Sept. 1859; BNF, NA Fr. 16272, Papiers Viardot, vol. 1, Lettres adressées à Pauline Viardot, f. 87, Delacroix to Pauline Viardot, 21 Sept. 1859.

82. BNF, NA Fr. 16272, Papiers Viardot, vol. 1, Lettres adressées à Pauline Viardot, f. 298, Ingres to Pauline Viardot, 5 Jan. 1862. On painters inspired by Viardot's *Orpheus* see Katrin Müller-Höcker, *Pauline Viardots Orpheus-Interpretation in der*

Berlioz-Fassung von Glucks Orphée, in *Viardot-Garcia-Studien*, vol. 5 (Hildesheim, 2016), pp. 225–8.

83. 'Pauline Viardot-Garcia to Julius Rietz, Letters of Friendship', *The Musical Quarterly*, vol. 2, no. 1, Jan. 1916, p. 44.

84. Fitzlyon, *Price of Genius*, p. 356.

85. Charlton (ed.), *Cambridge Companion to Grand Opera*, part IV, pp. 197 ff.

86. BNF, NA Fr. 16272, Papiers Viardot, vol. 1, Lettres adressées à Pauline Viardot, f. 102; Waddington, 'Dickens, Pauline Viardot, Turgenev', pp. 42–3.

87. Berlioz, *Correspondance générale*, vol. 6, p. 160.

88. Ibid., p. 223; Waddington, 'Viardot-Garcia as Berlioz's Counselor and Physician', pp. 396–7.

89. Peter Bloom and Hans Vaget, 'Berlioz und Wagner: Épisodes de la vie des artistes', *Archiv für Musikwissenschaft*, vol. 58. no. 1, 2001, pp. 1–22.

90. David Cairns, *Berlioz*, vol. 2: *Servitude and Greatness 1832–1869* (London, 1999), pp. 651 ff. Wagner, *My Life*, p. 498.

91. *PSS*, vol. 3, p. 205.

92. Ibid., vol. 4, p. 64.

93. Ibid., vol. 4, p. 211.

94. Ibid., vol. 4, pp. 64, 241.

95. BNF, Tourguéniev, Ivan, Manuscrits parisiens. Slave 88, XV, cote 25. See also, Andre Mazon, *Manuscrits parisiens d'Ivan Tourguénev, notices et extraits* (Paris, 1930), pp. 61–2, 68, 87.

5 EUROPE AT PLAY

1. HL, MUS 264 (365), Journal, 12 July 1863.

2. *PSS*, vol. 5, p. 175.

3. *Memoirs of Eugenie Schumann*, trans. Marie Busch (London, 1985), p. 109; NYPL, JOE 82-9, Letter from Pauline Viardot to Julius Rietz, 1 Jan. 1859.

4. *Revue et Gazette musicale de Paris*, 25 Aug. 1861, 12 Jan. 1862, 30 Mar. 1862.

5. *PSS*, vol. 3, p. 181.

6. *PSS*, vol. 3, pp. 214, 218; vol. 11, p. 223; Kovalevskii, 'Vospominaniia ob I. S. Turgeneve', p. 16.

7. Viardot, *Espagne et beaux-arts*, p. 380.

8. Cited in *Johannes Brahms in Baden-Baden und Karlsruhe* (Catalogue, Baden Landesbibliothek in Karlsruhe, 1983).

9. Klaus Fischer, 'Dernières traces de Tourguéniev à Baden-Baden', *Cahiers*, no. 6, 1982, p. 23; N. P. Generalova, *I. S. Turgenev: Rossiia i Evropa: Iz istorii russko evropeiskikh literaturnykh i obshchevstvennykh sviazei* (St Petersburg, 2003), p. 241.

10. Charles Clark, 'Baden-Baden in 1867', *Temple Bar*, 21 (Oct. 1867), pp. 384, 387; Ivan Turgenev, *Smoke*, trans. Michael Pursglove (London, 2013), p. 3.

11. Berlioz, *Correspondance générale*, vol. 4, no. 1627; Hector Berlioz, *Les Grotesques de la musique* (Paris, 1859), p. 121.

12. BNF, département Estampes et photographie, YD-1 (1863-04-01)-8, Catalogue des tableaux anciens et dessins formant la belle collection de M. Louis Viardot.

13. ANF, O/5/1698, 'Ordonnance de payement', f. 368; ANF, 20144790/129, Letter from Kiewert to the Chief Restorer of Painting at the Musée Impériale, 28 July 1857.

14. Julius Kraetz, 'Iwan Turgenjew: Seine Wohnsitze', *Baden-Baden: Beiträge zur Geschichte der Stadt und des Kurortes Baden-Baden*, no. 13, 1976: *Pauline Viardot – Iwan Turgenjew*; Gerhard Ziegengeist (ed.), *I. S. Turgenev und Deutschland: Materialien und Untersuchungen* (Berlin, 1965), p. 26; Lange-Brachmann and

Draheim (eds.), *Pauline Viardot*, p. 250; Patrick Waddington, 'Role of Courtavenel', p. 124.

15. Nicholas G. Zekulin, *The Story of an Operetta: Le Dernier Sorcier by Pauline Viardot and Ivan Turgenev* (Munich, 1989), pp. 11–14; *PSS*, vol. 7, p. 178.

16. *PSS*, vol. 5, p. 159, vol. 7, p. 82, vol. 9, pp. 17, 19, vol. 11, pp. 65, 79; Tamara Zviguilsky, 'Tourguéniev et sa fille, d'après leur correspondance', *Cahiers*, no. 12, 1988, p. 40.

17. *PSS*, vol. 7, pp. 139 ff., 170, 174, vol. 9, p. 43; Seljak, *Ivan Turgenevs Ökonomien*, pp. 190–94, 201–16.

18. *PSS*, vol. 4, p. 132, vol. 5, p. 157; Seljak, *Ivan Turgenevs Ökonomien*, pp. 131–2, 147.

19. GJ, vol. 2, p. 941.

20. Seljak, *Ivan Turgenevs Ökonomien*, pp. 134–7, 143, 151.

21. Ibid., p. 131; *PSS*, vol. 5, p. 219, vol. 6, pp. 8, 56, 69, vol. 7, p. 75, vol. 9, pp. 16, 26, 60.

22. OR RNB, f. 654, op. 1, d. 89, l. 3 (V. A. Rubinshtein, 'Otgoloski proshlogo. Vospominaniia').

23. NYPL, JOE 82-9, 10, Letter from Pauline Viardot to Julius Rietz, 1 Jan. 1859.

24. See Robert Priest, *The Gospel According to Renan: Reading, Writing, and Religion in Nineteenth-Century France* (Oxford, 2015), ch. 4.

25. L.V. [Louis Viardot], *Apologie d'un incrédule* (Paris, 1868), pp. 8, 10, 14–15.

26. OR RNB, f. 654, op. 1, d. 89, l. 6 (V. A. Rubinshtein, 'Otgoloski proshlogo. Vospominaniia').

27. *La France musicale*, no. 17, 26 Apr. 1863, p. 130.

28. Beatrix Borchard, *Pauline Viardot-Garcia: Fülle des Lebens* (Vienna, 2016), p. 108.

29. Ostrovskaia, *Vospominaniia o Turgeneve*, p. 5; Lange-Brachmann and Draheim (eds.), *Pauline Viardot in Baden-Baden und Karlsruhe*, p. 88.

30. Borchard, *Pauline Viardot-Garcia*, p. 232.

31. B. Litzmann (ed.), *Letters of Clara Schumann and Johannes Brahms, 1853–96*, 2 vols. (London, 1927), vol. 1, p. 171.

32. Ludwig Pietsch, 'Heimfahrt auf Umwegen', in *Iwan Turgenjew: Briefe an Ludwig Pietsch. Mit einem Anbang: Ludwig Pietsch über Turgenjew* (Berlin, 1968), p. 150.

33. Adelheid von Schorn, *Zwei Menschenhalter: Erinnerungen und Briefe aus Weimar und Rom* (Stuttgart, 1913), p. 153.

34. HL, MUS 264 (365), Journal, 23 July 1863.

35. Ostrovskaia, *Vospominaniia o Turgeneve*, pp. 13–14.

36. Alexandre Zviguilsky, 'Louise Héritte-Viardot 1841–1918', *Cahiers*, no. 15, 1991, pp. 103–12.

37. *PSS*, vol. 4, p. 241.

38. Gustave Dulong, *Pauline Viardot, tragédienne lyrique*, *Cahiers*, no. 8, 1984, p. 273.

39. See Alison F. Frank, 'The Air Cure Town: Commodifying Mountain Air in Alpine Central Europe', *Central European History*, vol. 45, no. 2, 2012, pp. 185–207.

40. Derek Scott, *Sounds of the Metropolis: The 19th-Century Popular Music Revolution in London, New York, Paris and Vienna* (London, 2011), pp. 131 ff.; Peter Kemp, *The Strauss Family* (London, 1989), pp. 66–7.

41. Heinrich Jacob, *Johann Strauss* (London, 1937), pp. 165–70; Hans Fantel, *Johann Strauss: Father and Son and Their Era* (Newton Abbot, 1971), pp. 123–9.

42. Michael Musgrave, *A Brahms Reader* (New Haven, 2000), p. 106.

43. Hervé Maneglier, *Paris impérial: La Vie quotidienne sous le Second Empire* (Paris, 1991), pp. 87–92; Roger Williams, 'Jacques Offenbach and Parisian Gaiety', *The Antioch Review*, vol. 17, no. 1, 1957, p. 121.

44. Weber, *Great Transformation*, pp. 208–31.

45. GJ, vol. 1, p. 1046.

46. François Caradec, *Le Café-concert* (Paris, 1980), p. 34; Patrice Higonnet, *Paris: Capital of the World* (Cambridge, Mass., 2002), trans. Arthur Goldhammer, p. 292; Maneglier, *Paris impérial*, pp. 175–6.

47. Maneglier, *Paris impérial*, pp. 179–80; T. J. Clark, *The Painting of Modern Life: Paris in the Art of Manet and His Followers*, rev. edn (London, 1990), pp. 206–34.

48. GJ, vol. 1, p. 632.

49. Nathalie Coutelet, '*Les Folies-Bergère*: une pornographie "select" ', *Romantisme*, no. 163, 2014/1, pp. 111–24.

50. Peter Bailey (ed.), *Music Hall: The Business of Pleasure* (Milton Keynes, 1986), pp. 16–17, 22–4; Derek Hudson, *Munby, Man of Two Worlds: The Life and Diaries of Arthur J. Munby, 1828–1910* (London, 1972), p. 119.

51. Irene Lawford-Hinrichsen, *Music Publishing and Patronage. C. F. Peters: 1800 to the Holocaust* (Kenton, 2000), p. 18; *A Short History of Cheap Music as Exemplified in the Records of the House of Novello, Ewer and Company* (London, 1887), pp. 78–9, 103–6; Derek Scott, *The Singing Bourgeois: Songs of the Victorian Drawing Room and Parlour*, 2nd edn (London, 2001), pp. 122–30; Paula Gillett, 'Entrepreneurial Women Musicians in Britain: From the 1700s to the Early 1900s', in William Weber (ed.), *The Musician as Entrepreneur, 1700–1914: Managers, Charlatans, and Idealists* (Bloomington, 2004), pp. 206–7.

52. Zekulin, *Story of an Operetta*, pp. 15–19; *PSS*, vol. 7, p. 31; Paul Viardot, *Souvenirs d'un artiste* (Paris 1910), p. 19.

53. On the Weimar premiere, see Klaus-Dieter Fischer and Nicholas Zekulin, *Die Beziehungen Pauline Viardots und Ivan S. Turgenevs zu Weimar*, in *Viardot-Garcia-Studien*, vol. 5 (Hildesheim, 2016), pp. 41–72.

54. Zekulin, *Story of an Operetta*, p. 26; *PSS*, vol. 7, p. 220.

55. BNF, NA 16274, Papiers de Pauline Viardot, vol. 3, Lettres adressées à Louis Viardot, ff. 192–4; Offenbach to Louis Viardot, 19 July 1868.

56. Alain Decaux, *Offenbach, roi du Second Empire* (Paris, 1958), pp. 142–3; Alexander Faris, *Jacques Offenbach* (London, 1980), pp. 102–4.

57. Robert Schipperges, 'Offenbach – Antisemitismus – Nazismus: Zu einigen Topoi der Rezeption', in Peter Csobádi et al. (eds.), *Das (Musik-)Theater in Exil und Diktatur: Vorträge und Gespräche des Salzburger Symposions 2003* (Salzburg, 2005), pp. 314–30.

58. GJ, vol. 3, p. 64.

59. Siegfried Kracauer, *Jacques Offenbach and the Paris of His Time* (New York, 2002), p. 163.

60. Jean-Claude Yon, *Jacques Offenbach* (Paris, 2000), p. 146.

61. Kracauer, *Jacques Offenbach*, pp. 204, 211–12; James Harding, *Jacques Offenbach: A Biography* (London, 1980), pp. 115–16; Williams, 'Jacques Offenbach and Parisian Gaiety', p. 122.

62. Jacques Offenbach, Henri Meilhac and Ludovic Halévy, *La Belle Hélène: Opérabouffe en trois actes* (Paris, 1864), p. 253.

63. Jacques Offenbach, Henri Meilhac and Ludovic Halévy, *La Vie parisienne: Opérabouffe en 5 actes ou 4 actes* (Paris, 1866), pp. 4, 45.

64. *PSS*, vol. 7, p. 217.

65. Ibid., p. 219.

66. Ibid.

67. Ibid., p. 218.

68. See Thomas Hall, *Planning Europe's Capital Cities: Aspects of Nineteenth-Century Urban Development* (London, 1997), pp. 344 ff. 69. *Mémoires du baron Haussmann*, 2nd edn, 3 vols. (Paris, 1890), vol. 2, pp. 199–200.

70. Alfred Delvau, *Les Plaisirs de Paris: Guide pratique et illustré* (Paris, 1867), p. 4; Charles Baudelaire, *The Painter of Modern Life and Other Essays*, trans. Jonathan Mayne (New York, 1964), p. 9. See further, Hazel Hahn Haejeong, 'Du flâneur au consommateur: spectacle et consommation sur les Grands Boulevards, 1840–1914', *Romantisme*, no. 134, 2006/4, pp. 67–78.

71. Yon, *Jacques Offenbach*, pp. 347, 359.

72. Williams, 'Jacques Offenbach and Parisian Gaiety', p. 127; Faris, *Jacques Offenbach*, p. 150.

73. Parturier, *Une amitié littéraire*, p. 154; *PSS*, vol. 7, p. 172.

74. Fantel, *Johann Strauss*, pp. 153, 56, 165–8.

75. Marguerite and Jean Alley, *A Passionate Friendship: Clara Schumann and Brahms* (London, 1956), p. 132.

76. For a listing of her compositions: Patrick Waddington, *The Musical Works of Pauline Viardot-Garcia (1821–1910): A Chronological Catalogue* (Upper Hutt, 2001).

77. *The Athenaeum*, 19 Jan. 1850, p. 79.

78. *NCI*, vol 1 (1971), p. xx; *LI*, p. 327; Franz Liszt, 'Pauline Viardot-Garcia', in *Gesammelte Schriften*, 6 vols. (Leipzig, 1881), vol. 3, p. 126.

79. *PSS*, vol. 1, p. 207, vol. 5, pp. 148, 184, 209, 215, 244, 249, vol. 6, p. 171, vol. 12, p. 60, vol. 14, p. 58.

80. Ibid., vol. 6, p. 146.

81. Thérèse Marix-Spire, 'Vicissitudes d'un opéra-comique: *La Mare au diable* de George Sand et de Pauline Viardot', *Cahiers*, vol. 3, 1979, pp. 66–7.

82. Nancy B. Reich, 'Women as Musicians: A Question of Class', in Ruth A. Solie (ed.), *Musicology and Difference: Gender and Sexuality in Music Scholarship*, (Berkeley, 1993), pp. 134–6.

83. Sebastian Hensel, *The Mendelssohn Family 1729–1847*, 4th rev. edn, 2 vols. (London, 1884), vol. 1, p. 82; *Letters of Felix Mendelssohn Bartholdy from 1833 to 1847*, ed. Paul Mendelssohn Bartholdy, trans. Lady Wallace (London, 1864), p. 113.

84. HL, MUS 264 (365), Pauline Viardot Journal, memoir dated 1889.

85. Marcia J. Citron, *Gender and the Musical Canon* (Cambridge, 1993), pp. 56–7; Borchard, '"Ma chère petite Clara"', p. 136.

86. Anna Eugénie Schoen-René, *America's Musical Inheritance* (New York, 1941), p. 134.

87. BMO, NLA 357, Pauline Viardot to Henri Heugel, 21 Feb. 1882.

88. Marix-Spire, 'Vicissitudes d'un opera-comique', p. 66.

89. Anton Chekhov, *Three Sisters*, in *Plays*, trans. Peter Carson (London, 2002), p. 265.

90. François-Joseph Fétis, *Biographie universelle des musiciens et bibliographie générale de la musique: Supplément et complément* (Paris, 1878), p. 314. See further, Bea Friedland, *Louise Farrenc, 1804–1875: Composer, Performer, Scholar* (Ann Arbor, 1980).

91. GJ, vol. 1, p. 941.

92. Gustave Flaubert, *Lettres inédites à Tourgueneff* (Monaco, 1946), p. 3.

93. Ibid.; *Lettres de Gustave Flaubert à George Sand* (Paris, 1884), p. 73

94. Flaubert, *Lettres inédites*, p. 21; *PSS*, vol. 8, p. 199.

95. *PSS*, vol. 10, pp. 146–7, vol. 15, p. 22.

96. Anton Fedyashin, *Liberals Under Autocracy: Modernization and Civil Society in Russia, 1866–1904* (Madison, 2012), p. 5; V. E. Kel'ner, *Chelovek svoego vremeni (M. M. Stasiulevich: izdatel'skoe delo i liberal'naia oppozitsiia)* (St Petersburg, 1993), p. 58.

97. Thierry Ozwald, 'Autour d'une collaboration littéraire: Les destins croisés de Mérimée et Tourguéniev', *Cahiers*, no. 15, 1991, pp. 79–101.

98. Rolf-Dieter Kluge, 'Ivan Turgenev und seine deutschen Freunde', in Dittmar Dahlmann, *Deutschland und Rußland: Aspekte kultureller und wissenschaftlicher Beziehungen im 19. und frühen 20. Jahrhundert* (Wiesbaden, 2004), p. 5.

99. Ibid., p. 136; Peter Brang, 'Tourguéniev et l'Allemagne', *Cahiers*, no. 7, 1983, p. 76; Toman, 'I. S. Turgenev i nemetskaia kul'tura', pp. 31–58; *PSS*, vol. 5, p. 12. On Wolfsohn and Glümer: Luis Sundkvist, 'Vil'gel'm Vol'fson, Kler fon Gliumer i pervye nemetskie perevody romana "Otsy i deti"', in NPG, vol. 4: *K 200-letiiu I. S. Turgeneva (1818–2018)* (Moscow, 2016), pp. 76–165.

100. *PSS*, vol. 8, pp. 191–2.

101. Ibid., vol. 9, pp. 94–5; 'M. Tourgueneff and His English Traducer', *Pall Mall Gazette*, 3 Dec. 1868.

102. OR RNB, f. 654, op. 1, d. 89, l. 7 (V. A. Rubinshtein, 'Otgoloski proshlogo. Vospominaniia'); Taylor, *Anton Rubinstein*, p. 107; *PSS*, vol. 11, p. 32.

103. V. V. Stasov, *Izbrannye sochineniia*, 2 vols. (Moscow, 1937), vol. 2, p. 557.

104. Ts. A. Kiui, *Izbrannye stat'i* (Leningrad, 1952), p. 43; Turgenev, *Smoke*, p. 89.

105. *PSS*, vol. 7, p. 130.

106. Benjamin Curtis, *Music Makes the Nation: Nationalist Composers and Nation Building in Nineteenth-Century Europe* (Amherst, 2008), pp. 128–9; John Tyrrel, *Czech Opera* (Cambridge, 1988), pp. 216–27.

107. See the classic work by Eric Hobsbawm and Terence Ranger (eds.), *The Invention of Tradition* (Cambridge, 1983).

108. Jonathan Bellman, 'Toward a Lexicon for the *Style hongrois*', *The Journal of Musicology*, vol. 9, no. 2, 1991, pp. 214–37; Lynn Hooker, *Redefining Hungarian Music from Liszt to Bartók* (Oxford, 2013), p. 139.

109. Joseph Frank, *Dostoevsky: The Miraculous Years 1865–1871* (Princeton, 1996), pp. 189–204; Anna Dostoevsky, *Dostoevsky Reminiscences*, trans. Beatrice Stillman (London, 1977), p. 130.

110. Turgenev, *Smoke*, pp. 3–4.

111. Frank, *Dostoevsky: The Miraculous Years*, pp. 212–13.

112. Ibid., pp. 215–16.

113. *PSS*, vol. 8, p. 87.

114. Fyodor Dostoevsky, *The Possessed*, trans. David Magarshack (London, 1973), pp. 452, 454, 474–5.

115. Frank, *Dostoevsky: The Miraculous Years*, p. 211; *PSS*, vol. 11, p. 86, vol. 12, p. 71.

116. Schapiro, *Turgenev*, p. 197.

117. *Letopis' zhizni i tvorchestva I. V. Turgeneva (1867–1870)* (Moscow, 1997), pp. 4, 33, 56; *PSS*, vol. 7, pp. 205, 207.

118. *PSS*, vol. 6, pp. 45–6.

119. HL, MUS 264 (365), Pauline Viardot Journal, 24 May 1868.

120. Ibid., Feb. 1869.

121. Frithjof Haas, *Hermann Levi: From Brahms to Wagner* (Toronto, 2012), pp. 51–5; Julien Tiersot (ed.), *Lettres françaises de Richard Wagner* (Paris, 1935), pp. 285–6.

122. Schoen-René, *America's Musical Inheritance*, pp. 69–71; *NCI*, vol. 1, p. 354.

123. Ziegengeist (ed.), *Turgenev und Deutschland*, pp. 279–80; Schapiro, *Turgenev*, pp. 191–2; *PSS*, vol. 9, p. 21, vol. 10, p. 44. See further: Karl-Dietrich Fischer, 'Turgenev und Richard Wagner', *Zeitschrift für Slawistik*, vol. 31, no. 2, 1986, pp. 228–32.

124. 'Pauline Viardot-Garcia to Julius Rietz', *The Musical Quarterly*, vol. 2, no. 1, Jan. 1916, p. 58.

125. Albert Goldman and Evert Sprinchorn (eds.), *Wagner on Music and Drama: A Selection from Richard Wagner's Prose Works*, trans. H. Ashton Ellis (London, 1970).

126. Max Horkheimer and Theodor Adorno, 'The Culture Industry: Enlightenment as Mass Deception', in *Dialectic of Enlightenment* (Stanford, 2002 [1944]). See

further, Nicholas Vazsonyi, *Richard Wagner: Self-Promotion and the Making of Brand* (Cambridge, 2010), p. 89 and passim.

127. Robert Hartford (ed.), *Bayreuth: The Early Years* (Cambridge 1980), pp. 16–28; Frederic Spotts, *Bayreuth: A History of the Wagner Festival* (New Haven, 1994), p. 40.

128. Haas, *Hermann Levi*, pp. 53–5; Lange-Brachmann and Draheim (eds.), *Pauline Viardot in Baden-Baden und Karlsruhe*, pp. 101–2.

129. Zekulin, *Story of an Operetta*, p. 58.

130. Heinz Becker and Gudrun Becker, *Giacomo Meyerbeer: A Life in Letters* (London, 1989), p. 14.

131. Zekulin, *Story of an Operetta*, pp. 58–9.

132. Rolf Kabel (ed.), *Eduard Devrient aus seinen Tagebüchern*, 2 vols. (Weimar, 1964), vol. 2, p. 567; *PSS*, vol. 10, p. 145; Zekulin, *Story of an Operetta*, pp. 54–5.

133. Zekulin, *Story of an Operetta*, pp. 56 ff.; *PSS*, vol. 10, p. 145.

134. Fischer and Zekulin, *Die Beziehungen Pauline Viardots*, p. 91.

135. *PSS*, vol. 10, pp. 192, 195.

136. Turgenev, *Sochinenii*, vol. 10, p. 313.

137. Litzmann (ed.), *Letters of Clara Schumann and Johannes Brahms*, vol. 1, p. 248.

138. *PSS*, vol. 10, pp. 216, 249; N. Mikhailov, 'Vitse-presidenta kongressa', in *Shakhmaty v SSSR* (Moscow, 1970), pp. 24–5.

139. *PSS*, vol. 10, pp. 231–2; *Turgenevskii sbornik*, p. 58.

140. *Memoirs of Eugénie Schumann*, p. 127.

141. *PSS*, vol. 10, pp. 233, 237–8.

142. Ibid., p. 239; Waddington, *Turgenev and England*, p. 141.

143. Decaux, *Offenbach*, pp. 208–9.

144. BNF NA 16274, Papiers de Pauline Viardot, vol. 3, Lettres adressées à Louis Viardot, George Sand to Louis Viardot, 8 Sept. 1870.

145. BMO, LA-VIARDOT PAULINE-66, Lettre de Pauline Viardot à Madame Crémieux.

146. HL, MUS 264 (365), Journal, 18 Oct. 1870.

147. *PSS*, vol. 10, p. 252.

6 THE LAND WITHOUT MUSIC

1. Waddington, *Turgenev and England*, p. 144.

2. Barbara Kendall-Davies, *The Life and Work of Pauline Viardot-Garcia*, vol. 2: *The Years of Grace, 1863–1910* (Amersham, 2013), p. 1; Litzmann (ed.), *Letters of Clara Schumann and Johannes Brahms*, vol. 1, p. 253; Viardot, *Souvenirs d'un artiste*, pp. 21–2.

3. Michèle Beaulieu, 'Louis-Claude Viardot, collectionneur et critique d'art', Société d'Histoire de l'Art Français, Séance du 4 février 1984, *Bulletin de la Société d'Histoire de l'Art Français*, 1984, pp. 252–3.

4. Stier, *Pauline Viardot-Garcia in Grossbritannien*, pp. 241–6.

5. HL, MUS 232/1, Gounod to Pauline Viardot, 31 Jan. 1864.

6. TCL, Houghton MSS, Q 47/1, Louis Viardot to Thomas Milner Gibson, 23 March 1871.

7. Herman Klein, *Thirty Years of Musical Life in London, 1870–1900* (London, 1903), pp. 34–41; Waddington, *Turgenev and England*, p. 145; *PSS*, vol. 10, p. 268.

8. *PSS*, vol. 11, pp. 18, 55.

9. *PSS*, vol. 11, p. 88. 10. Thomas C. Jones and Robert Tombs, 'The French Left in Exile: *Quarante*-Huitards and Communards in London, 1848–1880', in Martyn Cornick and Debra Kelly (eds.), *A History of the French in London: Liberty, Equality, Opportunity* (London, 2013), pp. 165–8, 235–7; Jerry White, *London in the Nineteenth Century: 'A Human Awful Wonder of God'* (London, 2007), pp. 142–3.

11. Jones and Tombs, 'French Left in Exile', pp. 170–71; B. Porter, *The Refugee Question in Mid-Victorian Politics* (Cambridge, 1979), pp. 182–3.

12. White, *London in the Nineteenth Century*, pp. 142–7; Lucio Sponza, *Italian Immigrants in Nineteenth-Century Britain: Realities and Images* (Leicester, 1988), pp. 2–4. On the German community in London, see Rosemary Ashton, *Little Germany: Exile and Asylum in Victorian England* (Oxford, 1986).

13. Christine Corton, *London Fog: The Biography* (London, 2015), ch. 5.

14. Flora Tristan, *Promenades dans Londres* (Paris, 1840), pp. 49–50.

15. Fabrice Bensimon, 'The French Exiles and the British', in Sabine Freitag (ed.), *Exiles from European Revolutions: Refugees in Mid-Victorian England* (New York, 2002), p. 91; Theodor Fontane, *A Prussian in Victorian London*, ed. John Lynch (London, 2014), p. 107.

16. Waddington, *Turgenev and England*, pp. 141–2.

17. GJ, vol. 1. p. 1138.

18. *Londres et son environs: Collection des Guides-Joannes* (Paris, 1882), p. 16.

19. Viardot, *Souvenirs de chasse*, pp. 53, 63.

20. TMS, p. 101; *LI*, p. 311.

21. Alexander Herzen, *My Past and Thoughts: The Memoirs of Alexander Herzen*, trans. Constance Garnett, 4 vols. (London, 1968), vol. 3, p. 1048. 22. Edward Carr, *The Romantic Exiles: A Nineteenth-Century Portrait Gallery* (London, 1949), p. 119; Edmondo De Amicis, *Memories of London*, trans. Stephen Parkin (London, 2014), pp. 63–4; Vallès cited in Higonnet, *Paris: Capital of the World*, p. 241.

23. Viardot, *Souvenirs de chasse*, p. 300.

24. Henry Taine, *Taine's Notes on England*, trans. Edward Hyams (London, 1957), p. 242.

25. Ian Buruma, *Anglomania: A European Love Affair* (New York, 1998), pp. 105–6; Litzmann (ed.), *Letters of Clara Schumann and Johannes Brahms*, vol. 1, p. 187; G. Karpeles (ed.), *Heinrich Heine's Memoirs*, trans. G. Cannan, 2 vols. (London 1910), vol. 1, pp. 192–3.

26. Iwo Zaluski and Pamela Zaluski, 'Chopin in London', *The Musical Times,* vol. 133, no. 1791, May 1992, p. 227.

27. Alley, *Passionate Friendship*, p. 160.

28. Davis, *Victorians and Germany*, pp. 248–9.

29. Jonathan Parry, *The Politics of Patriotism: English Liberalism, National Identity and Europe, 1830–1886* (Cambridge, 2006), pp. 9–10.

30. Lucy Riall, *Garibaldi: Invention of a Hero* (New Haven, 2007), pp. 336 ff.

31. Pemble, *Mediterranean Passion*, pp. 268–9.

32. Cited in Antoni Mączak, 'Gentlemen's Europe: Nineteenth-Century Handbooks for Travellers, *Annali d'Italianistica*, vol. 21: *Hodoeporics Revisited / Ritorno all'odeporica* (2003), p. 360.

33. See Linda Colley, *Britons: Forging the Nation 1707–1837* (New Haven, 1992).

34. Henry Mayhew, *German Life and Manners: As Seen in Saxony at the Present Day*, 2 vols. (London, 1864), vol. 1, pp. viii–ix.

35. Waddington, *Turgenev and England*, p. 203.

36. Sassoon, *Culture of the Europeans*, pp. 37–40.

37. Taine, *Taine's Notes on England*, p. 25.

38. Albinsson, 'Early Music Copyrights', p. 276; Franz Joseph Haydn, *The Collected Correspondence and London Notebooks of Joseph Haydn*, ed. H. C. Robbins Landon (Fair Lawn, 1959), p. 252.

39. Rudolf Evers (ed.), *Mendelssohn: A Life in Letters* (New York, 1986), p. 106; Cairns, *Berlioz*, vol. 2, p. 509.

40. Verdi, *Lettere*, p. 170.

41. Rosselli, *Singers of Italian Opera*, pp. 142–3.

42. Matthew Ringel, 'Opera in "The Donizettian Dark Ages": Management, Competition and Artistic Policy in London, 1861–70', Ph.D. diss., King's College London, 1996, p. 29.

43. Christophe Charle, 'La circulation des opéras en Europe au xixe siècle', *Relations internationales*, no. 155, 2013/3, pp. 11–31; Dideriksen, 'Repertory and Rivalry', pp. 286–8.

44. Henry Wyndham, *The Annals of Covent Garden Theatre*, 2 vols. (London, 1906), vol. 2, pp. 243–4.

45. Ibid., pp. 49–51, 71–3.

46. Henri Moulin, *Impressions de voyage d'un étranger à Paris: Visite à l'Exposition Universelle de 1855* (Mortain, 1856), p. 47.

47. Oscar Schmitz, *The Land without Music* (London, 1918), p. 26; Carl Engel, *An Introduction to the Study of National Music* (London, 1866), p. 3.

48. Guido Guerzoni, 'The British Painting Market 1789–1914', in M. North and W. Koln (eds.), *Economic History and the Arts* (Vienna, 1996), pp. 97–132; Bayer and Page, *Development of the Art Market in England*, p. 96.

49. M. F. MacDonald, P. de Montfort and N. Thorp (eds.), *The Correspondence of James McNeill Whistler, 1855–1903* (Glasgow, 2003), no. 08050.

50. Ross King, *The Judgement of Paris: The Revolutionary Decade That Gave the World Impressionism* (New York, 2006), pp. 239–40; Edward Morris, *French Art in Nineteenth-Century Britain* (London, 2005), pp. 156–7.

51. GJ, p. 596.

52. Assouline, *Discovering Impressionism*, p. 99.

53. Paul Durand-Ruel, *Memoirs of the First Impressionist Art Dealer (1831–1922)* (Paris, 2014), p. 122; John House, 'New Material on Monet and Pissaro in London,' *Burlington Magazine*, Oct. 1978, pp. 636–7; Morris, *French Art*, p. 157.

54. Caroline Corbeau-Parsons, 'Crossing the Channel', in Corbeau-Parsons (ed.), *The EY Exhibition. Impressionists in London: French Artists in Exile 1870–1904* (London, 2017), p. 19; Anne Robbins, 'Monet, Pissaro and Fellow French Painters in London, 1870–1', in ibid., p. 61.

55. Moulin, *Impressions*, p. 47.

56. Louis Viardot, *The Wonders of Sculpture* (London, 1872), pp. 271–2.

57. BNF, NA 16273, Lettres à Pauline Viardot, ff. 395–6, Turgenev to Pauline Viardot, 4 June 1879.

58. GJ, vol. 2, p. 369.

59. *PSS*, vol. 11, p. 15.

60. Ibid., p. 88.

61. BMO, LA-VIARDOT PAULINE-57, Pauline Viardot to François Schwab, 15 May 1871.

62. *PSS*, vol. 11, p. 102.

63. Ibid., p. 118.

64. Waddington, *Turgenev and England*, pp. 161–2.

65. *PSS*, vol. 11, p. 116; Waddington, *Turgenev and England*, pp. 115, 122–3.

66. Waddington, *Turgenev and England*, pp. 131, 130.

7 CULTURE WITHOUT BORDERS

1. *PSS*, vol. 11, p. 158; Waddington, 'Some Gleanings on Turgenev', p. 212.
2. *Vosp.*, pp. 318, 322; 'Vospominaniia A. I. Abarinovoi', *Istoricheskii vestnik*, vol. 83, Jan. 1901, p. 219.
3. Maria Ge, 'Vospominaniia (Iz znakomstva c Ivanom Sergeevichem Turgenevym)', *Novyi zhurnal dlia vsekh*, no. 2, 1915, p. 23; Maurice Guillemot, 'Un Russe de jadis', *Le Figaro*, 7 Nov. 1925; A. F. Koni, *Na zhiznennom puti*, 5 vols. (St Petersburg, 1912–29), vol. 2, p. 40; E. O. Repchanskaia, 'Moi vospominaniia o Viardot i ee otnosheniiakh k Turgenevu', *Angara* (Irkutsk), no. 1 (58), 1963, p. 117; Héritte-Viardot, *Une famille de grands musiciens*, p. 130.
4. P. D. Boborykin, 'U romanistov (Parizhskie Vpechatleniia)', *Slovo*, no. 11, 1878, p. 38; P. D. Boborykin, 'Turgenev doma i za granitsei', in *I. S. Turgenev v vospominaniiakh sovremennikov*, pp. 187–8.
5. APP BA art. 1287: Tourgeneff, Cabinet du Préfet: affaires générales, 106409, 'Rapports', 28 Oct. 1873, 3 Mar. 1880, 8 Sept. 1883.
6. Ibid., 10 Jan. 1877.
7. In October 1870, he had written to George Sand asking her to help him get elected as a republican deputy for the Indre *département*, where she lived: Sand, *Correspondance*, vol. 22, p. 208.
8. APP BA art. 1294: Viardot, Cabinet du Préfet: affaires générales, 128027, 'Rapports', 1 and 9 Dec.1874, 9 Oct. 1875.
9. Flaubert, *Correspondance*, vol. 5, p. 140.
10. Ibid., vol. 4, p. 723.
11. GJ, vol. 10, p. 75; Leon Edel (ed.), *Henry James Letters*, vol. 2: *1875–83* (London, 1974), pp. 16, 45.
12. Alphonse Jacobs (ed.), *Gustave Flaubert–George Sand: Correspondance* (Paris, 1981), pp. 222, 273.
13. *The George Sand–Gustave Flaubert Letters,* trans. A. L. McKenzie (New York, 1921), p. 289.
14. N.M., 'Cherty is parizhskoi zhizni', p. 314.
15. BNF, NA, 25877, pp. 1–2; B. Rees, *Camille Saint-Saëns: A Life* (London, 1999), p. 93.
16. Edel (ed.), *Henry James Letters*, vol. 2, p. 37.
17. Caroline Franklin Grout, *Heures d'autrefois: Mémoires inédits. Souvenirs intimes* (Rouen, 1999), pp. 84–5.
18. Elena Apreleva (E. Ardov), 'Iz vospominanii ob I. S. Turgeneve', *Russkie vedomosti*, 15 and 18 Jan. 1904; Viardot, *Souvenirs d'un artiste*, pp. 47–8.
19. Kovalevskii, 'Vospominaniia ob I. S. Turgeneve', p. 18.
20. L. N. Nazarova, 'Ochagi russkoi kul'tury v Parizhe', in NPG, vol. 1, pp. 7–9; Maria Ge, 'Vospominaniia', pp. 21–6.
21. GARF, f. 109, op. 1, d. 2159, l. 1 ff.
22. Ibid., p. 45; *PSS*, vol. 11, p. 223; Friang, *Pauline Viardot*, pp. 235–6.
23. Michael Strasser, 'The Société Nationale and Its Adversaries: The Musical Politics of *L'invasion germanique* in the 1870s', *19th-Century Music*, vol. 24, no. 3, 2001 (Spring), pp. 225–51.
24. *PSS*, vol. 13, p. 172; 'Vospominaniia A. I. Abarinovoi', pp. 220–21.
25. BMO, LA-VIARDOT PAULINE-67, Pauline Viardot to Théodore Dubois, 23 June 1877.
26. HL, MS Mus 232, Massenet to Pauline Viardot, 9 Apr. 1878; Jules Massenet, *Mes Souvenirs* (Paris, 1912), p. 17; Demar Irvine, *Massenet: A Chronicle of His Life and*

Times (New York, 1994), pp. 71–3; Alexandre Zviguilsky, 'Jules Massenet et Pauline Viardot d'après une correspondance inédite', *Cahiers*, no. 16, 1992, pp. 171, 177.

27. BMO, LA-VIARDOT PAULINE-67, Berlioz to Pauline Viardot, 20, 22 Feb. 1851.

28. Celsa Alonso, 'La Réception de la chanson espagnole dans la musique française du XIXe   siècle',   in François Lesure (ed.), *Échanges musicaux franco-espagnols, XVIIe–XIXe siècles* (Paris, 2000), pp. 123–60; Hervé Lacombe, 'L'Espagne à l'Opéra-Comique avant *Carmen: Du Guitarrero* de Halévy (1841) à *Don Cesar de Bazan* de Massenet (1872)', in Lesure (ed.), *Échanges musicaux*, pp. 161–94.

29. See Francesca Zantedeschi, 'Pan-National Celebrations and Provençal Regionalism', in Joep Leerssen and Ann Rigney (eds.), *Commemorating Writers in Nineteenth-Century Europe: Nation-Building and Centenary Fever* (London, 2014), pp. 134–51; Francesca Zantedeschi, 'Panlatinismes et visions d'Europe, 1860–1890', in Philippe Darriulat et al. (eds.), *Europe de papier: Projets européens au XIXe siècle* (Villeneuve d'Ascq, 2015), pp. 281–94.

30. See e.g. HL MUS 264, 77, Pauline Viardot to Sebastián Yradier, Paris, 23 July 1856.

31. Hervé Lacombe, *Georges Bizet: Naissance d'une identité créatrice* (Paris, 2000), p. 654.

32. NYPL, JOE 82-1, 38, Letter from Pauline Viardot to Julius Rietz, 12 June 1859; HL, MUS 264, 236–47; Julien Tiersot, 'Bizet and Spanish Music', *The Musical Quarterly*, vol. 13, no. 4, Oct. 1927, p. 581. For a musical analysis: Ralph P. Locke, 'Spanish Local Colour in Bizet's *Carmen*: Unexplored Borrowings and Transformations', in Mark Everist and Annegret Fauser (eds.), *Music, Theater, and Cultural Transfer: Paris, 1830– 1914* (Chicago, 2009), pp. 318–32.

33. Cited in Kerry Murphy, '*Carmen: Couleur locale* or the Real Thing?', in Everist and Fauser (eds.), *Music, Theater, and Cultural Transfer*, p. 301.

34. Winton Dean, *Georges Bizet: His Life and Work* (London, 1965), pp. 117–18.

35. P. I. Chaikovskii, *Polnoe sobranie sochinenii*, vol. 9 (Moscow, 1965), p. 195; Mina Curtiss, *Bizet and His World* (London, 1959), p. 430.

36. Elizabeth Kertesz and Michael Christoforidis, 'Confronting "Carmen" beyond the Pyrenees: Bizet's opera in Madrid, 1887–1888', *Cambridge Opera Journal*, vol. 20, no. 1, Mar. 2008, pp. 79–110; Murphy, 'Carmen', pp. 313–14.

37. BNF, NA, 16273, Papiers de Pauline Viardot, vol. II, Lettres adressés à Pauline Viardot (S–Z), Letter from Turgenev to Pauline Viardot, 10/22 Apr. 1880, ff. 411.

38. V. V. Stasov, 'Iz vospominaniia ob I. S. Turgeneva', in V. G. Fridliand and S. M. Petrov (eds.), *I. S. Turgenev v vospominaniiakh sovremennikov*, 2 vols. (Moscow, 1983), vol. 2, pp. 96–114; *PSS*, vol. 13, pp. 85, 87.

39. Rollo Myers, 'Claude Debussy and Russian Music', *Music & Letters*, vol. 39, no. 4, Oct. 1958, pp. 336–42; Edward Lockspeiser, 'Debussy, Tchaikovsky, and Madame von Meck', *The Musical Quarterly*, vol. 22, no. 1, Jan. 1936, pp. 38–44.

40. *PSS*, vol. 11, p. 80.

41. *P. I. Chaikovskii–S. I. Taneev: Perepiska (1874–1893)* (Moscow, 1951), p. 15; E. Blaramberg, 'Vospominaniia ob I. S. Turgeneve', in Fridliand and Petrov (eds.), *I. S. Turgenev v vospominaniiakh* sovremennikov', vol. 2, p. 192; *Vosp.*, p. 166.

42. Donald Mackenzie Wallace, *Russia*, 2 vols. (London, 1877); Anatole Leroy-Beaulieu, *L'Empire des tsars et les Russes*, 3 vols. (Paris, 1881–9).

43. V. V. Stasov, 'Vtoroi russkii kontsert', 'Polednye dva kontserta v Parizhe', *Sobranie sochinenii V. V. Stasova 1847–1886, Khudozhestvenyye stat'i*, vol. 3 (St Petersburg, 1894), pp. 331–9, and 342–50; Alexandre Zviguilsky, 'En marge d'une lettre inédite de Tchaikovsky à Edouard Colonne', *Cahiers*, no. 14, 1990, p. 154.

44. OR, f. 124, d. 2499, l. 2 (Ernst Karlovich Lipgart, 'Moi vospominaniia o Turgeneve'); *PSS*, vol. 14, pp. 30, 39, vol. 15, pp. 31, 78; Émile Zola, 'Le Salon de 1876',

in *Oeuvres complètes*, ed. Henri Mitterand, 15 vols. (Paris, 1966–9), vol. 10, p. 958.

45. OR, f. 124, d. 2499, l. 2 (Lipgart, 'Moi vospominaniia o Turgeneve').

46. IRL, f. 7, no. 12, ll. 55–6; *PSS*, vol. 13, kn. 1: *1880–1882*, p. 48; *Turgenevskii sbornik*, vol. 5, pp. 393–7.

47. I. S. Zil'bershtein, 'Vystavka khudozhnika V. Vereshchagina', in *Iz Parizhskogo arkhiva I. S. Turgeneva, Neizvestvnye proizvedeniia*, in *Literaturnoe nasledstvo*, vol. 73, kn. 1 (Moscow, 1964), pp. 291, 305, 312, 317–18; V. V. Stasov, 'Venskaia pechat' o Vereshchagine', and 'Vystavka Vereshchagina v Berline', *Sobranie sochinenii V. V. Stasova 1847–1886, Khudozhestvenyye stat'i, vol. 2 (St Petersburg, 1894), pp. 538–40, 563–4.

48. I. E. Repin, *Dalekoe blizkoe* (Moscow, 1960), p. 217; *I. E. Repin i V. V. Stasov: perepiska, 1871–[1906]*, 3 vols. (Moscow, 1948–50), vol. 1, p. 75.

49. *I. E. Repin i V. V. Stasov: perepiska, 1871–[1906]*, vol. 1, pp. 92–3; Gabriel Simonoff, 'Répine et Tourguéniev: des relations amicales difficiles', *Cahiers*, no. 19, 1995, pp. 23–7.

50. Simonoff, 'Répine et Tourguéniev', p. 89; *I. E. Repin i I. N. Kramskoǐ; perepiska, 1873–1885* (Moscow, 1949), pp. 99–100, 106; I. S. Zil'bershtein, *Repin i Turgenev* (Moscow–Leningrad, 1945), p. 44; Elizabeth Kridl Valkenier, 'Politics in Russian Art: The Case of Repin', *The Russian Review*, vol. 37, no. 1, Jan. 1978, p. 18.

51. Émile Bergerat, *Souvenirs d'un enfant de Paris*, vol. 2: *La Phase critique de la critique 1872–1880* (Paris, 1912), p. 189; Pierre Miquel, 'Les maîtres du paysage français dans la collection Tourguéniev', *Cahiers*, no. 5, 1981, p. 124; Steegmuller (ed. and trans.), *Letters of Gustave Flaubert*, p. 587.

52. *PSS*, vol. 13, p. 141, vol. 16, p. 23; Seljak, *Ivan Turgenevs Ökonomien*, pp. 137.

53. See Zvig., pp. 311, 315, 321.

54. *Vosp.*, pp. 222–3, 340–41; Bergerat, *Souvenirs d'un enfant*, vol. 2, p. 195.

55. Hilary Spurling, *The Unknown Matisse: A Life of Henri Matisse*, vol. 1: *1869–1908* (London, 1998), p. 123. *PSS*. vol. 13, kn. 2: *1882–1883*, pp. 24–7.

56. GJ, vol. 1, p. 822.

57. Ibid., vol. 2, p. 148. See also Robert Dessaix, *Twilight of Love: Travels with Turgenev* (New York, 2004), pp. 146–7.

58. Alexandre Zviguilsky, 'Tourguéniev à Bougival', *Cahiers*, no. 5, 1981, pp. 19–22; Zvig., p. 273; Jean-Claude Menou, 'Sauver, protéger, animer la datcha d'Ivan Tourguéniev et la villa de Pauline Viardot', *Cahiers*, no. 5, 1981, pp. 7–10; *PSS*, vol. 12, p. 161.

59. Communication by Paul-Louis Durand-Ruel and Flavie Durand-Ruel based on the 'Recueil d'Estampes' published by Durand-Ruel in 1873–5; Sylvie Patry (ed.), *Inventing Impressionism: Paul Durand-Ruel and the Modern Art Market* (London, 2015), p. 71.

60. Durand-Ruel, *Memoirs*, p. 117.

61. Merete Bodelsen, 'Early Impressionist Sales 1874–94 in the Light of Some Unpublished "Procès-Verbaux"', *The Burlington Magazine*, vol. 110, no. 783, June 1968, pp. 330–39; Patry (ed.), *Inventing Impressionism*, p. 39.

62. Lionello Venturi, *Les Archives de l'impressionnisme* (Paris, 1939), pp. 34, 115; Henry James, *Parisian Sketches: Letters to the New York Tribune* (New York, 1957), pp. 131, 166; Daniel Hannah, 'Henry James, Impressionism, and Publicity', *Rocky Mountain Review of Language and Literature*, vol. 61, no. 2, 2007 (Fall), pp. 28–43.63. Anne Distel, *Impressionism: The First Collectors*, trans. Barbara Perroud-Benson (New York, 1989), pp. 57–60.

64. *I. E. Repin i V. V. Stasov*, p. 132.

65. Émile Zola, 'M. Manet', in *Oeuvres complètes*, vol. 12, p. 802; F. W. J. Hemmings, 'Zola, Manet and the Impressionists (1875–1880)', *PMLA*, 93, 1959, p. 407.

66. Émile Zola, 'Une exposition: Les Peintres impressionnistes', in *Oeuvres complètes*, vol. 12, pp. 973–4.

67. GJ, vol. 2, p. 186 (14 Dec. 1868); Michel Robida, *Le Salon Charpentier et les impressionnistes* (Paris, 1958), p. 65.

68. Marcel Proust, *In Search of Lost Time*, vol. 6: *Time Regained*, trans. Andreas Mayor and Terence Kilmartin (London, 1996), p. 38.

69. Ibid., pp. 45, 71, 81–2.

70. Distel, *Impressionism*, pp. 95, 125–37, 177 ff., 195–7, 202, 207.

71. Assouline, *Discovering Impressionism*, pp. 81–93, 126; Patry (ed.), *Inventing Impressionism*, p. 28. On the role of reproduction in the internationalization of the art market: Paolo Serafini (ed.), *La Maison Goupil: Il successo italiano a Parigi negli anni dell'impressionismo* (Milan, 2003), pp. 57 ff.

72. *PSS*, vol. 15, p. 152, vol. 16, p. 199; *Zvig.*, pp. 312, 318.

73. Distel, *Impressionism*, pp. 83, 103–4.

74. *Collection de M. Ivan Tourguéneff et collection de M.X.* (Paris, 1878); Miquel, 'Les maîtres du paysage français', pp. 131–4; *PSS*, vol. 12, kn. 1: *1876–1878*, pp. 283, 310.

75. Francis Steegmuller, *Maupassant: A Lion in the Path.* (New York, 1972), pp. 64, 93.

76. Émile Zola, 'Flaubert et Tourgueneff', *Les Annales politiques et littéraires*, 12 November 1893, p. 307.

77. Edel (ed.), *Henry James Letters*, vol. 2, pp. 20, 52; Alphonse Daudet, *Trente ans de Paris* (Paris, 1888), p. 333.

78. On Flaubert's sociability and his image as a recluse, see Thierry Poyet, *La Gens Flaubert: La Fabrique de l'écrivain entre postures, amitiés et théories littéraires* (Paris, 2017), pp. 37–171.

79. Barbara Beaumont (ed.), *Flaubert and Turgenev: A Friendship in Letters. The Complete Correspondence* (New York, 1987), pp. 69, 71.

80. *PSS*, vol. 14, p. 146.81. Sylvain Kerandoux (ed.), *Gustave Flaubert, Guy de Maupassant: Correspondance (1873–1880)* (Rennes, 2009), p. 167.

82. Beaumont (ed.), *Flaubert and Turgenev*, p. 157.

83. Gustave Flaubert, *Oeuvres complètes: Correspondance*, ser. 7: *1873–1876*, (Paris, 1930), pp. 120, 138–40; *PSS*, vol. 13, pp. 77, 95.

84. Flaubert, *Correspondance*, vol. 5, p. 113.

85. OR RNB, f. 293 op. 1 d. 1466, l. 7; op. 3, d. 132, l. 1; Nikolai Zhekulin, 'Turgenev – Perevodchik Flobera: Legenda o Sv. Iuliane Milostivom', *Slavica Litteraria*, vol. 15, 2012/1, pp. 57–8, 68; *PSS*, vol. 15, kn. 2, pp. 68, 77.

86. Alain Pagès, 'La topographie du discours (Sur quelques textes de Zola publiés en 1879)', *Les Cahiers naturalistes*, no. 54, 1980, pp. 174–84.

87. P. Boborykin, *Stolytsi mira (Tridsat' let vospominanii)* (Moscow, 1911), pp. 183–9.

88. Vizetelly, *Emile Zola*, pp. 65, 114, 136; E. Halpérine-Kaminsky (ed.), *Ivan Tourguéneff d'après sa correspondance avec ses amis français* (Paris, 1901), pp. 189–90.

89. *PSS*, vol. 14, pp. 9, 28, 44, 66, 77, vol. 15, kn. 1, p. 17; *M. M. Stasiulevich i ero sovremenniki v ikh perepiskakh*, vol. 3, p. 610; M. Kleman, 'Zola v Rossii', *Literaturnoe nasledstvo*, 2, 1932, pp. 243, 245; Émile Zola, *Correspondance*, ed. B. H. Bakker, Colette Becker and Henri Mitterand, 10 vols. (Paris, 1978–1995), vol. 2: *1868–1877*, pp. 502, 557; Florence Montreynaud, 'La correspondence entre Zola et Stassioulevich, directeur du "Messenger de l'Europe" (Deuxième partie)', *Les Cahiers naturalistes*, no. 47, 1974, pp. 34–8.

90. Phillip Duncan, 'The Fortunes of Zola's *Parizhskie Pis'ma* in Russia', *Slavonic and East European Journal*, vol. 3, no. 2, 1959, p. 108; Kleman, 'Zola v Rossii', p. 235;

PSS, vol. 13, p. 95; *Vestnik Evropy*, vol. 10, no. 1, 1875, pp. 253–328, no. 2, pp. 694–774, no. 3, pp. 271–365.

91. Paul Alexis, *Émile Zola: Notes d'un ami* (Paris, 1882), p. 119.

92. Zola, *Correspondance*, vol. 2, pp. 453, 455, 457–8, 465–7; *PSS*, vol. 15, kn. 1, pp. 69, 238–9, vol. 15, kn. 2, p. 46.

93. GJ, vol. 3, p. 180. Translation taken from Edmond and Jules de Goncourt, *Pages from the Goncourt Journal*, ed. and trans. Robert Baldick (New York, 2007), p. 229.

94. HL, Mus 232, Letter from Jules Vallès to Turgenev, 13 Oct. 1877; A. Fifis, 'Al'fons Dode – Sotrudnik Petersburgskoi gazety "Novoe Vremia"', in NPG, vol. 1, pp. 210–12; *Vosp.*, p. 300; Zola, *Correspondance*, vol. 2, p. 553, vol. 3, p. 89; N. P. Generalova, 'Neopublikovannoe pis'mo k Turgenevu Zhiulia Vallesa (1877)', in NPG, vol. 4, pp. 629–30.

95. *M. M. Stasiulevich i ero sovremenniki v ikh perepiskakh*, vol. 3, pp. 193, 224; *PSS*, vol. 14, pp. 86, 163, 77–8, 90–91.

96. *PSS*, vol. 8, pp. 191–2, vol. 13, p. 98; Chevrel, D'hulst and Lombez (eds.), *Histoire des traductions*, pp. 620–21.

97. L. N. Tolstoi, *Polnoe sobranie sochinenii*, 90 vols. (Moscow–Leningrad, 1928–64), vol. 62, p. 446; Fet, *Moi vospominaniia*, pp. 369–71; Ostrovskaia, *Vospominaniia o Turgeneve*, p. 41.

98. Ilia Zilberstein, 'Le Roman *Guerre et Paix* et la France: Ivan Tourgueniev s'emploie à faire connaître l'oeuvre de Léon Tolstoï', in *Tolstoï aujourd'hui: Colloque international Tolstoï tenu à Paris du 10 au 13 Octobre 1978* (Paris, 1980), pp. 225–7; Ostrovskaia, *Vospominaniia o Turgeneve*, p. 40.

99. Tolstoi, *Polnoe sobranie sochinenii*, vol. 62, p. 446; *PSS*, vol. 12, kn. 1, p. 323.

100. Zilberstein, 'Le Roman *Guerre et Paix*', pp. 226–30; *PSS*, vol. 12, kn. 2, *1879–1880*, p. 197

101. Zilberstein, 'Le Roman *Guerre et Paix*', p. 230; Beaumont (ed.), *Flaubert and Turgenev*, pp. 174–5.

102. *PSS*, vol. 10, p. 381; Seljak, *Ivan Turgenevs Ökonomien*, p. 143; Rissa Tachnin and David H. Stam (compilers), *Turgenev in English: A Checklist of Works by and about Him* (New York, 1962), pp. 17–19.

103. *PSS*, vol. 12, pp. 48, 72, vol. 15, kn. 1, p. 157, vol. 15, kn. 2, p. 257, vol. 16, pp. 482–3.

104. Bachleitner, 'Produktion, Tausch und Übersetzung', in Barbier, ed., *Est–ouest*, p. 118; Dorrotaya Liptak, 'Die Sozialgeschichte der Literatur oder die übersetzte Literatur in den Wochenzeitschriften Prags und Budapests gegen Ende des 19. Jahrhunderts', in Barbier, ed., *Est–ouest*, p. 202.

105. Paul Aron and Pierre-Yves Soucy, *Les Revues littéraires belges de langue française de 1830 à nos jours* (Brussels, 1998), p. 17; Paul Aron, 'La Belgique francophone, carrefour du cosmopolitisme européen', in Jacqueline Pluet-Despatin, Michel Leyarie and Jean-Yves Mollier (eds.), *La Belle Époque des revues 1880–1914* (Paris, 2002), p. 329.

106. Carlos Serrano, 'Les Revues littéraires dans l'Espagne fin-de-siècle', in Pluet-Despatin, Leyarie and Mollier (eds.), *La Belle Epoque des revues*, p. 387.

107. Julian Schmidt, 'Iwan Turgenjev', in *Bilder aus dem geistigen Leben unserer Zeit* (Leipzig, 1870), pp. 428–71.

108. Kluge, *Ivan Turgenev und seine deutschen Freunde*, p. 126.

109. *PSS*, vol. 6, p. 111; Mikhail Alexeev, 'Lamartine et Tourguéniev', *Cahiers*, no. 14, 1990, p. 20; M. P. Alekseev and Iu.D. Levin, *Vil'iam Rol'ston – propagandist russkoi literatury i fol'klora* (St Petersburg, 1994), pp. 32–7.

110. Christine Richards, 'Occasional Criticism: Henry James on Ivan Turgenev', *Slavonic and East European Review*, vol. 78, no. 3, 2000, p. 463; Dale E. Peterson, *The Clement Vision: Poetic Realism in Turgenev and James* (Port Washington, 1975), pp. 10 ff.

111. Pauline Gacoin Lablanchy, 'Le vicomte Eugène-Melchior de Vogüé et l'image de la Russie dans la France de la IIIe République', *Bulletin de l'Institut Pierre Renouvin*, no. 39, 2014/1 (Spring), pp. 65–78; Edmund Gosse, *Portraits and Sketches* (London, 1913), pp. 243–63; F. W. J. Hemmings, *The Russian Novel in France 1885–1914* (Oxford, 1950), pp. 49–52.

112. Sylvain Briens, 'La mondialisation du théâtre nordique à la fin du XIXe siècle: Le fonds Prozor de la Bibliothèque nordique de Paris lu au prisme de la sociologie de l' acteur-réseau', *Revue de littérature comparée*, no. 354, 2015/2, pp. 137–50.

113. Franco Moretti, *Atlas of the European Novel 1800–1900* (London, 1998), p. 176.

114. Régnier, 'Littérature nationale, littérature étrangère', in Espagne and Werner, eds., *Philologiques III*, pp. 299–300.

115. Moretti, *Atlas of the European Novel*, pp. 184–5.

116. René Ternois, *Zola et ses amis Italiens* (Paris, 1967), p. 43; Pascale Casanova, *La République mondiale des lettres* (Paris, 1999), pp. 146–7.

117. A. Dezalay (ed.), *Zola sans frontières* (Strasbourg, 1996), p. 177.

118. Bard H. Bakker, 'Zola aux Pays-Bas, 1875–1885: Contribution à l'étude du naturalisme européen', *Revue des sciences humaines*, vol. XL, 1975, pp. 581–8; Joseph Hurt, 'The Reception of Naturalism in Germany', in Brian Nelson (ed.), *Naturalism in the European Novel: New Critical Perspectives* (Oxford, 1992), pp. 101–3.

119. Steegmuller (ed. and trans.), *Letters of Gustave Flaubert*, p. 624.

120. Émile Zola, 'L'Ouverture de l'Exposition Universelle', in *Oeuvres complètes*, vol. 10, pp. 342, 347–8; Zola, *Correspondance*, vol. 3, p. 32.

121. P. Boborykin, *Stolitsy mira: tridtsat' let vospominaniia* (Moscow, 1911), pp. 193–4.

122. Ibid., p. 194; Graham Robb, *Victor Hugo* (London, 1997), pp. 493–6

123. *LI*, p. xxviii.

124. Ibid., p. 494; E. M. Garshin, 'Vospominaniia o Turgeneve', *Istoricheskii vestnik*, no. 14, 1883, pp. 381–2.

125. *Congrès littéraire international de Paris, 1878. Présidence de Victor Hugo. Compte rendu in extenso et documents* (Paris, 1879), pp. 112–13.

126. Ibid., pp. 102–3.

127. *PSS*, vol. 8, pp. 76–81, 174, vol. 9, p. 94, vol. 11, p. 275, vol. 12, pp. 16, 52, 86–7, vol. 15, kn. 2, pp. 119–20.

128. Jac Ahrenberg, *Människor som jag känt: personliga minnen, utdrag ur bref och anteckningar*, 6 vols. (Helsingfors, 1904–14), vol. 3, pp. 75–7.

129. *PSS*, vol. 12, kn. 1: *1876–1878*, pp. 322, 326–7; M. P. Dragomanov, *Vospominaniia o znakomstve c I. S. Turgenevym* (Kazan, 1906), pp. 7–8.

130. *Congrès littéraire international de Paris, 1878*, pp. 186–90, 330–50; Patrick Waddington, 'I. S. Turgenev and the International Literary Congress of 1878', *New Zealand Slavonic Journal*, 1983, pp. 62–4; B. L. Chivilev, 'Otryvochnye vospominannia o Turgeneve', *Russkie vedomosti*, no. 270, 2 Sept. 1883; Kovalevskii, 'Vospominaniia ob I. S. Turgeneve', pp. 5–6; Dragomanov, *Vospominaniia*, p. 9.

131. *PSS*. vol. 12, kn. 1, p. 333; Flaubert, *Correspondance*, vol. 5, p. 398.

132. *PSS*. vol. 12, kn. 2: *1879–1880*, p. 81; Waddington, 'Turgenev and the International Literary Congress', p. 66.

133. Laurent Tissot, 'Naissance d'une Europe ferroviaire: la convention internationale de Berne (1890)', in *Les Entreprises et leurs réseaux: Hommes, capitaux, techniques et pouvoirs, XIXe–XXe siècles. Mélanges en l'honneur de François Caron* (Paris, 1998), pp. 283–95.

8 DEATH AND THE CANON

1. *PSS*, vol. 16, kn. 1, pp. 74, 92.
2. *Vosp.*, p. 536.
3. Samuel Fiszman, 'Ivan Turgenev's Unknown Letter and His Stay in Russia in 1879', *Slavic Review*, vol. 40, no. 1, 1981 (Spring), p. 82. On Turgenev's fears of arrest, see Vasili Vérechtchaguine, 'I. S. Tourguénieff, 1879–1883', *Cahiers*, no. 16, 1992, p. 48.
4. *Vosp.*, p. 538.
5. Ibid., p. 235.
6. Nora Gottlieb and Raymond Chapman (eds. and trans.), *Letters to an Actress: The Story of Turgenev and Marya Gavrilovna Savina* (London, 1973), p. 70.
7. Gottlieb and Chapman (eds. and trans.), *Letters to an Actress*, pp. 50 ff.
8. D. W. Martin, 'The Pushkin Celebrations of 1880: The Conflict of Ideals and Ideologies', *Slavonic and East European Review*, vol. 66, no. 4, Oct. 1988, p. 506; Marcus C. Levitt, *Russian Literary Politics and the Pushkin Celebration of 1880* (Cornell, 1989), pp. 3–4.
9. *PSS*, vol. 12, kn. 2 (Moscow, 1967), p. 247; Martin, 'Pushkin Celebrations', p. 506.
10. *Soch.*, pp. 341–50; Levitt, *Russian Literary Politics*, p. 125. *Turg*, vol. 12, kn. 2, p. 272.
11. David Magarshack, *Turgenev: A Life* (London, 1954), p. 295; Steegmuller, *Maupassant*, pp. 128–9.
12. Émile Zola, 'Gustave Flaubert', in *Oeuvres complètes*, ed. Henri Mitterand (Paris, 1966–9), vol. 11, pp. 124–6.
13. *PSS*, vol. 12, kn. 2: *1879–1880*, p. 322; André Billy, *The Goncourt Brothers*, trans. Margaret Shaw (London, 1960), pp. 258–60; GJ, vol. 3, p. 496.
14. GJ, vol. 3, pp. 497–8.
15. *Letopis' zhizni i tvorchestva F. M. Dostoevskogo*, 3 vols. (St. Petersburg, 1995), vol. 3, pp. 547, 558–9; Réné Fülöp-Miller, 'The Posthumous Life of Dostoevsky', *Russian Review*, vol. 15, no. 4, Oct. 1956, pp. 259–65.
16. Joseph Frank, *Dostoevsky: The Mantle of the Prophet, 1871–1881* (Princeton, 2003), pp. 752–4; *PSS*, vol. 13, kn. 1: *1880–1882*, pp. 56–7.
17. *Tombeau de Victor Hugo* (Paris, 1985), pp. 61, 164; Robb, *Victor Hugo*, pp. 522–3; Avner Ben-Amos, *Funeral, Politics, and Memory in Modern France, 1789–1996* (Oxford, 2000), p. 281.
18. Maurice Barrès, *Les Déracinés* (Paris, 1920), p. 443; Robb, *Victor Hugo*, pp. 527–9; Avner Ben-Amos, 'Les Funérailles de Victor Hugo', in Nora (ed.), *Lieux de Mémoire*, I: *La République* (Paris, 1984), pp. 499, 516.
19. APP BA art. 1294: Viardot, Cabinet du Préfet: affaires générales, 31 May 1878.
20. Jean-Marie Goulement and Éric Walter, 'Les Centenaires de Voltaire et de Rousseau', in Nora (ed.), *Lieux de Mémoire*, I, pp. 396, 409.
21. Jane Mayo Roos, 'Rodin's Monument to Victor Hugo: Art and Politics in the Third Republic', *The Art Bulletin*, vol. 68, no. 4, 1986, pp. 632–56; Ben-Amos, 'Funérailles de Victor Hugo', pp. 473–4.
22. Elizabeth Emery, *Photojournalism and the Origins of the French Writer House Museum (1881–1914): Privacy, Publicity, and Personality* (London, 2012), pp. 161–4, 175 ff.
23. Calculated from the database of 19th-Century Statues at http://romanticnationalism. net.
24. Marshall, 'Women Re-Read Shakespeare Country', p. 95; Julia Thomas, 'Shakespeare and Commercialism', in Gail Marshall (ed.), *Shakespeare in the Nineteenth Century* (Cambridge, 2012), p. 252.
25. *PSS*, vol. 10, p. 298.
26. See George Martin, 'Verdi, Politics and "Va Pensiero": The Scholars' Squabble', *The Opera Quarterly*, vol. 21, no. 1, Jan. 2005, p. 110. Contemporary accounts of the

funeral do not mention this singing of the 'Va Pensiero' chorus, but Martin cites an interview with Carlo Gatti, the Verdi scholar, who was at the funeral.

27. Roger Parker, *Studies in Early Verdi, 1832–1844: New Information and Perspectives on the Milanese Musical Milieu and the Operas from Oberto to Ernani* (New York, 1989), p. 139. See further Ann Smart, 'Liberty on (and off) the Barricades: Verdi's Risorgimento Fantasies', in Albert Ascoli and Krystyna von Henneberg (eds.), *Making and Remaking Italy: The Cultivation of National Identity around the Risorgimento* (Oxford, 2001).

28. Joep Leerson, 'Schiller 1859: Literary Historicism and Readership Mobilization', in J. Leerson and A. Rigney (eds.), *Commemorating Writers in Nineteenth-Century Europe: Nation-Building and Centenary Fever* (London, 2014), p. 27 (list of statues corrected from database of 19th-Century Statues at http://romanticnationalism.net).

29. An de Rider, 'Conscience 1883: Between Flanders and Belgium', in Leerson and Rigney, *Commemorating Writers*, pp. 188 ff.

30. S. Prawer, *Karl Marx and World Literature* (London, 2011), pp. 143–5; K. Marx and F. Engels, *The Communist Manifesto* (London, 1848).

31. L. E. Obolenskii, 'Literaturnye vospominaniia i kharakteristiki (1854–1892)' *Istoricheskii vestnik*, 1902, vol. 87 (Jan.–Mar.), pp. 504–5; *PSS*, vol. 12, kn. 2: *1879–1880*, p. 327.

32. BNF, NA Fr. Papiers de Pauline Viardot, 16275, Lettres adressées a Claudie et George Chamerot, Ivan Tourgénev et divers, ff. 257–8, Maupassant to Turgenev.

33. William Weber, 'Mass Culture and the Reshaping of European Musical Taste, 1770–1870', *International Journal of the Aesthetics and Sociology of Music*, vol. VIII, 1977, pp. 5–21.

34. Cooper, *Rise of Instrumental Music*, p. 157.

35. Taylor, *Anton Rubinstein*, p. 219; Weber, *Musician as Entrepreneur*, p. 118.

36. Georg Jäger, 'Der Musikalienverlag', in Jäger (ed.), *Geschichte des deutschen Buchhandels im 19. und 20. Jahrhundert: Das Kaiserreich 1871–1918*, vol 2 (Frankfurt am Main, 2003), pp. 7–61.

37. Lawford-Hinrichsen, *Music Publishing and Patronage* , pp. 18–20, 27.

38. Ringel, 'Opera in "The Donizettian Dark Ages" ', p. 58; *The Times*, 8 July 1861.

39. Ibid., pp. 73–4.

40. Albert Soubies, *Le Théâtre-Italien de 1801 à 1913* (Paris 1913), appendix table.

41. See Charle, 'Comparaisons et transferts', p. 31.

42. John Rosselli, 'Materiali per la storia socio-economica del San Carlo nel Ottocento', in Lorenzo Bianconi and Renato Bossa (eds.), *Musica e cultura a Napoli dal XV al XIX secolo* (Florence, 1983), p. 376; Jutta Toelle, *Bühne der Stadt: Mailand und das Teatro alla Scala zwischen Risorgimento und Fin de Siècle* (Munich, 2009), p. 81.

43. Katharine Ellis, 'Unintended Consequences: Theatre Deregulation and Opera in France, 1864–1878', *Cambridge Opera Journal*, vol. 22, no. 3, 2010, pp. 327–52; Katharine Ellis, 'Systems Failure in Operatic Paris: The Acid Test of the Théâtre-Lyrique', in Everist and Fauser (eds.), *Music, Theater, and Cultural Transfer*, pp. 53–5, 67.

44. Faith, *World the Railways Made*, p. 279.

45. Jutta Toelle, 'Der Duft der grossen weiten Welt: Ideen zur weltweiten Ausbreitung der italienischen Oper im 19. Jahrhundert', in Müller et al. (eds.), *Oper im Wandel der Gesellschaft*, p. 259.

46. Ibid., p. 71.

47. Jutta Toelle, *Oper als Geschäft: Impresari an italienischen Opernhäusern, 1860–1900* (Kassel, 2007), pp. 53–5; Toelle, *Bühne der Stadt*, p. 113.

48. Annegret Fauser, "Cette musique sans tradition": Wagner's Tannhäuser and Its French Critics', in Everist and Fauser (eds.), *Music, Theater, and Cultural Transfer*, p. 238.

49. Forti, 'Alle origini dell'industria musicale italiana', pp. 109–11.
50. Hans Busch (ed.), *Verdi's Aida: The History of an Opera in Letters and Documents* (Minneapolis, 1978), pp. 365, 397–400, 499–553; Toelle, *Bühne der Stadt*, p. 93.
51. Ibid., pp. 94 ff.
52. See Philipp Ther, 'Wie national war die Oper? Die Opernkultur des 19. Jahrhunderts zwischen nationaler Ideologie und europäischer Praxis', in Ther and Sachel (eds.), *Wie europäisch ist die Oper?*, pp. 110–11.
53. *Fellner & Helmer: Die Architekten der Illusion. Theaterbau und Bühnenbild in Europa: anlässlich des Jubiläums '100 Jahre Grazer Oper'* (Graz, 1999), pp. 10–11.
54. Toelle, *Bühne der Stadt*, p. 100; Annibale Alberti, *Verdi intimo, 1861–1886* (Milan, 1931), p. 17.
55. On the problems of data collection: Mark O'Neill, Sara Selwood and Astrid Swenson (2019): 'Looking Back: Understanding Visits to Museums in the UK and beyond since the Nineteenth Century', *Cultural Trends*, DOI: 10.1080/09548963.2019.1559472. On de Rijksmuseum: Ellinoor Bergvelt and Claudia Hörster, 'Kunst en publiek in de Nederlandse rijksmusea voor oude kunst (1800–1896): Een vergelijking met Bennets *Birth of the Museum*', *De Negentiende Eeuw*, vol. 34, no. 3, 2010, pp. 232–48; Claudia Hörster, 'Visiting the Trippenhuis: Social History of the Rijksmuseum Amsterdam 1800–1885', diss., Universiteit van Amsterdam, 2010. Figures for number of visitors communicated by Ellinoor Bergvelt. See also: Liesbet Nys, *De intrede van het publiek: Museumbezoek in België 1830–1914:* (Leuven, 2012); Bénédicte Savoy and Philippa Sissis (eds.), *Die Berliner Museumsinsel: Impressionen internationaler Besucher, 1830–1990. Eine Anthologie* (Vienna, 2013).
56. Louis Viardot, *Les Merveilles de la peinture* (Paris, 1868); *Les Merveilles de la sculpture. Ouvrage illustré … par Chapuis, etc.* (Paris, 1871); *Wonders of European Art. Illustrated by Reproductions by the Woodbury Permanent Process, and Wood Engravings* (London, 1871); *Wonders of Sculpture: Illustrated* (London, 1872); *A Brief History of the Painters of all Schools* (London, 1877).
57. Théophile Gautier, 'Le Musée ancien', *La Presse*, 10 Feb. 1849, p. 2.
58. McCauley, *Industrial Madness*, pp. 265–74. On the nineteenth-century cult of these two artists, see Alison McQueen, *The Rise of the Cult of Rembrandt: Reinventing an Old Master in Nineteenth-Century France* (Amsterdam, 2014); Berthold Hinz, *Dürers Gloria: Kunst, Kult, Konsum* (Berlin, 1971).
59. *Gérôme & Goupil: Art et entreprise* (Paris, 2000), p. 23; Alexandre Benois, *Memoirs*, trans. Moura Budberg (London, 1960), p. 103.
60. Anthony Hamber, 'Facsimile, Scholarship, and Commerce: Aspects of the Photographically Illustrated Art Book (1839–1880)', *Studies in the History of Art*, vol. 77: *Symposium Papers LIV: Art and the Early Photographic Album*, 2011, p. 144.
61. Austen Barron Bailey, 'Vetting the Canon: Galerie contemporaine, 1876–1884', *Studies in the History of Art*, vol. 77, *Symposium Papers LIV*, pp. 173–94 .
62. *Turgenevskii sbornik*, vol. 2, pp. 286–7; Kel'ner, *Chelovek svoego vremeni*, p. 95; Fedyashin, *Liberals Under Autocracy*, pp. 89–90.
63. Olivero, 'Paperback Revolution', in Spiers, ed., *Culture of the Publisher's Series*, vol. 1, p. 78.
64. Olivero, *L'Invention de la collection*, pp. 41, 166–9.
65. Alvaro Ceballos Viro, 'The Foreign Series of Herder Verlag by 1900: International Catholic Literature', in Spiers, ed., *Culture of the Publisher's Series*, vol. 2: *Nationalisms and the National Canon*, pp. 62–81.
66. Frederic Barbier, *L'Empire du livre: Le livre imprimé et la construction de l'Allemagne contemporaine (1815–1914)* (Paris, 1995), pp. 92–7; Bode, *Reclam*, pp. 14–15; Olivero, *L'Invention de la collection*, pp. 81–2.

67. Liptak, 'Sozialgeschichte der Literatur', pp. 203 ff.; Olivero, *L'Invention de la collection*, p. 107; Mariella Colin, 'La naissance de la littérature romanesque pour la jeunesse au xixe siècle en Italie; Entre l'Europe et la nation', *Revue de littérature comparée*, no. 304, 2002, pp. 507–18; Marisa Fernândez-Lépez, 'La naissance du roman hispanique à la lumière de ses modèles français, anglais et américain', *Revue de littérature comparée*, no. 304, 2002, pp. 493–505.

68. Simonetta Soldani and Gabriele Turi, *Fare gli Italiani: Scuola e cultura nell'Italia contemporanea*, 2 vols. (Bologna, 1993), vol. i, p. 50; Jean-François Botrel, *La Diffusion des livres en Espagne (1868–1914): Les libraires* (Madrid, 1988), p. 127; David Vincent, *The Rise of Mass Literacy: Reading and Writing in Modern Europe* (Oxford, 2000), p. 31.

69. Hermann Korte, 'Gymnasiale Kanonarchitektur und literarische Kanonisierungspraxis 1871 bis 1918 am Beispiel Westfalens', in Korte, Ilonka Zimmer and Hans-Joachim Jakob (eds.), *Der deutsche Lektürekanon an höheren Schulen Westfalens von 1871 bis 1918* (Frankfurt/M. 2011), pp. 11–122; Jana Mikota, 'For the Love of Words and Works: Tailoring the Reader for Higher Girls' Schools in Late Nineteenth-Century Germany', in Lynne Tatlock (ed.), *Publishing, Culture and the Reading Nation: German Book History in the Long Nineteenth Century* (Rochester, 2010), pp. 181–203.

70. M. Guiney, *Teaching the Cult of Literature in the French Third Republic* (London, 2004), pp. 102–5; Richard Altick, *The English Common Reader: A Social History of the Mass Reading Public 1800–1900* (Chicago, 1957), p. 185; Mary Hammond, *Reading, Publishing and the Formation of Literary Taste in England, 1880–1914* (Aldershot, 2006), p. 87.

71. Moretti, *Atlas of the European Novel*, p. 146.

72. Maurice Pellison, *Les bibliothèques populaires à l'étranger et en France* (Paris, 1906), p. 57; *The English Public Library, 1850–1939: Introduction to Heritage Assets* (English Heritage, 2014), p. 3.

73. Pellison, *Bibliothèques populaires*, p. 169; Eugène Morel, *Bibliothèques: Essai sur le développement des bibliothèques publiques et de la librairie dans les deux mondes* (Paris, 1908), pp. 128–9.

74. Pellison, *Bibliothèques populaires*, pp. 95–102; Giovanni Lazzari, *Libri e popolo: Politica della biblioteca pubblica in Italia dal 1861 ad oggi* (Naples, 1985), p. 45; Sassoon, *Culture of the Europeans*, p, 610.

75. Marie-Laure Malingre, 'Le roman dans les bibliothèques populaires au dix-neuvième siècle', in *Lectures et lecteurs au XIXe siècle: La Bibliothèque des Amis de l'instruction* (Paris, 1985), pp. 110–18.

76. *PSS*, vol. 12, kn. 2, *1879–1880*, pp. 48, 58, 428–9.

77. *PSS*, vol. 13, kn. 1, *1880–1882*, p. 245.

78. *Turgenevskii sbornik*, vol. 2, p. 331.

79. Patrick Waddington, *Turgenev's Mortal Illness: From Its Origins to the Autopsy* (Pinehaven, 1999), pp. 2–7, 14–15; Patrick Waddington, 'Turgenev's Last Will and Testament', *New Zealand Slavonic Journal*, no. 2, 1974, pp. 39–64.

80. M. K. Tenisheva, *Vpechatleniia moei zhizni* (Leningrad, 1991), p. 46.

81. Henri de Saint-Simon, 'Viardot et Tourgueneff', *Le Figaro*, 8 May 1883, pp. 1–2.

82. BMO, NLA 357, Pauline Viardot to unknown, 4 May 1883.

83. *PSS*, vol. 13, kn. 2, *1882–1883*, p. 180.

84. RGALI, f. 1573, op. 3, d. 1325, l. 27.

85. Waddington, *Turgenev's Mortal Illness*, pp. 58–60; *Vosp.*, pp. 409–11.

86. *Vosp.*, pp. 412, 420; M. M. Stasiulevich i ero sovremenniki v ikh perepiskakh, vol. 3, p. 230.

87. Waddington, *Turgenev's Mortal Illness*, p. 61; 'Pauline Viardot o konchine Turgeneva', *Knizhnye novosti*, no. 10, 1937, p. 55.

88. APP BA art. 1287: Tourgeneff, Cabinet du Préfet: affaires générales, 106409, Police reports on Turgenev funeral; 'Les obsèques de Tourguéneff', *La France*, 8 Sept. 1883, p. 3; H. de L., 'Nécrologie', *Le Clairon*, 8 Sept. 1883, p. 3.

89. *Vosp.*, p. 418.

90. *M. M. Stasiulevich i ero sovremenniki v ikh perepiskakh*, vol. 3, pp. 230–34, 273; Waddington, *Turgenev's Mortal Illness*, p. 57.

91. *M. M. Stasiulevich i ero sovremenniki v ikh perepiskakh*, vol. 3, p. 265; *Soch.*, p. 182.

92. L. D. Obolenskii, 'U groba Turgeneva', pp. 942–4; *Le XIXe siècle*, 3 Oct. 1883, p. 1; 'Ernest Renan, Tourguéniev et Pauline Viardot', *Cahiers*, no. 16, 1992, p. 25.

93. M. Stasiulevich, 'Iz vospominanii o poslednikh dniakh I. S. Turgeneva i ego pokhorony', in *I. S. Turgenev v vospominaniiakh sovremennikov*, vol. 2, pp. 420–24.

94. Ibid., pp. 424–7.

95. Ibid., p. 428; *Novoe vremia*, 28 Sept. (10 Oct.) 1883, pp. 1–2; *Iz Parizhskogo arkhiva I. S. Turgeneva, kniga pervaia, neizvestvnye proizvedeniia*, in *Literaturnoe Nasledstvo*, p. 328; Tamara Zviguilsky, *Le Musée Tourguéniev* (Bougival, 1993), p. 52.

EPILOGUE

1. Friang, *Pauline Viardot*, p. 252; Héritte-Viardot, *Une famille de grands musiciens*, p. 65.

2. BMD, 091 VIA, Pauline Viardot to Edmond Cottinet, 13 Jan. 1892; Borchard, *Pauline Viardot-Garcia*, p. 48.

3. *Dnevniki P. I. Chaikovskogo (1873–1891)* (St Petersburg, 1993), p. 64; Chaikovskii, *Polnoe sobranie sochinenii*, vol. 9, pp. 355–8, 383–4.

4. RGALI, f. 1573, op. 3, d. 1325, ll. 21, 26–9.

5. *Vosp.*, p. 169.

6. Ibid., pp. 353, 355.

7. M. A. Arzumanova, 'Zaveshchanie I. S. Turgeneva', in I. S. *Turgenev (1818–1883–1958): Stat'i i materiali* (Orel, 1960), pp. 264–86.

8. Kluge, 'Ivan Turgenev und seine deutschen Freunde', pp. 128–9.

9. Christophe Charle, 'Champ Littéraire francais et importations étrangères: de la vogue du roman russe à l'émergence d'un nationalisme littéraire (1886–1902)', in Espagne and Werner, eds., *Philologiques III*, p. 255; Phelps, *Russian Novel in English Fiction*, p. 39.

10. GJ, vol. 3, p. 67.

11. Henry James, *The House of Fiction: Essays on the Novel* (London, 1957), p. 170.

12. Chevrel, D'hulst and Lombez, eds., *Histoire des traductions*, pp. 257–8.

13. Béatrice Joyeux-Prunel, *Nul n'est prophète en son pays? L'internationalisation de la peinture des avant-gardes parisiennes, 1855–1914* (Paris, 2007), p. 61.

14. Comte de Saint-Simon, *De la réorganisation de la société européenne* (Paris, 1914), pp. 108–11.

15. Friedrich Nietzsche, *Human, All Too Human*, trans. Marion Faber and Stephen Lehmann (London, 1994); Nietzsche, *The Joyous Science*, trans. R. Kevin Hill (London, 2018); Nietzsche, *Beyond Good and Evil*, trans. R. Hollingdale (London, 2003), pp. 172–3.

16. Georg Brandes, 'Verdenslitteratur' (1899), in *Samlede Skrifter*, 18 vols. (Copenhagen, 1899–1910), vol. 12, pp. 23–8.

17. Paul Valéry, 'The Crisis of the Mind', in *The Outlook for Intelligence*, trans. Denise Folliot and Jackson Mathews (Princeton, 1989), pp. 26–8.

18. BNF, NA Fr. 17273, Papiers Pauline Viardot, vol. 2, ff. 10–11, Camille Saint-Saëns to Pauline Viardot, 19 Dec. 1909.
19. Borchard, *Pauline Viardot-Garcia*, p. 105.
20. BNF, VM BOB-21366, Lettres de Pauline Viardot à Gabriel Fauré, 1907–1910, nos. 299–305.
21. HL MUS 264 (366), Pauline Viardot Journal, 'La viellesse (la mienne)'.
22. See Richard Taruskin, *Stravinsky and the Russian Traditions*, 2 vols. (Oxford, 1996), vol. 1: *A Biography of the Works through Mavra*, pp. 637–45.
23. At least, there is no mention of a meeting in any of the relevant archives: BNF (Viardot, Boris Kochno), ANF (Viardot, Comtesse de Greffulhe, Princesse de Polignac), HL (Viardot), BMO (Viardot, Diaghilev), IRL (Diaghilev, Panaev-Kartseva), RGALI (Diaghilev) or NYPL (Gabriel Astruc Papers).
24. Héritte-Viardot, *Une famille de grands musiciens*, p. 65; *Les Annales politiques et littéraires*, no. 1405, 29 May 1910, p. 3.

Acknowledgements

I have been working on this book so long that I cannot now remember how the idea for it came about. It was only halfway through the project – about three or four years in – that I even thought a book was possible. The two people who most encouraged me in these early stages of research – my mother, Eva Figes, and my beloved agent, Deborah Rogers – have since died. I miss them terribly and wish they could have lived to see a work they inspired.

My new agent, Peter Straus, has been wonderfully supportive, as have my two editors, Simon Winder at Allen Lane and Sara Bershtel at Metropolitan, throughout the years when they saw nothing of my work and had only my assurances that it was slowly progressing.

The research for this book has been carried out without institutional support. I have no academies, trusts or councils to thank for academic grants or leave from teaching. So I am all the more grateful to my colleagues at Birkbeck for their friendship and encouragement, especially Filippo de Vivo, Fred Anscombe, Jan Rüger, Jessica Reinisch, Catharine Edwards, Chandak Sengoopta, Serafina Cuomo and Miriam Zukas for their feedback on my many applications for funding. Thanks are also due to Miles Taylor, Richard Evans, Chris Clark and Steve Smith, who generously acted as my academic referees.

I have been extremely fortunate in having the assistance of two outstanding young scholars: Antoine You, who helped with some of the detective work in the Paris archives; and Ella Saginadze, who tracked down materials for me in Moscow and St Petersburg. Thanks are also due to Claire Brodier, Maud Goodhart and Isabel Daykin, who each helped with a more specific task.

I am grateful to the following scholars for providing information on particular topics, in which they are far more expert than I am:

Alexandre Zviguilsky, Nicholas Žekulin, Agnès Penot, Laura Forti, Dagmar Paulus, Jennifer Davis, Julia Armstrong-Totten, Murat Siviloglu, James Radomski, Adam Zamoyski, Ellinoor Bergvelt and Claudia Hörster. Thanks as well to the many archivists who helped my research, among them, in particular: Vilma Zanotti (Archivo Storico Ricordi), Paul-Louis Durand-Ruel, Flavie Durand-Ruel (both at the Durand-Ruel Archive), Paul Beard (Royal Opera House Archives), James Kirwan (Trinity College Library), Mary Haegert and Susan Halpert (both at the Houghton Library).

I owe a special debt of gratitude to those dear people who generously read the early draft: Stella Tillyard, Hugh Macdonald, Barbara Diana, Miles Taylor, Marie-Pierre Rey, Peter Straus and Kate Figes. Their responses were invaluable, helping me to write the later drafts. In Sara Bershtel and Simon Winder I have what I think must be the finest editorial team in the English-speaking world. In their different ways their influence on my work has been immense.

I would also like to thank Cecilia Mackay, whose picture research for *The Europeans*, as on many of my other books, has been of the highest quality, and Mark Handsley, the best of copy-editors.

Finally, I thank my family – Stephanie, Lydia, Alice, Kate and Stoph – for their love and support. The book is dedicated to my sister, Kate, the single constant presence in my life, who joined me in reclaiming our German nationality following the UK's decision to leave the European Union.

That event, unforeseen (indeed, unthinkable) when I started working on this book, has added a real urgency to its writing. I hope the book will serve as a reminder of the unifying force of European civilization, which Europe's nations ignore at their peril.

London
January 2019

Index

Italic page numbers refer to illustrations in the text.

About the Author

ORLANDO FIGES is the author of nine books, including *A People's Tragedy*, *Natasha's Dance*, *The Whisperers*, and *The Crimean War*. He is a professor of history at Birkbeck, University of London, and a frequent contributor to the *New York Review of Books*. His books have won major prizes and been translated into over thirty languages. He lives in London and Umbria, Italy.